	Merchandise trade		Manufactured exports	High technology exports	Current account balance	Foreign direct investment	Official development assistance or official aid[a]	External debt		Domestic credit provided by banking sector	Net migration
	Exports	Imports						Total	Present value		
	$ millions 2006	$ millions 2006	% of total merchandise exports 2005	% of total manufactured exports 2005	$ millions 2006	$ millions 2005	$ per capita 2005	$ millions 2005	% of GNI 2005	% of GDP 2006	thousands 2000–05[a]
Mexico	250,292	268,169	77	20	−1,475	18,772	2	167,228	26	40	−3983
Moldova	1,033	2,585	39	3	−399	199	49	2,053	70	35	−250
Mongolia	1,529	1,489	21	0	84	182	83	1,327	63	25	−50
Morocco	12,559	23,302	65	10	1,110	1,552	22	16,846	34	90	−550
Mozambique	2,420	2,970	7	8	−761	108	65	5,121	28[c]	8	−20
Namibia	2,720	2,730	41	3	634	..	61	66	−1
Nepal	760	2,100	74	0	153	2	16	3,285	34	..	−100
Netherlands	462,083	416,121	68	30	57,448	40,416	188	110
New Zealand	22,449	26,441	31	14	−9,373	1,979	145	102
Nicaragua	1,035	2,977	11	5	−800	241	144	5,144	46	73	−210
Niger	540	800	8	3	−231	12	37	1,972	25[c]	8	−28
Nigeria	52,000	23,000	2	2	24,202	2,013	46	22,178	34	9	−170
Norway	121,505	64,120	17	17	56,074	3,285	10	84
Oman	22,340	10,730	6	2	4,717	715	12	3,472	14	35	−150
Pakistan	16,917	29,825	82	2	−3,608	2,183	11	33,675	30	42	−1,239
Panama	1,039	4,833	9	1	−378	1,027	6	9,765	90	91	8
Papua New Guinea	4,300	2,010	6	39	640	34	45	1,849	55	23	0
Paraguay	1,906	6,090	13	7	−22	64	9	3,120	54	18	−45
Peru	23,431	15,327	17	3	2,456	2,519	14	28,653	49	15	−510
Philippines	47,028	51,980	89	71	2,338	1,132	7	61,527	67	49	−900
Poland	109,731	124,178	78	4	−7,925	9,602	40	98,821	39	33	−200
Portugal	43,255	66,538	75	9	−18,281	3,200	163	276
Romania	32,458	51,160	80	3	−8,504	6,630	42	38,694	51	27	−270
Russian Federation	304,520	163,867	19	8	94,462	15,151	9	229,042	40	21	917
Rwanda	135	485	10	25	−52	8	64	1,518	18[c]	10	43
Saudi Arabia	208,867	64,995	9	1	87,131	..	1	47	285
Senegal	1,510	3,505	43	12	−513	54	59	3,793	34[c]	24	−100
Serbia	6,428	13,172	..	6	24	−339
Sierra Leone	220	390	−103	59	62	1,682	41[c]	11	472
Singapore	271,772[d]	238,652	81[d]	57	33,212	20,071	2	73	200
Slovak Republic	41,580	45,698	84	7	..	1,908	44	23,654	61	50	3
Slovenia	23,208	24,039	88	5	−959	541	31	76	22
South Africa	58,412	77,280	57[e]	7	−16,276	6,257	15	30,632	14	83	75
Spain	206,186	318,757	77	7	−106,344	22,789	178	2,846
Sri Lanka	6,860	10,226	70	1	−647	272	61	11,444	48	44	−442
Sudan	5,320	7,400	0	0	−2,768	2,305	50	18,455	88	19	−532
Sweden	147,266	126,301	79	17	23,643	10,679	125	152
Switzerland	147,457	141,373	93	22	63,494	15,420	188	100
Syrian Arab Republic	8,750	9,670	11	1	−1,061	427	4	6,508	27	32	200
Tajikistan	1,401	1,680	−21	54	37	1,022	41	15	−345
Tanzania	1,687	3,970	14	1	−536	473	39	7,763	22[c,f]	11	−345
Thailand	130,575	128,600	77	27	3,230	4,527	−3	52,266	32	101	231
Togo	630	1,200	58	0	−206	3	14	1,708	74	17	−4
Tunisia	11,513	14,865	78	5	−303	723	38	17,789	69	73	−29
Turkey	85,142	137,032	82	2	−23,155	9,805	6	171,059	59	59	−30
Turkmenistan	5,280	3,111	62	6	1,092	16	..	−10
Uganda	991	2,600	17	14	−131	257	42	4,463	29[c]	10	−5
Ukraine	38,368	45,035	69	4	2,531	7,808	9	33,297	53	46	−173
United Kingdom	443,358	600,833	77	28	−79,966	158,801	179	948
United States	1,037,320	1,919,574	82	32	−856,669	109,754	230	6,493
Uruguay	4,106	4,775	32	2	−457	711	4	14,551	116	32	−104
Uzbekistan	5,365	3,915	45	7	4,226	34	..	−300
Venezuela, RB	63,250	29,800	9	3	27,167	2,957	2	44,201	48	13	40
Vietnam	39,605	44,410	53	6	217	1,954	23	19,287	38	75	−200
West Bank and Gaza	304	9	11
Yemen, Rep.	8,100	5,840	4	5	1,215	−266	16	5,363	32	5	−100
Zambia	3,689	2,920	9	1	..	259	81	5,668	29	16	−82
Zimbabwe	1,920	2,100	28	1	..	103	28	4,257	85	93	−75
World	12,063,483t	12,278,444t	75w	22w	974,283s	17w	..s			167w	..
Low income	323,706	388,830	50	4	20,522	17	379,239		55	−4,690	
Middle income	3,305,551	2,934,082	64	21	260,273	15	2,363,139		77	−14,021	
Lower middle income	1,689,269	1,480,026	73	27	150,874	19	1,146,475		103	−9,750	
Upper middle income	1,615,598	1,450,813	57	16	109,399	3	1,216,664		53	−4,271	
Low & middle income	3,629,251	3,323,081	64	21	280,795	20	2,742,378		74	−18,711	
East Asia & Pacific	1,468,437	1,243,894	81	34	96,898	5	621,223		121	−3,847	
Europe & Central Asia	830,238	834,338	52	7	73,687	12	834,484		36	−1,730	
Latin America & Carribbean	661,934	601,583	54	15	70,017	11	727,628		57	−6,811	
Middle East & North Africa	280,881	210,805	20	3	13,765	88	152,724		52	−2,768	
South Asia	157,727	236,737	72	4	9,869	6	191,479		61	−2,484	
Sub–Saharan Africa	232,065	201,520	33	4	16,559	43	214,841		47	−1,070	
High income	8,435,922	8,960,432	78	22	693,488	0			195	18,604	

Note: Regional aggregates include data for economies that are not specified elsewhere. World and income group totals include aid not allocated by country or region. a. Annual average. b. Includes Luxembourg. c. Data are from debt sustainability analysis undertaken at part of the Heavily Indebted Poor Countries (HIPC) initiative. d. Includes re–exports. e. Data on total exports and imports refer to South Africa only. Data on export commodity shares refer to the South African Customs Union (Botswana, Lesotho, Namibia, and South Africa). f. GNI refers to mainland Tanzania only. g. World total computed by the UN sums to zero, but because the aggregates shown here refer to World Bank definitions, regional income group totals do not equal zero.

Introduction to International Economics

Second Edition

Dominick Salvatore

Fordham University

WILEY

John Wiley & Sons, Inc.

PUBLISHER	George Hoffman
ASSOCIATE PUBLISHER	Judith R. Joseph
ASSOCIATE EDITOR	Jennifer Conklin
EDITORIAL PROGRAM COORDINATOR	Sarah Vernon
EXECUTIVE MARKETING MANAGER	Amy Scholz
NEW MEDIA EDITOR	Allison Morris
SENIOR PRODUCTION EDITOR	Nicole Repasky
COVER DESIGNER	Madelyn Lesure
PRODUCTION MANAGEMENT SERVICES	Katie Boilard, Pine Tree Composition, Inc.

Cover Image: Hong Kong Convention Center at Night: Jeremy Woodhouse/Photodisc/Getty Images

This book was set in Palatino by Laserwords Private Limited, Chennai, India and printed and bound by R.R. Donnelley/Crawfordsville. The cover was printed by Phoenix Color.

This book is printed on acid-free paper. ⊗

To order books or for customer service please, call 1-800-CALL WILEY (225-5945).

ISBN-13: 978-0-470-40554-3

Printed in the United States of America

10 9 8 7 6 5 4 3 2 1

To My Mother

Preface

The aim of this text is to provide the student with an introduction to the field of international economics using many real-world case studies. This is to point out to the student the relevance and importance of studying international economics. The text seeks to explain how the world economy works, the major benefits that it provides to people and nations, and the most serious problems that it faces, all in a clear and realistic way that students with a limited background in economics can understand. This is the second edition of a text for a one-semester course in international economics for undergraduate economics and business programs whose students have only one or two courses in principles of economics. All of the features that made the first edition of this text such a great success are retained and extended in the second edition.

CHALLENGES FACING THE WORLD ECONOMY TODAY

The text sets out to present a simple but comprehensive, up-to-date, and clear exposition of the principles of international economics. These principles are essential for understanding, evaluating, and solving the important issues facing the United States and the world today.

These issues include:

1. Globalization of the world economy, rapid technological change, and increased international competition are causing widespread downsizing and job insecurity in the United States and in other advanced economies and leading to increasing demands for trade restrictions in the futile effort to protect industries and jobs from foreign competition.

2. The globalization of capital markets has led to volatile and misaligned exchange rates, unstable financial conditions, erosion of governments' control over domestic monetary matters, and frequent financial crises in developing and advanced economies alike, which threaten the stability of the entire international monetary system.

3. A low saving rate and excessive trade deficits in the United States, high structural unemployment in Europe and slow growth in Japan, as well as insufficient restructuring in transition economies of Central and Eastern Europe dampen the growth of international trade and the world economy, and lead to many trade disputes.

4. The deep poverty in many developing countries and the widening international inequalities pose serious moral, political, and developmental problems in the world today; and resource scarcity, environmental degradation, and climate change represent a great threat to continued growth and sustainable world development.

NEW TO THE SECOND EDITION

In Chapter 1, four new sections have been added to reflect the further globalization of the world economy. These are: We Live in a Global Economy, The Globalization Challenge, The International Flow of Labor and Capital, and International Organizations and the World Economy. Section 1.6 has been thoroughly revised to identify the major international economic (trade and financial) problems facing the United States and the world today, and so has the discussion in Chapter 16, which examines how they can be resolved.

The rapid globalization of the world economy is providing major benefits to most countries, but it is also presenting many challenges to poor countries that are unable to take advantage of globalization, as well as to the United States and other advanced countries, which face increasing competition from some emerging markets, especially China. These topics are discussed in several new sections and case studies in the trade and finance part of the text.

The dollar–euro exchange rate is much in the news these days as are the huge and unsustainable trade deficits of the United States. The relationship among U.S. trade deficits, trade protectionism and exchange rates is examined, both theoretically and empirically, and in all of its ramifications, in several trade and finance sections and case studies.

Besides its effect on international trade and international competitiveness, the continuing globalization of the world economy and liberalization of international capital markets have further eroded governments' control over national economic and financial matters. At the same time, international macroeconomic policy coordination has not progressed sufficiently to deal adequately with the potential problems and challenges that increased interdependence in world financial markets creates.

The second edition of the text also presents an in-depth analysis of the dangerous structural imbalances in the world economy and provides an evaluation of the policy options available to deal with them. The major imbalances in the world economy today are the huge trade and budget (twin) deficits of the United States, the high unemployment in Europe, the slow growth of Japan, the insufficient restructuring in transition economies of Central and Eastern Europe, the serious competitive challenge for both advanced and developing countries provided by the competition from China, the danger of financial and economic crises in emerging market economies, world poverty, resource scarcity, and the environment. All of these topics are addressed in this edition of the text.

The number of case studies has been increased to 83. Many are new and the others have been thoroughly revised.

The INTERNet section has been updated and expanded and gives the most important Internet site addresses or links to data sources, information, and analyses for the topics presented in each chapter to show the student how to access and use the wealth of information available on the Internet.

The Companion Site for the text has also been updated and expanded and presents for each chapter additional examples, cases, and theoretical points, as well as questions and problems that can be answered or solved using the Internet.

New sections in the second edition of the text include: We Live in a Global Economy; The Globalization Challenge; The International Flow of Labor and Capital; International Organizations and the World Economy; and Outsourcing, Offshoring, and Fear of Globalization. All other sections have been revised and updated.

New case studies include: Is India's Globalization Harming the United States?; Major Net Exporters and Importers of Capital; Economic Effects of the U.S. Quota on Sugar Imports; Job Loss Rates in U.S. Industries and Globalization; The New Economic Giants; The Deterioration in the U.S. Current Account Balance and Net International Investment Position; Interest Differentials, Exchange Rates, and the Monetary Approach; and The U.S. Subprime Mortgage Crisis and Sovereign Wealth Funds. Some case studies were dropped and all the other were thoroughly updated.

More international trade and finance data are included throughout the text that show the evolution of world trade and finance.

ORGANIZATION OF THE BOOK

The book is organized into six parts. Part One (Chapters 2–4) deals with trade theory (i.e., the basis and the gains from trade). Part Two (Chapters 5 and 6) deals with trade policy (i.e., obstructions to the flow of trade and their effects). Part Three (Chapters 7–9) examines economic integration, economic development, and international resource flows. Part Four (Chapters 10–12)

deals with the measurement of a nation's balance of payments, foreign exchange markets, and exchange rate determination. Part Five (Chapters 13–14) examines open-economy macroeconomics or the relationships between the domestic economy and the rest of the world. Part Six (Chapters 15 and 16) examines the operation of the present international monetary system. In a typical course in international economics, instructors may drop the chapters in Part Three, leaving 12 chapters plus the introductory material. This will allow them to cover one chapter per week during the course.

For the Student

- *An example is utilized in all chapters that deal with the same basic concepts discussed in the text.* This feature is unique to this text. For example, the same graphical and numerical model is used in all chapters from Chapters 2 through 6 (the chapters that deal with trade theory and policy). This greatly reduces the real burden on the student, who will not have to start with a new example every time.
- *Actual numbers are used in the examples and the graphs are presented on scale.* This makes the various concepts and theories more concrete, accessible, and pertinent to the student. It also makes the graphs easier to read and to understand.
- *There are 83 case studies* (from three to eight per chapter) that show the relevance and importance of international economics.
- *The sections in each chapter are numbered for easier referencing.* All of the graphs and diagrams are carefully explained in the text and then summarized in the captions.
- The judicious use of *color and shading* enhances the readability of the text and aids the student in understanding the principles involved.

 Each chapter includes:

- **Learning Objectives** that identify the most important material for students to understand while reading each chapter.
- **Key Terms** that are introduced in bold-face type with their definition appearing in the margin. A glossary of all these terms is provided at the end of the book.
- **Concept Checks** that summarize the most important concepts introduced in the text. Being able to use these questions in studying helps the student in the learning process.

- A **Summary** paragraph that reviews each section of the text.
- **Review Questions and Problems** that ask the student to calculate a specific measure or explain a particular event.
- **Appendices** that develop more difficult material than what is presented in the chapter.
- **Selected Bibliographies** that are included along with specific mention of the topics they deal with. An authors index is included at the end of the book for reference.
- An **INTERNet** section at the end of each chapter that provides Internet site addresses or links to data sources, information, and analyses of the topics presented in each chapter. This shows the student how to access and use the wealth of information available on the Internet.

 Also included are:

- A **web site** for the book that presents additional examples, cases, and theoretical points and includes questions, as well as problems, that can be answered or solved using the Internet. The web site will be updated continuously to reflect important new developments in the international economy as they unfold.
- A **Study Guide** that is prepared by Professor Arthur Raymond of Muhlenberg College is available for students. This provides the student an extensive review of key concepts, numerous additional illustrative examples, and practice problems and exercise sets.
- A **Schaum Outline** on the *Theory and Problems of International Economics* (4th edition, 1996), prepared by the author, that can be purchased in most bookstores. This provides a problem-solving approach to the topics presented in the traditional way in this and other international economics texts.

For the Instructor

- An **Instructor's Manual**, prepared by the author, is available which includes chapter objectives and lecture suggestions, answers to the end-of-chapter problems, a set of 15 multiple-choice questions with answers, and additional problems and essays for each part of the text.
- **PowerPoints** for each chapter, prepared by Carol Stivender of the University of North Carolina, Charlotte.

ACKNOWLEDGMENTS

This text grew out of the undergraduate courses in international economics that I have taught at Fordham University over the past 30 years. I am very fortunate to have had many excellent students whose questions and comments contributed to the clarity of this text.

I owe a great intellectual debt to my brilliant former teachers of international economics, Professor Arthur I. Bloomfield and Professor Michael Michaely. I have received much useful advice from Professors Robert Baldwin (University of Wisconsin), Jagdish Bhagwati (Columbia University), Alan Blinder (Princeton University), William Branson (Princeton University), Phillip Cagan (Columbia University), Richard Cooper (Harvard University), W. M. Corden (Johns Hopkins University), the late Rudi Dornbusch (MIT), Martin Feldstein (Harvard University and National Bureau of Economic Research), Ronald Findlay (Columbia University), Gerald Helleiner (University of Toronto), Lawrence Klein (University of Pennsylvania), Ronald McKinnon (Stanford University), Robert Mundell (Columbia University), Edmund Phelps (Columbia University), Jeffrey Sachs (Columbia University), T.N. Srinivasan (Yale University), Robert Stern (University of Michigan), Joseph Stiglitz (Columbia University), and Lawrence Summers (former U.S. Treasury Secretary and President of Harvard University).

I have also received assistance in preparing this edition of the text by various people in a number of well-known international and national organizations: Michael Mussa, Vito Tanzi, and George Tavlas, formerly of the International Monetary Fund; Michael Finger and David Tarr of the World Bank; Fred Campano, Karl Sauvant, and Douglas Walker, formerly of the United Nations; Robert Balckhurst and Ake Linden of the World Trade Organization (WTO); Antonio Costa, formerly of the European Bank for Reconstruction and Development and now the Chief Anticorruption Officer of the United Nations; André Sapir of the European Economic Community; Per M. Wijkman of the European Free Trade Association; Donald Rousslang of the U.S. International Trade Commission; Victor Fuchs and Robert E. Lipsey of the National Bureau of Economics Research; Morris Morkre of the Federal Trade Commission; Larry Mishel of the Economic Policy Institute; Jacob Frenkel, former Governor of the Bank of Israel and former Vice-President of Merrill Lynch; Luca Bonardi of KPMG; and Michael Halloran of Ernst & Young.

The following Professors reviewed the text and made many valuable suggestions:

Richard T. Baillie
Michigan State University

Nicola Borri
Boston University

Gregory Brock
Georgia Southern University

Ralf Hepp
Fordham University

William Holmes
Temple University

Baybars Karacaovali
Fordham University

Kwan S. Kim
University of Notre Dame

David Lehr
Longwood College

Susan Linz
Michigan State University

Emre Ozsoz
Fashion Institute of Technology

William H. Phillips
University of South Carolina

Jaishankar Raman
Valparaiso University

Rupert Rhodd
Florida Atlantic University

Fred J. Ruppel
Eastern Kentucky University

Sunil Sapra
California State University, Los Angeles

Jeffrey K. Sarbaum
University of North Carolina at Greensboro

Anthony Scaperlanda
Northern Illinois University

Robert Scully
Barry University

Kishor Thanawala
Villanova University

Fred Campano, Clive Daniels, Edward Dowling, Nick Gianaris, Darryl McLeod, Erick Rengifo, Henry Schwalbenberg, and Greg Winczewski, my colleagues at Fordham University, have also provided much useful advice. My graduate assistants Liana Gabor, Jenifer Murray, Yuman Omor, Mariana Barrientos Ossio, Angela Solikova, and Rossen Trendafilov provided much help with many aspects of the project.

Finally, I would like to express my gratitude to George Hoffman, the Publisher at Wiley; Judith Joseph, the Associate Publisher; Jennifer Conklin,

the Associate Editor; Sarah Vernon, the Editorial Program Coordinator; Nicole Repasky, the Senior Production Editor; Amy Scholz, the Executive Marketing Manager; and the entire staff at Wiley for their kind and skillful assistance; and to Giuseppina Cannariato and Angela Bates, the department secretaries, for their efficiency and cheerful dispositions.

Dominick Salvatore
Distinguished Professor of Economics
Fordham University
New York 10458
Tel. 718-817-4045
Fax 718-817-5578
e-mail: salvatore@fordham.edu

Brief Contents

Contents

PART ONE: INTERNATIONAL TRADE THEORY 29

PART TWO: INTERNATIONAL TRADE POLICY 115

PART FIVE: OPEN-ECONOMY MACROECONOMICS 335

Case Studies

Introduction to the Global Economy

After studying this chapter, you should be able to:

- Understand the meaning and importance of globalization
- Describe the relationship between international trade and a nation's standard of living
- Understand why the international flow of people (migration) and capital is also an indicator of economic integration and globalization of the world economy
- Describe the subject matter of international economics
- Identify the major international economic problems

CHAPTER OUTLINE

KEY TERMS

Globalization	Microeconomics
Anti-globalization movement	Macroeconomics
Interdependence	Open-economy macroeconomics
International trade theory	International finance
International trade policy	World Trade Organization (WTO)
Balance of payments	World Bank
Foreign exchange markets	International Monetary Fund (IMF)
Adjustment in the balance of payments	United Nations (UN)

1.1 WE LIVE IN A GLOBAL ECONOMY

We live in a globalized world. We can connect instantly with any corner of the world by cellular phone, e-mail, instant messaging, teleconferencing, and we can travel anywhere incredibly fast. Tastes are converging (i.e., more and more people all over the world generally would like the same things) and many goods we consume are either made abroad or have many imported parts and components. Many of the services we use are

increasingly provided by foreigners as, for example, when a radiography taken in a New York hospital is evaluated across the world in Bangalore (India) and when H&R Block sends our tax returns abroad for processing. Even small companies that until a few decades ago faced only local or regional competition now must compete with firms from across the world.

Although not as free as the flow of international trade in goods and services, millions of workers at all skill levels have migrated and can migrate around the world, and thousands of jobs have moved from advanced countries to such emerging markets as India and China.

Finance has also globalized: We can invest in companies anywhere in the world and purchase financial instruments (stocks and bonds) from any company from almost anywhere in the world. Many pension funds are in fact invested abroad and a financial crisis in one financial center quickly spreads across the world at the click of a mouse. We can exchange dollars for euros and most other currencies easily and quickly but the rates at which we exchange our currency often change frequently and drastically. In short, tastes, production, competition, labor markets, and financial markets are rapidly globalizing, and this affects all of us deeply as consumers, workers, investors, and voters—yes, we live in a global economy (see Case Studies 1-1 and 1-2).

1.2 THE GLOBALIZATION CHALLENGE

Globalization The increasing integration of economies around the world, particularly through trade and financial flows, but also through the movement of ideas and people, facilitated by the revolution in telecommunications and transportation.

Globalization is a revolution which in terms of scope and significance is comparable to the Industrial Revolution, but while the industrial revolution took place over a century, today's global revolution is taking place under our very eyes in a decade or two. Globalization, of course, is not new. Roman coins circulated throughout the empire 2000 years ago and so did even earlier the Chinese currency in China. More recently, the world has experienced three periods of rapid globalization: 1870–1914, 1945–1980, and 1980 to the present.

Globalization in 1870–1914 resulted from the industrial revolution in Europe and the opening up of new, resource-rich, but sparsely populated lands in North America (the United States and Canada), South America (Argentina, Chile and Uruguay), Australia and New Zealand, and South Africa. These lands received millions of immigrants and vast amounts of foreign investments, principally from England, to open up new lands to food and raw material production. These so-called "regions of recent settlement" grew rapidly during this period by exporting increasing amounts of food and raw materials to Europe in exchange for manufactured goods. This period of modern globalization came to an end with the breakout of World War I in 1914.

The second period of rapid globalization started with the end of World War II in 1945 and extended to about 1980. It was characterized by the rapid

CASE STUDY 1-1

The Dell PC Is Anything But American!

Headquartered in Round Rock, Texas, Dell co-ordinates a global production network in 34 countries in the Americas, Europe, and Asia. For most PCs sold in the United States, Dell performs only the final assembly domestically and relies on outside suppliers and contract manufacturers for components, peripherals, printed circuit board (PCB) assemblies, and subassemblies (box builds). The reason is that most parts and components are cheaper to produce in other parts of the world and are thus imported (see Table 1.1). Neither high value components nor very low value components (such as power supplies or keyboards) have to be made close to Dell's assembly plants. Only some midlevel components (such as motherboards and other PCB assemblies), which are too expensive to ship by air to meet volatility in demand and too risky to hold in inventory, are produced locally, but even that is not always the case. In 2004, IBM sold its PC business to Lenovo of China. In 2008, more than 90 percent of all the parts and components going into HP's PCs were made outside the United States.

Table 1.1. *Locations and Companies That Supply Specific Parts and Components for Dell's PCs*

Part/Component	Location	Companies
Monitors	Europe and Asia	Phillips, Nokia, Samsung, Sony, Acer
PCBs	Asia, Scotland, and Eastern Europe	SCI, Celestica
Drives	Asia, mainly Singapore	Seagate, Maxtor, Western Digital
Printers	Europe (Barcelona)	Acer
Box builds	Asia and Eastern Europe	Hon Hai/Foxteq
Chassis	Asia and Ireland	Hon Hai/Foxteq

Source: J. Dedrick and K. L. Kraemer, "Dell Computer: Organization of a Global Production Network" and "Globalization of the Personal Computer Industry: Trends and Implications," *Working Paper*, Irvine, CA: Center for Research on Information Technology and Organization (CRITO), University of California, Irvine, 2002; "Lenovo Buys IBM's PC Unit for $1.75 Billion," *Financial Times*, December 9, 2004, p. 16; and "The Laptop Trail," *The Wall Street Journal*, June 9, 2005, p. 31.

increase of international trade as a result of the dismantling of the heavy trade protection that had been put in place during the great Depression that started in the United States in 1929 and during World War II. What is different about the present globalization revolution (since 1980) is its speed, depth, and immediacy resulting from the tremendous improvements in telecommunications and transportation, massive international capital flows resulting from elimination of most restrictions on their flow across national boundaries, as well as by the participation of most countries of the world. This is what makes today's globalization that much more pervasive and dramatic than earlier periods of globalization.

CASE STUDY 1-2

What Is an "American" Car?

Strange as it may seem, the question of what is an American car may be difficult to answer. Should a Honda Accord produced in Ohio be considered American? What about a Chrysler minivan produced in Canada (especially when Chrysler was owned by Germany's MercedesChrysler)? Is a Kentucky Toyota or Mazda that uses nearly 40 percent of imported Japanese parts American? Clearly, it is becoming more and more difficult to define what is American, and opinions differ widely.

For some, any vehicle assembled in North America (the United States, Canada, and Mexico) should be considered American because these vehicles use mostly U.S.-made parts. But the United Auto Workers union views cars built in Canada and Mexico as taking away U.S. jobs. Some regard automobiles produced by Japanese-owned plants in the United States as American because they provide jobs for Americans. Others regard production by these Japanese "transplants" as foreign, because (1) the jobs they create were taken from the U.S. automakers, (2) they use nearly 40 percent imported Japanese parts, and (3) they remit profits to Japan. What if Japanese transplants increased their use of American parts to 75 percent or 90 percent? Was the Ford Probe, built for Ford by Mazda in Mazda's Michigan plant, American?

It is difficult to decide exactly what is an American car—even after the American Automobile Labeling Act of 1992, which requires all automobiles sold in the United States to indicate what percentage of the car's parts are domestic or foreign. One could even ask if this question is relevant at all in a world growing more and more interdependent and globalized. In order to be competitive, automakers must purchase parts and components wherever they are cheaper and better made, and they must sell automobiles throughout the world to achieve economies of mass production. Ford designs its automobiles in six nations (the United States, the United Kingdom, Germany, Italy, Japan, and Australia), has production facilities in 30 locations (3 in North America, 3 in South America, 7 in Asia, and 17 in Europe), and employs more workers outside than in the United States. In fact, the automotive and many other industries are rapidly moving toward a handful of truly global, independent companies.

Sources: "Honda's Nationality Proves Troublesome for Free-Trade Pact," *The New York Times*, October 9, 1992, p. 1; "Want a U.S. Car? Read the Label," *The New York Times*, September 18, 1994, Section 3, p. 6; "Made in America? Not Exactly: Transplants Use Japanese Car Parts," *The Wall Street Journal*, September 1, 1995, p. A3B; "And Then There Were Five," *U.S. News & World Report*, March 4, 2000, p. 46; and "Defining an American Car," August 2007, http://autos.msn.com/advice/article.aspx?contentid=4021986.

As all revolutions, however, today's globalization brings many benefits and advantages but also has some disadvantages or harmful side effects. In fact, there is a great deal of disagreement as to the extent and type of advantages and disadvantages. Does getting cheaper and/or better products and service from abroad justify sacrificing domestic jobs? Why are some people in some countries very rich and obese while others dismally poor and starving?

What is meant by globalization? What are its **advantages and disadvantages?**

Although labor migration generally leads to the more efficient utilization of labor, it also leads to job losses and lower wages for less skilled labor in advanced nations and harms (i.e., it is a "brain drain" for) the nations of emigration. Similarly, financial globalization and unrestricted capital flows lead to the more efficient use of capital throughout the world, as well as provide opportunities for higher returns and risk diversification for individuals and corporations. But they also seem to lead to periodic international financial crises, like the ones that started in Asia in 1997 and affected most other developing countries, and the subprime housing mortgage crisis that started in the United States in 2007 and affected the entire world. Finally, are we running out of resources such as petroleum, other minerals, water? Is the world headed for a climate disaster?

These disadvantages and negative aspects of globalization have given rise to a rethinking of the age-old belief in free trade as the best policy and to a strong anti-globalization movement, which blames globalization for many human and environmental problems throughout the world, and for sacrificing human and environmental well-being to the corporate profits of multinationals. Globalization is being blamed for world poverty and child labor in poor countries, job losses and lower wages in rich countries, as well as environmental pollution and climate change throughout the world. While there is some truth in these accusations, an in-depth economic analysis will show that often the primary cause of many of the serious problems facing the world today lies elsewhere.

Anti-globalization movement The loose organization that blames globalization for many human and environmental problems throughout the world and for sacrificing human and environmental well-being to the corporate profits of multinationals (Sect. 6.10).

Globalization has many social, political, legal, and ethical aspects, and so economists need to work closely with other social and physical scientists, as well as with the entire civil society, to give globalization a more human face (i.e., have all nations and people share its benefits). Globalization is important because it increases efficiency in the production of material things; it is inevitable because we cannot hide or run away from it. But we would like globalization also to be sustainable and humanizing, and ultimately "fair." This requires a profound change in world governance. Such is the challenge facing humanity today and in the next decade.

All of these topics and many more are either directly or indirectly the subject matter of international economics that are covered in this text (see Case Study 1-3).

Companies such as IBM, Citigoup, and Morgan Stanley point out that outsourcing high-skill and high-wage jobs to India (and other emerging markets, especially China) where they can be done more cheaply keeps them internationally competitive, leads to lower prices for their products and services to American consumers, and is necessary for them to take advantage of fast-growing emerging markets. Transferring abroad many high-skill and high-paying jobs, as well as the crucial technologies on which they are based, inevitably causes great concern in the United States, not only

CASE STUDY 1-3

Is India's Globalization Harming the United States?

The outsourcing of low-skilled service industry jobs (such as answering customer inquiries) from advanced countries to low-wage countries, such as India, reduces costs and prices in advanced countries, and it does not create much concern. In recent years, however, many high-skill and high-pay jobs in such diverse fields as computing and aircraft engineering, investment banking, and pharmaceutical research have been transferred to India and other emerging markets, creating great concern in advanced nations, especially the United States. Table 1.2 shows the outsourcing of high-tech services and jobs to India by some U.S. multinationals in 2008.

Table 1.2. *Globalizing India*

U.S. Company	Global Work Force	Work Force in India	Percentage in India	Outsourced Services
Accenture	146,000	27,000	18.5	By the end of 2008, the company expects to have more workers in India than in the U.S.
I.B.M.	356,000	52,000	14.6	Independent development of software solutions for Indian and global clients
Citigroup	327,000	22,000	6.7	Analysis of U.S. stocks and evaluation of creditworthiness of U.S. companies

Source: "India's Edge Goes Beyond Outsourcing," *The New York Times*, April 4, 2008, p. C1.

for the loss of good U.S. jobs, but also for the U.S. ability to remain the world technological leader.

1.3 INTERNATIONAL TRADE AND THE NATION'S STANDARD OF LIVING

The United States, stretching across a continent and rich in a variety of human and natural resources, can produce, relatively efficiently, most of the products it needs. Contrast this with the situation of small industrial countries, such as Switzerland or Austria, which have a few very specialized resources, produce and export a much smaller range of products, and import all the rest. Even large industrial countries such as Japan, Germany, France, England, Italy, and Canada rely crucially on international trade. For developing nations, exports provide employment opportunities and earnings to pay for the many

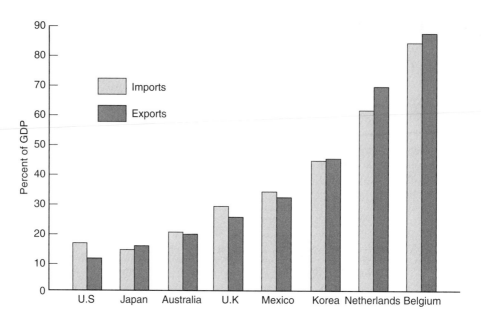

FIGURE 1.1. Imports and Exports as a Percentage of GDP in Various Countries in 2007.
International trade (imports and exports) is even more important to smaller developed countries and to developing countries than it is to the United States.
Source: International Monetary Fund, *International Financial Statistics* (Washington, D.C.: May 2008).

Interdependence
The (economic) relationships among nations.

products that they cannot produce at home and for the advanced technology they need.

A rough measure of the economic relationship among nations, or their interdependence, is given by the ratio of their imports and exports of goods and services to their gross domestic product (GDP). The GDP refers to the total value of all goods and services produced in the nation. Figure 1.1 shows that imports and exports as a percentage of GDP are much larger for smaller industrial and developing countries than they are for the United States. Thus, international trade is even more important to most other nations than it is to the United States.

Even though the United States relies to a relatively small extent on international trade, a great deal of its high standard of living depends on it. First of all, there are many commodities—coffee, bananas, cocoa, tea, scotch, cognac—that the country does not produce at all. In addition, the United States has no deposits of such minerals as tin, tungsten, and chromium, which are important to certain industrial processes, and it has only dwindling reserves of petroleum, copper, and many other minerals. Much more important *quantitatively* for the nation's standard of living are

How important is
international trade to
a nation's standard of
living?

the many products that could be produced domestically but only at a higher
cost than abroad. We will see later that these account for most of the *benefits
or gains from trade*.

Nevertheless, the United States could probably withdraw from world
trade and still survive without too drastic a decline in its standard of living.
The same cannot be said of such nations as Japan, Germany, England, or
Italy—not to speak of Switzerland or Austria. Even Russia and China, which
for political and military reasons valued self-sufficiency very highly in the
past, have now come to acknowledge their need to import high-technology
products, foreign capital, and even grains, soybeans, and other agricultural
commodities, and at the same time be able to export large quantities of their
goods and services in order to pay for all the imports they need.

In general, the economic interdependence among nations has been
increasing over the years, as measured by the more rapid growth of world
trade than world production (see Figure 1.2). This has certainly been the case
for the United States during the past four decades (see Case Study 1-4). The
only exception to world trade rising, and rising faster than world GDP, was
in 2001. In 2001, world GDP rose slightly but world trade actually declined
by 1 percent (the first such a decline since 1982–1983). To a large extent
this was due to the economic recession in the United States in 2001 and

**FIGURE 1.2. Growth of World Production and Trade, 1996–2006 (annual
percentage changes).**
International trade grew much faster than world production since 1996, except in
2001.
Source: World Trade Organization, *World Trade Report* (Geneva, 2007), p. 2.

CASE STUDY 1-4

Rising Importance of International Trade to the United States

After remaining at between 4 and 5 percent during most of the 1960s, merchandise imports and exports as percentages of gross domestic product (GDP) rose sharply in the United States during the 1970s. Figure 1.3 shows that imports as a percentage of U.S. GDP increased from about 5 percent during the late 1960s to a high of 17 percent in 2007. Exports increased from about 5 percent in the late 1960s to a high of 11.9 percent in 2007. Thus international trade has become more important to the United States (i.e., the United States has become more interdependent with the world economy) during the past four decades. Figure 1.3 also shows that the share of imports in GDP exceeded the share of exports since 1976, and the excess widened sharply during the first half of the 1980s and then again from 1996. This led to huge U.S. trade deficits and persistent demands for protection of domestic markets and jobs against foreign competition by American industry and labor.

 Concept Check Is international trade becoming more important to the United States?

YEAR	2000	2001	2002	2003	2004	2005	2006	2007
IMPORTS	15.0	13.8	13.7	14.1	15.4	16.3	16.9	17.0
EXPORTS	11.2	10.2	9.6	9.5	10.1	10.5	11.1	11.9

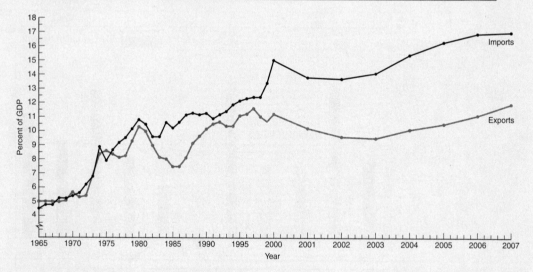

FIGURE 1.3. **Imports and Exports as a Percentage of U.S. GDP, 1965–2007.**
The share of merchandise imports and exports in U.S. GDP increased sharply since the early 1970s. Thus, international trade has become increasingly important to the United States. During the first half of the 1980s, and again from 1996, U.S. imports greatly exceeded U.S. exports and resulted in huge trade deficits.

Source: International Monetary Fund, *International Financial Statistics Yearbook* (Washington, D.C.: various issues).

the fear of terrorism following the September 11, 2001, attack on the World Trade Center in New York City. In all likelihood, trade will continue to serve as a strong stimulus to world growth in the future. (The appendix to this chapter provides data on the commodity and geographic concentration of international trade, as well as on the world's leading exporters and importers of goods and services; Case Study 10-1 gives the major commodity exports and imports of the United States, and Case Study 10-2 its major trade partners).

But there are many other crucial ways in which nations are interdependent, so that economic events and policies in one nation significantly affect other nations (and vice versa). For example, if the United States stimulates its economy, part of the increased demand for goods and services by its citizens spills into imports, which stimulate the economies of other nations that export those commodities. On the other hand, an increase in interest rates in the United States will attract funds (capital) from abroad. As we will see in Part Four of the text, this inflow of funds to the United States, by itself, tends to increase the international value of the dollar, which in turn stimulates U.S. imports and discourages U.S. exports. This then leads to a trade deficit, which dampens economic activity in the United States and stimulates economic activity abroad.

Finally, trade negotiations that reduce trade barriers across nations not only lead to an increase in the exports of high-technology goods (such as computers), and thus to an increase in employment and wages in those industries in the United States, but also lead to an increase in imports of shoes and textiles, thereby reducing employment and wages in those sectors.

1.4 THE INTERNATIONAL FLOW OF LABOR AND CAPITAL

Besides trade in goods and services, the international flow of people (migration) and capital across national boundaries is another measure or indicator of economic integration and globalization in the world economy.

There are today about 190 million people in the world who live in a country other than the one in which they were born—nearly 60 percent of them are in rich countries (about 36 million in Europe and 38 million in the United States). People migrate primarily for economic reasons (i.e., to improve their standard of living and provide more opportunities for their children), but some do so to escape political and religious oppression. The 38 million foreign-born people who live in the United States represent 12.6 percent of the U.S. population. Of these, over 11 million, or nearly 30 percent, entered the nation illegally. Most nations impose restrictions on immigration to reduce the inflow of low-skilled people (while often encouraging the immigration of highly skilled and technical people). Migration is generally more restricted and regulated than the international

flow of goods, services and capital. (International labor migration is examined in detail in Section 9.10.)

In general, capital flows more freely across national boundaries than people. Financial or portfolio capital (bank loans and bonds) generally move to nations and markets where interest rates are higher, and foreign direct investments in plants and firms flows to nations where expected profits are higher. This leads to the more efficient use of capital and generally benefits both lenders and borrowers. During the 1970s, Middle Eastern nations deposited a great deal of their huge earnings from petroleum exports in New York and London banks, which then lent (recycled) them to Latin American and Asian governments and corporations. During the 1980s, Japan invested a large chunk of its huge export earnings in financial assets and real estate and set up corporate subsidiaries in the United States.

Since the mid-1980s, the United States has become an increasingly large net borrower from the rest of the world to cover its excess of spending over production (see Case Study 1-5). Global banks established branches in major international monetary centers around the world (New York, London, Frankfurt, Tokyo, Singapore), nearly \$2 trillion (about 14 percent of the size of the US GDP or economy) of foreign currencies are exchanged each day by around the clock trading in world financial centers, and newly established sovereign funds (financial institutions owned by Middle Eastern petroleum exporting nations, Singapore, China, Russia and Brazil) are making huge investments of all kinds all over the world. Financial markets are globalized as never before. (International capital flows are examined in detail in Chapter 9.)

> **Concept Check**
>
> Why is globalization important? Why is it inevitable?

International trade theory Analyzes the basis and the gains from trade.

International trade policy Examines the reasons for and effects of trade restrictions.

Balance of payments A summary statement of all the international transactions of the residents of a nation with the rest of the world during a particular period of time, usually a year.

Foreign exchange markets The framework for the exchange of one national currency for another.

1.5 THE SUBJECT MATTER OF INTERNATIONAL ECONOMICS

International economics deals with the economic and financial interdependence among nations. It analyzes the flow of goods, services, payments, and monies between a nation and the rest of the world, the policies directed at regulating these flows, and their effect on the nation's welfare. This economic and financial interdependence is affected by, and in turn influences, the political, social, cultural, and military relations among nations.

Specifically, international economics deals with international trade theory, international trade policy, the balance of payments and foreign exchange markets, and open-economy macroeconomics. International trade theory analyzes the basis for and the gains from trade. International trade policy examines the reasons for and the effects of trade restrictions. The balance of payments measures a nation's total receipts from and the total payments to the rest of the world, while foreign exchange markets is the institutional framework for the exchange of one national currency for others. Finally, open-economy macroeconomics deals with the mechanisms of

CASE STUDY 1-5

Major Net Exporters and Importers of Capital

Table 1.3 shows data on the major net exporters and importers of capital in 2007. Practically all nations export and import capital as their investors take advantage of foreign lending and investment opportunities, cover risk, and diversify their portfolios. Nations that export more capital than they import are the net capital exporters on the world scene, while those that import more capital than they export are

the net capital importers. From the table we see that China is by far the largest net capital exporter, followed by Japan and Germany. The United States, on the other hand, is by far the largest net capital importer. The United States is simply spending too much and living beyond its means—a situation that the United States needs to correct.

Table 1.3. *Major Net Exporters and Importers of Capital in 2007*

Net Exporters of Capital	Percent of World Capital Exports	Net Importers of Capital	Percent of World Capital Imports
China	21.4	United States	49.4
Japan	12.6	Spain	9.3
Germany	11.0	United Kingdom	9.1
Saudi Arabia	6.0	Australia	3.4
Russia	4.5	Italy	3.2
Switzerland	4.2	Greece	2.9
Norway	3.6	Turkey	2.5
Other	36.6	Other	20.2

Source: IMF, *International Financial Statistics*, 2008.

Adjustment in the balance of payments The operation and effects of the mechanisms for correcting balance-of-payments disequilibria.

Concept Check

What is the subject matter of international economics?

adjustment in the balance of payments disequilibria (deficits and surpluses). More importantly, it analyzes the relationship between the internal and the external sectors of the economy of a nation, and how they are interrelated or interdependent with the rest of the world economy under different types of international monetary systems.

International trade theory and policies are the microeconomic aspects of international economics because they deal with *individual* nations treated as single units and with the (relative) price of *individual* commodities. On the other hand, since the balance of payments deals with *total* receipts and payments, as well as with adjustment and other economic policies that affect the level of *national* income and the *general* price of the nation as a whole, they represent the macroeconomic aspects of international economics. These are often referred to as open-economy macroeconomics or international finance.

Microeconomics
The study of individual units, such as a particular nation and the relative price of a single commodity.

Macroeconomics
The study of the whole or the aggregate, such as the total receipts and payments of a nation and the general price index.

Open-economy macroeconomics or International finance The study of foreign exchange markets, the balance of payments, and adjustment to balance-of-payments disequilibria.

International economic relations differ from interregional economic relations (i.e., the economic relations among different parts of the same nation), thus requiring somewhat different tools of analysis and justifying international economics as a distinct branch of economics. That is, nations usually impose some restrictions on the flow of goods, services, and factors across their borders, but not internally. In addition, international flows are to some extent hampered by differences in language, customs, and laws. Furthermore, international flows of goods, services, and resources give rise to payments and receipts in foreign currencies, which change in value over time.

The field of international economics has enjoyed a long, continuous, and rich development over the past two centuries, with contributions from some of the world's most distinguished economists, from *Adam Smith* to *David Ricardo, John Stuart Mill, Alfred Marshall, John Maynard Keynes*, and *Paul Samuelson*. Other special branches of economics are of more recent vintage, and none can claim such a distinguished list of contributors and background.

1.6 CURRENT INTERNATIONAL ECONOMIC PROBLEMS

In this section, we briefly identify the most important international economic problems facing the world today. These are the problems that the study of international economic theories and policies can help us understand, and evaluate suggestions for their resolution. The most serious international trade problem facing the world today is the rising protectionism in advanced countries in the context of a rapidly globalizing world. The most serious international monetary problems are the excessive volatility of exchange rates (i.e., the very large fluctuations in the international value of national currencies) and their large and persistent misalignments (i.e., the fact that exchange rates can be far out of equilibrium for long periods of time), as well as the danger of frequent international financial crises. Other serious international economic problems are the deep structural imbalances in the United States, slow growth in Europe and Japan, and insufficient restructuring in the transition economies of Central and Eastern Europe; the deep poverty in many developing countries; and resource scarcity, environmental degradation, and climate change and the danger they pose for continued growth and sustainable world development. A brief description of these problems follows.

1. Trade Protectionism in Advanced Countries in a Rapidly Globalizing World

In the study of the pure theory of international trade in Part One (Chapters 2–4), we will see that the best policy for the world as a whole

is free trade. With free trade, each nation will specialize in the production of the commodities that it can produce most efficiently and, by exporting some of them, obtain more of the other commodities than it could produce at home. In the real world, however, most nations impose some restrictions on the free flow of trade. Although invariably justified on national welfare grounds, trade restrictions are usually advocated by and greatly benefit a small minority of producers in the nation at the expense of the mostly silent majority of consumers. The problem is now exacerbated by the increasing competitive challenge that advanced countries face from the leading emerging market economies, particularly China and India. Widespread fears of large job losses have led to calls for protection from foreign competition in advanced countries, especially the United States. The challenge for advanced countries is how to remain competitive, avoid major job losses, share in the benefits of globalization, and avoid increased protectionism. How advanced countries can meet this challenge is examined in Part Two (Chapters 5 and 6) of the text.

2. Excessive Fluctuations and Misalignment in Exchange Rates and Financial Crises

In the study of international finance in Part Four (Chapters 10–12), we will see that exchange rates have exhibited excessive fluctuations and volatility, as well as persistent misalignments or disequilibria. Periodic financial crises have also led to financial and economic instability and dampened growth in advanced and emerging markets alike—witness the financial crisis that started in Southeast Asia in 1997 and the United States in 2007. These can disrupt the pattern of international trade and specialization and can lead to unstable international financial conditions throughout the world. They have also led to renewed calls for reforms of the present international monetary system and for more international coordination of economic policies among the leading economies (examined in Chapters 15 and 16 in Part Six of the text).

3. Structural Imbalances in the United States, Slow Growth in Europe and Japan, and Insufficient Restructuring in Transition Economies

The United States faces deep structural imbalances in the form of excessive spending and inadequate national saving. This means that the United States is simply living beyond its means by borrowing excessively abroad. The result is a huge and unsustainable trade deficit, a depreciated dollar, and unstable financial conditions. Europe faces inflexible labor markets and Japan serious inefficiencies in its distribution system, which slows their growth. Transition economies (the former communist countries of Central and Eastern Europe)

require additional economic restructuring in order to establish full-fledged market economies and achieve more rapid growth. Inadequate growth in these areas slows the growth of the entire world economy and leads to calls for protectionism. Thus, we see how national and regional challenges quickly become global economic problems in our interdependent world. Part Four of the text (dealing with open-economy macroeconomics) examines the policies available to address these challenges.

4. Deep Poverty in Many Developing Countries

Even though many developing countries, especially China and India, are now growing very rapidly, some of the poorest developing nations, particularly those of sub-Saharan Africa, face deep poverty, unmanageable international debts, economic stagnation, and widening international inequalities in living standards. There are today more than 1 billion people (about one-sixth of the world population) who live on less than $1 a day! A world where millions of people starve each year is not only unacceptable from an ethical point of view, but it can hardly be expected to be peaceful and tranquil. Chapters 8 and 16 will examine why international inequalities in standards of living between the rich and many of the poorest developing countries of the world are so large and widening, and what can be done to stimulate growth in the world's poorest countries.

Concept Check

What are the major inter-national economic problems-facing the world economy today?

5. Resource Scarcity, Environmental Degradation, Climate Change, and Sustainable Development

Growth in rich countries and development in poor countries are now threatened by resource scarcity, environmental degradation, and climate change. In the face of rapidly growing demand, particularly by China and India, and supply rigidities in producing nations, the price of petroleum and other raw materials has risen sharply during the past few years, and so has the price of food. In many leading emerging market economies protection of the environment takes a back seat to the growth imperative. Environmental pollution is dramatic in some parts of China, and the Amazon forest is rapidly being destroyed. And we are witnessing very dangerous climate changes that may have increasingly dramatic effects on life on earth. These problems can only be adequately analyzed and addressed by a joint effort of all the sciences, a major world-wide cooperative effort, and a change in world governance.

1.7 INTERNATIONAL INSTITUTIONS AND THE WORLD ECONOMY

The world economic, financial, and political system is regulated by four specialized international institutions: the World Trade Organization, World

Bank, International Monetary Fund, and United Nations. In this section we briefly describe their function.

World Trade Organization (WTO) The international organization that regulates international trade in goods and services.

World Trade Organization (WTO). The Geneva-based international organization to which most nations of the world belong with authority over international trade in goods and services. Specifically, it deals with the rules of trade between nations, negotiates and implements new trade agreements, adjudicates (i.e., rules) over trade disputes among its members, and is in charge of policing member countries' adherence to all the WTO agreements. The WTO came into existence on January 1, 1995 as the successor of the General Agreement on Tariffs and Trade (GATT), which was created in 1948. The GATT and the WTO sponsored eight successful multilateral trade negotiations that sharply reduced tariffs and other trade barriers. The WTO was the host to new negotiations, under the Doha Development Agenda (DDA) launched in 2001, but it failed in July 2008.

World Bank The bank that provides loans to developing countries for developing programs and poverty reduction.

World Bank. (also called the International Bank for Reconstruction and Development or IBRD). The internationally supported bank established after World War II that provides loans to developing countries for development programs (e.g., bridges, roads, schools) with the stated goal of reducing poverty. Immediately after World War II, the bank also made loans to developed countries for reconstruction from the war devastation. Over time, most of the bank's loans have been for development purposes, although it also makes some loans for other post-conflict reconstruction, reconstruction after natural disasters, response to humanitarian emergencies, and post-conflict rehabilitation in needy developing and transition economies.

International Monetary Fund (IMF) The organization that oversees that rules in international finance are followed.

International Monetary Fund (IMF). The Washington, D.C.–headquartered international organization that oversees that member nations follow a set of agreed-upon rules of conduct in international finance and provides borrowing facilities for nations with temporary balance of payments difficulties. Specifically, it oversees the global financial system by following the macroeconomic policies of its member countries, in particular those with an impact on exchange rates and the balance of payments. It also offers financial and technical assistance to its members, making it an international lender of last resort.

United Nations The international organization to facilitate cooperation in international law, security, economic development, social progress, and human rights.

Concept Check

What is the function of each of the major international economic organizations?

United Nations (UN). The 192-member international organization with headquarters in New York City whose stated aims are to facilitate cooperation in international law, international security, economic development, social progress, and human rights issues. The UN was founded in 1945 to replace the League of Nations, to stop wars between nations, and to provide a platform for peacefully resolving international disagreements.

1.8 ORGANIZATION OF THE TEXT

This text is organized into six parts. Part One (Chapters 2–4) deals with international trade theory. It starts with the explanation of the important theory of comparative advantage in Chapter 2, it examines the basis for and the gains from trade with the standard trade model in Chapter 3, and it presents the modern theories on international trade based on factor endowments, economies of scale, and imperfect competition in Chapter 4.

Part Two (Chapters 5–6) deals with international trade policies. Chapter 5 examines tariffs, while Chapter 6 deals with nontariff trade barriers, the political economy of protectionism, and the history of commercial policies of the United States and in other nations over the past decades.

Part Three (Chapters 7–9) deals with international trade and investment relations. Chapter 7 deals with economic integration among a group of nations; Chapter 8 examines economic growth and the effects of international trade on economic development, while Chapter 9 discusses international resource movements and multinational corporations.

Part Four (Chapters 10–12) deals with the balance of payments, foreign exchange markets, and exchange rate determination. A clear grasp of these three chapters is crucial for understanding Part Five, on the adjustment to balance-of-payments disequilibria and open-economy macroeconomics. Chapter 10 deals with the measurement of a nation's balance of payments; Chapter 11 examines the operation of foreign exchange markets, while Chapter 12 discusses the forces that determine exchange rates and the reasons for great volatility.

Part Five (Chapters 13–14) examines the various mechanisms for adjusting balance-of-payments disequilibria, which are often referred to as "open-economy macroeconomics." Chapter 13 examines the adjustment mechanism that operates through variations in domestic and foreign prices and incomes. Chapter 14 deals with adjustment policies by changing taxes, interest rates, and exchange rates.

Part Six (Chapters 15–16) examines the operation of the international economy. Chapter 15 compares fixed and flexible exchange rate systems, examines the European Monetary System, and discusses international macroeconomic policy coordination. Chapter 16 examines the operation of the international monetary system and it offers possible solutions for the major international economic problems facing the world today.

Besides the numerous examples and current events woven throughout the text to illustrate a theory or a point, from three to seven specific case studies are presented in each chapter of the text. These real-world cases are generally short and to the point, and serve to reinforce understanding of and to highlight the most important topics presented in the chapter. Important terms are printed in boldface when they are first introduced and explained (as in this chapter) and are then collected with their definitions in

the general Glossary at the end of the text. The selected bibliography gives the most important references for the topics examined in the chapter, while INTERNet provides international economics Internet site addresses or links with information on where to access additional information.

SUMMARY

1. The world today is in the midst of a revolution based on the globalization of tastes, production, labor markets, and financial markets. Globalization is important because it increases efficiency; it is inevitable because international competition requires it. Globalization is being blamed for increased world income inequalities, child labor, environmental pollution, and other problems, and it has given rise to a strong anti-globalization movement.

2. The United States relies on international trade to obtain many products that it does not produce and some minerals of which it has no deposits, or dwindling domestic reserves. More important *quantitatively* for the nation's standard of living are the many products that could be produced domestically but only at a higher cost than abroad. International trade is even more crucial to the well-being of other nations.

3. Besides trade, the international flow of people (migration) and capital across national boundaries are other measures of economic integration of the world economy. There are today about 190 million people in the world who live in a country other than the one in which they were born, of which about 38 million are in the United States. Huge amounts of capital (in the form of bank loans, bonds, and foreign direct investments in plants and firms) move across national boundaries each year.

4. International economics deals with the pure theory of trade, the theory of commercial policy, growth and the international movement of resources, the balance of payments, foreign exchange markets, and adjustment in the balance of payments or open-economy macroeconomics. The first three topics are the microeconomic aspects of international economics; the latter three are the macroeconomic aspects, also known as international finance.

5. The major international economic problems facing the world today are (1) trade protectionism in advanced countries in a rapidly globalizing world, (2) excessive volatility and large disequilibria in exchange rates, as well as frequent international financial crises, (3) the need for economic restructuring in Europe, Japan, and in the former communist countries of Central and Eastern Europe, (4) deep poverty in many developing countries, and (5) resource scarcity, environmental degradation, and climate change.

6. The world's economic, financial, and political systems are regulated by four specialized international institutions: the World Trade Organization, World Bank, International Monetary Fund, and United Nations.

7. This text is organized into six parts. Part One (Chapters 2–4) deals with international trade theory. Part Two (Chapters 5–6) discusses international trade policies. Part Three (Chapters 7–9) examines international trade and investment relations. Part Four (Chapters 10–12) deals with the balance of payments, foreign exchange markets, and exchange rate determination. Part Five (Chapters 13–14) discusses the various mechanisms for adjusting balance-of-payments disequilibria or open-economy macroeconomics. Part Six (Chapters 15–16) examines the operation of the international economy and plans to improve its functioning. Three to seven specific case studies are presented in each chapter to highlight the relevance of the study of international economics in the world today.

REVIEW QUESTIONS AND PROBLEMS

1. What is the meaning of globalization? What is its advantage and disadvantage? Why is there an anti-globalization movement?

2. How do international economic relations differ from interregional (i.e., within a country) economic relations?

3. How can we get a rough measure of the economic interdependence of each nation with the rest of the world?

4. Why does the United States rely less on international trade than most other developed nations?

5. What would happen to the U.S. standard of living if the United States withdrew completely from international trade?

6. What is the benefit and cost of immigration to the United States?

7. Why does capital flow across national boundaries?

8. What are the major international economic problems facing the world today?

9. Which are the most important international institutions? What is the function of each?

10. How do the problems facing the world today affect the United States? You personally?

International Trade Data, Sources, and Information

In this appendix, we present basic data on the commodity and geographic concentration of international trade, as well as on the world's leading exporters and importers of goods and services. We also provide sources of additional international data and information on current events.

A1.1 INTERNATIONAL TRADE DATA

Table 1.4 shows the commodity composition of world merchandise (goods) trade in 2006. It shows that of the total world merchandise exports of $12,083 billion, $945 billion or 7.8 percent were in agricultural products, $2,277 billion (or 18.8 percent) were in fuels and mining products (of which $1,771 billion or 14.7 percent were in fuels), and $8,257 billion or 68.3 percent were in manufactures (of which $1,451 billion or 12.0 percent were in office and telecom equipment, $1,248 billion or 10.3 percent in chemical, and $1,016 billion or 8.4 percent in automotive products). Thus, more than two-thirds of total world merchandise exports were manufactures, 18.8 percent in fuels and mining products, and 7.8 percent in agricultural products.

Table 1.5 shows the geographic composition of world merchandise trade in 2006. It shows that of the total of $12,083 billion world merchandise exports, $1,678 billion or 14.2 percent originated in North America (of which $1,038 billion or 8.6 percent in the United States), $430 billion or 3.6 percent

Table 1.4. *Commodity Composition of World Merchandise Trade, 2006 (billion dollars and percentage share of world total)*

Category	Value of Exports	Percent of World Exports
Agricultural products	$ 945	7.8
Fuels and mining products	2,277	18.8
Fuels	1,771	14.7
Manufactures	8,257	68.3
Iron and steel	374	3.1
Chemicals	1,248	10.3
Office and telecom equipment	1,451	12.0
Automotive products	1,016	8.4
Textiles	219	1.8
Clothing	311	2.6
Other	604	5.0
Total merchandise exports	12,083	100.0

Source: WTO, *International Trade* (Geneva, 2007), Table II.1.

originated in South and Central America (of which $138 billion or 1.1 percent in Brazil), $4,963 billion or 42.1 percent originated in Europe (of which $1,112 billion or 9.2 percent in Germany), $426 billion or 3.6 percent came from the Commonwealth of Independent States or CIS (of which $305 billion or 2.5 percent from the Russian Federation), $363 billion or 3.1 percent originated in Africa (of which $58 billion or 0.5 percent from South Africa), $646 billion or 5.5 percent (mostly petroleum) originated in the Middle East, and $3,278 billion or 27.8 percent came from Asia (of which $969 billion or 8.0 percent from China, $650 billion or 5.4 percent from Japan, and $1,131 billion or 9.6 percent from the Six East Asian Traders). Thus, Europe and Asia were by far the world's largest exporters, followed by North America. Table 1.5 also shows the geographic composition of world merchandise imports in 2006.

Table 1.6 shows the geographic destination of the merchandise exports of various regions in 2006. The first column of the table shows that 38.4 percent of the merchandise exports of North America went to North America (these are U.S. exports to Canada and Mexico, and Canadian and Mexican exports to the United States and to each other), 5.7 percent went to South and Central America, 18.3 percent went to Europe, 1.0 percent went to the Commonwealth of Independent States (CIS), 3.4 percent went to Africa, 3.1 percent to the Middle East, and 30.1 went to Asia. The second column of Table 1.6 shows that North America was the main trade partner of South and Central America (outside the region), followed by Asia and Europe. The third column shows that 71.3 percent of European trade is within or intra-regional trade. As expected, Europe represents by far the largest trade partner of the Commonwealth of Independent States (CIS), as well as Africa,

Table 1.5. *Geographical Composition of World Merchandise Trade, 2006 (billion dollars and percentage share of world total)*

Region or Country	Value of Exports	Share (%)	Value of Imports	Share (%)
North America	$1,678	14.2	$2,607	21.0
United States	1,038	8.6	1,919	15.5
Canada	390	3.2	358	2.9
Mexico	250	2.1	268	2.2
South and Central America	430	3.6	373	3.0
Brazil	138	1.1	96	0.8
Europe	4,963	42.1	5,350	43.1
Germany	1,112	9.2	909	7.3
France	490	4.1	535	5.0
United Kingdom	448	3.7	619	5.0
Italy	411	3.4	437	3.5
Commonwealth Indep. States (CIS)[a]	426	3.6	285	2.3
Russian Federation	305	2.5	164	1.3
Africa	363	3.1	298	2.4
South Africa	58	0.5	77	0.6
Middle East	646	5.5	385	3.1
Asia	3,278	27.8	3,103	25.0
China	969	8.0	792	6.4
Japan	650	5.4	580	4.7
India	120	1.0	175	1.4
Six East Asian Traders[b]	1,131	9.6	1,068	8.6
World	12,083	100.0	12,413	100.0

[a]Armenia, Azerbaijan, Belarus, Georgia, Kazakhstan, Kyrgyz Republic, Moldova, Russian Federation, Tajikistan, Turkmenistan, Ukraine, and Ubzbekistan.

[b]Rep. of Korea, Malaysia, Philippines, Chinese Taipei, Thailand, Singapore.

Note: The values may not add up to 100 because of rounding.

Source: WTO, *Annual Report* (Geneva, 2007), Table I.6, I.7, and I.8.

while the Middle East exports (mostly petroleum) primarily to Europe, Asia and the United States.

Table 1.7 ranks the world's leading merchandise exporting and importing countries in 2006. The table shows that the world's top exporters and importers are the largest industrial countries and China, with Germany leading the list of the world exporters and the United States leading the list of the world importers. China moved very rapidly in the ranks of the largest world merchandise exporters and importers and now occupies third place, after Germany and the United States, in both categories.

Table 1.8 shows the world's leading exporting and importing countries of commercial services in 2006. The ranking is similar to that for merchandise trade, except for China that ranks eighth in exports and sixth in imports.

Table 1.6. *Geographical Destination of Merchandise Exports, 2006 (percentages)*

	North America	South & Central America	Europe	Commonwealth Independent States (CIS)[a]	Africa	Middle East	Asia	World
North America	38.4%	28.4%	5.5%	2.8%	7.7%	11.0%	11.1%	14.2
South & Central America	5.7	29.5	1.7	2.1	4.0	2.1	2.2	3.6
Europe	18.3	17.6	71.3	48.7	42.6	33.8	12.9	42.1
Commonwealth of Independent States (CIS)	1.0	2.0	4.8	27.7	2.0	3.5	1.6	3.6
Africa	3.4	3.0	2.9	0.5	11.6	1.7	2.6	3.1
Middle East	3.1	1.2	2.0	1.0	7.4	18.8	12.0	5.5
Asia	30.1	18.4	11.8	17.1	24.7	29.2	57.7	27.8
World	100.0	100.0	100.0	100.0	100.0	100.0	100.0	100.0

[a] Armenia, Azerbaijan, Belarus, Georgia, Kazakhstan, Kyrgyz Republic, Moldova, Russian Federation, Tajikistan, Turkmenistan, Ukraine, and Ubzbekistan.

Note: The values may not add up to 100.0% because of incomplete coverage and rounding.

Source: WTO, *International Trade Statistics* (Geneva, 2007), Table III.3.

To be noted is that trade in commercial services is now more than one-fifth of merchandise trade and has been growing more rapidly than the latter as a reflection of the shift toward services in most countries, especially the advanced countries.

Table 1.7. *Leading Exporters and Importers of Merchandise, 2006 (billion dollars and percentage share of world total)*

	Exporters				Importers		
Rank	Country	Value	Share (%)	Rank	Country	Value	Share (%)
1	Germany	$1,112.0	9.2	1	United States	$1,919.4	15.5
2	United States	1,038.3	8.6	2	Germany	908.6	7.3
3	China	968.9	8.0	3	China	791.5	6.4
4	Japan	649.9	5.4	4	United Kingdom	619.4	5.0
5	France	490.4	4.1	5	Japan	579.6	4.7
6	Netherlands	462.4	3.8	6	France	534.9	4.3
7	United Kingdom	448.3	3.7	7	Italy	437.4	3.5
8	Italy	410.6	3.4	8	Netherlands	416.4	3.4
9	Canada	389.5	3.2	9	Canada	357.7	2.9
10	Belgium	369.2	3.1	10	Belgium	353.7	2.9
Total of above[a]		6,339.5	52.5	Total of above[a]		6,918.6	55.2
World[a]		12,083.0	100.0	World[a]		12,413.0	100.0

[a] Includes significant re-exports or imports for re-export.

Source: WTO, *Annual Report* (Geneva, 2007), Table I.8.

Table 1.8. *Leading Exporters and Importers of Commercial Services, 2007 (billion dollars and percentage share of world total)*

	Exporters				Importers		
Rank	*Country*	*Value*	*Share (%)*	*Rank*	*Country*	*Value*	*Share (%)*
1	United States	$388.8	14.1	1	United States	$307.8	11.6
2	United Kingdom	227.5	8.3	2	Germany	219.1	8.3
3	Germany	168.8	6.1	3	United Kingdom	172.0	6.5
4	Japan	122.5	4.4	4	Japan	144.0	5.4
5	France	114.5	4.2	5	France	108.8	4.1
6	Spain	105.5	3.8	6	China	100.3	3.8
7	Italy	97.5	3.5	7	Italy	98.4	3.7
8	China	91.4	3.3	8	Ireland	78.4	3.0
9	Netherlands	82.5	3.0	9	Netherlands	78.1	2.9
10	India	73.8	2.7	10	Spain	77.9	2.9
Total of above		1,472.8	53.5	Total of above		1,384.8	52.2
World		2,755.0	100.0	World		2,650.0	100.0

Source: WTO, *Annual Report* (Geneva, 2007), Table I.10.

A1.2 SOURCES OF ADDITIONAL INTERNATIONAL DATA AND INFORMATION

The most important sources of national and international trade and financial data, as well as for current events, are the following.

Published by the U.S. Government

Economic Report of the President (Washington, D.C.: U.S. Government Printing Office, annual) contains chapters on recent economic events, as well as time series data on the U.S. economy (including international trade and finance).

Statistical Abstract of the United States (Washington, D.C.: U.S. Department of Commerce, annual) includes a large amount of data on the United States, as well as comparative international statistics.

Survey of Current Business (Washington, D.C.: U.S. Department of Commerce, monthly) contains summary data on international trade by commodity group and geographic area, as well as other domestic and international data.

Published by International Organizations

Direction of Trade Statistics (Washington, D.C.: International Monetary Fund, quarterly and annual) includes detailed data on the exports and imports of each of 186 countries to and from every other country of the world.

International Financial Statistics (Washington, D.C.: International Monetary Fund, monthly and annual) includes a great variety of economic data on 212 countries.

International Trade Statistics (Geneva: World Trade Organization, annual) gives trade data on each of 147 member countries and various groupings of nations.

OECD Economic Outlook (Paris: Organization for Economic Cooperation and Development, June and December of each year) contains analyses of recent events and OECD projections about future economic activity, as well as summary data tables on the 30 member countries and groups of countries.

World Economic Outlook (Washington, D.C.: International Monetary Fund, April and October of each year) contains analyses of recent events and IMF projections about future economic activity, as well as summary data tables on the leading industrial countries and groups of countries.

World Development Report (Oxford University Press, for the World Bank, annual) contains economic and social data for developing countries, as well as analysis of recent events and projections for the future.

Current Events Sources

Chicago Tribune (daily)	*Business Week* (weekly)
Los Angeles Times (daily)	*Forbes* (biweekly)
New York Times (daily)	*Fortune* (biweekly)
Washington Post (daily)	*IMF Survey* (biweekly)
Financial Times (daily)	*The Economist* (weekly)
Wall Street Journal (daily)	

SELECTED BIBLIOGRAPHY

- J. Stiglitz, *Globalization and Its Discontents* (New York: Norton, 2003).

- J. Bhagwati, *In Defense of Globalization* (New York: Oxford University Press, 2004).

- T. Friedman, *The World Is Flat: Further Updated and Expanded* (New York: Farrar, Straus, Giroux, 2007).

For a discussion of the operation of the present international trading system, see:

- P. Krugman, *Pop Internationalism* (Cambridge, Mass.: MIT Press, 1996).

- J. N. Bhagwati, *Free Trade Today* (Princeton, N.J.: Princeton University Press, 2002).

A discussion of the operation of the present international monetary system is found in:

- R. Solomon, *Money on the Move* (Princeton, N.J.: Princeton University Press, 1999).
- P. B. Kenen, *The International Financial Architecture* (Washington, D.C.: Institute for International Economics, 2001).
- D. Salvatore, ed., "The Dollar, the Euro, and the International Monetary System," Special Issue of the *Journal of Policy Modeling*, June 2005 (with the participation of some of the world's leading experts).

Globalization and the problem of poverty in the world today are discussed in:

- The World Bank, *Globalization, Growth and Poverty* (Washington, D.C.: The World Bank, 2002).
- J. Sachs, *The End of Poverty* (New York: Penguins Press, 2005).
- D. Salvatore, "Economic Growth, Cross-Country Inequality, and World Poverty during Globalization," *Journal of Policy Modeling*, June 2007, pp. 635–642.

INTERNet

The Internet site addresses for the International Monetary Fund (IMF), World Trade Organization (WTO), Organization for Economic Cooperation and Development (OECD), World Bank, and United Nations, which contain a wealth of trade and financial information and data (including the reports listed in the Selected Bibliography) are, respectively:

http://www.imf.org

http://www.wto.org

http://www.oecd.org

http://worldbank.org

http://unstats.un.org/unsd

Extensive recent and historical data on U.S. exports, imports, and trade balances with individual countries can be found in:

http://www.census.gov/ftp/pub/foreign-trade/www

The web site for the Institute for International Economics, which publishes many reports and analyses on international trade and international finance, is:

http://www.iie.com

International Trade Theory

Part One (Chapters 2–4) deals with international trade theory. It starts with the explanation of the important theory of comparative advantage in Chapter 2, it examines the basis for and the gains from trade with the standard trade model in Chapter 3, and it presents the modern theories on international trade based on factor endowments, economies of scale, and imperfect competition in Chapter 4.

Comparative Advantage

After studying this chapter, you should be able to:

- Explain the mercantilists' views on trade
- Explain how trade can be based on absolute advantage
- Understand the law of comparative advantage
- Understand the relationship between opportunity costs and relative commodity prices
- Show the basis and the gains from trade under constant costs

CHAPTER OUTLINE

KEY TERMS

Basis for trade	Labor theory of value
Gains from trade	Opportunity cost theory
Pattern of trade	Production possibility frontier
Mercantilism	Constant opportunity costs
Absolute advantage	Relative commodity prices
Laissez-faire	Complete specialization
Law of comparative advantage	Small-country case

2.1 INTRODUCTION

In this chapter, we examine the development of trade theory from the seventeenth century through the first part of the twentieth century. This historical approach is useful not because we are interested in the history of economic thought, as such, but because it is a convenient way of introducing the concepts and theories of international trade from the simple to the more complex and realistic.

The basic questions that we seek to answer in this chapter are:

Basis for trade The forces that give rise to trade between two nations. This was absolute advantage according to Adam Smith and comparative advantage according to David Ricardo.

1. What is the basis for trade and what are the gains from trade? Presumably (and as in the case of an individual), a nation will voluntarily engage in trade only if it benefits from trade. But how are gains from trade generated? How large are the gains and how are they divided among the trading nations?

2. What is the pattern of trade? That is, what commodities are traded and which commodities are exported and imported by each nation?

Gains from trade The increase in consumption in each nation resulting from specialization in production and trading.

We begin with a brief discussion of the economic doctrine known as mercantilism that prevailed during the seventeenth and eighteenth centuries. We then go on to discuss the theory of absolute advantage, developed by Adam Smith. It remained for David Ricardo, however, writing some 40 years after Smith, to truly explain the pattern and the gains from trade with his law of comparative advantage. The law of comparative advantage is one of the most important laws of economics, with applicability to nations, as well as to individuals, and useful for exposing many serious fallacies in apparently logical reasoning.

Pattern of trade The commodities exported and imported by each nation.

One difficulty remained. Ricardo had based his *explanation* of the law of comparative advantage on the *labor theory of value*, which was subsequently rejected. In the first part of the twentieth century, Gottfried Haberler came to Ricardo's "rescue" by explaining the law of comparative advantage in terms of the opportunity cost theory, as reflected in production possibility frontiers or transformation curves.

For simplicity, our discussion will initially refer to only two nations and two commodities. In the appendix to this chapter, the conclusions will be generalized to trade in more than two commodities and more than two nations.

2.2 MERCANTILISTS' VIEWS ON TRADE

Economics, as an organized science, originated with the publication of *The Wealth of Nations* in 1776 by Adam Smith. However, writings on international trade preceded this date in such countries as England, Spain, France, Portugal, and the Netherlands as they developed into modern national states. Specifically, during the seventeenth and eighteenth centuries a group of men (merchants, bankers, government officials, and even philosophers) wrote essays and pamphlets on international trade that advocated the economic philosophy of mercantilism.

Mercantilism The body of writings prevailing during the seventeenth and eighteenth centuries that postulated that the way for a nation to become richer was to restrict imports and stimulate exports. Thus, one nation could gain only at the expense of other nations.

Mercantilists maintained that the way for a nation to become rich and powerful was to export more than it imported. The resulting export surplus would then be settled by an inflow of bullion, or precious metals, primarily gold and silver. The more gold and silver a nation had, the richer and more powerful it was. Thus, the government had to do all in its power to stimulate

the nation's exports and discourage and restrict imports (particularly the import of luxury consumption goods). However, since all nations could not simultaneously have an export surplus and the amount of gold and silver was fixed at any particular point in time, one nation could gain only at the expense of other nations. The mercantilists thus preached economic nationalism, believing that national interests were basically in conflict.

The mercantilists measured the wealth of a nation by the stock of precious metals it possessed. In contrast, today we measure the wealth of a nation by its stock of human, man-made, and natural resources available for producing goods and services. The greater this stock of useful resources, the greater the *flow* of goods and services to satisfy human wants, and the higher the standard of living in the nation.

There were, however, more rational reasons for the mercantilists' desire to accumulate precious metals. Remember that mercantilists were writing primarily for their nation's rulers and to enhance national power. With more gold, rulers could maintain larger and better armies and consolidate their power at home; improved armies and navies also made it possible for them to acquire more colonies. In addition, more gold meant more money (i.e., more gold coins) in circulation and greater business activity. Furthermore, by encouraging exports and restricting imports, the government would encourage the development of new industries and encourage national output and employment.

Concept Check

What were the mercantilists' views on trade? Are these ideas still alive today?

In any event, mercantilists advocated strict government control over all economic activity and preached economic nationalism because they believed that a nation could gain in trade only at the expense of other nations (i.e., they regarded trade as a zero-sum game). These views are important for two reasons. First, the ideas of Adam Smith, David Ricardo, and other classical economists who followed can best be understood as reactions to the mercantilists' views on trade and on the role of government. Second, today there seems to be a resurgence of neo-mercantilism, as nations plagued by slow growth and high levels of unemployment seek to restrict imports in an effort to stimulate domestic production and employment (this is examined in detail in Chapter 6). In fact, aside from England during the period 1815–1914, no Western nation has ever been completely free of mercantilist ideas (see Case Study 2-1).

2.3 TRADE BASED ON ABSOLUTE ADVANTAGE: ADAM SMITH

Smith started with the simple truth that for two nations to *voluntarily* trade with each other, both nations must gain. If one nation gained nothing or lost, it would simply refuse to trade. But how does this mutually beneficial trade take place and from where do these gains from trade come?

CASE STUDY 2-1

Mercantilism Is Alive and Well in the Twenty-First Century

Although most nations claim to be in favor of free trade, most of them continue to impose many restrictions on international trade. Most industrial nations restrict imports of agricultural commodities, textiles, shoes, steel, and many other products in order to protect domestic employment. They also provide subsidies to some of their high-tech industries, such as computers and telecommunication, deemed essential for the international competitiveness of the nation and its future growth. Developing countries are even more protective of domestic industries. As overt protection (in the form of tariffs and quotas) has been reduced or eliminated over the years through multilateral negotiations, other less explicit types of protection (such as tax benefits and subsidies for research and development) have been increased. This is evidenced by the numerous trade disputes that have arisen over the years.

During the past few years, there have been disputes between the United States and the European Union (EU) on the latter's prohibition of U.S. beef exports from cattle raised with hormones and on genetically modified foods; on the EU preferences for banana imports from African countries at the expense of bananas from Central American plantations (owned by American business interests); on EU subsidies to Airbus Industrie for the development of its new super jumbo jet that will take sales away from the Boeing's 747; on the tax rebates that the U.S. government provided to some exporters; and on the 30 percent tariff that the United States imposed in 2002 on imported steel. There are similarly many other trade disputes between the United States, Japan, other developed and developing countries, and among all these countries with one another. Indeed, the list of protected products is long and varied. Trade restrictions are demanded to protect domestic jobs from foreign competition and to encourage domestic high-tech industries—all classic mercantilist arguments. This proves that mercantilism, though declining, is alive and well in the twenty-first century.

Source: J. N. Bhagwati, *Free Trade Today* (Princeton, N.J.: Princeton University Press, 2002); D. A. Irwin, *Free Trade Under Fire* (Princeton, N.J.: Princeton University Press, 2002); and D. Salvatore, ed., *Protectionism and World Welfare* (New York: Cambridge University Press, 1993).

Absolute advantage
The greater efficiency that one nation may have over another in the production of a commodity. This was the basis for trade for Adam Smith.

Concept Check

How is absolute advantage determined?

According to Adam Smith, trade between two nations is based on absolute advantage. When one nation is more efficient than (or has an absolute advantage over) another in the production of one commodity but is less efficient than (or has an absolute disadvantage with respect to) the other nation in producing a second commodity, then both nations can gain by each specializing in the production of the commodity of its absolute advantage and exchanging part of its output with the other nation for the commodity of its absolute disadvantage. By this process, the resources of both nations are utilized most efficiently and the output of both commodities will rise. The increase in the output of both commodities measures the gains from specialization in production available to be divided or shared between the two nations through trade.

For example, because of climatic conditions, Canada is efficient in growing wheat but inefficient in growing bananas (hothouses would have to be used). On the other hand, Nicaragua is efficient in growing bananas but inefficient in growing wheat. Thus, Canada has an absolute advantage over Nicaragua in the cultivation of wheat but an absolute disadvantage in the cultivation of bananas. The opposite is true for Nicaragua. Under these circumstances, Canada would specialize in the production of wheat (i.e., produce more than needed domestically) and exchange some of it for (surplus) bananas grown in Nicaragua. As a result, both more wheat and more bananas would be grown and consumed, and both Canada and Nicaragua would gain.

Thus, while the mercantilists believed that one nation could gain only at the expense of other nations and advocated strict government control of all economic activity and trade, Adam Smith (and the other classical economists who followed him) believed that all nations would gain from free trade and strongly advocated a policy of laissez-faire (i.e., as little government interference with the economic system as possible). Free trade would lead to the most efficient use of world resources and would maximize world welfare. There were to be only a few exceptions to the policy of laissez-faire and free trade. One of these was the protection of industries important for national defense.

> **Laissez-faire** The policy of minimum government interference in or regulation of economic activity, advocated by Adam Smith and other classical economists.

In view of this belief, it seems paradoxical that today most nations impose many restrictions on the free flow of international trade. Trade restrictions are invariably rationalized in terms of national welfare. In reality, they are advocated by the few industries and their workers who benefit from the restrictions but hurt consumers, who will have to pay higher prices for competing domestic goods. These issues will be examined in detail in Part Two.

Absolute advantage can be examined with a simple numerical example. Table 2.1 shows that one hour of labor time produces six bushels of wheat in the United States but only one in the United Kingdom. On the other hand, one hour of labor time produces four yards of cloth in the United States but five in the United Kingdom. Thus, the United States is more efficient than, or has an absolute advantage over, the United Kingdom in the production of wheat, while the United Kingdom is more efficient than, or has an absolute advantage over, the United States in the production of cloth. With trade, the

Table 2.1. *Absolute Advantage*

	U.S.	U.K.
Wheat (bushels/hour)	6	1
Cloth (yards/hour)	4	5

United States would specialize in the production of wheat and exchange part of it for British cloth. The opposite is true for the United Kingdom.

If the United States exchanges six bushels of wheat (6W) for six yards of British cloth (6C), the United States gains 2C or saves one-half hour or 30 minutes of labor time (since the United States can only exchange 6W for 4C domestically). Similarly, the 6W that the United Kingdom receives from the United States is equivalent to or would require six hours of labor time to produce in the United Kingdom. These same six hours can produce 30C in the United Kingdom (6 hours times 5 yards of cloth per hour). By being able to exchange 6C (requiring a little over one hour to produce in the United Kingdom) for 6W with the United States, the United Kingdom gains 24C, or saves almost five hours of work.

The fact that the United Kingdom gains much more than the United States is not important at this point. What is important is that both nations can gain from specialization in production and trade. (We will see in Section 2.6 how the rate at which commodities are exchanged for one another is determined and how the gains from trade are divided among the trading nations.)

Absolute advantage, however, can explain only a very small part of world trade today, such as some of the trade between developed and developing countries. Most of world trade, especially trade among developed countries, cannot be explained by absolute advantage. It remained for David Ricardo, with the law of comparative advantage, to truly explain the basis for and the gains from trade. Indeed, absolute advantage will be seen as only a special case of the more general theory of comparative advantage.

2.4 TRADE BASED ON COMPARATIVE ADVANTAGE: DAVID RICARDO

Law of comparative advantage It postulates that a nation should specialize in and export the commodity in which its absolute disadvantage is smaller (this is the commodity of its comparative advantage), and should import the other commodity.

In 1817 Ricardo published his *Principles of Political Economy and Taxation*, in which he presented the law of comparative advantage. This is one of the most important and unchallenged laws of economics, with many practical applications. In this section, we will define the law of comparative advantage and restate it with a simple numerical example. In the next section, we will prove it by demonstrating that both nations can indeed gain by each specializing in the production and exportation of the commodity of its comparative advantage.

According to the law of comparative advantage, even if one nation is less efficient than (has an absolute disadvantage with respect to) the other nation in the production of *both* commodities, there is still a basis for mutually beneficial trade. The first nation should specialize in the production of and export the commodity in which its absolute disadvantage is smaller (this is the commodity of its *comparative advantage*) and import the commodity in which its absolute disadvantage is greater (this is the commodity of its *comparative disadvantage*).

Concept Check

Can you state the law of comparative advantage in your own words?

Table 2.2. *Comparative Advantage*

	U.S.	U.K.
Wheat (bushels/hour)	6	1
Cloth (yards/hour)	4	2

The statement of the law can be clarified by looking at Table 2.2. The only difference between Tables 2.2 and 2.1 is that the United Kingdom now produces only two yards of cloth per hour instead of five. Thus, the United Kingdom now has an absolute disadvantage in the production of both wheat and cloth with respect to the United States.

However, since U.K. labor is only half as productive in cloth but six times less productive in wheat with respect to the United States, *the United Kingdom has a comparative advantage in cloth*. On the other hand, the United States has an absolute advantage in both wheat and cloth with respect to the United Kingdom, but since its absolute advantage is greater in wheat (6:1) than in cloth (4:2), *the United States has a comparative advantage in wheat*.

To summarize, the U.S. absolute advantage is greater in wheat, and so the United States has a comparative advantage in wheat. The U.K. absolute disadvantage is smaller in cloth, so its comparative advantage lies in cloth. According to the law of comparative advantage, both nations can gain if the United States specializes in the production of wheat and exports some of it in exchange for British cloth. (At the same time, the United Kingdom specializes in the production and exporting of cloth.)

Note that in a two-nation, two-commodity world, once it is determined that one nation has a comparative advantage in one commodity, then the other nation must necessarily have a comparative advantage in the other commodity.

2.5 GAINS FROM TRADE WITH COMPARATIVE ADVANTAGE

To prove the law of comparative advantage, we must be able to show that the United States and the United Kingdom can both gain by each specializing in the production and exporting the commodity of its comparative advantage.

To start with, we know that the United States would be indifferent to trade if it received only 4C from the United Kingdom in exchange for 6W, since the United States can produce exactly 4C domestically by utilizing the resources released in giving up 6W (see Table 2.2). And the United States would certainly not trade if it received less than 4C for 6W. Similarly, the United Kingdom would be indifferent to trade if it had to give up 2C for each 1W it received from the United States, and it certainly would not trade if it had to give up more than 2C for 1W.

To show that both nations can gain, suppose the United States could exchange 6W for 6C with the United Kingdom. The United States would then gain 2C (or save one-half hour of labor time) since the United States could only exchange 6W for 4C domestically. To see that the United Kingdom would also gain, note that the 6W that the United Kingdom receives from the United States would require six hours of labor time to produce in the United Kingdom. The United Kingdom could instead use these six hours to produce 12C and give up only 6C for 6W from the United States. Thus, the United Kingdom would gain 6C or save three hours of labor time. Once again, the fact that the United Kingdom gains more from trade than the United States is not important at this point. What is important is that both nations can gain from trade even if one of them (in this case the United Kingdom) is less efficient than the other in the production of *both* commodities.

Concept Check

How can the law of comparative advantage be explained with a lawyer and secretary?

We can convince ourselves of this by considering a simple example from everyday life. Suppose a lawyer can type twice as fast as her secretary. The lawyer then has an absolute advantage over her secretary in both the practice of law and typing. However, since the secretary cannot practice law without a law degree, the lawyer has a greater absolute advantage or a comparative advantage in law, and the secretary has a comparative advantage in typing. According to the law of comparative advantage, the lawyer should spend all of her time practicing law and let her secretary do the typing. For example, if the lawyer earns $100 per hour practicing law and must pay her secretary $10 per hour to do the typing, she would actually lose $80 for each hour that she typed. The reason for this is that she would save $20 (since she can type twice as fast as her secretary) but forgo earning $100 in the practice of law.

Returning to the United States and the United Kingdom, we see that both nations would gain by exchanging 6W for 6C. However, this is not the only rate of exchange at which mutually beneficial trade can take place. Since the United States could exchange 6W for 4C domestically (in the sense that both require 1 hour to produce), the United States would gain if it could exchange 6W for more than 4C from the United Kingdom. On the other hand, in the United Kingdom 6W = 12C (in the sense that both require 6 hours to produce). Anything less than 12C that the United Kingdom must give up to obtain 6W from the United States represents a gain from trade for the United Kingdom. To summarize, the United States gains to the extent that it can exchange 6W for more than 4C from the United Kingdom. The United Kingdom gains to the extent that it can give up less than 12C for 6W from the United States. Thus, the range for mutually advantageous trade is

$$4C < 6W < 12C$$

The spread between 12C and 4C (i.e., 8C) represents the total gains from trade available to be shared by the two nations by trading 6W. For example, we have seen that when 6W are exchanged for 6C, the United States gains 2C and the United Kingdom 6C, making a total of 8C. The closer the rate of

exchange is to 4C = 6W (the *domestic*, or *internal*, rate in the United States—see Table 2.2), the smaller is the share of the gain going to the United States and the larger is the share of the gain going to the United Kingdom. On the other hand, the closer the rate of exchange is to 6W = 12C (the domestic, or internal, rate in the United Kingdom), the greater is the gain of the United States relative to that of the United Kingdom.

For example, if the United States exchanged 6W for 8C with the United Kingdom, both nations would gain 4C, for a total gain of 8C. If the United States could exchange 6W for 10C, it would gain 6C and the United Kingdom only 2C. (Of course, the gains from trade are proportionately greater when more than 6W are traded.) In Section 2.10 we will see how this rate of exchange is actually determined in the real world by demand as well as supply considerations. The rate of exchange will also determine how the total gains from trade are actually shared by the trading nations. Up to this point, all we have wanted to do was to prove that mutually beneficial trade can take place even if one nation is less efficient than the other in the production of both commodities.

Only if the absolute disadvantage that one nation has with respect to another nation is the same in both commodities, there will be no comparative advantage and no trade. For example, if one hour of labor time produced 3W instead of 1W in the United Kingdom (see Table 2.2), the United Kingdom would be exactly half as productive as the United States in both wheat and cloth. Then the United Kingdom would not be willing to give up more than 4C to obtain 6W from the United States because the United Kingdom can produce either 6W or 4C with two hours of work domestically. Under these circumstances, no mutually beneficial trade can take place. This situation, however, would be quite coincidental and rare.

2.6 COMPARATIVE ADVANTAGE WITH MONEY

According to the law of comparative advantage (and disregarding the exception noted earlier), even if one nation (the United Kingdom in this case) has an absolute disadvantage in the production of both commodities with respect to the other nation (the United States), there is still a basis for mutually beneficial trade. But how, you may ask, can the United Kingdom export anything to the United States if it is less efficient than the United States in the production of both commodities? The answer is that wages in the United Kingdom will be sufficiently lower than wages in the United States so as to make the price of cloth (the commodity in which the United Kingdom has a comparative advantage) lower in the United Kingdom, and the price of wheat lower in the United States *when both commodities are expressed in terms of the currency of either nation.* Let us see how this works.

Suppose that the wage rate in the United States is $6 per hour. Since one hour of labor time produces 6W in the United States (see Table 2.2),

the price of a bushel of wheat is $P_w = \$1$. On the other hand, since one hour of work produces 4C, $P_c = \$1.50$ (from $6/4C$). Suppose that at the same time the wage rate in England is £1 per hour (the symbol "£" stands for pound, the U.K. currency). Since one hour produces 1W in the United Kingdom (see Table 2.2), $P_w = £1$ in the United Kingdom. Similarly, since one hour produces 2C, $P_c = £0.5$. If the exchange rate between the pound and the dollar is £1 = \$2, then $P_w = £1 = \$2$ and $P_c = £0.5 = \$1$ in the United Kingdom. Table 2.3 shows the dollar price of wheat and cloth in the United States and the United Kingdom at the exchange rate of £1 = \$2.

From Table 2.3 we can see that the dollar price of wheat (the commodity in which the United States has a comparative advantage) is lower in the United States than in the United Kingdom. On the other hand, the dollar price of cloth (the commodity in which the United Kingdom has a comparative advantage) is lower in the United Kingdom. (The result would be similar if the price of both commodities had been expressed in pounds.)

Concept Check

Can you explain the law of comparative advantage in terms of money?

With the dollar price of wheat lower in the United States, businesspeople would buy wheat there and sell it in the United Kingdom, where they would buy cloth to sell in the United States. Even though U.K. labor is half as productive as U.S. labor in cloth production (see Table 2.2), U.K. labor receives only one-third of the U.S. wage rate (£1 = \$2 as opposed to \$6 in the United States), so that the dollar price of cloth is lower in the United Kingdom. To put it differently, the inefficiency of U.K. labor relative to U.S. labor in cloth production is more than compensated for by the lower wages in the United Kingdom. As a result, the dollar price of cloth is less in the United Kingdom, so that the United Kingdom can export cloth to the United States. This is always the case as long as the U.K. wage rate is between one-sixth and one-half of the U.S. wage rate (the same as the productivity difference between the United Kingdom and the United States in the production of wheat and cloth).

Thus, the argument that could be advanced in the United States that it needs to protect the high wages and standard of living of its workers against cheap British labor is generally false. Similarly faulty is the opposing argument that could be advanced in the United Kingdom that its labor needs protection against more efficient U.S. labor. These arguments are certainly inconsistent, and both are basically false (see Case Study 2-2).

Table 2.3. *Dollar Price of Wheat and Cloth in the United States and the United Kingdom at* £1 = \$2

	U.S.	U.K.
Price of one bushel of wheat	\$1.00	\$2.00
Price of one yard of cloth	\$1.50	\$1.00

CASE STUDY 2-2

The Petition of the Candlemakers

Sometimes satire and ridicule are more effective than theory and logic in influencing public opinion. For example, exasperated by the spread of protectionism under the prevailing mercantilist philosophy of the time, French economist Frédéric Bastiat (1801–1851) overwhelmed the proponents of protectionism by satirically extending their arguments to their logical and absurd conclusions. Nowhere is this more brilliantly accomplished than in the fictitious petition of the French candlemakers, written by Bastiat in 1845, and excerpted as follows.

We are suffering from the intolerable competition of a foreign rival, placed, it would seem, in a condition so far superior to ours for the production of light, that he absolutely *inundates* our *national market* at a price fabulously reduced. The moment he shows himself, our trade leaves us—all of our consumers apply to him; and a branch of native industry, having countless ramifications, is all at once rendered completely stagnant. This rival . . . is not other than the sun.

What we pray for is, that it may please you to pass a law ordering the shutting up of all windows, sky-lights, dormerwindows,

curtains, blinds, bull's eyes; in a word all openings, holes, chinks, clefts, and fissures, by or through which the light of the sun has been in use to enter houses, to the prejudice of the meritorious manufactures with which we flatter ourselves we have accommodated our country—a country which, in gratitude, ought not to abandon us now to a strife so unequal. . .

Does it not argue to the greatest inconsistency to check as you do the importation of coal, iron, cheese, and goods of foreign manufacture, merely because and even in proportion as their price approaches zero, while at the same time you freely admit, and without limitation, the light of the sun, whose price is during the whole day at zero?

If you shut up as much as possible all access to natural light, and create a demand for artificial light, which of our French manufactures will not be encouraged by it? If more tallow is consumed, then there must be more oxen and sheep; and, consequently, we shall behold the multiplication of artificial meadows, meat, wool, hides, and above all, manure, which is the basis and foundation of all agricultural wealth.

Source: Frédéric Bastiat, *Economic Sophisms* (Edinburgh: Oliver and Boyd, 1873), pp. 49–53, abridged.

2.7 COMPARATIVE ADVANTAGE AND OPPORTUNITY COSTS

Labor theory of value The theory that the cost or price of a commodity is determined by or can be inferred exclusively from its labor content.

Ricardo based his law of comparative advantage on the labor theory of value, which postulates that the value or price of a commodity depends exclusively on the amount of labor going into the production of the commodity. This implies (1) that either labor is the only factor of production or that labor is used in the same fixed proportion in the production of all commodities and (2) that labor is homogeneous (i.e., of only one type). Since neither of these

assumptions is true, the explanation of comparative advantage should not be based on the labor theory of value.

Specifically, labor is not the only factor of production, nor is it used in the same fixed proportion in the production of all commodities. For example, much more capital equipment per worker is required to produce some products (such as steel) than to produce other products (such as textiles). In addition, there is usually some possibility of substitution between labor, capital, and other factors in the production of most commodities. Furthermore, labor is obviously not homogeneous but varies greatly in training, productivity, and wages. At the very least, we should allow for different productivities of labor. Indeed, this is how the Ricardian theory of comparative advantage has been tested and confirmed empirically (see Case Study 2–3).

The theory of comparative advantage, however, need not be based on the labor theory of value, but can be explained on the basis of the opportunity cost theory (which is acceptable). It was left to Haberler in 1936 to explain or base the theory of comparative advantage on the opportunity cost theory. In this form, the law of comparative advantage is sometimes referred to as the *law of comparative cost.*

Opportunity cost theory The theory that the cost of a commodity is the amount of a second commodity that must be given up to release just enough resources to produce one more unit of the first commodity.

According to the opportunity cost theory, the cost of a commodity is the amount of a second commodity that must be given up to release just enough resources to produce one additional unit of the first commodity. No assumption is made here that labor is the only factor of production or that labor is homogeneous. Nor is it assumed that the cost or price of a commodity depends on or can be inferred exclusively from its labor content. Consequently, the nation with the lower opportunity cost in the production of a commodity has a comparative advantage in that commodity (and a comparative disadvantage in the second commodity).

For example, since the United States must give up two-thirds of a unit of cloth to release just enough resources to produce one additional unit of wheat domestically, *the opportunity cost of wheat is two-thirds of a unit of cloth* (i.e., $1W = 2/3C$ in the United States). If $1W = 2C$ in the United Kingdom, then the opportunity cost of wheat (in terms of the amount of cloth that must be given up) is lower in the United States than in the United Kingdom, and the United States would have a comparative (cost) advantage over the United Kingdom in wheat. In a two-nation, two-commodity world, the United Kingdom would then have a comparative advantage in cloth.

Concept Check

What is the relationship between opportunity costs and comparative advantage?

According to the law of comparative advantage, the United States should specialize in producing wheat and export some of it in exchange for British cloth. This is exactly what we concluded earlier with the law of comparative advantage based on the labor theory of value, but now our explanation is based on the opportunity cost theory.

CASE STUDY 2-3

Labor Productivities and Comparative Advantage

The first empirical test of the theory of comparative advantage based on labor productivities and costs was conducted by *MacDougall* in 1951 and 1952, using labor productivity and export data for 25 industries in the United States and the United Kingdom for the year 1937. Since wages were twice as high in the United States as in the United Kingdom, MacDougall argued that costs of production would be lower in the United States in those industries where American labor was more than twice as productive as British labor. These would be the industries in which the United States had a comparative advantage with respect to the United Kingdom and in which it would undersell the United Kingdom in the rest of the world. On the other hand, the United Kingdom would have a comparative advantage and undersell the United States in those industries where the productivity of British labor was more than one-half as productive as American labor. MacDougall's empirical results showed that this was indeed true for 20 out of the 25 industries that he studied.

The positive relationship between labor productivity and exports for the United States and the United Kingdom was confirmed by subsequent studies by *Balassa* using 1950 data and *Stern* using 1950 and 1959 data. More recently, the Ricardian trade model was confirmed by *Golub* for trade between the United States and Japan using 1990 data for 33 industries and by Golub and *Hsieh* for trade between the United States and nine other countries (Japan, Germany, the United Kingdom, France, Italy, Canada, Australia, Mexico, and Korea) using data for 39 sectors from 1972 to 1991. Thus, production costs other than labor costs, demand considerations, political ties, and various obstructions to the flow of international trade did not seem to break the link between relative labor productivity and export shares.

Source: G.D.A. MacDougall, ''British and American Exports: A Study Suggested by the Theory of Comparative Costs,'' *Economic Journal*, December 1951, p. 703; R. Stern, ''British and American Productivity and Comparative Costs in International Trade,'' *Oxford Economic Papers* October 1962, pp. 275–296; B. Balassa, ''An Empirical Demonstration of Classical Comparative Cost Theory,'' *Review of Economics and Statistics*, August 1962, pp. 231–238; S. S. Golub, *Comparative and Absolute Advantage in the Asia-Pacific Region* (San Francisco: Federal Reserve Bank of San Francisco, Center for Pacific Basin Monetary and Economic Studies 1995), p. 46; and S. S. Golub and C. T. Hsieh, ''Classical Ricardian Theory of Comparative Advantage Revisited,'' *Review of International Economics*, May 2000, pp. 221–234.

Production possibility frontier A curve showing the various alternative combinations of two commodities that a nation can produce by fully utilizing all of its resources with the best technology available to it.

2.8 PRODUCTION POSSIBILITY FRONTIER WITH CONSTANT COSTS

Opportunity costs can be illustrated with the production possibility frontier, or transformation curve. The production possibility frontier is a curve that shows the alternative combinations of the two commodities that a nation can produce by fully utilizing all of its resources with the best technology available to it.

Table 2.4. *Production Possibility Schedules for Wheat and Cloth in the United States and the United Kingdom*

United States		United Kingdom	
Wheat	*Cloth*	*Wheat*	*Cloth*
180	0	60	0
150	20	50	20
120	40	40	40
90	60	30	60
60	80	20	80
30	100	10	100
0	120	0	120

Table 2.4 gives the (hypothetical) production possibility schedules of wheat (in million bushels/year) and cloth (in million yards/year) for the United States and the United Kingdom. We see that the United States can produce 180W and 0C, 150W and 20C, or 120W and 40C, down to 0W and 120C. For each 30W that the United States gives up, just enough resources are released to produce an additional 20C. That is, 30W = 20C (in the sense that both require the same amount of resources). Thus, the opportunity cost of one unit of wheat in the United States is 1W = 2/3C (the same as in Table 2.2) and remains constant. On the other hand, the United Kingdom can produce 60W and 0C, 50W and 20C, or 40W and 40C, down to 0W and 120C. The United Kingdom can increase its output by 20C for each 10W it gives up. Thus, the opportunity cost of wheat in the United Kingdom is 1W = 2C and remains constant.

The United States and United Kingdom production possibility schedules given in Table 2.4 are graphed as production possibility frontiers in Figure 2.1. Each point on a frontier represents one combination of wheat and cloth that the nation can produce. For example, at point *A*, the United States produces 90W and 60C. At point *A'*, the United Kingdom produces 40W and 40C.

Points inside, or below, the production possibility frontier are also possible but are inefficient, in the sense that the nation either has some idle resources and/or is not using the best technology available to it. On the other hand, points above the production frontier cannot be achieved with the resources and technology currently available to the nation.

The downward, or negative, slope of the production possibility frontiers in Figure 2.1 indicates that if the United States and the United Kingdom want to produce more wheat, they must give up some of their cloth production. The fact that the production possibility frontiers of both nations are straight lines reflects the fact that their opportunity costs are constant. That is, to produce each additional 1W, the United States must give up 2/3C and the United Kingdom must give up 2C, *no matter from which point on its production possibility frontier each nation starts.*

Concept
Check

What is the shape
of the production
possibility frontier
with constant costs?

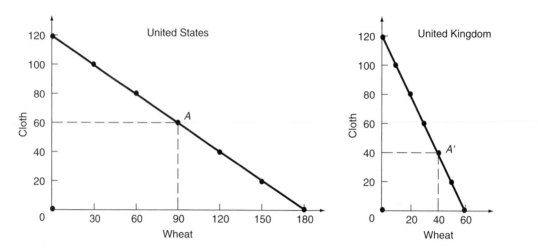

FIGURE 2.1. The Production Possibility Frontiers of the United States and the United Kingdom.
The U.S. and U.K. production frontiers are obtained by plotting the values in Table 2.4. The frontiers are downward, or negatively sloped, indicating that as each nation produces more wheat, it must give up some cloth. Straight-line production possibility frontiers reflect constant opportunity costs.

Constant opportunity costs The constant amount of a commodity that must be given up to produce each additional unit of another commodity.

Constant opportunity costs arise when (1) resources or factors of production are either perfect substitutes for each other or used in fixed proportion in the production of both commodities, and (2) all units of the same factor are homogeneous or exactly of the same quality. Then, as each nation transfers resources from the production of cloth to the production of wheat, it will not have to use resources that are less and less suited to wheat production, no matter how much wheat it is already producing. The same is true for the production of more cloth. Thus, we have constant costs in the sense that the same amount of one commodity must be given up to produce each additional unit of the second commodity.

While opportunity costs are constant in each nation, they differ among nations, providing the basis for trade. Constant costs are not realistic, however. They are discussed only because they serve as a convenient introduction to the more realistic case of increasing costs, discussed in the next chapter.

2.9 OPPORTUNITY COSTS AND RELATIVE COMMODITY PRICES

We have seen that the opportunity cost of wheat is equal to the amount of cloth that the nation must give up to release just enough resources to produce

one additional unit of wheat. This is given by the (absolute) slope of the production possibility frontier, or transformation curve, and is sometimes referred to as the *marginal rate of transformation.*

Figure 2.1 shows that the (absolute) slope of the U.S. transformation curve is $^{120}/_{180} = ^2/_3 =$ the opportunity cost of wheat in the United States, and remains constant. The slope of the U.K. transformation curve is $^{120}/_{60} = 2 =$ the opportunity cost of wheat in the United Kingdom, and remains constant. On the assumptions that prices equal costs of production and that the nation does produce both some wheat and some cloth, the opportunity cost of wheat is equal to the price of wheat relative to the price of cloth (P_w/P_c).

Thus, $P_w/P_c = ^2/_3$ in the United States, and inversely $P_c/P_w = ^3/_2 = 1.5$. In the United Kingdom, $P_w/P_c = 2$, and $P_c/P_w = ^1/_2$. The lower P_w/P_c in the United States ($^2/_3$ as opposed to 2 for the United Kingdom) is a reflection of the U.S. comparative advantage in wheat. Similarly, the lower P_c/P_w in the United Kingdom ($^1/_2$ as opposed to the United States $^2/_3$) reflects the U.K. comparative advantage in cloth. Note that under constant costs, P_w/P_c is determined exclusively by production, or supply, considerations in each nation. Demand considerations do not enter at all in the determination of relative commodity prices.

> **Relative commodity prices** The price of one commodity divided by the price of another commodity. This equals the opportunity cost of the first commodity and is given by the absolute slope of the production possibility frontier.

To conclude, we can say that the difference in relative commodity prices between the two nations (given by the difference in the slope of their transformation curves) is a reflection of their comparative advantage and provides the basis for mutually beneficial trade.

2.10 BASIS FOR AND GAINS FROM TRADE UNDER CONSTANT COSTS

In the absence of trade, a nation can only consume the commodities that it produces. As a result, the nation's production possibility frontier also represents its *consumption frontier*. Which combination of commodities the nation actually chooses to produce and consume depends on the people's tastes, or demand considerations.

For example, in the absence of trade, the United States might choose to produce and consume combination *A* (90W and 60C) on its production possibility frontier (see Figure 2.2), and the United Kingdom might choose combination *A'* (40W and 40C).

With trade possible, the United States would specialize in the production of wheat (the commodity of its comparative advantage) and produce at point *B* (180W and 0C) on its production possibility frontier. Similarly, the United Kingdom would specialize in the production of cloth and produce at *B'* (0W and 120C). If the United States then exchanges 70W for 70C with the United Kingdom, it ends up consuming at point *E* (110W and 70C), and the United Kingdom ends up consuming at *E'* (70W and 50C). Thus, the United States gains 20W and 10C from trade (compare point *E* with point *A* in

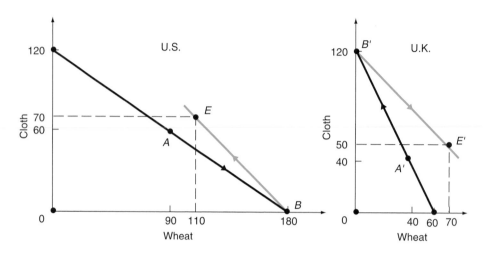

FIGURE 2.2. The Gains from Trade.
In the absence of trade, the United States produces and consumes at *A*, and the United Kingdom at *A'*. With trade, the United States specializes in the production of wheat and produces at *B*, while the United Kingdom specializes in the production of cloth and produces at *B'*. By exchanging 70W for 70C with the United Kingdom, the United States ends up consuming at *E* (and gains 20W and 10C), while the United Kingdom ends up consuming at *E'* (and gains 30W and 10C).

Figure 2.2), and the United Kingdom gains 30W and 10C (compare point *A'* with point *E'*).

The increased consumption of both wheat and cloth in both nations was made possible by the increased output that resulted as each nation specialized in the production of the commodity of its comparative advantage. That is, in the absence of trade, the United States produced 90W and the United Kingdom 40W, for a total of 130W. With specialization in production and trade, 180W are produced (all in the United States). Similarly, in the absence of trade, the United States produced 60C and the United Kingdom 40C, for a total of 100C. With specialization in production and trade, 120C are produced (all in the United Kingdom).

Concept Check

Can you show the basis and the gains from trade with constant costs?

It is this increase in output of 50W and 20C resulting from specialization in production that is shared by the United States and the United Kingdom and represents their gains from trade. Recall that in the absence of trade, the United States would not specialize in the production of wheat because it also wanted to consume some cloth. Similarly, the United Kingdom would not specialize in the production of cloth in the absence of trade because it also wanted to consume some wheat.

Note that with 70W exchanged for 70C, $P_w/P_c = 1$. At $P_w/P_c > 1$, the United States would want to export more wheat than the United Kingdom

wants to import at that high price of wheat, and P_w/P_w would fall to 1. On the other hand, if $P_w/P_c < 1$, the United States would want to export less wheat than the United Kingdom would like to import at that low price of wheat, and so P_w/P_c would rise to 1. At $P_w/P_c = 1$ the amount of wheat that the United States wants to export is exactly equal to the amount of wheat that the United Kingdom would like to import at that price. Thus, $P_w/P_c = 1$ is the *equilibrium relative commodity price with trade*.

Complete specialization The utilization of all of a nation's resources in the production of only one commodity with trade. This usually occurs under constant costs.

Finally, note that with constant costs, there is complete specialization in production in both countries, and the equilibrium-relative commodity price of each commodity is between the pretrade relative commodity price in each nation. The only exception arises if one of the two countries is too small to be able to satisfy the other nation's demand for the small country's export commodity. In that case, only the small nation will specialize completely, and trade will take place at the pretrade relative commodity prices in the large country. All of the gains from trade will then go to the small country. This is the small-country case and shows "the importance of being unimportant." (This benefit, however, is not without cost since the small nation faces the risk of a possible future reduction in demand for the only commodity it produces.) What happens here is that the large nation will gain from specialization and trade with other large nations, and the small nation "just rides along."

Small-country case The situation where trade takes place at the pretrade-relative commodity prices in the large nation so that the small nation receives all of the benefits from trade.

SUMMARY

1. This chapter examined the development of trade theory from the mercantilists to Smith, Ricardo, and Haberler and sought to answer two basic questions: (a) What is the basis for and what are the gains from trade? (b) What is the pattern of trade?

2. The mercantilists believed that a nation could gain in international trade only at the expense of other nations. As a result, they advocated restrictions on imports, incentives for exports, and strict government regulation of all economic activities.

3. According to Adam Smith, trade is based on absolute advantage and benefits both nations. (The discussion assumes a two-nation, two-commodity world.) That is, when each nation specializes in the production of the commodity of its absolute advantage and exchanges part of its output for the commodity of its absolute disadvantage, both nations end up consuming more of both commodities. Absolute advantage, however, explains only a small portion of international trade today.

4. David Ricardo introduced the law of comparative advantage. This postulates that even if one nation is less efficient than the other nation in the production of both commodities, there is still a basis for mutually beneficial trade. The less efficient nation should specialize in the production and export of the commodity in which its absolute disadvantage is less. This is the commodity of its comparative advantage. Ricardo, however, explained

the law of comparative advantage in terms of the labor theory of value, which is unacceptable. Despite this, the Ricardian trade model is confirmed empirically when expressed in terms of relative labor productivities.

5. Gottfried Haberler came to the "rescue" by explaining the law of comparative advantage in terms of the opportunity cost theory. This states that the cost of a commodity is the amount of a second commodity that must be given up in order to release just enough resources to produce one additional unit of the first commodity. The opportunity cost of a commodity is equal to the relative price of that commodity and is given by the (absolute) slope of the production possibility frontier. A straight-line production possibility frontier reflects constant opportunity costs.

6. In the absence of trade, a nation's production possibility frontier is also its consumption frontier. With trade, each nation can specialize in producing the commodity of its comparative advantage and exchange part of its output for the commodity of its comparative disadvantage from the other nation. By so doing, both nations end up consuming more of both commodities than without trade. With complete specialization, the equilibrium-relative commodity prices will be between the pretrade-relative commodity prices prevailing in each nation.

REVIEW QUESTIONS AND PROBLEMS

1. What were the mercantilists' views on trade? How were their views different from those of Adam Smith? What is the relevance of all this today?

2. What was the basis for and the pattern of trade according to Adam Smith? How were gains from trade generated? What policies did Smith advocate in international trade? What did he think was the proper function of government in the economic life of the nation?

3. In what way was Ricardo's law of comparative advantage superior to Smith's theory of absolute advantage? How do gains from trade arise with comparative advantage? How can a nation that is less efficient than another nation in the production of all commodities export anything to the second nation?

4. Table 2.5, on page 51, shows bushels of wheat and the yards of cloth that the United States and the United Kingdom can produce with one hour of labor time under four different hypothetical situations. In each case, identify the commodity in which the United States and the United Kingdom have
 (a) an absolute advantage or disadvantage.
 (b) comparative advantage or disadvantage.

5. Suppose that, in Case B in Table 2.5, the United States exchanges 4W for 4C with the United Kingdom.
 (a) How much does the United States gain in terms of C?
 (b) How much does the United Kingdom gain in terms of C?
 (c) What is the range for mutually beneficial trade?

Table 2.5. *Production Possibilities in the United States and the United Kingdom*

	Case A		Case B		Case C		Case D	
	U.S.	*U.K.*	*U.S.*	*U.K.*	*U.S.*	*U.K.*	*U.S.*	*U.K.*
Wheat (bushels/hour)	4	1	4	1	4	1	4	2
Cloth (yards/hour)	1	2	3	2	2	2	2	1

 (d) How much would each nation gain in terms of C if they exchanged 4W for 6C instead?

6. Using the information for Case B in Table 2.5, assume that labor is the only factor of production and is homogeneous (i.e., all of one type).
 (a) What is the cost in terms of labor content of producing wheat and cloth in the United States and the United Kingdom?
 (b) What is the dollar price of wheat and cloth in the United States if the wage rate is $6?
 (c) What is the pound price of wheat and cloth in the United Kingdom if the wage rate is £1?

7. How would you counter the argument that the United States needs to restrict textile imports in order to save American jobs?

8. Why is Ricardo's explanation of the law of comparative advantage unacceptable? What acceptable theory can be used to explain the law?

9. What is the relationship between opportunity costs and the production possibility frontier of a nation? How does the production possibility frontier look under constant opportunity costs? What is the relationship between the opportunity cost of a commodity and the relative price of that commodity? How can they be visualized graphically?

10. Assume that the data in Case B in Table 2.5 refer to millions of bushels of wheat and of yards of cloth.
 (a) Plot on graph paper the production frontiers of the United States and the United Kingdom.
 (b) What is the relative price of wheat (i.e., P_w/P_c) in the United States and in the United Kingdom under autarky (no trade)?
 (c) What is the relative price of cloth (i.e., P_c/P_w) in the United States and in the United Kingdom under autarky (no trade)?
 (d) Assuming that the no-trade or autarky point is 3W and 3/4C (in million units) in the United States and 1/2W and 1C in the United Kingdom. Assuming also that with the opening of trade the United States exchanges 1W for 1C with the United Kingdom. Show graphically for the United States and the United Kingdom the autarky (or no-trade) point of production and consumption, the point of production and consumption with trade, and the gains from trade.

Comparative Advantage with More than Two Commodities and Nations

We now extend the theory of comparative advantage first to the case of more than two commodities and then to the case of more than two nations. In each case, we will see that the theory of comparative advantage is easily generalized.

A2.1 COMPARATIVE ADVANTAGE WITH MORE THAN TWO COMMODITIES

Table 2.6 shows the dollar and the pound cost, or price, of five commodities in the United States and the United Kingdom.

To determine which commodities will be exported and imported by the United States and the United Kingdom, we must first express all commodity prices in terms of the same currency and then compare prices in the two nations. For example, if the exchange rate between the dollar and the pound is £1 = $2, the dollar prices of the commodities in the United Kingdom are:

Commodity	A	B	C	D	E
Dollar price in the U.K.	12	8	6	4	2

Table 2.6. *Commodity Prices in the United States and United Kingdom*

Commodity	Price in the U.S.	Price in the U.K.
A	$2	£6
B	4	4
C	6	3
D	8	2
E	10	1

At this exchange rate, the dollar prices of commodities A and B are lower in the United States than in the United Kingdom; commodity C is equally priced in the two nations; and the dollar prices of commodities D and E are lower in the United Kingdom. As a result, the United States will export commodities A and B to the United Kingdom and import commodities D and E from the United Kingdom. Commodity C will not be traded.

Now assume that the exchange rate between the dollar and the pound is £1 = $3. The dollar price of the commodities in the United Kingdom would be:

Commodity	A	B	C	D	E
Dollar price in the U.K.	18	12	9	6	3

At this higher exchange rate, the dollar prices of commodities A, B, and C are lower in the United States, while the dollar prices of commodities D and E are lower in the United Kingdom. Thus, the United States would export commodities A, B, and C to the United Kingdom and import commodities D and E from the United Kingdom. Note that commodity C, which was not traded at the exchange rate of £1 = $2, is now exported by the United States at the exchange rate of £1 = $3.

Finally, if the exchange rate were £1 = $1, the dollar prices of the commodities in the United Kingdom would be:

Commodity	A	B	C	D	E
Dollar price in the U.K.	6	4	3	2	1

In this case, the United States would export only commodity A to the United Kingdom and import all other commodities, with the exception of commodity B (which would not be traded because it is now equally priced in the two nations).

If the exchange rate between the dollar and the pound is flexible and is determined exclusively by trade forces, then the actual exchange rate

between the dollar and the pound will settle at the level at which *the value of U.S. exports to the United Kingdom exactly equals the value of the U.S. imports from the United Kingdom*. Once this equilibrium exchange rate is established, we will be able to determine exactly which commodities are exported by the United States and which are exported by the United Kingdom. Each nation will then have a comparative advantage in the commodities that it exports at the particular equilibrium exchange rate established.

What we can say on the basis of Table 2.6 is that the U.S. comparative advantage is greatest in commodity A, and the United States must export at least this commodity. For this to be possible, the exchange rate between the dollar and the pound must be £ 1 > \$0.33. The United Kingdom's comparative advantage is highest in commodity E, so that the United Kingdom must export at least commodity E. For this to be possible, the exchange rate between the dollar and the pound must be £ 1 < \$10. This discussion can be generalized to cover any number of commodities.

A2.2 COMPARATIVE ADVANTAGE WITH MORE THAN TWO NATIONS

Suppose that, instead of two nations and five commodities, we have two commodities (wheat and cloth) and five nations (A,B,C,D, and E). Table 2.7 ranks these nations from lowest to highest in terms of their internal P_w/P_c values. With trade, the equilibrium P_w/P_c will settle somewhere between 1 and 5. That is, $1 < P_w/P_c < 5$.

If the equilibrium $P_w/P_c = 3$ with trade, Nations A and B will export wheat to Nations D and E in exchange for cloth. Nation C will not engage in international trade in this case because its pretrade P_w/P_c equals the equilibrium P_w/P_c with trade. Given a trade equilibrium $P_w/P_c = 4$, Nations A, B, and C will export wheat to Nation E in exchange for cloth, and Nation D will not engage in international trade. If the equilibrium $P_w/P_c = 2$ with trade, Nation A will export wheat to all the other nations, with the exception of Nation B, in exchange for cloth.

This discussion can easily be extended to any number of countries and commodities. Thus, the conclusions reached on the basis of our simple model with only two nations and two commodities can be generalized and are applicable to the case of many nations and many commodities.

Table 2.7. *Ranking of Nations in Terms of Internal P_w/P_c*

Nation	A	B	C	D	E
P_w/P_c	1	2	3	4	5

SELECTED BIBLIOGRAPHY

For a problem-solving approach to the material covered in this chapter, with many examples and solved problems, see:

- D. Salvatore, *Theory and Problems of International Economics*, 4th ed. (New York: McGraw-Hill, 1996), chs. 1, 2 (sects. 2.1 to 2.3).

The preclassical mercantilist view on international trade is found in:

- E. F. Heckscher, *Mercantilism*, Vols. I and II (London: Allen & Unwin, 1935).
- P. C. Newman, A. D. Gayer, and M. H. Spencer, *Source Readings in Economic Thought* (New York: Norton, 1954), pp. 24–53.

For Smith's and Ricardo's views on international trade, see:

- A. Smith, *The Wealth of Nations* (New York: The Modern Library, 1937), Book I, ch. 3; Book IV, chs. 1–3, 6–8.
- D. Ricardo, *The Principles of Political Economy and Taxation* (Homewood, Ill.: Irwin, 1963), ch. 7.

An excellent exposition of the classical theory of comparative advantage can be found in:

- G. Haberler, *The Theory of International Trade* (London: W. Hodge & Co., 1936), chs. 9–10.
- J. Viner, *Studies in the Theory of International Trade* (New York: Harper & Brothers, 1937), ch. 7.

For empirical tests of the Ricardian trade model, see:

- G. D. A. MacDougall, "British and American Exports: A Study Suggested by the Theory of Comparative Costs," *Economic Journal*, December 1951 (Part I: pp. 697–724) and September 1952 (Part II: pp. 487–521).
- S. S. Golub and C. T. Hsieh, "The Classical Ricardian Theory of Comparative Advantage Revisited," *Review of International Economics*, May 2000.

INTERNet

For trade policies of all the member countries of the World Trade Organization, see:

http://www.wto.org

For information and analyses on international trade theory and policies, generally supporting a liberal trading system, published by the Institute for International Economics, see:

http://www.iie.com

The case against free trade made by the Public Citizen Global Trade Watch, an organization created by Ralph Nader (the consumer advocate), is found at:

http://www.citizen.org/trade/index.cfm

The Standard Trade Model

After studying this chapter, you should be able to:

- Draw a production possibility frontier with increasing costs
- Draw a set of community indifference curves
- Show a nation in equilibrium without international trade under increasing costs
- Show the basis and the gains from trade with increasing costs
- Explain the meaning of the terms of trade
- Explain the relationship between international trade and deindustrialization in the United States and other advanced countries

CHAPTER OUTLINE

KEY TERMS

Increasing opportunity costs	Equilibrium-relative commodity price with trade
Marginal rate of transformation (MRT)	
Community indifference curve	Incomplete specialization
Marginal rate of substitution (MRS)	Terms of trade
Autarky	Deindustrialization
Equilibrium-relative commodity price in isolation	Offer curve
	Reciprocal demand curve

3.1 INTRODUCTION

This chapter extends our simple trade model of the previous chapter to the more realistic case of increasing opportunity costs. Tastes or demand preferences are introduced with community indifference curves. We then see

how these forces of supply and demand determine the equilibrium-relative commodity price in each nation in the absence of trade under increasing costs. This will also indicate the commodity of comparative advantage of each nation.

Afterwards, we examine how, with trade, each nation gains by specializing in the production of the commodity of its comparative advantage and exporting some of its output in exchange for the commodity of its comparative disadvantage, and how the terms of trade of each country are determined. Finally, we discuss the problem of deindustrialization that many advanced countries believe they are facing.

In this and in the following chapters, it will be convenient to generalize the presentation and deal with Nation 1 and Nation 2 (instead of the United States and United Kingdom) and commodity X and commodity Y (instead of wheat and cloth). The optional appendix to this chapter shows how the equilibrium-relative commodity prices can also be obtained with the use of offer curves.

3.2 THE PRODUCTION FRONTIER WITH INCREASING COSTS

Increasing opportunity costs The increasing amounts of one commodity that a nation must give up to release just enough resources to produce each additional unit of another commodity. This is reflected in a production frontier that is concave from the origin.

It is more realistic for a nation to face increasing, rather than constant, opportunity costs. Increasing opportunity costs mean that the nation must give up more and more of one commodity to release just enough resources to produce each additional unit of another commodity. Increasing opportunity costs result in a production frontier that is concave (rather than a straight line). Figure 3.1 shows the hypothetical production frontier of commodities X and Y for Nation 1 and Nation 2.

Suppose that Nation 1 wants to produce more of commodity X, starting from point *A* on its production frontier in the left panel of Figure 3.1. Since at point *A* the nation is already utilizing all of its resources with the best technology available, the nation can only produce more of X by reducing the output of commodity Y. (In Chapter 2, we saw that this is the reason production frontiers are negatively sloped.)

The left panel of Figure 3.1 shows that for each additional batch of 20X that Nation 1 produces, it must give up more and more Y. The increasing opportunity costs in terms of Y that Nation 1 faces are reflected in the longer and longer downward arrows next to the vertical axis of the figure and result in a production frontier that is concave.

Concept Check

What is the shape of the production possibility frontier with increasing costs?

Nation 1 also faces increasing opportunity costs in the production of Y. This could be demonstrated graphically by showing that Nation 1 has to give up increasing amounts of X for each additional batch of 20Y that it produces. However, instead of showing this for Nation 1, we demonstrate increasing opportunity costs in the production of Y with the production frontier of Nation 2 shown in the right-hand panel of Figure 3.1.

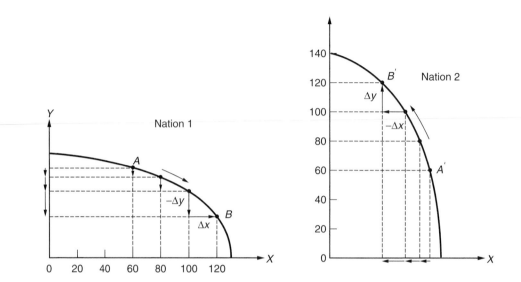

FIGURE 3.1. Production Frontiers of Nation 1 and Nation 2 with Increasing Costs.
Concave production frontiers reflect increasing opportunity costs. Nation 1 must give up more and more of Y for each additional batch of 20X that it produces. This is illustrated by downward arrows of increasing length on the vertical axis in the left panel. Similarly, Nation 2 incurs increasing opportunity costs in terms of forgone X (illustrated by the increasing length of the leftward arrows on the horizontal axis in the right panel) for each additional batch of 20Y it produces.

Moving upward from point A' along the production frontier of Nation 2, we observe leftward arrows of increasing length along the horizontal axis, reflecting the increasing amounts of X that Nation 2 must give up to produce each additional batch of 20Y.

3.3 THE MARGINAL RATE OF TRANSFORMATION

Marginal rate of transformation (MRT) The amount of one commodity that a nation must give up to produce each additional unit of another commodity. This is another name for the opportunity cost of a commodity and is given by the slope of the production frontier at the point of production.

The Marginal rate of transformation (MRT) of X for Y refers to the amount of Y that a nation must give up to produce each additional unit of X. Thus, MRT is another name for the opportunity cost of X (the commodity measured along the horizontal axis in Figure 3.1) and is given by the slope of the production frontier at the point of production.

For example, if the slope of the production frontier (MRT) of Nation 1 in the left panel of Figure 3.1 is equal to $1/4$ at point A, this means that Nation 1 must give up $1/4$ of a unit of Y to release just enough resources to produce one additional unit of X at this point. Similarly, if the slope, or MRT, equals 1 at point B, this means that Nation 1 must give up one unit of Y to produce one additional unit of X at this point.

Thus, a movement from point *A* down to point *B* along the production frontier of Nation 1 involves an increase in the slope (MRT) from $1/4$ (at point *A*) to 1 (at point *B*) and reflects the increasing opportunity costs in producing more X. This is in contrast to the case of a straight-line production frontier (as in Chapter 2), where the opportunity cost of X is constant regardless of the level of output and is given by the constant value of the slope (MRT) of the production frontier.

But how do increasing opportunity costs arise and why are they more realistic than constant opportunity costs? Increasing opportunity costs arise because resources or factors of production are (1) not homogeneous (i.e., all units of the same factor are not identical or of the same quality) and (2) not used in the same fixed proportion or intensity in the production of all commodities. This means that as the nation produces more of a commodity, it must utilize resources that become progressively less efficient or less suited for the production of that commodity. As a result, the nation must give up more and more of the second commodity to release just enough resources to produce each additional unit of the first commodity.

Concept Check

Why do increasing costs arise?

For example, suppose some of a nation's land is flat and suited for growing wheat, and some is hilly and better suited for grazing and milk production. Suppose that the nation originally specialized in wheat but now wants to concentrate on producing milk. By transferring its hilly areas from wheat growing to grazing, the nation gives up very little wheat and obtains a great deal of milk. Thus, the opportunity cost of milk in terms of the amount of wheat given up is initially small. But if this transfer process continues, eventually flat land, which is better suited for wheat growing, will have to be used for grazing. As a result, the opportunity cost of milk in terms of wheat will rise, and the production frontier will be concave.

The difference in the production frontiers of Nation 1 and Nation 2 in Figure 3.1 is due to the fact that the two nations have different factor endowments or resources at their disposal and/or use different technologies in production. In the real world, the production frontiers of different nations will usually differ, since practically no two nations have identical factor endowments (even if they could have access to the same technology).

As the supply or availability of factors and/or technology changes over time, a nation's production frontier shifts. These changes are examined in Chapter 8, which deals with economic growth and its effect on international trade.

3.4 COMMUNITY INDIFFERENCE CURVES

So far, we have discussed production, or supply, considerations in a nation, as reflected in its production frontier. We now introduce the tastes, or demand preferences, of the nation. These are given by community (or social) indifference curves.

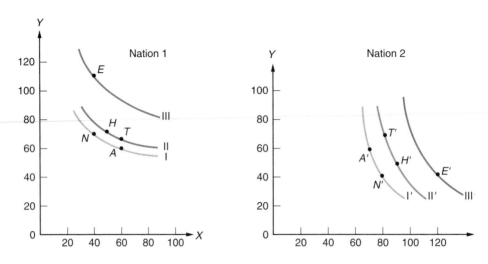

FIGURE 3.2. Community Indifference Curves for Nation 1 and Nation 2.
A community indifference curve shows the various combinations of commodity X and Y that yield equal
satisfaction to the community or nation. A higher curve refers to a higher level of satisfaction. Community
indifference curves are downward, or negatively, sloped and convex. The declining slope of the curve
reflects the diminishing marginal rate of substitution (MRS) of X for Y in consumption.

**Community indif-
ference curve** The
curve that shows the
various combinations
of two commodities
yielding equal satis-
faction to the com-
munity or nation.
Community indif-
ference curves are
negatively sloped,
convex from the ori-
gin, and should not
cross.

A community indifference curve shows the various combinations of
two commodities that yield equal satisfaction to the community or nation.
Higher curves refer to greater satisfaction, lower curves to less satisfaction.
Community indifference curves are negatively sloped and convex (the
same as the individual's indifference curves discussed in principles of
economics courses). Figure 3.2 shows three hypothetical indifference curves
for Nation 1 and Nation 2. They differ on the assumption that tastes, or
demand preferences, are different in the two nations.

For example, points N and A give equal satisfaction to Nation 1, since
they are both on indifference curve I in the left panel of Figure 3.2. Points
H and T refer to a higher level of satisfaction, since they are on a higher
indifference curve (II). Even though point H involves more of Y but less of X
than point A, satisfaction is greater at H because it is on indifference curve II.
Point E refers to still greater satisfaction, since it is on indifference curve III.
For Nation 2, $A' = N' < H' < E'$.

Note that the community indifference curves in Figure 3.2 are negatively
sloped. This is always the case because as a nation consumes more of X, it
must consume less of Y if the nation is to have the same level of satisfaction
(i.e., remain on the same level of satisfaction). Thus, as Nation 1 moves from
N to A on indifference curve I in the left panel of Figure 3.2, it consumes
more of X but less of Y. Similarly, as Nation 2 moves from A' to N' on

indifference curve *I'* in the right panel of the figure, it consumes more of X but less of Y. If a nation continued to consume the same amount of Y as it increased its consumption of X, the nation would necessarily move to a higher indifference curve.

Marginal rate of substitution (MRS)
The amount of one commodity that a nation could give up in exchange for one extra unit of a second commodity and still remain on the same indifference curve. It is given by the slope of the community indifference curve at the point of consumption and declines as the nation consumes more of the second commodity.

Concept Check

Can you explain the characteristics of community indifference curves?

The marginal rate of substitution (MRS) of X for Y in consumption refers to the amount of Y that a nation could give up for one extra unit of X *and still remain on the same indifference curve*. This is given by the (absolute) slope of the community indifference curve at the point of consumption and declines as the nation moves down the curve. For example, the (absolute) slope, or MRS, of indifference curve I is greater at point *N* than at point *A* (see the left panel of Figure 3.2). Similarly, the slope, or MRS, of indifference curve *I'* is greater at point *A'* than at *N'* in the right panel of Figure 3.2.

The decline in MRS or absolute slope of an indifference curve is a reflection of the fact that the more of X and the less of Y a nation consumes, the more valuable to the nation is a unit of Y at the margin compared with a unit of X. Therefore, the nation can give up less and less of Y for each additional unit of X it wants.

Declining MRS means that community indifference curves are convex. Thus, while *increasing* opportunity cost in production is reflected in *concave* production frontiers, a *declining* marginal rate of substitution in consumption is reflected in *convex* community indifference curves. To be useful, community indifference curves must also not intersect (cross). A point of intersection would refer to equal satisfaction on two different community indifference curves, which is inconsistent with their definition. Thus, the indifference curves of Nation 1 and Nation 2 in Figure 3.2 are drawn as nonintersecting.

3.5 EQUILIBRIUM IN ISOLATION

In Section 3.2, we discussed production frontiers, which illustrate the production, or supply, conditions in a nation. In Section 3.4, we examined community indifference curves, which reflect the tastes, or demand preferences, in a nation. We will now see how the interaction of these forces of supply and demand determine the equilibrium point, or point of maximum social welfare, in a nation in isolation (i.e., in the absence of trade).

In the absence of trade, a nation is in equilibrium when it reaches the highest indifference curve possible given its production frontier. This occurs at the point where a community indifference curve is tangent to the nation's production frontier. The common slope of the two curves at the tangency point gives the internal equilibrium relative commodity price in the nation and reflects the nation's comparative advantage. Let us see this for Nations 1 and 2.

Figure 3.3 brings together the production frontiers of Figure 3.1 and the community indifference curves of Figure 3.2. In the left panel of Figure 3.3, we see that indifference curve *I* is the highest indifference curve that Nation 1

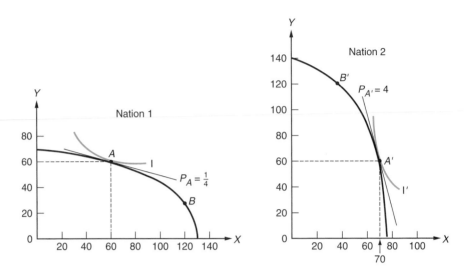

FIGURE 3.3. Equilibrium in Isolation.
Nation 1 is in equilibrium, or maximizes its welfare, in isolation by producing and consuming at point A, where its production frontier reaches (is tangent to) indifference curve I (the highest possible). Similarly, Nation 2 is in equilibrium at point A', where its production frontier is tangent to indifference curve I'. The equilibrium relative price of X in Nation 1 is given by the slope of the common tangent to its production frontier and indifference curve I at point A. This is $P_A = \frac{1}{4}$. For Nation 2, $P_{A'} = 4$. Since the relative price of X is lower in Nation 1 than in Nation 2, Nation 1 has a comparative advantage in commodity X and Nation 2 in commodity Y.

Autarky The absence of trade, or isolation.

can reach with its production frontier. Thus, Nation 1 is in equilibrium, or maximizes its welfare, when it produces and consumes at point A in the absence of trade, or autarky. Similarly, in the right panel of Figure 3.3 we see that Nation 2 is in equilibrium at point A', where its production frontier is tangent to indifference curve I'. Note that in the absence of trade a nation can only consume what it produces.

Equilibrium-relative commodity price in isolation The relative commodity price at which a nation is maximizing its welfare in isolation. It is given by the slope of the common tangent to the nation's production frontier and indifference curve at the autarky point of production and consumption.

Since community indifference curves are convex and drawn as nonintersecting, there is only one point of tangency, or equilibrium. We can be certain that one such equilibrium point exists because there are an infinite number of indifference curves (even though we drew only three of them for each nation in Figure 3.2). Points on lower indifference curves are possible, but would not maximize the nation's welfare. On the other hand, the nation cannot reach higher indifference curves with the resources and technology presently available.

The equilibrium-relative commodity price in isolation is given by the slope of the common tangent to the nation's production frontier and indifference curve at the autarky point of production and consumption.

Concept
Check

How do we deter-
mine the comparative
advantage of a
nation?

Thus, the equilibrium-relative price of X in isolation is $P_A = P_X/P_Y = {}^1\!/_4$ in Nation 1 and $P_{A'} = P_X/P_Y = 4$ in Nation 2 (see Figure 3.3). Relative prices are different in the two nations because their production frontiers and indifference curves differ in shape and location.

Since in isolation $P_A < P_{A'}$, Nation 1 has a comparative advantage in commodity X and Nation 2 in commodity Y. It follows that both nations can gain if Nation 1 specializes in the production of and exports commodity X in exchange for commodity Y from Nation 2. How this takes place will be seen in the next section.

3.6 THE BASIS AND THE GAINS FROM TRADE WITH INCREASING COSTS

We have seen in Figure 3.3 that in the absence of trade the equilibrium-relative price of X is $P_A = {}^1\!/_4$ in Nation 1 and $P_{A'} = 4$ in Nation 2. Thus, Nation 1 has a comparative advantage in commodity X and Nation 2 in commodity Y. With trade, Nation 1 should now specialize in the production and export of commodity X in exchange for commodity Y from Nation 2. How this takes place is illustrated by Figure 3.4.

Starting from point A (the equilibrium point in isolation in the left panel of Figure 3.4), as Nation 1 specializes in the production of X and moves *down* its production frontier, it incurs increasing opportunity costs in the production of X. This is reflected in the increasing *slope* of its production frontier. Starting from point A' in the right panel of Figure 3.4, as Nation 2 specializes in the production of Y and moves *upward* along its production frontier, it experiences increasing opportunity costs in the production of Y. This is reflected in the *decline in the slope* of its production frontier (a reduction in the opportunity cost of X, which means a *rise* in the opportunity cost of Y).

This process of specialization in production continues until relative commodity prices (the slope of the production frontiers) become equal in the two nations. The common relative price (slope) with trade will be somewhere between the pretrade relative prices of ${}^1\!/_4$ and 4, at the level at which trade is balanced. In Figure 3.4, this is $P_B = P_{B'} = 1$.

With trade, Nation 1 moves from point A down to point B in production in the left panel of Figure 3.4. By then exchanging 80X for 80Y with Nation 2 (see trade triangle BCE), Nation 1 ends up consuming at point E (40X and 110Y) on its indifference curve III (as compared with point A on indifference curve I). Thus, Nation 1 gains from specialization in production and trade. Indifference curve III is the highest level of satisfaction that Nation 1 can reach with trade at $P_X/P_Y = 1$. Line BE is called the *trading possibilities line* or, simply, the *trade line* because trade takes place along this line.

Similarly, Nation 2 moves from point A' up to point B' in production (see the right panel of Figure 3.4), and, by exchanging 80Y for 80X with Nation 1 along trade line $B'E'$ (see trade triangle $B'C'E'$), it ends up consuming at point

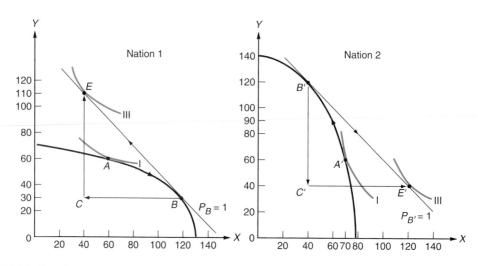

FIGURE 3.4. The Gains from Trade with Increasing Costs.
With trade, Nation 1 moves from point A to point B in production in the left panel. By then exchanging 80X for 80Y with Nation 2 (see trade triangle BCE), Nation 1 ends up consuming at point E (on indifference curve III) as compared with autarky point A on indifference curve I. Similarly, Nation 2 moves from A' to B' in production in the right panel. By then exchanging 80Y for 80X with Nation 1 (see trade triangle $B'C'E'$), Nation 2 ends up consuming at point E' on higher indifference curve III' as compared with autarky point A' on indifference curve I'. $P_B = P_{B'} = 1$ is the equilibrium-relative price—the price at which trade is balanced.

Concept Check

Can you show the gains from trade with increasing costs?

E' (120X and 40Y) on its indifference curve III' (as compared with point A' on indifference curve I'). Thus Nation 2 also gains from specialization in production and trade.

 Note that with specialization in production and trade, each nation can consume outside its production frontier (which also represented its no-trade consumption frontier). This was not possible without specialization and trade.

3.7 EQUILIBRIUM-RELATIVE COMMODITY PRICES WITH TRADE

Equilibrium-relative commodity price with trade The common relative commodity price in two nations at which trade is balanced.

The equilibrium-relative commodity price with trade is the common relative price in both nations at which trade is balanced. In Figure 3.4, this is $P_B = P_{B'} = 1$. At this relative price, the amount of X that Nation 1 wants to export (80X) equals the amount of X that Nation 2 wants to import (80X). Similarly, the amount of Y that Nation 2 wants to export (80Y) exactly matches the amount of Y that Nation 1 wants to import (80Y). Any other relative price could not persist because trade would be unbalanced.

Note that even though Nation 1 consumes less of commodity X at point E (40X) than at point A (60X), it consumes so much more of commodity Y (130Y instead of 30Y—see Figure 3.4) as to make the nation better off with trade than without trade (i.e., Nation 1 moves from community indifference curve I to III with trade). Thus, the benefit of consuming more of Y exceeds the loss of consuming less of X, and so Nation 1 is better off with trade than without trade. The reason that Nation 1 consumes less of commodity X and so much more of commodity Y with trade is that the relative price of Y has fallen while the relative price of X has risen so much with trade. The same type of reasoning applies to Nation 2.

In Figure 3.4, the equilibrium-relative commodity price was determined by trial and error; that is, various relative prices were tried until the one that balanced trade was found. The optional appendix to this chapter shows how the equilibrium-relative price with trade can be determined more rigorously by deriving and making use of (1) the demand and supply curve for each commodity in each nation and (2) offer curves.

Incomplete specialization The continued production of both commodities in both nations with increasing costs, even in a small nation with trade.

Finally, note that under increasing costs (as compared with the case of constant costs) there is incomplete specialization (i.e., neither nation specializes completely in production—see Case Study 3-1).

CASE STUDY 3-1

Specialization and Export Concentration in Selected Countries

Because of increasing costs, no nation specializes completely in the production of only one product in the real world. The closest to complete specialization in production and trade that any nation comes is Kuwait, where petroleum exports represented 92.9 percent of the total value of its exports in 2006. For Argentina, another developing nation with highly specialized natural resources, food exports represent 45.8 percent of its total exports. Table 3.1 shows that the largest export product for the United States, the 25-member European Union (EU-25), Germany (the largest economy of the EU), and Japan represents less than one-quarter of their total exports.

Table 3.1. *Leading Export as a Percentage of Total Exports of Selected Countries in 2006*

United States	Office and telecommunications equipment	13.2
European Union	Chemicals	15.0
Japan	Automotive products	21.5
Germany	Automotive products	22.1
Korea	Office and telecommunications equipment	25.7
Argentina	Food	45.8
Kuwait	Fuels	92.9

Source: WTO, *International Trade Statistics* (Geneva, 2007).

3.8 TERMS OF TRADE

Terms of trade
The ratio of the index price of a nation's export to its import commodities.

Concept Check

What does a deterioration in a nation's terms of trade mean?

The terms of trade of a nation are defined as the ratio of the price of its export commodity to the price of its import commodity. Since in a two-nation world, the exports of a nation are the imports of its trade partner, the terms of trade of the latter are equal to the inverse, or reciprocal, of the terms of trade of the former.

For example, since Nation 1 exports commodity X and imports commodity Y, the terms of trade of Nation 1 is then given by P_X/P_Y, which equals 1 in Figure 3.4. On the other hand, since Nation 2 exports commodity Y and imports commodity X, the terms of trade of Nation 2 is given by P_Y/P_X, which is equal to 1 (because the reciprocal or inverse of $P_X/P_Y = 1$, the terms of trade of Nation 1 is also equal to 1).

As supply and demand considerations change over time, the volume and the terms of trade will change. An increase or improvement in the nation's terms of trade is usually regarded as beneficial to the nation in the sense that the prices that the nation receives for its exports rise relative to the prices that it pays for its imports. In a two-nation world, an improvement in the

CASE STUDY 3-2

The Terms of Trade of the G-7 Countries

Table 3.2 gives the terms of trade of the Group of 7 largest advanced or industrial countries (G-7) for selected years from 1990 to 2007. The terms of trade were measured by dividing the index of export unit value by the index of import unit value, taking 2000 as 100. Table 3.2 shows that from 1990 to 2007 the terms of trade declined for the United States, Japan, and Germany, and increased for the other four countries, especially for Canada, primarily because of the sharp increase since 2004 in the price of petroleum (of which Canada is a major exporter).

Table 3.2. *The Terms of Trade of Industrial Countries, Selected Years, 1990–2007 (Export Unit Value ÷ Import Unit Value; 2000 = 100)*

	1990	1995	2000	2005	2007
United States	101.1	103.2	100.0	97.2	96.6
Canada	97.2	97.2	100.0	111.3	120.1
Japan	83.9	114.9	100.0	83.3	71.8
Germany	109.3	107.5	100.0	105.3	97.1
United Kingdom	101.1	101.1	100.0	104.9	104.2
France	100.1	106.5	100.0	110.6	101.4
Italy	94.0	96.0	100.0	101.1	97.6

Source: Elaborated from IMF, *International Financial Statistics* (Washington, D.C., 2008).

terms of trade of one nation necessarily involves a deterioration in the trade partner's terms of trade. For example, if over time the terms of trade of Nation 1 increased from 1 to 2, this would mean a deterioration in Nation 2's terms of trade from 1 to $1/2$.

In a world of many (rather than just two) traded commodities, the terms of trade of a nation are given by the ratio of the price index of its exports to the price index of its imports. This ratio is usually multiplied by 100 in order to express the terms of trade in percentages. These terms of trade are often referred to as the commodity or net barter terms of trade to distinguish them from other measures of the terms of trade presented in Chapter 8 in connection with trade and development. Case Study 3-2 shows the terms of trade of the G-7 countries, and Case Study 3-3 gives the terms of trade of industrial and developing countries for selected years over the 1990–2007 period.

CASE STUDY 3-3

The Terms of Trade of Industrial and Developing Countries

Table 3.3 gives the terms of trade of industrial countries, developing countries as a whole, as well as of Asian, Middle Eastern, European, and Western hemispheric developing countries for selected years from 1990 to 2006 (data for 2007 were not yet available when this edition went to press). The terms of trade were measured by dividing the index of export unit value by the index of import unit value, with 2000 as 100.

Table 3.3 shows that the terms of trade declined slightly from 1990 to 2006 for both industrial and developing countries as a group, but they declined sharply for Asian and Western hemisphere developing countries, and increased a little for Africa and a great deal for European developing countries, but especially for the Middle Eastern (primarily because of the sharp increase in the price of their petroleum exports since 2004).

Table 3.3. *The Terms of Trade of Industrial and Developing Countries, Selected Years, 1990–2006 (Export Unit Value/Import Unit Value; 2000 = 100)*

	1990	*1995*	*2000*	*2005*	*2006*
Industrial countries	99.8	104.8	100.0	101.3	99.0
Developing countries	103.0	101.9	100.0	99.4	100.5
Africa	100.4	102.8	100.0	107.9	105.2
Asia	106.8	106.8	100.0	91.5	89.2
Europe	68.7	105.5	100.0	102.1	99.8
Middle East	109.0	68.4	100.0	140.4	155.9
Western Hemisphere	129.6	107.1	100.0	104.3	108.7

Source: Elaborated from IMF, *International Financial Statistics* (Washington, D.C., various issues).

3.9 SPECIALIZATION, TRADE, AND DEINDUSTRIALIZATION

We have seen that the specialization in production that takes place with international trade involves producing more of the commodities in which the nation has a comparative advantage and less of the commodities in which the nation has a comparative disadvantage. This leads to job creation in those domestic sectors and industries in which the nation has a comparative advantage but to job losses in those domestic industries in which the nation has a comparative disadvantage. On balance, we know that more jobs are created than are lost, and the jobs created are in sectors and industries in

CASE STUDY 3-4

Job Losses in High U.S. Import-Competing Industries

Table 3.4 shows the number of workers who lost their jobs (i.e., were displaced) in various high import-competing industries in the United States between 1979 and 1999. High import-competing industries were broadly defined as those in the top 25 percent in import shares. From the table, we see that almost 6.5 million workers lost their jobs in these industries over the 1979–1999 period, with the electrical machinery and apparel industries leading the list, with 1,181,000 and 1,136,000 jobs lost, respectively. As Case 3–5 shows, however, only a small fraction of these job losses were due to imports and outsourcing.

Table 3.4. *Job Losses in High Import-Competing Industries*

Industry	Job Lost (thousands)	Industry	Job Lost (thousands)
Electrical machinery	1,181	Toys and sporting goods	156
Apparel	1,136	Primary metals other than steel	133
Motor vehicles	918	Photographic equipment	68
Electronic computing equipment	513	Leather products	57
Radio and television	395	Office and accounting machines	41
Steel	361	Pottery and related products	24
Construction machinery	351	Watches and clocks	9
Tires and other rubber products	193	Leather, tanning and finishing	5
Footwear	184	Other industries	406
Scientific instruments	164	Total	6,454
Textiles	159		

Source: L. G. Kletzer, *Job Loss from Imports:* Measuring the Costs (Washington, D.C.: Institute for International Economics, 2001), pp. 18–19.

International Trade and Deindustrialization in the United States, the European Union, and Japan

Since the 1970s, most advanced economies have been concerned with the problem of *deindustrialization*, as reflected in their declining share of manufacturing employment. Table 3.5 shows the relative importance of the different factors accounting for deindustrialization in all industrial countries as a group, in the United States, in the European Union, and in Japan, from 1970 to 1994.

Table 3.5 shows that the average share of manufacturing employment declined by about 10 percentage points in all industrial countries as a group, in the United States and in the European Union, and by about 4 percentage points in Japan. The table also shows that most of this decline, however, resulted from

the growth of labor productivity (which made possible higher levels of output with less labor), the decline in the rate of investments, and other domestic forces. International trade actually resulted in an increase in industrial employment (the negative signs indicated the opposite of deindustrialization), except in the United States. This, however, does not take into consideration that the huge U.S. trade deficits now lead to many more job losses than gains in the United States. Furthermore, the electronic revolution is increasing fears that millions of U.S. jobs are at risk of being shipped out of the country. This topic is explored in detail in Part Two of the text (Chapters 5 and 6).

Table 3.5. *Factors Responsible for Deindustrialization*

	Industrial Countries	United States	European Union	Japan
Share of manufacturing Employment (in percent)				
1970	27.6	26.4	30.4	27.0
1994	18.0	16.0	20.2	23.2
Change	−9.6	−10.4	−10.2	−3.8
Percentage change due to:				
Productivity growth	65.6	65.4	59.8	157.9
Investment	18.8	3.8	20.6	71.1
Trade	(−) 2.1	9.6	(−) 2.9	(−) 30.0
Other	17.7	21.2	22.5	(−) 51.7
Total	100.0	100.0	100.0	100.0

Source: International Monetary Fund, *Staff Studies for the World Economic Outlook* (Washington, D.C., December 1997), p. 68; R. E. Scott, "Costly Trade with China," *Briefing Paper #188*, Economic Policy Institute, October 9, 2007; and "Pain from Free Trade Spurs Second Thoughts," *The Wall Street Journal*, March 28, 2008, p. A1.

which the nation is more efficient and thus pay higher wages than in the jobs that are lost. Nevertheless, the workers and the labor unions in the sectors and industries suffering job losses invariably demand trade protection through their government representatives in order to save domestic jobs. These trade policies are examined in Part Three (Chapters 5–6) of the text. We will see that nations should in general resist these pressures and only provide assistance to workers to retrain for other jobs in expanding industries or to move to other parts of the nation where more jobs are being created. Case Study 3-4 provides an estimate of the jobs lost in high U.S. import-competing industries during the last two decades of the last century.

As we will see in Case Study 3-5, however, most of the jobs lost in these industries were not due to imports but to purely internal or domestic causes, such as technological change, changes in consumer demand, and economic restructuring. High import-competing industries did, however, experience a higher job loss than other manufacturing industries because of imports. This is evident from the fact that although high import-competing industries accounted for 30 percent of manufacturing employment, they experienced 38.4 percent of manufacturing jobs losses over the 1979–1999 period.

Deindustrialization
The decline in the relative importance of manufacturing and in the share of manufacturing employment.

Since the 1970s, the United States and other advanced economies have been concerned with the problem of deindustrialization, as reflected in its declining share of manufacturing employment. But, as pointed out in Case Study 3-5, this phenomenon was due mainly to increases in labor productivity and other internal causes rather than to foreign trade, as it was sometimes claimed. Indeed, advanced countries have been shifting their production and economies away from industry and toward the service sectors, which now represent more than half of their GDP. Therefore, it would be more appropriate to refer to advanced economies as "service economies" rather than "industrial economies."

Concept Check

What is the relationship between specialization, trade, and deindustrialization?

SUMMARY

1. This chapter extended our simple trade model to the more realistic case of increasing opportunity costs. It also introduced demand preferences in the form of community indifference curves. It then went on to examine how the interaction of these forces of demand and supply determines each nation's comparative advantage and sets the stage for specialization in production and mutually beneficial trade.

2. Increasing opportunity costs mean that the nation must give up more and more of one commodity to release just enough resources to produce each additional unit of another commodity. This leads to a concave production frontier. The slope of the production frontier gives the marginal rate of transformation (MRT). Increasing opportunity costs arise because resources are not homogeneous and are not used in the same fixed proportion in the production of all commodities. Production frontiers differ because of different factor endowments and/or technology in different nations.

3. A community indifference curve shows the various combinations of two commodities that yield equal satisfaction to the nation. Higher curves refer to a greater level of satisfaction. Community indifference curves are negatively sloped, convex, and noncrossing. The slope of indifference curves gives the marginal rate of substitution (MRS) in consumption, or the amount of one commodity that a nation could give up for each extra unit of the other commodity and still remain on the same indifference curve.

4. In the absence of trade, a nation is in equilibrium when it reaches the highest indifference curve possible with its production frontier. This occurs at the point where a community indifference curve is tangent to the nation's production frontier. The common slope of the two curves at the tangency point gives the internal equilibrium-relative commodity price in the nation and reflects the nation's comparative advantage.

5. With trade, each nation specializes in producing the commodity of its comparative advantage and faces increasing opportunity costs. Specialization in production proceeds until relative commodity prices in the two nations are equalized at the level at which trade is in equilibrium. By then trading with one another, each nation ends up consuming on a higher indifference curve than in the absence of trade. With increasing costs, specialization in production is incomplete.

6. The terms of trade of a nation are given by the ratio of the price index of its exports to the price index of its imports, multiplied by 100 in order to express the terms of trade in percentages. An increase in the nation's terms of trade is usually regarded as beneficial to the nation in the sense that the prices that the nation receives for its exports rise relative to the prices that it pays for its imports.

7. International trade results in job gains in industries in which the nation has a comparative advantage, but in job losses in industries in which the nation has a comparative disadvantage. This leads to demands to restrict imports to save domestic jobs. In general, only assistance to workers to retrain for other jobs should be provided. Advanced economies have been concerned by deindustrialization, as reflected in declining shares of manufacturing employment. This, however, was due mainly to increases in labor productivity and other internal causes rather than to foreign trade.

REVIEW QUESTIONS AND PROBLEMS

1. (a) What is the reason for increasing opportunity costs?
 (b) Why do the production frontiers of different nations have different shapes?
2. On one set of axes, sketch a concave production frontier.
 (a) Starting near the midpoint on the production frontier, use arrows to show that the nation incurs increasing opportunity costs in producing more of X (the commodity measured along the horizontal axis) and in producing more of Y.

(b) How does the slope of the production frontier change as the nation produces more of X? More of Y?

(c) What do these changes reflect?

3. (a) On one set of axes, sketch a community indifference curve tangent to the fairly flat section of a concave production frontier. On a second set of axes, sketch another (different) community indifference curve tangent to the fairly steep portion of another (different) concave production frontier.

(b) Draw in the line showing the equilibrium-relative commodity price in isolation in each nation.

(c) Which is the commodity of comparative advantage for each nation?

(d) Under what (unusual) condition would there be no such thing as comparative advantage or disadvantage between the two nations?

4. (a) On the graphs of Problem 3, show, for each nation with trade, the direction (by an arrow on the production frontier) of specialization in production and the equilibrium point of production and consumption.

(b) How much does each nation gain in consumption compared with its autarky point?

5. (a) What is meant by the equilibrium-relative commodity price of a nation in isolation?

(b) How is this price determined in each nation?

(c) How does it define the nation's comparative advantage?

6. (a) How can Nation 2 be better off at point E' than at point A' if it consumes only 40Y at point E' as compared with 60Y at point A'?

(b) Why does Nation 2 consume less of Y at point E' than at point A'?

7. (a) Why is there incomplete specialization in production (even in a smaller nation) with increasing opportunity costs?

(b) How are the results under increasing costs different from the fixed-costs case?

8. On one set of axes, draw a single concave production frontier with two different community indifference curves tangent to the single production frontier, on the assumption that two nations are identical in production but have different tastes. Indicate on your figure the autarky equilibrium-relative commodity price in each nation and show the process of specialization in production and mutually beneficial trade.

9. Suppose that the terms of trade of a nation improved from 100 to 110 over a given period of time.
(a) By how much did the terms of trade of its trade partner deteriorate?

(b) In what sense can this be said to be unfavorable to the trade partner?

(c) Does this mean that the welfare of the trade partner has definitely declined?

10. During the negotiations for NAFTA (North American Free Trade Agreement among the United States, Canada, and Mexico) in the early 1990s, opponents argued that the United States would lose many jobs to Mexico because of the much lower wages in Mexico. What was wrong with this line of reasoning?

The Equilibrium-Relative Commodity Price with Trade and the Terms of Trade

In this appendix, we show how the equilibrium-relative commodity price with trade shown in Figure 3.4 can be determined by deriving and making use of (1) the demand and supply curve for each commodity in each nation and (2) the offer curve of each nation.

A3.1 THE EQUILIBRIUM-RELATIVE COMMODITY PRICE WITH TRADE, WITH DEMAND AND SUPPLY

In this appendix we show how the equilibrium-relative commodity price with trade in Figure 3.4 can be determined by deriving and making use of the demand and supply curve for each commodity of Nation 1 and Nation 2.

In Figure 3.4, the equilibrium-relative commodity price was determined by trial and error; that is, various relative prices were tried until the one that balanced trade was found. In this section we show how the equilibrium-relative price with trade can be determined more rigorously by deriving and making use of the demand and supply curve for each commodity in each nation. This is shown in Figure 3.5.

The left panel of Figure 3.5 shows how to derive the supply curve and the demand curve for commodity X in Nation 1. The supply curve of commodity

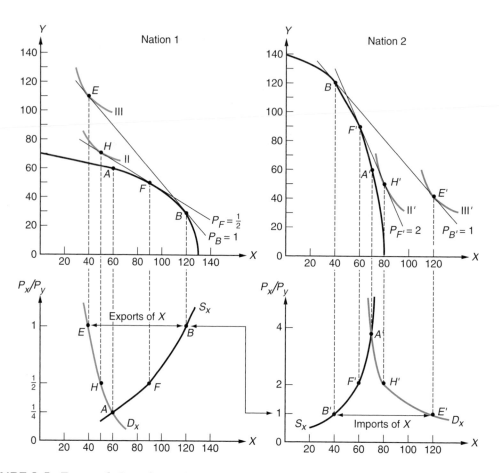

FIGURE 3.5. Demand, Supply, and Equilibrium-Relative Commodity Prices with Trade.
Supply curve *AFB* for commodity X in Nation 1 (S_X) in the left bottom panel is derived from production points A, F, and B, respectively, at $P_X/P_Y = \frac{1}{4}$, $P_X/P_Y = \frac{1}{2}$, and $P_X/P_Y = 1$ on the production frontier of Nation 1 in the top panel. Nation 1's demand curve *AHE* in the left bottom panel (D_X) is derived, respectively, from tangency points of community indifferences and trade lines at points A, H, and E in the top panel. S_X and D_X for Nation 2 in the right panel are derived in an analogous way. From both bottom panels, we see that only at $P_X/P_Y = 1$ would the quantity of exports of commodity X supplied by Nation 1 exactly match the quantity demanded of imports of commodity X of Nation 2. Thus, $P_X/P_Y = 1$ is the equilibrium-relative commodity prices with trade.

X (S_X) in Nation 1 in the bottom panel is derived from production points at various relative prices on the production frontier of Nation 1 in the top panel. Specifically, Nation 1 produces 60X at point A, where price line $P_X/P_Y = \frac{1}{4}$ (not shown in the figure to avoid unnecessarily complicating the figure) is tangent to the production frontier in the top panel. This gives point A on

supply curve S_X in the bottom panel (where P_X/P_Y is measured along the vertical axis). Nation 1 produces 90X at point F, where price line $P_X/P_Y = \frac{1}{2}$ is tangent to the production frontier in the top panel. This gives point F on supply curve S_X in the bottom panel. Finally, at $P_X/P_Y = 1$, Nation 1 produces 120X at point B, where price line $P_X/P_Y = 1$ is tangent to the production frontier in the top panel. This gives point B on supply curve S_X in the bottom panel. Joining points AFB gives Nation 1's supply curve of commodity X (S_X) in the bottom part of the figure. Note that as P_X/P_Y increases, Nation 1 produces more of commodity X.

The demand curve of commodity X (D_X) in Nation 1 shown in the bottom left-hand panel of Figure 3.5 is derived from tangency points of a community indifference curve and a trade line in the top panel. Specifically, Nation 1 demands 60X at point A in the top panel, where price line $P_X/P_Y = \frac{1}{4}$ is tangent to indifference curve I (as in Figure 3.3, but not shown in Figure 3.5 to avoid unnecessarily complicating the figure). This gives point A on demand curve D_X in the bottom panel. At $P_X/P_Y = \frac{1}{2}$, Nation 1 is in equilibrium or maximizes welfare at point H, where indifference curve II is tangent to trade line FH. This gives point H on D_X in the bottom panel. Finally, at $P_X/P_Y = 1$, Nation 1 is in equilibrium or maximizes welfare at point E, where indifference curve III is tangent to trade line BE. This gives point E on D_X in the bottom panel. Joining points AHE gives the demand curve of commodity X (D_X) in the bottom panel of the figure. Note that as P_X/P_Y increases, Nation 1 consumes less of commodity X, as postulated by the law of demand. The supply curve (S_X) and demand curve (D_X) of Nation 2 in the bottom right-hand panel of Figure 3.5 is derived in an analogous manner and is left for the student as an exercise.

Examining only the bottom panels of Figure 3.5, we see in the left panel that at $P_X/P_Y = \frac{1}{4}$, Nation 1 wants to consume at home all the 60X it produces (point A) and would export nothing. At $P_X/P_Y = \frac{1}{2}$, Nation 1 would produce 90X (point F) and consume 50X (point H), and thus it would be willing to export 40X *(FH)*. At $P_X/P_Y = 1$, Nation 1 would produce 120X (point B) and consume 40X (point E), and thus it would be willing to export 80X *(BE)*. On the other hand, the right panel shows that at $P_X/P_Y = 4$, Nation 2 would consume all the 70X it produces (point A') and would import nothing. At $P_X/P_Y = 2$, Nation 2 would consume 80X (point H') and produce 60X (point F'), and thus it would be willing to import 20X *(H'F')*. At $P_X/P_Y = 1$, Nation 1 would consume 120X (point E') and produce 40X (point B'), and thus it would be willing to import 80X *(E'B')*.

Concept Check

How do we determine the equilibrium-relative commodity prices with trade?

From both bottom panels of Figure 3.5, we see that only at $P_X/P_Y = 1$ would the quantity of exports of commodity X *supplied by Nation 1* exactly match the quantity *demanded of imports* of commodity X of Nation 2. No other relative price could persist because trade would be unbalanced. The same could be shown for commodity Y. Thus, $P_X/P_Y = 1$ is the equilibrium-relative commodity prices with trade.

A3.2 OFFER CURVES AND THE TERMS OF TRADE

In this appendix we derive the offer curve of Nation 1 and Nation 2 and show how the equilibrium-relative commodity price with trade and their terms of trade are determined at the intersection of their offer curves.

Offer curve A curve that shows how much of its import commodity a nation demands to be willing to supply various amounts of its export commodity, or the willingness of the nation to import and export at various relative commodity prices.

The offer curve (also called the reciprocal demand curve) of a nation shows how much of its import commodity the nation demands to be willing to supply various amounts of its export commodity. Thus, offer curves incorporate elements of both demand and supply. The offer curve of a nation can be derived from the nation's production frontier, its indifference map, and the various hypothetical relative commodity prices at which trade could take place. This is shown in Figure 3.6.

In the top left-hand panel of Figure 3.6, Nation 1 starts at the no-trade (or autarky) point A, as in Figure 3.3. If trade takes place at $P_B = P_X/P_Y = 1$, Nation 1 moves to point B in production, trades 80X for 80Y with Nation 2, and reaches point E on its indifference curve III (as in Figure 3.4). This gives point E in the top right-hand panel of Figure 3.6.

Reciprocal demand curve Another name for the offer curve.

At $P_F = P_X/P_Y = \frac{1}{2}$ (see the top left panel of Figure 3.6), Nation 1 would move instead from point A to point F in production, exchange 40X for 20Y with Nation 2, and reach point H on its indifference curve II. This gives point H in the right panel. Joining the origin with points H and E and other points similarly obtained, we generate Nation 1's offer curve in the right panel. This shows how much imports of commodity Y Nation 1 requires to be willing to export various quantities of commodity X. Note that Nation 1's offer curve bulges toward the X-axis (the commodity of its comparative advantage) and shows that to induce Nation 1 to export more of commodity X, P_X/P_Y must rise. Thus, at $P_F = \frac{1}{2}$, Nation 1 would export 40X, and at $P_B = 1$, it would export 80X.

The offer curve of Nation 2 is derived in an analogous manner in the middle panels of Figure 3.6. In the middle left panel of Figure 3.6, Nation 2

FIGURE 3.6. *(opposite page)* **Offer Curves and Terms of Trade.**
The offer curve of Nation 1 is derived in the top panel from Nation 1's production frontier, its indifference map, and the various hypothetical relative commodity prices at which trade could take place. The offer curve of Nation 2 is derived in an analogous manner in the middle panel. The intersection of the offer curves of Nation 1 and Nation 2 at point E in the bottom panel defines equilibrium $P_X/P_Y = P_B = P_{B'} = 1$. At P_B, Nation 1 offers 80X for 80Y (point E on Nation 1's offer curve), Nation 2 offers exactly 80Y for 80X (point E' on Nation 2's offer curve), and trade is in equilibrium. $P_B = P_X/P_Y = 1$ are Nation 1's terms of trade. $P_{B'} = P_Y/P_X = 1$ are Nation 2's terms of trade.

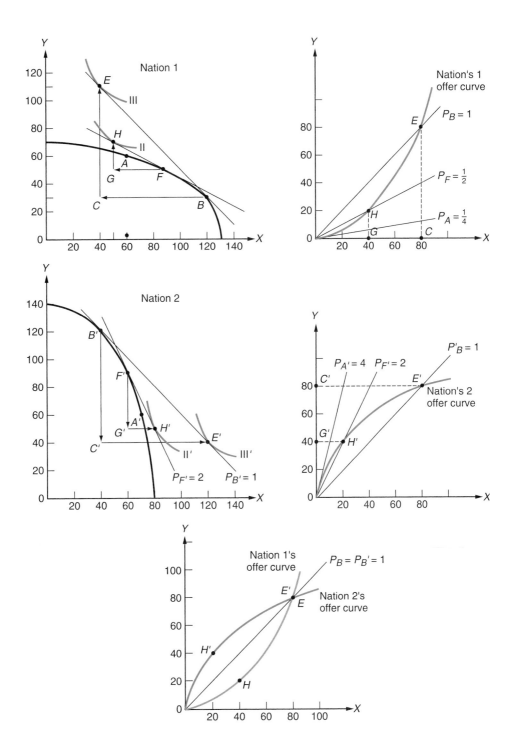

starts at the autarky equilibrium point A', as in Figure 3.3. If trade takes place at $P_{B'} = P_X/P_Y = 1$, Nation 2 moves to point B' in production, exchanges 80Y for 80X with Nation 1, and reaches point E' on its indifference curve III'. Trade triangle $B'C'E'$ in the left panel of Figure 3.6 corresponds to trade triangle $O'C'E'$ in the right panel, and we get point E' on Nation 2's offer curve.

At $P_{F'} = P_X/P_Y = 2$ in the left panel, Nation 2 would move instead to point F' in production, exchange 40Y for 20X with Nation 1, and reach point H' on its indifference curve II'. Trade triangle $F'G'H'$ in the left panel corresponds to trade triangle $O'G'H'$ in the right panel, and we get point H' on Nation 2's offer curve. Joining the origin with points H' and E' and other points similarly obtained, we generate Nation 2's offer curve in the right panel. Note that Nation 2's offer curve bulges toward the Y-axis (the commodity of its comparative advantage) and shows that to induce Nation 2 to export more of commodity Y, the relative price of Y must rise. This means that its reciprocal (i.e., P_X/P_Y) must fall. Thus, at $P_{F'} = 2$, Nation 2 would export 40Y and at $P_{B'} = 1$, it would export 80Y.

The offer curves of Nation 1 and Nation 2 intersect at point E in the bottom panel of Figure 3.6, defining equilibrium $P_X/P_Y = P_B = P_{B'} = 1$. At P_B, Nation 1 offers 80X for 80Y (point E' on Nation 1's offer curve), and Nation 2 offers exactly 80Y for 80X (point E' on Nation 2's offer curve). Thus, trade is in equilibrium at P_B. $P_B = P_X/P_Y = 1$ are Nation 1's terms of trade. $P_{B'} = P_Y/P_X = 1$ are Nation 2's terms of trade.

At any other P_X/P_Y, trade would not be in equilibrium. For example, at $P_F = \frac{1}{2}$, the 40X that Nation 1 would export (see point H in the bottom panel of Figure 3.6) falls far short of the imports of commodity X demanded by Nation 2 at this relatively low price of X (to show it we would have to extend Nation 2's offer curve until it intersected price line $P_F = \frac{1}{2}$, also not shown in the figure). The excess import demand for commodity X at $P_F = \frac{1}{2}$ by Nation 2 tends to drive P_X/P_Y up. As this occurs, Nation 1 will supply more of commodity X for export (i.e., Nation 1 will move up its offer curve), while Nation 2 will reduce its import demand for commodity X (i.e., Nation 2 will move down its offer curve) until supply and demand become equal at P_B. The pressure for P_F to move toward P_B could also be explained in terms of commodity Y and arises at any other P_X/P_Y, such as $P_F \neq P_B$.

SELECTED BIBLIOGRAPHY

For a problem-solving approach to the material covered in this chapter, with many examples and solved problems, see:

• D. Salvatore, *Theory and Problems of International Economics*, 4th ed. (New York: McGraw-Hill, 1996), ch. 2 (sects. 2.4 and 2.5) and ch. 3.

For a classic diagrammatic presentation of cost conditions in international trade, see:

- G. Haberler, *The Theory of International Trade* (London: W. Hodge & Co., 1936), ch. 12.

For an exposition of the gains from trade, see:

- P. Kenen, "Distribution, Demand and Equilibrium in International Trade: A Diagrammatic Analysis," *Kyklos*, December 1959, pp. 629–658. Reprinted in R. E. Caves and H. G. Johnson, *Readings in International Economics* (Homewood, Ill.: Irwin, 1968), pp. 90–98.

The changing pattern of comparative advantage in the United States and other industrial nations is examined in:

- R. Z. Lawrence, *Can America Compete?* (Washington, D.C.: Brookings Institution, 1984).
- M. E. Porter, *The Comparative Advantage of Nations* (New York: The Free Press, 1990).
- M. E. Porter, *On Competition* (Cambridge, Mass.: Harvard Business School Press, 1998).

Job losses in high import-competing industries are examined in:

- L. G. Kletzer, *Job Loss from Imports: Measuring the Costs* (Washington, D.C.: Institute for International Economics, 2001).
- B. Bradford and L. G. Kletzer, "Fear of Offshoring: The Scope of Potential Impact of Exports and Imports of Services," *Policy Brief*, Peterson Institute, January 2008.

INTERNet

Information and data on the comparative advantage of nations, specialization and export concentration, and deindustrialization are published by the World Trade Organization (WTO), the United Nations, the International Monetary Fund, and the World Bank and can be found at:

http://www.wto.org

http://unstats.un.org/unsd

http://www.imf.org

http://worldbank.org

For deindustrialization, see:

http://www.imf.org/external/pubs/ft/issues10

http://www.imf.org/external/pubs/ft/wp/WP9742.PDF

The Heckscher–Ohlin and Other Trade Theories

After studying this chapter, you should be able to:

- Know what the factor proportion or the Heckscher–Ohlin theory postulates
- Explain how international trade affects the income distribution in a nation
- Explain how international trade can be based on economies of scale
- Know how product differentiation can be a basis for international trade
- Understand the technological gap and product cycle models of trade
- Understand how transportation costs affect international trade
- Understand the relationship between environmental standards and trade

CHAPTER OUTLINE

KEY TERMS

Heckscher–Ohlin (H–O) theory

Heckscher–Ohlin (H–O) theorem

Factor-proportions or factor-endowment theory

Revealed comparative advantage

Factor- price equalization theorem

Stolper-Samuelson theorem

Specific-factors model

Leontief paradox

Increasing returns to scale

Outsourcing

International economies of scale

Differentiated products

Intra-industry trade

Technological gap model

Product cycle model

Transport or logistics costs

Nontraded goods and services

Environmental standards

4.1 INTRODUCTION

In this chapter, we extend the standard trade model that we examined in Chapter 3 in three important directions. *First*, we explain the basis of (i.e., what determines) comparative advantage. We have seen in Chapter 3

that the difference in relative commodity prices between two nations is evidence of their comparative advantage and forms the basis for mutually beneficial trade. We now go one step further and explain the reason, or cause, for the difference in relative commodity prices and comparative advantage between the two nations.

The *second* way we extend our trade model is to analyze the effect that international trade has on the earnings of factors of production in the two trading nations. That is, we want to examine the effect of international trade on the earnings of labor and capital, as well as on international differences in earnings. These two important questions, left unanswered by the standard trade model, are explained in this chapter by the Heckscher–Ohlin (H–O) or factor-proportions theory.

The *third* way we extend our trade model is to examine other trade theories that base international trade on economies of scale, product differentiation, or technological differences among nations. We conclude the chapter by examining transportation costs and the effect of environmental standards on international trade. The optional appendix to this chapter presents the specific-factors and intra-industry trade models.

4.2 FACTOR ENDOWMENTS AND THE HECKSCHER–OHLIN THEORY

In 1919 *Eli Heckscher*, a Swedish economist, published an article entitled "The Effect of Foreign Trade on the Distribution of Income." The article went largely unnoticed for over ten years until *Bertil Ohlin*, another Swedish economist and former student of Heckscher, picked it up, clarified, built on it, and in 1933 published his famous book *Interregional and International Trade*, which represents a major extension of the standard trade model presented in Chapter 3.

In Chapter 3, we saw that the difference in relative commodity prices and comparative advantage between two nations was based on the difference in production frontiers (resulting from a difference in the relative abundance of factors of production and/or technology) and a difference in the community indifference curves (tastes) in the two nations—see Figures 3.3 and 3.4. This difference in production frontiers and community indifference curves was the basis for the difference in relative commodity prices and comparative advantage in the two nations.

Heckscher–Ohlin (H–O) theory The theory that postulates that (1) a nation exports commodities intensive in its relatively abundant and cheap factor and (2) international trade brings about equalization in returns to homogeneous factors across countries.

The Heckscher–Ohlin (H–O) theory focuses on the difference in the relative abundance of factors of production in various nations as the most important determinant of the difference in relative commodity prices and comparative advantage. The *Heckscher–Ohlin (H–O) theory* can be expressed in the form of two theorems: the so-called *H–O theorem* (which deals with and

predicts the pattern of trade) and the *factor–price equalization theorem* (which deals with the effect of international trade on factor prices). In this section we discuss the H–O theorem. The factor–price equalization theorem will be discussed in Section 4.4.

Heckscher–Ohlin (H–O) theorem The part of the Heckscher–Ohlin theory that postulates that a nation will export the commodity intensive in its relatively abundant and cheap factor and import the commodity intensive in its relatively scarce and expensive factor.

The Heckscher–Ohlin (H–O) theorem postulates that *a nation will export the commodity whose production requires the intensive use of the nation's relatively abundant and cheap factor and import the commodity whose production requires the intensive use of the nation's relatively scarce and expensive factor.* In short, the relatively labor-rich nation exports the relatively labor-intensive commodity and imports the relatively capital-intensive commodity.

Of all the possible reasons for differences in relative commodity prices and comparative advantage among nations, the H–O theorem isolates the difference in relative factor abundance, or *factor endowments*, among nations as the basic cause or determinant of comparative advantage and international trade. For this reason, the H–O theory is often referred to as the factor-proportions or factor-endowment theory. That is, each nation specializes in the production of and exports the commodity intensive in its relatively abundant and cheap factor and imports the commodity intensive in its relatively scarce and expensive factor.

Factor-proportions or **factor-endowment theory** See Heckscher–Ohlin theory.

Thus, the H–O theorem *explains* comparative advantage rather than assuming it (as was the case for classical economists). The H–O theorem postulates that the difference in relative *factor* abundance and relative *factor* prices is the *cause* of the pretrade difference in relative commodity prices between two nations. This difference in *relative* factor and *relative* commodity prices is then translated into a difference in *absolute* factor and commodity prices between the two nations (as outlined in Section 2.6). It is this difference in absolute commodity prices in the two nations that is the *immediate* cause of trade.

Concept Check

Why is the Heckscher–Ohlin theory often referred to as the factor proportion theory?

That is, a businessperson does not have to know the H–O theory or the cause of the different dollar price of different commodities in the two nations to trade. He or she simply buys the good in the nation where it is cheaper and sells it in the nation where it is more expensive. But the difference in the dollar price of commodities in the two nations is based on a difference in relative commodity prices (i.e., P_X/P_Y) in the two nations, which is itself based on a difference in relative factor prices (say, the price of labor in relation to the price of capital), which depends (according to the H–O theory) on the relative abundance of factors (say labor and capital) in the two nations.

4.3 THE FORMAL HECKSCHER–OHLIN MODEL

To show the H–O model graphically, assume that Nation 1 is the *labor-abundant country* (i.e., Nation 1 has more labor in relation to capital than Nation 2) and that commodity X is the relatively *labor-intensive commodity*

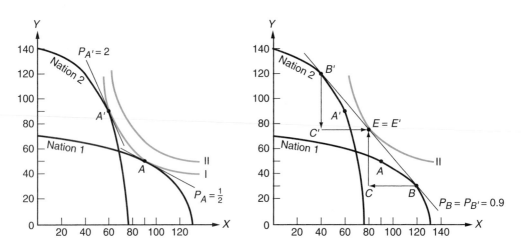

FIGURE 4.1. The Heckscher–Ohlin Model.
Indifference curves I and II are common to both nations because of the assumption of equal tastes. Indifference curve I is tangent to the production frontier of Nation 1 at point A and tangent to the production frontier of Nation 2 at point A'. This defines the no-trade equilibrium-relative commodity price of $P_A = \frac{1}{2}$ in Nation 1 and $P_{A'} = 2$ in Nation 2 (see the left panel). Since $P_A < P_{A'}$, Nation 1 has a comparative advantage in commodity X and Nation 2 in commodity Y. With trade (see the right panel), Nation 1 produces at point B and by exchanging 40X for 45Y reaches point E in consumption (see trade triangle BCE). Nation 2 produces at point B' and by exchanging 45Y for 40X reaches point E' (which coincides with E—see trade triangle $B'C'E'$). Both nations gain from trade because they consume on higher indifference curve II.

(i.e., the ratio of labor to capital, L/K, in the production of X is greater than in the production of Y). This gives a production frontier for Nation 1 that is relatively flatter and wider than the production frontier of Nation 2. This is shown in the left panel of Figure 4.1.

In the left panel of Figure 4.1, we have plotted the production frontiers of Nation 1 and Nation 2 on the same set of axes. (These are the production frontiers used in Chapter 3.) Since Nation 1 is the L-abundant nation and commodity X is the L-intensive commodity, Nation 1's production frontier is skewed toward the horizontal axis, which measures commodity X. On the other hand, since Nation 2 is the K-abundant nation and commodity Y is the K-intensive commodity, Nation 2's production frontier is skewed toward the vertical axis, measuring commodity Y. The production frontiers are plotted on the same set of axes so that the difference in their shape is more clearly evident and because this will facilitate the illustration of the Heckscher–Ohlin model.

Suppose that in the absence of trade the two nations have the same tastes or community indifference curves. Nation 1 will then be in equilibrium at

point A, where indifference curve I is tangent to its production frontier, while Nation 2 will be in equilibrium at point A' where indifference curve I is tangent to its own production frontier (see the left panel of Figure 4.1). Since $P_X/P_Y = P_A = \frac{1}{2}$ in Nation 1 is lower than $P_X/P_Y = P_{A'} = 2$ in Nation 2 in the absence of trade, Nation 1 has a comparative advantage in commodity X while Nation 2 has a comparative advantage in commodity Y.

With trade (see the right panel of Figure 4.1, Nation 1 specializes in the production of commodity X and moves from point A to point B in production. By then exchanging 40X for 45Y with Nation 2 at $P_X/P_Y = P_B = 0.9$ (40/45), Nation 1 reaches point E in consumption (see trade triangle BCE), which is on higher indifference curve II. Nation 2 specializes in the production of commodity Y and moves from point A' to point B' in production. By then exchanging 45Y for 40X with Nation 1 at $P_X/P_Y = P_B = P_{B'} = 0.9$, Nation 2 reaches point E' in consumption (see trade triangle $B'C'E'$), which is on higher indifference curve II. Both nations gain from trade because they consume on higher indifference curve II, as compared with consuming on indifference curve I in the absence of trade.

The H–O theorem isolates the difference in the *physical* availability or supply of factors of production among nations (in the face of equal tastes and technology) to explain the difference in relative commodity prices and trade among nations. Note, however, that the H–O model does not require that tastes and technology be exactly the same in the two nations for these results to follow. It only requires that they be broadly similar, so that it is the difference in factor supplies or endowments among nations that is the *primary* cause of the difference in relative commodity prices and trade among them.

Case Study 4-1 examines the pattern of revealed comparative advantage and disadvantage of various countries or regions based on differences in factor endowments. Revealed comparative advantage or disadvantage is measured by exports minus imports in each product category, as a percentage of the total manufactured exports of the nation or region. The index can range from +1 to −1. A positive coefficient indicates a revealed comparative *advantage* while a negative coefficient indicates a revealed comparative *disadvantage*. The absolute value (i.e., the value disregarding the sign) of the estimated coefficient then indicates the degree or strength of the comparative advantage or disadvantage.

4.4 FACTOR–PRICE EQUALIZATION AND INCOME DISTRIBUTION

The factor–price equalization theorem of the H–O model postulates that *international trade will bring about equalization in the returns to homogeneous or identical factors across nations.* What this means is that international trade will cause the wages of the same type of labor (i.e., labor with the same

Concept Check

Can you show the factor proportion or Heckscher–Ohlin theory graphically?

Revealed comparative advantage The revealed comparative advantage of a nation or region is measured by the excess in the percentage of total exports over the percentage of total imports in each major commodity group for the nation or region.

Factor–price equalization (H–O) theorem The part of the H–O theory that predicts, under highly restrictive assumptions, that international trade will bring about equalization in relative and absolute returns to homogeneous factors across nations.

CASE STUDY 4-1

The Revealed Comparative Advantage of Various Countries and Regions

Table 4.1 gives the revealed comparative advantage or disadvantage in capital-intensive, skill-intensive, and unskilled-intensive manufactured goods of various nations, groups of nations, or regions in 1993. It shows that the United States, the European Union, and Japan have a comparative advantage in capital-intensive and skill-intensive commodities, but a comparative disadvantage in unskilled-intensive commodities—just as it could be predicted by their relative-factor endowments. Canada has a comparative advantage in capital-intensive commodities but a comparative disadvantage in skilled-intensive and unskilled-intensive commodities. All other countries or regions have a comparative advantage in unskilled-intensive commodities and a comparative disadvantage in capital-intensive and skill-intensive commodities (except for Mexico).

Table 4.1. *Revealed Comparative Advantage of Various Countries and Regions*

Country/Region	Capital	Skilled	Unskilled
United States	0.11	0.06	−0.30
European Union	0.03	0.01	−0.06
Japan	0.07	0.15	−0.50
Canada	0.19	−0.25	−0.03
Rest of OECD[a]	0.00	−0.01	0.01
Mexico	−0.05	−0.02	0.01
Rest of Latin America	−0.16	−0.23	0.47
China	−0.24	−0.25	0.44
India	−0.04	−0.64	0.37
Hong Kong, South Korea, Taiwan, Singapore	−0.11	−0.03	0.14
Rest of Asia	−0.33	−0.05	0.40
Eastern Europe (Including Russia)	−0.08	−0.31	0.36
OPEC[b]	−0.09	−0.29	0.45
Rest of the world	−0.17	−0.18	0.40

[a]OECD = Organization for Economic Cooperation and Development, which includes all the other industrial countries.
[b]OPEC = Organization of Petroleum Exporting Countries.
Source: W. R. Cline, *Trade and Income Distribution*, op. cit., p. 192.

level of training, skills, and productivity) to be the same in all trading nations (in the absence of trade restriction, transportation costs, and other assumptions). Similarly, international trade will cause the return or earnings of homogeneous capital (i.e., capital of the same productivity and risk) to be the same in all trading nations. Both relative and absolute factor prices are equalized.

From Section 4.3, we know that in the absence of trade the relative price of commodity X is lower in Nation 1 than in Nation 2 because the relative price of labor, or wage rate, is lower in Nation 1. As Nation 1 specializes in the production of commodity X (the *L*-intensive commodity) and reduces its production of commodity Y (the *K*-intensive commodity), the relative demand for labor rises, causing wages to rise, while the relative demand for capital falls, causing the price of capital or the interest rate to fall. The exact opposite occurs in Nation 2. That is, as Nation 2 specializes in the production of Y and reduces its production of commodity X with trade, its demand for labor falls, causing the wage rate to fall, while its demand for capital rises, causing the interest rate to rise.

Thus, international trade causes the wage rate to rise in Nation 1 (the low-wage nation) and to fall in Nation 2 (the high-wage nation) and reduces the pretrade difference in wages between the two nations. Similarly, international trade causes the interest rate to fall in Nation 1 (the *K*-expensive nation) and to rise in Nation 2 (the *K*-cheap nation), thus reducing the pretrade difference in interest rates between the two nations. As long as wages and interest rates differ between the two nations, trade continues to expand, but its expansion reduces the difference in wage and interest rates. International trade continues to expand until wages and interest rates are completely equalized between the two nations. This is true not only for relative but also absolute or real wages and interest rates. That is, free international trade continues to expand until the real wages for the same type of labor in the two nations and the real rate of interest for the same type of capital in the two nations are completely equalized (in the absence of trade restriction, transportation costs, and other assumptions).

Concept Check

How does international trade affect factor prices and income distribution?

The equalization of relative and absolute factor prices between the two nations as a result of free trade implies that the real *income* of labor will rise and the real *income* of owners of capital will fall in Nation 1 (the nation with relatively abundant and cheap labor and relative scarce and expensive capital) and the real income of labor will fall and the real income of owners of capital will rise in Nation 2 (the nation with expensive labor and cheap capital). This is the conclusion of the Stolper–Samuelson theorem. More generally, the Stolper–Samuelson theorem postulates that free international trade reduces the real income of the nation's relatively scarce factor and increases the real income of the nation's relatively abundant factor.

Stolper–Samuelson theorem It postulates that free international trade reduces the real income of the nation's relatively scarce factor and increases the real income of the nation's relatively abundant factor.

Since in developed nations (e.g., the United States, Germany, Japan, France, Britain, Italy, Canada) labor is the relatively scarce factor and capital is the relatively abundant factor (as in our Nation 2), international trade tends to reduce the real income of labor and increase the real income of owners of capital. This is why labor unions in developed nations generally favor trade restrictions. On the other hand, since in less developed nations (e.g., India, Egypt, Korea, Mexico) capital is the relatively scarce factor, international

trade will reduce the real income of capital owners and increase the real income of labor.

But with international trade causing real wages and the real income of labor to fall in a labor-scarce and capital-abundant nation such as the United States, shouldn't the U.S. government restrict trade? The answer is almost invariably no. The reason is that the loss that trade causes to labor (particularly unskilled labor—see Case Study 4-2) is less than the gain received by owners of capital. With an appropriate redistribution policy of taxes on owners of capital and subsidies to labor, both broad classes of factors of production can benefit from international trade. Such a redistribution policy can take the form of retraining for other jobs the labor displaced by imports, tax relief for labor, and provisions for more social services. We will return to this important question in our discussion of trade policies in Chapters 5 and 6.

Specific-factors model The model to analyze the effect of a change in commodity price on the returns of factors in a nation when at least one factor is not mobile between industries.

This conclusion holds only if labor and capital are completely mobile between the different industries or sectors in each economy. Suppose, instead, that labor was mobile, but capital was not. That is, suppose that some type of capital (such as agricultural machinery) could be used only in or was *specific* to the production of one good (say, food), while another type of capital (such as industrial machinery) could be used only in or were specific to the production of another good (say, cloth), then we have the specific-factors model. This postulates that the opening of trade leads to (1) an increase in the return or earnings of capital specific or used to produce the nation's export commodity, (2) a reduction in the return of capital specific or used in the nation's import-competing industry, and (3) ambiguous results (i.e., to an increase or a decrease) in the return or earnings of labor (the mobile factor). The specific-factors model is more likely to be applicable in the short run (when some factors are likely to be specific) than in the long run when all factors are variable and less likely to be specific. The specific-factors model is presented in optional Appendix A4.1.

Concept Check

When is the specific-factors model applicable?

Finally, note that international trade acts as a substitute for the international mobility of factors of production in its effect on factor prices. Specifically, with perfect mobility (i.e., with complete information and no legal restrictions or transportation costs), labor would migrate from the low-wage nation to the high-wage nation until wages in the two nations became equal. Similarly, capital would move from the low-interest to the high-interest nation until the rate of interest was equalized in the two nations. While trade operates on the demand for factors, factor mobility operates on the supply of factors. In either case, the result is complete equalization in the returns to homogeneous factors. With some (rather than perfect) international mobility of factors, a smaller volume of international trade would be required to bring about equality in factor returns between the two nations.

CASE STUDY 4-2

Has International Trade Increased U.S. Wage Inequalities?

Has international trade increased wage inequalities between skilled and unskilled workers in the United States and other industrial countries? The answer is yes, but it was probably not a major cause. First, some facts. Between 1979 and 1993, average real wages declined by more than 20 percent for U.S. high school graduates but rose by 11 percent for college graduates, resulting in a large increase in skilled–unskilled workers' real wage inequalities. According to another study, the real wage differential between college and high school graduates in the United States increased by 63 percent between 1973 and 1996. The question is how much did international trade contribute to this increase?

Here there are wide disagreements. Some economists, such as *Rodrik* (1997), argue that the growth of manufactured exports from newly industrializing economies (NIEs) was the major cause of the increased wage inequalities in the United States and unemployment in Western Europe during the past two decades. Other economists, such as *Cline* (1997), however, point out that industrial countries' nonpetroleum imports from low-wage countries are only about 3 percent of their GDP and, hence, it could

not possibly have been the major cause of the large fall in the real wages of unskilled workers in the United States and the large increase in unemployment (because of more rigid wages) in Western Europe. They acknowledge that international trade certainly contributed to the unskilled workers' problems in industrial countries, but that it played only a minor role (i.e., it may have been responsible for no more than 10 to 15 percent) in the increase in U.S. skilled–unskilled real wage inequalities. Most of the increase in unskilled–skilled real wage inequalities was probably due to technological changes, such as automation and the computerization of many jobs, which sharply reduced the demand for unskilled workers in the United States and Europe.

The weight of evidence seems to be with this latter view—international trade may have sped up the introduction of labor-saving innovations, but it may have had only a small *direct* impact on the demand and wages of unskilled labor in industrial nations. Table 4.2 shows that international trade contributed only 10.1 percent to the increase in wage inequalities in the United States in 1995. Most of the increase in wage inequality was due to other factors.

Table 4.2. *Sources of Wage Inequalities in the United States*

Source of Wage Inequality	Contribution (in percent)
Technological change	37.7
Trade	10.1
Stagnant minimum wage	7.2
Decline of unions	4.4
Immigration	2.9
Unexplained	37.7

Source: "At the Heart of the Trade Debate: Inequity," *The Wall Street Journal*, October 31, 1997, p. A2.

4.5 EMPIRICAL TESTS OF THE HECKSCHER–OHLIN THEORY

Concept Check

Why is the Leontief paradox important for the H-O theory?

Leontief paradox
The empirical finding that U.S. import substitutes were more *K* intensive than U.S. exports. This is contrary to the H–O trade model, which predicts that, as the most *K*-abundant nation, the United States should import *L*-intensive products and export *K*-intensive products.

The first empirical test of the Heckscher–Ohlin model was conducted by *Leontief* in 1951 using U.S. data for the year 1947. Since the United States was the most *K*-abundant nation in the world, Leontief expected to find that it exported *K*-intensive commodities and imported *L*-intensive commodities. The results of Leontief's test were startling. The U.S. import substitutes were about 30 percent more *K* intensive than U.S. exports. That is, the United States seemed to export *L*-intensive commodities and import *K*-intensive commodities. This was the opposite of what the H–O model predicted, and it became known as the Leontief paradox.

One possible source of bias and reason for the paradox was that Leontief used a two-factor model (*L* and *K*), thus abstracting from other factors such as natural resources (soil, climate, mineral deposits, forests, etc.). Classifying a commodity that was intensive in natural resources as either *K* or *L* intensive (with a two-factor model) was clearly inappropriate. Leontief also included in his measure of capital only physical capital (such as machinery, other equipment, buildings, and so on), completely ignoring human capital. *Human capital* refers to the education, job training, and health embodied in workers, which increase their productivity. Subsequent empirical tests that included human capital and excluded natural resources removed or eliminated the paradox.

Recent research using data on many sectors, for many countries, over many years, and allowing for differences in technology and factor productivities among countries provided confirmation of the H–O model, especially when considering that countries could specialize in a particular subset or group of commodities that were best suited to their specific factor endowments (see *Salvatore*, 2007, Sect. 5.6). An increasing amount of trade, however, is today based on economies of scale, product differentiation, and technological differences across countries. These are discussed in the rest of the chapter and complement the basic H-O model in explaining the pattern of world trade.

With regard to factor-price equalization (H–O theorem II), even casual observation clearly indicates that trade has not equalized the earnings or returns to identical factors across countries. Thus, wages are much higher for doctors, engineers, technicians, mechanics, secretaries, and laborers in the United States and Germany than in Mexico and China. But the reason for this is that many of the simplifying assumptions (such as all countries using exactly the same technology, no trade restrictions, etc.) on which the H–O theory rests do not hold in the real world, and many other forces (such as more rapid technological change) may proceed more rapidly in some countries than in others. Under these circumstances, it is more realistic to expect international trade to reduce (rather than eliminate)

international difference in the returns to homogeneous o:
across countries—and this has certainly occurred for com
and benefits) across industrial countries over the past deca
the hourly compensation of production workers in Japane
increased from 48 percent of U.S. hourly compensation in :
in 2006; in the United Kingdom it rose from 54 percent to 1

4.6 ECONOMIES OF SCALE AND INTERNATIONAL TRADE

Even if two nations face identical production and demand conditions (i.e., they have identical production frontiers and community indifference curves) so that relative commodity prices are identical in the two nations before trade (i.e., there is no comparative advantage or disadvantage), there is still a basis for mutually beneficial trade between the two nations based on increasing returns to scale.

Increasing returns to scale The production situation where output grows proportionately more than the increase in inputs or factors of production. For example, doubling all inputs more than doubles output.

Increasing returns to scale refer to the production situation where output grows proportionately more than the increase in inputs or factors of production. For example, output may more than double with a doubling of inputs. Increasing returns to scale may occur because at a larger scale of operation a greater division of labor and specialization becomes possible. That is, as each worker specializes in performing a simple repetitive task, labor productivity increases. Furthermore, a larger scale of operation permits the introduction of more specialized and productive machinery than would be feasible at a smaller scale of operation. About a third of all goods-producing industries are characterized by increasing returns to scale in the world today.

Figure 4.2 shows how mutually beneficial trade can be based on increasing returns to scale. If the two nations are assumed to be identical in every respect, we can use a single production frontier and a single indifference map to refer to both nations. Increasing returns to scale result in production frontiers that are *convex*, or inward-bending. Here, as each nation specializes in the production of a commodity, the relative price of the commodity diminishes, rather than increases (as in the increasing costs case examined earlier). With identical production frontiers and indifference maps, the no-trade equilibrium relative commodity prices in the two nations are also identical. In Figure 4.2, this is $P_X/P_Y = P_A$ in both nations and is given by the slope of the common tangent to the production frontier and indifference curve I at point A.

With trade, Nation 1 could specialize completely in the production of commodity X and produce at point B. Nation 2 would then specialize completely in the production of commodity Y and produce at point B'. By then exchanging 60X for 60Y with each other, each nation would end up consuming at point E on indifference curve II, thus gaining 20X and 20Y. These gains from trade arise from economies of scale in the production of

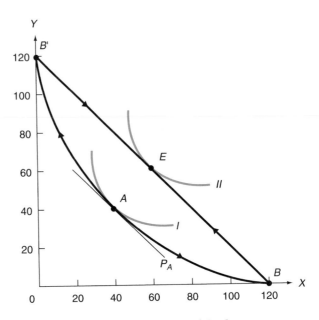

FIGURE 4.2. **Trade Based on Economies of Scale.**

With identical and convex to the origin (because of economies of scale) production frontiers and indifference maps, the no-trade equilibrium-relative commodity price in the two nations is identical and given by P_A. With trade, Nation 1 could specialize completely in the production of commodity X and produce at point B. Nation 2 would then specialize completely in the production of commodity Y and produce at point B'. By then exchanging 60X for 60Y with each other, each nation would end up consuming at point E on indifference curve II, thus gaining 20X and 20Y.

Concept Check

How can international trade be based on increasing economies of scale?

only one commodity in each nation. In the absence of trade, the two nations would not specialize in the production of only one commodity because each nation wants to consume both commodities.

Note that the no-trade equilibrium point A is unstable in the sense that if, for whatever reason, Nation 1 moves to the right of point A along its production frontier, the relative price of X (the slope of the production frontier) will fall and will continue to fall until Nation 1 becomes completely specialized in the production of commodity X. Similarly, if Nation 2 moves to the left of point A along its production frontier, P_X/P_Y will rise (so that its inverse, P_Y/P_X, falls) until Nation 2 becomes completely specialized in the production of commodity Y.

Several additional aspects of this analysis and Figure 4.2 must be clarified. First of all, it is a matter of complete indifference as to which of the two nations specializes in the production of commodity X or commodity Y. In the real world, this may result from historical accident. Second, the two nations

Outsourcing A firm's purchase of parts and components abroad, rather than itself producing them at home, in order to keep costs down in a global world economy.

need not be identical in every respect for mutually beneficial trade to result from increasing returns to scale. Third, during the past decade or so, there has been a sharp increase in international trade in parts and components, or outsourcing, as well as in setting up of production facilities abroad, and these have been the source of new and significant international economies of scale (see Case Study 4-3).

Finally, and somewhat related to economies of scale, is the hypothesis advanced by *Linder* in 1961 that a nation exports those manufactured products for which a large domestic market exists. These are products that appeal to the *majority* of the population. In the process of satisfying such a market, the nation acquires the necessary experience and efficiency to be

CASE STUDY 4-3

The New International Economies of Scale

Today, more and more products manufactured by international corporations have parts and components made in many different nations (see Case Study 1-1). The reason is to minimize production costs. For example, the motors of some Ford Fiestas are produced in the United Kingdom, the transmissions in France, the clutches in Spain, and the parts are assembled in Germany for sales throughout Europe. Similarly, Japanese and German cameras are often assembled in Singapore to take advantage of cheaper labor there.

Foreign "sourcing" of inputs is often not a matter of choice to earn higher profits, but simply a requirement to remain competitive. Firms that do not look abroad for cheaper inputs face loss of competitiveness in world markets and even in the domestic market. U.S. firms now spend more than $100 billion on outsourcing and by doing so they cut costs by 10–15 percent. Outsourcing now accounts for more than one-third of total manufacturing costs by Japanese firms, and this saves them more than 20 percent of production costs.

Firms must constantly explore sources of cheaper inputs and overseas production in order to remain competitive in our rapidly

shrinking world. Indeed, this process can be regarded as manufacturing's *new international economies of scale* in today's global economy. Just as companies were forced to rationalize operations within each country in the 1980s, they now face the challenge of integrating the operations for their entire system of manufacturing around the world to take advantage of these new international economies of scale. What is important is for the firm to focus on its core competency, produce only those components that are indispensable to the company's competitive position over subsequent product generations, and outsource other components in which outside suppliers have a distinctive production advantage. These new international economies of scale are likely to become even more important in the future as we move closer and closer to a truly global economy.

Source: "Manufacturing's New Economies of Scale," *Harvard Business Review*, May–June 1992, pp. 94–102; "How to Think Strategically About Outsourcing," *Harvard Management Update*, May 2000, pp. 4–6; and D. Salvatore, "The U.S. Challenge to European Firms," *European Journal of International Management*, Vol. 1, No.1, 2007, pp. 69–80.

International economies of scale The increased productivity resulting from the firm's integration of its entire system of manufacturing operations around the world.

able subsequently to export these commodities to other nations with similar tastes and income levels. The nation will then import those products that appeal to its low- and high-income *minorities*. According to this *"preference similarity"* or *"overlapping demands"* hypothesis, trade in manufactures is likely to be largest among countries with similar tastes and income levels. While confirmed for his native Sweden, Linder's hypothesis has not been confirmed for other nations. It also cannot explain, for example, why China exports artificial Christmas trees in the absence of a domestic market for these products.

4.7 TRADE BASED ON PRODUCT DIFFERENTIATION

A large portion of the output of modern economies today involves differentiated rather than homogeneous products. Thus, a Chevrolet is not identical to a Toyota, a Volkswagen, or a Renault. As a result, a great deal of international trade can and does involve the exchange of differentiated products of the same industry or broad product group. That is, a great deal of international trade is intra-industry trade in differentiated products, as opposed to inter-industry trade in completely different products.

Differentiated products The somewhat different products (such as automobiles, cigarettes, and soaps) produced by different manufacturers in the same industry or general product group.

Intra-industry trade arises in order to take advantage of important economies of scale in production. That is, international competition forces each firm or plant in industrial countries to produce only one, or at most a few, varieties and styles of the same product rather than many different varieties and styles. This is crucial in keeping unit costs low. With few varieties and styles, more specialized and faster machinery can be developed for a continuous operation and a longer production run. The nation then imports other varieties and styles from other nations. Intra-industry trade benefits consumers because of the wider range of choices (i.e., the greater variety of differentiated products) available at the lower prices made possible by economies of scale in production.

Intra-industry trade International trade in the differentiated products of the same industry or broad product group.

Even before the formation of the European Union, plant size in most industries was about the same in Europe and the United States. However, unit costs were much higher in Europe, primarily because European plants produced many more varieties and styles of a product than did their American counterparts. As tariffs were eliminated and trade expanded within the European Union, each plant specialized in the production of only a few varieties and styles of a product, and unit costs fell sharply.

Concept Check

How can international trade be based on product differentiation?

Two interesting considerations must be made with respect to the intra-industry trade models developed by *Elhanan Helpman, Paul Krugman, Kelvin Lancaster*, and others since 1979. First, although trade in the H–O model is based on comparative advantage or differences in factor

endowments (labor, capital, natural resources, and technology) among nations, intra-industry trade is based on product differentiation and economies of scale. While trade based on comparative advantage is likely to be larger when the difference in factor endowments among nations is greater, intra-industry trade is likely to be larger among industrial economies of similar size and factor proportions (when factors of production are broadly defined).

Second, in contrast to the H–O model, which predicts that trade will lower the return of the nation's scarce factor, with intra-industry trade based on economies of scale, it is possible for all factors to gain. This may explain why the formation of the European Union and the great postwar trade liberalization in manufactured goods met little resistance by interest groups. This is to be contrasted to the strong objections raised by labor in industrial countries against liberalizing trade with some of the most advanced of the developing countries because this trade, being of the inter- rather than of the intra-industry trade type, could lead to the collapse of entire industries (such as the textile industry) and involve lower real wages and massive reallocations of labor to other industries in industrial nations.

Concept Check

What is the difference between inter- and intra-industry trade?

The tentative conclusion that can be reached, therefore, is that comparative advantage seems to determine the pattern of *inter-industry trade*, while economies of scale in differentiated products give rise to *intra-industry trade*. Both types of international trade occur in today's world. The more dissimilar are factor endowments (as between developed and developing countries), the more important are comparative advantage and *inter-industry* trade. On the other hand, *intra-industry* trade is likely to be dominant the more similar are factor endowments (as among developed countries).

Recent empirical tests of the H-O theory discussed in Section 4.5, however, showed that by allowing for differences in technology and factor prices across countries, for the existence of nontraded goods and transportation costs, and by utilizing more disaggregated factor endowments and trade data, and considering that countries could specialize in a particular subset or group of commodities that were best suited to their specific factor endowments, we realize that a great deal of intra-industry trade is in fact based on international differences in factor endowments and comparative costs. Thus, there seems to be much less conflict between intra-industry and the H–O theories than might appear at first sight.

That is, a great deal of intra-industry trade is consistent with trade based on differences in factor endowments and comparative costs. For example, the importation of a computer from Mexico by the United States may in fact involve the re-export of U.S. computer chips produced with highly skilled U.S. labor, as well as the export of other less skilled Mexican labor embodied in the computers assembled in border plants, known as *maquiladoras* (see Case Study 4-4). The appendix to this chapter presents a formal model of intra-industry trade.

CASE STUDY 4-4

Growth of Intra-Industry Trade

Table 4.3 presents data on the share of intra-industry trade in manufactured products of industrial countries in 1988–1991 and 1996–2000. The intra-industry trade index ranges in value from 0 (with no such trade) to 1 (when all of a nation's trade is intra-industry trade). The table shows that in 1996–2000, France had the highest level of intra-industry trade (77.5), followed by Canada (76.2) and Austria (74.2). For the other G-7 countries, the United Kingdom had an index of 73.7,

Germany 72.0, the United States 68.5, Italy 64.7, and Japan 47.6. The highest indexes were for European countries (except for Norway and Greece) and the lowest were for Pacific and developing countries (except for Mexico). The highest percentage growth in the index between the two periods was for Hungary, Korea, Mexico, and Japan. For some countries (such as Belgium/Luxembourg, Greece and Ireland), the index actually declined.

Table 4.3. *Manufacturing Intra-Industry Trade as a Percentage of Total Manufacturing Trade in Selected Countries*

Country	1988–1991	1996–2000	Country	1988–1991	1996–2000
France	75.9	77.5	Denmark	61.6	64.8
Canada	73.5	76.2	Italy	61.6	64.7
Austria	71.8	74.2	Poland	56.4	62.6
United Kingdom	70.1	73.7	Portugal	52.4	61.3
Mexico	62.5	73.4	Korea	41.4	57.5
Hungary	54.9	72.1	Ireland	58.6	54.6
Switzerland	69.8	72.0	Finland	53.8	53.9
Germany	67.1	72.0	Japan	37.6	47.6
Belgium/Luxembourg	77.6	71.4	New Zealand	37.2	40.6
Spain	68.2	71.2	Turkey	36.7	40.0
Netherlands	69.2	68.9	Norway	40.0	37.1
United States	63.5	68.5	Greece	42.8	36.9
Sweden	64.2	66.6	Australia	28.6	29.8

Source: OECD, "Intra-Industry Trade," *Economic Outlook* (Paris: OECD, June 2002), pp. 159–163.

4.8 TECHNOLOGICAL GAP AND PRODUCT CYCLE MODELS

Apart from differences in the relative availability of labor, capital, and natural resources (stressed by the Heckscher–Ohlin theory) and the existence of economies of scale and product differentiation, dynamic changes in

Technological gap model The hypothesis that a portion of international trade is based on the introduction of new products or processes.

technology among nations can be a separate determinant of international trade. These are examined by the technological gap and product cycle models. Since time is involved in a fundamental way in both of these models, they can be regarded as *dynamic extensions* of the static H–O model.

According to the technological gap model, a great deal of the trade among industrialized countries is based on the introduction of new products and new production processes. As the sole producer of these products, the innovating firm and nation have a temporary monopoly in these products. Such a temporary monopoly is often based on patents and copyrights, which are granted to encourage inventions.

As the most technologically advanced nation, the United States exports a large number of new high-technology products. As they acquire the new technology, however, foreign producers eventually conquer markets abroad, and even the U.S. market for the product, because of their lower labor costs. In the meantime, U.S. producers may have introduced still newer products and production processes, and they may be able to export these products based on the new technological gap established. A shortcoming of this model, however, is that it does not explain the size of technological gaps and does not explore the reason that technological gaps arise in the first place or exactly how they are eliminated over time.

Product cycle model The hypothesis, advanced by Vernon, that new products introduced by industrial nations and produced with skilled labor eventually become standardized and can be produced in other nations with less skilled labor.

A generalization and extension of the technological gap model is the product cycle model developed by *Vernon* in 1966. According to this model, when a new product is introduced, it usually requires highly skilled labor to produce. As the product matures and acquires mass acceptance, it becomes standardized; it can then be produced by mass production techniques and less skilled labor. Therefore, comparative advantage in the product shifts from the advanced nation that originally introduced it to less advanced nations, where labor is relatively cheaper. This may be accompanied by foreign direct investments from the innovating nation to nations with cheaper labor.

According to the product cycle model, a product goes through five stages: (1) the introduction of the product, (2) expansion of production for export, (3) standardization and beginning of production abroad through imitation, (4) foreign imitators underselling the nation in third markets, and (5) foreigners underselling the innovating firms in their home market as well.

Concept Check

How can trade be based on technological gaps and product cycles?

Vernon pointed out that high-income and labor-saving products are most likely to be introduced in rich nations because (1) the opportunities for doing so are greatest there, (2) the development of these new products requires proximity to markets so as to benefit from consumer feedback in modifying the product, and (3) there is a need to provide service. While the technological gap model emphasizes the time lag in the *imitation* process, the product cycle model stresses the *standardization* process. According to these models, the most highly industrialized economies are expected to export nonstandardized products embodying new and more advanced technologies and import products embodying old or less advanced technologies.

A classic example of the product cycle model is provided by the experience of U.S. and Japanese radio manufacturers since World War II. Immediately after the war, U.S. firms dominated the international market for radios, based on vacuum tubes developed in the United States. However, within a few years, Japan was able to capture a large share of the market by copying U.S. technology and utilizing cheaper labor. The United States recaptured technological leadership with the development of transistors. But, once again, in a few short years, Japan imitated the technology and was able to undersell the United States. Subsequently, the United States reacquired its ability to compete successfully with Japan by introducing printed circuits. It remains to be seen whether this latest technology will finally result in radios being labor or capital intensive and whether the United States will be able to stay in the market—or whether both the United States and Japan will eventually be displaced by still cheaper producers in such nations as Korea and Singapore.

In a 1967 study, *Gruber, Mehta*, and *Vernon* found a strong correlation between expenditures on research and development (R&D) and export performance. The authors took expenditures on research and development as a proxy for the temporary comparative advantage that firms and nations acquire in new products and new production processes. As such, these results tend to support both the technological gap model and the closely related product cycle model. By turning out new products and technologies very rapidly, the United States ranks as the most competitive economy in the world (see Case Study 4–5).

Note that in these models trade is originally based on new technology developed by the relatively abundant factors in industrialized nations (such as highly skilled labor and expenditures on research and development). Subsequently, through imitation and product standardization, less developed nations gain a comparative advantage based on their relatively cheaper labor. As such, trade can be said to be based on changes in relative factor abundance (technology) among nations over time. Therefore, the technological gap and product cycle models can be regarded as extensions of the basic H–O model into a technologically dynamic world, rather than as alternative trade models. In short, the product cycle model tries to explain *dynamic* comparative advantage for new products and new production processes, as opposed to the *basic* H–O model, which explains *static* comparative advantage. We return to this source of growth and change in comparative advantage over time in Section 8.2.

4.9 TRANSPORTATION COSTS AND INTERNATIONAL TRADE

So far we have implicitly assumed that transportation costs are zero. We now relax this assumption and see that transportation costs affect international

CASE STUDY 4-5

The United States as the Most Competitive Economy in the World

Table 4.4 shows the 22 top-ranked nations in international competitiveness in 2008, as measured by the Switzerland-based Institute for Management Development (IMD). International competitiveness was defined as the ability of a country or company to generate more wealth for its people than its competitors in world markets. International competitiveness was calculated as the weighted average of more than 300 competitiveness criteria grouped into four large categories: (1) economic performance (macro-economic evaluation of the domestic economy); (2) government performance (extent to which government policies are conducive to competitiveness); (3) business efficiency (extent to which enterprises perform

in an innovative and profitable way); (4) infrastructure (extent to which basic, technological, scientific and human resources meet the needs of business).

As Table 4.4 shows, the United States occupies the number one position, followed by Singapore and Hong Kong SAR. Canada is 8th, Germany is 16th, China is 17th, the United Kingdom 21st, and Japan 22nd. To be sure, there is another competitiveness ranking (by the World Economic Forum, also based in Switzerland), which ranks the United States first, followed by Switzerland, Denmark, Sweden, Germany, Finland, Singapore, Japan, United Kingdom, and the Netherlands in the top 10 positions.

Table 4.4. *International Competitiveness Rankings in 2008*

Rank	Country	Rank	Country
1	United States	12	Ireland
2	Singapore	13	Taiwan, China
3	Hong Kong SAR	14	Austria
4	Switzerland	15	Finland
5	Luxembourg	16	Germany
6	Denmark	17	China
7	Australia	18	New Zealand
8	Canada	19	Malaysia
9	Sweden	20	Israel
10	Netherlands	21	United Kingdom
11	Norway	22	Japan

Source: IMD, 2008.

trade directly by affecting the price of the traded commodity in the exporting and importing countries, and indirectly by affecting the international location of production and industry.

Transportation or logistics costs include freight charges, warehousing costs, costs of loading and unloading, insurance premiums, and interest charges while goods are in transit. We will use the term transportation costs

Transport or logistics costs Freight charges, warehousing costs, costs of loading and unloading, insurance premiums, and interest charges while goods are in transit (Sect. 6.6).

to include all the costs of transferring goods from one location (nation) to another.

A homogeneous good will be traded internationally only if the pretrade price difference in the two nations exceeds the cost of transporting the good from one nation to the other. Consideration of transportation costs explains why most goods and services are not traded at all internationally. These are referred to as nontraded goods and services. They are the goods and services for which transportation costs exceed price differences across nations. Thus, cement is not traded internationally except in border areas because of its high weight-to-value ratio. Similarly, the average person does not travel from New York to London simply to get a haircut.

Nontraded goods and services Those goods and services that are not traded internationally because the cost of transporting them exceeds the international price difference.

In general, the price of nontraded commodities is determined by domestic demand and supply conditions, while the price of traded commodities is determined by world demand and supply conditions. The great reduction in transportation costs that resulted from using refrigerated trucks and ships converted many nontraded into traded goods. For example, grapes and other fruits and vegetables found in many Boston, Chicago, New York, and Philadelphia stores during winter are shipped from South America. In the past, high transportation costs and spoilage prevented this. Similarly, the development of containerized cargo shipping (i.e., the packing of goods in very large, standardized containers) greatly reduced the cost of handling and transporting goods, turning many previously nontraded commodities into traded ones.

In Figure 4.3, the common vertical axis measures the dollar price of commodity X in Nation 1 and in Nation 2. Increasing quantities of commodity X are measured by a movement to the right from the common origin (as usual) for Nation 2. Increasing quantities of commodity X for Nation 1 are instead measured by a movement to the left from the common origin. Note that Nation 1's demand curve for commodity X (D_X) is negatively inclined (slopes downward), while its supply curve of commodity X (S_X) is positively inclined, *as we move from the origin to the left*, as we should, for Nation 1.

In the absence of trade, Nation 1 produces and consumes 50X at the equilibrium price of $P_X = \$5$ (given by the intersection of D_X and S_X in Nation 1). Nation 2 produces and consumes 50X at $P_X = \$11$. With the opening of trade, Nation 1 will export commodity X to Nation 2. As it does, P_X rises in Nation 1 and falls in Nation 2. With free trade and no transportation costs, the equilibrium price of commodity X is $8 at which the desired exports of commodity X by Nation 1 equal the desired imports of commodity X by Nation 2. Figure 4.3 shows that at $P_X = \$8$, Nation 1 will produce 80X, consume domestically 20X, and export 60X to Nation 2, while the exact opposite occurs in Nation 2.

With a transportation cost of $2 per unit, P_X in Nation 2 will exceed P_X in Nation 1 by $2. This cost will be shared by the two nations so as to balance trade. This occurs in Figure 4.3 when $P_X = \$7$ in Nation 1 and $P_X = \$9$ in

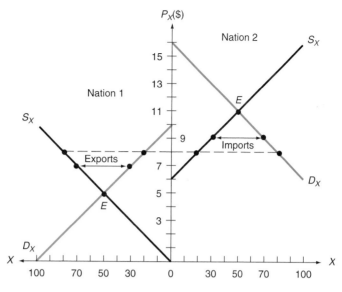

FIGURE 4.3. Partial Equilibrium Analysis of Transportation Costs.
The common vertical axis measures the dollar price of commodity X in the two nations. A movement to the left from the common origin measures increasing quantities of commodity X for Nation 1. In the absence of trade, Nation 1 will produce and consume 50X at $P_X = \$5$. Nation 2 will produce and consume 50X at $P_X = \$11$. With transportation costs of \$2 per unit, $P_X = \$7$ in Nation 1 and $P_X = \$9$ in Nation 2. At $P_X = \$7$, Nation 1 will produce 70X, consume 30X, and export 40X. At $P_X = \$9$, Nation 2 will produce 30X, import 40X, and consume 70X.

Concept Check

What is the relationship between transportation costs and international trade?

Nation 2. At $P_X = \$7$, Nation 1 will produce 70X, consume domestically 30X, and export 40X to Nation 2. At $P_X = \$9$, Nation 2 will produce 30X, import 40X, and consume 70X.

Note that in the absence of transportation costs, $P_X = \$8$ in both nations and 60X are traded. Thus, transportation costs reduce the level of specialization in production and also the volume and gains from trade. Finally, because of the way Figure 4.3 was drawn, the cost of transportation is shared equally by the two nations. In general, the more steeply inclined D_X and S_X are in Nation 1 relative to Nation 2, the greater is the share of transportation costs paid by Nation 1.

4.10 ENVIRONMENTAL STANDARDS AND INTERNATIONAL TRADE

Industrial location and international trade are also affected by different environmental standards in different nations. Environmental standards refer

Environmental standards The level of pollution accepted in various countries.

to the levels of air pollution, water pollution, thermal (i.e., heat) pollution, and pollution resulting from garbage disposal that a nation allows. Environmental pollution results whenever the environment is used (abused) as a convenient and cheap dumping ground for all types of waste products arising from the production, consumption, or disposal of goods and services.

Environmental pollution can lead to serious trade problems because the price of traded goods and services often does not fully reflect social environmental costs. A nation with lower environmental standards can in effect use the environment as a resource endowment or as a factor of production in attracting polluting firms from abroad and achieving a comparative advantage in polluting goods and services.

For example, U.S. labor opposed NAFTA out of fear that many jobs would be lost in the United States as a result of U.S. firms migrating to Mexico to take advantage of much more lax environmental laws and lower clean-up costs. Indeed, environmental considerations were so strong that a side agreement on the environment had to be added to ensure the passage of NAFTA by the U.S. Congress. Thus, it is easy to see how a nation can use environmental policies to seek to offset the cost advantage that other countries might enjoy because of lower environmental standards in the nation and to impose its own environmental preferences on other nations.

Concept Check

What is the relationship between environmental standards and trade?

During the past three decades polluting or dirty industries and their exports have expanded faster than clean industries and their exports in poor developing countries. As a country develops and becomes richer, pollution usually diminishes because production generally moves toward cleaner activities and because people demand a cleaner environment. Fast-growing economies with liberal trade policies (such as Chile) have also experienced less pollution-intensive growth than closed economies (such as Bolivia and El Salvador).

Strong antipollution regulations that slow growth may not, therefore, be justified during the early stages of development. Also not justified are strong uniform international environmental standards. As long as different nations have different social priorities and environmental objectives, it is not efficient to impose uniform international standards. As nations grow richer, they voluntarily adopt more "environmentally friendly" approaches to economic development and become increasingly concerned about "sustainable development" so as to meet their own needs without compromising those of future generations.

The *High-Level Symposium on Trade and the Environment* held in Geneva in March 1999 strongly recommended that future trade agreements be subjected to environmental impact assessments, just like the United States now requires on domestic projects. Disputes about different national environmental standards and international trade are likely to become more frequent and louder in the years to come and to figure prominently in future trade negotiations. Indeed, the anti-global movement uses antipollution as one

of its main arguments against globalization (the others are sweatshops and exploitation of labor by multinationals). Most available studies suggest that the effect of international trade on the environment is rather small and varies across countries.

In July 2001, a historic accord that set targets for industrialized countries to cut emission of greenhouse gases that contribute to global warming was signed by 178 countries, thus keeping alive the *Kyoto Protocol* on climate change originally signed in 1997. The Kyoto protocol was ratified by 141 countries and came into effect in 2005. As of May 2007, 172 countries had ratified the protocol. The United States, on the other hand, refused to sign the agreement, calling its targets arbitrary and too costly for the United States to comply.

SUMMARY

1. The Heckscher–Ohlin theory presented in this chapter extends our trade model of Chapter 3 to explain the basis of (i.e., what determines) comparative advantage and to examine the effect of international trade on the earnings of factors of production. These two important questions were left largely unanswered by classical economists. This chapter also examines other complementary trade theories that base international trade on economies of scale, product differentiation, or technological differences among nations.

2. The Heckscher–Ohlin, or factor-endowment, theory can be expressed in terms of two theorems. According to the Heckscher–Ohlin (H–O) theorem, a nation will export the commodity intensive in its relatively abundant and cheap factor and import the commodity intensive in its relatively scarce and expensive factor. According to the factor–price equalization theorem, international trade will bring about equalization in the returns or earnings to homogeneous or identical factors across nations.

3. The Stolper–Samuelson theorem postulates that free international trade reduces the real income of the nation's relatively scarce factor and increases the real income of the nation's relatively abundant factor. If some factors are specific (i.e., can only be used in some industries, as often occurs in the short run), the specific-factors model postulates that trade will have an ambiguous effect on the nation's mobile factor, benefits the immobile factor that is specific to the nation's export commodities or sectors, and harms the immobile factor that is specific to the nation's import-competing commodities or sectors.

4. Out of all the possible forces that could cause a difference in pretrade-relative commodity prices between nations, Heckscher and Ohlin isolate the difference in factor endowments (in the face of equal technology and tastes) as the basic determinant or cause of comparative advantage. International trade can also be a substitute for the international mobility of factors in equalizing the returns of identical factors across nations.

5. The first empirical test of the H–O model was conducted by Leontief in 1951 using 1947 U.S. data. Leontief found that U.S. import substitutes were about 30 percent more K intensive than U.S. exports. Since the United States was the most K-abundant nation, this result was the opposite of what the H–O model predicted and became known as the Leontief paradox. Recent studies provide strong support of the basic H–O model.

6. Even if two nations are identical in every respect, there is still a basis for mutually beneficial trade based on economies of scale. When each nation specializes in the production of one commodity, the combined total world output of both commodities will be greater than without specialization when economies of scale are present. With trade, each nation then shares in these gains.

7. A large portion of international trade today involves the exchange of differentiated products. Such intra-industry trade arises in order to take advantage of important economies of scale in production, which result when each firm or plant produces only one or a few styles or varieties of a product. The more similar nations are in factor endowments, the greater is the importance of intra- relative to inter-industry trade.

8. According to the technological gap model, a firm exports a new product until imitators in other countries take away its market. In the meantime, the innovating firm will have introduced a new product or process. According to the related product cycle model, a product goes through five stages: the introduction of the product, expansion of production for export, standardization and beginning of production abroad through imitation, foreign imitators underselling the nation in third markets, and foreigners underselling the innovating firms in their home market as well. The technological gap and product cycle models can be regarded as extensions of the basic H–O model into a technologically dynamic world.

9. With costs of transportation, only those commodities whose pre-trade price difference exceeds the cost of transporting them will be traded. When trade is in equilibrium, the relative price of traded commodities in the two nations will differ by the cost of transporting them. Transportation costs also affect international trade by affecting the location of production and industry. Environmental standards also affect the location of industry and international trade.

REVIEW QUESTIONS AND PROBLEMS

1. (a) What does the Heckscher–Ohlin theorem postulate?
 (b) Which force does Heckscher and Ohlin identify as the basic determinant of comparative advantage and trade?
 (c) In what way does the Heckscher–Ohlin theory represent an extension of the standard trade model presented in the previous chapter?

2. Starting with the production frontiers for Nation 1 and Nation 2 shown in Figure 4.1, show graphically that even with a small difference in tastes in the two nations, Nation 1 would continue to have a comparative advantage in commodity X.

3. (a) What does the factor–price equalization theorem postulate?

 (b) What does the Stopler–Samuelson theorem postulate?

 (c) What does the specific-factors theorem postulate?

 (d) What is its relationship to the international mobility of factors of production?

4. (a) What is meant by the Leontief paradox?

 (b) How was the paradox resolved or explained?

 (c) What is the status of the H–O theory today?

5. In what way can international trade with developing countries be said to have contributed to increased wage inequalities in the United States during the past 20 years?

6. (a) What is meant by economies of scale?

 (b) How can economies of scale be the basis for international trade?

 (c) What is meant by the "new international economies of scale"?

7. (a) What is meant by product differentiation and intra-industry trade?

 (b) How does inter-industry trade arise?

 (c) What are the benefits of intra-industry trade?

8. (a) How can international trade take place according to the technological gap model?

 (b) What criticisms are leveled against this model?

 (c) What are the various stages in a product life cycle?

9. Draw a figure similar to Figure 4.3, showing that transportation costs fall more heavily on the nation with the steeper demand and supply curves for the traded commodity.

10. How do different environmental standards affect industry location and international trade?

The Specific-Factors and Intra-Industry Trade Models

In this appendix, we present the specific-factors model and a formal intra-industry trade model. These models are more advanced than the material presented in the chapter and are optional.

A4.1 THE SPECIFIC-FACTORS MODEL

Suppose that in Nation 1 (the L-abundant nation) labor is mobile between industries but capital is not. Since labor is mobile, the wage of labor will be the same in the production of commodities X and Y in Nation 1. The equilibrium wage and the amount of labor employed in the production of X and Y in Nation 1 are given by the intersection of the value of the marginal product of labor curve in the production of X and Y. From microeconomic theory, we know that the value of the marginal product of labor in the production of X is equal to the price of commodity X times the marginal physical product of labor in the production of X. The marginal physical product of labor is the increase in output per unit increase in labor. That is, $VMPL_X = (P_X)(MPL_X)$. Similarly, $VMPL_Y = (P_Y)(MPL_Y)$. We also know that if a firm employs more labor with a given amount of capital, VMP_L declines because of the law of diminishing returns. Finally, to maximize profits, firms will employ labor until the wage they must pay equals the value of the marginal product of labor (i.e., until $w = VMP_L$).

We can show the no-trade equilibrium wage and employment of labor in the production of commodities X and Y in Nation 1 with the aid of Figure 4.4. In the figure, the horizontal axis measures the total supply of labor available to Nation 1, and the vertical axis measures the wage rate. To begin with, concentrate on the $VMPL_X$ curve (which is read from left to right, as usual) and on the $VMPL_Y$ curve (which is read from right to left). The equilibrium wage rate is ED and is determined at the intersection of the $VMPL_X$ and $VMPL_Y$ curves. The wage rate is identical in the production of X and Y because of perfect labor mobility in the nation between the two industries. The amount OD of labor is used in the production of X, and the remainder, or DO', is used in the production of Y.

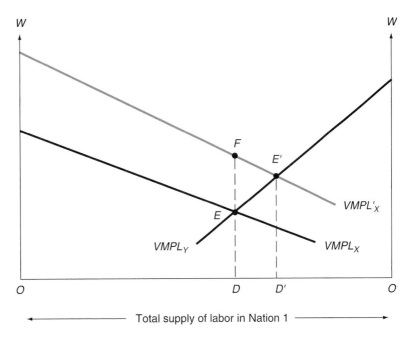

FIGURE 4.4. Specific-Factors Model.
Labor is mobile between the two industries, but capital is not. The horizontal axis measures the total supply of L available to Nation 1, and the vertical axis the wage rate (W). Before trade, the intersection of the $VMPL_X$ and $VMPL_Y$ curves determines $w = ED$ in the two industries. OD of L is used in the production of X and DO' in Y. With trade, P_X/P_Y increases and shifts $VMPL_X$ up to $VMPL'_X$, W rises from ED to $E'D'$, and DD' of L shifts from Y to X. Since W rises less than P_X, W falls in terms of X but rises in terms of Y (since P_Y is unchanged). With more L used with fixed K in the production of X, $VMPK_X$ and r increase in terms of both X and Y. With less L used with fixed K in Y, $VMPK_Y$ and r fall in terms of both commodities.

Since Nation 1 (the L-abundant nation) has a comparative advantage in commodity X (the L-intensive commodity), the opening of trade increases P_X/P_Y. Since $VMPL_X = (P_X)(MPL_X)$, the increase in P_X shifts the $VMPL_X$ curve upward proportionately, by EF, to $VMPL'_X$. The wage rate increases less than proportionately, from ED to $E'D'$, and DD' units of labor shift from the production of Y to the production of X. Since W increases by less than the increase in P_X, W falls in terms of X but rises in terms of Y (since P_Y is unchanged). Thus, the effect of the increase in P_X on the real income of labor is ambiguous and depends on spending patterns. Workers who consume mainly commodity X will be worse off, while those who consume mainly commodity Y will be better off.

The rewards (r) to the specific factor (capital) change unambiguously, however. Since the specific capital in the production of commodity X has more labor to work with, $VMPK_X$ and r increase in terms of both commodities X and Y. On the other hand, since less labor is used with the fixed capital in the production of commodity Y, $VMPK_Y$ and r fall in terms of commodity X, and therefore in terms of commodity Y as well.

Thus, with the opening of trade, the real income of the immobile capital (the nation's scarce factor) rises in the production of X and falls in the production of Y, while real wages (which are equal in the production of both commodities) fall in terms of commodity X and rise in terms of commodity Y. This is the result we obtain in the short run with the specific-factors model when capital is specific to or immobile between the two industries of the nation.

Generalizing the specific-factors model, we can say that trade will have an ambiguous effect on each nation's mobile factors, benefit the immobile factors specific to the nation's export sectors, and harm the immobile factors specific to the nation's import-competing sectors. This is what we can expect in the *short run* when some factors are specific or immobile (i.e., they can only be used in some industries). In the long run, of course, when all inputs are mobile among all industries of a nation, the Heckscher–Ohlin model postulates that the opening of trade will lead to an increase in the real income or return of the inputs used intensively in the nation's export sectors and to a reduction in the real income or return of the inputs used intensively in the production of the nation's import-competing sectors.

A4.2 A MODEL OF INTRA-INDUSTRY TRADE

Figure 4.5 presents a formal model of intra-industry trade. In Figure 4.5, D represents the demand curve faced by a firm for the differentiated products that it sells. Since each firm sells a differentiated product, the demand curve is downward or negatively sloped, but it is fairly elastic (i.e., D has a small inclination) because the products sold by each firm are very similar. With D fairly elastic, even a small change in price leads to a large change in the

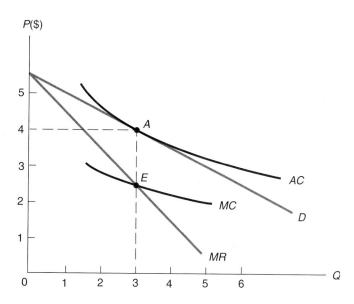

FIGURE 4.5. Production and Pricing under Monopolistic Competition.
D is the demand curve for the product sold by a firm, while *MR* is the corresponding marginal revenue curve. *D* is downward sloping because the product is differentiated. As a result, *MR* < *P*. The best level of output for the monopolistically competitive firm is 3 units and is given by point *E*, at which *MR = MC*. At *Q* = 3, *P = AC* = $4 (point *A*) and the firm breaks even (i.e., earns only a normal return on investment in the long run). *AC* is the average cost curve of the firm. *AC* is downward sloping because of economies of scale.

Monopolistic competition The form of market organization where there are many firms selling a differentiated product and entry into or exit from the industry is relatively easy.

firm's sales. The form or market organization where (as in this case) there are many firms selling a differentiated product and entry into or exit from the industry is easy is called monopolistic competition.

Because the firm must lower the price (*P*) if it wants to increase sales, the marginal revenue curve of the firm *(MR)* is below the demand curve (*D*), so that *MR* < *P*. For example, *D* shows that the firm can sell 2 units at *P* = $4.50 and have a total revenue of $9 or sell 3 units at *P* = $4 and have a total revenue of $12. Thus, the change in total revenue or *MR* = $3, compared with *P* = $4 for the third unit of the commodity sold.

By producing a large amount of only one type (rather than many varieties) of the product, the firm also faces increasing returns to scale in production, so that its average cost curve *(AC)* is also downward sloping (i.e., *AC* declines as output increases). As a result, the firm's marginal cost curve *(MC)* is below the *AC* curve. The reason for this is that for *AC* to decline, *MC* must be smaller than *AC*.

The best level of output for the firm is 3 units and is given by point E, where the MR and MC curves intersect (see Figure 4.5). At a smaller level of output, MR (i.e., the extra revenue) exceeds MC (i.e., the extra cost) and it pays for the firm to expand output. On the other hand, at an output greater than 3 units, $MR < MC$, and it pays for the firm to reduce output. Thus, the best level of output (Q) is 3 units. The firm will then charge the price of $4, shown by point A on the D curve. Furthermore, since more firms are attracted to the industry in the long run whenever firms in the industry earn profits, the demand curve facing this firm (D) is tangent to its AC curve, so that $P = AC = \$4$ at $Q = 3$. This means that the firm breaks even (i.e., it earns only a normal return on investment in the long run).

We can now examine the relationship between inter-industry and intra-industry trade. To do this, suppose that Nation 1 has a relative abundance of labor and commodity X is labor intensive, while Nation 2 has a relative abundance of capital and commodity Y is capital intensive. If commodities X and Y are homogeneous, Nation 1 will then export commodity X and import commodity Y, while Nation 2 will export commodity Y and import commodity X—as postulated by the Heckscher–Ohlin theory. This is inter-industry trade and reflects comparative advantage only.

On the other hand, if there are different varieties of commodities X and Y (i.e., commodities X and Y are differentiated), Nation 1 will still be a net exporter of commodity X (this is inter-industry trade, which is based on comparative advantage), but it will also import some varieties of commodity X and export some varieties of commodity Y (this is intra-industry trade, which is based on product differentiation and economies of scale).

Similarly, while Nation 2 will still be a net exporter of commodity Y, it will also import some varieties of commodity Y and export some varieties of commodity X. The net exports of X and Y by Nations 1 and 2, respectively, reflect inter-industry trade, which is based on comparative advantage. On the other hand, the fact that Nation 1 also imports some varieties of commodity X and exports some varieties of commodity Y, while Nation 2 also imports some varieties of commodity Y and exports varieties of commodity X (i.e., the fact that there is an interpenetration of each other's market in each product) reflects intra-industry trade, which is based on product differentiation and economies of scale.

Thus, when products are homogeneous, we have only inter-industry trade. On the other hand, when products are differentiated, we have both inter- and intra-industry trade. The more similar nations are in factor endowments and technology, the smaller is the importance of inter- relative to intra-industry trade, and vice versa. Since industrial nations have become more similar in factor endowments and technology over time, the importance of intra- relative to inter-industry trade has increased. As pointed out earlier,

however, a great deal of intra-industry trade is also based on differences in international factor endowments (when factors are defined less broadly and in a more disaggregated way).

SELECTED BIBLIOGRAPHY

For a problem-solving approach to the material covered in this chapter, see:

- D. Salvatore, *Theory and Problems of International Economics*, 4th ed. (New York: McGraw-Hill, 1996), ch. 4.

For a more advanced and complete treatment of the Hecksher–Ohlin Theory, see:

- D. Salvatore, *International Economics*, 9th ed. (Hoboken, N.J.: Wiley, 2007), chs. 4 and 5.

The original work on the Heckscher–Ohlin theory is:

- B. Ohlin, *Interregional and International Trade* (Cambridge, Mass.: Harvard University Press, 1983).

On the effect of international trade on U.S. wage inequalities in the United States, see:

- W. Cline, *Trade and Income Distribution* (Washington, D.C.: Institute for International Economics, 1997).
- D. Rodrik, *Has Globalization Gone Too Far?* (Washington, D.C.: Institute for International Economics, 1997).

For intra-industry trade, see:

- D. Greenaway and C. R. Milner, *The Economics of Intra-Industry Trade* (Oxford: Basil Blackwell, 1986).
- M. E. Porter, *On Competition* (Cambridge, Mass.: Harvard Business School Press, 1998).
- D. Salvatore, *Managerial Economics in a Global Economy*, 6th ed. (New York: Oxford University Pess, 2007), chs 6–7.

For transport costs, see:

- World Bank, *From Natural Resources to the Knowledge Economy: Trade and Job Quality* (Washington, D.C.: World Bank, 2002), ch. 2.

For the relationship between environmental pollution, industry location, and international trade, see:

- P. R. Portney, "Environmental Problems and Policy: 2000–2050," *Journal of Economic Perspectives*, Winter 2000, pp. 199–206.

- World Bank, *International Trade and Climate Change* (Washington, D.C.: 2007).

INTERNet

A great deal of trade statistics for the United States by country and region can be found through the home page of the U.S. Department of Commerce, International Trade Administration, at:

http://www.ita.doc.gov/td/industry/otea

Trade statistics for European countries are provided by EuroStat (the Statistical Office of the European Communities) by clicking "external trade" at:

http://europa.eu.int/comm/eurostat

The hourly compensation of U.S. workers in manufacturing and how it compares with that of foreign workers is found from the home page of the Bureau of Labor Statistics, Foreign Labor Statistics, at:

http://www.bls.gov/home.htm

The capital stock per worker of many countries is found on the University of Pennsylvania web site at:

http://pwt.econ.upenn.edu

Data on the international competitiveness of nations are available from the Institute for Management Development and the World Economic Forum at:

http://www.imd.ch/wcy

http://www.weforum.org

Trade statistics that can be used to measure inter- and intra-industry trade are provided by the U.S. Census Bureau at:

http://www.census.gov/foreign-trade/sitc1/

International trade statistics by country and product group are available from the International Trade Center (ITC) by selecting "Countries" and then "Trade Statistics Aggregates" at:

http://www.intracen.org

PART TWO

International Trade Policy

Part Two (Chapters 5 and 6) deals with international trade or commercial policies. Chapter 5 examines tariffs, the most important of the trade restrictions historically. Chapter 6 extends the discussion to other trade restrictions, evaluates the justification usually given for trade restrictions, and summarizes their history.

Trade Restrictions: Tariffs

After studying this chapter, you should be able to:

- Describe the effect of a tariff on consumers and producers
- Identify the costs and benefits of a tariff on a small nation
- Describe the effects of a tariff on a large nation
- Describe an optimum tariff and retaliation
- Understand the meaning of tariff structure

CHAPTER OUTLINE

KEY TERMS

Trade or commercial policies

Import tariff

Export tariff

Ad valorem tariff

Specific tariff

Compound tariff

Consumption effect of a tariff

Production effect of a tariff

Trade effect of a tariff

Revenue effect of a tariff

Consumer surplus

Rent or producer surplus

Protection cost or deadweight loss of a tariff

Terms of trade effect of a tariff

Optimum tariff

Prohibitive tariff

Nominal tariff

Rate of effective protection

5.1 INTRODUCTION

We have seen in Part One that free trade maximizes world output and benefits all nations. However, practically all nations impose some restrictions on the free flow of international trade. In this chapter, we analyze the effects of a tariff on production, consumption, trade, and welfare in the nation imposing the tariff and on its trade partner(s). Chapter 6 will then extend our presentation to nontariff barriers to trade and to the political economy of protectionism.

Section 5.2 of this chapter examines the different types of tariffs. Section 5.3 analyzes the general effects of a tariff in a *small nation*. Section 5.4 shows the effects of a tariff on consumer and producer surplus, while Section 5.5 measures the costs and benefits of a tariff in the nation. Section 5.6 measures the costs and benefits of a tariff in a *large nation*, while section 5.7 discusses the size of an optimum tariff and foreign retaliation. Finally, section 5.8 examines the theory of tariff structure. The optional appendix to this chapter presents a more advanced analysis of a tariff using offer curves.

5.2 TYPES OF TARIFFS

Trade or commercial policies The regulations governing a nation's commerce or international trade.

Since the restrictions and regulations that a nation imposes on international trade deal with the nation's trade or commerce, they are generally known as trade or commercial policies. We will see that although trade restrictions are invariably rationalized in terms of national welfare, in reality they are usually advocated by those special groups in the nation that stand to benefit from such restrictions.

Import tariff A tax or duty on imports.

Export tariff A tax or duty on exports.

The tariff has been the most important type of trade restriction historically. A tariff is a tax or duty levied on the traded commodity as it crosses a national boundary. An import tariff is a duty on the imported commodity, while an export tariff is a duty on the exported commodity. Import tariffs are more important than export tariffs, and most of our discussion will deal with import tariffs. Export tariffs are prohibited by the U.S. Constitution but are often applied by developing countries on their traditional exports (such as Ghana on its cocoa and Brazil on its coffee) to get better prices and raise revenues. Developing nations rely heavily on export tariffs to raise revenues because of their ease of collection. On the other hand, industrial countries invariably impose tariffs or other trade restrictions to protect some (usually labor-intensive) industry, while using mostly income taxes to raise revenues.

Ad valorem tariff A tariff expressed as a fixed *percentage* of the value of a traded commodity.

Specific tariff A tariff expressed as a fixed *sum* per unit of a traded commodity.

Tariffs can be ad valorem, specific, or compound. The ad valorem tariff is expressed as a fixed percentage of the value of the traded commodity. The specific tariff is expressed as a fixed sum per physical unit of the traded commodity. Finally, a compound tariff is a combination of an ad valorem and a specific tariff.

Compound tariff A combination of an ad valorem and a specific tariff.

For example, a 10 percent ad valorem tariff on bicycles would result in the payment to customs officials of the sum of $10 on each $100 imported bicycle and the sum of $20 on each $200 imported bicycle. On the other hand, a specific tariff of $10 on imported bicycles means that customs officials collect the fixed sum of $10 on each imported bicycle regardless of its price. Finally, a compound duty of 5 percent ad valorem and a specific duty of $10 on imported bicycles would result in the collection by customs officials of the sum of $15 on each $100 bicycle and $20 on each $200 imported bicycle.

Concept Check

What are the different types of tariffs?

The United States uses the ad valorem and the specific tariff with about equal frequency, whereas European countries rely mainly on the ad valorem tariff. Most of our presentation in this chapter will be in terms of ad valorem import tariffs.

Tariffs have been sharply reduced since the end of Word War II and now average 5 percent or less on industrial products in developed nations (see Case Study 5-1), but they are much higher in developing nations (see Case Study 5-2). Trade in agricultural commodities is still subject to relatively high trade barriers. These are discussed in the next chapter.

CASE STUDY 5-1

Average Tariff on Industrial Products in Major Developed Countries

Table 5.1 gives the average tariff imposed by the United States, the European Union, Japan, and Canada (i.e., by the leading developed countries and the European Union) on various industrial products in 2006. The table shows that the highest tariff is invariably imposed on imports of clothing, textiles, and leather products (also on fish and fish products in the European Union and Japan), but the average tariff level is less than 5 percent. The average tariff on imports of industrial products is even lower in other developed countries. It is 0.6 percent in Norway, 2.1 percent in Switzerland, 2.4 in Iceland 3.2. It is 3.9 percent in Australia.

Table 5.1. *Tariffs on Industrial Products in the United States, the European Union, Japan, and Canada in 2006 (percentages)*

	United States	*European Union*	*Japan*	*Canada*
Wood, paper, etc.	0.4	1.1	0.9	1.1
Textiles	7.9	6.6	5.5	6.9
Clothing	11.5	11.5	9.2	17.0
Leather, footwear, etc.	4.3	4.2	15.0	5.6
Chemicals	2.8	4.6	2.5	2.8
Transport equipment	3.1	4.1	0.0	5.8
Non-electrical machinery	1.2	1.7	0.0	1.5
Electrical machinery	1.7	2.5	0.2	2.4
Mineral & metals	1.7	1.9	1.0	1.7
Manufactures, other	2.1	2.4	1.1	2.8
Fish & fish products	1.1	10.3	5.7	1.0
Petroleum	2.1	2.7	0.7	2.7
Average	3.3	4.5	3.5	4.3

Source: World Trade Organization, *Annual Report 2007* (Geneva: WTO, 2007), Part 2.

CASE STUDY 5-2

Average Tariffs on Industrial Products in Some Major Developing Countries

Table 5.2 gives the tariff imposed by Brazil, Mexico, Russia, Korea, China, and India on various industrial products in 2006. The table shows that the lowest tariffs are imposed by Korea and the highest by India, with China, Russia, Brazil, and Mexico occupying an intermediate position. All six countries, however, have much higher tariffs than developed countries. The average tariff on industrial products in 2006 was 4.7 for Turkey, 7.9 for South Africa, and 12.6 in Argentina.

Table 5.2. *Tariffs on Industrial Products in Brazil, Mexico, Korea, Thailand, and India in 2006 (percentages)*

	Brazil	*Mexico*	*Russia*	*Korea*	*China*	*India*
Wood, paper, etc.	11.0	12.3	15.4	2.4	4.9	13.5
Textiles	16.8	16.1	12.4	9.2	9.7	20.2
Clothing	20.0	35.0	21.7	12.6	16.1	22.4
Leather, footwear, etc.	14.7	18.1	12.6	7.9	13.0	15.4
Chemicals	8.3	9.8	7.1	5.8	6.7	15.0
Transport equipment	18.1	17.3	11.0	5.4	11.6	24.8
Non-electrical machinery	12.8	8.3	7.5	6.0	8.3	14.3
Electrical machinery	14.1	11.3	10.3	6.0	8.7	12.3
Mineral & metals	9.9	11.4	10.5	4.8	7.7	15.4
Manufactures, other	15.6	12.7	13.8	6.4	11.7	13.9
Fish & fish products	10.1	16.6	14.4	16.1	11.0	30.0
Petroleum	0.3	8.7	5.0	5.1	4.5	14.0
Average	12.6	13.3	11.1	6.6	9.0	16.4

Source: World Trade Organization, *Annual Report 2007* (Geneva: WTO, 2007), Part 2.

5.3 EFFECTS OF A TARIFF IN A SMALL NATION

We now want to examine the effects of an import tariff on the nation imposing the tariff. We will do this first for a small nation and then (in Section 5.6) for a large one. A small nation is here defined as one that does not affect the world price of the commodity it imports. That is, the small nation can import all it wants at the given world price of the commodity. We can analyze the effects of the import tariff with the aid of Figure 5.1.

In Figure 5.1, D_X is the demand curve and S_X is the supply curve of commodity X in the nation. In the absence of trade, the intersection of D_X

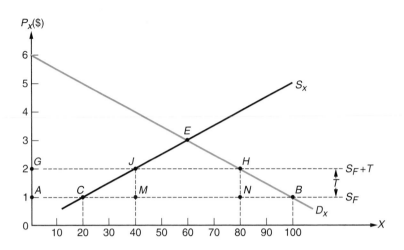

FIGURE 5.1. Effects of a Tariff in a Small Nation.
D_X and S_X represent the nation's demand and supply curves of commodity X. At the free trade price of $P_X = \$1$, the nation consumes 100X *(AB)*, of which 20X *(AC)* is produced domestically and 80X *(CB)* is imported. With a 100-percent import tariff on commodity X, P_X rises to \$2 for individuals in the nation. At $P_X = \$2$, the nation consumes 80X *(GH)*, of which 40X *(GJ)* is produced domestically and 40X *(JH)* is imported. Thus, the consumption effect of the tariff is (–) 20X *(BN)*; the production effect is 20X *(CM)*; the trade effect equals (–) 40X *(BN + CM)*; and the revenue effect is \$40 *(MJHN)*.

Consumption effect of a tariff The reduction in domestic consumption of a commodity resulting from the increase in its price due to a tariff.

Production effect of a tariff The increase in domestic production of a commodity resulting from the increase in its price due to a tariff.

Trade effect of a tariff The reduction in the volume of trade in the commodity resulting from a tariff.

and S_X defines equilibrium point E, at which 60X is demanded and supplied at $P_X = \$3$ in the nation. With free trade at the world price of $P_X = \$1$, the nation will consume 100X *(AB)*, of which 20X *(AC)* is produced domestically and the remainder of 80X *(CB)* is imported. The horizontal dashed line S_F represents the free trade foreign supply curve of commodity X to the nation on the assumption that the nation is too small to affect the world price by its trading.

If the nation now imposes a 100 percent ad valorem tariff on the imports of commodity X, P_X in the nation will rise to \$2 (the same as on the world market). At $P_X = \$2$, the nation consumes 80X *(GH)*, of which 40X *(GJ)* is produced domestically and the remainder of 40X *(JH)* is imported. The horizontal dashed line $S_F + T$ represents the new tariff-inclusive foreign supply curve of commodity X to the nation.

Thus, the consumption effect of the tariff (i.e., the reduction in domestic consumption) equals (–) 20X *(BN)*; the production effect (i.e., the expansion of domestic production resulting from the tariff) equals 20X *(CM)*; the trade effect (i.e., the decline in imports) equals 40X *(BN + CM)*; and the

Revenue effect of a tariff The revenue collected by the government from the tariff.

revenue effect (i.e., the revenue collected by the government) equals $40 ($1 on each of the 40X imported, or *MJHN*).

Note that for the same $1 increase in P_X in the nation as a result of the tariff, the more elastic and flatter D_X is, the greater is the consumption effect (see the figure). Similarly, the more elastic S_X is, the greater is the production effect. Thus, the more elastic D_X and S_X are in the nation, the greater is the trade effect of the tariff (i.e., the greater is the reduction in the nation's imports of commodity X) and the smaller is the revenue effect of the tariff.

Concept Check

What are the effects of a tariff on a small nation?

5.4 EFFECT OF A TARIFF ON CONSUMER AND PRODUCER SURPLUS

The increase in the price of commodity X from $P_X = \$1$ to $P_X = \$2$ as a result of the 100 percent tariff imposed by the nation on its imports of commodity X leads to a reduction in consumer surplus and an increase in producer surplus. These are examined in Figure 5.2 and then used in the next section to obtain a monetary measure of the costs and benefits of the tariff.

The left panel of Figure 5.2 shows that the loss of consumer surplus resulting from the tariff is equal to shaded area $AGHB = \$90$. The reason for this is as follows. Before the imposition of the tariff, consumers in the nation consume 100X at $P_X = \$1$. Consumers pay for each unit as much as they are willing to pay for the last, or 100th, unit of commodity X (given by point B on D_X). Consumers, however, receive more satisfaction and would therefore be willing to pay higher prices for earlier units of commodity X, as indicated by the height of the demand curve for each unit of the commodity consumers buy rather than go without it.

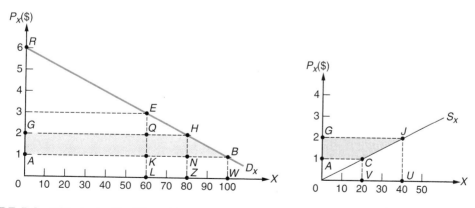

FIGURE 5.2. Effect of a Tariff on Consumer and Producer Surplus.
The left panel shows that a tariff that increases the price of commodity X from $P_X = \$1$ to $P_X = \$2$ results in a reduction in consumer surplus from $ARB = \$250$ to $GRH = \$160$, or by shaded area $AGHB = \$90$. The right panel shows that the tariff increases producer surplus by shaded area $AGJC = \$30$.

Consumer surplus
The difference between what consumers are willing to pay for a specific amount of a commodity and what they actually pay for it.

The difference between what consumers would be willing to pay for each unit of the commodity (indicated by the height of Dx at that point) and what they actually pay for that unit (the same as for the last unit that they purchase) is called consumer surplus. Thus, consumer surplus is the difference between what consumers would be willing to pay for each unit of the commodity and what they actually pay. Graphically, consumer surplus is measured by the area under the demand curve above the going price.

For example, the left panel of Figure 5.2 shows that consumers in the nation would be willing to pay $LE = \$3$ for the 60th unit of commodity X. Since they only pay $1, they receive a consumer surplus of $KE = \$2$ on the 60th unit of commodity X they purchase. Similarly, for the 80th unit of commodity X, consumers would be willing to pay $ZH = \$2$. Since they only pay $ZN = \$1$, they receive a consumer surplus of $NH = \$1$ on the 80th unit of X that they purchase. For the 100th unit of commodity X, consumers would be willing to pay $WB = \$1$. Since this is equal to the price that they actually pay, the consumer surplus for the 100th unit of X is zero. With the total of 100X being purchased at $P_X = \$1$ in the absence of the import tariff, the total consumer surplus in the nation is equal to $ARB = \$250$ ($5 times 100 divided by 2). This is the difference between what consumers would have been willing to pay ($ORBW = \$350$) and what they actually pay for 100X ($OABW = \$100$).

Concept Check

What are the effects of a tariff on consumer surplus?

When the nation imposes a 100 percent import tariff, the price of commodity X rises from $P_X = \$1$ to $P_X = \$2$ and purchases of commodity X fall from 100X to 80X. With the tariff, consumers pay $OGHZ = \$160$ for 80X. The consumer surplus thus shrinks from $ARB = \$250$ (with $P_X = \$1$ before the tariff) to $GRH = \$160$ (when $P_X = \$2$ with the tariff), or by $AGHB = \$90$ (the shaded area in the left panel of Figure 5.2). The imposition of the 100 percent import tariff by the nation thus leads to a reduction in consumer surplus.

Rent or producer surplus A payment that need not be made in the long run in order to induce producers to supply a specific amount of a commodity or factor services.

The right panel of Figure 5.2 shows that the increase in rent or producer surplus resulting from the tariff is given by shaded area $AGJC = \$30$. The reason for this is as follows. At free trade $P_X = \$1$, domestic producers produce 20X and receive $OACV = \$20$ in revenues. With the tariff and $P_X = \$2$, they produce 40X and receive $OGJU = \$80$. Of the $60 increase ($AGJC + VCJU$) in the revenue of producers, $VCJU = \$30$ (the unshaded area under the S_X curve between 20X and 40X) represents the increase in their costs of production, while the remainder (shaded area $AGJC = \$30$) represents the increase in rent or producer surplus. This is defined as a payment that need not be made in the long run in order to induce domestic producers to supply the additional 20X with the tariff. The increase in rent or producer surplus resulting from the tariff is sometimes referred to as the subsidy effect of the tariff.

Concept Check

What are the effects of a tariff on producer surplus?

5.5 COSTS AND BENEFITS OF A TARIFF IN A SMALL NATION

The concept and measure of consumer and producer surplus can now be used to measure the costs and benefits of the tariff in monetary terms in the nation. These are shown in Figure 5.3, which summarizes and extends the information provided by Figures 5.1 and 5.2.

Figure 5.3 shows that when the nation imposes a 100 percent import tariff, the price of commodity X increases from $P_X = \$1$ to $P_X = \$2$, consumption falls from $AB = 100X$ to $GH = 80X$, production increases from $AC = 20X$ to $GJ = 40X$, imports decline from $CB = 80X$ to $JH = 40X$, and the government of the nation collects $MJHN = \$40$ in import duties (as in Figure 5.1). Furthermore, consumer surplus declines by $AGHB = \$90$ (as in the left panel of Figure 5.2), and producer surplus increases by $AGJC = \$30$ (as in the right panel of Figure 5.2).

Figure 5.3 shows that of the reduction of the consumer surplus of $AGHB = a + b + c + d = \$90$ $MJHN = c = \$40$ is collected by the government as tariff revenue, $AGJC = a = \$30$ is redistributed to domestic producers of commodity X in the form of increased producer surplus or rent, while the

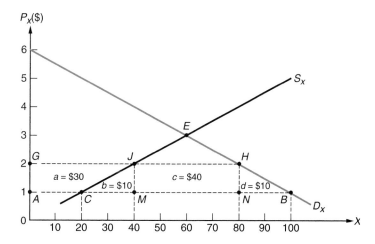

FIGURE 5.3. Costs and Benefits of a Tariff in a Small Nation.
With a 100-percent import tariff on commodity X, P_X rises from $1 to $2 in the nation. This reduces the consumer surplus by $AGHB = a + b + c + d = \$30 + \$10 + \$40 + \$10 = \$90$. Of this, $MJHN = c = \$40$ is collected by the government as tariff revenue, $AGJC = a = \$30$ is redistributed to domestic producers of commodity X in the form of increased rent or producer surplus, while the remaining $20 (the sum of the areas of triangles $CJM = b = \$10$ and $BHN = d = \$10$) represents the protection cost, or deadweight loss, to the economy.

Protection cost or deadweight loss of a tariff The real losses in a nation's welfare because of inefficiencies in production and distortions in consumption resulting from a tariff.

remaining $20 (the sum of the areas of triangles $CJM = b = \$10$ and $BHN = d = \$10$) represents the protection cost, or deadweight loss, to the economy.

The production component ($CJM = b = \$10$) of the protection cost, or deadweight loss, arises because, with the tariff, some domestic resources are transferred from the more efficient production of exportable commodity Y (not shown in the figures) to the less efficient production of importable commodity X in the nation. The consumption component ($BHN = d = \$10$) of the protection cost, or deadweight loss, arises because the tariff artificially increases P_X in relation to P_Y and distorts the pattern of consumption in the nation.

Thus, the tariff redistributes income from domestic consumers (who pay a higher price for the commodity) to domestic producers of the commodity (who receive the higher price) and from the nation's abundant factor (producing exportables) to the nation's scarce factor (producing importables). This leads to inefficiencies, referred to as the protection cost, or deadweight loss, of the tariff. By dividing the loss of consumer surplus by the number of jobs "saved" in the industry because of the tariff (or equivalent rate of protection), we can calculate the cost per domestic job saved (see Case Studies 5-3 and 5-4).

Concept Check

What are the costs and benefits of a tariff on a small nation?

5.6 COSTS AND BENEFITS OF A TARIFF IN A LARGE NATION

We now examine the effects of an import tariff in a large nation—defined as a nation that affects the world price of the commodity by its trading. We will see that part of the tariff will fall on domestic consumers (in the form of the higher price they pay for the import commodity) and part will fall on foreign producers (in the form of the lower price they receive for the commodity). The reason is that the decline in the demand for the import of the commodity by a large nation (as a result of the increase in price due to the tariff) is significant and leads to a reduction in the price that foreign producers can charge for the commodity. The *incidence or burden* of the import tariff then falls partly on consumers in the large nation imposing the tariff and partly on foreign producers that export the commodity. This is shown in Figure 5.4.

Figure 5.4 is similar to Figure 5.3, except that the vertical or price axis has been expanded. The free trade price of commodity X is still $1.00, and the nation still imposes a $1.00 import tariff. But now, because the nation is large, the price that domestic consumers pay for the commodity increases only to $1.75 (instead of $2.00 when the nation is small), and foreign producers of the commodity receive $0.75 instead of $1.00. The $1.00 difference between the price of $1.75 paid by domestic consumers and the $0.75 price received by foreign producers is collected by the government of the nation imposing the import tariff.

The Welfare Effects of Liberalizing Trade in Some U.S. Products

Table 5.3 shows the welfare effect of removing trade protection (the tariff or its equivalent, as a percentage of the world price of the product) in 1990 on some specific products on which U.S. protection remained high (despite very low overall average tariff rates). The consumer cost refers to the reduction in consumer surplus resulting from the tariff ($AGHB = a + b + c + d$ in Figure 5.3). The tariff revenue is the revenue collected from the tariff by the U.S. government ($MJHN = c$ in Figure 5.3). Producer gain refers to the increase in the producer surplus resulting from the tariff ($AGJC = a$ in Figure 5.3). The deadweight loss is the protection cost of the tariff ($CJM + BHN$ in Figure 5.3). The table also shows the cost per domestic job "saved" by the tariff. This is obtained by dividing the consumer cost (i.e., reduction in consumer surplus) of the tariff by the number of domestic jobs saved as a result of the tariff.

For example, Table 5.3 shows that the tariff of 20 percent that the United States imposed on imports of rubber footwear (the third line from the bottom in Table 5.3) resulted in a $208 million cost to U.S. consumers, $141 million in tariff revenues collected by the U.S. government, $55 million in producer gain, and $12 million of deadweight loss. The table also shows that the cost of each job saved in the production of rubber footwear in the United States (as compared with the free trade situation) was about $122,000 ($208 million divided by the 1,705 jobs saved). Note the high cost of tariff protection to U.S. consumers even for relatively unimportant products and the very high cost of preserving each job in U.S. import-competing industries.

Table 5.3. *Economic Effect of U.S. Import Tariffs on Selected Products in 1990*

Product	Tariff (%)	Consumer Cost (million $)	Tariff Revenue (million $)	Producer Gain (million $)	Deadweight Cost (million $)	Consumer Cost per job (thousand $)
Ceramic tiles	19.0	139	92	45	2	401
Costume jewelry	9.0	103	51	46	5	97
Frozen concentrated orange juice	30.0	281	145	101	35	57
Glassware	11.0	266	95	162	9	180
Luggage	16.5	211	169	16	26	934
Rubber footwear	20.0	208	141	55	12	122
Women's footwear	10.0	376	295	70	11	102
Women's handbags	9.0	103	51	46	5	97

Source: G. C. Hufbauer and K. A. Elliott, *Measuring the Cost of Protection in the United States* (Washington, D.C.: Institute for International Economics, 1994), pp. 8–13.

CASE STUDY 5-4

The Welfare Effects of Liberalizing Trade in Some EU Products

Table 5.4 shows the welfare effect of removing trade protection (the tariff or its equivalent, as a percentage of the world price of the product) in 1990 on some specific products on which European Union (EU) protection remained high (despite very low overall average tariff rates). The interpretation of the table is identical to the U.S. case. The only difference is that benefits and costs are here measured in euros (€), the new currency of 12 of the then 15 members of the European Union (this will be discussed in the finance part of the text). Since at the time of this writing, the value of €1 was approximately $1.10, the equivalent dollar values would be about 10 percent higher than the euro values shown in Table 5.4.

For example, Table 5.4 shows that the tariff (or its equivalent) of 22.9 percent that the European Union imposed on imports of chemical fibers (the first line in Table 5.4) resulted in a €580 (about $638) million cost to EU consumers, €362 ($398) million in tariff revenues collected by the EU governments, €139 ($153) million in producer gain, and €79 ($87) million of deadweight loss. The table also shows that the cost of each job saved in the production of chemical fibers in the European Union (as compared with the free trade situation) was about €526,000 or about $579,000 (€580 million divided by the 1,103 jobs saved). Note the high cost of tariff protection to EU consumers even for relatively unimportant products and the very high cost of preserving each job in EU import-competing industries.

Table 5.4. *Economic Effect of EU Protection on Selected Elected Products in 1990*

Product	Tariff Equivalent (%)	Consumer Cost (million €)	Tariff Revenue (million €)	Producer Gain (million €)	Deadweight Cost (million €)	Consumer Cost per Job (thousand €)
Chemical fibers	22.9	580	362	139	79	526
Videocassettes	30.2	313	165	82	67	420
Integrated circuits	47.6	2,187	548	139	564	366
Photocopiers	33.7	314	242	5	66	3,483
Steel	21.9	1,626	229	397	333	316
Passenger cars	17.1	2,101	979	278	276	569
Textiles	21.4	7,096	1,742	2,678	668	180
Clothing	31.3	7,103	1,696	1,712	1,079	214

Source: P. A. Messerlin, *Measuring the Cost of Protection in Europe* (Washington, D.C.: Institute for International Economics, 2001), pp. 46–47, 54–55.

We can now measure the costs and benefits of the tariff on the large nation imposing the tariff. Since the price of the imported commodity increases for domestic consumers from $1.00 to $1.75, the loss of consumer surplus is equal to $AG'H'B = a' + b' + c' + d'$, of which a' is the increase in producer's

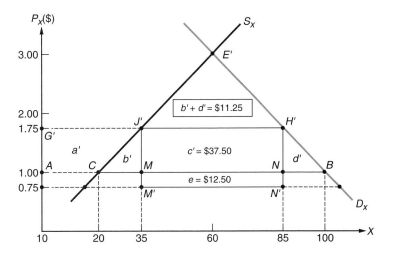

FIGURE 5.4. Costs and Benefits of a Tariff in a Large Nation.
When the large nation imposes a 100 percent import tariff on commodity X, P_X rises from $1.00 to $1.75 for domestic consumers and falls from $1.00 to $0.75 for foreign producers. Since the protection cost or deadweight loss to the nation ($b' + d' = \$11.25$) is smaller than the terms of trade effect of the tariff ($e = \$12.50$), the large nation gains from the imposition of a tariff.

surplus, c' is the tariff revenue collected by the government from domestic consumers, and $b' + d'$ is the protection cost, or deadweight loss, of the tariff to the nation. Now the welfare loss to the nation is $b' = \$5.625$ (15 times $0.75, divided by 2) plus $d' = \$5.625$, for a total of $11.25. Note that since the price to domestic consumers increases only by $0.75, the protection or deadweight loss of the tariff is less than for the small nation (where the price

of the import commodity increased by the full $1.00 value of the import tariff and the welfare loss was $20).

From Figure 5.4, we see that the government of the large nation also collects $0.25 on each of the $J'H' = 50X$ imported from foreign producers (in the form of the lower price that they now receive) for a total of $MM'N'N = e = \$12.50$. This is the terms of trade effect of the tariff. Since the tariff revenue that the government collects from foreign producers ($e = \$12.50$) exceeds the protection or deadweight loss of the tariff ($b' + d' = \$11.25$), the large nation as a whole is better off with the tariff than without the tariff.

Had the opposite been the case, the large nation would have experienced a net welfare loss. It all depends on which of the two effects is larger. In general, the more elastic or flatter are the demand and supply curves of the importable commodity in the nation imposing the tariff, the smaller is the burden or incidence of a tariff on domestic consumers and the larger

is the burden on foreign producers, and the more likely it is that the large nation will experience a net welfare gain from the tariff.

5.7 THE OPTIMUM TARIFF AND RETALIATION

Optimum tariff
The rate of tariff that maximizes the benefit resulting from improvement in the nation's terms of trade against the negative effect resulting from reduction in the volume of trade.

Prohibitive tariff
A tariff sufficiently high to stop all international trade so that the nation returns to autarky.

Concept Check

Why does the use of an optimum tariff usually lead to retaliation?

We saw in the previous section that when a large nation imposes an import tariff, the volume of trade declines but the nation's terms of trade improve. The decline in the volume of trade, by itself, tends to reduce the nation's welfare, while the improvement in its terms of trade, by itself, tends to increase the nation's welfare.

The optimum tariff is the tariff that maximizes the net benefit resulting from the improvement in the nation's terms of trade against the negative effect resulting from reduction in the volume of trade. That is, starting from the free trade position, as the nation increases its tariff rate, its welfare increases up to a maximum (the optimum tariff) and then declines as the tariff rate is raised past the optimum. With a high enough or prohibitive tariff, the nation will eventually be pushed back toward the autarky point.

However, in a two-nation world, as the terms of trade of the nation imposing the tariff improve, those of the trade partner deteriorate since they are the inverse, or reciprocal, of the terms of trade of the tariff-imposing nation. Facing both a lower volume of trade and deteriorating terms of trade, the trade partner's welfare will definitely decline. As a result, the trade partner is likely to retaliate and impose an optimum tariff on its own. While recapturing most of its losses with the improvement in its terms of trade, retaliation by the trade partner will definitely reduce the volume of trade still further. The first nation may then itself retaliate. In the end, all nations will end up losing all or most of the gains from trade (this is shown graphically in the appendix to this chapter).

Note that even when the trade partner does not retaliate when one nation imposes the optimum tariff, the gains of the tariff-imposing nation are less than the losses of the trade partner, so that the world as a whole is worse off than under free trade. It is in this sense that free trade maximizes world welfare.

Nominal tariff A tariff (such as an ad valorem one) calculated on the price of a final commodity.

Rate of effective protection The tariff calculated on the domestic value added in the production of a commodity.

5.8 THEORY OF TARIFF STRUCTURE

The tariff we have discussed until now is the nominal tariff. This is calculated on the value or price of the imported commodity. From the nominal tariff we can calculate the rate of effective or actual protection provided to the domestic industry. The rate of effective protection is the actual tariff calculated on the domestic value added or in the processing of the commodity taking place in the nation. Very often, a nation imports a raw material duty free or imposes a lower tariff rate on the importation of the raw material than on the importation of the final commodity produced with the imported

input. The nation does this in order to encourage domestic processing and employment. For example, a nation may import wool duty free but impose a tariff on the importation of cloth in order to stimulate the domestic production of cloth and domestic employment.

When this is the case, the *rate of effective protection* (calculated on the domestic value added) exceeds the nominal tariff rate (calculated on the market price of the commodity). *Domestic value added* equals the price of the final commodity minus the cost of the imported inputs going into the production of the commodity. While the nominal tariff rate is important to consumers (because it indicates by how much the price of the final commodity increases as a result of the tariff), the effective tariff rate is important to producers (because it indicates how much protection is actually provided to the domestic processing of the import-competing commodity). An example will clarify the distinction between the nominal and effective tariff rates.

Concept Check

What is the difference between a nominal and an effective tariff?

Suppose that $80 of imported wool goes into the domestic production of a suit. Suppose also that the free trade price of the suit is $100 and the nation imposes a 10 percent nominal tariff on each imported suit, but not on the imported wool used in the production of each suit. The price of suits to domestic consumers would then be $110. Of this, $80 represents imported wool, $20 is domestic value added, and $10 is the tariff. The $10 tariff collected on each imported suit represents a 10 percent nominal tariff rate since the nominal tariff is calculated on the price of the final commodity (i.e., $10/$100 = 10 percent) but corresponds to a 50 percent effective tariff rate because the *effective tariff* is calculated on the value added domestically to the suit (i.e., $10/$20 = 50 percent).

While consumers are only concerned with the fact that the $10 tariff increases the price of the suits they purchase by $10 or 10 percent, producers view this $10 tariff as being 50 percent of the $20 portion of the suit produced domestically. To them, the $10 tariff provides 50 percent of the value of domestic processing. This represents a much greater degree of protection (five times more) than the 10 percent nominal tariff rate on the suit seems to indicate. It is this effective rate of tariff protection that is important to producers in stimulating the domestic production of suits in competition with imported suits. Whenever the imported input is admitted duty free or at a lower tariff rate than on the final commodity produced with the imported input, the effective rate of protection will exceed the nominal tariff rate on the commodity.

Clearly, the nominal tariff rate can be very deceptive and does not give even a rough idea of the degree of protection actually provided to domestic producers of the import-competing product. Furthermore, most industrial nations have a "cascading" tariff structure with very low or zero nominal tariffs on raw materials and higher rates the greater the degree of processing (see Case Study 5-5). This "tariff escalation" makes the rate

CASE STUDY 5-5

Rising Tariff Rates with the Degree of Domestic Processing

Figure 5.5 shows that industrial countries imposed an average import tariff of about 2.1 percent on raw materials, 5.3 percent on semi-manufactures, and 9.1 percent on finished products before the completion of the Uruguay Round of multilateral trade negotiations in 1993. Although average tariff rates on imports at all stages of processing have fallen during the past decade as a result of the implementation of the Uruguay Round, the figure shows that the cascading tariff structure or the tariff escalation with the stage of processing remains. Thus, as the effective rate of protection exceeds the nominal tariff rate by larger percentages, the greater is the degree of domestic processing.

FIGURE 5.5. Pre- and Post-Uruguay Round Cascading Tariff Structure in Industrial Countries.
Source: W. Martin and L. A. Winters, *The Uruguay Round* (Washington, D.C.: World Bank, 1995), p. 11.

of effective protection on a final commodity with imported inputs much greater than the nominal tariff rate would indicate. As Case Study 5-6 shows, the highest tariff rates in developed nations are often found on simple labor-intensive commodities, such as textiles, in which developing nations have a comparative advantage and, as such, are of crucial importance to their development. (These questions will be analyzed in detail in Chapter 8.) As we will see in the next chapter, the rate of effective protection plays a crucial role during trade negotiations, especially between developed and developing countries.

CASE STUDY 5-6

Structure of Tariffs on Industrial Products in the United States, EU, Japan, and Canada

Table 5.5 gives the post-Uruguay Round tariff levels on imports of raw materials, semi-manufactures, and finished products in the United States, the European Union, Japan, and Canada. Transport equipment, non-electrical machinery, electrical machinery, and other manufactured goods have the single tariff levels indicated in Table 5.1 (independently of the stage of processing), and so they are not included in Table 5.5. The table shows the cascading tariff structure on many industrial products imported in the leading developed countries. The increase in the tariff with the stage of processing is greatest on imports of textiles and clothing, leather, rubber, and travel goods. It is also prevalent in metals, fish, and fish products (except for Japan), and in mineral products (except for Canada). For chemicals, wood, pulp, paper, and furniture, the situation is mixed. The tariff structure in other developed countries is similar.

Table 5.5. *Cascading Tariff Structure on Imports of Industrial Products in the United States, European Union, Japan, and Canada (percentages)*

	United States			European Union		
	Raw Materials	Semi-manufactures	Finished Products	Raw Materials	Semi-manufactures	Finished Products
Wood, pulp, paper, and furniture	0.0	0.7	0.7	0.0	1.0	0.5
Textiles and clothing	2.8	9.1	9.1	2.6	6.6	9.7
Leather, rubber, and travel goods	0.0	2.3	11.7	0.1	2.4	7.0
Metals	0.8	1.1	2.9	0.0	1.2	2.8
Chemicals and photo. supplies	0.0	4.1	2.3	0.0	5.2	3.4
Mineral products	0.6	1.3	5.3	0.0	2.4	3.7
Fish and fish products	0.7	1.7	4.0	11.2	13.3	14.1
	Japan			Canada		
	Raw Materials	Semi-manufactures	Finished Products	Raw Materials	Semi-manufactures	Finished Products
Wood, pulp, paper, and furniture	0.1	1.9	0.6	0.2	0.9	1.9
Textiles and clothing	2.6	5.9	8.3	2.5	11.1	14.5
Leather, rubber, and travel goods	0.1	10.4	20.7	0.3	5.7	10.3
Metals	0.0	1.0	0.9	0.1	1.7	5.2
Chemicals and photo. supplies	0.0	2.9	1.0	0.0	4.7	3.9
Mineral products	0.2	0.5	1.8	2.7	1.0	4.4
Fish and fish products	5.2	10.4	7.9	0.6	0.3	4.6

Source: WTO, *Market Access: Unfinished Business* (Geneva: WTO, 2001), pp. 36–39.

SUMMARY

1. Although free trade maximizes world welfare, most nations impose some trade restrictions that benefit special groups in the nation. The most important type of trade restriction historically is the tariff. This is a tax or duty on imports or exports. The ad valorem tariff is expressed as a percentage of the value of the traded commodity, whereas the specific tariff is a fixed sum per unit. The two are sometimes combined into a compound tariff. The most common is the ad valorem import tariff. These have generally declined over the past 50 years and today average less than 5 percent on industrial products in developed nations.

2. For a small nation, the domestic price of the importable commodity rises by the full amount of the tariff. The import tariff reduces the domestic consumption of the commodity, increases domestic production, reduces imports, leads to tariff revenue, and redistributes income from domestic consumers (who pay a higher price for the commodity) to domestic producers (who receive a higher price). A tariff leads to inefficiencies referred to as protection cost or deadweight loss.

3. When a large nation imposes an import tariff, the burden or incidence of the tariff falls partly on domestic consumers (in the form of a higher price they pay for the import commodity) and partly on foreign producers (in the form of the lower price they receive for the commodity). If the welfare loss to the nation resulting from the decline in the volume of trade is smaller than the welfare benefit that the nation receives from the improvement in its terms of trade, the nation as a whole benefits from the tariff.

4. The optimum tariff is the tariff that maximizes the net benefit resulting from the improvement in the nation's terms of trade against the negative effect resulting from reduction in the volume of trade. When a nation imposes an optimum tariff, the trade partner's welfare declines because of the lower volume of trade and the deterioration in its terms of trade. The trade partner is likely to retaliate, and in the end both nations are likely to lose as a result of the reduction in the volume of trade.

5. The appropriate measure of the degree of protection actually provided to domestic producers is given by the rate of effective protection. This is the tariff rate calculated on the value added in the production of the commodity in the nation. When the nation imposes a nominal tariff on the importation of a commodity but none or a lower nominal tariff on the imported inputs used in the production of a commodity, the rate of effective protection is higher than the nominal tariff rate. Rates of effective protection in industrial nations are generally much higher than the corresponding nominal rates and increase with the degree of processing.

REVIEW QUESTIONS AND PROBLEMS

1. Suppose that the small nation of Figure 5.1 imposed a 150 percent (rather than 100 percent) ad valorem tariff on the imports of commodity X. Draw a figure similar to Figure 5.1 and determine
 (a) The level of consumption, production, imports, and tariff revenue on commodity X.
 (b) The consumption, production, trade, and revenue effects of the tariff.

2. For the nation of Problem 1:
 (a) Determine the dollar value of the consumer surplus before and after the imposition of the tariff.
 (b) Of the increase in the revenue of producers with the tariff (as compared with their revenues under free trade), how much represents increased production costs? Increased rent, or producer surplus?
 (c) What is the dollar value of the protection cost, or deadweight loss, of the tariff?

3. Suppose that the nation in Problems 1 and 2 was large rather than small and that two-thirds of the import tariff fell on domestic consumers and one-third on foreign producers. Determine the net welfare effect of the tariff on the nation.

4. Suppose that for the nation in Figure 5.4 half of the burden of the tariff fell on domestic consumers and the other half on foreign producers. Determine the net welfare effect of the tariff on the nation.

5. What is meant by the optimum tariff? What is its relationship to changes in the nation's terms of trade and volume of trade?

6. Why are other nations likely to retaliate when a nation imposes an optimum tariff (or, for that matter, any import tariff)? What is likely to be the final outcome resulting from the process of retaliation?

7. Why does world welfare decline if one nation imposes an optimum tariff and the other nation does not retaliate with a tariff of its own?

8. (a) What is the difference between a nominal tariff and an effective tariff? How is the rate of effective protection measured?
 (b) What is the usefulness of the concept of effective protection?

9. (a) What is the tariff structure of industrial nations?
 (b) Why is this of special concern to developing nations?

10. Suppose that a nation reduces import tariffs on raw materials and intermediate products but not on finished products. What effect will this have on the rate of effective protection in the nation?

Optimum Tariff and Retaliation with Offer Curves

When a nation imposes a tariff, its offer curve rotates away from the axis measuring its export commodity by the amount of the import tariff. The reason is that for any amount of the export commodity, importers now want sufficiently more of the import commodity to also cover (i.e., pay for) the tariff.

For example, we see in the left panel of Figure 5.6 (repeated from the bottom of Figure 3.6 in the Appendix to Chapter 3) that if Nation 1 imposed a 200 percent ad valorem tariff on its imports of commodity Y, its offer curve would rotate from offer curve 1 to offer curve 1′, which is 200 percent or three times as distant from the X-axis as offer curve 1 (compare, for example, point H to point E′ in the figure.)

Before the imposition of the tariff, the intersection of offer curve 1 and offer curve 2 defined equilibrium point E, at which Nation 1 exchanged 80X for 80Y with Nation 2 at the terms of trade of $P_X/P_Y = 1$. After the imposition of the tariff, the intersection of offer curve 1′ and offer curve 2 defines the new equilibrium point E′ at the terms of trade of $P_X/P_Y = 1.5$. The imposition of a tariff has reduced the volume of trade but it improved Nation 1's terms of trade. The reduction in the volume of trade, by itself, tends to reduce Nation 1's welfare, while the improvement in its terms of trade tends to increase Nation 1's welfare. Whether the nation's welfare actually rises or falls depends on the net effect of these two opposing forces.

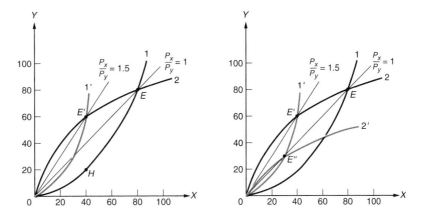

FIGURE 5.6. The Optimum Tariff and Retaliation.
In the left panel, the intersection of offer curves 1 and 2 defines free trade equilibrium point E and $P_X/P_Y = 1$. If Nation 1's optimum tariff is 200 percent, its offer curve rotates to offer curve $1'$, giving new equilibrium point E'. The volume of trade has declined but Nation 1's terms of trade has improved from $P_X/P_Y = 1$ to $P_X/P_Y = 1.5$. Since Nation 2 loses, it is likely to retaliate with an import tariff of its own, which rotates its offer curve to offer $2'$ (see the right panel), giving new equilibrium point E''. Nation 2 has now recaptured all the loss in its terms of trade but the volume of trade has shrunk considerably, so that both nations suffer a welfare loss.

The optimum tariff is the tariff that maximizes the net benefit resulting from the improvement in the nation's terms of trade against the negative effect resulting from the reduction in the volume of trade. Suppose that the optimum tariff is the 200 percent import tariff that rotates Nation 1's offer curve from offer curve 1 to offer curve $1'$. The increase in welfare benefit that Nation 1 receives from its optimum tariff, however, comes at the expense of Nation 2, which loses, both because of the reduction in the volume of international trade and the deterioration in its terms of trade (from $P_Y/P_X = 1$ to $P_Y/P_X = 0.67$, the reciprocal or inverse of Nation 1's terms of trade of $P_X/P_Y = 1.5$ at point E').

Nation 2 is likely to retaliate and impose an import tariff of its own to recapture the loss in its terms of trade. This can be shown by the clockwise rotation of Nations 2's offer curve from offer curve 2 to offer curve $2'$, which intersects Nation 1's offer curve $1'$ at point E'' at $P_Y/P_X = P_X/P_Y = 1$. Nation 2's terms of trade are now the same as before Nation 1 imposed the optimum tariff, but the volume of trade has shrunk considerably from 80X for 80Y to 30X for 30Y. As a result, both nations have suffered a welfare loss and are worse off with tariffs than with free trade. This type of analysis is called general equilibrium analysis because it shows the effect of a tariff on both nations and both commodities.

SELECTED BIBLIOGRAPHY

For a problem-solving approach to the theory of tariffs, see:

- D. Salvatore, *Theory and Problems of International Economics*, 4th ed. (New York: McGraw-Hill, 1996), ch.6.

For a more advanced treatment of the theory of tariffs, see:

- D. Salvatore, *International Economics*, 9th ed. (Hoboken, N.J.: Wiley, 2007), ch.8.

A general discussion of tariffs and commercial policies is found in:

- J. N. Bhagwati, *Protectionism* (Cambridge, Mass.: MIT Press, 1988).
- D. A. Irwin, *Free Trade Under Fire* (Princeton, N.J.: Princeton University Press, 2001).
- J. Bhagwati, *Free Trade Today* (Princeton, N.J.: Princeton University Press, 2002).

For the structure of tariffs, see:

- World Trade Organization, *Annual Trade Report 2007* (Geneva: WTO, 2007).

For measures of the cost of protection, see:

- G. H. Hufbauer and K. A. Elliott, *Measuring the Cost of Protection in the United States* (Washington, D.C.: Institute for International Economics, 1994).
- P. Messerlin, *Measuring the Cost of Protection in the European Union* (Washington, D.C.: Institute for International Economics, 2001).
- Y. Sazanami, S. Urata, and H. Kawai, *Measuring the Cost of Protection in Japan* (Washington, D.C.: Institute for International Economics, 1999).

INTERNet

For international trade policies in the United States, visit the Internet site for the Economic Report of the President (and click on the most recent year to get the latest Report), and the Internet site of the State Department, the United States Trade Representative, and the U.S. International Trade Commission, respectively, at:

http://www.gpoaccess.gov/eop

http://www.state.gov

http://www.ustr.gov

http://www.usitc.gov

For international trade policies around the world, see the Internet site of the World Trade Organization (WTO), the European Union, the Canadian Department of Foreign Affairs, respectively, at:

http://www.wto.org

http://mkaccdb.eu.int

http://www.infoexport.gc.ca

Nontariff Trade Barriers and the Political Economy of Protectionism

After studying this chapter, you should be able to:

- Know what is an import quota and other nontariff trade barriers
- Know the meaning of dumping and export subsidies
- Explain the political economy of protectionism
- Know what is outsourcing, offshoring, and fear of globalization
- Know what are strategic trade and industrial policies
- Describe the general U.S. commercial policy over the postwar period
- Describe the Uruguay Round and identify current international trade problems

CHAPTER OUTLINE

KEY TERMS

Quota

Nontariff trade barriers (NTBs)

New protectionism

Voluntary export restraints (VERs)

Technical, administrative, and other regulations

International cartel

Dumping

Persistent dumping

Predatory dumping

Sporadic dumping

Trigger-price mechanism

Export subsidies

Export-Import Bank

Foreign Sales Corporations

Countervailing duties (CVDs)

Scientific tariff

Infant-industry argument

Offshoring

Strategic trade policy

Industrial policy

Smoot–Hawley Tariff Act

Trade Agreements Act of 1934

Most-favored-nation principle

Bilateral trade

General Agreement on Tariffs and Trade (GATT)

Multilateral trade negotiations

Peril-point provisions

Escape clause

National security clause

Trade Expansion Act of 1962

Trade Adjustment Assistance (TAA)

Kennedy Round

Trade Reform Act of 1974

Tokyo Round

Trade and Tariff Act of 1984

Omnibus Trade and Competitiveness
 Act of 1988

Uruguay Round

World Trade Organization (WTO)

Trade promotion authority or "fast
 track"

Doha Round

Game theory

6.1 INTRODUCTION

Although tariffs have historically been the most important form of trade restriction, there are many other types of trade barriers, such as import quotas, voluntary export restraints, and antidumping actions. As tariffs were negotiated down during the postwar period, the importance of nontariff trade barriers has greatly increased.

In this chapter, we analyze the effect of nontariff trade barriers and the political economy of protectionism. Section 6.2 examines the effects of an import quota and compares them to those of an import tariff. Section 6.3 deals with other nontariff trade, such as voluntary export restraints and other regulations. Section 6.4 deals with dumping and export subsidies. In Section 6.5, the various arguments for protection are presented, from the clearly fallacious ones to those that seem to make some economic sense. Section 6.6 discusses outsourcing, offshoring, and fear of globalization. Section 6.7 examines strategic trade and industrial policies. Section 6.8 surveys the history of U.S. commercial or trade policy. Finally, Section 6.9 summarizes the outcome of the Uruguay Round of trade negotiations, while Section 6.10 discusses the outstanding trade problems facing the world today and the launching of the Doha Round. The appendix examines strategic trade and industrial policies with game theory.

6.2 IMPORT QUOTAS

Quota A direct *quantitative* restriction on trade.

A quota is a direct quantitative restriction on the amount of a commodity allowed to be imported or exported in a nation. In this section, we examine import quotas. Export quotas (in the form of voluntary export restraints) are examined in the next section. Import quotas can be used to protect a domestic industry or agriculture and for balance-of-payments reasons. Import quotas

were very common in Western Europe immediately after World War II. Since then they have been used by practically all industrial nations to protect their agriculture and by developing nations to stimulate the import substitution of manufactured products and for balance-of-payments reasons.

The effects of an import quota can be examined with Figure 6.1, which is almost identical to Figure 5.1, used to analyze the effects of an import tariff. In Figure 6.1 D_X is the demand curve and S_X is the supply curve of commodity X for the nation. With free trade at the world price of P_X = $1, the nation consumes 100X *(AB)*, of which 20X *(AC)* is produced domestically and the remainder of 80X *(CB)* is imported. An import quota of 40X *(JH)* would raise the domestic price of X to P_X = $2, exactly as with a 100 percent ad valorem import tariff (see Figure 5.1). The reason is that only at P_X = $2 does the quantity demanded of 80X *(GH)* equal the 40X *(GJ)* produced domestically plus the 40X *(JH)* allowed by the import quota. Thus, consumption is reduced by 20X *(BN)* and domestic production is increased by 20X *(CM)* with an import quota of 40X *(JH)*, exactly as with the 100 percent import tariff. If the government also auctioned off import licenses to the

Concept
Check

What is the effect of
an import quota?

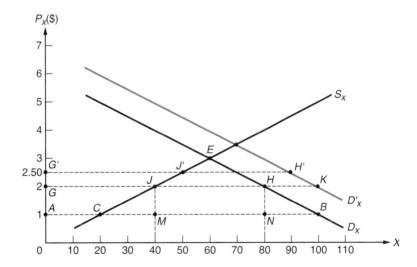

FIGURE 6.1. Effects of an Import Quota.
D_X and S_X represent the nation's demand and supply curves of commodity X. Starting from the free trade P_X = $1, an import quota of 40X *(JH)* would result in P_X = $2 and consumption of 80X *(GH)*, of which 40X *(GJ)* is produced domestically. If the government auctioned off import licenses to the highest bidder in a competitive market, the revenue effect would also be $40 *(JHNM)*, as with a 100-percent import tariff. With a shift in D_X to D'_X and an import quota of 40X *(J'H')*, consumption would rise from 80X to 90X *(G'H')*, of which 50X *(G'H')* would be produced domestically.

highest bidder in a competitive market, the revenue effect would be $40 ($1 on each of the 40X of the import quota), given by area *JHNM*. Then the import quota of 40X would be equivalent in every respect to an "implicit" 100 percent import tariff.

With an upward shift of D_X to D'_X, the *given import quota* of 40X ($J'H'$) would result in the domestic price of X rising to $P_X = \$2.50$, domestic production rising to 50X ($G'J'$), and domestic consumption rising from 80X to 90X ($G'H'$). On the other hand, with the given 100 percent import tariff (in the face of the shift from D_X to D'_X), the price of X would remain unchanged at $P_X = \$2$ and so would domestic production at 20X (GJ), but domestic consumption would rise to 100X (GK) and imports to 60X (JK).

The shift of D_X to D'_X in Figure 6.1 points to one of several important differences between an import quota and an equivalent (implicit) import tariff. With a given import quota, an increase in demand will result in a higher domestic price and greater domestic production than with an equivalent import tariff. On the other hand, with a given import tariff, an increase in demand will leave the domestic price and domestic production unchanged but will result in higher consumption and imports (see Figure 6.1).

A second important difference between an import quota and an import tariff is that the quota involves the distribution of import licenses. If the government does not auction off these licenses in a competitive market, firms that receive them will reap monopoly profits. In that case, the government must decide the basis for distributing licenses among potential importers of the commodity. Such choices may be based on arbitrary official judgments rather than on efficiency considerations. Since import licenses result in monopoly profits, potential importers are likely to devote a great deal of effort to lobbying and even bribing government officials to obtain them (in so-called rent-seeking activities).

Finally, an import quota limits imports to the specified level with *certainty*, while the trade effect of an import tariff may be uncertain. The reason is that the shape or elasticity of D_X and S_X is often not known, making it difficult to estimate the import tariff required to restrict imports to a desired level. Furthermore, foreign *exporters* may absorb all or part of the tariff by increasing their efficiency of operation or accepting lower profits. As a result, the actual reduction in imports may be less than anticipated. Exporters cannot do this with an import quota since the *quantity* of imports allowed into the nation is clearly specified by the quota. It is for this reason, and also because an import quota is less "visible," that domestic producers strongly prefer import quotas to import tariffs. However, since import quotas are more restrictive than equivalent import tariffs, society should generally resist these efforts. As we will see in Section 6.8, one of the provisions of the Uruguay Round was to change import quotas and other nontariff barriers into equivalent tariffs (a process known as "tariffication"). Case Study 6-1 examines the economic effects of the U.S. quota on sugar imports.

Concept Check

How does an import quota compare with an import tariff?

Economic Effects of the U.S. Quota on Sugar Imports

The United States restricts sugar imports into the United States with a quota of 1.4 million tons per year. The quota more than doubles the price of sugar to U.S. consumers and leads to a loss of consumer surplus of about $1.7 billion per year (measured by the sum of areas $a' + b' + c' + d'$, as indicated in Figure 5.4), of which $0.9 billion accrues to U.S. sugar producers in the form of producer surplus (area a' in Figure 5.4), $0.4 billion goes to foreign sugar exporters to the United States in the form of the higher price that they receive (area c' in Figure 5.4), and $0.4 billion represent the deadweight loss from the production and consumption distortions in the United States as a result of the quota (the sum of areas $b' + d'$ in Figure 5.4). Thus, the net total loss to the United States as a result of its sugar quota is about $0.8 billion (the $1.7 billion loss of consumer surplus minus the gain in producer surplus of $0.9 billion).

Dividing the total loss of consumer surplus of $1.7 billion by the nearly 300 million people now living in the United States, means that on average every American spends about $6 more on sugar per year than in the absence of the quota. Most Americans, of course, do not know of the quota and would not much care about it since it increases their expenditure on sugar by only a few dollars per year. But with fewer than 1000 large sugar producers in the United States, the sugar quota raises their average profits by about $1 million per year. (No wonder American sugar interests lobby the federal government so strenuously to keep the quota in place!) Since removing the sugar quota is estimated to lead to about 7,000 jobs lost in the U.S. sugar industry (18.5 percent loss of employment of the 38,000 jobs in the U.S. sugar growing industry—see Case Study 6-7), this means that the *consumer cost* of each job saved in the U.S. sugar-growing industry is about $243,000 (the loss of the consumer surplus of $1.7 billion from the U.S. sugar quota divided by the 7,000 jobs saved).

Source: USITC, *The Economic Effects of Significant U.S. Import Restraints* (Washington, D.C.: February 2007), pp. XXII and XVIII; and "Sugar's Sweetheart Deal," *The New York Times*, October 30, 2007, p. 24.

6.3 OTHER NONTARIFF TRADE BARRIERS

Nontariff trade barriers (NTBs) Trade restrictions other than tariffs, such as voluntary export restraints; technical, administrative, and other regulations; as well as those arising from international cartels, dumping, and export subsidies.

Trade barriers other than import tariffs and quotas include voluntary export restraints and technical, administrative, and other regulations. Trade restrictions also result from the existence of international cartels and from dumping and export subsidies. During the past two decades, these nontariff trade barriers (NTBs), or new protectionism, have become more important than tariffs as obstructions to the flow of international trade and represent a major threat to the world trading system. In this section, we examine voluntary export restraints, technical, administrative, and other regulations, as well as international cartels, while leaving a discussion of dumping and export subsidies for the next section.

New protectionism
New forms of nontariff trade barriers.

Voluntary export restraints (VERs)
Refer to an importing country inducing another country to "voluntarily" reduce its exports of a commodity to the importing nation under the threat of higher all-around trade restrictions.

Concept Check

What are other nontariff trade barriers? What are their effects?

Technical, administrative, and other regulations Nontariff trade barriers such as safety, health, labeling requirements, and border taxes.

Voluntary export restraints (VERs) refer to the case where an importing country induces another nation to reduce its exports of a commodity "voluntarily," under the threat of higher all-round trade restrictions, when these exports threaten an entire domestic industry. Voluntary export restraints have been negotiated since the 1950s by the United States, the European Union, and other industrial nations to curtail exports of textiles, steel, electronic products, automobiles, and other products from Japan, Korea, and other nations. These are the mature industries that faced sharp declines in employment in the industrial countries during the past three decades. VERs allowed the United States and other industrial nations making use of them to save at least the appearance of continued support for the principle of free trade. The Uruguay Round (discussed in Section 6.8) required the phasing out of all VERs and prohibited the imposition of new ones.

When successful, VERs have all the economic effects of equivalent import quotas, except for being administered by the exporting country, and so the revenue effect or rents are captured by foreign exporters or their government. An example of this is provided by the "voluntary" restraint on Japanese automobile exports to the United States negotiated in 1981 (see Case Study 6-2).

Voluntary export restraints are less effective in limiting imports than import quotas because the exporting nations agree only reluctantly to curb their exports. Foreign exporters also tended to fill their quota with higher quality and higher priced units of the product over time. Furthermore, only major supplier countries usually are involved, thus leaving the door open for other nations to replace part of the exports of the major suppliers.

International trade is also hampered by numerous technical, administrative, and other regulations. These include *safety regulations* for automobile and electrical equipment, *health regulations* for the hygienic production and packaging of imported food products, and *labeling requirements* showing origin and contents. While many of these regulations serve legitimate purposes, some (such as the French ban on scotch advertisements and the British restriction on the showing of foreign films on British television) are only thinly veiled disguises for restricting imports.

Other trade restrictions have resulted from laws requiring governments to buy from domestic suppliers (the so-called government procurement policies). For example, under the "Buy American Act" passed in 1933, U.S. government agencies gave a price advantage of up to 12 percent (50 percent for defense contracts) to domestic suppliers. As part of the Tokyo Round of trade liberalization discussed in Section 6.8, the United States and other nations agreed on a government procurement code to bring these practices and regulations into the open and give foreign suppliers a fair chance.

Much attention has also been given in recent years to *border taxes*. These are rebates for internal *indirect taxes* given to exporters of a commodity and imposed (in addition to the tariff) on importers of a commodity. Examples of

Voluntary Export Restraints on Japanese Automobiles to the United States and Europe

From 1977 to 1981, U.S. automobile production fell by about one-third, the share of imports rose from 18 to 29 percent, and nearly 300,000 autoworkers in the United States lost their jobs. In 1980 the Big Three U.S. automakers (GM, Ford, and Chrysler) suffered combined losses of $4 billion. As a result, the United States negotiated an agreement with Japan that limited Japanese automobile exports to the United States to 1.68 million units per year from 1981 to 1983 and to 1.85 million units for 1984 and 1985. Japan "agreed" to restrict its automobile exports out of fear of still more stringent import restrictions by the United States.

U.S. automakers generally used the time from 1981 to 1985 wisely to lower breakeven points and improve quality, but the cost improvements were not passed on to consumers, and Detroit reaped profits of nearly $6 billion in 1983, $10 billion in 1984, and $8 billion in 1985. Japan gained by exporting higher priced autos and earning higher profits. The big loser was the American public, which had to pay about $660 more for U.S.-made automobiles and $1,300 for Japanese cars in 1984. The total cost of the agreement to U.S. consumers has been estimated to be $15.7 billion from 1981 through 1984 and 44,000 U.S. automakers' jobs were saved at the cost of more than $100,000 each.

Since 1985, the United States has not asked for a renewal of the VER agreement, but Japan unilaterally limited its auto exports (to 2.3 million from 1986 to 1991 and 1.65 million afterward) in order to avoid more trade friction with the United States. From the late 1980s, Japan invested heavily to produce automobiles in the United States in so-called transplant factories, and by 1996 Japan was producing more than 2 million cars in the United States and had captured 23 percent of the U.S. auto market. By 2007, Japanese automakers' share of the U.S. market had reached 35 percent (between domestic production and imports). Following the U.S. lead, Canada and Germany also negotiated restrictions on Japanese exports (France and Italy already had very stringent quotas). A 1991 agreement to limit the Japanese share of the European Union's auto market to 16 percent expired at the end of 1999, when the share of Japanese cars (imports and production in Europe) was 11.4 percent of the European market. That share exceeded 13 percent in 2007 and was expected to continue to rise in the future.

Source: U.S. International Trade Commission, *A Review of Recent Developments in the U.S. Automobile Industry, Including an Assessment of the Japanese Voluntary Restraint Agreements* (Washington, D.C.: February 1985); "Japanese Cars Set Europe Sales Record," *The Japan Times*, January 16, 2005, p. 1; and "Once Again We're Driving What's Not Made Here," *The New York Times*, September 30, 2007, p. 3.

indirect taxes are excise and sales taxes in the United States and the value-added tax (VAT) in Europe. Since most government revenues are raised through direct taxes (such as income taxes) in the United States and through indirect taxes (such as the value-added tax) in Europe, United States exporters receive much lower rebates than European exporters (or no rebate at all) and are thus at a competitive disadvantage. *International commodity agreements* and *multiple exchange rates* also restrict trade. However, as the

International cartel
An organization of suppliers of a commodity located in different nations (or a group of governments) that agrees to restrict output and exports of the commodity with the aim of maximizing or increasing the total profits of the organization. An international cartel that behaves as a monopolist is called a centralized cartel.

Concept Check

How was OPEC able to sharply increase petroleum prices?

Dumping The export of a commodity at below cost or at a lower price than sold domestically.

Persistent dumping The *continuous* tendency of a domestic monopolist to maximize total profits by selling the commodity at a lower price abroad than domestically; also called international price discrimination.

Predatory dumping The *temporary* sale of commodity at a lower price abroad in order to drive foreign producers out of business, after which prices are raised to take advantage of the newly acquired monopoly power abroad.

former are of primary concern to developing nations and the latter relate to international finance, they are discussed in Chapter 8 and Chapter 14, respectively.

Another type of NTBs are international cartels. An international cartel is an organization of suppliers of a commodity located in different nations (or a group of governments) that agrees to restrict output and exports of the commodity with the aim of maximizing or increasing the total profits of the organization. Although *domestic* cartels are illegal in the United States and restricted in Europe, the power of *international* cartels cannot easily be countered because they do not fall under the jurisdiction of any one nation.

The most notorious of present-day international cartels is OPEC (Organization of Petroleum Exporting Countries), which, by restricting production and exports, succeeded in quadrupling the price of crude oil between 1973 and 1974. Another example is the International Air Transport Association, a cartel of major international airlines that met annually until 2007 to set international airfares and policies. An international cartel is more likely to be successful if there are only a few international suppliers of an essential commodity for which there are no close substitutes. OPEC fulfilled these requirements very well during the 1970s. When there are many international suppliers, however, it is more difficult to organize them into an effective cartel. Similarly, when good substitutes for the commodity are available, the attempt by an international cartel to restrict output and exports in order to increase prices and profits would only lead buyers to shift to substitute commodities. This explains the failure of, or inability to set up, international cartels in minerals other than petroleum and tin, and agricultural products other than sugar, coffee, cocoa, and rubber. Cartels often break up because of cheating by cartel members and encouraging some producers to stay out or break away from the cartel.

6.4 DUMPING AND EXPORT SUBSIDIES

Trade barriers may also result from dumping and export subsidies. Dumping is the export of a commodity at below cost or at a lower price than the commodity is sold domestically. Dumping is classified as persistent, predatory, and sporadic. Persistent dumping, or international price discrimination, refers to the *continuous* sale of the commodity at a higher price in the domestic market (which is, to some extent, insulated from foreign competition by transportation costs and trade barriers) than internationally (where it must meet the competition of foreign producers). The incentive for persistent dumping is the higher profits it provides to domestic producers.

Predatory dumping is the *temporary* sale of a commodity at below cost or at a lower price abroad than at home in order to drive foreign producers out of business, after which prices are raised to maximize profits. Sporadic dumping

Sporadic dumping The *occasional* sale of a commodity at a lower price abroad than domestically in order to sell an unforeseen and temporary surplus of the commodity abroad without having to reduce domestic prices.

is the *occasional* sale of a commodity at below cost or at a lower price abroad than domestically in order to unload an unforeseen and temporary surplus of the commodity without having to reduce domestic prices.

Trade restrictions to counteract *predatory* dumping are justified to protect domestic industries from unfair competition from abroad. These restrictions usually take the form of *antidumping* duties to offset price differentials. Since it is often difficult to determine the type of dumping, however, domestic producers invariably demand protection against any form of dumping. By so doing, they discourage imports (the "harassment thesis") and increase their own production and profits (rents).

Over the past three decades, Japan was accused of dumping steel and television sets in the United States and European nations of dumping cars, steel, and other products. Many industrial nations and the European Union persistently dump agricultural commodities arising from their farm support programs. When dumping is proved, the violating nation or firm often chooses to raise its price rather than face antidumping duties. Only eight countries had antidumping laws in 1980 compared with 96 (including many developing countries) in 2007.

Concept Check

What are the different types of dumping?

Trigger-price mechanism The antidumping mechanism introduced by the United States in 1978 to protect its steel industry by imposing a duty on underpriced imported steel to make its price equal to that of the lowest cost foreign producer.

In 1978, the United States introduced a trigger-price mechanism under which a charge that steel was being imported into the United States at prices below those of the lowest cost foreign producer (Korea in the late 1980s) was subject to a speedy antidumping investigation. If dumping was proved, the U.S. government would provide quick relief to the domestic steel industry in the form of a duty that would bring the price of the imported steel to equal that of the lowest cost country. Since 1992, when the voluntary export restraints on steel exports to the United States expired, U.S. steel producers have filed hundreds of antidumping suits against foreign steel producers, which resulted in bitter disputes.

In 1985, U.S. producers filed antidumping suits against Japanese exporters of computer chips (the brain of computers and most modern-day machinery). An agreement was reached in 1986 under which Japan would stop dumping chips in the United States and around the world. Charging continued dumping, however, the United States imposed a 100 percent import duty on $300 million worth of Japanese exports to the United States in 1987. The tariff was removed in 1991 when Japan renegotiated the semiconductor agreement under which Japan agreed to help foreign (U.S.) producers increase their share of the Japanese chip market from 8 percent in 1986 to 20 percent by 1992. Disagreements continued, however, when U.S. chip producers failed to achieve the agreed-upon 20 percent market share in Japan in 1994. In 1996, the agreement was renewed, but it required only that the U.S. and Japanese computer chip industries monitor each other's market without any market-sharing requirement.

On average, about one-half of antidumping investigations are terminated without any measure being imposed and the rest end with the imposition of

CASE STUDY 6-3

Antidumping Measures

Table 6.1 gives the countries with the most antidumping measures in force on June 30, 2006. It shows that the United States was the heaviest user, with 262 measures out of the total of 1,279 in force. India was the second heaviest user, with 177 actions. It was followed by the European Union (154), China (88), Turkey (81), South Africa (71), Mexico (70), Argentina (64), Brazil (49), Canada (49), and Australia (47).

Products exported from China were the subject of the most antidumping investigations (64) initiated from July 1, 2005 to June 30, 2006, followed by products exported by the European Union and the United States (13 each), Malaysia (12), Thailand (11), Taiwan (China) and Korea (10 each), India and Indonesia (8 each), and Japan (7).

Table 6.1. *Antidumping Measures in Force on June 30, 2006*

Country	Antidumping Measures in Force	Country	Antidumping Measures in Force
United States	262	Argentina	64
India	177	Brazil	49
European Union	154	Canada	49
China	88	Australia	47
Turkey	81	Philippines	34
South Africa	71	Total	1,279
Mexico	70		

Source: WTO, *Annual Report* (WTO: Geneva, 2007), Table II-4.

Export subsidies
The granting of tax relief and subsidized loans to potential exporters, and low-interest loans to foreign buyers of the nation's exports.

Export-Import Bank
A U.S. government agency that extends subsidized loans to foreigners to finance U.S. exports.

a duty or with the exporter increasing the price of the export commodity. The number of antidumping measures in force rose from 880 at the end of 1997 to 1,279 in mid-2006. Case Study 6-3 gives the total antidumping measures in force in various countries in mid-2006.

Export subsidies are direct payments (or the granting of tax relief and subsidized loans) to the nation's exporters or potential exporters and/or low-interest loans to foreign buyers to stimulate the nation's exports. As such, export subsidies can be regarded as a form of dumping. Although export subsidies are illegal by international agreement, many nations provide them in disguised and not-so-disguised forms.

For example, all major industrial nations give foreign buyers of the nation's exports low-interest loans to finance the purchase through agencies such as the U.S. Export–Import Bank. These low-interest credits finance about 2 percent of U.S. exports but a much larger percentage of Japan's,

France's, and Germany's exports. Indeed, this is one of the most serious trade complaints that the United States has against other industrial countries today. The amount of the subsidy provided can be measured by the difference between the interest that would have been paid on a commercial loan and what was in fact paid at the subsidized rate.

Foreign sales corporations The overseas subsidiaries set up by U.S. corporations to take advantage of partial exemption from U.S. tax laws.

Another example is provided by the U.S. foreign sales corporations provisions of the U.S. tax code. These have been used since 1971 by some 3,600 U.S. corporations (including Boeing, Microsoft, and Caterpillar) to set up overseas subsidiaries to enjoy partial exemption from U.S. tax laws on income earned from exports. This provision saved American companies from $4 to $5 billion in taxes each year. In 1999, the World Trade Organization (WTO) ruled that such tax relief was a form of export subsidy and ordered the United States to repeal it. The United States appealed and lost, and so in 2004 it repealed the provision to avoid $4 billion in sanctions.

Concept Check

How are countervailing duties related to trade protectionism?

Particularly troublesome are the very high support prices provided by the European Union (EU) to maintain its farmers' income under its common agricultural policy (CAP). These high farm subsidies lead to huge agricultural surpluses and subsidized exports, which take export markets away from the United States and other countries, and are responsible for some of the sharpest trade controversies between the United States and the European Union (see Case Study 6-4).

Countervailing duties (CVDs) Tariffs imposed on imports to offset subsidies by foreign governments.

Serious controversies also arise from the subsidies that the EU provides to its aircraft (Airbus) industry and Japan's Ministry of International Trade and Industry (MITI) to its computer and other high-tech industries. Countervailing duties (CVDs) are often imposed on imports to offset export subsidies by foreign governments. Case Study 6-5 examines the extent of nontariff barriers on the imports of the United States, the European Union, Japan, and Canada.

6.5 THE POLITICAL ECONOMY OF PROTECTIONISM

In this section, we analyze the various arguments for protection. These range from clearly fallacious propositions to arguments that can stand up, with some qualification, to close economic scrutiny.

One *fallacious* argument is that trade restrictions are needed to *protect domestic labor against cheap foreign labor*. This argument is not valid because even if domestic wages are higher than wages abroad, domestic labor *costs* can still be lower if the productivity of labor is sufficiently higher domestically than abroad. If not, expensive-labor nations can still specialize in the production and export capital- and technology-intensive commodities (refer to Section 2.4).

Scientific tariff The tariff rate that would make the price of imports equal to domestic prices so as to allow domestic producers to meet foreign competition.

Another *fallacious* argument for protection is the scientific tariff. This is the tariff rate that would make the price of imports equal to domestic prices and (so the argument goes) allow domestic producers to meet foreign

CASE STUDY 6-4

Agricultural Subsidies in Developed Nations

Table 6.2 gives the assistance that developed nations provided to their agriculture, both in billions of U.S. dollars and as a percentage of the value of agricultural output in 2004 and 2006. The table shows that in 2006, the European Union spent the most on agricultural subsidies ($138.0 billion), followed by Japan ($40.7 billion) and the United States ($29.3 billion). As a percentage of total agricultural output, the United States spent one-third as much as the European Union, about a fifth of that of Japan, and half that of Canada.

Among the smaller developed nations, New Zealand and Australia provided the smallest percentage assistance (1 percent and 6 percent, respectively) while Switzerland and Norway provided the largest (63 and 65 percent, respectively) in 2006. For all industrial countries, the assistance averaged 27 percent in 2006 (down from 30 percent in 2004). Agricultural subsidies are responsible for some of the sharpest trade controversies in the world today and were responsible for the long delay in concluding the Uruguay Round of trade negotiations and in getting the Doha Round under way (see Sections 6.8 and 6.9).

Table 6.2. *Agricultural Subsidies in Developed Nations and the European Union, 2004 and 2006*

Country	Billions of U.S. Dollars		Subsidy as a Percentage of Agricultural Output	
	2004	*2006*	*2004*	*2006*
United States	46.5	29.3	16	11
European Union	133.4	138.0	36	32
Japan	48.7	40.7	56	53
Canada	5.7	7.5	21	23
Australia	1.1	1.4	4	6
New Zealand	0.3	0.1	1	1
Norway	3.0	3.0	67	65
Switzerland	5.8	5.0	68	63
All developed countries	279.5	272.0	30	27

Source: OECD, *Agricultural Policies in OECD Countries: Monitoring and Evaluation* (OECD: Paris, 2005 and 2007), Table 2.

competition. However, this would eliminate international price differences and trade in commodities subject to such "scientific" tariffs.

Two *questionable* arguments are that protection is needed (1) to reduce domestic unemployment and (2) to cure a deficit in the nation's balance of payments (i.e., the excess of the nation's expenditures abroad over its foreign earnings). Protection would reduce domestic unemployment and a balance-of-payments deficit by leading to the substitution of imports with

CASE STUDY 6-5

Pervasiveness of Nontariff Barriers

Table 6.3 gives the pervasiveness of all types of nontariff trade barriers (volutary export restraints, antidumping measures, technical and other regulations, and countervailing duties) in effect in the United States, in the European Union, Japan, and Canada in 1996. The pervasiveness of nontariff trade barriers is measured by the percentage of tariff lines affected. For example, 2.8 percent of the U.S. food, beverage, and tobacco trade was affected by some type of nontariff trade barriers in 1996, as compared with 17.2 percent in the European Union, 5.9 percent in Japan, and 0.4 percent in Canada.

From the table, we see that by far the most protected sector in all countries or region is textile and apparel. On an overall basis, the trade-weighted percentage of nontariff trade barriers on all manufactured products was 17.9 percent in the United States, 13.4 percent in the European Union, 10.3 percent in Japan, and 7.8 percent in Canada. These averages are likely to be lower today as a result of the implementation of the provisions of the Uruguay Round, but more recent data are not available. Smaller developed nations made much less use of nontariff trade barriers than larger nations.

Table 6.3. *Pervasiveness of Nontariff Barriers in Large Developed Nations*

Product	Percent of Tariff Lines Affected			
	United States	*European Union*	*Japan*	*Canada*
Food, beverage, and tobacco	2.8	17.2	5.9	0.4
Textiles and apparel	67.5	75.2	31.9	42.9
Wood and wood products	0.6	0.0	0.0	3.2
Paper and paper products	1.1	0.7	0.0	0.4
Chemicals, petroleum products	3.3	2.9	0.9	0.6
Nonmetallic mineral products	3.6	0.0	0.0	0.0
Basic metal industries	30.4	0.6	5.1	1.7
Fabricated metal products	5.9	0.0	0.0	2.2
Other manufacturing	1.7	0.0	0.0	0.9
Average manufacturing	17.9	13.4	10.3	7.8

Source: WTO, *Market Access: Unfinished Business* (WTO: Geneva, 2001), p. 21.

Infant-industry argument The argument that temporary trade protection is needed to set up an industry and to protect it during its infancy against competition from more established and efficient foreign firms.

domestic production. However, these are *beggar-thy-neighbor* measures that come at the expense of other nations, which are likely to retaliate and cause all nations to lose in the end. Domestic unemployment and a deficit in a nation's balance of payments should be corrected with appropriate domestic monetary, fiscal, and trade policies (discussed in Chapter 14) rather than with trade restrictions.

One qualified argument for protection is the infant-industry argument to allow a nation to develop an industry in which it has a potential comparative

advantage. *Temporary* trade protection is then justified to establish and protect the domestic industry during its "infancy" until it can grow and meet foreign competition. For this argument to be valid, however, protection must be temporary, and the return in the grown-up industry must be sufficiently high to also offset the higher prices paid by domestic consumers of the commodity during the period of infancy.

Several important qualifications must be made with regard to the infant-industry argument for protection. First, this argument is more justified for developing nations (where capital markets may not function properly) than for industrial nations. Second, it is usually difficult to identify which industry or potential industry qualifies for this treatment, and experience has shown that protection, once given, is difficult to remove. Third, and most important, what trade protection (say, in the form of an import tariff) can do, an equivalent production *subsidy* to the infant industry can do better. The reason is that a purely *domestic distortion* should be overcome with a *purely domestic policy* (such as a direct production subsidy to the infant industry) rather than with a trade policy that also distorts relative prices and domestic consumption. A production subsidy is also a more direct form of aid that is easier to remove than an import tariff. One practical difficulty is that a subsidy requires revenues rather than generating them as, for example, an import tariff does.

The same general principle also holds for other types of domestic distortion. For example, suppose that an industry generates an *external economy* (i.e., a benefit to society at large, say, by training workers who then leave to work in other industries). There is then likely to be underinvestment in the industry (because the industry does not receive the full benefit from its investments). One way to encourage the industry and confer greater external economies on society would be to restrict imports. But this also increases the price of the product to domestic consumers. A better policy would, again, be to provide a direct subsidy to the industry. Similarly, a direct tax would also be better than a tariff to discourage activities (such as automobile travel) that give rise to *external diseconomies* (pollution) because the tax does not distort relative prices and consumption.

Trade restrictions are often advocated to protect domestic industries important for national defense. But even in this case, direct production subsidies are generally better than tariff protection. The closest we come to a truly valid economic argument for protection is the *optimum tariff* discussed in Section 5.7. That is, if a nation is large enough to affect its terms of trade, the nation can exploit its market power and improve its terms of trade and welfare with an optimum tariff. However, as we have seen, this is a beggar-thy-neighbor policy and other nations are likely to retaliate and lead to losses all around.

It is clear that by increasing the commodity price, trade protection benefits producers and harms consumers (and usually the nation as a

Concept
Check

How must the
infant-industry
argument be
qualified?

whole). However, since producers are few and stand to gain a great deal from protection, they have a strong incentive to lobby the government to adopt protectionist measures. On the other hand, since the losses are diffused among many consumers, each of whom loses very little from the protection, they are not likely to effectively organize to resist protectionist measures. Thus, there is a bias in favor of protectionism. For example, the U.S. sugar quota raises individual expenditures on sugar by about $8 per person per year in the United States. But with a U.S. population of 300 million people, the quota generates about $2.4 billion in rents to the few thousand sugar producers in the country.

Concept Check

Which groups in a nation usually get trade protection?

In industrial countries, protection is more likely to be provided to labor-intensive industries employing unskilled, low-wage workers who would have great difficulty in finding alternative employment if they lost their present jobs. Some empirical support has also been found for the *pressure-group* or *interest-group* theory, which postulates that industries that are highly organized (such as the automobile industry) receive more trade protection than less organized industries. Industries that produce consumer products are also generally able to obtain more protection than industries producing intermediate products because the former can exercise *countervailing* power and block protection by the latter, which would increase input prices and lead to higher consumer prices.

6.6 OUTSOURCING, OFFSHORING, AND FEAR OF GLOBALIZATION

Offshoring This refers to a firm producing in its own plants abroad some of the parts and components that it uses in its products.

In Section 4.6 we defined *outsourcing* as a firm's purchase of parts and components abroad, rather than itself producing them at home, in order to keep its costs down in the globalized world economy. This differs from offshoring, which refers instead to a firm producing in its own plants abroad (foreign direct investment) some of the parts and components that it uses in its products. In Case Study 1-1, we saw that Dell outsources most of the parts and components it uses to produce its PCs. On the other hand, IBM produced about one-third of the parts and components that it used to build its Thinkpad laptop (before it sold it to Lenovo of China) in the United States, offshored another third of the parts and components from IBM plants overseas, and outsourced the rest from foreign producers.

Outsourcing and/or offshoring are undertaken by firms in order to remain internationally competitive. That is, in todays's globalized world a firm must purchase or make the parts and components it needs to produce its goods wherever in the world they are made or can be made cheaper and or better. If it does not, the firm will lose the international market to more efficient domestic and foreign competitors and eventually it can lose the domestic market as well. Of course, the national government could provide the firm with trade protection in the form of a tariff, quota, or a

subsidy to avoid outsourcing or offshoring and keeping jobs at home, but this is not allowed by WTO rules. As we have seen, nations often do try to protect domestic industries and jobs, and this is the source of serious trade disputes.

Furthermore, trade protection increases the price of the product to domestic consumers and reduces the international competitiveness of other domestic producers that use the output of the protected industry in its own production. For example, if Brazil encourages its computer industry by trade protection and, as a result, builds computers that are more expensive and less efficient than American or Japanese ones, the Brazilian consumers will pay more for less efficient domestic computers and the Brazilian steel industry, which uses computers for its production, will lose international competitiveness vis-à-vis foreign steel producers which are not so handicapped. Of course, Brazil may justify protection as a strategic policy to create the computer industry because it deems it necessary for its future development and in the expectation that trade protection can be removed when its computer industry will become internationally competitive (this is discussed in the next section).

The fact remains, however, that outsourcing and offshoring, while necessary for the firm to lower costs and remain internationally competitive, does lead to some job losses and the fear of even greater losses in the future. But as we have seen in Case Study 3-4, most of the de-industrialization and manufacturing jobs lost in the United States and in other advanced nations during the past decade or two resulted from technological changes that increased labor productivity and reduced the use of labor rather than because of imports. Nevertheless, a growing number of economists, while remaining believers that free trade is the best policy for the world as a whole, are expressing a rising concern that the revolution in telecommunications and transportation is making possible the export of an increasing number of high-skill and high-wage jobs not only in manufacturing, but a growing range of services that until recently were regarded as secure (See Case Study 6-6 and Case Study 1-3).

 Concept Check

What is the "fear of globalization"? Is it justified?

The belief is starting to take hold that most of the benefits from international trade and openness (globalization) that before accrued mostly to advanced nations now seem to flow primarily to some of the most dynamic emerging market economies, such as China and India. Accordingly, the international economic system needs fixing or reforming to prevent the loss of many high-skill jobs in advanced countries and thus counter the increasingly vocal calls for protectionism. Although there are other concerns and fears regarding globalization (see Section 1.2), this is the most serious concern and complaint about the globalization of the world economy today, and the one that can lead to potentially most damaging reactions.

Job Loss Rates in U.S. Industries and Globalization

Table 6.4 shows that from 2003 to 2005, the percentage of jobs lost in U.S. manufacturing was three times higher than in U.S. service industries. But in all sectors (except professional and business services) job losses were much higher in the nontradable sectors (and thus not caused by increased imports, outsourcing, or offshoring) than in the tradable sectors. This confirms what was said in Case Study 4-3.

That is, that most job losses in the United States resulted from technological changes that raised labor productivity rather than international trade and affected mostly low-skilled industrial workers. The fear, however, is that the electronic revolution may now result in millions of high-skilled U.S. service jobs being shipped abroad.

Table 6.4. *U.S. Job Loss Rates by Industry, 2003–2005 (percent)*

Industry	Overall	Tradable	Nontradable
Manufacturing	12	12	17
Information	4	4	15
Financial services	4	3	12
Professional & business services	4	6	3

Source: A. Bradword and L. G. Kletzer, "Fear of Offshoring: The Scope and Potential Impact of Imports and Exports of Services," *Policy Brief*, Petersen Institue, January 2008; P. Samuelson, "Where Ricardo and Mill Rebut and Confirm Arguments of Mainstream Economists Supporting Globalization," *Journal of Economic Perspectives*, Summer 2004, pp. 135–146; J. Bhagwati, "The Free Trade Perspective Lives On," *The Financial Times*, October 9, 2007, p. 11; A. Blinder, "Pain from Free Trade Spurs Second Thoughts," *The Wall Street Journal*, March 28, 2008, p. A1; D. T. Coe, "Jobs on Another Shore," *Finance and Development*, March 2008, pp. 48-52; and L. Summers, "America Needs to Make a New Case for Trade," *The Financial Times*, April 28, 2008, p. 11.

6.7 STRATEGIC TRADE AND INDUSTRIAL POLICIES

Strategic trade policy The argument that an activist trade policy in oligopolistic markets subject to extensive external economies can improve a nation's welfare.

Strategic trade policy is a relatively recent development advanced in favor of an activist trade policy and protectionism. According to this argument, a nation can create a comparative advantage (through temporary trade protection, subsidies, tax benefits, and cooperative government–industry programs) in such fields as semiconductors, computers, telecommunications, and other industries that are deemed crucial to future growth in the nation. These high-technology industries are subject to high risks, require large-scale production to achieve economies of scale, and give rise to extensive external economies when successful. Strategic trade policy suggests that

by encouraging such industries, the nation can reap the large external economies that result from them and enhance its future growth prospects. This is similar to the infant-industry argument in developing nations, except that it is advanced for industrial nations to acquire a comparative advantage in some crucial high-tech industry.

Industrial policy
An activist policy by the government to stimulate the development and growth of some (usually high-tech) industry in an industrial nation.

Examples of strategic trade and industrial policy are provided by semiconductors in the 1970s and 1980s in Japan and by the development of the Concorde (the supersonic aircraft) and Airbus in Europe in the 1970s. Semiconductors in Japan are usually given as the textbook case of successful strategic trade and industrial policy. The market for semiconductors (such as computer chips) was dominated by the United States in the 1970s. Starting in the mid-1970s, Japan's powerful Ministry of Trade and Industry (MITI) targeted the development of this industry by financing research and development, granting tax advantages for investments in the industry, and fostering government–industry cooperation, while protecting the domestic market from foreign (especially U.S.) competition.

These policies are credited for Japan's success in nearly wresting control of the semiconductor market from the United States in the mid-1980s. Most economists remain skeptical, however, and attribute Japan's stunning performance in this field primarily to other forces, such as greater educational emphasis on science and mathematics, higher rates of investment, and a willingness to take a long-run view of investments rather than stressing quarterly profits, as in the United States. In Europe, the Concorde was a technological feat but a commercial disaster, and Airbus Industrie would not have survived without heavy government subsidies.

Concept Check

Have strategic trade and industrial policies been generally effective?

There are also serious difficulties in carrying strategic industrial and trade policies. First, it is extremely difficult to pick winners (i.e., choose the industries that will provide large external economies in the future) and devise appropriate policies to successfully nurture them. Second, since most leading nations undertake strategic trade policies at the same time, their efforts are largely neutralized, so that the potential benefits to each may be small. Third, when a country does achieve substantial success with a strategic trade policy, this comes at the expense of other countries (i.e., it is a beggar-thy-neighbor policy), which are likely to retaliate. Faced with all these practical difficulties, even supporters of strategic trade policy grudgingly acknowledge that *free trade is still the best policy*, after all. That is, free trade may be suboptimal in theory, but it is optimal in practice. The appendix to this chapter examines strategic trade policies with game theory.

While not generally opposed to industrial targeting and strategic trade policies domestically, the United States did retaliate against countries that adopted these policies to the detriment of U.S. economic interests. An example was the semiconductor agreement that the United States negotiated with Japan in 1991 discussed earlier. On a broader scale, the United States and

Japan engaged in negotiations (called the Structural Impediments Initiative, or SII) during the mid-1990s aimed, among other things, at opening the entire Japanese distribution system more widely to U.S. firms. During the 1990s, the United States also demanded a sharp reduction in subsidies granted to Airbus Industrie by the governments of France, Germany, England, and Spain, to agriculture by the European Union, and since the turn of the new century on subsidies for Airbus's development of its new super jumbo aircraft. Furthermore, the United States has requested that other countries, such as Brazil, China, and India, remove excessive restrictions against specific U.S. exports and demanded protection for its intellectual property (such as patented materials) from unauthorized and uncompensated use. Case Study 6.7 provides an estimate of the economic benefits to the United States from removing all import restraints.

6.8 HISTORY OF U.S. COMMERCIAL POLICY

Smoot–Hawley Tariff Act Raised average import duties in the United States to the all-time high of 59 percent in 1932.

This section surveys the history of U.S. commercial policy. It starts by examining the Trade Agreements Act of 1934 and then discussing the importance of the General Agreement on Tariffs and Trade (GATT). Next we examine the 1962 Trade Expansion Act and the results of the Kennedy Round of trade negotiations. Subsequently, we discuss the Trade Reform Act of 1974 and the outcome of the Tokyo Round of trade negotiations. Finally, we examine the 1984 and the 1988 Trade Acts.

Trade Agreements Act of 1934 Authorized the President to negotiate with other nations mutual tariff reductions of up to 50 percent under the most-favored-nation principle.

The Trade Agreements Act of 1934. During the early 1930s, world trade in general and U.S. exports in particular fell sharply because of (1) greatly reduced economic activity throughout the world as a result of the Great Depression and (2) passage in 1930 of the Smoot–Hawley Tariff Act, under which the average import duty in the United States reached the all-time high of 59 percent in 1932. The aim was to stimulate domestic employment, but it provoked retaliation by other countries, and this led to the collapse of world trade (American imports in 1932 were only 31 percent of their 1929 level, and exports fell even more).

Most-favored-nation principle The extension to all trade partners of any reciprocal tariff reduction negotiated by the United States with any other nation.

To reverse the trend toward sharply reduced world trade, the U.S. Congress passed the Trade Agreements Act of 1934, which authorized the President to negotiate *mutual* tariff reductions by as much as 50 percent of the rates set under the Smoot–Hawley Tariff Act. Tariff reductions were to be based on the most-favored-nation principle, which extended to all trade partners any *reciprocal* tariff reduction negotiated by the United States with any of its trade partners. This bilateral trade approach, however, faced the serious shortcoming that tariff reductions were negotiated, for the most part, only in commodities that *dominated* bilateral trade.

Bilateral trade Trade between any two nations.

Economic Effects of Removing All Import Restraints on Various U.S. Sectors

Table 6.5 shows the projected economic effects on employment, output, imports, exports, and price in 2011 from simultaneously removing all significant restraints on U.S. imports in various sectors. All effects are measured in terms of percentage changes in the sector affected. For example, the first row of the table under "Sugar" shows that the removal of all restrictions on sugar is projected to reduce the U.S. employment in that sector by 18.5 percent, reduce output by 3.1, increase U.S. sugar imports by 318.4, increase U.S. sugar exports by 131.4 percent, and lead to a price reduction of sugar in the United States of 3.4 by 2011.

From the table, we see that the largest percentage reduction in employments are in sugar (18.5) and in textile and mill goods (15.3). The total welfare effect of the removal of all significant restraints on U.S. imports (not shown in the table and resulting mostly from the reduction in the price for the particular product) was $3,688 million, distributed as follows: textile and apparel, $1,885 million; sugar, $811 million; dairy, $573 million; and footwear and leather products, $249 million.

Table 6.5. *Economic Effects of Removing All U.S. Import Restraints in Various Sectors, 2011 (percentage)*

Sector	Employment	Output	Imports	Exports	Price
Food and agricultural sectors					
Sugar	−18.5	−3.1	318.4	131.4	−3.4
Dairy	−2.4	−2.6	131.9	30.9	−1.1
Canned tuna	−8.5	−15.1	12.3	4.6	−5.5
Tobacco	−0.2	−0.3	14.9	1.8	−0.1
Textile and apparel sectors					
Textile and mill goods	−15.3	−11.1	3.5	−38.6	−0.5
Textile products	−0.6	−1.2	3.1	−5.0	−1.2
Apparel	−4.0	−5.4	3.1	−31.9	−1.9
Other manufacturing sectors					
Ceramic wall and floor tiles	−5.6	−5.3	2.8	0.4	−0.1
Costume jewelry	−3.3	−2.7	5.8	0.7	−1.6
Cutlery and hand tools	−1.1	−1.1	4.3	0.7	−0.8
Footwear and leather products	−2.9	−2.2	4.4	1.3	−4.2
Glass and glass products	−0.4	−0.4	6.1	5.2	−0.6
Pens, pencils, and parts	−2.9	−2.3	4.6	1.6	−1.1
Table and kitchenware	−2.5	−2.4	2.9	0.2	−1.8

Source: USITC, *The Economic Effects of Significant U.S. Import Restraints* (Washington, D.C.: February 2007), p. XXII.

General Agreements on Tariffs and Trade (GATT) An international organization devoted to the promotion of freer trade through multilateral trade negotiations.

Multilateral trade negotiations Trade negotiations among many nations.

Peril-point provisions A protectionist device that prevented the president from negotiating any tariff reduction that would cause serious damage to a domestic industry.

Escape clause A protectionist device that allowed any industry that claimed injury from imports to petition the International Trade Commission, which could then recommend to the president to revoke any negotiated tariff reduction.

National security clause A protectionist device that prevented any tariff reduction (even if already negotiated) that would hurt industries important for national defense.

Trade Expansion Act of 1962 Granted the President authority to negotiate across-the-board tariff reductions of up to 50 percent of their 1962 level and replaced the no-injury principle with adjustment assistance.

The General Agreement on Tariffs and Trade (GATT). The General Agreement on Tariffs and Trade (GATT) was an international organization, created in 1947 and headquartered in Geneva (Switzerland), devoted to the promotion of freer trade through multilateral trade negotiations. GATT rested on (1) the principle of *nondiscrimination*, or the unconditional acceptance of the most-favored-nation principle; (2) the elimination of *nontariff* trade barriers (such as quotas), except for agricultural products and for nations in balance-of-payments difficulties; and (3) consultation among nations in solving trade disputes within the GATT framework. By 1993, a total of 123 nations (including the United States and all major countries, with the exception of the countries of the former Soviet Union and China) were signatories of the GATT and covered over 90 percent of world trade.

Initial success in lowering tariffs under GATT auspices were limited by the protectionist measures adopted by the U.S. Congress during the 1950s. These were (1) the peril-point provisions, which prevented the president from negotiating any tariff reduction that would cause serious damage to a domestic industry; (2) the escape clause, which allowed any domestic industry that claimed injury from imports to petition the International Trade Commission (the U.S. Tariff Commission until 1975) to recommend to the president to revoke any *negotiated* tariff reduction—a rising share of imports in an industry was sufficient to "prove" injury; and (3) the national security clause, which prevented tariff reductions (even if already negotiated) when they would hurt industries important for national defense.

The 1962 Trade Expansion Act and the Kennedy Round. The Trade Expansion Act of 1962 replaced the product-by-product approach of the Trade Agreements Act, authorized the president to negotiate across-the-board tariff reductions of up to 50 percent of their 1962 level, and provided Trade Adjustment Assistance (TAA) to displaced workers (in the form of retraining and moving assistance) and to firms (in the form of tax relief, low-cost loans, and technical help) injured by tariff reductions. Under the authority of this act, the United States negotiated the Kennedy Round of multilateral trade negotiation in 1967, which lowered average tariff rates on industrial products to less than 10 percent in industrial nations.

The Trade Reform Act of 1974 and the Tokyo Round. The Trade Reform Act authorized the president to negotiate (1) tariff reductions of up to 60 percent and removal of tariffs of 5 percent or less and (2) a code of conduct for nations in applying nontariff trade barriers to reduce their restrictive effect. The act also liberalized the criteria for adjustment assistance. Under the authority of the act, the United States participated in the multilateral tariff negotiations known as the Tokyo Round, which were concluded in 1979 and resulted in average tariff reductions (phased over an eight-year period, starting in 1980) of 31 percent for the United States, 27 percent for the European Union, and 28 percent for Japan.

Trade Adjustment Assistance The provision of the Trade Expansion Act of 1962 (and continued in subsequent trade acts) which provides assistance to displaced workers and firms injured by trade liberalization.

Concept Check

Can you briefly describe U.S. commercial policies since the end of World War II?

Trade Reform Act of 1974 Granted the President authority to negotiate tariff reductions of up to 60 percent of their post–Kennedy Round level and to negotiate reductions in nontariff trade barriers.

Tokyo Round The multilateral trade negotiations that were completed in 1979 (under the authority of the 1974 Trade Reform Act) in which agreement was reached to cut average tariff rates by about 30 percent and to adopt a uniform international code of conduct for applying nontariff trade barriers.

The Trade and Tariff Act of 1984. This had three major provisions: (1) It authorized the president to negotiate international agreements for the protection of intellectual property rights and to lower barriers to trade in services, high-technology products, and direct investments; (2) it extended the Generalized System of Preferences (GSP), which granted preferential access to the exports of developing countries to the United States (see Section 8.6); and (3) it provided authority for negotiation in the Uruguay Round that started in 1986 (see Section 6.8).

The Omnibus Trade and Competitiveness Act of 1988. This called on the U.S. Special Trade Representative (USTR) to set a rigorous schedule for negotiating reductions in trade barriers with countries that heavily restricted U.S. exports and required retaliation if negotiations failed.

Figure 6.2 summarizes the history of average tariff rates on dutiable imports in the United States from 1900 to 2004. Tariffs in the other leading

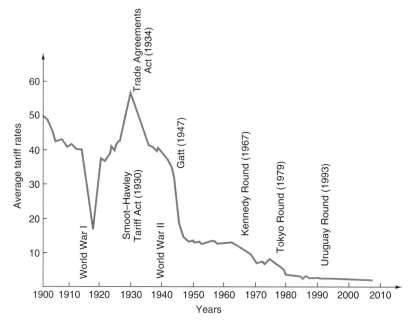

FIGURE 6.2. U.S. Average Tariff Rates on Dutiable Imports, 1900–2003. Average tariff rates on dutiable imports in the United States ranged from the high of 59 percent, reached in 1932 under the Smoot–Hawley Tariff Act of 1930, to less than 5 percent in 2003.

Source: Historical Abstract of the United States (Washington, D.C.: U.S. Government Printing Office, 1972); and *Statistical Abstract of the United States* (Washington, D.C.: U.S. Government Printing Office, 2004) for years since 1971.

developed nations have shown similar declines and are now comparable to U.S. rates (see Table 5.1).

6.9 THE URUGUAY ROUND

Uruguay Round
The multilateral trade negotiations started in 1986 and completed at the end of 1993 aimed at reversing the trend of rising nontariff trade barriers. It replaced the GATT with the World Trade Organization (WTO), brought services and agriculture into the WTO, and improved the dispute settlement mechanism.

In December 1994, the Uruguay Round, the eighth and most ambitious round of multilateral trade negotiations in history in which 123 countries participated, was completed after seven years of tortuous negotiations. Disagreements between the United States and the European Union (EU), especially France, on reducing agricultural subsidies delayed its conclusion for three years. The aim of the Uruguay Round was to check the proliferation of the new protectionism and reverse its trend; bring services, agriculture, and foreign investments into the negotiations; negotiate international rules for the protection of intellectual property rights; and improve the dispute settlement mechanism by ensuring more timely decisions and compliance with GATT rulings. The agreement was signed by the United States, and most other countries on April 15, 1994, and took effect on July 1, 1995. The major provisions of the accord were the following:

1. *Tariffs.* Tariffs on industrial products are to be reduced from an average of 4.7 percent to 3 percent, and the share of goods with zero tariffs is to increase from 20–22 percent to 40–45 percent; tariffs were removed altogether on pharmaceuticals, construction equipment, medical equipment, paper products, and steel.

2. *Quotas.* Nations are to replace quotas on agricultural imports and imports of textiles and apparel with less restrictive tariffs by the end of 1999, for agriculture, and by the end of 2004 for textiles and apparel; tariffs on agricultural products are to be reduced by 24 percent in developing nations and by 36 percent in developed nations; tariffs on textiles are to be cut by 25 percent.

3. *Antidumping.* The agreement provides for tougher and quicker action to resolve disputes resulting from the use of antidumping laws, but it does not ban their use.

4. *Subsidies.* The volume of subsidized agricultural exports is to be reduced by 21 percent over a six-year period; government subsidies for industrial research are limited to 50 percent of applied research costs.

5. *Safeguards.* Nations may temporarily raise tariffs or other restrictions against an import surge that severely harms a domestic industry, but it bars countries from administering health and safety standards unless based on scientific evidence and not simply to restrict trade. For example, a nation can only keep out beef imports from cattle raised with growth hormones by showing that the beef so produced is unsafe for human consumption.

6. *Intellectual property.* The agreement provides for 20-year protection of patents, trademarks, and copyrights, but it allows a 10-year phase-in period for patent protection in pharmaceuticals for developing countries.

7. *Services.* The United States failed to secure access to the markets of Japan, Korea, and many developing nations for its banks and security firms, and did not succeed in having France and the European Union lift restrictions on the showing of American films and TV programs in Europe.

8. *Other industry provisions.* The United States and Europe agreed to continue talking about further limiting government subsidies to civil aircraft makers, opening up the distance telephone market, and limiting European subsidies to steelmakers; the United States also indicated that it intended to continue negotiating the further opening of the Japanese computer chip market.

9. *Trade-related investment measures.* The agreement phases out the requirement that foreign investors (such as automakers) buy supplies locally or export as much as they import.

10. *World Trade Organization.* The agreement also called for the replacement of the General Agreement on Tariffs and Trade (GATT) secretariat with the World Trade Organization (WTO) in Geneva with authority not only in trade in industrial products but also in agricultural products and services. Trade disputes are also to be settled by a vote of two-thirds or three-quarters of the nations rather than unanimously as under GATT (which meant that the guilty nation could block any action against it).

World Trade Organization (WTO) The organization set up at the Uruguay Round to replace the General Agreement on Tariffs and Trade (GATT) secretariat with authority over trade in industrial goods, agricultural commodities, and services, and with greater authority to settle trade disputes.

Concept Check

What were the major provisions of the Uruguay Round?

The Uruguay Round is estimated to increase world trade by about 20 percent (with one-quarter of the increase in trade in manufactures and the rest in agriculture), and to have generated total gains in world income of $349 billion ($164 billion from liberalizing trade in agriculture, $130 billion from manufactures and $55 billion from services), with developing countries receiving 42 percent of the total gains (mostly from liberalization of trade in manufactures), which is roughly double their share of world GDP.

During 1996 and 1997, multilateral agreements to open up trade in telecommunications, financial services, and information technology (that were not reached at the Uruguay Round) were concluded. Over time, these agreements could provide larger gains in trade volumes than the entire Uruguay Round treaty. In 1999, the European Union reached a free trade agreement with Mexico (which became effective in July 2000) that ended all tariffs on their bilateral trade by 2007.

It has been estimated that the implementation of the Uruguay Round increased world welfare by $73 billion, of which $58.3 billion of the gains went to developed countries and $19.2 billion to developing countries. During 1996 and 1997, multilateral agreements to open up trade in telecommunications, financial services, and information technology (that were not reached at the Uruguay Round) were concluded. Over time, these agreements could

provide larger gains in trade volumes than the entire Uruguay Round treaty. In 1999, the European Union reached a free trade agreement with Mexico (which became effective in July 2000) that ended all tariffs on their bilateral trade by 2007. In December 2001, China was admitted as the 144th member of the WTO and by June 2008, total membership stood at 152.

Trade promotion authority or **"fast track"** Legislation granting to the president of the United States the right to negotiate global trade agreements with other nations that allowed no amendments, but only an up-or-down vote by Congress to ratify or reject the agreement.

In August 2002, Congress granted the President trade promotion authority, formerly known as "fast track," to negotiate broad trade agreements that allowed no amendments, but only an up-or-down vote by Congress to ratify or reject the agreement. The purpose of this legislation was to assure foreign governments that Congress would act expeditiously on any agreement that they negotiate with the U.S. government. The legislation also required the president to consider environmental protection, labor rights, and antidumping laws in his negotiations, and it provided up to $1.2 billion a year in health insurance and other benefits to workers who lose their jobs, and added farmers and ranchers to the list of those eligible. Fast track, however, was not renewed after it expired in 2007.

Doha Round The multilateral trade negotiations launched in November 2001 in Doha (Qatar) with the aim of providing greater trade access by developing countries in developed countries' markets, but which failed in July 2008.

Since 2001, the United States has reached free trade agreements (FTAs) with Australia, Bahrain, Chile, Jordan, Morocco, Peru, and Singapore, and signed CAFTA (the Central American Free Trade Agreement) with Costa Rica, El Salvador, Guatemala, Honduras, Nicaragua, and Santo Domingo. In 2008, the United States was negotiating similar FTAs with South Korea, Panama, and Colombia. Case Study 6-8 provides a summary of the eight rounds of successful multilateral trade negotiations conducted under the auspices of the GATT since 1947, as well as the new (ninth) Doha Round sponsored by the WTO, which was announced in November 2001 in Doha, the capital of the Gulf state of Qatar, and failed in July 2008 because of disagreement on agricultural protectionism between the United States and China and India.

6.10 OUTSTANDING TRADE PROBLEMS AND THE DOHA ROUND

Despite the great benefits resulting from the successful completion of the Uruguay Round, many serious trade problems remain. *One problem* is the serious trade disputes between the United States and the European Union (EU) on the subsidies that the EU grants Airbus on the development of new aircraft (a complaint that the EU answered by launching a complaint of its own against the indirect subsidies that Boeing received from government military contracts). The United States also disputes the EU's ban on U.S. exports of hormone-raised beef and genetically modified (biotech) food. In fall 2005, the United States and the European Union also severely restricted China's rapidly growing exports of knit fabrics and other textile products. In 2007, the United States renewed tariff protection to domestic steel producers

The Multilateral Rounds of Trade Negotiations

Table 6.6 provides a summary of the year, the place and name of the trade round, the number of participating countries, the subject covered, and the weighted percentage tariff reduction achieved. From the table we see that the most significant rounds sponsored by the

GATT were those of 1947 (Geneva), 1964–1967 (Kennedy Round), 1973–1979 (Tokyo Round), and 1986–1994 (Uruguay Round). The Doha Round launched by the WTO in 2001 failed in July 2008.

Table 6.6. *The GATT Trade Rounds, 1947–1993 and the WTO Round, 2001–2008*

Year	Place/Name	Number of Participating Countries	Subject Covered	Weighted Percentage Tariff Reduction
1947	Geneva	23	Tariffs	26
1949	Annecy	13	Tariffs	3
1950–51	Torquay	38	Tariffs	4
1955–56	Geneva	26	Tariffs	3
1961–62	Geneva (Dillon Round)	26	Tariffs	4
1964–67	Geneva (Kennedy Round)	62	Tariffs and antidumping measures	38
1973–79	Geneva (Tokyo Round)	102	Tariffs, nontariff measures, multilateral agreements	33
1986–94	Geneva (Uruguay Round)	123	Tariffs, nontariff measures, agriculture, services, textiles, intellectual property, dispute settlement, creation of WTO	38
2001–08	Doha (Doha Round)	144	Liberalize global trade in agriculture, industrial goods, and services	Failed

Source: WTO, *Annual Report*, 2007.

against steel imports from China, Japan, Brazil, Mexico, and India—and the European Union is threatening to do the same. The United States, EU, and Canada are in a dispute with China on restrictions on their export auto parts, Korea on Japanese duties on Korean exports of memory chips to Japan, Brazil and the United States on cotton trades, the United States and the EU on trade in bananas, and so on.

A *second problem* is that subsidies and tariffs on agricultural products remain very high; antidumping measures and safeguards are still possible and frequently abused, and so the potential for serious trade disputes remains.

A *third trade problem* is the tendency for the world to break up into three major trading blocs: the European Union (EU), the North America Free Trade Area (NAFTA), and a (much less defined) Asian bloc (trading blocs are examined in detail in the next chapter). Although these trading blocs could be regarded as building blocks of a freer trading system, they can also become stumbling blocks and lead to more bilateral deals, protectionism, and interbloc trade conflicts.

The *fourth problem* is the call by some developed countries, such as the United States and France, for the establishment of labor and environmental standards. These are supposed to ensure a "leveling of working conditions" between developed and developing countries and avoid "social dumping" by the latter (i.e., developing countries competing unfairly by denying their workers basic rights and decent wages and working conditions). The danger is that the movement to establish labor and environmental standards can easily be captured by protectionistic forces. The same is true for environmental standards (see Section 4.10). Trade-related competition policies (such as subsidies and regulations) as well as *trade-related investment measures (TRIMs)* also need to be dealt with more adequately than they have been in the Uruguay Round.

Concept Check

What are the major trade problems facing the world today?

An attempt was made to launch a Millennium Round of trade negotiations at the WTO Trade Conference held in Seattle in December 1999. The attempt failed because (1) developing countries were adamantly opposed to putting labor and environmental standards on the agenda for the new round; (2) the European Union and Japan objected to the U.S. desire to put on the agenda the complete liberalization of trade in agricultural products; and (3) the United States objected to discussing competition and investment policies that the European Union wanted. All this came up in the face of large demonstrations organized by a strong anti-globalization movement (refer to Section 1.2).

In November 2001, the Doha Round was launched in Doha, Qatar. The agenda included (1) the further liberalization of production and trade in agriculture, industrial products, and services, and (2) the further tightening of rules for antidumping measures and safeguards, as well as investment and competition policies. From the very beginning, developing nations were reluctant to make concessions because they felt that the Uruguay Round failed to deliver a great deal of what it promised them, and insisted on making the Doha Round a true "development round." The Doha Round was supposed to be concluded by the end of 2004, but after seven years of negotiations the round failed in July 2008 as the result of a clash between the United States, and China and India, over agricultural protectionism.

SUMMARY

1. A quota is a direct quantitative restriction on imports or exports. An import quota has the same consumption and production effects as an (equivalent) import tariff. If the government auctions off import licenses to the highest bidder in a competitive market, the revenue effect also is the same. The adjustment to any shift in demand or supply occurs in the domestic price with an import quota and in the quantity of imports with a tariff. If import licenses are not auctioned off, they lead to monopoly profits and possible corruption. An import quota is in general more restrictive than an equivalent import tariff.

2. Voluntary export restraints refer to the case where an importing nation induces another nation to curb its exports of a commodity "voluntarily," under the threat of higher all-around trade restrictions. When successful, their economic impact is the same as that of an equivalent import quota, except for the revenue effect, which is now captured by foreign suppliers. Voluntary export restraints are no longer allowed.

3. Trade restrictions can also result from dumping and export subsidies. Dumping is the export of a commodity at below cost or at a lower price than it is sold domestically. Dumping can be persistent, predatory, or sporadic. Countervailing duties (CVDs) are tariffs imposed on imports to offset subsidies by foreign governments.

4. The argument that tariffs are needed to protect domestic labor against cheap foreign labor and the "scientific tariff" are clearly false. Two questionable beggar-thy-neighbor arguments are that protection is needed to reduce domestic unemployment and a deficit in the nation's balance of payments. A more valid argument for protection is the infant-industry argument. However, what trade protection can do, direct subsidies and taxes can do better in overcoming purely domestic distortions. The same is true for industries important for national defense. The closest we come to a valid economic argument for protection is the optimal tariff (which, however, invites retaliation). Trade protection in the United States is usually given to low-wage workers and to large, well organized industries producing consumer products.

5. Outsourcing and offshoring are causing fear of globalization. Outsourcing refers to a firm's purchase of parts and components abroad, while offshoring to a firm producing parts and components in its own plant abroad. Both are undertaken by firms in order to remain internationally competitive by giving rise to the fear of globalization or the transfer of a large number of high-skill U.S. jobs abroad.

6. Strategic trade and industrial policy is another qualified argument for protection. It suggests that by encouraging high-tech industries, a nation

can reap the large external economies that result from them and enhance its future growth prospects. Strategic trade and industrial policy does face, however, many practical difficulties because it is difficult for nations to pick winners and because it invites retaliation. Thus, free trade may still be the best policy after all.

7. The Smoot–Hawley Tariff Act of 1930 resulted in the all-time-high average import duty in the United States of 59 percent in 1932, provoking foreign retaliation. The Trade Agreements Act of 1934 authorized the president to negotiate mutual tariff reductions of up to 50 percent under the most-favored-nation principle. A serious disadvantage was its bilateral approach. The General Agreement on Tariffs and Trade (GATT) was devoted to freer trade based on nondiscrimination, consultation, and removal of nontariff trade barriers, except in agriculture and in nations experiencing balance-of-payments difficulties. Under the authority of the 1962 Trade Expansion Act, the United States negotiated tariff reductions averaging 35 percent on industrial products in the Kennedy Round completed in 1967 and replaced the no-injury doctrine with adjustment assistance. Under the authority of the Trade Reform Act of 1974, the United States negotiated tariff reductions averaging 31 percent in the Tokyo Round completed in 1979, and accepted a code of conduct for nominal trade barriers. The 1988 Trade Act strengthened U.S. retaliatory procedures against nations that greatly restrict U.S. exports.

8. The Uruguay Round was completed in December 1994. It called for the reduction of average tariffs on industrial goods from 4.7 percent to 3 percent, for quotas to be replaced by tariffs, and for antidumping and safeguards to be tightened. The agreement also called for the reduction in agricultural export subsidies and industrial subsidies, and for the protection of intellectual property. During 1996 and 1997, agreements were reached to open up trade in telecommunications, financial services, and information technology. In July 2000, the EU–Mexico free trade agreement became effective; in December 2001, China became the 144th member of WTO; in August 2002, Congress granted the president trade negotiating authority or fast track; in 2002, the United States negotiated a free trade agreement with several countries.

9. The major trade problems facing the world today are (1) the serious trade disputes among the United States, the European Union, and Japan; (2) the high trade protectionism, especially in the agriculture and textile industries, which are of great importance to developing countries, and the abuse of antidumping and safeguards; (3) the breaking up of the world into a few major trading blocks, and a serious anti-globalization movement that has come into existence. All these problems were taken up by the Doha Round launched in November 2001 which, however, failed in July 2008.

REVIEW QUESTIONS AND PROBLEMS

1. (a) What are the effects of an import quota?

 (b) How are they similar to and different from the effects of an equivalent import tariff?

2. Starting with D_X and S_X and $P_X = \$1$ with free trade in Figure 6.1, analyze the effects of an import quota of 20X if D_X shifts down to D''_X in such a way that D''_X is parallel to D_X and crosses S_X at $P_X = \$2.50$.

3. Starting with D_X and S_X and $P_X = \$1$ with free trade in Figure 6.1, analyze the effects of a negotiated export quota of 20X. How are the effects of the negotiated export quota similar to and different from those of an equivalent import tariff or quota?

4. (a) What is an international cartel? How do their operations restrict trade?

 (b) What was the most successful international cartel during the 1970s? Why did its power sharply decline in the 1980s and 1990s?

5. (a) What is meant by dumping?

 (b) What are the different types of dumping?

 (c) Why does dumping usually lead to trade restrictions?

6. (a) What is the infant-industry argument for protection?

 (b) How must this argument be qualified?

7. (a) What is the difference between outsourcing and offshoring?

 (b) What is the "fear of globalization"? Is it justified?

8. (a) What is meant by strategic and industrial trade policy?

 (b) What is its relevance today?

9. (a) What were the main provisions of the Uruguay Round?

 (b) What were its main accomplishments?

10. (a) What are the outstanding trade problems facing the world today?

 (b) Why do we need the Doha Round?

Strategic Trade and Industrial Policies with Game Theory

In this appendix we use game theory to examine strategic trade and industrial policy. We can best show this by an example. Suppose that Boeing and Airbus are both deciding whether to produce a new aircraft. Suppose also that because of the huge cost of developing the new aircraft, a single producer would have to have the entire world market for itself to earn a profit of, say, $100 million. If both producers produce the aircraft, each loses $10 million. This information is shown in Table 6.7. The case where both firms produce the aircraft and each incurs a loss of $10 million is shown in the first row and first column (the top left-hand corner) of Table 6.7. If only Boeing produces the aircraft, Boeing makes a profit of $100 million, while Airbus makes a zero profit (the first row and second column, or top right-hand corner of the table). On the other hand, if Boeing does not produce the aircraft while Airbus does, Boeing makes zero profit while Airbus makes a profit of $100 million (the second row and first column, or bottom left-hand corner of the table). Finally, if neither firm produces the aircraft, each makes a zero profit (the second row and the second column, or bottom right-hand corner of the table).

Suppose that for whatever reason, Boeing enters the market first and earns a profit of $100 million. Airbus is now locked out of the market because it could not earn a profit. This is the case shown in the first row and second column (the top right-hand corner) of the table. If Airbus entered the market,

Game theory A method of choosing the optimal strategy in conflict situations.

Table 6.7. *Two-Firm Competition and Strategic Industrial Policy*

	Airbus	
	Produce	*Don't Produce*
Produce	−10, −10	100, 0
Don't Produce	0, 100	0, 0

both firms would incur a loss (and we would have the case shown in the first row and first column, or top left-hand corner of the table). Suppose that now European governments give a subsidy of $15 million per year to Airbus. Then Airbus will produce the aircraft even though Boeing is already producing the aircraft because with the $15-million subsidy, Airbus would turn a loss of $10 million into a profit of $5 million. Without a subsidy, however, Boeing will then go from making a profit of $100 million (without Airbus in the market) to incurring a loss of $10 million afterwards. (We are still in the first row and first column, or top left-hand corner of the table, but with the Airbus entry changed from −10 without the subsidy to +5 with the subsidy.) Because of its unsubsidized loss, Boeing will then stop producing the aircraft, thus eventually leaving the entire market to Airbus, which will then make a profit of $100 million without any further subsidy (the second row and first column, or bottom left-hand corner of the table).

The U.S. government could, of course, retaliate with a subsidy of its own to keep Boeing producing the aircraft. Except in cases of national defense, however, the U.S. government is much less disposed to grant subsidies to firms than are European governments. While the real world is much more complex than this, we can see how a nation could overcome a market disadvantage and acquire a strategic comparative advantage in a high-tech field by using an industrial and strategic trade policy. In fact, in 2000 Airbus decided to go ahead and build its super-jumbo A380 capable of transporting 550 passengers to be ready by 2006 at a development cost of over $10 billion, and thus compete head-on with the Boeing 747 (which has been in service since 1969 and can carry up to 475 passengers). The A380 came into service with a delay of two years in 2008 and huge costs overruns.

One serious shortcoming of this analysis is that it is usually very difficult to forecast accurately the outcome of government industrial and trade policies (i.e., get the data to fill a table such as Table 6.7). Even a small change in the table could completely alter the results. For example, suppose that if both Airbus and Boeing produce the aircraft, Airbus incurs a loss of $10 million (as before), but Boeing now makes a profit of $10 million (without any subsidy), say, because it is more efficient. Then, even if Airbus produces the aircraft with the subsidy, Boeing would remain in the market because it makes a profit without any subsidy. Then Airbus would require a subsidy indefinitely, year after year, in order to continue to produce the aircraft. In

this case, giving a subsidy to Airbus does not seem to be such a good idea. Thus, it is extremely difficult to correctly carry out this type of analysis. We would have to correctly forecast the precise outcome of different strategies, and this is very difficult to do. This is why most economists would say that free trade may still be the best policy after all!

SELECTED BIBLIOGRAPHY

For a more advanced treatment of the theory of tariffs, see:

- D. Salvatore, *International Economics*, 9th ed. (Hoboken, N.J.: Wiley, 2007), ch. 9.

A general discussion of the new protectionism is found in:

- D. Salvatore, ed., *Protectionism and World Welfare* (New York: Cambridge University Press, 1993).
- P. R. Krugman, "Is Free Trade Passé?" *Journal of Economic Perspectives*, Fall 1987, pp. 131–144.
- C. Fred Bergsten, "Fifty Years of Trade Policy: The Policy Lessons," *The World Economy*, January 2001, pp. 1–14.
- J. Bhagwati, *Free Trade Today* (Princeton, N.J.: Princeton University Press, 2002).
- J. Stiglitz, *Globalization and Its Discontents* (New York: Norton, 2003).
- J. Bhagwati, *In Defense of Globalization* (New York: Oxford University Press, 2004).
- I. M., Destler, *American Trade Policies*, 4th ed. (Washington, D.C.: Institute for International Economics, 2005).
- T. Friedman, *The World Is Flat: Further Updated and Expanded* (New York: Farrar, Straus, & Giroux, 2007).
- World Trade Organization, *World Trade Report 2007* (Geneva: WTO, 2007).

For the Uruguay and Doha Rounds of multilateral trade negotiations, see:

- W. McKibbin and D. Salvatore, "The Global Economic Consequences of the Uruguay Round," *Open Economies Review*, April 1995, pp. 111–129.
- A. McGuirk, "The Doha Development Agenda," *Finance and Development*, September 2002, pp. 4–7.

INTERNet

For international trade policies in the United States, visit the Internet site for the Economic Report of the President (and click on the most recent year to get the latest report), and the Internet site of the State Department, the United

States Trade Representative, and the U.S. International Trade Commission, respectively, at:

http://www.gpoaccess.gov/eop

http://www.state.gov

http://www.ustr.gov

http://www.usitc.gov

For international trade policies around the world, see the Internet site of the World Trade Organization (WTO), the European Union, the Canadian Department of Foreign Affairs, respectively, at:

http://www.wto.org

http://mkaccdb.eu.int

http://www.infoexport.gc.ca

For a discussion of "fast track", see:

http://www.citizen.org/trade/fasttrack/index.cfm

http://www.iie.com/publications/newsreleases/newsrelease.cfm?id=33

http://www.globalexchange.org/campaigns/ftaa/fasttrack/why.html

http://www.cnie.org/nle/crsreports/03Apr/IB10084.pdf

For dumping cases dealt with by the Canadian International Trade Tribunal, see:

http://www.citt.gc.ca

For information on the Export-Import Bank, see:

http://www.exim.gov

For government support of R&D in the United States, Japan, and Korea, see the web site of the National Science Foundation and Sematech for the United States, the Statistics Center of the Management and Coordination Agency for Japan, and the World Bank site for Korea, respectively at:

http://www.nsf.gov/statistics/fedfunds/

http://www.sematech.org

http://www.stat.go.jp/english/index.htm

http://www.worldbank.org/research/journals/wbro/obsfeb00/art3.htm

A strong anti-globalization view is found in:

http://www.nologo.org

For international environmental laws, see:

http://www2.spfo.unibo.it/spolfo/ENVLAW.htm

PART THREE

International Trade and Investment Relations

Part Three (Chapters 7–9) deals with international trade and investment relations. Chapter 7 examines economic integration, such as free trade areas and customs unions. Chapter 8 examines the relationship between international trade and economic development, while Chapter 9 deals with international resource (capital and people) movements and multinational corporations.

Economic Integration

After studying this chapter, you should be able to:

- Identify the different types of economic integration schemes
- Understand the meaning of trade creation and trade diversion
- Describe the dynamic benefits of economic integration
- Know what is the European Union
- Describe the European Free Trade Association and Mercosur
- Explain what is NAFTA
- Describe attempts at economic integration among developing countries
- Describe economic integration in Central and Eastern Europe

CHAPTER OUTLINE

KEY TERMS

Preferential trade arrangements

Free trade area

Customs union

Common market

Economic union

Duty-free zones or free economic zones

Trade creation

Trade diversion

Tariff factories

European Union (EU)

Variable import levies

European Free Trade Association (EFTA)

Trade deflection

European Economic Area (EEA)

North American Free Trade Agreement (NAFTA)

Southern Common Market (Mercosur)

Council of Mutual Economic Assistance (CMEA) or (COMECON)

State trading companies

Centrally planned economies

Bilateral agreements

Bulk purchasing

Central and Eastern European Countries (CEEC)

Newly Independent States (NIS)

Commonwealth of Independent States (CIS)

Central European Free Trade Association (CEFTA)

Baltic Free Trade Area (BFTA)

7.1 INTRODUCTION

In this chapter, we examine economic integration in general and customs unions in particular. The theory of economic integration refers to the commercial policy of discriminatively reducing or eliminating trade barriers only among the nations joining together.

In Section 7.2 we examine the different forms of economic integration. Section 7.3 deals with static welfare effects of customs unions, while Section 7.4 examines the dynamic effects of customs unions. Section 7.5 then examines the European Union; Section 7.6 deals with the European Free Trade Association; Section 7.7 discusses the North American Free Trade Agreement; Section 7.8 deals with attempts at economic integration among developing countries; and Section 7.9 examines economic integration among Central and Eastern European countries and the former Soviet Republics.

Preferential trade arrangements The loosest form of economic integration; provides lower barriers to trade among participating nations than on trade with nonparticipating nations. An example is the British Commonwealth Preference Scheme.

7.2 FORMS OF ECONOMIC INTEGRATION

The degree of economic integration ranges from preferential trade arrangements to free trade areas, customs unions, common markets, and economic unions.

Preferential trade arrangements provide lower barriers on trade among participating nations than on trade with nonmember nations. This is the loosest form of economic integration. The best example of a preferential trade arrangement is the *British Commonwealth Preference Scheme*, established in 1932 by the United Kingdom with members and some former members of the British Empire.

A free trade area is the form of economic integration wherein all barriers are removed on trade among members, but each nation retains its own barriers to trade with nonmembers. The best examples are the *European Free Trade Association (EFTA)*, formed by the United Kingdom, Austria, Denmark, Norway, Portugal, Sweden, and Switzerland in 1960; the *North American Free Trade Agreement (NAFTA)*, formed by the United States, Canada, and Mexico in 1993; and the *Southern Common Market (Mercosur)* formed by Argentina, Brazil, Paraguay, and Uruguay in 1991.

A customs union allows no tariffs or other barriers on trade among members (as in a free trade area), and in addition it harmonizes trade policies (such as the setting of common tariff rates) toward the rest of the world. The most famous example is the *European Union (EU)*, or *European Common Market*, formed in 1957 by West Germany, France, Italy, Belgium, the Netherlands, and Luxembourg.

A common market goes beyond a customs union by also allowing the free movement of labor and capital among member nations. The EU achieved the status of a common market in 1993.

Free trade area Removes all barriers on trade among members, but each nation retains its own barriers on trade with nonmembers. The best examples are the EFTA, NAFTA, and Mercosur.

Customs union Removes all barriers on trade among members and harmonizes trade policies toward the rest of the world. The best example is the European Union (EU).

Common market Removes all barriers on trade among members, harmonizes trade policies toward the rest of the world, and also allows the free movement of labor and capital among member nations. An example is the European Union (EU) since January 1, 1993.

What are the different
types of economic
integration?

Economic union
Removes all barriers on trade among
members, harmonizes trade policies
toward the rest of the
world, allows the free
movement of labor
and capital among
member nations, and
also harmonizes or
unifies the monetary,
fiscal, and tax policies
of its members.

Duty-free zones or
free economic zones
Areas set up to
attract foreign investments by allowing
raw materials and
intermediate products duty free.

Trade creation
Occurs when some
domestic production
in a member of the
customs union is
replaced by lower
cost imports from
another member
nation. This increases
welfare.

An economic union goes still further by harmonizing or even unifying the monetary and fiscal policies of member states. This is the highest form of economic integration. An example is *Benelux*, which is the economic union of Belgium, the Netherlands, and Luxembourg, formed after World War II (and now part of the EU). An example of a *complete* economic and monetary union is the United States.

An interesting recent development that can be analyzed with the same concepts used to analyze customs unions is duty-free zones or free economic zones. These are areas set up to attract foreign investments by allowing the importation of raw materials and intermediate products duty free.

The discussion in this chapter generally concerns customs unions, but most of what is said about customs unions also refers to other forms of regional economic association.

7.3 TRADE CREATION AND TRADE DIVERSION IN CUSTOMS UNIONS

The formation of a customs union has both static and dynamic effects on the countries involved. In this section we analyze the static effects, leaving a discussion of the dynamic effects for Section 7.5. The static welfare effects resulting from the formation of a customs union are measured by the extent to which it leads to trade creation and trade diversion. These are examined with Figure 7.1.

In Figure 7.1, D_X and S_X are Nation 2's domestic demand and supply curves of commodity X, while S_1 and S_3 are the free trade, perfectly elastic (horizontal), supply curves of Nation 1 and Nation 3, respectively. With a nondiscriminatory 100 percent tariff on imports of commodity X, Nation 2 imports commodity X from Nation 1 at $P_X = \$2$, along $S_1 + T$ curve (rather than producing it at home, or importing it from Nation 3 with the tariff, at $P_X = \$3$). At $P_X = \$2$, Nation 2 consumes 80X *(GH)*, with 40X *(GJ)* produced domestically and 40X *(JH)* imported from Nation 1. Nation 2 also collects \$40 *(JHNM)* in tariff revenues (exactly as in Figure 5.3).

If Nation 2 now forms a customs union with Nation 3 (i.e., removes the tariff on the imports from Nation 3 only), Nation 2 finds it cheaper to import commodity X from Nation 3 at $P_X = \$1.50$ (without the tariff) than importing it from Nation 1 (with the tariff). At $P_X = \$1.50$, Nation 2 consumes 90X *(G'B')*, with 30X *(G'C')* produced domestically and 60X *(C'B')* imported from Nation 3. In this case, Nation 2 collects no tariff revenue. The expansion of trade from $GH = 80X$ to $G'B' = 90X$ resulting from the formation of the customs union is called trade creation, and this increases the welfare of Nation 1.

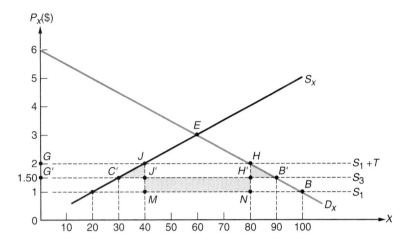

FIGURE 7.1. Trade Creation and Trade Diversion in a Customs Union.
D_X and S_X represent Nation 2's domestic demand and supply curves of commodity X, while S_1 and S_3 are the free-trade perfectly elastic supply curves of commodity X of Nation 1 and Nation 3, respectively. With a nondiscriminatory 100 percent tariff, Nation 2 imports 40X (*JH*) at $P_X = \$2$ from Nation 1. By forming a customs union with Nation 3, Nation 2 imports 60X (*C'B'*) at $P_X = \$1.50$ from Nation 3. The welfare gain in Nation 2 from pure trade creation is $5 (given by the sum of the areas of the two shaded triangles). The welfare loss from trade diversion proper is $20 (the area of the shaded rectangle). Thus, this trade-diverting customs union leads to a net welfare loss of $15 for Nation 2.

Concept Check

What is the difference between trade creation and trade diversion?

Trade diversion Occurs when lower cost imports from outside the union are replaced by higher cost imports from another union member. By itself, this reduces welfare.

The imports of commodity X into Nation 2, however, have now been *diverted* from the more efficient producers in Nation 1 (which can produce commodity X at the *cost* of $1) to the less efficient producers in Nation 3 (which produces commodity X at the *cost* of $1.50) because the tariff discriminates against the imports from Nation 1 (which is outside the union). This is trade diversion. Trade diversion, by itself, reduces the welfare of Nation 2 because it shifts production from more efficient producers outside the customs union to less efficient producers inside the union.

Since the formation of a customs union usually results in *both* trade creation and trade diversion, the welfare of the nation forming or joining a customs union can increase or decrease, depending on the relative strength of these two opposing forces. In Figure 7.1, the welfare gain of Nation 2 resulting from pure trade creation is given by the sum of the areas of shaded triangles *C'JJ'* and *B'HH'*, which is equal to $5. The welfare loss in Nation 2 resulting from the diversion of the initial 40X (*JH*) of imports from lower cost Nation 1 (but subject to the import tariff) to higher cost Nation 3 (not subject

to the import tariff) is given by the area of shaded rectangle $MJ'H'N$, which equals $20.

Specifically, of the gain in consumer surplus of $G'GHB'$ resulting from the formation of the customs union, $G'GJC'$ represents a transfer from producer to consumer surplus in Nation 2 and therefore washes out (i.e., leaves no net gain or loss for Nation 2 as a whole). Of the $JMNH$ ($40) tariff revenue collected by Nation 2 before the formation of the customs union with Nation 3, $J'JHH'$ is transferred to consumers in Nation 2 in the form of the lower price of commodity X after the formation of the customs union. This leaves shaded triangles $C'JJ'$ and $B'HH'$ as the net gain to Nation 2. From this, however, we must deduct the still unaccounted loss of tariff revenue by Nation 2 given by shaded rectangle $MNH'J'$.

Since the area of the shaded rectangle ($20) in Figure 7.1 measuring the welfare loss from trade diversion exceeds the sum of the areas of the shaded triangles ($5) measuring the welfare gain from trade creation, this customs union leads to a net welfare loss of $15 for Nation 2. The welfare of nonmembers also declines because their economic resources can only be utilized less efficiently than before trade was diverted away from them. Had the sum of the areas of the two shaded triangles been larger than the area of the shaded rectangle in Figure 7.1, Nation 2's welfare would have increased. This is more likely to occur the closer the S_3 curve is to the S_1 curve (i.e., the smaller is the relative inefficiency of Nation 3, which is in the union, with respect to Nation 1, which is not in the union. The figure showing this is left as an end-of-chapter problem.)

Had Nation 2 formed a customs union with Nation 1 instead of with Nation 3, there would have been only trade creation and no trade diversion (this would be equivalent to having free trade) and benefits for all three nations. Nation 2 and Nation 1 would gain from specialization in production and increased international trade based on comparative advantage. Nation 3 would also benefit because some of the increased income in the customs union would spill over into a demand for more of its imports. The question then arises as to why Nation 2 formed a customs union with Nation 3 instead of with Nation 1. The answer is that customs unions are formed not only for economic reasons but for political considerations, and also depend on the geographical proximity of nations.

The several attempts to measure (along the lines discussed earlier) the static welfare effects resulting from the formation of a customs union all came up with surprisingly small *net static* welfare gains. For the European Union these gains were estimated to be in the range of 1 to 2 percent of GDP. There are, however, other *static* welfare gains resulting from the formation of a customs union. These are the savings from the elimination of customs officers, border patrols, and so on, as well as the increased bargaining power that the customs union is likely to have in international negotiations in

Concept Check

What is the effect of trade creation and trade diversion?

relation to all the member nations separately. This has certainly been the case for the European Union.

7.4 DYNAMIC BENEFITS FROM CUSTOMS UNIONS

Besides the static welfare effects previously discussed, the nations forming a customs union are likely to receive several important *dynamic* benefits. These are due to increased competition, economies of scale, stimulus to investment, and better utilization of economic resources. These will be examined in turn.

The greatest dynamic benefit from the formation of a customs union is the *increased competition* that is likely to result. That is, in the absence of a customs union, producers are likely to grow sluggish and complacent behind trade barriers. But when a customs union is formed and trade barriers among member nations are eliminated, producers in each nation must become more efficient to meet the competition of other producers within the union, merge, or go out of business. All of these efforts will cut costs of production to the benefit of consumers. A customs union must, however, be careful (by passing and enforcing antitrust legislation) that larger and more efficient firms will not restrict competition.

A second possible dynamic benefit from the formation of a customs union is *economies of large-scale production*. However, it must be pointed out that even a small nation that is not a member of any customs union can overcome the smallness of its domestic market and achieve substantial economies of scale in production by exporting to the rest of the world. For example, it was found that plants in many major industries in such relatively small nations as Belgium and the Netherlands were already of comparable size to U.S. plants before they joined the EU and thus already enjoyed substantial economies of scale by producing for the domestic market and for export. Nevertheless, significant additional economies were achieved after the formation of the EU by reducing the range of differentiated products manufactured in each plant and increasing "production runs" (refer to Section 4.7).

Tariff factories
Direct investments made in a nation or other economic unit (such as a customs union) to avoid import tariffs.

Another possible benefit is the *stimulus to investment* to take advantage of the enlarged market and to meet the increased competition. The formation of a customs union is also likely to spur outsiders to set up production facilities within the customs union to avoid the (discriminatory) trade barriers imposed on nonunion products. These are the so-called tariff factories. The massive investments that U.S. firms made in Europe after 1955 and again after 1986 can be explained by their desire not to be excluded from this rapidly growing market. Finally, in a customs union that is also a common market, the free communitywide movement of labor and capital is likely to result in better utilization of the economic resources of the entire community.

These dynamic gains resulting from the formation of a customs union are believed to be much greater than the static gains discussed earlier and

What are the
dynamic benefits
from customs
unions?

to be very significant. Indeed, the United Kingdom joined the EU in 1973 primarily because of them. Recent empirical studies seem to indicate that these dynamic gains are about five to six times larger than the static gains.

7.5 THE EUROPEAN UNION

European Union (EU) The customs union formed by West Germany, France, Italy, Belgium, the Netherlands, and Luxembourg that came into existence in 1958, and expanded to 15 nations with the joining of the United Kingdom, Denmark, and Ireland in 1973, Greece in 1981, Spain and Portugal in 1986, and Austria, Finland, and Sweden in 1995.

The European Union (EU), then called the European Common Market, was founded by the Treaty of Rome, signed in March 1957 by West Germany, France, Italy, Belgium, the Netherlands, and Luxembourg, and came into being on January 1, 1958. The common external tariff was set at the average of the 1957 tariffs of the six nations. Free trade in industrial goods within the EU and a common price for agricultural products were achieved in 1968, and restrictions on the free movement of labor and capital were reduced by 1970. Membership increased to 15 after the United Kingdom, Denmark, and Ireland joined in 1973, Greece in 1981, Spain and Portugal in 1986, and Austria, Finland, and Sweden in 1995. On January 1, 1993, the EU removed all remaining restrictions on the free flow of goods, services, and resources (including labor) among its members, thus becoming a single unified market. The expanded Union represents the largest trading bloc in the world (see Case Study 7-1). Intra-EU trade has been estimated to be double what it would have been in the absence of integration. More than half of this trade expansion has been in intra-industry trade (see Section 4.7).

The formation of the EU significantly expanded trade in industrial goods with nonmembers. This was due to (1) the very rapid growth of the EU, which increased its demand for imports of industrial products from outside the union, and (2) the reduction to very low levels of the average tariff on imports of industrial products as a result of the Kennedy and Tokyo Rounds (initiated by the United States, which feared trade diversion). On the other hand, the formation of the EU resulted in trade diversion in agricultural commodities, particularly in temperate products, such as grain from the United States.

What is the European
Union?

Variable import levies The import duties levied by the EU on imports of agricultural commodities and equal to the difference between the high farm prices established by the EU and the lower world prices.

The development of a *common agricultural policy (CAP)* was particularly troublesome for the EU. The final outcome sacrificed consumers' interests to those of EU farmers in general, and French farmers in particular, by setting relatively high farm prices. The EU imposes tariffs (called variable import levies) so as always to make the price of imported agricultural products equal to the high common agricultural prices set by EU. The high farm support price level has also led to huge agricultural surpluses within the EU, high storage costs, and subsidized exports (see Section 6.4 on export subsidies and Case Study 6-4), and was responsible for some of the sharpest trade disputes with the United States and at the Uruguay Round (see Section 6.9).

Economic Profile of the EU, NAFTA, and Japan

Table 7.1 provides an economic profile of the European Union (EU), the North American Free Trade Area (NAFTA), and Japan in 2006. The table shows that the EU (15) has 88 percent of NAFTA's population and 89 percent of its gross national income (GNI). Comparable percentages for EU-27 are 112 and 95. Total EU-27 merchandise exports and extra–EU-27 merchandise exports (i.e., exports to the rest of the world) are, respectively, 273 percent

and 89 percent of total NAFTA exports. Corresponding figures for total EU-27 imports and extra–EU-27 imports are, respectively 186 percent and 68 percent. Japan has 26 percent of EU-27 population, 33 percent of its GNI, 43 percent of extra–EU-27 exports, and 33 percent of extra–EU-27 imports. With respect to NAFTA, Japan has 29 percent of its population, 32 percent of its GNI, 39 percent of its exports, and 23 percent of its imports.

Table 7.1. *The EU, NAFTA, and Japan*

Country	Population (millions)	GNI (billions)	Exports (billions)	Imports (billions)
EU(15)	388.5	$13,794.8	$4,154.1	$4,238.3
Of which				
Germany	82.6	3,018.0	1,112.0	908.6
U.K.	60.5	2,425.2	448.3	619.4
France	61.3	2,297.8	490.4	534.9
Italy	58.9	1,875.6	410.6	437.4
Spain	43.9	1,200.7	205.5	316.4
New Entrants	103.4	857.4	426.0	495.4
Of which				
Poland	38.1	312.2	110.3	126.0
Total EU(27)	491.9	14,652.2	4,580.1	4,733.7
Extra–EU(27)	—	—	1,498.0	1,733.6
Canada	32.6	1,177.4	389.5	357.7
Mexico	105.3	820.3	250.4	268.2
United States	302.8	13,446.0	1,038.3	1,919.4
Total NAFTA	440.7	15,443.7	1,678.2	2,545.3
Japan	128.0	4,900.0	649.9	579.6

EU(15) includes: Austria, Belgium, Denmark, Finland, France, Germany, Greece, Ireland, Italy, Luxembourg, Netherlands, Portugal, Spain, Sweden, and the United Kingdom. New Entrants (12) are: Bulgaria, Czech Republic, Estonia, Hungary, Latvia, Lithuania, Malta, Poland, Romania, Slovak Republic, Slovenia; Bulgaria and Romania entered the EU in January 2008 but are included in the 2006 data in the table.

Source: World Bank, *World Development Report*, 2008; and WTO, *International Trade Statistics*, 2007.

At the *Lomé Convention* in 1975, the EU eliminated most trade barriers on imports from 46 developing nations in Africa, the Caribbean, and the Pacific region that were former colonies of EU countries. The treaty was renewed every five years (1980, 1985, 1990, and 1995), and the number of associate states (AS) rose to 71. Earlier, in 1971, the EU had granted generalized tariff preferences to imports of manufactured and semimanufactured products from developing nations. But textiles, steel, consumer electronics, shoes, and many other products of great importance to developing nations were excluded. Preferences were extended to trade in tropical products in the Tokyo Round in 1979. However, since these preferences fell short of the complete elimination of trade barriers granted to former colonies, a bitter controversy arose because of the alleged trade diversion. Quotas and tariffs on developing countries' exports are now scheduled to be gradually reduced as a result of the Uruguay Round completed in 1994 (see Section 6.9). In February 2000, *Lomé IV* expired and was replaced by a new agreement, the *Cotonou Agreement*, signed in Cotonou, Benin, in June 2000. The new agreement had the same general purpose as the Lomé Convention. The EU replaced the *Cotonou Agreement* in January 2008 with "new partnership agreements (NPAs) based on reciprocity" with the 79 countries involved, broken into six regional groups.

As pointed out earlier, the static welfare benefits resulting from the formation of the EU were estimated to be 1 to 2 percent of GDP, while the dynamic benefits were estimated to be much larger (see Case Study 7-2). Perhaps the greatest benefit has been political, resulting from unifying into a single economic community, nations such as Germany and France, that were once bitter enemies. The United States has been of two minds on European unity, supportive yet wary of losing influence. In 1986, the EU amended the *Treaty of Rome* with the *Single European Act*, which provided for the removal of all remaining barriers to the free flow of goods, services, and resources among members. This was actually achieved with the *EU 1992 Program*, which turned the EU into a single unified market at the beginning of 1993. This led to the pouring in of foreign direct investments into the EU out of fear of increased protectionism against outsiders.

Other highlights in the operation of the EU are: (1) Member nations adopted a common *value-added tax system*, under which a tax is levied on the value added to the product at each stage of its production and passed on to the consumer. (2) The *Commission* (the executive body of the EU headquartered in Brussels) proposes laws, monitors compliance with treaties, and administers common policies such as antitrust policies. (3) The *Council of Ministers* (whose members represent their own national governments) makes final decisions but only on the recommendation of the Commission. There is also a *European Parliament* (with 626 members elected by direct vote in the member nations every five years but without much legislative power at present) and a *Court of Justice* (with power to rule on the constitutionality of the decision of

Gains from the Single EU Market in 1992

At the beginning of 1993, all remaining restrictions to the free flow of goods, services, capital, and labor among member nations were eliminated so that the EU became a single, unified market. Over time, this was expected to result in substantial efficiency gains and other benefits to the EU. Table 7.2 shows that the EU's gross domestic product (GDP) was expected to increase by 0.2 percent from the removal of nontariff trade barriers, 2.2 percent from the removal of production barriers, 1.65 percent from economies of scale, and 1.25 percent

from intensified competition, for an overall total (one-time) gain of 5.3 percent of the EU's GDP in 1988. This was equivalent to about $265 billion. In addition, the overall rate of inflation was expected to fall by 6.1 percent and 1.8 million additional jobs were expected to be created, thereby reducing the average rate of unemployment in the EU by 1.5 percentage points. The EU92 Program also induced large foreign direct investments from the United States and Japan in anticipation of a possible increase in EU protectionism against outsiders.

Table 7.2. *Gains from the Single EU Market*

	Percent of 1988 EU's GDP
Gains from	
Removal of nontariff trade barriers	0.20
Removal of production barriers	2.20
Economies of scale	1.65
Intensified competition	1.25
Overall total gains	5.30

Source: P. Cecchini, *The European Challenge: 1992* (Aldershot, England: Wildwood House, 1988).

Concept
Check

Can you describe
the operation of the
European Union?

the Commission and the Council). (4) Plans have also been drawn for full monetary union, including harmonization of monetary and fiscal policies, and eventual full political union (see Section 16.4).

 In May 2004, ten countries, mostly from the former communist bloc in Central and Eastern Europe, became members of the European Union. The ten countries are Poland, Hungary, Czech Republic, Slovak Republic, Slovenia, Estonia, Lithuania, Latvia, Malta, and Cyprus. Bulgaria and Romania joined in 2008 and others, such as Turkey, are negotiating accession. With the admission of the 12 new members, the European Union has a population of 492 million, exceeding NAFTA's 441 million, and a gross national income (GNI) 95 percent that of NAFTA.

7.6 THE EUROPEAN FREE TRADE ASSOCIATION

European Free Trade Association (EFTA)
The free trade area that was formed in 1960 by the United Kingdom, Austria, Denmark, Norway, Portugal, Sweden, and Switzerland.

Trade deflection
The entry of imports from the rest of the world into the low-tariff member of a free trade area to avoid the higher tariffs of other members.

Concept Check

Which nations are now members of the European Free Trade Association?

European Economic Area (EEA) The free trade area formed by the 12 members of the EU and 5 of the 7 members of the EFTA on January 1, 1994.

In 1960, the free trade area known as the European Free Trade Association (EFTA) was formed by the "outer seven" nations: the United Kingdom, Austria, Denmark, Norway, Portugal, Sweden, and Switzerland, with Finland becoming an associate member in 1961. The EFTA achieved free trade in industrial goods in 1967, but only a few special provisions were made to reduce barriers on trade in agricultural products.

The maintenance by each nation of its own trade barriers against nonmembers can lead to the problem of trade deflection. This refers to the entry of imports from the rest of the world into the low-tariff member of the association to avoid the higher tariffs of other members. To combat trade deflection requires checking the original source and the final country of destination of all imports. The problem, of course, does not arise in a customs union because of its common external tariff, and it is much less serious in preferential trade arrangements, where only small tariff preferences are granted to members.

Iceland acceded the EFTA in 1970, Finland became a full member in 1986, and Liechtenstein, a part of the Swiss customs area, in 1991. However, in 1972, the United Kingdom and Denmark left the EFTA and, together with Ireland, joined the EU, as did Portugal in 1986. Thus, in 1991, the EFTA had seven members (Austria, Finland, Iceland, Liechtenstein, Norway, Sweden, and Switzerland), with headquarters in Geneva.

On January 1, 1994, the EFTA joined the EU to form the European Economic Area (EEA), a customs union that will eventually allow the free movement of most goods, services, capital, and people among the 17 member nations (Switzerland and Liechtenstein rejected the treaty in December 1992 and Liechtenstein cannot join without Switzerland), with a combined population of 385 million people. In 1995, Austria, Finland, and Sweden left the EFTA and joined the EU, leaving the EFTA with only four members (Switzerland, Norway, Iceland, and Liechtenstein).

7.7 U.S. FREE TRADE AGREEMENTS AND THE NORTH AMERICAN FREE TRADE AGREEMENT

In September 1985, the United States negotiated a free trade agreement with Israel. This was the first bilateral trade agreement signed by the United States. It provided for bilateral reductions in tariff and nontariff barriers to trade in goods between the two countries. Trade in services was also liberalized, and some provisions were made for the protection of intellectual property rights.

Although the United States and Canada have had a free trade agreement in autos since 1965, a comprehensive economywide, free trade agreement had proved elusive for over a century. In 1988, such a free trade agreement was

finally negotiated. By the time the pact went into effect in January 1, 1989, Canada was already by far the largest trading partner of the United States, with two-way yearly trade of about $150 billion (75 percent of which was already duty-free). The pact called for the elimination of most of the remaining tariff and nontariff trade barriers between the two countries by 1998. As a result of the agreement, Canada was estimated to have grown 5 percent faster and the United States 1 percent faster than in the absence of the agreement, and hundreds of thousands of jobs were created on both sides of the border.

The pact also established for the first time a set of rules governing trade in services, with each country agreeing to treat each other's service sector in the same way it treated its own and reducing the red tape for accountants, lawyers, engineers, and other professionals in crossing the border. In addition, the pact dropped all remaining restrictions on the shipment of energy between the two countries and reduced restrictions on investments in each other's market.

North American Free Trade Agreement (NAFTA) The agreement to establish a free trade area among the United States, Canada, and Mexico that came into existence on January 1, 1994.

In September 1993, the United States, Canada, and Mexico signed the North American Free Trade Agreement (NAFTA), which took effect on January 1, 1994. This agreement is eventually to lead to free trade in goods and services over the entire North American area. NAFTA is also to phase out many other barriers to trade and reduce barriers to cross-border investment among the three countries. With $40 billion of exports to and $41 billion of imports from the United States in 1993, Mexico was already the United States' third largest trading partner after Canada and Japan at the time the agreement took effect. The main impact of NAFTA was on trade between the United States and Mexico. (Canada only joined in the negotiations to ensure that its interests were protected.)

The implementation of NAFTA benefits the United States by increasing competition in product and resource markets, as well as by lowering the prices of many commodities to U.S. consumers. In fact, between 1994 and 2008, two-way trade between the United States and Mexico almost doubled. Because the U.S. economy is more than 15 times larger than Mexico's economy, the U.S. gains from NAFTA as a proportion of its GDP were much smaller than Mexico's. Furthermore, with wages more than six times higher in the United States than in Mexico, NAFTA was expected to lead to a loss of unskilled jobs, but an increase of skilled jobs, for an overall net increase in employment in the United States. A 2002 study puts the net gain in U.S. employment at between 90,000 and 160,000 as a result of NAFTA. A more recent study, however, indicated a much smaller net gain in U.S. employment or even a small net loss of jobs. Low-wage areas of the United States (such as Alabama and Arkansas) suffered while high-wage areas gained, but with a 15-year phase-in period and about $3 billion assistance to displaced workers, the harm to workers in low-income areas in the United States was minimized.

Free trade access to Mexico allows U.S. industries to import labor-intensive components from Mexico and keep other operations in the United States rather than possibly losing all jobs in the industry to low-wage countries. Some of the jobs that Mexico gained have not in fact come from the United States but from other countries, such as Malaysia, where wages are now roughly equal to Mexico's. As a condition for congressional approval of NAFTA, the United States also negotiated a series of supplemental agreements with Mexico governing workplace and environmental standards (to prevent U.S. firms from moving their operations to Mexico to take advantage of much more lax labor and environmental regulations), as well as to protect some American industries against import surges that might threaten them.

The implementation of NAFTA benefited Mexico by leading to greater export-led growth resulting from increased access to the huge U.S. market and by increasing inward foreign direct investments. Mexico suffered a net loss of jobs and incomes in agriculture, but these losses were more than matched by net increases in industry. With time, increasing employment opportunities and rising wages in industry are also expected to reduce the pressure for Mexicans to emigrate to the United States. Mexico's ability to benefit from NAFTA has been limited, however, by weak economic institutions and inadequate structural reforms of the economy.

Concept Check

What have been the effects of NAFTA on the United States and Mexico?

In 1993, the United States launched the Enterprise for the Americas Initiative (EAI), which led to the formation of the Free Trade Area of the Americas (FTAA) in 1998, whose ultimate goal is hemispheric free trade among the 34 democratic countries of North and South America. Negotiations are proving to be difficult and are not expected to succeed anytime soon. Since 2001, the United States has also signed free trade agreements (FTAs) with Australia, Bahrain, Chile, Jordan, Morocco, Peru, and Singapore, and signed CAFTA (the Central American Free Trade Agreement with Costa Rica, El Salvador, Guatemala, Honduras, Nicaragua, Santo Domingo, and Peru). In 2008, the United States was negotiating similar agreements with South Korea, Panama, and Colombia.

The European Union and other countries were also active in signing FTAs so that by 2008, there were more than 250 of them from just about 50 in 1990. Today, most countries belong to multiple FTAs. This spaghetti-bowl proliferation of bilateral and regional FTAs is regarded by some as a stumbling block to a freer multilateral trading system.

7.8 ATTEMPTS AT ECONOMIC INTEGRATION AMONG DEVELOPING COUNTRIES

The success of the EU encouraged many attempts at economic integration among groups of developing nations as a means of stimulating the rate of

economic development. Most of these attempts, however, met with only limited success or failed. Examples are:

1. The Central American Common Market (CACM), established by Costa Rica, El Salvador, Guatemala, Honduras, and Nicaragua in 1960, which was dissolved in 1969 and revived in 1990.

2. The Latin American Free Trade Association (LAFTA), established in 1960 by Mexico and most of South America, and its subgroup (the Andean Community of Nations, formed by Bolivia, Ecuador, Chile, Colombia, Peru, and Venezuela in 1969), which hoped to accelerate the process of integration and establish a common market; in 1980, the LAFTA was superseded by the Latin American Integration Association (LAIA).

Southern Common Market (Mercosur)
The South American Common Market formed by Argentina, Brazil, Paraguay, and Uruguay in 1991.

3. The Southern Common Market (Mercosur), formed by Argentina, Brazil, Paraguay, and Uruguay in 1991, became a customs union in 1995, and was joined, as associate members, by Bolivia and Chile in 1996 and by Peru in 2003.

4. The Free Trade Area of the Americas (FTAA) established in 1998 with the goal of free trade among the 34 democratic countries of North and South America.

5. The Caribbean Free Trade Association (CARIFTA), set up in 1968 and transformed into a common market (CARICOM) in 1973 with the membership of Antigua and Barbuda, Bahamas, Barbados, Belize, Dominica, Grenada, Guyana, Jamaica, Montserrat, St. Kitts-Nevis, St. Lucia, St. Vincent and the Grenadines, Suriname, and Trinidad and Tobago.

6. The East African Community (EAC), established in 1967 by Kenya, Tanzania, and Uganda.

7. The West African Economic and Monetary Union (UEMOA–WAEMU), which includes Benin, Burkina Faso, Côte d'Ivoire, Guinea Bissau, Mali, Niger, Senegal, and Togo.

8. The 12-member Southern Africa Development Community (SADC), extending from Angola, Botswana, Democratic Republic of Congo, Lesotho, Malawi, Madagascar, Mauritius, Mozambique, Namibia, South Africa, Swaziland, Tanzania, Zambia, Zimbabwe.

9. The Association of South East Asian Nations (ASEAN), which includes Brunei, Darussalam, Cambodia, Indonesia, Laos, Malaysia, Philippines, Singapore, Thailand, and Vietnam, though primarily a political association, in 1977 decided that it would also move toward a common market.

These customs unions are (or were) to a large extent explicitly trade diverting to encourage industrial development. Perhaps the greatest stumbling block to successful economic integration among groups of developing nations is the uneven distribution of benefits among members.

Since benefits are likely to accrue mainly to the most advanced nations in the group, lagging nations are likely to withdraw, causing the attempt at economic integration to fail. One way to avoid this difficulty is to provide investment assistance through industrial planning (i.e., assign some industries to each member nation). Although this tactic was tried in the Central American Common Market, the effort failed nevertheless, and the union dissolved in 1969 (although, as noted earlier, it was revived in 1990).

Another difficulty is that many developing nations are not willing to relinquish part of their newly acquired sovereignty to a supranational community body, as is required for successful economic integration. Other difficulties arise from lack of good transportation and communication among member nations, the great distance that often separates members, and the basically complementary nature of their economies and competition for the same world markets for their agricultural exports. For these reasons, economic integration among developing countries cannot be said to have been successful in most cases. One success story is Mercosur (see Case Study 7-3).

Starting in 2003, Mercosur, under the leadership of Brazil, sought to negotiate a free trade agreement with the Andean Community of Nations, as well as with other South American nations, in order to increase its bargaining strength vis-à-vis the United States in pursuing free trade for all of the Americas under the Free Trade Area of the Americas (FTAA). Case Study 7-4 shows the changes in the patterns of trade with economic integration.

Concept Check

Can you describe the attempts at economic integration among developing countries?

Council of Mutual Economic Assistance (CMEA or COMECON) The organization of Communist bloc nations formed by the Soviet Union in 1949 to divert trade from Western nations and achieve a greater degree of self-sufficiency among communist nations.

7.9 ECONOMIC INTEGRATION IN CENTRAL AND EASTERN EUROPE AND IN THE FORMER SOVIET REPUBLICS

In 1949, the Soviet Union formed the Council of Mutual Economic Assistance (CMEA or COMECON) with the communist bloc nations in Eastern Europe (Bulgaria, Czechoslovakia, East Germany, Hungary, Poland, and Romania) plus Mongolia (Cuba, North Korea, and Vietnam joined later). The purpose of this agreement was to divert trade from Western nations and achieve a greater degree of self-sufficiency among communist nations. Under this arrangement, most CMEA members imported oil and natural gas from the Soviet Union in exchange for industrial and farm products.

State trading companies The state organizations in centrally planned economies handling trade in specific product lines.

In CMEA member countries, the state decided and controlled all international transactions through a number of state trading companies, each handling some product line. Under such a system, the types and amounts of goods imported were determined by the requirements of the national plan over and above domestically available products (i.e., to close the gap in the "material balance"). The state then decided which goods to export in order

CASE STUDY 7-3

Economic Profile of Mercosur

Table 7.3 provides an economic profile of Mercosur or the Southern Common Market, which was formed in 1991 by Argentina, Brazil, Paraguay, and Uruguay. Chile and Bolivia became associate members of Mercosur in 1996, and Peru in 2003. The table shows that in 2006 the population of Mercosur was 237.7 million, gross national income (GNI) was $1,110.2 million, total merchandise exports were $190.0 billion, and total merchandise imports were $140.8 billion. Mercosur (now the third largest market in the world after NAFTA and the EU) became a customs union at the beginning of 1995 (with a common external tariff averaging 14 percent and free trade on 95 percent of intra-bloc trade), and a common market (also with the free flow of resources) in 2006.

Table 7.3. *Mercosur*

Country	Population (millions)	GNI (billions)	Exports (billions)	Imports (billions)
Argentina	39.1	$201.4	$46.6	$34.2
Brazil	189.3	882.8	137.5	95.9
Paraguay	6.0	8.4	1.9	5.9
Uruguay	3.3	17.6	4.0	4.8
Mercosur	237.7	1,110.2	190.0	140.8
United States	302.8	13,446.0	1,038.3	1,919.4
NAFTA	440.7	15,443.7	1,678.2	2,545.3
EU(27)	491.9	14,652.2	4,580.1	4,733.7
Extra-EU(27)	—	—	1,498.0	1,733.6
Japan	128.0	4,900.0	649.9	579.6

Source: World Bank, *World Development Report*, 2008; WTO, *International Trade Statistics*, 2007.

Centrally planned economies
Economies in which factors of production are owned by the government and prices are determined by government directives.

to pay for the required imports. Political considerations played at least as important a role as economic considerations in such trade, while comparative advantage and relative commodity prices did not have any direct role. In fact, these centrally planned economies (i.e., economies where prices are not determined by market forces but by government directives) generally emphasized self-sufficiency and tended to regard international trade as a necessary evil to close the material balance and obtain goods and services (such as high-technology products) that the nation could not supply for itself or within CMEA.

CASE STUDY 7-4

Changes in Trade Patterns with Economic Integration

Table 7.4 shows the value of total merchandise exports, intra-regional trade agreement (RTA) exports, and intra-RTA exports as a percentage of the total RTA exports of the EU, NAFTA, and Mercosur in 1990, 1995, 2000, 2005, and 2006. The table shows that the EU has the largest percentage of intra-RTA trade and Mercosur has the smallest. However, intra-RTA trade grew faster in Mercosur between 1990 and 1995 (i.e., in the four years after its creation in 1991) and in NAFTA from 1995 to 2000 (i.e., after its creation in 1994). Intra-Mercosur trade as a percentage of its total trade was 12.9 in 2005 and 13.6 in 2006, down from 20.1 in 2000, because of the economic crisis in Brazil and Argentina between 2001 and 2002. By 2003, however, intra-Mercosur trade had resumed its growth.

Table 7.4. *Total and Intra-EU, NAFTA, and Mercosur Merchandise Exports in 1990, 1995, 2000, 2005 and 2006 (billion dollars and percentages)*

EU Exports (in billion dollars)			
Year	Total	Intra-EU	Intra-EU as Percentage of Total
1990 (EU-15)	$1,482.4	$ 979.7	66.1
1995 (EU-15)	1,936.8	1,295.3	66.9
2000 (EU-15)	2,251.0	1,392.3	61.9
2005 (EU-27)	4,042.0	2,673.5	66.1
2006 (EU-27)	4,580.1	3,082.1	67.3

NAFTA Exports (in billion dollars)			
Year	Total	Intra-NAFTA	Intra-NAFTA as Percentage of Total
1990	$ 561.9	$239.6	42.8
1995	856.5	394.3	46.0
2000	1,224.9	681.6	55.6
2005	1,479.3	824.4	55.7
2006	1,678.2	902.4	53.8

Mercosur Exports (in billion dollars)			
Year	Total	Intra-Mercosur	Intra-Mercosur as Percentage of Total
1990	$46.4	$4.1	8.9
1995	70.5	14.5	20.5
2000	84.6	17.7	20.1
2005	163.8	21.1	12.9
2006	190.0	25.8	13.6

Source: WTO, *International Trade Statistics*, 2007.

Concept Check

What was economic integration in Eastern Europe before the collapse of communism?

Bilateral agreements Agreements between two nations regarding quantities and terms of specific trade transactions.

Bulk purchasing An agreement to purchase a specified amount of a commodity for a year or a number of years.

Central and Eastern European Countries (CEEC) Includes Albania, Bosnia and Herzegovina, Bulgaria, Croatia, the Czech Republic, the Federal Republic of Yugoslavia, Hungary, the former Yugoslav Republic (FYR), Macedonia, Poland, Romania, the Slovak Republic, and Slovenia.

Newly Independent States (NIS) Includes Armenia, Azerbaijan, Belarus, Estonia, Georgia, Kazakhstan, the Kyrgyz Republic, Latvia, Lithuania, Moldova, Russia, Tajikistan, Turkmenistan, Ukraine, and Uzbekistan.

Trade among CMEA economies was generally conducted on the basis of bilateral agreements and bulk purchasing. Bilateral agreements often involved *barter trade* and *countertrade*, in which one good was exchanged for another, or at least the attempt was made to balance trade with each nation individually. The reason was that any surplus of "convertible" rubles (the unit of account in CMEA trade) could not be spent to import goods and services from any nation other than the one from which the surplus was accumulated. For example, if Poland exported more than it imported from the Soviet Union, Poland could only use the surplus rubles accumulated to purchase Soviet goods. Bulk purchasing referred to the agreement of a state trading company to purchase a specified quantity of a commodity for a year or for a number of years from a state trading company of another nation.

After 1989, communist regimes collapsed all over Eastern Europe, and in the Soviet Union, East and West Germany were reunited, Yugoslavia disintegrated, and the Soviet Union dissolved. These momentous political changes were triggered, at least in part, by the economic failures of central planning. All 12 Central and Eastern European Countries (CEEC) and the 15 Newly Independent States (NIS) of the former Soviet Union have and are continuing to restructure their economies and their foreign trade along market lines. This is a monumental task, after many decades of central planning and gross inefficiencies. The establishment of a market economy required (1) freeing prices and wages from government control (so that market forces of demand and supply would freely allocate resources); (2) transferring productive resources from government to private ownership (i.e., privatizing the economy); (3) opening the economy to competition and liberalizing international trade (i.e., replacing state trading with trade based on market principles); and (4) establishing the legal and institutional framework necessary for the functioning of a market economy (such as property rights, a Western-style banking system, a capital market, cost accounting, business law, etc.).

In the majority of countries, severe economic dislocations in the form of increasing unemployment, high inflation, huge budget deficits, unsustainable international debts, and disrupted trade relations accompanied the collapse of traditional central planning. To date, Poland, Hungary, the Czech Republic (which arose from the breakup of Czechoslovakia into the Czech and the Slovak Republics in 1992), Slovenia (which broke away from the former Yugoslavia in 1991), and Estonia (a Baltic State and former Soviet Republic) have made the most progress toward restructuring their economies and are growing rapidly. Other CEEC nations are lagging somewhat behind, and most NIS nations (including Russia) are only about halfway through the process. Particularly difficult has been the privatization of large industries and the establishment of the institutions required for a democratic society and a market economy.

Commonwealth of Independent States (CIS) The organization formed by most of the former Soviet Republics when the Soviet Union was dissolved at the end of 1991.

Central European Free Trade Association (CEFTA) The agreement signed by Poland, Hungary, the Czech Republic, and Slovakia in 1992 calling for the establishment of free trade among its members within ten years (subsequently anticipated for 1997).

Baltic States Free Trade Area (BFTA) The agreement among the Baltic States of Estonia, Latvia, and Lithuania setting up a free trade area among themselves.

Concept Check

What is the extent of economic integration in Central and Eastern Europe now?

Since 1989 there has been a shift in the direction of CEEC and NIS trade. In 1980, 51 percent of CEEC and NIS exports went to other CEEC and NIS countries, 28 percent to industrial countries, and 21 percent to developing countries. By the year 2002, these values had changed to 26 percent, 62 percent, and 12 percent, respectively. Most CEEC have had and most NIS countries are having serious difficulties expanding trade with the West because of the generally low quality of their manufactured products and protectionism in industrial countries. For the restructuring process to be successful, however, CEEC and NIS countries need large amounts of foreign aid from industrial countries, easier access for their exports in industrial markets, and huge foreign direct investments (FDI) and inflows of modern technology from industrial countries.

At the end of 1991, the Soviet Union was formally dissolved, and, under the leadership of Russia, most former Soviet Republics (now called the Newly Independent States, or NIS) formed the Commonwealth of Independent States (CIS). In 1991, the EU signed association agreements with Poland, Hungary, and Czechoslovakia, giving those countries free trade access to the EU, except in some important products, such as steel, textile, and agricultural products. By 1996, the agreement had been extended to ten CEEC nations. In 1992, Poland, Hungary, the Czech Republic, and Slovakia formed the Central European Free Trade Association (CEFTA), and the Baltic States of Estonia, Latvia, and Lithuania formed the Baltic Free Trade Area (BFTA) in preparation for admission into the EU.

In March 1998, the Czech Republic, Estonia, Hungary, Poland, and Slovenia began negotiations to become members of the European Union, and in February 2000, Bulgaria, Latvia, Lithuania, Romania, and the Slovak Republic followed suit. In 2004, ten Central and Eastern European countries (Poland, Hungary, Czech Republic, Slovakia, Slovenia, Estonia, Lithuania, Latvia, Malta, and Cyprus) became EU members and Bulgaria and Romania joined in 2008. Albania, the countries of former Yugoslavia (Bosnia-Herzogovina, Croatia, Serbia, Montenegro, Macedonia, with the exception of Slovenia), as well as Turkey have started negotiations for admission into the EU. The former Soviet Republics (Russia, Armenia, Azerbaijan, Belarus, Georgia, Kazakhstan, Kyrgyz Republic, Moldova, Tajikistan, Turkmenistan, Ukraine, and Uzbekistan—with the exception of the Baltic States of Estonia, Latvia, and Lithuania) are further behind in their restructuring process and are not in line to join the EU.

SUMMARY

1. Economic integration refers to the commercial policy of discriminatively reducing or eliminating trade barriers only among the nations joining together. The degree of economic integration ranges from preferential trade

arrangements to free trade areas, customs unions, common markets, and economic unions.

2. A preferential trade arrangement (such as the British Commonwealth Preference Scheme) reduces barriers on trade among participating nations only. A free trade area (e.g., EFTA and NAFTA) removes all barriers on trade among members, but each nation retains its own barriers on trade with nonmembers. A customs union (e.g., the EU) goes further by also adopting a common commercial policy toward the outside world. A common market (the EU since 1993 and Mercosur in the future) goes still further by allowing the free movement of labor and capital among member nations. An economic union harmonizes (e.g., Benelux) or even unifies (e.g., the United States) the monetary and fiscal policies of its members.

3. The static welfare effects of customs unions are measured in terms of trade creation and trade diversion. Trade creation arises because a customs union leads to an increase in international trade. This increases welfare of the country forming a customs union. A customs union is also likely to result in trade diversion when lower cost imports from outside the union are replaced by higher cost imports from another union member (because of the tariff preference accorded to union members). By itself, trade diversion reduces welfare because it shifts production away from comparative advantage. The formation of a customs union usually leads to both trade creation and trade diversion and may increase or reduce welfare, depending on the relative strength of these two opposing forces.

4. Besides the static welfare gains, the nations forming a customs union are likely to receive significant dynamic benefits from increased competition, economies of scale, stimulus to investment, and better utilization of economic resources.

5. The EU was formed in 1958 by West Germany, France, Italy, Belgium, the Netherlands, and Luxembourg. They were joined by the United Kingdom, Denmark, and Ireland in 1973; Greece in 1981; Spain and Portugal in 1986; and Austria, Finland, and Sweden in 1995. In 2004, ten more nations joined the EU. These are Poland, Hungary, Czech Republic, Slovak Republic, Slovenia, Estonia, Lithuania, Latvia, Malta, and Cyprus. Bulgaria and Romania may join in 2007, but no timetable has been established for Turkey's accession. Free trade in industrial goods among the original members and common agricultural prices were achieved in 1968, and a full common market at the beginning of 1993. The EU led to trade expansion in industrial goods, but trade diversion in agricultural products. Development of a common agricultural policy was particularly difficult. The static gains resulting from the formation of the EU are in the range of 1 to 2 percent of GDP, but the dynamic gains are much greater.

6. An example of a free trade area is the EFTA, which was established in 1960 and joined the EU in a customs union in summer 1993. The members of the EFTA are now only Switzerland, Norway, Iceland, and Liechtenstein.

7. The United States negotiated free trade agreements with Israel in 1985, Canada in 1988, Jordan in 2001, Singapore and Chile in 2003, and Australia, Morocco, and six Central American countries at the beginning of 2004. In 1993, the United States, Canada, and Mexico signed the North American Free Trade Agreement (NAFTA). Free trade areas face the problem of trade deflection.

8. The many attempts at economic integration among developing nations have had only limited success, except the Southern Common Market, or Mercosur. Its members are Brazil, Argentina, Paraguay, and Uruguay, with Chile, Bolivia, and Peru as associate members.

9. The restructuring of the former communist countries of Central and Eastern Europe and the former Soviet Republics along market lines and their integration into the world economy was one of the greatest challenges that the world faced during the past decade, and it has still not been completed. Most Central and Eastern European countries joined the EU in 2004.

REVIEW QUESTIONS AND PROBLEMS

1. Suppose that the autarky price of commodity X is $10 in Nation A, $8 in Nation B, and $6 in Nation C, and Nation A is too small to affect prices in Nation B or C by trading. If Nation A initially imposes a nondiscriminatory ad valorem tariff of 100 percent on its imports of commodity X from Nations B and C, will Nation A produce commodity X domestically or import it from Nation B or Nation C?

2. Starting with the given of Problem 1:
 (a) If Nation A subsequently forms a customs union with Nation B, will Nation A produce commodity X domestically or import it from Nation B or Nation C?
 (b) Will this customs union lead to any trade diversion? Why?

3. Suppose that the autarky prices of commodity X in Nations A, B, and C are the same as in Problem 1, and Nation A is too small to affect prices in Nations B and C by trading. If Nation A initially imposes a nondiscriminatory ad valorem tariff of 50 percent (rather than 100 percent) on imports of commodity X from Nations B and C, will Nation A produce commodity X domestically or import it from Nation B or Nation C?

4. Starting with the given of Problem 3:
 (a) If Nation A subsequently forms a customs union with Nation B, will Nation A produce commodity X domestically or import it from Nation B or Nation C?
 (b) Will this customs union lead to any trade diversion? Why?

5. (a) Draw a figure illustrating the case of a customs union that leads to both trade creation and trade diversion but results in a net welfare gain for the country joining the union.

(b) Using the figure that you have drawn for Problem 5, measure the net welfare gain of the nation joining this customs union.

6. What are the factors that determine whether a customs union that leads to both trade creation and trade diversion results in a net increase or decrease in the welfare of a member nation?

7. What dynamic benefits are the nations forming a customs union likely to receive?

8. Draw a figure showing what happens if Country A forms a customs union with country Country B only, but the tariff-inclusive prices in Country C are less than the free trade prices in Country B.

9. Explain why the 1988 U.S.–Canada Free Trade Agreement created much less controversy in the United States than NAFTA, which included Mexico.

10. Indicate the possible cost and benefit to the United States from the movement to a single unified market by the European Union at the beginning of 1993.

SELECTED BIBLIOGRAPHY

The theory of regional trade agreements is examined in:

- A. Panagariya, "Preferential Trade Liberalization: The Traditional Theory and New Development," *Journal of Economic Literature*, June 2000, pp. 287–331.

For a detailed analysis and estimation of the welfare effects resulting from the European Union (the former European Community), see:

- P. Messerlin, *Measuring the Cost of Protection in the European Union* (Washington, D.C.: Institute for International Economics, 2001).

For the impact of the North American Free Trade Agreement, see:

- L. Klein and D. Salvatore, "Welfare Effects of the North American Free Trade Agreement," *Journal of Policy Modeling*, April 1995, pp. 163–176.
- G. C. Hufbauer and J. J. Schott, *NAFTA Revisited* (Washington, D.C.: Institute for International Economics, 2005).

For Mercosur, the South American Common Market, see:

- Inter-American Development Bank, *Integration and Trade in the Americas* (Washington, D.C.: Inter-American Development Bank, 2008).

For customs unions among developing countries, see:

- The World Bank, *Global Economic Prospects* (Washington, D.C.: The World Bank, May 1998).

For economic reforms and trade among Eastern European countries and the former Soviet Union, see:

- L. Orlowsky and D. Salvatore, eds., *Trade and Payments in Central and Eastern Europe's Transforming Economies* (Westport, Conn.: Greenwood Press, 1997).
- D. Salvatore, "The EU's Eastern Enlargment," *Empirica*, July 2001, pp. 1–21.
- EBRD, *Transition Report* (London: EBRD, 2008).

INTERNet

For information on the European Union, see:

http://mkaccdb.eu.int

For NAFTA's impact on the United States, Canada, Mexico, and other nations, see:

http://lanic.utexas.edu/la/mexico/nafta

http://www.citizen.org/trade/nafta/index.cfm

Information on Mercosur is found at:

http://europa.eu.int/comm/external_relations/mercosur/intro

Information on the Free Trade Area of the Americas (FTAA) is found at:

http://www.alca-ftaa.org

For the Asia-Pacific Economic Cooperation (APEC), a regional organization that promotes free trade and economic cooperation among 21 countries, see:

http://www.apec.org

Information on the ten-member Association of Southeast Asian Nations (ASEAN) is found in:

http://www.aseansec.org/home.htm

Information on international trade, economic restructuring, and regional trade agreements in former communist countries is found at:

http://www.ebrd.com/pubs/econo/series/tr.htm

Growth and Development with International Trade

After studying this chapter, you should be able to:

- Describe how growth and development takes place over time
- Understand the relationship between trade theory and economic development
- Identify the contribution of international trade to economic development
- Understand the relationship between the terms of trade and development
- Explain how instability in export earnings affects development
- Compare the effects of import substitution and export orientation in development
- Describe the current trade problems facing developing countries

CHAPTER OUTLINE

KEY TERMS

Balanced growth

Engine of growth

Regions of recent settlement

Vent for surplus

Endogenous growth theory

High-performance Asian economies
 (HPAEs)

Commodity, or net barter, terms of trade

Income terms of trade

Immiserizing growth

Export instability

Marketing boards

International commodity agreements

Buffer stocks

Export controls

Purchase contracts

Import-substitution industrialization
 (ISI)

Export-oriented industrialization

BRICs (Brazil, Russia, India, and China)

Foreign debt

Newly industrialized economies (NIEs)

Export pessimism

New International Economic Order
 (NIEO)

United Nations Conferences on Trade
 and Development (UNCTAD)

8.1 INTRODUCTION

With the exception of a handful of nations in North America, Western Europe, Japan, Australia, and New Zealand, most nations of the world are classified as less developed or, to put it more positively, as developing countries. In relation to developed (or more developed) countries, the average developing country is characterized by a low (and sometimes extremely low) average real per capita income, a relatively high proportion of the labor force in agriculture or other primary activities, such as mineral extraction, a low life expectancy, a high rate of illiteracy, and a high rate of population growth. There is, however, no sharp dichotomy between developed and developing nations but a fairly continuous spectrum from the very rich to the very poor.

In the past, the economic relationship between developed and developing nations was characterized by developing nations exporting primarily food and raw materials in exchange for manufactured goods from developed nations. This is still the case for the poorest developing nations, but not for the more advanced developing nations. In 1980, manufactured products were only 25 percent of developing country exports, but by 2008 that figure exceeded 80 percent.

Although the level and rate of economic development depend primarily on internal conditions in developing nations, most economists today believe that international trade can contribute significantly to the development process. This was not always the case. Until the 1980s, a sizable and influential minority of economists strongly believed that international trade and the functioning of the present international economic system hindered rather than facilitated development through secularly declining terms of trade and widely fluctuating export earnings of the developing nations. These economists contended that standard international trade theory based on comparative advantage was completely irrelevant for developing nations and the development process. Therefore, they advocated industrialization through import substitution (i.e., the domestic production of manufactured goods previously imported) and generally placing less reliance on international trade for development. They also advocated reforms of the present international economic system to make it more responsive to the special needs of developing countries.

In this chapter, we will examine all of these topics. In Section 8.2, we illustrate the effect of a change in factor endowments on the nation's production frontier and growth. In Section 8.3, we examine the relevance of international trade theory in the process of economic development. Section 8.4 then examines the contribution that international trade can make to economic development. Section 8.5 deals with the terms of trade and their effect on growth and development. Section 8.6 examines immiserizing growth; Section 8.7 deals with the relationship between export instability and economic development; Section 8.8 discusses the choice of development

strategy through import substitution or through exports. Section 8.9 examines the recent move toward trade liberalization in developing countries. Finally, Section 8.10 reviews the major problems facing developing countries today.

8.2 GROWTH AND DEVELOPMENT OVER TIME

Over time, nations grow through increases in the size in their labor force (L), the accumulation of capital (investments), including human capital (K), and improvements in technology or technical progress (T). An increase in the endowment of labor and capital and/or technical progress over time causes the nation's production frontier to shift outward. The type and degree of the shift depend on the rate at which L, K, and T grow.

We will examine growth for a nation producing two commodities (commodity X, which is L intensive, and commodity Y, which is K intensive) under constant returns to scale and with technology remaining constant. If L and K grow at the same rate, the nation's production frontier will shift out evenly in all directions at the rate of factor growth. The slope of the old and new production frontiers (before and after factor growth) will be the same at any point where they are cut by a ray from the origin. This is the case of **balanced growth**.

Balanced growth
Equal rates of factor growth and technological progress in the production of both commodities.

If instead only L grows, the output of both commodity X and Y grows because L is used in the production of both commodities. However, the output of commodity X (the L-intensive commodity) grows faster than the output of commodity Y (the K-intensive commodity). The opposite is true if only the endowment of K grows. If L and K grow at different rates, the outward shift in the nation's production frontier can similarly be determined. The same would be true as a result of technological progress. Figure 8.1 shows growth in a nation experiencing various types of factor growth.

The left panel of Figure 8.1 shows the case of balanced growth when the amount of L and K available to Nation 1 (from Figure 3.1) increases by 50 percent. With constant returns to scale, the maximum amount of each commodity that the nation can produce also increases by 50 percent, from 130X and 70Y to 195X and 105Y. Note that the shape of the expanded production frontier is identical to the shape of the production frontier before growth, so that the slope of the two production frontiers, or P_X/P_Y, is the same at such points as B and B', where they are cut by a ray from the origin.

The right panel repeats Nation 1's production frontier before growth (with intercepts of 130X and 70Y) and shows two additional production frontiers—one with only L increasing by 50 percent (solid line) and the other with only K increasing by 50 percent (dashed line). When only L increases by 50 percent, the production frontier shifts more along the X-axis, measuring the L-intensive commodity. If only K increases by 50 percent, the production frontier shifts more along the Y-axis, measuring the K-intensive commodity.

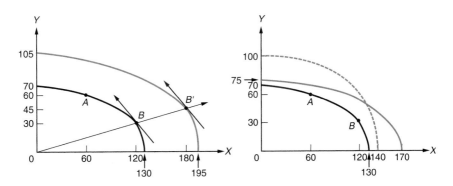

FIGURE 8.1. Growth of Labor and Capital over Time.
The left panel shows the case of balanced growth, with L and K doubling under constant returns to scale and unchanged technology. The two production frontiers have identical shapes and the same slope, or P_X/P_Y, along any ray from the origin. The right panel shows the case when only L or only K doubles. When only L doubles, the output of commodity X (the L-intensive commodity) grows proportionately more than the output of Y (but less than doubles). Similarly, when only K doubles, the output of Y grows proportionately more than that of X, but less than doubles (see the dashed production frontier).

Note that when only L doubles, the maximum output of commodity X does not increase by 50 percent (i.e., it only rises from 130X to 170X). For X to increase by 50 percent, both L and K must increase by 50 percent. Similarly, when only K increases by 50 percent, the maximum output of commodity Y increases by less than 50 percent (from 70Y to 100Y).

When both L and K grow at the same rate and we have constant returns to scale and unchanged technology in the production of both commodities, the productivity, and therefore the returns of L and K, remain the same after growth as they were before growth took place. If the dependency rate (i.e., the ratio of dependents to the total population) also remains unchanged, Nation 1's real per capita income and standard of living would remain unchanged. If only L grows (or L grows proportionately more than K), the ratio of capital to labor (K/L) available to the nation will fall and so will the productivity of L, the returns to L, and real per capita income. If, on the other hand, only the endowment of K grows (or K grows proportionately more than L), K/L will rise and so will the productivity of L, the returns to L, and real per capita income. Similar effects arise with different types of technical progress.

Concept Check

How does growth and development take place over time?

8.3 TRADE THEORY AND ECONOMIC DEVELOPMENT

According to traditional trade theory, if each nation specializes in the production of the commodity of its comparative advantage, world output

will be greater and, through trade, each nation will share in the gain. With the present distribution of factor endowments and technology between developed and developing nations, the theory of comparative advantage thus prescribes that developing nations should continue to specialize in the production of and export raw materials, fuels, minerals, food, and simple L-intensive commodities to developed nations in exchange for more sophisticated manufactured products.

While this may maximize their welfare in the short run, many developing nations believed that this pattern of specialization and trade relegated them to a subordinate position vis-à-vis developed nations and kept them from reaping the dynamic benefits of industry and from maximizing their welfare in the long run. The dynamic benefits (to be distinguished from the static benefits from comparative advantage) resulting from industrial production are a more trained labor force, more innovations, higher and more stable prices for the nation's exports, and higher income for its people. With developing nations specializing in primary commodities and simple L-intensive commodities while developed nations specializing in more sophisticated manufactured products, all or most of these dynamic benefits of industry and trade are believed to accrue to developed nations, leaving developing nations poor, undeveloped, and dependent. This belief was reinforced by the observation that all developed nations are primarily industrial, while most developing nations are, for the most part, primarily agricultural or engaged in mineral extraction or the production of simple manufactures.

Thus, traditional trade theory was attacked for being static and irrelevant to the development process. According to this thesis, traditional trade theory involves adjustment to existing conditions, while development necessarily requires changing existing conditions. In short, traditional trade theory was believed to maximize welfare at one point in time or in the short run but not over time or in the long run.

These are serious charges, which, if true, would indeed make traditional trade theory irrelevant to the process of economic development. However, as shown in Section 8.2, traditional trade theory can readily be extended to incorporate changes in factor supplies and technology over time. What this means is that a nation's pattern of development is not determined once and for all, but must be recomputed as underlying conditions change or are expected to change over time in the nation. For example, as a developing nation accumulates capital and improves its technology, its comparative advantage shifts away from primary products and simple manufactured goods to more sophisticated goods and services. To some extent, this has already occurred in Brazil, Korea, Taiwan, Mexico, and many other developing nations. As a result, traditional trade theory remains very much relevant to developing nations and the development process.

Concept Check

How does trade affect growth and development?

Engine of growth
The view that exports were the leading sector that propelled the economies of the regions of recent settlement into rapid growth and development during the nineteenth century.

Regions of recent settlement The mostly empty and resource-rich lands that Europeans settled during the nineteenth century, such as the United States, Canada, Argentina, Uruguay, Australia, New Zealand, and South Africa.

It must be pointed out, however, that today international trade cannot be the engine of growth, or serve as the most important force in economic development, that it was during the nineteenth century for the regions of recent settlement (the United States, Canada, Australia, New Zealand, Argentina, Uruguay, and South Africa). The reason is that the demand for food, raw materials, and simple manufactured products is not growing as rapidly today as it was during the nineteenth century, and many developing countries today are not as well endowed with natural resources in relation to their population (except for petroleum-exporting nations) as were the regions of recent settlement a century ago. International trade, however, does remain a necessary condition for development. No one forced China to open up to the world economy, but without such opening China would not have received the capital and technology, and it would not have had the markets that allowed it to grow so rapidly during the past decade.

8.4 THE CONTRIBUTIONS OF TRADE TO DEVELOPMENT

Even though international trade cannot be an "engine of growth" today, there are many ways (besides the static gains from comparative advantage) that it can contribute to the economic growth of today's developing nations. Some of these are:

1. Trade can lead to the full utilization of otherwise underemployed domestic resources. That is, through trade, a developing nation can move from an inefficient production point inside its production frontier, with unutilized resources because of insufficient internal demand, to a point on its production frontier with trade. For such a nation, trade would represent a

Vent for surplus
The view that exports could be an outlet for the potential surplus of agricultural commodities and raw materials in some developing countries.

vent for surplus, or an outlet for its potential surplus of agricultural commodities and raw materials. This has indeed occurred in many developing nations, particularly those in Southeast Asia and West Africa, during the past decades.

2. By expanding the size of the market, trade makes possible division of labor and economies of scale. This is especially important and has actually taken place in the production of light manufactures in small economies such as Taiwan, Hong Kong, and Singapore.

3. International trade is the vehicle for the transmission of new ideas, new technology, and new managerial and other skills.

4. Trade also stimulates and facilitates the international flow of capital from developed to developing nations. In the case of foreign direct investments, where the foreign firm retains managerial control over its investment, the foreign capital is likely to be accompanied by foreign skilled personnel to operate it (foreign direct investments are examined in Chapter 9).

5. In several large developing nations, such as Brazil and India, the importation of new manufactured products has stimulated domestic demand until efficient domestic production of these goods became feasible.

6. International trade is an excellent antimonopoly weapon because it stimulates greater efficiency by domestic producers in order for them to meet foreign competition. This is particularly important to keep low the cost and price of intermediate or semifinished products that are used as inputs in the domestic production of other commodities.

Critics of international trade can match this impressive list of benefits with an equally impressive list of the allegedly harmful effects of trade. However, since a developing nation can refuse to trade if it gains nothing or loses, the presumption is that it must also gain from trade. It is true that when most of the gains from trade accrue to developed nations, there is a great deal of dissatisfaction and justification for demands to rectify the situation, but this should not be construed to mean that trade is actually harmful. One can, of course, always find cases where, on balance, international trade has actually hindered economic development. However, in most cases it can be expected to provide invaluable assistance to the development process. This conclusion has been confirmed by many empirical studies.

Recent developments in endogenous growth theory provide an even more convincing and rigorous theoretical basis for the positive relationship between international trade and economic growth and development. Specifically, endogenous growth theory postulates that lowering trade barriers will speed up the rate of economic growth and development in the long run by allowing developing nations to absorb the technology developed in advanced nations at a faster rate than with a lower degree of openness and by increasing the benefits that flow from research and development (R&D) (see Case Study 8-1).

Endogenous growth theory The theory that seeks to identify in detail and rigorously the actual channels or the ways by which freer trade leads to faster long-run economic growth and development.

 Concept Check

What contribution can international trade make to the development of a nation?

8.5 THE TERMS OF TRADE AND ECONOMIC DEVELOPMENT

In Section 3.8, we defined the terms of trade of a nation as the ratio of the price of its export commodity to the price of its import commodity. In a world of many commodities, we can define the commodity, or net barter, terms of trade (N) as the ratio of the price index of the nation's exports (P_X) to the price index of its imports (P_M) multiplied by 100 (to express the terms of trade in percentages). That is:

Commodity, or net barter, terms of trade The ratio of the price index of the nation's exports to the price index of its imports times 100.

$$N = (P_X/P_M)\,100 \qquad (8\text{-}1)$$

For example, if we take 1980 as the base year ($N = 100$), and we find that by the end of 2003 the nation's P_X fell by 5 percent (to 95), while its P_M

The East Asian Miracle of Growth and Trade

Table 8.1 shows the average growth rate of real GDP and trade in the high-performance Asian economies (HPAEs). These include Hong Kong, Korea, Singapore, and Taiwan (the so-called four "tigers," which started rapid growth in the 1960s), as well as Malaysia, Indonesia, Thailand, and especially China, which followed them in the high-growth path in the 1970s and 1980s. Because of its spectacular growth, China is a class by itself. Data on Taiwan (Chinese Taipei) were not available.

The table shows that real GDP grew at the average rate of 6.9 percent in the HPAEs during the 1980–1990 decade and 7.7 percent in the 1990–1995 period. The growth of real GDP in China was even greater—10.2 percent and 12.8 percent, respectively. At these rates, the growth of real GDP would double every ten years or so in the HPAEs and every six or seven years in China.

Table 8.1 also shows that the rate of growth of exports was even greater than the growth of GDP. The growth of exports is certain to have provided a great stimulus to the growth of GDP and in turn to have been stimulated by it. There were, of course, other forces at work that contributed to the extraordinary growth of HPAEs and China. These were extremely high rate of savings and investments, significant improvement in education and training, the rapid rate of adoption of new technologies, and the shift from agrarian to industrial economies. This "East Asian miracle" of growth and trade has to be compared with much lower average growth rates of real GDP and exports for all developing countries and for industrial countries (see Table 8.1).

In July 1997, however, Thailand suddenly plunged into a deep economic crisis that quickly spread to the other HPAEs (with the exception of China, which had maintained tight control over its economy). The cause of the crisis was excessive borrowing of short-term funds in dollars and yen on international capital markets and using a great deal of these funds for real estate speculation and other unproductive investments. When local banks and firms were unable to repay their loans, foreign banks refused to extend new loans. Local banks then stopped making loans to local businesses, causing many of them to fail and plunging the nations into deep recession. At the height of the crisis in 1997–1998, the real GDP of Korea, Hong Kong, Thailand, and Malaysia declined by more than 5 percent and by nearly 15 percent in Indonesia. By 1998–1999, however, the worst of the crisis was over and growth had resumed, but at lower than the pre-crisis levels (except for China). Today, Asia is once again the most dynamic economic region in the world, accounting for close to half of global growth.

Table 8.1. *Average Growth of Real GDP and Trade in HPAEs, 1980–1995 (percentage)*

	Growth of Real GDP		Growth of Exports	
	1980–1990	*1990–1995*	*1980–1990*	*1990–1995*
Korea	9.4	7.2	12.0	13.4
Hong Kong	6.9	5.6	14.4	13.5
Singapore	6.4	8.7	10.0	13.3
Thailand	7.6	8.4	14.0	14.2
Indonesia	6.1	7.6	5.3	21.3
Malaysia	<u>5.2</u>	<u>8.7</u>	<u>10.9</u>	<u>14.4</u>
Average	6.9	7.7	11.1	15.0
China	10.2	12.8	11.5	15.6
Developing countries	2.8	2.1	7.3	5.2
Industrial countries	3.2	2.0	5.2	6.4

Source: World Bank, *World Bank Development Report*, 1997–2008.

High-performance Asian economies (HPAEs) Hong Kong, Korea, Singapore, and Taiwan; characterized by rapid growth in gross domestic product (GDP), in industrial production, and in manufactured exports. Also called newly industrialized economies (NIEs).

rose by 10 percent (to 110), then this nation's commodity terms of trade declined to

$$N = (95/110)\,100 = 86.36$$

This means that between 1980 and 2003 the nation's export prices fell by about 14 percent in relation to its import prices.

There is also another type of terms of trade called the income terms of trade. A nation's income terms of trade (I) are given by

$$I = (P_X/P_M)\,Q_X \qquad (8\text{-}2)$$

Income terms of trade The ratio of the price index of the nation's exports to the price index of its imports times the index of the nation's volume of exports.

where Q_X is an index of the *volume* of exports. Thus, I measures the nation's export-based capacity to import. Returning to our example, if Q_X rose from 100 in 1980 to 120 in 2003, then the nation's income terms of trade rose to

$$I = (95/110)120 = (0.8636)(120) = 103.63$$

This means that from 1980 to 2003 the nation's capacity to import (based on its export earnings) increased by 3.63 percent (even though P_X/P_M declined).

The change in the income terms of trade is very important for developing nations, since they rely to a large extent on imported capital goods for their development. If a nation's N and I increase, the nation is clearly better off as a result of trade. If both N and I fall, the nation is worse off. If N falls but I rises, the nation is better off in the sense that they can afford to purchase more imports.

According to *Raul Prebisch* and *Hans Singer*, the *commodity terms of trade* of developing nations deteriorated from 1870 to 1938. The reason they gave was that most or all of the productivity increases that took place in developed nations were passed on to their workers in the form of higher wages and income (because labor was relatively scarce and labor unions strong), while most or all of the productivity increases that took place in developing nations were reflected in lower prices. Thus, developed nations, so the argument went, had the best of both worlds. They retained the benefits of their own productivity increases in the form of higher wages and income for their workers, and at the same time they reaped most of the benefits from the productivity increases taking place in developing nations through the lower prices that they were able to pay for the agricultural exports of developing nations.

Although Prebisch's and Singer's conclusions and reasoning were strongly criticized by other economists, a 2002 study by *P. Cashin* and *C. J. McDermott* did find that real primary commodity (raw materials, food, and minerals) prices deteriorated by about 1 percent per year from 1862 to 1999. They also found evidence of a rising amplitude of price fluctuations since the early 1900s and more frequent fluctuations since the early 1970s. Thus, what is important is the type of products that each developing nation

CASE STUDY 8-2

Changes in Commodity Prices over Time

Table 8.2 shows the change in commodity price indices in selected years 1990 to 2007. Setting the price in 2000 equal to 100, the table shows that from 1990 to 2007, the price index of all primary commodities rose from 93.0 to 213.4, or by 98 percent, with the price of non-fuel commodities rising 49.3 percent and that of energy 82.2 percent. Among non-fuel commodities, the increase was least in raw materials, most for metals, with food and beverages in between. From 2005, the price of food and beverages also started to rise rapidly. The data show that the terms of trade of primary exporters depend very much on the type of commodities exported. (See Table 3.3 for the change in terms of trade of developing countries as a whole, and of Asia, Africa, Europe, the Middle East, and the Western Hemisphere).

Table 8.2. *Changes in Commodities Prices, Selected Years, 1990–2007 (2000 = 100)*

Commodity	1990	1995	2000	2004	2005	2006	2007	% Change 1990–2007
All primary commodities	73.0	86.1	100.0	127.2	158.1	190.8	213.4	98.0
Non-fuel commodities	106.6	125.8	100.0	118.4	125.6	154.8	176.6	49.3
Food	111.2	126.6	100.0	122.9	121.8	134.6	155.1	33.0
Beverages	102.1	154.2	100.0	111.9	132.1	143.2	162.9	45.9
Raw materials	94.3	123.7	100.0	100.9	101.5	110.4	115.9	20.6
Metals	122.0	122.1	100.0	130.3	159.5	249.1	292.4	82.2
Energy	85.5	64.0	100.0	134.9	186.3	222.1	245.3	96.6

Source: IMF, *International Financial Statistics* (Washington, D.C.: various issues).

Concept Check

How have changes in the terms of trade affected economic development?

exports. For example, a developing nation that exported mostly food and beverages experienced terms of trade rising very little or declining, while a developing nation that exported primarily raw materials or energy products experienced a large increase in their terms of trade (see Case Study 8-2). Furthermore, most studies found that, regardless of the secular movement in the *commodity terms of trade*, the overall *income terms of trade* of developing nations as a group have increased substantially over time because of sharply rising volumes of exports.

8.6 IMMISERIZING GROWTH

If growth in a nation leads to more exports but its commodity terms of trade deteriorate very much, the nation's welfare may decline. This situation

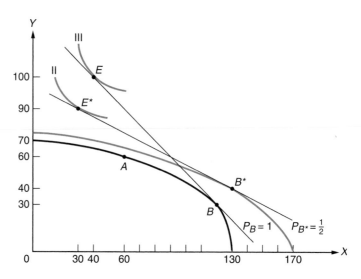

FIGURE 8.2. Immiserizing Growth.
With an increase in the supply of labor only, Nation 1's production frontier shifts out proportionately more along the horizontal axis, which measures commodity X (the L-intensive commodity), than along the Y-axis, as in Figure 8.1 With growth, Nation 1 exports more of X but its terms of trade deteriorate from $P_X/P_Y = P_B = 1$ to $P_X/P_Y = P_B^* = \frac{1}{2}$. Nation 1 will then consume at point E^* on indifference curve II with growth as compared with point E on indifference curve III before growth. Growth is immiserizing for this nation (i.e., Nation 1 is poorer after growth than before).

Immiserizing growth The situation where a nation's terms of trade deteriorate so much as a result of growth that the nation is worse off after growth than before, even if growth without trade tends to improve the nation's welfare.

was called immiserizing growth by *Jagdish Bhagwati*, the trade economist who first discussed this possibility. Immiserizing growth is illustrated in Figure 8.2.

Figure 8.2 shows that with a 50 percent increase in the supply of labor, Nation 1's production frontier expands much more along the horizontal axis measuring commodity X (the L-intensive commodity) than along the vertical axis measuring commodity Y (the K-intensive commodity), as in the right panel of Figure 8.1. Figure 8.2 shows that the increase in the export of commodity X by Nation 1 with growth reduces its terms of trade from $P_X/P_Y = P_B = 1$ (as in Figure 3.4) to $P_X/P_Y = P_B^* = \frac{1}{2}$. Consumption falls from point E on indifference curve III to point E^* on indifference curve II. Growth is immiserizing for this nation (i.e., Nation 1 is poorer after growth than before).

Although possible, immiserizing growth is seldom experienced in the real world. As we have seen in the previous section, with a sufficient increase in the volume of trade, the nation is usually better off even if it suffers a deterioration in its commodity terms of trade.

Concept
Check

Has growth been generally immiserizing?

8.7 EXPORT INSTABILITY AND ECONOMIC DEVELOPMENT

Independent of possibly deteriorating *long-term* or secular terms of trade, developing nations may also face such a large *short-run fluctuations* in their export prices and earnings as to seriously hamper their development efforts. Large short-run fluctuations in the export prices and earnings of developing nations were believed to be due to both inelastic and unstable demand and supply curves for their exports.

The demand for many primary exports of developing nations is price inelastic because individual households in developed nations spend only a small fraction of their income on such commodities as coffee, tea, cocoa, and sugar. Consequently, when the prices of these commodities change, households do not significantly change the purchases of these commodities, resulting in price-inelastic demand curves. Similarly, the demand for many minerals is price inelastic because few substitutes are available for them. At the same time, the demand for the primary exports of developing nations is unstable because of business cycle fluctuations in developed nations.

Turning to the supply side, we find that the supply of the primary exports of developing nations is price inelastic (i.e., the quantities supplied do not respond very much to changes in their prices) because of internal rigidities and inflexibilities in resource uses in most developing nations, especially in the case of tree crops that involve long gestation periods. Supply curves are unstable or shifting because of weather conditions, pests, and so on.

Because of wildly fluctuating export prices, the export *earnings* of developing nations can also vary significantly from year to year. When export earnings rise, exporters increase their consumption expenditures, investments, and bank deposits, but reduce them just as much when export earnings fall. This alternation of boom and bust periods renders development planning (which depends on imported machinery, fuels, and raw materials) much more difficult.

In a well known study published in 1966, *MacBean* found that while export instability was somewhat larger for developing nations than for developed nations during the postwar period, this did not seem to have interfered much with their development efforts. Most (but not all) subsequent studies seem to confirm MacBean's results for later periods.

Despite this, many developing countries have in the past demanded international commodity agreements in order to stabilize and increase their export earnings. Stabilizing export earnings, however, could be accomplished with purely domestic schemes, such as marketing boards. These operate by purchasing the output of domestic producers at the stable prices set by the board, which would then export the commodities at

Concept Check

How has instability in export earnings affected economic development?

Export instability Short-run fluctuations in export prices and earnings.

Marketing boards National schemes set up by several developing nations after World War II to stabilize export prices for individual producers of an agricultural commodity.

fluctuating world prices. In good years, domestic prices would be set below world prices so that the board would accumulate funds, which it would then disburse in bad years by paying domestic producers prices higher than world prices. Examples are the cocoa marketing board of Ghana and the rice marketing board of Burma (now Myanmar) set up after World War II. Only a few of these marketing boards, however, succeeded because of the great difficulty in correctly anticipating the domestic prices that would average out world prices over time and because of corruption.

Developing nations have been more interested in international commodity agreements than in setting up marketing boards because the former also offered the possibility of *increasing* their export prices and earnings. There are three basic types of international commodity agreements: buffer stocks, export controls, and purchase contracts. Buffer stocks involve the purchase of the commodity (to be added to the stock) when the commodity price falls below an agreed minimum level, and the sale of the commodity out of the stock when the commodity price rises above the established maximum price. Examples are the *International Tin Agreement*, the *International Cocoa Agreement*, and the *International Natural Rubber Agreement*. Most of these, however, collapsed after a few years of operation.

Export controls seek to regulate the quantity of a commodity exported by each nation in order to stabilize its price. The *International Sugar Agreement* and the *International Coffee Agreement* were based on export controls. These agreements also did not work well or collapsed. One export control scheme that is doing very well is *OPEC (the Organization of Petroleum Exporting Countries)*.

Purchase contracts are long-term multilateral agreements that stipulate a minimum price at which importing nations agree to *purchase* a specified quantity of the commodity and a maximum price at which exporting nations agree to *sell* specified amounts of the commodity. An example is the *International Wheat Agreement*, which was signed in 1949, but became inoperative in the early 1970s.

In general, and with the exception of the International Coffee Agreement during some years, international commodity agreements have either failed or had very limited success. One reason for this is the very high cost of operating them and the general lack of support by developed nations, which would have to shoulder most of the burden of setting up and running them. Almost always, the resources required to operate international commodity agreements could very likely be used more profitably for truly developmental purposes. With the sharp increase in most commodity prices since 2005, discussion of most schemes to stabilize and increase the export earning of developing countries have all but ended.

International commodity agreements Organizations of producer and consumer nations attempting to stabilize and increase the prices and earnings of the primary exports of developing nations.

Buffer stocks The type of international commodity agreement that involves the purchase of the commodity (to be added to the stock) when the commodity price falls below an agreed minimum price, and the sale of the commodity out of the stock when the commodity price rises above the established maximum price.

Export controls The type of international commodity agreement that seeks to regulate the quantity of the commodity exported by each nation.

Purchase contracts Long-term multilateral agreements that stipulate the minimum price at which importing nations agree to purchase a specified quantity of the commodity and a maximum price at which exporting nations agree to sell specified amounts of the commodity.

8.8 IMPORT SUBSTITUTION VERSUS EXPORT ORIENTATION

During the 1950s, 1960s, and 1970s, most developing nations made a deliberate attempt to industrialize rather than continuing to specialize in the production of primary commodities (food, raw materials, and minerals) for export, as prescribed by traditional trade theory. Industrialization was relied upon to provide (1) faster technological progress, (2) the creation of high-paying jobs to relieve the serious unemployment and underemployment problems faced by most developing nations, (3) greater backward and forward linkages in the production process, (4) rising terms of trade and more stable export prices and earnings, and (5) relief from balance-of-payments difficulties that result because the demand of developing nations for manufactured products rises faster than their export earnings. The desire of developing nations to industrialize is natural in view of the fact that all rich nations are primarily industry and service oriented while most poor nations are primarily agricultural.

Import-substitution industrialization (ISI) The industrialization policy that many developing nations followed during the 1950s, 1960s, and 1970s involving the replacement of imports of industrial goods with domestically produced goods.

Having decided to industrialize, developing nations had to choose between industrialization through import substitution or an export orientation. Both strategies have advantages and disadvantages. An import-substitution industrialization (ISI) strategy has three main advantages: (1) The market for the industrial product already exists, as evidenced by imports of the commodity, so that risks are reduced in setting up an industry to replace imports. (2) It is easier for developing nations to protect their domestic market against foreign competition than to force developed nations to lower trade barriers against their manufactured exports. (3) Foreign firms are induced to establish so-called tariff factories to overcome the tariff wall of developing nations.

Against these advantages are the following disadvantages: (1) Domestic industries can grow accustomed to protection from foreign competition and have no incentive to become more efficient. (2) Import substitution can lead to inefficient industries because of the smallness of the domestic market in many developing nations. (3) After the simpler manufactured imports are replaced by domestic production, import substitution becomes more and more difficult and costly (in terms of the higher protection and inefficiency) as more capital-intensive and technologically advanced imports have to be replaced by domestic production.

Export-oriented industrialization The policy of industrialization pursued by some developing nations that involves increasing the output of manufactured goods for export.

Export-oriented industrialization also has advantages and disadvantages. The advantages include: (1) It overcomes the smallness of the domestic market and allows a developing nation to take advantage of economies of scale. This is particularly important for the many developing countries that are both very poor and small. (2) Production of manufactured goods for export requires and stimulates efficiency throughout the economy. This is especially important when the output of an industry is used as an input of another

domestic industry. (3) The expansion of manufactured exports is not limited (as in the case of import substitution) by the growth of the domestic market.

On the other hand, there are two serious disadvantages from an export-orientation strategy: (1) It may be very difficult for developing nations to set up export industries because of the competition from the more established and efficient industries in developed nations. (2) Developed nations often provide a high level of effective protection for their industries producing simple labor-intensive commodities in which developing nations already have or can soon acquire a comparative advantage.

During the 1950s, 1960s, and 1970s, most developing nations, particularly the larger ones, strongly opted for a policy of import substitution to industrialize. They protected their infant industries or stimulated their birth with effective tariff rates that rose sharply with the degree of processing. This was done at first to encourage the relatively simple step of assembling foreign parts, in the hope that subsequently more of these parts and intermediary products could be produced domestically (backward linkage). Heavy protection of domestic industries also stimulated the establishment of tariff factories in developing nations.

Concept Check

Is export orientation better than import substitution?

The policy of industrialization through import substitution generally met with only limited success or with failure. It often led to (1) inefficient domestic industries and very high prices for domestic consumers, (2) excessive capital intensity and relatively little labor absorption, and (3) the neglect of agriculture and other primary sectors, with the result that many developing nations experienced a decline in their earnings from traditional exports, and some (such as Brazil) were even forced to import some food products that they had previously exported.

The overall result was that those developing nations (such as India, Pakistan, and Argentina) that stressed industrialization through import substitution fared much worse and grew at a much slower rate than those developing economies (such as Hong Kong, Korea, and Singapore) that from the early 1950s followed an export-oriented strategy (see Case Study 8-3). It must be pointed out, however, that a policy of import substitution may be of some benefit in the early stages of development (especially for larger developing nations), while an export orientation becomes an absolute necessity later in the development process. Thus, rather than being alternatives, the strategy of import substitution and export orientation could profitably be applied to some extent sequentially, especially in the larger developing nations. This is, in fact, what Korea did.

8.9 TRADE LIBERALIZATION AND GROWTH IN DEVELOPING COUNTRIES

Starting in the 1980s, many developing nations that had earlier followed an import-substitution industrialization (ISI) strategy began to liberalize

The Growth of GDP of Rich Countries, Globalizers, and Nonglobalizers

Table 8.3 shows that globalizing developing countries grew much faster than rich countries and nonglobalizers during the past two-and-a-half decades, but less rapidly during the 1960s and 1970s. Globalizers were those developing countries that experienced a rapid increase in the ratio of international trade to GDP and sharply reduced their average tariff rates. Growth was measured as the weighted average increase of real GDP.

Table 8.3. *Average Growth of Real GDP of Rich Countries, Globalizers, and Non-Globalizers, 1960s–2000s (percentage)*

	1960s	*1970s*	*1980s*	*1990s*	*2000–6*
Rich countries	4.7	3.1	2.3	2.2	2.1
Globalizers	1.4	2.9	3.5	5.0	6.1
Nonglobalizers	2.4	3.3	0.8	1.4	2.3

Source: D. Dollar and A. Kraay, "Trade Growth and Poverty," *World Bank Research Paper*, March 2001, p. 38; and World Bank, *World Development Report*, 2008.

Concept
Check

Why have many
developing countries
liberalized trade in
recent decades?

trade and adopt an outward orientation. The reforms were spurred by the debt crisis that began in 1982 (see Section 8.10) and the evident success of the outward-oriented countries. In general, the reforms involved a dramatic reduction and simplification in average tariff rates and in quantitative import restrictions. These, in turn, resulted in a much higher degree of openness of international trade, a sharp increase in the ratio of manufactures in total exports (see Case Study 8-4), and higher rates of growth.

The World Bank greatly facilitated the planning and carrying out of trade liberalization programs in developing counties with technical assistance and loans. The World Bank began its lending for structural adjustment in 1980, and by 1995 it had lent more than $20 billion to more than 60 countries for the purpose of implementing structural or sectoral reforms. The largest number of loans went to sub-Saharan African countries, but since these loans were generally small, a much larger amount went to other developing countries. The fact that many of the liberalizing developing countries joined the World Trade Organization (WTO) consolidated the reforms already undertaken and encouraged further reforms. These are likely to increase productivity and growth in developing countries during this decade. In fact, new economic giants have emerged and are emerging among developing countries, the

Manufactures in Total Exports of Selected Developing Countries

Table 8.4 gives the percentage of manufactured exports in the total merchandise exports of selected developing countries in Africa, Asia, and Latin America in 1983 and 2006. The table shows that the structure of exports of all the countries in the table changed dramatically toward manufactures during the period examined. This was especially true for S. Africa and Malaysia (where manufactures as a percentage of the nation's total merchandise exports tripled) and in Egypt, Thailand, Argentina, Chile, and Mexico (where it doubled). Thus, the stereotype of developing countries exporting raw materials and foods and importing manufactured goods is no longer true. Even the conclusion that most manufactured exports of developing countries are simple, labor-intensive products is no longer valid, especially for the most advanced of the developing countries, such as Malaysia and Brazil (among the countries listed in the table).

Table 8.4. *Manufactures as Percent of Total Merchandise Exports, Selected Developing Countries, 1983 and 2006*

Africa	1983	2006	Asia	1983	2006	L. America	1983	2006
Egypt	12	31	India	52	70	Argentina	16	31
Kenya	15	21	Malaysia	25	75	Brazil	39	54
S. Africa	18	57	Pakistan	63	82	Chile	7	14
Tunisia	44	78	Thailand	31	77	Mexico	37	77

Source: World Bank, *World Development Report*, 2008.

BRICs Brazil, Russia, India, and China, the new economic giants, which provide increasing competition to the traditional giants (United States, EU, and Japan).

so-called BRICs (Brazil, Russia, India, and China), which provide increasing competition to the traditional giants (the United States, the European Union, and Japan—see Case Study 8-5).

8.10 CURRENT PROBLEMS FACING DEVELOPING COUNTRIES

The most serious problems facing developing countries today are: (1) the conditions of stark poverty prevailing in many countries, particularly those of sub-Saharan Africa; (2) the unsustainable foreign debt of some of the poorest developing countries; and (3) the remaining trade protectionism of developed countries against developing countries' exports. Let us briefly examine each of these problems.

The New Economic Giants

New economic giants are emerging among developing countries in the world economy today. These are the BRICs (Brazil, Russia, India, and China). China is already an economic giant, India is on the way; Brazil and Russia are following. Table 8.5 provides data on the size and economic importance of the new emerging economic giants in relation to the traditional ones: the United States, the European Union, and Japan. The best measure of the economic size of an economy is its gross national income (GNI) at purchasing power parity (PPP), which takes into account the difference in the purchasing power of money in various countries.

The data in the table show that China and India are the super-giants in terms of population, as Russia is in land area. The GNI (PPP) of the 27 countries of the European Union (EU-27) and the United States are the largest, followed by China, Japan, and India. Russia and Brazil are much smaller. In terms of per capita

income (per capita GNI at PPP—a measure of the standard of living in each nation), the United States is clearly first, followed by Japan, and EU-27. Russia, China, Brazil, and India follow, with much lower per capita incomes, especially India. Except for Brazil, however, the new giants (especially China) are growing much more rapidly than the traditional ones and are expected to surpass the United States and EU-27 in 30–40 years *with continued growth at current rates*. In terms of per capita incomes, it would take much longer.

Even more important than economic size and growth rates, however, is the rising competitive challenge that the new giants are providing to the traditional giants, on both world markets and in their own domestic market, in a widening range of increasingly sophisticated products (especially China) and services (especially India).

Table 8.5. *The Economy of the New and Traditional Economic Giants in 2006*

	Population (million)	Land Area (sq. km.)	GNI* (billion $)	Per Capita GNI ($)*	Average Growth Rate (%) (2000–2006)
China	1,312	9,598	6,119	4,660	9.8
Russia	143	17,075	1,815	12,740	6.4
India	1,110	3,287	2,726	2,460	7.4
Brazil	189	8,547	1,648	8,700	3.0
USA	303	9,629	13,196	44,070	2.8
EU (15)	389	3,210	12,498	32,211	1.3
EU (27)	492	4,308	13,919	28,348	1.8
Japan	128	378	4,196	32,840	1.4

*Purchasing power parity (PPP).

Source: World Bank, *World Development Indicators*, 2008; and *World Development Report*, 2008.

Table 8.6. *Population and Economic and Health Indicators, 1990–2006*

| Country/Region | Population in 2006 (millions) | Income per Capita | | Infant Mortality Rate per 1,000 Live Births | | Life Expectancy at Birth (years) | |
		Dollars* 2006	Growth Rate 2000–2006 (% per year)	1990	2006	1990	2006
Low and middle income	5,507	4,436	5.7	69	54	63	66
Sub-Saharan Africa	782	1,681	4.7	109	94	50	50
East Asia and Pacific	1,899	4,359	8.6	42	24	67	71
of which, China	1,312	4,660	9.8	36	20	69	72
South Asia	1,499	2,289	4.7	86	62	59	64
of which India	1,110	2,460	7.4	80	57	59	64
Europe and Central Asia	461	9,791	5.8	40	22	69	69
Middle East and N. Africa	311	6,710	4.2	58	34	64	70
Latin America and Caribbean	556	8,682	3.1	43	22	68	73
High-income economies	1,031	34,933	2.3	9	6	76	79
World	6,538	9,202	3.0	63	50	65	68

*Purchasing power parity (PPP).

Source: World Bank, *World Development Indicators*, 2008.

1. Poverty in Developing Countries

Table 8.6 gives the population and the per capita income in terms of PPP of various groups of countries in 2006, as well as the growth in real per capita income from 2000 to 2006, and infant mortality and life expectancy in 1990 and 2006. The table shows that the average per capita income of all developing economies was $4,436 in 2006, as compared with $34,933 in high-income developed economies, but the average growth rate of per capita income was much higher in developing countries, especially in East Asia and the Pacific, than in developed countries between 2000 and 2006. Even sub-Saharan Africa achieved a respectable average growth rate between 2000 and 2006 after two previous decades of negative growth. The table also shows that infant mortality is much higher and life expectancy much lower in low-income developing countries than in high-income developed countries, but major improvements were made in both measures, except in sub-Saharan Africa and in the developing countries of Europe and Central Asia, from 1990 to 2006.

Concept Check

What is the extent of poverty in the world today?

Despite the fact that the number of poor people in the world (defined by the World Bank as people who live on less than one dollar per day) has been cut in half during the past two-and-half decades of rapid globalization, there are still more than one billion poor people in the world today and more than 20,000 children die of starvation each day. The recent sharp increase in world food prices is now threatening to undo the achievements of the past in reducing world poverty and is a tragedy for the world poor.

2. The Foreign Debt Problem of Developing Countries

Foreign debt The hundreds of billions of dollars that developing countries owe to commercial banks in developed countries and that they find difficult to repay or even service (i.e., pay interest on).

During the 1970s and early 1980s, developing countries accumulated a total foreign debt exceeding $1 trillion, which they found very difficult to service (i.e., repay the principal or even the interest on the debt). When Mexico was unable to service (pay the interest on) its foreign debt in August 1982, the world was plunged into a foreign debt crisis. As part of the deal to renegotiate their debts, developing nations were required by the International Monetary Fund (IMF) to adopt austerity measures to reduce imports and to cut inflation, wage increases, and domestic programs. By 1994 the foreign debt problem was more or less resolved (i.e., made manageable) for middle-income developing countries but not for the poorest heavily indebted developing countries (most of which are in sub-Saharan Africa). In June 1999, the Group of 7 leading industrial nations wrote off up to 90 percent of the debt that the world's most indebted nations owed to their governments.

Concept Check

How serious is the foreign debt problem of developing countries?

The financial crisis in East Asia in 1997–1998, Russia in 1998, Brazil in 1999 and 2002, and Turkey and Argentina since the latter part of the last decade caused the foreign debt of these nations to shoot up. This required rescue packages (promises of financial aid) by the IMF, the World Bank, and private banks to Korea, Indonesia, Brazil, Russia, Thailand, Turkey, and Argentina (Argentina, nevertheless, defaulted on its $140 billion foreign debt in December 2001). Despite the fact that by 2006 the foreign debt problem of most developing countries had improved, it still remained serious for some of them (see Case Study 8-6).

3. Trade Problems of Developing Countries

Newly industrialized economies (NIEs) Hong Kong, Korea, Singapore, and Taiwan. Characterized by rapid growth in gross domestic product (GDP), in industrial production, and in manufactured exports; also called high-performance Asian economies (HPAEs).

Export pessimism The feeling that developing countries' exports to developed countries cannot grow rapidly because of the latter's increased protectionism.

During the 1980s, developed countries, beset by slow growth and large unemployment, increased the trade protection they provided to some of their large industries (such as textiles, steel, shipbuilding, consumer electronic products, television sets, shoes, and many other products) against imports from developing countries. These were the very industries in which developing countries had gained or were gaining a comparative advantage. A great deal of the new protectionism was directed especially against the manufactured exports of the high-performance Asian economies (HPAEs), then called newly industrialized economies (NIEs). These economies (Hong Kong, Korea, Singapore, and Taiwan) were characterized by rapid growth in gross domestic product (GDP), in industrial production, and in manufactured exports. By 1993, nearly a third of developing countries' exports to industrial countries were restricted by quotas and other nontariff trade barriers (NTBs).

Had the trend toward increased protectionism continued, it could have led to a revival (and justification) of export pessimism and a return to inward-looking policies in developing countries. Fortunately, the Uruguay

CASE STUDY 8-6

The Foreign Debt Burden of Developing Countries

Table 8.7 shows the total foreign debt, the foreign debt as a percentage of GNI, and the foreign debt service (interest and amortization payments on the debt) as a percentage of exports for all developing countries together and for developing countries in each geographical region in 1980 (i.e., before the 1982 official start of the debt crisis), in 1990 (near the height of the debt crisis), and in 2006. From the table, we see that the total foreign debt of all developing countries was $580 billion in 1980 (the largest component of which was the $257 billion foreign debt of the Latin American and Caribbean countries). The total debt increased sharply to $1,422 billion by 1990, and it was $2,984 billion in 2006.

Table 8.7 also shows that the total foreign debt as a percentage of GNI increased sharply from 1980 to 1990, but then it declined, except for Europe and Central Asia (because of the disruptions arising from the collapse of communism). The foreign debt service as a percentage of exports also increased from 1980 to 1990 (except for East Asia and the Pacific and for Latin America and the Caribbean), but it then declined in all regions, except for Europe and Central Asia. Although less serious than in the 1980 and 1990s, many developing nations were still facing serious foreign debt problems in 2006 despite the fact that the rich countries cancelled $55 billion of the debt owed by the poorest developing countries at the end of 2005.

Table 8.7. *Developing Countries' Foreign Debt Indicators, 1980, 1990, 2006*

	Total Debt (billion $)			Debt as % of GNI			Debt Service as % of Exports		
	1980	1990	2006	1980	1990	2006	1980	1990	2006
All developing countries	580	1,422	2,984	21	35	26	13	19	13
Sub-Saharan Africa	61	177	174	24	63	26	7	13	11
East Asia and Pacific	65	239	660	16	36	18	27	19	5
South Asia	38	129	227	16	32	20	12	29	8
Europe and Central Asia	76	218	1,047	8	18	43	7	15	20
Middle East and N. Africa	83	183	141	22	46	22	6	16	10
Latin America and Caribbean	257	475	734	36	45	26	36	24	23

Source: World Bank, *World Development Indicators,* 2008.

Concept Check

What are the most serious trade problems facing developing countries today?

Round was successfully completed in 1994 (see Section 6.9) and led to a reduction in trade restrictions and protectionism. Although most of the liberalization that took place was in trade among developed countries, developing countries also benefited. The *Doha Round* (see Section 6.10), launched in November 2001, was supposed to be a "development round" by dealing with the trade demands of developing countries, but it failed in July 2008.

New International Economic Order (NIEO) The demands made by developing nations as a group at the United Nations for the removal of the alleged inequities in the operation of the present international economic system and for specific steps to be taken to facilitate their development.

United Nations Conferences on Trade and Development (UNCTAD) Special conferences held under the auspices of the United Nations at which developing nations advanced their demands for NIEO.

In June 1974, the General Assembly of the United Nations called for the establishment of a New International Economic Order (NIEO). This called for (1) the renegotiation of the international debt of developing countries and the reduction in interest payments, (2) the establishment of international commodity agreements, (3) preferential access in developed nations' markets to all the manufactured exports of developing nations, (4) removing trade barriers on agricultural products in developed nations, (5) increasing the transfer of technology to developing nations and regulating multinational corporations, (6) increasing the yearly flow of foreign aid to developing nations to 0.7 percent of rich nations' income, and (7) allowing developing nations a greater role in international decision making. Most of these same demands had been made previously at various United Nations Conferences on Trade and Development (UNCTAD). However, the slowdown in the world economy during the 1980s and early 1990s led most industrial countries to turn inward to address their own internal problems of slow growth and unemployment, and to the demise of the NIEO as a hotly debated issue.

Nevertheless, growth has increased and poverty fallen in many developing countries during the past two-and-a-half decades of rapid globalization. There is also an increased awareness in the world today that the major cause of poverty in some of the poorest developing countries is internal and due to wars, corruption, political instability, disease, and natural calamities. In 2000 the World Bank sponsored the *Millennium Development Goals (MDG)*, which proposed a program for rich countries to help the poorest developing countries stimulate growth, reduce poverty, and promote sustainable development.

SUMMARY

1. Over time, nations grow as a result of the growth of their labor force (L), the accumulation of capital (K) or investments, and improvements in technology. With constant returns to scale, unchanged technology, and L and K growing at the same rate (balanced growth), the nation's production frontier will shift out evenly in both directions at the rate of factor growth, and output per worker will remain constant. If L grows faster than K, the nation's production frontier will shift proportionately more in the direction of the L-intensive commodity, and output per worker will decline. The opposite is true if K grows faster than L.

2. Traditional trade theory can be extended to incorporate changes in factor endowments and technology. Although the level and the rate of economic development depend primarily on internal conditions in developing nations, international trade can contribute significantly to the development process.

3. Because of less favorable demand and supply conditions, international trade today is not the engine of growth that it was for the regions of recent

settlement in the nineteenth century, but it is still crucial for economic development.

4. The commodity, or net barter, terms of trade (N) measure the movement over time in the nation's export prices relative to its import prices. The income terms of trade (I) measure the nation's export-based capacity to import. Prebisch and Singer have argued that N has a tendency to decline for developing nations because most of their productivity increases are passed on in the form of lower prices for their agricultural exports. Empirical studies indicate that N has declined over the past century but I has increased substantially for developing nations.

5. Growth could result in such a large deterioration in a developing nation's terms of trade as to make it worse off after growth than before (immiserizing growth).

6. Developing nations face larger short-run fluctuations in their export prices and earnings than developed nations because of price-inelastic and unstable demand for supply of their exports. However, this did not seem to have been detrimental to their economic development. In the past, developing nations demanded international commodity agreements to stabilize and increase their export prices and earnings. These involve buffer stocks, export controls, or purchasing agreements. Only a very few of these are in operation today, and none seems particularly effective. The large expenditures that would be required to set up and run international commodity agreements would in all likelihood not represent the best use of resources.

7. During the 1950s, 1960s, and 1970s, most developing nations made a deliberate attempt to industrialize through the policy of import substitution. The results were generally inefficient industries, excessive capital intensity, little labor absorption, and neglect of agriculture.

8. Since the late 1980s, many developing nations have shifted toward an export-oriented strategy and have been paying more attention to their agriculture, and they have experienced more rapid growth and development.

9. The most serious problems facing developing countries today are (1) the conditions of stark poverty prevailing in many countries, particularly those of sub-Saharan Africa, (2) the unsustainable foreign debt of many of the poorest developing countries, and (3) the protectionism in developed countries against developing countries' exports. Developing countries sought to overcome these problems by demanding a New International Economic Order (NIEO). This has not occurred. In 2000 the World Bank sponsored the *Millennium Development Goals (MDG)*, which proposed a program for rich countries to help the poorest developing countries stimulate growth, reduce poverty, and promote sustainable development.

REVIEW QUESTIONS AND PROBLEMS

1. (a) Why do some economists regard traditional international trade theory as irrelevant to the development process?

 (b) How can this charge be answered?

2. Starting with Nation 1's pre-growth production frontier in the left panel of Figure 8.1, draw a new production frontier for Nation 1 showing that:
 (a) The amount of both capital and labor available to Nation 1 doubles.

 (b) Only the amount of capital doubles.

 (c) Only the amount of labor doubles.

3. Draw a hypothetical production frontier for a developing nation that measures primary commodities along the horizontal axis and manufactured goods along the vertical axis. Show on your figure the effect on the nation's production frontier of an improvement in the technology only in primary production.

4. What effect is an improvement in the technology of primary production only likely to have on the terms of trade of a developing country? Why?

5. Draw a figure showing how trade could be a vent for surplus.

6. Taking the index of export prices, import prices, and the volume of exports in a developing nation to be all equal to 100 in 1980, what would the following be in 2003:
 (a) The commodity terms of trade of this nation if the index of its export prices rises by 10 percent but the index of its import prices rises by 20 percent?

 (b) This nation's income terms of trade if the index of export volume grows to 130 by 2003?

 (c) Is the nation better or worse off in 2003 as compared with 1980 from all these changes? Why?

7. With respect to immiserizing growth, explain
 (a) how it can take place in a developing country and

 (b) why it did not seem to have occurred in most developing countries over the past two decades.

8. Draw a figure showing that when the supply of a commodity increases, its equilibrium price will fall by a greater amount the more price-inelastic is the demand curve for the commodity.

9. (a) Why has the New International Economic Order demanded by developing countries not been established?

 (b) In what way did the implementation of the Uruguay Round help developing nations? In what way did it not?

10. Explain the reason rich nations should and should not forgive all of the foreign debt of the poorest developing countries.

SELECTED BIBLIOGRAPHY

Analysis of the relationship between trade, growth, and economic development is found in:

- D. Salvatore, *International Economics*, 9th ed. (Wiley, 2007), chs. 7 and 11.
- D. Salvatore, "International Trade Policies, Industrialization, and Economic Development," *International Trade Journal*, Spring 1996, pp. 21–47.
- D. Greenaway, W. Morgan, and P. Wright, "Trade Liberalization and Growth in Developing Countries," *Journal of Development Economics*, February 2002, pp. 229–244.

For a discussion and measurement of the commodity terms of trade and export instability, and their effect on economic development, see:

- P. Cashin and C. J. McDermott, "The Long-Run Behavior of Commodity Prices: Small Trends and Big Variability," *IMF Staff Papers*, vol. 49, no. 2, 2002, pp. 175–199.
- United Nations, *Trade and Development Report* (Geneva: UNCTAD, 2008).

The classics on import substitution are:

- H. Bruton, "A Reconsideration of Import Substitution," *Journal of Economic Perspectives*, June 1998, pp. 903–936.

For conditions in and policies toward developing countries, see:

- E. Grilli and D. Salvatore, eds., *Handbook of Economic Development* (Westport, Conn.: Greenwood Press, 1994).
- World Bank, *World Development Report* (Washington, D.C.: World Bank, 2008).

The importance of the Uruguay Round to developing countries is examined in:

- W. Martin and L. A. Winters, eds., *The Uruguay Round and the Developing Countries* (Washington, DC: World Bank, 1995).

The agenda for the Doha Round of trade negotiations is examined in:

- A. McGuirk, "The Doha Development Agenda," *Finance and Development*, September 2002, pp. 4–7.

Globalization and the problem of poverty are discussed in:

- The World Bank, *Globalization, Growth and Poverty* (Washington, D.C.: The World Bank, 2002).
- J. Sachs, *The End of Poverty* (New York: Penguin Press, 2005).

- D. Salvatore, "Economic Growth, Cross-Country Inequality, and World Poverty during Globalization," *Journal of Policy Modeling*, June 2007, pp. 635–642.

INTERNet

The data and other information used in this chapter are found in the *2008 World Bank's World Development Report*, the International Monetary Fund's (IMF) 2008 *International Financial Statistics* and the *April 2008 World Economic Outlook*, the United Nations Conference on Trade and Development (UNCTAD's) *2008 Trade and Development Report*, and the United Nations Development Program's (UNDP's) *2007–2008 Human Development Report*. All reports except International Financial Statistics are on the Internet, respectively, at:

http://www.worldbank.org/html/wdr/wdr2008

http://www.imf.org/external/pubs/ft/weo/2008/01/index.htm

http://www.unctad.org/en/docs/tdr2008_en.pdf

http://hdr.undp.org/en/reports/global/hdr2007-2008/

International Resource Movements and Multinational Corporations

After studying this chapter, you should be able to:

- Understand the different types of foreign investments
- Describe the motives for international portfolio investments
- Describe the motives for foreign direct investments
- Identify the effects of international capital flows on investing and host countries
- Understand the reasons for the existence of multinational corporations
- Identify the effects of multinational corporations in the home and host countries
- Understand the motives and effects of international labor migration

CHAPTER OUTLINE

KEY TERMS

Portfolio investments	Vertical integration
Direct investments	Multinational corporations (MNCs)
Portfolio theory	Transfer pricing
Risk diversification	Brain drain
Horizontal integration	

9.1 INTRODUCTION

So far, we have dealt almost exclusively with commodity trade and have assumed no international resource movement. However, capital, labor, and technology do move across national boundaries. In some ways, international trade and movements of productive resources can be regarded

as substitutes for one another. For example, a relatively capital-abundant and labor-scarce country, such as the United States, could either export capital-intensive commodities or export capital itself, and either import labor-intensive products or allow the immigration of workers from countries with plentiful labor supplies. As in the case of international trade, the movement of productive resources from nations with relative abundance and low remuneration to nations with relative scarcity and high remuneration has a tendency to equalize factor returns internationally and generally increases welfare. Since multinational corporations are an important vehicle for the international flows of capital, labor, and technology, we also devote a great deal of attention to this relatively new and crucial type of economic enterprise.

In Section 9.2, we examine the different types of foreign investments. In Section 9.3, we present some data on international capital flows. In Sections 9.4 and 9.5, we examine, respectively, the motives for international portfolio and direct investments. Section 9.6 examines the effects of international capital flows on investing and host countries. In Section 9.7, we discuss the reasons for the existence of multinational corporations. Sections 9.8 and 9.9 examine the problems created by multinational corporations in the home and host countries, respectively. Finally, Section 9.10 deals with international labor migration. The appendix shows how to measure the effects of international capital inflows and migration.

9.2 TYPES OF FOREIGN INVESTMENTS

Portfolio investments The purchase of purely financial assets, such as bonds and stocks (if the stock purchase represents less than 10 percent of the stock of a corporation), usually arranged through banks and investment funds.

There are two main types of foreign investments: portfolio investments and direct investments. Portfolio investments are purely financial assets, such as bonds, denominated in a national currency. With bonds, the investor simply lends capital to get fixed payouts or a return at regular intervals and then receives the face value of the bond at a prespecified date. Most foreign investments prior to World War I were of this type and flowed primarily from the United Kingdom to the "regions of recent settlement," such as the United States and Canada, for railroad construction and the opening up of new lands and sources of raw materials. The U.S. government also defines as a portfolio investment stock purchases that involve less than 10 percent of the voting stock of a corporation (a purchase of 10 percent or more of the voting stock of a corporation is regarded as a direct investment). With stocks, the investor purchases equity, or a claim on the net worth of the firm. Portfolio or financial investments take place primarily through financial institutions such as banks and investment funds. International portfolio investments collapsed after World War I and have only revived since the 1960s.

Direct investments Real investments in factories, capital goods, land, and inventories where both capital and management are involved and the investor retains control over the use of the invested capital.

Direct investments, on the other hand, are real investments in factories, capital goods, land, and inventories where both capital and management are involved and the investor retains control over the use of the invested capital. Direct investment usually takes the form of a firm starting a subsidiary or

Concept
Check

What are the different types of international capital flows?

taking control of another firm (e.g., by purchasing a majority of the stock). Any purchase of 10 percent or more of the stock of a firm, however, is defined as direct investment by the U.S. government. In the international context, direct investments are usually undertaken by multinational corporations engaged in manufacturing, resource extraction, or services. Direct investments are now as important as portfolio investments as forms or channels of international private capital flows.

9.3 DATA ON INTERNATIONAL CAPITAL FLOWS

We now present some data on the size and composition of U.S. capital investments in foreign nations and foreign capital investments in the United States from 1950 to 2006.

We can see from Table 9.1 that both U.S. private holdings of foreign long-term securities (stocks and bonds) and foreign private holdings of U.S. long-term securities increased very rapidly from 1950 to 2006, with the former a little higher than the latter at the end of 2006. Table 9.1 also shows the value of U.S. *direct* investments abroad and foreign *direct* investments in the United States at the end of various years. Foreign direct investments are valued at historical cost and current or replacement cost (the latter available only from 1976). The need to supplement the historical values of foreign direct investments with those at current cost arises because most U.S. foreign direct investments occurred in the 1960s and 1970s and require significantly larger adjustments for the cumulative effects of inflation than foreign direct investments in the United States, which occurred mostly since the 1980s. Table 9.1 shows that both the stock of U.S. direct investments abroad and foreign direct investments in the United States also increased very rapidly

Table 9.1. *U.S. Foreign Long-Term Private International Investment Position in Selected Years, 1950–2006 (billions of U.S. dollars, at historical-cost and current-cost basis, at year end)*

Year	1950	1960	1970	1980	1985	1990	1995	2000	2006
U.S. assets abroad									
Foreign securities	4.3	9.5	20.9	62.5	119.4	342.3	1,203.9	2,425.5	5,604.5
Direct investments at									
Historical cost	11.8	31.9	75.5	214.5	230.3	421.5	711.6	1,316.2	2,454.7
Current cost	—	—	—	388.1	371.0	616.7	885.5	1,531.6	2,936.0
Foreign assets in the U.S.									
U.S. securities	2.9	9.3	34.8	74.1	207.9	460.6	969.8	2,623.0	5,372.4
Direct investments at									
Historical cost	3.4	6.9	13.3	83.0	184.6	403.7	535.6	1,256.9	1,843.9
Current cost	—	—	—	127.1	247.2	505.3	680.1	1,421.0	2,151.6

Source: U.S. Department of Commerce, *Survey of Current Business* (Washington, D.C.: U.S. Government Printing Office, July 2008, pp. 18–19 and p. 23, and previous issues).

Table 9.2. *U.S. Direct Investments Abroad by Area in Selected Years, 1950–2006 (billions of U.S. dollars, at historical-cost basis, at year end)*

Year	Total	Canada	Europe	Latin America	Asia and Pacific	of which Japan	Others
1950	11.8	3.6	1.7	4.6	0.3	0.0	1.6
1960	31.9	11.2	7.0	8.4	1.2	0.3	4.1
1970	78.2	22.8	24.5	14.8	8.3	1.5	7.8
1980	215.6	45.0	96.5	38.9	25.3	6.2	9.9
1985	230.3	46.9	105.2	28.3	35.3	9.2	14.6
1990	421.5	68.4	204.2	72.5	63.6	21.0	12.8
1995	711.6	81.4	363.5	122.8	126.0	39.2	17.9
2000	1,316.2	132.5	687.3	266.6	207.1	57.1	22.7
2006	2,454.7	230.0	1,341.1	427.4	405.5	92.4	50.7

Source: U.S. Department of Commerce, *Survey of Current Business* (Washington, D.C.: U.S. Government Printing Office, July 2008, p. 32 and previous issues).

from 1950 to 2006 and were higher at current cost than at historical cost at the end of 2006.

Table 9.2 shows that from 1950 and 2006, the stock of U.S. direct investments in Europe grew much more rapidly than the stock of U.S. direct investments in Canada and Latin America. This was due to the rapid growth of the European Union and the desire on the part of the United States to avoid the common external tariff imposed by the EU on imports from outside the EU. Note that U.S. direct investments in Latin America were actually lower in 1985 than in 1980 as a result of the international debt problem of the Latin American countries (discussed in Section 8.10). Also note that U.S. direct investments in Japan increased less than elsewhere since 1995 because of stagnation in Japan during the 1990s and 2000s.

Table 9.3 separates U.S. direct investments abroad and foreign direct investments in the United States into manufacturing, finance (excluding depository institutions), and others (mostly services other than financial services). Data on finance are available only since 1985. The table shows that direct investments in finance and other categories grew much more rapidly than direct investments in manufacturing since 1985. Case Study 9-1 shows the yearly flows of foreign direct investments into the United States from 1980 to 2006.

Concept Check

How much in international capital inflows and outflows has the United States had?

9.4 MOTIVES FOR INTERNATIONAL PORTFOLIO INVESTMENTS

The basic motive for international portfolio investments is to earn higher returns abroad. Thus, residents of one country purchase bonds of another country if the returns on bonds are higher in the other country. This is

Table 9.3. *U.S. Foreign Direct Investment Position in Selected Years, 1950–2006 (billions of U.S. dollars, at historical-cost basis, at year end)*

Year	1950	1960	1970	1980	1985	1990	1995	2000	2006
U.S. investments abroad									
Manufacturing	3.8	11.1	31.0	89.3	94.7	168.0	250.3	343.9	466.7
Finance	—	—	—	—	22.5	109.4	228.7	257.2	497.3
Other	8.0	20.8	44.5	126.1	113.1	149.6	238.5	715.1	1,490.7
Total	11.8	31.9	75.5	215.4	230.3	427.0	717.5	1,316.2	2,454.7
Foreign investments in the U.S.									
Manufacturing	1.1	2.6	6.1	33.0	59.6	152.8	214.5	480.6	581.1
Finance	—	—	—	—	35.5	70.4	115.6	217.0	258.7
Other	2.3	4.3	7.2	50.0	89.5	171.7	205.5	559.3	1,004.1
Total	3.4	6.9	13.3	83.0	184.6	394.9	535.6	1,256.9	1,843.9

Source: U.S. Department of Commerce, *Survey of Current Business* (Washington, D.C.: U.S. Government Printing Office, July 2008, pp. 34–35 and previous issues).

the simple and straightforward outcome of yield maximization and tends to equalize returns internationally. According to the basic (two-nation) Heckscher–Ohlin model, returns on capital are originally higher in the nation having the lower overall relative capital–labor ratio. Residents of one country may also purchase stock in a corporation in another country if they expect the future profitability of the foreign corporation to be greater than that of domestic corporations. (For simplicity, here we ignore the greater transaction and other costs usually involved in holding foreign securities.)

The problem with this explanation is that it cannot account for *observed* two-way capital flows. That is, if returns on securities are lower in one nation than in another nation, this could explain the flow of capital investments from the former nation to the latter, but is inconsistent with the simultaneous flow of capital in the opposite direction, which is often observed in the real world (see Tables 9.1 and 9.3).

To explain two-way international capital flows, the element of risk must be introduced. That is, investors are interested not only in the rate of return but also in the risk associated with a particular investment. The risk with bonds consists of bankruptcy and the variability in their market value. With stocks, the risk consists of bankruptcy, even greater variability in market value, and the possibility of lower than anticipated returns. Thus, investors maximize returns for a given level of risk and generally accept a higher risk only if returns are higher.

For example, suppose that we deal with stocks and measure risk by the variability (variance) of returns about the average. Suppose also that both stocks A and B have a rate of return of 30 percent on average, but there is a 50-50 chance that the yield will be either 20 percent or 40 percent on stock A and 10 percent or 50 percent on stock B. Stock B is then clearly riskier

CASE STUDY 9-1

Fluctuations in Foreign Direct Investment Flows to the United States

Table 9.4 shows that the level of foreign direct investments (FDI) in the United States was $16.9 billion in 1980. It declined to $10.4 billion in 1983 (a recession year) before rising to $68.3 billion in 1989. Afterwards, it declined to $19.8 billion in 1992 (another recession year) and then rose to the all-time high of $321.3 billion in 2000. It declined between 2001 and 2003 because of recession in 2001 and slow growth in 2002 and 2003, and it was $242.0 in 2006. Thus, flows of FDI to the United States seem to be cyclical, rising during periods of high growth and falling during periods of recession or slow growth.

During the second half of the 1980s, many Americans became concerned that foreigners, particularly the Japanese, were "buying up" America. These fears subsided during the early 1990s, as slow growth and recession made FDI in the United States less attractive to foreigners. With the resumption of rapid growth in 1993, FDI in the United Stated shot up again to much higher levels than during the late 1980s, but with the United States doing much better in international competitiveness than in the 1980s (see Case Study 4–5), the new upsurge in FDI did not cause much concern and was actually welcomed as contributing to rapid growth in the U.S. economy. Foreign acquisitions

of high-tech American firms in recent years, however, is causing some anxiety that this could undermine U.S. international competitiveness and threaten national security.

Table 9.4. *Foreign Direct Investment Flows to the United States in Selected Years, 1980–2006 (billions of U.S. dollars)*

Year	FDI	Year	FDI
1980	16.9	1994	46.1
1981	25.2	1995	57.8
1982	12.6	1996	86.5
1983	10.4	1997	105.6
1984	24.5	1998	179.0
1985	19.7	1999	289.4
1986	35.4	2000	321.3
1987	58.5	2001	167.0
1988	57.7	2002	84.4
1989	68.3	2003	63.8
1990	48.5	2004	146.0
1991	23.2	2005	112.6
1992	19.8	2006	242.0
1993	51.4		

Source: U.S. Department of Commerce, *Survey of Current Business* (Washington, D.C.: U.S. Government Printing Office, July 2008, pp. 66–67).

Concept Check

What are the motives for international portfolio investments?

than stock A. Since both stocks have the same yield on the average, investors should purchase stock A to minimize risks.

However, if the yield on stock A falls when the yield on stock B rises and vice versa (i.e., if changes in yields are inversely, or negatively, correlated over time), then by holding both stocks, the investor can still receive a yield of 30 percent on average but with a much lower risk. That is, the risk of a lower than average yield on stock A at any point is more or less matched by the tendency for the yield on stock B to be higher than average at the same

How can risk
diversification ex-
plain two-way in-
ternational portfolio
investments?

Portfolio theory
Maintains that by
investing in securities
with yields that are
inversely related over
time, a given yield
can be obtained at
a smaller risk or a
higher yield can be
obtained at the same
level of risk for the
portfolio as a whole.

Risk diversification
Investments in
securities with yields
that are inversely, or
negatively, correlated
or investments in
different lines of
products in order
to spread and thus
reduce the overall
risks of the total
investments.

time. As a result, the risk of a portfolio including *both* stock A and stock B is substantially reduced.

Portfolio theory thus tells us that by investing in securities with yields that are inversely related over time, a given yield can be obtained at a smaller risk or a higher yield can be obtained for the same level of risk for the portfolio as a whole. Since yields on foreign securities (depending primarily on the different economic conditions abroad) are more likely to be inversely related to yields on domestic securities, a portfolio including both domestic and foreign securities can have a higher average yield and/or lower risk than a portfolio containing only domestic securities.

To achieve such a balanced portfolio, a two-way capital flow may be required. For example, if stock A (with the same average yield but lower risk than stock B) is available in one country, while stock B (with yields inversely related to the yields on stock A) is available in another country, investors in the first nation must also purchase stock B (i.e., invest in the second nation), and investors in the second nation must also purchase stock A (i.e., invest in the first nation) to achieve a balanced portfolio. Risk diversification can thus explain two-way international portfolio investments.

Throughout the preceding discussion, it was implicitly assumed that investors know precisely the average return on stocks and their variability. In reality, this is seldom known in advance. Thus, investors must determine for themselves (from their market knowledge and intuition) what the average returns and variabilities are likely to be in deciding which stocks to purchase. Since different individuals can have different expectations for the same stocks, it is possible that some investors in each nation think that stocks in the other nation are a better buy. This provides an additional explanation for two-way international portfolio investments.

9.5 MOTIVES FOR DIRECT FOREIGN INVESTMENTS

The motives for direct investments abroad are generally the same as for portfolio investments—that is, to earn higher returns (possibly resulting from higher growth rates abroad, more favorable tax treatment, or greater availability of infrastructures) and to diversify risks. Indeed, it has been found that firms with a strong international orientation (either through exports or through foreign production and/or sales facilities) are more profitable and have a much smaller variability in profits than purely domestic firms.

Although these reasons are sufficient to explain international portfolio investments, they leave unanswered the basic question of why the residents of a nation do not borrow from other nations and themselves make real investments in their own nation rather than accept *direct* investments from abroad. There are several possible explanations for this. The most important is that many large corporations often have some unique production knowledge or managerial skill that could easily and profitably be utilized abroad and

Horizontal integration The production abroad of a differentiated product that is also produced at home.

over which the corporation wants to retain direct control. In such a situation, the firm will make direct investments abroad. This involves horizontal integration, or the production abroad of a differentiated product that is also produced at home.

For example, IBM has a particular computer technology over which it wants to retain direct control but which it can easily duplicate abroad so as to serve the foreign market better (by adapting to local conditions) than through exports. IBM does not want to license foreign producers because it wants to retain complete control over its trade secrets and patents and to ensure consistent quality and service. Even if IBM were willing to negotiate licensing agreements with foreign producers, this would not be feasible in view of the very rapid rate of technological innovations in the field. The situation is basically the same for Xerox, Gillette, Toyota, and many other multinational corporations, and it is the motive behind most direct foreign investments in manufacturing in developed nations.

Vertical integration The expansion of a firm backward to supply its own raw materials and intermediate products and/or forward to provide its own sales or distribution networks.

Another important reason for direct foreign investments is to obtain control of a needed raw material and thus ensure an uninterrupted supply at the lowest possible cost. This is referred to as vertical integration and was the form of most direct foreign investments in developing countries and in some mineral-rich developed countries. Thus, American and foreign corporations own mines in Canada, Jamaica, Venezuela, Australia, and other nations, and foreigners own some coal mines in the United States. Vertical integration involving multinational corporations can also go forward into the ownership of sales or distribution networks abroad, as is the case with most of the world's major automobile producers.

Still other reasons for direct foreign investments are to avoid tariffs and other restrictions that nations impose on imports or to take advantage of various government subsidies to encourage direct foreign investments. Examples of the former are the large-scale direct investments made by U.S. firms in the EU countries and some direct foreign investments in manufacturing in developing nations. Examples of the latter are the direct foreign investments made in developing nations and in depressed regions of some developed nations. Other possible reasons for direct foreign investments are to enter a foreign market so as to share in the profits, to purchase a promising foreign firm to avoid its future competition and the possible loss of export markets, or because only a large foreign multinational corporation can obtain the necessary financing to enter the market.

Concept Check

What are the motives for direct foreign investments?

Two-way direct foreign investments can then be explained by some industries being more advanced in one nation (such as the computer industry in the United States), while other industries are more efficient in other nations (such as the automobile industry in Japan). Direct foreign investments have been greatly facilitated (in a sense made possible) by the very rapid advances in transportation (i.e., jet travel) and communications (i.e., international telephone lines and international data transmission and processing) that

have occurred since the end of World War II. These advances permit the headquarters of multinational corporations to exert immediate and direct control over the operations of their subsidiaries around the world, and thus facilitate and encourage direct investments abroad.

The regional distribution of foreign direct investments around the world also seems to depend on geographical proximity or established trade relations. For example, the United States is the main supplier of foreign direct investments to Latin America, Bangladesh, Pakistan, the Philippines, and Saudi Arabia; foreign direct investments from the European Union flow mostly to Ghana and Morocco in Africa, Brazil in Latin America, India, Sri Lanka, and Vietnam in Asia, and to the former communist countries in Eastern Europe; and Japan is the main supplier of foreign direct investments to South Korea, Singapore, Taiwan, and Thailand. Case Study 9-2 shows the outward and inward stock of foreign direct investment in various regions and selected countries and years.

9.6 EFFECTS OF INTERNATIONAL CAPITAL FLOWS ON INVESTING AND HOST COUNTRIES

We now examine the welfare effects of international capital flows on the investing and host countries. If capital is free to move internationally, it will flow from the nation of lower returns to the nation of higher returns until returns have been equalized in the two countries. This leads to greater efficiency in the use of capital internationally and higher world output and welfare (see Appendix A9.1 for a graphical proof). This is similar to the export of capital-intensive commodities from relatively capital-abundant countries. The capital-rich nation is now exporting capital instead of capital-intensive commodities and importing labor instead of labor-intensive commodities. Just as trade based on comparative advantage increases the efficiency in the use of world resources and increases world welfare, so does the export of capital by capital-rich countries to capital-poor countries.

Specifically, assuming two factors of production (capital and labor), both fully employed before and after the capital transfer, the investing country will experience an increase in the average return on capital but a decrease in the average return to labor decreases (because each unit of labor will now have less capital to work with). Thus, while the investing country as a whole gains from investing abroad, there is a redistribution of domestic income from labor to capital. It is for this reason that organized labor in the United States is opposed to U.S. investments abroad. On the other hand, while the host country also gains from receiving foreign investments, these investments lead to a redistribution of domestic income from capital to labor. If we allow for less than full employment, foreign investments tend to depress the level of employment in the investing country and increase it in the host country

CASE STUDY 9-2

The Stock of Foreign Direct Investments around the World

Table 9.5 shows the outward and inward stock of foreign direct investment (i.e., the stock of foreign direct investment made and received) by region and selected country in 1990, 2000, and 2006. The table shows that in 2006 the United States had the largest outward and inward stock of foreign direct investment (FDI). For the outward stock of FDI, the United States was followed by the United Kingdom, France, Germany, the Netherlands, Switzerland, Spain, Belgium, Japan, Canada, and Italy, in that order.

For the inward stock of FDI, the United States was followed by the United Kingdom,

France, Belgium and Luxembourg, the Netherlands, Germany, Canada, and Spain. In 2006, the outward stock of FDI of developing countries was about one-seventh that of developed countries, while their stock of inward FDI was a little over one-third that of developed countries. Of the total inward stock of FDI of all developing countries, 72 percent was in Asia (with Hong Kong having by far the largest share) and 24 percent was in Latin America. The inward stock of FDI of Africa and South-Eastern Europe and CIS (Commonwealth of Independent States) was small (see the table).

Table 9.5. *Stock of Outward and Inward FDI by Region and Selected Country in 1990, 2000, and 2006 (billions of U.S. dollars)*

	Outward			Inward		
	1990	*2000*	*2006*	*1990*	*2000*	*2006*
Developed countries	1,669	5,329	10,711	1,414	4,031	8,454
United States[a]	431	1,316	2,384	395	1,257	1,789
United Kingdom	229	898	1,487	204	439	1,135
France	110	445	1,080	87	260	783
Germany	152	542	1,005	111	272	502
Netherlands	107	305	653	69	244	451
Switzerland	66	232	545	34	87	207
Spain	16	168	508	66	156	443
Belgium	41	180	462	58	195	603
Japan	201	278	450	10	50	108
Canada	85	238	449	113	213	385
Italy	60	180	376	60	121	295
Developing countries	146	859	1,600	365	1,708	3,156
Asia	66	610	1,152	198	1,069	1,927
Hong Kong (China)	12	388	689	45	455	769
Singapore	8	57	118	30	113	210
China	4	28	73	21	193	293
Latin America	60	204	388	105	481	909
Brazil	41	52	87	37	103	222
Mexico	3	8	35	22	97	229
Africa	20	44	60	59	151	315
South-Eastern Europe and CIS	0	22	164	0	71	389
World	1,815	6,209	12,474	1,779	5,810	11,999

[a]U.S. values differ a little from those in Tables 12.1 to 12.3 because of different data collection methods.

Source: UNCTAD, *World Investment Report* (Geneva: United Nations, 2007).

and, once again, can be expected to be opposed by labor in the former and to increase employment and benefit labor in the latter.

International capital transfers also affect the balance of payments of the investing and host countries. A nation's balance of payments measures its total receipts from and total expenditures in the rest of the world. In the year in which the foreign investment takes place, the foreign expenditures of the investing country increase and cause a balance-of-payments deficit (an excess of expenditures abroad over foreign receipts). This was certainly a major contributor to the huge balance-of-payments deficits of the United States during the 1960s and led to restrictions on U.S. foreign investments from 1965 to 1974. Of course, the counterpart to the worsening in the investing nation's balance of payments is the improvement in the host nation's balance of payments in the year in which it receives the foreign investment.

However, the initial capital transfer and increased expenditures abroad of the investing country are likely to be mitigated by increased exports of capital goods, spare parts, and other products of the investing country, and by the subsequent flow of profits to the investing country. It has been estimated that, on average, the "payback" period for the initial capital transfer is between five and ten years. Another effect to consider in the long run is whether foreign investments will lead to the replacement of the investing country's exports and even to imports of commodities previously exported. Thus, while the immediate effect on the balance of payments is negative in the investing country and positive in the host country, the long-run effects are less certain. Since foreign investments for most developed countries are two-way (see Sections 9.4 and 9.5), these short-run and long-run balance-of-payments effects are mostly neutralized, except for a nation such as Japan, with investments abroad greatly exceeding foreign investments received and for developing countries that are primarily recipients of foreign investments and chronically face serious balance-of-payments difficulties (see Case Study 9-2).

Concept Check

What are the effects of international capital flows on investing and host countries?

Another important welfare effect of foreign investments on both the investing and host countries results from different rates of taxation and foreign earnings in various countries. Thus, if corporate taxes are 35 percent of earnings in the United States but only 25 percent in England, it is only natural for U.S. firms to invest in England or reroute foreign sales through subsidiaries there in order to pay the lower tax rate. Because most nations, including the United States, are signatories of double-taxation agreements (to avoid double taxation—on equity grounds), the United States would collect a tax of only 10 percent on foreign earnings (the difference between the domestic tax rate of 35 percent and the foreign tax rate of 25 percent) when foreign earnings are repatriated. As a result, the tax base and the amount of taxes collected decline in the investing and rise in the host country.

Foreign investments, by affecting output and the volume of trade of both investing and host countries, are also likely to affect the terms of trade. However, how the terms of trade will change depends on conditions in both

nations, and not much can be said a priori. Finally, foreign investments may affect the investing nation's technological lead and the host country's control over its economy and ability to conduct its own independent economic policy. Since these and other effects of international capital transfers usually result from the operations of multinational corporations, they are examined in the next section.

9.7 REASONS FOR THE EXISTENCE OF MULTINATIONAL CORPORATIONS

Multinational corporations (MNCs) Firms that own, control, or manage production and distribution facilities in several countries.

One of the most significant international economic developments of the postwar period is the proliferation of multinational corporations (MNCs). These are firms that own, control, or manage production facilities in several countries. Today MNCs account for about 25 percent of world output, and *intrafirm* trade (i.e., trade among the parent firm and its foreign affiliates) is estimated to be about one-third of total world trade in manufacturing. Some MNCs, such as General Motors and Exxon, are truly giants, with yearly sales in the tens of billions of dollars and exceeding the total national income of all but a handful of nations. Furthermore, most international direct investments today are undertaken by MNCs. In the process, the parent firm usually provides its foreign affiliates with managerial expertise, technology, parts, and a marketing organization in return for some of the affiliates' output and earnings. In this section, we examine the reasons for the existence of MNCs.

The basic reason for the existence of MNCs is the competitive advantage of a global network of production and distribution. This competitive advantage arises in part from vertical and horizontal integration with foreign affiliates. By *vertical* integration, most MNCs can ensure their supply of foreign raw materials and intermediate products and circumvent (with more efficient *intrafirm* trade) the imperfections often found in foreign markets. They can also provide better distribution and service networks. By *horizontal* integration through foreign affiliates, MNCs can better protect and exploit their monopoly power, adapt their products to local conditions and tastes, and ensure consistent product quality.

The competitive advantage of MNCs is also based on economies of scale in production, financing, research and development (R&D), and the gathering of market information. The large output of MNCs allows them to carry division of labor and specialization in production much further than smaller national firms. Product components requiring only unskilled labor can be produced in low-wage nations and shipped elsewhere for assembly. Furthermore, MNCs and their affiliates usually have greater access, at better terms, to international capital markets than do purely national firms. They can also concentrate R&D in one or a few advanced nations best suited for these purposes because of the greater availability of technical personnel

and facilities. Finally, foreign affiliates funnel information from around the world to the parent firm, placing it in a better position than national firms to evaluate, anticipate, and take advantage of changes in comparative costs, consumers' tastes, and market conditions generally.

The large corporation invests abroad when expected profits on additional investments in its industry are higher abroad. Since the corporation usually has a competitive advantage and knows its industry best, it does not usually consider the possibility of higher returns in every other domestic industry before it decides to invest abroad. That is, differences in expected rates of profits domestically and abroad in the particular industry are of crucial importance in a large corporation's decision to invest abroad. This explains, for example, Toyota automotive investments in the United States and IBM computer investments in Japan. All of these factors imply that MNCs are *oligopolists* selling for the most part *differentiated products*, often developed as described by the *technological gap* and *product cycle models*, and produced under strong *economies of scale* (see Section 4.8). Examples of the products sold by MNCs are motor vehicles, petroleum products, electronics, metals, office equipment, chemicals, and food.

MNCs are also in a much better position to control or change to their advantage the environment in which they operate than are purely national firms. For example, in determining where to set up a plant to produce a component, an MNC can and usually does "shop around" for the low-wage nation that offers the most incentives in the form of tax holidays, subsidies, and other tax and trade benefits. The sheer size of most MNCs in relation to most host nations also means the MNCs are in a better position than purely national firms to influence the policies of local governments and extract benefits. Furthermore, MNCs can buy up promising local firms to avoid future competition and are in a much better position than purely domestic firms to engage in other practices that restrict local trade and increase their profits. MNCs, through greater diversification, also face lower risks and generally earn higher profits than purely national firms.

Transfer pricing
The overpricing or underpricing of products in the intrafirm trade of multinational corporations in an attempt to shift income and profits from high- to low-tax nations.

Finally, by artificially overpricing components shipped *to* an affiliate in a higher-tax nation and underpricing products shipped *from* the affiliate in the high-tax nation, an MNC can minimize its tax bill. This is called transfer pricing and can arise in intrafirm trade as opposed to trade among independent firms or conducted at "arm's length."

Concept Check

What are the reasons for the existence of multinational corporations?

In the final analysis, it is a combination of all or most of these factors that gives MNCs their competitive advantage vis-à-vis purely national firms and explains the proliferation and great importance of MNCs today. That is, by vertical and horizontal integration with foreign affiliates, by taking advantage of economies of scale, and by being in a better position than purely national firms to control the environment in which they operate, MNCs have become the most prominent form of private international economic organization in existence today. Case Study 9-3 examines the world's largest MNCs.

CASE STUDY 9-3

The World's Largest Multinational Industrial Corporations

Table 9.6 gives the home nation of the parent firm, the major industry, the level of yearly sales, and the percentage of those sales made outside the home country for the world's largest industrial multinational corporations (MNCs) with 2005 sales in excess of $90 billion. From the table we see that 6 of these 15 MNCs have headquarters in the United States, 2 each in Japan and Germany, and 1 each in UK/Netherlands, the United Kingdom, Germany/United States, France, and Italy. Six each are in petroleum and motor vehicles, 2 in electronics, and 1 in computers. British petroleum has the highest percentage of foreign sales (79.0), and the simple percentage average of foreign to total sales for all the firms is 55.5.

Table 9.6. *The World's Largest Industrial Multinational Corporations in 2005*

Rank	Company	Home Nation	Industry	Yearly Sales (billion $)	Percentage of Foreign Sales
1	Exxonmobil Corporation	United States	Petroleum	359.0	69.2
2	Royal Dutch/Shell Group	United Kingdom/ Netherlands	Petroleum	306.7	60.0
3	British Petroleum	United Kingdom	Petroleum	253.6	79.0
4	Chevron Corporation	United States	Petroleum	193.6	51.6
5	General Motors	United States	Motor vehicles	192.6	33.9
6	DaimlerChrysler	Germany/ United States	Motor vehicles	186.5	41.3
7	Toyota Motor Corporation	Japan	Motor vehicles	186.2	63.2
8	Total	France	Petroleum	178.3	74.6
9	Ford Motor Company	United States	Motor vehicles	177.1	45.4
10	Mitsubishi Corporation	Japan	Motor vehicles	168.7	17.6
11	General Electric	United States	Electronics	149.7	40.0
12	Volkswagen Group	Germany	Motor vehicles	118.6	72.4
13	Siemens AG	Germany	Electronics	96.0	67.1
14	ENI	Italy	Petroleum	91.8	55.4
15	IBM	United States	Computers	91.1	61.6

Source: United Nations, *World Investment Report*, 2007.

9.8 PROBLEMS CREATED BY MULTINATIONAL CORPORATIONS IN THE HOME COUNTRY

While MNCs, by efficiently organizing production and distribution on a worldwide basis, can increase world output and welfare, they can also create problems in both the home and host countries. The most controversial of the alleged harmful effects of MNCs on the *home* nation is the loss of domestic jobs resulting from foreign direct investments. These are likely to be unskilled and semiskilled production jobs in which the home nation has a comparative disadvantage. It is for this reason that organized labor in the United States and other major home nations opposes direct foreign investments by MNCs. However, some clerical, managerial, and technical jobs are also likely to be created in the headquarters of the MNC in the home nation as a result of foreign direct investments. Even if the number of jobs lost exceeds the number created, it may be that the home nation would have lost these jobs anyway to foreign competitors and would have had no jobs created at home without the direct foreign investment. The extent to which this may be true depends, of course, on the type of direct foreign investment and the circumstances under which it takes place. See Case Study 9-4 for the employment of workers abroad by U.S. MNCs.

A related problem is the export of advanced technology to be combined with other cheaper foreign factors to maximize corporate profits. It is claimed that this may undermine the technological superiority and future of the home nation. However, against this possible harmful effect is the tendency of MNCs to concentrate their R&D in the home nation, thus allowing it to maintain its technological lead. Whether or not MNCs, on balance, undermine the technological superiority of the home country is a hotly debated question to which no clear-cut answer is yet possible.

Another possible harmful effect of MNCs on the home country can result from transfer pricing and similar practices, and from shifting their operations to lower tax nations, which reduce tax revenues and erode the tax base of the home country. This results from common international taxing practice. Specifically, the host country taxes the subsidiary's profits first. To avoid double taxation of foreign subsidiaries, the home country then usually taxes only repatriated profits (if its tax rate is higher than in the host country), and only by the difference in the tax rates.

An example will clarify this point. Suppose that the corporate profit tax is 40 percent in the home country and 30 percent in the host country, and the before-tax risk-adjusted profit rate is 20 percent abroad but 16 percent at home. The MNC will then invest abroad. When 20 percent is earned abroad, the host country gets 6 percent in taxes (at the 30 percent tax rate) and the MNC retains 14 percent. When the MNC repatriates this 14-percent profit, the home country will tax it at the rate of 10 percent (the difference between the domestic and the foreign corporate tax profit rate). Thus, the home

Concept Check

What problems can multinational corporations create for the home country?

CASE STUDY 9-4

Employment of U.S. MNCs Abroad

Table 9.7 shows the number and percentage of workers employed abroad by U.S. MNCs in various nations in 2005. The table shows that U.S. MNCs employed 10.3 million workers abroad in 2005, of which 41.7 percent were in Europe, 25.2 percent in Asia and the Pacific, and 19.7 percent in Latin America and other countries of the Western Hemisphere. The United Kingdom and Canada had the largest number among industrial countries (with 12.1 percent and 10.7 percent of the total, respectively). Mexico came first among developing nations and third among all nations (with 10.0 percent of the total). To be noted that foreign-based MNCs employed 5.1 million workers in the United States in 2005 and, as pointed out in Section 9.8, not all jobs created abroad by U.S. MNCs come at the expense of domestic jobs in the United States.

Table 9.7. *Number of Workers Employed Abroad by U.S. MNCs in 2005 (in thousands)*

Region/Country	Employment	Percentage of Total
Canada	1,107	10.7
Europe, of which	4,306	41.7
United Kingdom	1,252	12.1
Germany	632	6.1
France	620	6.0
Asia and Pacific, of which	2,604	25.2
Japan	555	5.4
China	547	5.3
Australia	321	3.1
Latin America and other Western Hemisphere, of which	2,036	19.7
Mexico	1,037	10.0
Brazil	430	4.2
Africa, of which	179	1.7
Middle East	73	0.7
All countries	10,333	100.0

Source: U.S. Department of Commerce, *Survey of Current Business*, November 2007, p. 58.

country gets only 1.4 percent, and only when the profits are repatriated. The reinvestment of profits abroad in the MNC's affiliate thus amounts to an interest-free loan from the home country. If the corporate profit tax rates of the home and host countries were equal, the home country would collect no

tax at all even when the MNC repatriates its profits. Had the MNC invested in the home country to begin with and earned a profit of 16 percent, the home country would have collected a tax of 6.4 percent (at the 40 percent tax rate). Thus, MNCs reduce tax revenues and erode the tax base of the home country.

Finally, because of their access to international capital markets, MNCs can circumvent domestic monetary policies and make government control over the economy in the home nation more difficult. These alleged harmful effects of MNCs are of crucial importance to the United States, since it is home for about one-third of the largest MNCs. In general, home nations do impose some restrictions on the activities of MNCs, either for balance-of-payments reasons or, more recently, for employment reasons.

9.9 PROBLEMS CREATED BY MULTINATIONAL CORPORATIONS IN THE HOST COUNTRY

Host countries have even more serious complaints against MNCs than home countries. First and foremost is the allegation that MNCs dominate their economies. This is certainly true for Canada, where almost 60 percent of the total capital in manufacturing is owned or controlled by foreigners (40 percent by Americans). It is also true for some of the smaller developing nations. Foreign domination is felt in many different ways in host countries, including (1) the unwillingness of a local affiliate of an MNC to export to a nation deemed unfriendly to the home nation or the requirement to comply with a *home*-nation law prohibiting such exports; (2) the borrowing of funds abroad to circumvent tight domestic credit conditions and the lending of funds abroad when interest rates are low at home; and (3) the effect on national tastes of large-scale advertising for such products as Coca-Cola, McDonald's, and so on.

Another alleged harmful effect of MNCs on the host country is the siphoning off of R&D funds to the home nation. While this may be more efficient for the MNC and the world as a whole, it also keeps the host country technologically dependent. This is especially true and serious for developing nations. MNCs may also absorb local savings and entrepreneurial talent, thus preventing them from being used to establish domestic enterprises that might be more important for national growth and development. The extent to which this occurs, however, is not clear. MNCs may also extract from host nations most of the benefits resulting from their investments, either through tax and tariff benefits or through tax avoidance. In developing nations, foreign direct investments by MNCs in mineral and raw material production have often given rise to complaints of foreign exploitation in the form of low prices paid to host nations, the use of highly capital-intensive production techniques inappropriate for labor-abundant developing nations, lack of training of local labor, overexploitation of natural resources, and creating highly dualistic "enclave" economies.

Most of these complaints are to some extent true, particularly in the case of developing host countries, and they have led many host nations to regulate foreign investments in order to mitigate the harmful effects and increase the possible benefits. Thus, Canada imposed higher taxes on foreign affiliates with less than 25 percent Canadian interest. India specifies the sectors in which direct foreign investments are allowed and sets rules to regulate their operation. Some developing nations allow only *joint ventures* (i.e., local equity participation) and set rules for the transfer of technology and the training of domestic labor, impose limits on the use of imported inputs and the remission of profits, set environmental regulations, and so on. In the extreme, the host nation can nationalize foreign production facilities. However, this is likely to seriously reduce the future flow of direct foreign investments to the nation.

Concept Check

What problems can multinational corporations create for the host country?

Even in the United States, the home of about a third of the largest MNCs, great concern was expressed over foreign control at the height of foreign direct investment flows during the late 1980s. This concern then vanished in the light of the sharp reduction in foreign direct investments in the early 1990s (see Case Study 9-1). Efforts are currently in progress within the EU, OECD, the UN, and UNCTAD to devise an international code of conduct for MNCs. However, since the interests of home and host countries are generally in conflict, it is virtually impossible for such an international code to be very specific. As a result, it is unlikely to succeed in severely restricting most of the abuses of and problems created by MNCs in home and host countries. The Uruguay Round removed only some of the domestic restrictions on FDI.

9.10 MOTIVES AND WELFARE EFFECTS OF INTERNATIONAL LABOR MIGRATION

Labor is generally less mobile internationally than capital. However, great waves of immigrants moved from Europe to the New World during the nineteenth century. This relieved population pressures in Europe and contributed significantly to the rapid growth and development of the New World, especially the United States. International labor migration can take place for economic as well as non-economic reasons. Some of the international migrations that occurred in the nineteenth century and earlier were certainly motivated by the desire to escape political and religious oppression in Europe. However, most international labor migration, particularly since the end of World War II, has been motivated by the prospect of earning higher real wages and income abroad.

The decision to migrate for economic reasons can be analyzed in the same manner and with the same tools as any other investment decision. Specifically, migration, just like any other type of investment, involves both costs and benefits. The costs include the expenditures for transportation and the loss of wages during time spent relocating and searching for a job in the

new nation. In addition, there are many other less quantifiable costs, such as the separation from relatives, friends, and familiar surroundings; the need to learn new customs and often a new language; and the risks involved in finding a job, housing, and so on in a new land. Many of these non-economic costs are greatly reduced by the fact that migrations usually occur in waves and in chains, with many migrants moving together and/or to areas with an already substantial number of earlier migrants from the same place of origin.

The economic benefits of international migration can be measured by the higher real wages and income that the migrant worker can earn abroad during his or her remaining working life, over and above what he or she could have earned at home. Other benefits may be greater educational and job opportunities for the migrants' children. From the excess of returns over costs, an internal rate of return for the migration decision can be estimated, just as for any other type of investment. If this rate of return is sufficiently high to also overcome the non-economic costs associated with migration, then the worker will migrate. Of course, in the real world workers seldom, if ever, have the information to carry out this type of cost-benefit analysis explicitly. Nevertheless, they behave as if they did. This is confirmed by the fact that migrants invariably move from low-wage to high-wage nations. Furthermore, younger workers migrate more readily than older workers because, among other things, they have a longer remaining working life over which to benefit from the higher wages abroad.

Concept Check

What are the motives for and effect of international labor migration?

In general, immigration is good for the country of immigration and emigration because it leads to a more efficient utilization of labor resources (the proof of this is found in Appendix A9.2). But, at least in the short run, native workers receive lower wages than without immigration, while employers gain by being able to pay lower wages. This explains why labor in the United States is generally opposed to immigration while business favors it. In a recent study *George Borjas* (see the Selected Bibliography) estimated that a 10 percent increase in the supply of labor through immigration reduces the wages of native workers by 3 or 4 percent.

So far, we have implicitly assumed that migrants are unskilled. Many of them, however, are skilled and highly trained. Indeed, more and more U.S. high-tech industries, from semiconductors to biotechnology, are depending on immigrant scientists and engineers to remain competitive in the increasingly global marketplace. The problem of the migration of highly skilled workers for the country of emigration is vividly conveyed by the term brain drain. The brain drain is often encouraged by national immigration laws that facilitate the immigration of skilled persons but generally impose serious obstacles to the immigration of unskilled workers. For example, the U.S. H1-B visa program established in 1990 allowed each year 65,000 educated foreigners to fill specialized American jobs, largely in the high-tech industry, for a period of six years if an employer petitions the U.S. Immigration and

Brain drain The migration of highly skilled and trained people from developing nations and from other industrial nations to the United States.

U.S. Immigration and Debate over Immigration Policy

Table 9.8 shows the number of people immigrating to the United States and their percentage of the U.S. population for each decade from 1901 to 2006. The table shows that the number of immigrants into the United States reached almost 9 million, representing over 10 percent of the U.S. population in the 1901–1910 decade. It fell drastically during the 1931–1940 decade because of the Great Depression and the outbreak of World War II. Immigration rose again after World War II and surpassed 9 million in the 1991–2000 decade (but represented only 2.7 percent of the population because of rapid growth of the U.S. population during the past century). With legal immigration rising steeply, the U.S. Congress is considering bills to restrict it (except for highly skilled people).

In 2006, 38.4 million Americans were born elsewhere. This represented 10.1 percent of the entire population for that year, which was higher than in any other year since World War II (the all-time high was 14.7 percent in 1910). The U.S. Census data indicate that nearly 21 percent of recent immigrants over the age of 25 have bachelors' degrees (as compared with about 15 percent for native Americans), but 36 percent do not have a high school diploma (as compared with 17 percent of those born in the United States). Thus, the majority of recent immigrants are either very educated or have little education.

Table 9.8. *U.S. Immigration, 1901–2006*

	Total	
Years	Number	Rate*
1901–1910	8,795	10.4
1911–1920	5,736	5.7
1921–1930	4,107	3.5
1931–1940	528	0.4
1941–1950	1,035	0.7
1951–1960	2,515	1.5
1961–1970	3,322	1.7
1971–1980	4,499	2.0
1981–1990	7,256	3.0
1991–2000	9,081	3.4
2001–2006	6,168	3.5

*Per 1,000 of U.S. population.

Source: *U.S. Statistical Abstract*, 2008, Table 45.

Naturalization Service on their behalf. There are now about 900,000 H1-B employees in the United States.

There is then the problem of illegal migration. This has become a burning issue in the United States, where millions of illegal immigrants work in the underground economy at below minimum wages and with few if any social benefits. In 1986, the United States passed the *Immigration Reform and Control Act of 1986*, which provided (1) amnesty and the possibility of acquiring legal residence and eventual citizenship to illegal aliens who could demonstrate that they had resided in the United States continuously since before January 1, 1982, and (2) fines for employers ranging from $250 to $10,000 for each illegal alien that they hired. By 1995, about 2.5 million aliens had applied for legal status. But this was only one-fifth of the total number of illegal aliens estimated to be in the United States.

In 2005 immigrants represented nearly 23 percent of the *labor force* of Australia, 22 percent of that of Switzerland, 19 percent of Canada, 12 percent of the United States, 10 percent of France, and 8 percent of the United Kingdom. Case Study 9-5 provides historical data on U.S. immigration and summarizes the debate over immigration policy.

SUMMARY

1. In this chapter we examined the effects of international flows of capital, labor, and technology. In some ways, these are substitutes for international commodity trade.

2. Portfolio investments, such as the purchase of bonds, are purely financial assets and take place primarily through banks and investment funds. Direct investments are real investments in factories, capital goods, land, and inventories where both capital and management are involved and the investor retains control over use of the invested capital. International direct investments are usually undertaken by multinational corporations.

3. U.S. private holdings of foreign long-term securities (bonds and stocks) and foreign private holdings of U.S. long-term securities increased sharply from 1950 to 2002. The same is true for foreign direct investments. From 1950 and 2002, the stock of U.S. direct investments in Europe grew much more rapidly than the stock of U.S. direct investments in Canada and Latin America. U.S. direct investments abroad and foreign direct investments in the United States in manufacturing, finance, and services grew much more rapidly than in petroleum. The surge in foreign direct investments in the United States during the second half of the 1990s did not cause as much concern as did that of the second half of the 1980s.

4. The basic motives for international portfolio investments are yield maximization and risk diversification. The latter is also required to explain two-way capital movements.

5. Direct foreign investments are also undertaken for yield maximization and risk diversification, but require additional explanations. These are (1) to exploit abroad some unique production knowledge or managerial skill (horizontal integration), (2) to gain control over a foreign source of a needed raw material or a foreign marketing outlet (vertical integration), (3) to avoid import tariffs and other trade restrictions and/or to take advantage of production subsidies, (4) to enter a foreign market to share in its profits, (5) to acquire a foreign firm in order to avoid future competition, or (6) because of unique ability to obtain financing.

6. International capital transfers increase the national income of both the investing and host countries, but in the investing nation the relative share going to capital rises and the share going to labor falls, while the opposite occurs in the host or receiving nation. In the short run, the balance of payments tends to worsen in the investing nation and improve in the

host nation. In the long run, the balance-of-payments effects of foreign investments on the investing and host nations are less clear cut. Nations with high corporate tax rates encourage investments abroad and thereby lose tax revenues. The terms of trade are also likely to be affected by foreign investments.

7. Multinational corporations have grown to be the most prominent form of private international economic organization today. The basic reason for their existence is the competitive advantage of a global network of production and distribution.

8. Some of the alleged problems created by multinational corporations in the home country are the export of domestic jobs, erosion of the home nation's technological advantage, avoidance of domestic taxes through transfer pricing, and reduced government control over the domestic economy.

9. Host countries complain of loss of sovereignty and domestic research activity, tax avoidance, the utilization of inappropriate technology, and most benefits flowing to the home nation. As a result, most host nations have adopted policies to reduce these alleged harmful effects and increase the possible benefits.

10. International labor migration can occur for economic and non-economic reasons. When the decision to migrate is economic, it can be evaluated in terms of costs and benefits, just as any other investment in human and physical capital. International migration increases real wages in the nation of emigration while it reduces them in the nation of immigration. These changes are accompanied by a net increase in world output. The migration of highly skilled and trained people confers special benefits on the nation of immigration but represents a brain drain on the nation of emigration.

REVIEW QUESTIONS AND PROBLEMS

1. In what sense are international flows of productive resources a substitute for international commodity trade?

2. (a) What is meant by portfolio investments? Through what institutions are they usually undertaken internationally?

 (b) What is meant by direct investments? By what organizations are they usually undertaken internationally?

3. (a) What are the basic motives for international portfolio investments?

 (b) What additional reasons are required to explain direct foreign investments?

4. Determine whether the following statement is true or false and explain why: "The profitability of a portfolio of many securities can never exceed the yield of the highest yield security in the portfolio but it can have a risk lower than the lowest risk security."

5. What is the effect of capital outflows on
 (a) the share of national income going to capital and labor?
 (b) national income?

6. What are some of the problems created by multinational corporations in the home country?

7. (a) What are some of the problems created by multinational corporations in the host country?
 (b) How have host countries attempted to limit the alleged harmful effects and increase the beneficial effects of multinational corporations?

8. Update Table 9.6 for the most recent year for which data are available. How has the ranking of the world's largest corporations changed since 2002?

9. Explain why the rate of return on U.S. direct investment in developing nations often exceeds the rate of return on investment on U.S. direct investments in developed nations.

10. (a) What are the motives for the international migration of workers?
 (b) What is the effect of migration on the nation of immigration and on the nation of emigration?

Analysis of Effects of International Capital Flows and Migration

In this appendix we examine the effects of international capital flows on the investing and host countries and of international labor migration.

A9.1 ANALYSIS OF EFFECTS OF INTERNATIONAL CAPITAL FLOWS ON INVESTING AND HOST COUNTRIES

We have seen in Section 9.6 that if capital is free to move internationally, it will flow from the nation in which its returns are lower to the nation in which the returns are higher. This increases the efficiency in the use of capital and, hence, world output and welfare. We now want to rigorously prove this proposition. In order to isolate the effect of capital flows, we assume that there is no trade in goods or migration of labor.

In Figure 9.1, we examine a world of only two nations (Nation 1 and Nation 2) with a total combined capital stock of OO'. Of this total capital stock, OA belongs to Nation 1 and $O'A$ belongs to Nation 2. The $VMPK_1$ and $VMPK_2$ curves give the value of the marginal product of capital in Nation 1 and Nation 2, respectively, for various levels of investments. From microeconomic theory, we know that the value of the marginal product of capital is equal to the price of the commodity produced with the capital times

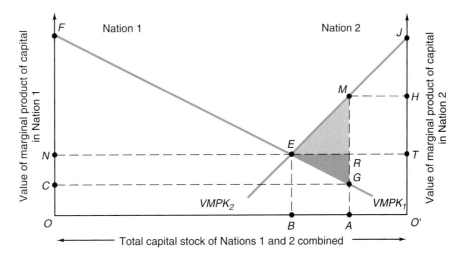

FIGURE 9.1. Output and Welfare Effects of International Capital Transfers

Of the total capital stock of OO', Nation 1 holds OA and its total output is $OFGA$, while Nation 2 holds $O'A$ and its total output is $O'JMA$. The transfer of AB of capital from Nation 1 to Nation 2 equalizes the return on capital in the two nations at BE. This increases world output by EGM (the shaded area), of which EGR accrues to Nation 1 and ERM to Nation 2. Of the increase in total domestic product of $ABEM$ in Nation 2, $ABER$ goes to foreign investors, leaving ERM as the net gain in domestic income in Nation 2.

the marginal product of capital. Under competitive conditions, the value of the marginal product of capital represents the return, or yield, on capital.

In isolation, Nation 1 invests its entire capital stock OA domestically at a yield of OC. The total product (which can be measured by the area under the value of the marginal product curve) is thus $OFGA$, of which $OCGA$ goes to owners of capital in Nation 1 and the remainder of CFG goes to other cooperating factors, such as labor and land. Similarly, Nation 2 in isolation invests its entire stock $O'A$ domestically at a yield of $O'H$. Total product is $O'JMA$, of which $O'HMA$ goes to owners of capital in Nation 2 and the remainder of HJM goes to other cooperating factors.

Let us assume that free international capital movements are allowed. Since the return on capital is higher in Nation 2 *(O'H)* than in Nation 1 *(OC)*, AB of capital flows from Nation 1 to Nation 2 so as to equalize at BE (= ON = $O'T$), the rate of return on capital in the two nations. Total *domestic product* in Nation 1 is now $OFEB$, to which must be added $ABER$ as the total return on foreign investments, giving a total *national income* of $OFERA$ (ERG greater than before foreign investments). With free international capital flows, the

total return on capital in Nation 1 increases to *ONRA*, while the total return on other cooperating factors decreases to *NFE*.

The inflow of *AB* of foreign capital into Nation 2 lowers the rate of return on capital from *O'H* to *O'T*. Total domestic product in Nation 2 grows from *O'JMA* to *O'JEB*. Of the increase in total product of *ABEM*, *ABER* goes to foreign investors, so that *ERM* remains as the *net gain* in total product accruing to Nation 2. The total return to domestic owners of capital falls from *O'HMA* to *O'TRA*, while the total return to other cooperating factors rises from *HJM* to *TJE*.

From the point of view of the world as a whole (i.e., the two nations combined), total product increased from *OFGA* + *O'JMA* to *OFEB* + *O'JEB*, or by *ERG* + *ERM* = *EGM* (the shaded area of the figure). Thus, international capital flows increase the efficiency in the allocation of resources internationally and increase world output and welfare. Note that the steeper the $VMPK_1$ and $VMPK_2$ curves are, the greater is the total gain from international capital flows.

A9.2 ANALYSIS OF EFFECTS OF INTERNATIONAL LABOR MIGRATION

The welfare effects of international labor migration on the nations of emigration and immigration can be analyzed with the same diagrammatic technique used to analyze the welfare effects of international capital movements. In Figure 9.2, the supply of labor is *OA* in Nation 1 and *O'A* in Nation 2. The $VMPL_1$ and $VMPL_2$ curves give the value of the marginal revenue product of labor in Nation 1 and Nation 2, respectively. Under competitive conditions, *VMPL* represents the real wages of labor.

Before migration, the wage rate is *OC* and total product is *OFGA* in Nation 1. In Nation 2, the wage rate is *O'H* and total product is *O'JMA*. Now let us assume free international labor migration. Since wages are higher in Nation 2 *(O'H)* than in Nation 1 *(OC)*, *AB* of labor migrates from Nation 1 to Nation 2 so as to equalize wages in the two nations at *BE* (= *ON* = *O'T*). Thus, wages rise in Nation 1 and fall in Nation 2 (and for that reason immigration is generally opposed by organized labor). On the other hand, total product falls from *OFGA* to *OFEB* in Nation 1 and rises from *O'JMA* to *O'JEB* in Nation 2, for a net gain in world output of *EGM* (the shaded area in the figure). Note that there is a redistribution of national income toward labor in Nation 1 (the nation of emigration) and toward nonlabor resources in Nation 2. Nation 1 may also receive some remittances from its migrant workers. Note also that if *AB* of labor had been unemployed in Nation 1 before migration, the wage rate would have been *ON* and the total product *OFEB* in Nation 1 with and without migration, and the net increase in world output with migration would have been *ABEM* (all accruing to Nation 2).

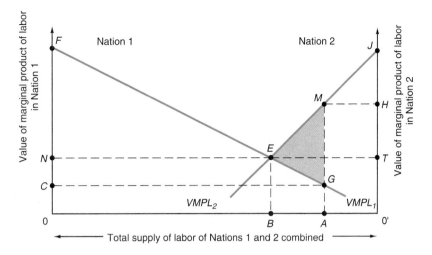

FIGURE 9.2. Output and Welfare Effects of International Labor Migration
With a supply of labor of *OA*, Nation 1 has a real wage rate of *OC* and a total output of *OFGA*. With a supply of labor of *O'A*, Nation 2 has a real wage rate of *O'H* and a total output of *O'JMA*. The migration of *AB* of labor from Nation 1 to Nation 2 equalizes real wages in the two nations at *BE*. This reduces total output to *OFEB* in Nation 1 and increases it in Nation 2 to *O'JEB*, for a net increase in world output of *EGM* (the shaded area).

SELECTED BIBLIOGRAPHY

For data on foreign investments, see:

- Department of Commerce, *U.S. Survey of Current Business* (Washington, D.C.: U.S. Government Printing Office, Monthly.

- OECD, *International Direct Investment Statistics Yearbook* (Paris: OECD, 2007).

- UN, *World Investment Report* (New York: UN, 2007).

The motives and consequences of foreign direct investments are examined in:

- International Monetary Fund, *Determinants and Systemic Consequences of International Capital Flows* (Washington, D.C.: IMF, 1991).

- B. A. Blonigen, "A Review of the Empirical Literature on FDI Determinants," *NBER Working Paper No. 11299*, April 2005.

On multinational corporations, see:

- B. Ricker and D. Ricker, "Are U.S. Multinationals Exporting Jobs?" *NBER Working Paper No. 5958*, September 1997.

On transfer pricing, see:

- T. A. Gresik, "The Taxing Task of Taxing Transnationals," *Journal of Economic Literature*, September 2001, pp. 800–838.
- D. Salvatore, *Managerial Economics in a Global Economy*, 6th ed. (New York: Oxford University Press, 2007), Section 11–6.

The motives and welfare effects of international labor migrations are examined in:

- G. J. Borjas, "Reexamining the Impact of Immigration on the U.S. Labor Market," *Quarterly Journal of Economics*, November 2003, pp. 1335–1374.
- C. Ozden and M. Schiff, eds., *International Migration, Remittances, and the Brain Drain* (Washington, D.C.: World Bank, 2006).
- OECD, *Trends in International Migration* (Paris: OECD, 2007).

INTERNet

The data on foreign direct investments are published by the United Nations in the *World Investment Report* (yearly), the OECD in the *International Investment Statistics Yearbook*, and by the Bureau of Economic Analysis in *Survey of Current Business* in the July issue of each year. The web sites for these organizations are listed below. The United Nations makes available on the Internet only parts of the *World Investment Report* and so does the OECD for its *International Investment Statistics Yearbook*. The Bureau of Economic Analysis does provide data on international direct investments on the web site indicated below.

http://www.unctad.org and click on *World Investment Report*.

http://www.oecd.org and click on *International Investment Statistics Yearbook*.

http://bea.doc.gov and click on *Survey of Current Business*, July issue.

For articles on transfer pricing see the OECD site:

http://www.oecd.org and click transfer pricing

http://www.econ.iastate.edu/classes/econ355/choi/mnc.htm

Information on immigration to the United States is found on the web site of the U.S. Immigration and Naturalization Service (INS) at:

http://uscis.gov

The Balance of Payments, Foreign Exchange Markets, and Exchange Rates

Part Four (Chapters 10, 11, and 12) deals with balance of payments, foreign exchange markets, and exchange rate determination. A clear grasp of the material in these three chapters is crucial for understanding Parts Five and Six, which cover adjustment to balance-of-payments disequilibria, open-economy macroeconomics, and the functioning of the present international monetary system. Chapter 10 examines the meaning, function, and measurement of the balance of payments and defines the concepts of deficit and surplus in a nation's balance of payments. Chapter 11 deals with foreign exchange markets and their operation. Chapter 12 examines exchange rate theories and exchange rate determination.

Balance of Payments

After studying this chapter, you should be able to:

- Understand what the balance of payments is and what it measures
- The meaning of credits and debits, and double-entry bookkeeping
- Describe the international transactions of the United States
- Understand the meaning of disequilibrium in international transactions
- Know how to measure a deficit or a surplus in a nation's balance of payments
- Describe the change in the balance of payments of the United States over the years
- Describe the evolution of the U.S. international investment position

CHAPTER OUTLINE

KEY TERMS

Balance of payments	Capital account
Credit transactions	Deficit in the balance of payments
Debit transactions	Official reserve account
Capital inflow	Surplus in the balance of payments
Capital outflow	Official settlements balance
Double-entry bookkeeping	Autonomous transactions
Unilateral transfers	Accommodating transactions
Statistical discrepancy	International investment position
Current account	

10.1 INTRODUCTION

In Parts One to Three of the text, we dealt with the "real," as opposed to the monetary, side of the economy. Money was not explicitly considered, and the discussion was in terms of relative commodity prices. We now begin our examination of the monetary aspects of international economics, or international finance. Here, money is explicitly brought into the picture, and commodity prices are expressed in terms of domestic and foreign currency

units. We begin our discussion of international finance by examining the balance of payments.

In Section 10.2, we discuss the meaning and use of the balance of payments and the reason nations measure it. In Section 10.3 we present some balance of payments accounting principles. Section 10.4 explains the meaning of double-entry bookkeeping that is used in measuring the balance of payments. Section 10.5 presents and analyzes the international transactions of the United States for the year 2007. Section 10.6 examines accounting balances and disequilibrium in the international transactions of the United States. Section 10.7 then examines the concept and measurement of a balance-of-payments deficit or surplus. Section 10.8 briefly reviews the post-war balance-of-payments history of the United States. Finally, Section 10.9 examines the international investment position of the United States.

10.2 THE BALANCE OF PAYMENTS: DEFINITION AND USE

Balance of payments A summary statement of all the transactions of the residents of a nation with the rest of the world during a particular period of time, usually a year.

The balance of payments is a summary statement in which, in principle, all the transactions of the residents of a nation with the residents of all other nations are recorded during a particular period of time, usually a calendar year. The United States and some other nations also keep such a record on a quarterly basis. The main purpose of the balance of payments is to inform the government of the international position of the nation and to help it in its formulation of monetary, fiscal, and trade policies. Governments also regularly consult the balance of payments of important trade partners in making policy decisions. The information contained in a nation's balance of payments is also indispensable to banks, firms, and individuals directly or indirectly involved in international trade and finance.

The definition of the balance of payments just given requires some clarification. First of all, it is obvious that the literally millions of transactions of the residents of a nation with the rest of the world cannot appear *individually* in the balance of payments. As a *summary statement*, the balance of payments aggregates all merchandise trade into a few major categories. Similarly, only the net balance of each type of international capital flow is included. Furthermore, the balance of payments includes some transactions in which the residents of foreign nations are not directly involved—for example, when a nation's central bank sells a portion of its foreign currency holdings to the nation's commercial banks.

An international transaction refers to the exchange of a good, service, or asset (for which payment is usually required) between the residents of one nation and the residents of other nations. However, gifts and certain other transfers (for which no payment is required) are also included in a nation's balance of payments. The question of who is a resident of a nation also requires some clarification. Diplomats, military personnel, tourists, and

workers who temporarily migrate are residents of the nation in which they hold citizenship. Similarly, a corporation is the resident of the nation in which it is incorporated, but its foreign branches and subsidiaries are not. Some of these distinctions are, of course, arbitrary and may lead to difficulties. For example, a worker may start by emigrating temporarily and then decide to remain abroad permanently. International institutions such as the United Nations, the International Monetary Fund (IMF), the World Bank, and the World Trade Organization (WTO) are not residents of the nation in which they are located. Also to be remembered is that the balance of payments has a time dimension. Thus, it is the flow of goods, services, gifts, and assets between the residents of a nation and the residents of other nations during a particular period of time, usually a calendar year.

10.3 BALANCE-OF-PAYMENTS ACCOUNTING PRINCIPLES: CREDITS AND DEBITS

Credit transactions Transactions that involve the receipt of payments from foreigners. These include the export of goods and services, unilateral transfers from foreigners, and capital inflows.

Debit transactions Transactions that involve payments to foreigners. These include the import of goods and services, unilateral transfers to foreigners, and capital outflows.

Capital inflow An increase of foreign assets in the nation or a reduction in the nation's assets abroad.

International transactions are classified as credits or debits. Credit transactions are those that involve the receipt of payments from foreigners. Debit transactions are those that involve the making of payments to foreigners. Credit transactions are entered with a positive sign, and debit transactions are entered with a negative sign in the nation's balance of payments.

Thus, the export of goods and services, unilateral transfers (gifts) received from foreigners, and capital inflows are entered as credits (+) because they involve the receipt of payments from foreigners. On the other hand, the import of goods and services, unilateral transfers or gifts made to foreigners, and capital outflows involve payments to foreigners and are entered as debits (−) in the nation's balance of payments.

Capital inflows can take either of two forms: an increase in foreign assets in the nation or a reduction in the nation's assets abroad. For example, when a U.K. resident purchases a U.S. stock, foreign assets in the United States increase. This is a capital inflow to the United States and is recorded as a credit in the U.S. balance of payments because it involves the receipt of a payment from a foreigner. A capital inflow can also take the form of a reduction in the nation's assets abroad. For example, when a U.S. resident sells a foreign stock, U.S. assets abroad decrease. This is a capital inflow to the United States (reversing the capital outflow that occurred when the U.S. resident purchased the foreign stock) and is recorded as a credit in the U.S. balance of payments because it too involves the receipt of a payment from foreigners.

The definition of capital inflows to the United States as increases in foreign assets in the United States or reductions in U.S. assets abroad can be confusing and is somewhat unfortunate, but this is the terminology actually used in all U.S. government publications. Confusion can be avoided by remembering that when a foreigner purchases a U.S. asset (an increase in

foreign assets in the United States), this involves the receipt of a payment from foreigners. Therefore, it is a capital inflow, or credit. Similarly, when a U.S. resident sells a foreign asset (a reduction in U.S. assets abroad), this also involves a payment from foreigners; therefore, it too represents a capital inflow to the United States and a credit. Both an increase in foreign assets in the United States and a reduction in U.S. assets abroad are capital inflows, or credits, because they both involve the receipt of payment from foreigners.

Capital outflow A decrease of foreign assets in the nation or an increase in the nation's assets abroad.

On the other hand, capital outflows can take the form of either an increase in the nation's assets abroad or a reduction in foreign assets in the nation because both involve a payment to foreigners. For example, the purchase of a U.K. treasury bill by a U.S. resident increases U.S. assets abroad and is a debit because it involves a payment to foreigners. Similarly, the sale of its U.S. subsidiary by a German firm reduces foreign assets in the United States and is also a debit because it involves a payment to foreigners. (The student should study these definitions and examples carefully, since mastery of these important concepts is crucial to understanding what follows.)

Concept Check

Are capital inflows credits or debits? Why?

To summarize, the export of goods and services, the receipt of unilateral transfers, and capital inflows are credits (+) because they all involve the receipt of payments from foreigners. On the other hand, the import of goods and services, unilateral transfers to foreigners, and capital outflows are debits (−) because they involve payments to foreigners.

10.4 DOUBLE-ENTRY BOOKKEEPING

Double-entry bookkeeping
The accounting procedure whereby each (international) transaction is entered twice, once as a credit and once as a debit of an equal amount.

In recording a nation's international transactions, another accounting procedure known as double-entry bookkeeping is used. This means that each international transaction is recorded twice, once as a credit and once as a debit of an equal amount. The reason for this is that in general every transaction has two sides. We sell something, and we receive payment for it. We buy something, and we have to pay for it.

For example, suppose that a U.S. firm exports $500 of goods to be paid for in three months. The United States first credits goods exports for $500 since this goods export will lead to the receipt of a payment from foreigners. The *promise of the payment* from foreigners is then entered as a capital debit because it represents a capital outflow from the United States. That is, by agreeing to wait three months for payment, the U.S. exporter is extending credit to, and has acquired a claim on, the foreign importer. This is an increase in U.S. assets abroad and a debit. The entire transaction is entered as follows in the U.S. balance of payments:

	Credit (+)	Debit (−)
Goods exports	$500	
Capital outflow		$500

As another example of double-entry bookkeeping, suppose that a U.S. resident visits London and spends $200 on hotels, meals, and so on. The U.S. resident is purchasing travel services from foreigners requiring a payment. (This is similar to a U.S. import.) Thus, the U.S. debits travel services for $200. The payment itself is then entered as a credit because it represents an increase in foreign claims on the United States. Specifically, we can think of the $200 in British hands as "securities" giving the United Kingdom a claim on U.S. goods and services, equivalent to an increase in foreign assets in the United States. Therefore, it is a capital inflow to the United States and is recorded as a capital credit of $200. The entire transaction is entered as follows in the U.S. balance of payments:

	Credit (+)	Debit (−)
Travel services purchased from foreigners		$200
Capital inflow	$200	

As a third example, assume that the U.S. government gives a U.S. bank balance of $100 to the government of a developing nation as part of the U.S. aid program. The United States debits unilateral transfers for the $100 gift given (payment made) to foreigners. The payment itself is the U.S. bank balance given to the government of the developing nation. This represents an increase in foreign claims on, or foreign assets in, the United States and is recorded as a capital inflow, or credit, in the U.S. balance of payments. The entire transaction is thus:

Unilateral transfers
Gifts or grants extended to or received from abroad.

	Credit (+)	Debit (−)
Unilateral transfers made		$100
Capital inflow	$100	

As a fourth example, suppose that a U.S. resident purchases a foreign stock for $400 and pays for it by increasing foreign bank balances in the United States. The purchase of the foreign stock increases U.S. assets abroad. This is a capital outflow from the United States and is recorded as a capital debit of $400 in the U.S. balance of payments. The increase in foreign bank balances in the United States is an increase in foreign assets in the United States (a capital inflow to the United States) and is entered as a credit in the U.S. balance of payments. The result would be the same if the U.S. resident paid for the foreign stock by reducing bank balances abroad. (This would be a reduction in U.S. assets abroad, which is also a capital inflow to

the United States and a credit.) Note that both sides of this transaction are financial:

	Credit (+)	Debit (−)
Capital outflow (the purchase of the foreign stock by the U.S. resident)		$400
Capital inflow (the increase in foreign bank balances in the U.S.)	$400	

Finally, suppose that a foreign investor purchases $300 of U.S. treasury bills and pays by drawing down his bank balances in the United States by an equal amount. The purchase of the U.S. treasury bills increases foreign assets in the United States. This is a capital inflow to the United States and is recorded as a credit in the U.S. balance of payments. The drawing down of U.S. bank balances by the foreigner is a reduction in foreign assets in the United States. This is a capital outflow from the United States and is recorded as a capital outflow of the U.S. balance of payments:

	Credit (+)	Debit (−)
Capital inflow (the purchase of U.S. treasury bills by a foreigner)	$300	
Capital outflow (the reduction in foreign bank balances in the U.S.)		$300

If we assume that these five transactions are all the international transactions of the United States during the year, then the U.S. balance of payments is as follows:

	Credit (+)	Debit (−)
Goods	$500	
Services		$200
Unilateral transfers		100
Capital, net		200
Total debits and credits	$500	$500

The net capital debit balance of −$200 is obtained by adding together the seven capital entries (−$500, $200, $100, −$400, $400, $300, −$300) previously examined separately. Total debits equal total credits because of double-entry bookkeeping.

10.5 THE INTERNATIONAL TRANSACTIONS OF THE UNITED STATES

Table 10.1 presents a summary of the international transactions of the United States for 2007. In the table, credits are entered with positive signs and debits with negative signs.

Table 10.1 shows that the United States exported $2,464 billion of goods and services (including the income receipts on U.S. assets abroad) in 2007. Goods exports of $1,148 billion included automobiles, chemicals, agricultural products, semiconductors, and civilian aircraft (see Case Study 10-1). Service exports of $497 billion included travel and transportation services provided to foreigners, as well as fees and royalties received from foreigners. U.S. residents also earned $818 billion in interest and dividends on their foreign investments. Note that while a capital or financial outflow from the United States is recorded as a debit under capital (an increase in U.S.-owned assets abroad), the earnings received from abroad for the services of U.S. assets abroad (i.e., foreign investments) are recorded here with the export of other services. The income receipts on U.S. assets abroad are recorded separately from other services because of their importance.

On the other hand, the United States imported goods and services (including income payments on foreign assets in the United States) for $3,082 billion in 2007. Goods imports included automobiles, petroleum, apparel and household goods, household appliances, computers, and many other products. The $378 billion imports of services included the travel and transportation services purchased by U.S. residents from other nations, fees and royalties paid to foreigners, as well as $736 billion the interest and dividends paid on foreign investments in the United States. Note that the inflow of foreign capital into the United States is recorded as a credit under capital (an increase of foreign-owned assets in the United States), while the payments made to foreigners for the services of the foreign capital invested in the United States are recorded as a debit with other imported services in the U.S. balance of payments.

The United States made net unilateral transfers to foreigners of (−)$113 billion during 2007. These included net U.S. government economic and military grants to foreign nations (−$33 billion), net U.S. government pensions and other transfers to foreign nations (−$7 billion) and net private remittances and other transfers (−$72 billion). Private remittances and other transfers refer to the immigrant remittances to relatives "back home" and other private gifts. Since more of these private transfers were made to foreigners than were received by U.S. residents from abroad, the United States had a net debit entry of (−)$72 billion for private remittances and other transfers in 2007.

Concept Check

What was the U.S. balance in goods, services and income in 2007?

Table 10.1. *Summary of U.S. International Transactions for 2007 (billions of dollars)*

	Credits	Debits
Exports of goods, services, and income	+2,464	
Goods	+1,148	
Services	+497	
Income receipts on U.S. assets abroad	+818	
Imports of goods, services, and income		−3,082
Goods		−1,968
Services		−378
Income payments on foreign assets in the U.S.		−736
Unilateral transfers, net		−113
U.S. government grants		−33
U.S. government pensions and other transfers		−7
Private remittances and other transfers		−72
U.S.-owned assets abroad, net (increase/financial outflow (−)		−1,290
U.S. official reserve assets, net		0
U.S. government assets, other than official reserve assets, net		−22
U.S. private assets, net		−1,268
Direct investment		−333
Foreign securities		−289
Nonbank claims		−1
Bank claims		−645
Foreign-owned assets in the United States, net (increase/financial inflow (+)	+2,058	
Foreign official assets in the United States, net	+411	
Other foreign assets in the United States, net	+1,647	
Direct investment in the United States,	+238	
U.S. treasury securities	+157	
U.S. securities other than U.S. treasury securities	+574	
U.S. currency	−11	
Nonbank liabilities	+156	
Bank liabilities	+533	
Statistical discrepancy	−41	
Memoranda		
Balance on goods trade		−819
Balance on services	+119	
Balance on goods and services		−700
Balance on income	+82	
Balance on goods, services, and income		−618
Unilateral current transfers, net		−113
Balance on current account		−731

Source: U.S. Department of Commerce, *Survey of Current Business* (Washington, D.C.: U.S. Government Printing Office, July 2008), pp. 66–67.

The Major Goods Exports and Imports of the United States

Table 10.2 shows the value of the major goods exported and imported by the United States in 2007. The major U.S. exports were automobiles, chemicals, agricultural products, semiconductors, and civilian aircraft. U.S. imports were dominated by petroleum, automobiles, apparel and household goods, household appliances, and computers. From Table 10.2, we see that the United States had an export surplus in chemi-

cals, agricultural products, semiconductors, civilian aircraft, and medical products. These are the products in which the United States has a (revealed) comparative advantage. The United States had an import surplus (and comparative disadvantage) in petroleum, automobiles, apparel and household goods, household appliances, computers, electrical generating machinery, and telecommunications.

Table 10.2. *Major Goods Exports and Imports of the United States in 2007 (billions of dollars)*

Exports	Value	Imports	Value
Automobiles	$121.0	Petroleum	$331.0
Chemicals	94.5	Automobiles	258.9
Agricultural products	92.1	Apparel and household goods	117.4
Semiconductors	50.4	Household appliances	112.0
Civilian aircraft	48.8	Computers	105.2
Computers	45.5	Agricultural products	62.1
Electrical generating machinery	41.3	Chemicals	56.2
Medical products	35.2	Electrical generating machinery	55.1
Telecommunications	30.3	Telecommunications	44.1
Household appliances	28.5	Civilian aircraft	34.4

Source: U.S. Department of Commerce, *Survey of Current Business* (Washington, D.C.: U.S. Government Printing Office, July 2008), pp. 80–83.

Table 10.1 also shows that the stock of U.S.-owned assets abroad increased (a capital outflow of the United States and a debit) by the net amount of (−)$1,290 billion during 2007. There was no change in the stock of U.S. official reserve assets (mostly gold and foreign currencies), a net increase in the stock of U.S. government assets other than official reserve assets of (−)$22 billion, and a net increase of (−)$1,268 billion in the stock of U.S. *private* assets abroad. The latter included a net increase in U.S. foreign direct investments abroad of (−)$333 billion, a net increase in U.S. holdings of foreign securities of (−)$289 billion, a net increase in U.S. nonbank claims on foreigners of (+)$1 billion, and a net increase in U.S. bank claims on foreigners of (−)$645 billion.

The stock of foreign-owned assets in the United States increased (a capital inflow to the United States and a credit) by the net amount of (+)$2,058 billion

Did the U.S. have a net capital inflow or outflow in 2007?

in 2007. This included a net increase in the stock of foreign official assets in the United States of (+)$411 billion and a net increase in other (than official) foreign assets in the United States of (+)$1,647 billion. The latter included a net increase of (+)$238 billion in foreign direct investments in the United States, (+)$157 billion in foreign holdings of U.S. treasury securities, (+)$574 billion U.S. securities other than U.S. treasury securities, (+)$156 billion in U.S. nonbank liabilities to foreigners, (+)$533 billion in U.S. bank liabilities to foreigners, and a net *decrease* of (−)$11 billion in U.S. currency.

When we sum the total credits of (+)$2,464 billion for U.S. exports of goods, services, and income and the (+)$2,058 billion net increase in foreign-owned assets in the United States, we get the overall credit total of (+)$4,522 billion for the U.S. international transactions during 2007. On the other hand, adding up the debits of (−)$3,082 billion for the U.S. imports of goods, services, and income, the (−)$113 billion for the net unilateral transfers, and the (−)$1,290 billion for the net increase in U.S.-owned assets abroad, we get the overall debit total of (−)$4,485 billion. Since the overall credit total of (+)$4,522 billion exceeds the overall debit total of (−)$4,485 billion by $37 billion (with a $4 billion rounding error), there is a debit entry called statistical discrepancy of (−)$41 billion in Table 10.1. This entry is required to make the total credits (including the statistical discrepancy) equal to the total debits, as required by double-entry bookkeeping.

Statistical discrepancy The entry made in a nation's balance of payments to make total credits equal to total debits, as required by double-entry bookkeeping.

Note that a statistical discrepancy results from incorrectly recording or from not recording at all only one side of some transactions. (If both sides of a transaction are reported incorrectly or are not reported at all, no statistical discrepancy between total debits and total credits would arise because of double-entry bookkeeping.) Statistical discrepancies are particularly likely to arise in recording short-term international private capital flows. Thus, the (−)$41 billion statistical discrepancy is likely to reflect unrecorded net short-term private capital *outflows* from the United States during 2007. The memoranda items at the bottom of Table 10.1 are discussed next.

10.6 ACCOUNTING BALANCES AND DISEQUILIBRIUM IN INTERNATIONAL TRANSACTIONS

The first accounting balance in the memoranda at the bottom of Table 10.1 is the balance on goods trade. In 2007, the United States exported $1,148 billion and imported $1,968 billion of goods, for a net debit balance on goods trade of (−)$819 billion. On the other hand, the United States had a net credit balance on services of $119 billion (from the $497 billion export of services minus the $378 billion import of services). Thus, the United States had a net debit balance on goods and services of (−)$700 billion. The United States also had a net surplus balance of (+)$82 billion on investment income (from the

$818 billion interest and dividends earned on U.S. investment abroad minus the $736 billion income payments on foreign assets in the United States). The United States, therefore, had a net debit balance on goods, services, and income of (−)$618 billion.

Adding the net debit balance of (−)$113 billion of unilateral transfers to the net debit balance of (−)$618 billion on goods, services, and income, we get the current account net debit balance of (−)$731 billion. Thus, the current account lumps together all sales and purchases of currently produced goods and services, investment incomes, and unilateral transfers and provides the link between the nation's international transactions and its national income. Specifically, a current account surplus stimulates domestic production and income, while a current account deficit dampens domestic production and income. (This link between the nation's international trade and current account and its national income will be examined in detail in Chapter 13.)

The change in U.S.-owned assets abroad and foreign-owned assets in the United States, other than official reserve assets, gives the capital account of the United States. This measures the change in the stock of all nonreserve financial assets. The justification for excluding official reserve assets from the capital account is that changes in reserves reflect government policy rather than market forces.

The capital account of the United States shows a net increase in U.S.-owned *private* assets abroad (a capital outflow of the United States) of (−)$1,290 billion (from the total of −$1,290 billion minus the $0 billion net increase in U.S. official reserve assets) and a net increase in foreign-owned *private* assets in the United States (a capital inflow to the United States) of $1,647 billion (from the total of $2,058 billion minus the +$411 billion net *increase* in foreign official assets in the United States). Thus, the United States had a net credit balance (a net capital inflow) in its capital account of (+)$357 billion in 2007.

Current account
The account that includes all sales and purchases of currently produced goods and services, income on foreign investments, and unilateral transfers.

Capital account
The change in U.S. assets abroad and foreign assets in the United States, other than official reserve assets.

Concept Check

What were the U.S. current and capital account balances in 2007?

10.7 MEASURING DEFICITS OR SURPLUSES IN THE BALANCE OF PAYMENTS

By adding the current and capital account balances, as well as the statistical discrepancy balance (because, as we said earlier, it represents mostly unrecorded private capital flows), we get the nation's balance of payments. That is,

Current account balance + Capital account balance +
Statistical discrepancy = Balance of payments

Deficit in the balance of payments The excess of debits over credits in the current and capital accounts, or autonomous transactions.

If total debits exceed total credits in the nation s current and capital accounts and statistical discrepancy, the nation has a deficit in the balance of payments equal to net debit balance. It means that the nation spent that much more than it earned abroad during the year. This deficit must

Official reserve account It measures the change in U.S. official reserve assets and the change in foreign official reserve assets in the United States.

Surplus in the balance of payments The excess of credits over debits in the current and capital accounts, or autonomous transactions.

Official settlements balance The net credit or debit balance in the official reserve account.

Autonomous transactions International transactions that take place for business or profit motives and independently of balance-of-payments considerations.

Accommodating transactions Transactions in official reserve assets required to balance international transactions.

then be settled (i.e., paid for or financed) with an equal net *credit* balance (remember that the balance of payments as a whole must balance because of double-entry bookkeeping) in the official reserves account, which holds the nation's international reserves. On the other hand, a nation has a surplus in the balance of payments if its total credits exceed its total debits in the current and capital accounts and statistical discrepancy. This means that the nation earned that much more than it spent abroad during the year. The net credit balance gives the size of the surplus and is settled by an equal net *debit* balance in the nation's official reserve account. The balance in the official reserve account is called the official settlements balance.

All transactions in the current and capital accounts (including the statistical discrepancy) are called autonomous transactions because they take place for business or profit motives (except for unilateral transfers) and independently of balance-of-payments considerations. On the other hand, transactions in official reserve assets included in the official reserve account are called accommodating transactions because they result from and are needed to balance international transactions. The autonomous transaction balance (balance of payments) plus the accommodating transactions balance (official settlements balance) must equal zero because of double-entry bookkeeping.

From Table 10.1 and the discussion in the previous section, we see that during 2007 the United States had a net debit balance of (−)$731 billion in its current account, a net credit balance of (+)$357 billion in its capital account, and a net credit balance of (−)$41 billion of statistical discrepancy. This gives a net debit balance or balance of payments *deficit* of $411 billion (including a $3 billion rounding error) for the United States in 2007. This balance of payments deficit was settled by an increase in foreign official assets in the United States of (+)$411 billion (see Table 10.1).

10.8 THE POSTWAR BALANCE OF PAYMENTS OF THE UNITED STATES

Concept Check

What was the U.S. balance of payments surplus or deficit in 2007?

In this section, we present a brief balance-of-payments history of the United States with the aid of Table 10.3. From Table 10.3, we see that the U.S. positive trade balance on goods of the 1960s became negative in the 1970s (except for 1973 and 1975) and deteriorated sharply thereafter, reaching the peak of (−)$838 billion in 2006. To a large extent, this reflected the sharp rise in the price of imported petroleum products during the 1970s, the high international value of the dollar in the 1980s, the more rapid growth of the United States than Europe and Japan during the 1990s, and the sharp increase in the price of petroleum since 2004. Case Study 10-2 gives the major trade partners of the United States and the balance of trade on merchandise

Table 10.3. *Summary of U.S. International Transactions: 1960–2007 (billions of dollars)*

Year	Balance on Goods Trade	Balance on Goods, Services, and Income	Balance on Current Account	Balance of Payments (−) Deficit, (+) Surplus
1960	5	7	3	−3
1965	5	10	3	−1
1970	2	8	2	−10
1975	9	25	18	−6
1980	−26	11	2	−15
1985	−122	−96	−118	1
1990	−111	−52	−79	−34
1995	−174	−75	−114	−110
2000	−455	−359	−417	−43
2005	−787	−639	−729	−259
2006	−838	−696	−788	−488
2007	−819	−619	−731	−411

Source: U.S. Department of Commerce, *Survey of Current Business* (Washington, D.C.: U.S. Government Printing Office, July 1996 and July 2008), pp. 66–67.

(goods) of the United States with each of them in 2007, while Case Study 10-3 examines the evolution of the U.S. trade deficit with China since 1985.

Table 10.3 also shows that the deterioration in the U.S. trade balance in goods, services, and income was a little less than the deterioration in the U.S. trade balance in goods alone because of the U.S. trade surplus in services and income. Adding the negative balance on U.S. unilateral transfers resulted in the U.S current account deteriorating even more than the balance on goods, services, and income.

Concept Check

How has the U.S. balance of payments changed since 1980?

The last column of Table 10.3 gives the U.S. balance of payments. It shows that the United States had its first large balance-of-payments deficit (of $10 billion) in 1970. The deficit rose sharply in 1971, when it reached $30 billion (not shown in Table 10.3). Since 1973 the United States has had a deficit in its international transactions in every year, except 1979, 1982, 1985, 1989, 1998, and 2001. The U.S. balance-of-payments deficit exceeded $30 billion in each year in 1977–1978, 1986–1988, and 1990. It reached $110 billion in 1995, the maximum of $488 billion in 2006, and it was $411 billion in 2007.

Three things must be kept in mind in examining a nation's balance of payments. First, too much attention is generally placed on the balance on goods and on short-term data. The reason is that data on the quarterly trade balance on goods are the first to become available. It is also dangerous to extrapolate for the year based on quarterly data. Even the notion of a positive trade balance on goods being favorable is somewhat misleading because a positive trade balance means that the nation has fewer goods to consume domestically. On the other hand, a large and persistent trade deficit (like the one that United States has, which now exceeds 6 percent of GNI) is not

CASE STUDY 10-2

The Major Trade Partners of the United States

Table 10.4 shows the value of U.S. exports and imports of goods and services, and the net balance with its ten major trade partners in 2007. The table shows that the largest trade partners of the United States in 2007 were Canada, Mexico, China, Japan, Germany, and the United Kingdom. The table also shows that the United

States had a huge trade deficit with China and this is the source of sharp trade disagreements (see Case Study 10-3). The United States also had large deficits with Japan, Mexico, Canada, and Germany in 2007, but clearly the U.S. trade deficit with China dominated.

Table 10.4. *U.S. Trade in Goods and Services and Net Balance with Its Major Trade Partners in 2007 (billions of dollars)*

Country	Exports	Imports	Net Balance
Canada	$249.7	$320.3	$−72.6
Mexico	136.0	213.6	−77.6
China	65.1	321.7	−256.6
Japan	60.9	146.0	−85.1
Germany	49.0	94.3	−45.3
United Kingdom	48.7	56.4	−7.7
South Korea	33.6	47.5	−13.9
Netherlands	32.7	18.4	−14.3
France	27.1	41.5	−14.4
Taiwan (China)	26.0	38.5	−12.5

Source: U.S. Department of Commerce, *Survey of Current Business* (Washington, D.C.: U.S. Government Printing Office, July 2008), pp. 74–79.

sustainable in the long run, even for so rich a country as the United States. This problem will be examined in Chapter 13.

Second, it is important to keep in mind that international transactions are closely interrelated rather than independent, so that an attempt to reduce the U.S. trade deficit with respect to a nation such as Japan or China is likely to reduce the U.S. surplus with respect to Brazil, because Brazil pays for U.S. goods partly through natural resource exports to Japan and China.

Finally, it must be pointed out that measuring the deficit (or surplus) in the balance of payments (as well as the concept itself) is strictly correct only under a fixed exchange rate system (as we had from the end of World War II until 1973), and not under a flexible exchange rate system or a managed exchange rate system (that we have had since then). The reason for this is explained in Chapter 11, which deals with exchange rates. Knowledge of how the balance of payments is measured is important, however, because

CASE STUDY 10-3

The Exploding U.S. Trade Deficit with China

Figure 10.1 shows the value of U.S. good exports and imports from China from 1985 to 2007. During this period, U.S. imports from China grew much faster than U.S. exports to China, and resulted in a very large and fast-rising U.S. trade deficit with China (equal to $256.6 billion in 2007). Since 2000, China has replaced Japan as the nation with which the

United States has the largest trade deficit and the most trade disputes. Although it is normal for a large and rapidly growing developing country such as China to have a trade surplus, the huge size and extremely rapid growth of its trade surplus vis-à-vis the United States is creating major difficulties in U.S.–China trade relations.

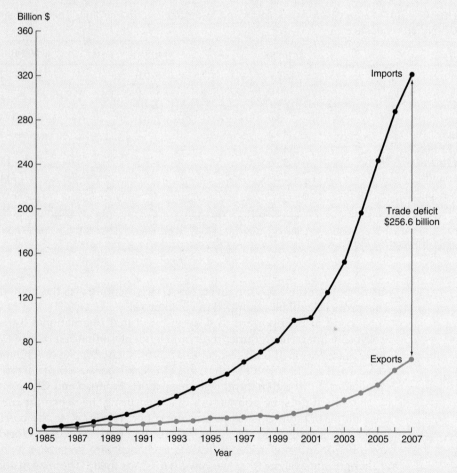

FIGURE 10.1. **U.S. Exports and Imports in Goods with China, 1985–2007 (billions of dollars).** U.S. imports from China grew much faster than U.S. exports to China and resulted in huge and rapidly growing U.S. trade deficits with China.
Source: U.S. Department of Commerce, *Survey of Current Business* (Washington, D.C.: U.S. Government Printing Office, various issues).

it shows how the national economy is connected to the rest of the world economy though flows of trade, capital, and labor. (International trade is an alternative to labor migration, and labor migration affects the growth of the economy and leads to the large international flow of emigrant remittances.)

10.9 THE INTERNATIONAL INVESTMENT POSITION OF THE UNITED STATES

International invest-ment position The total amount and the distribution of a na-tion's assets abroad and foreign assets in the nation at year end; also called the balance of interna-tional indebtedness.

While a nation's balance of payments measures the international *flow* of goods, services, and capital *during a one-year period*, the international investment position measures the total amount and the distribution of a nation's assets abroad and foreign assets in the nation at the end of the year. Thus, the balance of payments represents a flow concept, and the international investment position (often called the *balance of international indebtedness*) represents a stock concept.

The statement of a nation's international investment position can be used to project the future flow of income or earnings from the nation's foreign investments and the flow of payments on foreign investments in the nation. Furthermore, with some adjustments, adding the nation's capital flows during a particular year to its international investment position at the end of the *previous* year should give the international investment position of the nation at the end of that particular year.

Table 10.5 gives the international investment position of the United States at the end of 1980, 1990, 2000, and 2006, with foreign direct investments

Table 10.5. *The U.S. International Investment Position, Selected Years: 1980–2006 (at current cost, billions of dollars at year end)*

	1980	1990	2000	2006
Net U.S. international investment position	$366	$−223	$−1,331	$−2,226
U.S. assets abroad	930	2,179	6,239	14,381
Official reserve assets	171	175	128	220
Other U.S. government assets	66	84	85	72
Private assets	693	1,920	6,025	12,850
Direct investments	388	617	1,531	2,936
Other	305	1,303	4,494	9,914
Foreign assets in U.S.	564	2,402	7,569	16,607
Official assets	176	373	1,031	2,826
Private assets	388	2,029	6,539	12,602
Direct investments	127	505	1,421	2,152
Other	261	1,524	5,118	12,450

Source: U.S. Department of Commerce, *Survey of Current Business* (Washington, D.C.: U.S. Government Printing Office, July 2003 and July 2008), pp. 21–22 and 18–19, respectively.

CASE STUDY 10-4

The Deterioration of U.S. Current Account Balance and Net International Investment Position

Figure 10.2 shows the sharp increase in the U.S. current account deficit after 1997 and its net international investment position after 1999. The figure shows that the U.S. net investment position became negative (making the U.S. a net debtor nation) in 1986 and increased so rapidly after 1999 as to make the United States the world's most indebted nation in 2006.

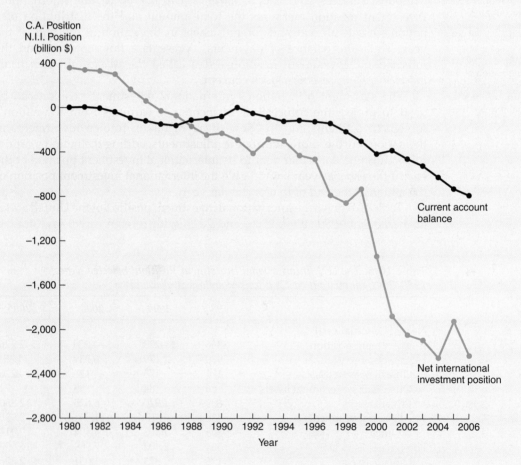

FIGURE 10.2. U.S. Current Account Balance and Net International Investment Position, 1980–2006 (billion dollars).

The United States had small current account surpluses only in 1980, 1981, and 1991, and current account deficits in all other years. U.S. current account deficits became very large and increased rapidly after 1997. The U.S. net international investment position was positive until 1986 and negative thereafter, and it increased sharply after 1999.

Source: U.S. Department of Commerce, *Survey of Current Business* (Washington, D.C.: U.S. Government Printing Office, July 2008), pp. 18–19 and 66–67.

CASE STUDY 10-5

The United States as a Debtor Nation

The shift of the United States from net creditor to debtor nation in 1986 gave rise to a lively debate among economists, politicians, and government officials on the benefits and risks of this development. On the benefit side, large foreign investments allowed the United States to finance about half of its budget deficit during the mid-1980s without the need for higher interest rates and more "crowding out" of private investments. A portion of foreign investments also went into businesses, farms, real estate, and other property, which made more rapid growth possible in the United States. It has been estimated that foreign investments created about 2.5 million additional jobs in the United States during the 1980s, and also helped spread some new and more efficient managerial techniques from abroad.

To the extent that foreign investments went into directly productive activities with returns greater than the interest and dividend payments flowing to foreign investors, this investment was beneficial to the United States. On the other hand, the portion of foreign investments that simply went to finance larger U.S. consumption expenditures led to the interest and dividend payments to foreign investors, and represents a real burden or drain on future consumption and growth in the United States. As the largest and richest nation in the world, there is no question that the United States could repay its foreign debt if called upon to do so. At about 19 percent of its gross national income (GNI), the U.S. foreign debt is smaller than that of much poorer developing nations. It is the burden that the foreign debt imposes on future

generations, as well as the siphoning of capital from poorer nations, that is more troublesome.

There is also the danger that foreigners, for whatever reason, may suddenly withdraw their funds. This would lead to a financial crisis and much higher interest rates in the United States. Rising income payments to foreigners on their investments also means a worsening of the U.S. current account balance in the future. This also drains resources and reduces growth in the rest of the world. On a more general level, some people fear that foreign companies operating in the United States can transfer advanced American technology abroad, which could also lead to some loss of domestic control over political and economic matters in the United States. There is a bit of irony in all of this—these were the very complaints usually heard from Canada, European nations, and developing countries with regard to the large U.S. investments in their countries during the 1950s, 1960s, and 1970s. With the great concern often voiced during the second half of the 1980s about the dangers of foreign investments to the United States, the tables seemed to have turned. Such fears all but disappeared during the 1990s (when most nations eagerly sought to attract foreign direct investments), only to resurface in this decade.

Source: "A Note on the United States as a Debtor Nation," *Survey of Current Business* (Washington, D.C.: U.S. Government Printing Office, June 1985), p. 28; and "The International Investment Position of the United States," *Survey of Current Business* (July 2003 and 2007).

valued at current (i.e., replacement) cost. From the table, we see that the U.S. net international investment position deteriorated sharply, from +$366 billion at the end of 1980 to −$223 billion in 1990, −$1,331 billion in 2000, and −$2,226 at the end of 2006. The amount of U.S.-owned assets abroad

increased 15.5 times, from $930 billion in 1980 to $14,381 billion in 2006. Foreign-owned assets in the United States increased at double the rate (29.4 times), from $564 billion in 1980 to $16,607 billion in 2006. Case Study 10-4 compares the deterioration in the U.S. current account with that of its net investment position from 1980 to 2006.

Two important points can be made with regard to Table 10.5. First, the United States became a net debtor nation in 1985 (see Case Study 10-4, page 276), for the first time since 1914. For one of the richest nations in the world, this distinction seems somewhat inappropriate. Second, U.S. private assets abroad were much larger than foreign assets in the United States in 1980, but smaller in 2006. As a result, the United States became a large (in fact the largest) debtor nation in the 1990s (see Case Study 10-5, page 277). Thirdly, the stock of U.S. direct investments abroad declined from 3.1 times the value of the stock of foreign direct investments in the United States in 1980 to 1.4 in 2006. Other U.S. private assets abroad (mostly foreign securities and bank claims) were also higher than other foreign investments in the United States in 1980, but lower in 2006.

Concept Check

How much has the U.S. international investment position deteriorated since 1980?

SUMMARY

1. The balance of payments is a summary statement of all the transactions of the residents of a nation with the rest of the world during a particular period of time, usually a year. Its main purpose is to inform monetary authorities of the international position of the nation and to aid banks, firms, and individuals engaged in international trade and finance in their business decisions.

2. International transactions are classified as credits or debits. Credit transactions are those that involve the receipt of payments from foreigners. Debit transactions are those that involve payments to foreigners. The export of goods and services, unilateral transfers from foreigners, and capital inflows are credits and are entered with a positive sign. The import of goods and services, unilateral transfers to foreigners, and capital outflows are debits and are entered with a negative sign.

3. In a nation's balance of payments, each transaction is recorded twice, once as a credit and once as a debit of an equal amount. This is known as double-entry bookkeeping. This ensures that total credits equal total debits (including the statistical discrepancy) for the balance of payments statement as a whole.

4. In 2007, U.S. exports of goods and services as well as income receipts on U.S. assets abroad amounted to $2,464 billion, while U.S. imports of goods and services and income payments on foreign assets were (−)$3,082 billion. The United States also made net unilateral transfers to foreigners equal to (−)$113 billion. This gave a net current account deficit of (−)$731 billion. The United States had a net capital outflow (including official reserve assets) of

(−)$1,290 billion and a net capital inflow of (+)$2,058 billion. A statistical discrepancy credit entry of (−)$41 billion was necessary to make total credits equal to total debits, as required by double-entry bookkeeping.

5. The change in U.S.-owned assets abroad and foreign-owned assets in the United States, other than official reserve assets, gives the U.S. capital account. This showed a net credit balance (a net capital inflow) of (+)$357 billion in 2007.

6. All transactions in the current and capital accounts are called autonomous transactions. If total debits on these autonomous items exceed total credits, the nation has a deficit in its balance of payments equal to the net debit balance. The deficit is then settled by an equal net credit balance on the accommodating items in the official reserve account. The opposite is the case for a balance of payments surplus. This measure of the balance of payments is called the official settlements balance. In 2007, the United States had a balance of payments deficit of $413 billion.

7. The United States had its first large balance of payments deficit in 1970 and this was followed by a much larger deficit in 1971. Since 1973 the United States has had a deficit in its international transactions in every year, except 1979, 1982, 1985, 1989, 1998, and 2001. The U.S. balance-of-payments deficit exceeded $30 billion in each year in 1977–1978, 1986–1988, and 1990. It reached $110 billion in 1995, the maximum of $488 billion in 2006, and it was $411 billion in 2007.

8. The international investment position, or balance of indebtedness, measures the total amount and distribution of a nation's assets abroad and foreign assets in the nation at year-end. Its usefulness is in projecting the future flow of income from U.S. foreign investments and payments on foreign investments in the United States. In 1986, the United States became a net debtor nation for the first time since 1914 and is now the largest debtor nation in the world.

REVIEW QUESTIONS AND PROBLEMS

1. Indicate how each of the following international transactions is entered into the U.S. balance of payments with double-entry bookkeeping:
 (a) A U.S. resident imports $500 worth of merchandise from a U.K. resident and agrees to pay in three months.
 (b) After the three months, the U.S. resident pays for his imports by drawing down his bank balances in London.
 (c) What is the net effect of transactions (a) and (b) on the U.S. balance of payments if they occur during the same year?

2. Indicate how each of the following international transactions is entered into the U.S. balance of payments with double-entry bookkeeping:
 (a) The U.S. government gives a $100 cash balance in a U.S. bank to a developing nation as part of the U.S. foreign aid program.

 (b) The developing nation uses the $100 bank balance to import $100 worth of food from the United States.

 (c) What is the net effect of transactions (a) and (b) on the U.S. balance of payments if they occur during the same year?

3. Indicate how the following transactions are entered into the U.S. balance of payments with double-entry bookkeeping:

 (a) The U.S. government gives $100 worth of food aid to a developing nation.

 (b) What is the difference in their effect on the balance of payments between transaction (a) in this problem, on one hand, and the net result of transactions (a) and (b) in Problem 2, on the other?

4. Indicate how the following transaction is entered into the U.S. balance of payments with double-entry bookkeeping: A U.S. resident purchases a $1,000 foreign stock and pays for it by drawing down her bank balances abroad.

5. Indicate how the following transaction is entered into the U.S. balance of payments with double-entry bookkeeping: A U.S. resident receives a dividend of $100 on her foreign stock and deposits it into her bank account abroad.

6. Indicate how the following transaction is entered into the U.S. balance of payments with double-entry bookkeeping: A foreign investor purchases $400 of U.S. treasury bills and pays by drawing down his bank balances in the United States.

7. Indicate how the following transaction is entered into the U.S. balance of payments with double-entry bookkeeping: At maturity (during the same year), the foreign investor of Problem 6 receives $440 for the principal and interest earned and deposits these dollars in his bank account in his own nation.

8. Indicate how the following transaction is entered into the U.S. balance of payments with double-entry bookkeeping:

 (a) A U.S. commercial bank exchanges $800 worth of pounds sterling for dollars at the Federal Reserve Bank of New York.

 (b) What effect does this transaction have on the official settlements balance of the United States?

9. Update Table 10.1 for the most recent year.

10. With regard to the United States becoming a net debtor nation in 1986, indicate its:

 (a) benefits

 (b) risks

SELECTED BIBLIOGRAPHY

For a problem-solving approach to the material covered in this chapter, see:

• D. Salvatore, *Theory and Problems of International Economics*, 4th ed. (New York: McGraw-Hill, 1996), ch. 7.

Data on U.S. international transactions are presented in:

- U.S. Department of Commerce, Bureau of Economic Analysis, *Survey of Current Business* (Washington, D.C.: U.S. Government Printing Office, monthly).

For international transactions of members of the International Monetary Fund as well as discussion of the statistical discrepancy in the world's current account balances, see:

- International Monetary Fund, *Balance of Payments Statistics Yearbook* (Washington, D.C.: IMF, yearly).

For the U.S.–Japan trade problem, see:

- D. Salvatore, The Japanese Trade Challenge and the U.S. Response (Washington, D.C.: Economic Policy Institute, 1990).
- W. R. Cline, Predicting External Imbalances for the United States and Japan (Washington, D.C.: Institute for International Economics, 1995).

For the U.S.–China trade problem, see:

- Federal Reserve Bank of New York, "The Growing U.S. Trade Imbalance with China," *Current Issues in Economics and Finance* (New York: May 1997).

Surveys of postwar changes in the structure of U.S. trade and investment position are found in:

- D. Salvatore, "Trade Protection and Foreign Direct Investment in the United States," *Annals of the American Academy of Political and Social Science*, July 1991, pp. 91–105.
- C. L. Mann, "Perspectives on the U.S. Current Account Deficit and Sustainability," *Journal of Economic Perspectives*, Summer 2002, pp. 131–152.
- Lawrence J. Kotlikoff, "Is the United States Bankrupt?" *Federal Reserve of Bank of St.Louis Review*, July/August 2006, pp. 235–249.
- United Nations, *World Investment Report* (New York and Geneva: United Nations, 2008).

INTERNet

Data on the international transactions and the international investment position of the United States are found on the Bureau of Economic analysis web site:

http://www.bea.gov by clicking International Data

Data on current account balances and ratio of current account balance to GDP for each nation are found in the *World Economic Outlook*, published in

April and October of each year by the International Monetary Fund, whose web site is:

http://www.imf.org by clicking on "World Economic Outlook"

The *Survey of Current Business* with data on U.S. international transactions and U.S. international investment position are found in the July and August issue of each year at:

http://www.bea.gov by clicking Survey of Current Business

Information and data on the international situation of the United States are also provided in the *Economic Report of the President*, published yearly. For the 2008 *Report*, see:

http://www.gpoaccess.gov/eop/

The data on foreign direct investments are published by the United Nations in the *World Investment Report* (yearly) in

http://www.unctad.org/en/docs/wir2007_en.pdf, for the complete 2007 World Investment Report

The Foreign Exchange Market and Exchange Rates

After studying this chapter, you should be able to:

- Understand the meaning and functions of the foreign exchange market
- Understand the meaning of the equilibrium exchange rate
- Know the cross exchange rate, effective exchange rate, and arbitrage
- Understand the relationship of the exchange rate and the balance of payments
- Know what the spot and forward exchange rates are
- Know what exchange futures and options are
- Understand what foreign exchange risks are and how they arise
- Understand the meaning of hedging, speculation, and interest arbitrage

CHAPTER OUTLINE

KEY TERMS

Foreign exchange market	Foreign exchange options
Vehicle currency	Foreign exchange risk
Seigniorage	Hedging
Exchange rate	Speculation
Euro	Stabilizing speculation
Depreciation	Destabilizing speculation
Appreciation	Interest arbitrage
Cross exchange rate	Uncovered interest arbitrage
Effective exchange rate	Covered interest arbitrage
Arbitrage	Covered interest arbitrage parity (CIAP)
Spot rate	Eurocurrency
Forward rate	Eurocurrency market
Forward discount	Offshore deposits
Forward premium	Eurobonds
Foreign exchange futures	Euronotes

11.1 INTRODUCTION

Foreign exchange market The framework for the exchange of one national currency for another.

The foreign exchange market is the market in which individuals, firms, and banks buy and sell foreign currencies or foreign exchange. The foreign exchange market for any currency—say, the U.S. dollar—is composed of all the locations (such as London, New York, Zurich, Tokyo, Singapore, Sydney, and Hong Kong SAR) where dollars are bought and sold for other currencies. These different monetary centers are connected electronically and are in constant contact with one another, thus forming a single international foreign exchange market.

In Section 11.2, we examine the functions of the foreign exchange market. In Section 11.3, we define foreign exchange rates. In Section 11.4 we examine cross exchange rates, effective exchange rates, and arbitrage. In Section 11.5, we examine the relationship between the exchange rate and the nation's balance of payments. Spot and forward rates are discussed in Section 11.6 and foreign exchange futures and options are examined in Section 11.7. Section 11.8 then deals with foreign exchange risks, Section 11.9 with hedging, and Section 11.10 with speculation. Finally, Section 11.11 examines interest arbitrage

11.2 FUNCTIONS OF THE FOREIGN EXCHANGE MARKET

By far the principal function of foreign exchange market is the transfer of funds or purchasing power from one nation and currency to another. This is usually accomplished by an electronic transfer and increasingly through the Internet. With it, a domestic bank instructs its correspondent bank in a foreign monetary center to pay a specified amount of the local currency to a person, firm, or account.

The demand for foreign currencies arises when tourists visit another country and need to exchange their national currency for the currency of the country they are visiting, when a domestic firm imports from other nations, when an individual invests abroad, and so on. On the other hand, a nation's supply of foreign currencies arises from foreign tourist expenditures in the nation, from export earnings, from receiving foreign investments, and so on. For example, suppose a U.S. firm exporting to the United Kingdom is paid in pounds sterling (the U.K. currency). The U.S. exporter will exchange the pounds for dollars at a commercial bank. The commercial bank will then sell these pounds for dollars to a U.S. resident who is going to visit the United Kingdom, to a U.S. firm that wants to import from the United Kingdom and pay in pounds, or to a U.S. investor who wants to invest in the United Kingdom and needs the pounds to make the investment.

Thus, a nation's commercial banks operate as *clearinghouses* for the foreign exchange demanded and supplied in the course of foreign transactions by

the nation's residents. In the absence of this function, a U.S. importer needing British pounds, for instance, would have to locate a U.S. exporter with pounds to sell. This would be very time-consuming and inefficient and would essentially be equivalent to reverting to barter trade. Those U.S. commercial banks that find themselves with an oversupply of pounds will sell their excess pounds (through the intermediary of *foreign exchange brokers*) to commercial banks that happen to be short of pounds to satisfy their customers' demand. In the final analysis, a nation pays for its tourist expenditures abroad, its imports, its investments abroad, and so on with its foreign exchange earnings from tourism, exports, and the receipt of foreign investments.

If the nation's total demand for foreign exchange exceeds its total foreign exchange earnings, the rate at which currencies exchange for one another will have to change (as explained in the next section) to equilibrate the total quantities demanded and supplied. If such an adjustment in the exchange rates were not allowed, the nation's commercial banks would have to borrow from the nation's central bank. The nation's central bank would then act as the "lender of last resort" and draw down its foreign exchange reserves (a balance-of-payments deficit of the nation). On the other hand, if the nation generated an excess supply of foreign exchange in the course of its business transactions with other nations (and if adjustment in exchange rates were not allowed), this excess supply would be exchanged for the national currency at the nation's central bank, thus increasing the nation's foreign currency reserves (a balance-of-payments surplus).

Thus, four *levels* of agents or participants can be identified in the foreign exchange market. At the bottom, or at the first level, are such traditional users as tourists, importers, exporters, investors, and so on. These are the immediate users and suppliers of foreign currencies. At the next, or second, level are the commercial banks, which act as clearinghouses between users and earners of foreign exchange. At the third level are foreign exchange brokers, through whom the nation's commercial banks even out their foreign exchange position (the so-called *interbank or wholesale market*). Finally, at the fourth and highest level is the nation's central bank, which acts as the seller or buyer of last resort when the nation's total foreign exchange earnings and expenditures are unequal. The central bank then either draws down its foreign exchange reserves or adds to them.

Because of the special position of the U.S. dollar as an international currency, U.S. importers and U.S. residents wishing to make investments abroad could pay in dollars. Then it would be U.K. exporters and investment recipients who would have to exchange dollars for pounds in the United Kingdom. Similarly, U.S. exporters and U.S. recipients of foreign investments may require payment in dollars. Then it would be U.K. importers or investors who have to exchange pounds for dollars in London. This makes

foreign monetary centers relatively larger than they might otherwise might have been.

Vehicle currency
A currency, such as the U.S. dollar and the euro, used for international transactions and to denominate international contracts.

Seigniorage The benefit accruing to a nation when its currency is used as an international currency.

But the dollar is more than an international currency. It is a vehicle currency; that is, the dollar is also used for transactions that do not involve the United States at all, as, for example, when a Braziliian importer uses dollars to pay a Japanese exporter. The same is true for the euro, the newly established currency of the European Monetary Union or EMU. The United States receives a seigniorage benefit when the dollar is used as a vehicle currency. This arises from and amounts to an interest-free loan from foreigners to the United States on the amounts of dollars held abroad. More than 60 percent of the U.S. currency is now held abroad.

The Bank for International Settlements (BIS) in Basel, Switzerland, estimated that the total of foreign exchange trading or "turnover" for the world as a whole averaged $3.2 trillion *per day* in 2007, up from $1.2 trillion in 2001 and $1.9 trillion in 2004. This is more than one-quarter the average *yearly* volume of world trade and about one-fifth of the U.S. gross domestic product (GDP) in 2007. London is by far the largest foreign exchange market in the world, with about $1,360 billion of transactions per day, or 34 percent of total turnover. New York is second with $660 billion or nearly 17 percent of the total. Zurich, Tokyo, and Singapore follow with each about $240 billion or 6 percent of the total. Then come Sydney and Hong Kong SAR with about $170 billion or 4 percent of the total; the rest was in other smaller markets. Most of these foreign exchange transactions take place through debiting and crediting bank accounts rather than through actual currency exchanges. For example, a U.S. firm will pay for the import of goods from England by debiting his or her account at a U.S. bank. The latter will then instruct its correspondent bank in England to credit the account of the British exporter with the pound value of the goods.

Another function of the foreign exchange market is the credit function. Credit is usually needed when goods are in transit and also to allow the buyer time to resell the goods and make the payment. In general, exporters allow 90 days for the importer to pay. However, the exporter usually discounts the importer's obligation to pay at his or her commercial bank. As a result, the exporter receives payment right away, and the bank will eventually collect the payment from the importer when due. Still another function of foreign exchange markets is to provide the facilities for hedging and speculation (discussed in Sections 11.9 and 11.10). Today, about 90 percent of foreign exchange trading reflects purely financial transactions and only about 10 percent trade financing.

Concept Check

What are functions of the foreign exchange market?

With electronic transfers, foreign exchange markets have become truly global in the sense that currency transactions now require only a few seconds to execute and can take place 24 hours per day. As banks end

their regular business day in San Francisco and Los Angeles, they open in Singapore, Hong Kong, Sydney, and Tokyo; by the time the latter banks wind down their regular business day, banks open in London, Zurich, Paris and Frankfurt; and before the latter close, New York and Chicago banks open.

Case Study 11-1 examines the U.S. dollar as the dominant international currency, while Case Study 11-2 discusses the birth of the euro.

CASE STUDY 11-1

The U.S. Dollar as the Dominant International Currency

Today the U.S. dollar is the dominant international currency, serving as a unit of account, medium of exchange, and store of value not only for domestic transactions but for private and official international transactions. Since its creation at the beginning of 1999, the euro (the common currency of 15 member countries of the European Union) has become the second most important international currency (see Case Study 11-2).

Table 11.1 shows the relative importance of the dollar, the euro, and other major currencies in the world economy in 2007. The table shows that 43.2 percent of foreign exchange trading was in dollars, as compared with 18.5 percent in euros, 8.3 percent in Japanese yen, and smaller percentages in other currencies. Table 11.1 also shows that 56.7 percent of international bank loans, 33.7 percent of international bond offerings, and 52.0 percent of international trade invoicing were denominated in U.S. dollars. Also, 63.9 percent of foreign exchange reserves were held in U.S. dollars, as compared with much smaller percentages for the euro and other currencies.

Table 11.1. *Relative International Importance of Major Currencies in 2007 (in percentages)*

	Foreign Exchange Trading[a]	International Bank Loans[a]	International Bond Offering[a]	Trade Invoicing[b]	Foreign Exchange Reserves[c]
U.S. dollar	43.2	56.7	33.7	52.0	63.9
Euro	18.5	22.5	41.9	24.8	26.5
Japanese yen	8.3	3.6	3.0	4.7	2.9
Pound sterling	7.5	6.5	13.5	5.4	4.7
Swiss franc	3.4	2.1	2.4	na	0.2
Other currencies	19.1	8.6	5.5	13.1	0.8

[a]Bank of International Settlements, *Triennial Central Bank Survey* (Basel: BIS, March 2007) and BIS data set.
[b]P. Bekx "The Implications of the Introduction of the Euro for Non-EU Countries," *Euro Paper No. 26*, July 1998. Data are for 1995. More recent data are not available.
[c]IMF, *Annual Report* (Washington, D.C.: IMF, 2008).

The Birth of a New Currency: The Euro

On January 1, 1999, the euro (€) came into existence as the single currency of 11 of the 15 member countries of the European Monetary Union or EMU (Austria, Belgium, Germany, Finland, France, Ireland, Italy, Luxembourg, Spain, Portugal and the Netherlands). Greece was admitted at the beginning of 2001, Slovenia in 2007, and Cyprus and Malta in 2008—making the number of EMU countries equal to 15. Britain, Sweden, and Denmark chose not to participate, but reserved the right to join later. This was the first time that a group of sovereign nations voluntarily gave up their currency in favor of a common currency, and it ranks as one of the most important economic events of the postwar period.

From the start, the euro became an important international currency because the EMU (1) is almost as large an economic unit and a larger trading unit than the United States, (2) has a large, well developed, and growing financial market, which is increasingly free of controls, and (3) and has a good inflation performance

that keeps the value of the euro stable. But it is not likely that the euro will displace the dollar as the leading international currency anytime soon because (1) most primary commodities are priced in dollars; (2) most non-EMU countries are likely to continue to use the dollar for most of their international transactions for the foreseeable future, with the exception of the former communist nations in Central and Eastern Europe (which are candidates for admission into the EMU) and the former French colonies in West and Central Africa; and (3) sheer inertia, which favors the incumbent (the dollar). The most likely situation will be that the euro will share the leading position with the dollar in the future.

Source: D. Salvatore, "The Euro: Expectations and Performance," *Eastern Economic Journal*, Winter 2002, pp. 121–136; and D. Salvatore, "Euro," *Princeton Encyclopedia of the World Economy* (Princeton, N.J.: Princeton University Press, 2008).

11.3 EQUILIBRIUM EXCHANGE RATES

Euro The common currency adopted at the beginning of 1999 by 11 of the 15 member countries of the European Union.

Exchange rate The domestic currency price of the foreign currency.

In order to examine how exchange rates are determined, assume for simplicity that there are only two economies, the United States and the European Monetary Union (EMU), with the dollar ($) as the domestic currency and the euro (€) as the foreign currency. The exchange rate between the dollar and the euro (R) is equal to the number of dollars needed to purchase one euro. That is, $R = \$/€$. For example, if $R = \$/€ = 1$, this means that one dollar is required to purchase one euro.

If exchange rates are more or less free to fluctuate (as is the case today), the dollar price of the euro (R) is determined, just like the price of any commodity, by the intersection of the market demand and supply curves for euros. This is shown in Figure 11.1, where the vertical axis measures the dollar price of the euro, or the exchange rate, $R = \$/€$, and the horizontal

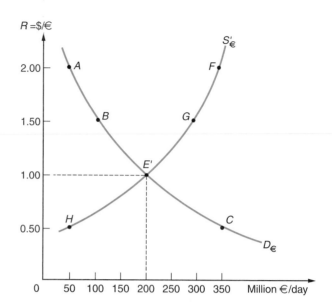

FIGURE 11.1. The Exchange Rate with Flexible Exchange Rates.
The vertical axis measures the dollar price of the euro ($R = \$/\text{€}$), and the horizontal axis measures the quantity of euros. With flexible exchange rates, the equilibrium exchange rate is $R = 1$, at which the quantity demanded and the quantity supplied are equal at €200 million per day. This is given by the intersection at point E of the U.S. demand and supply curves for euros. At a higher exchange rate, a surplus of euros would result that would tend to lower the exchange rate toward the equilibrium rate. At an exchange rate lower than $R = 1$, a shortage of euros would result that would drive the exchange rate up toward the equilibrium level.

axis measures the quantity of euros. The market demand and supply curves for euros intersect at point E, defining the equilibrium exchange rate of $R = 1$, at which the quantity of euros demanded and the quantity supplied are equal at €200 million per day. At a higher exchange rate, the quantity of euros supplied exceeds the quantity demanded, and the exchange rate will fall toward the equilibrium rate of $R = 1$. At an exchange rate lower than $R = 1$, the quantity of euros demanded exceeds the quantity supplied, and the exchange rate will be bid up toward the equilibrium rate of $R = 1$.

The U.S. demand for euros is negatively inclined, indicating that the lower the exchange rate (R), the greater the quantity of euros demanded by U.S. residents. The reason is that the lower the exchange rate (i.e., the fewer the number of dollars required to purchase a euro), the cheaper it is for U.S. residents to import from and invest in the European Monetary Union, and thus the greater the quantity of euros demanded by U.S. residents. On the other hand, the U.S. supply of euros is usually positively inclined

(see Figure 11.1), indicating that the higher the exchange rate (R), the greater the quantity of euros earned by U.S. residents and supplied to the United States. The reason is that at higher exchange rates, EMU residents receive more dollars for each of their euros. As a result, they find U.S. goods and investments cheaper and more attractive and spend more in the United States, thus supplying more euros to the United States.

Depreciation An increase in the domestic currency price of the foreign currency.

If the U.S. demand curve for euros shifted up (e.g., as a result of increased U.S. tastes for EMU goods) and intersected the U.S. supply curve for euros at point G (see Figure 11.1), the equilibrium exchange rate would be $R = 1.50$, and the equilibrium quantity of euros would be €300 million per day. The dollar is then said to have depreciated, since it now requires $1.50 (instead of the previous $1) to purchase one euro. Depreciation thus refers to an increase in the domestic price of the foreign currency. On the other hand, if the U.S. demand curve for euros shifted down so as to intersect the U.S. supply curve for euros at point H (see Figure 11.1), the equilibrium exchange rate would fall to $R = 0.5$ and the dollar would be said to have appreciated (because fewer dollars are now required to purchase one euro). Appreciation thus refers to a decline in the domestic price of the foreign currency. Of course, an appreciation of the domestic currency means a depreciation of the foreign currency and vice versa.

Concept Check

Under what conditions does a currency depreciate or appreciate?

Appreciation A decrease in the domestic currency price of the foreign currency.

The exchange rate could also be defined as the foreign-currency price of a unit of the domestic currency. This is the inverse, or reciprocal, of our previous definition. Since in the previous case we examined, the dollar price of the euro is $R = 1$, its inverse is also 1. If the dollar price of the euro were instead $R = 2$, then the euro-price of the dollar would be $1/R = 1/2$, or it would take half a euro to purchase one dollar. Although this definition of the exchange rate is sometimes used, we will use the previous one, or the dollar price of the euro (R), unless clearly stated to the contrary. In the real world, the particular definition of the exchange rate being used is generally spelled out to avoid confusion. Case Study 11-3 presents actual foreign exchange quotations for various currencies as they appear in *The Wall Street Journal*.

11.4 CROSS EXCHANGE RATES, EFFECTIVE EXCHANGE RATES, AND ARBITRAGE

So far, for simplicity we have dealt with only two currencies. In reality, there are numerous exchange rates, one between any pair of currencies. Thus, besides the exchange rate between the U.S. dollar and the euro, there is an exchange rate between the U.S. dollar and the British pound (£), between the U.S. and the Canadian dollar (C$), between the British pound and the euro (€), the euro and the Swiss franc (SF), and between each of these currencies and the Japanese yen (¥). Once the exchange rate between each of a pair of currencies with respect to the dollar is established, however, the exchange

CASE STUDY 11-3

Foreign Exchange Quotations

Table 11.2 gives the exchange or spot rate for various currencies with respect to the U.S. dollar for Wednesday August 13, 2008—defined first as the dollar price of the foreign currency (often referred to as in *direct* or "American" terms) and then as the foreign currency price of the dollar (i.e., in *indirect* or "European" terms). For example, next to the Euro area, we find that the direct spot rate was $1.4928/€1.

On the same line, we find that the indirect or euro price of the dollar was €0.6699/$1. The last column of the table, headed "U.S. $ vs. YTD chg (%)", shows the percentage change in the exchange rate year to date (YTD); that is, from the beginning of the year. For example, the table shows that the dollar depreciated by (−)2.2 percent vis-à-vis the euro from the beginning of 2008 to August 13, 2008.

Table 11.2. *Foreign Exchange Quotation, August 13, 2008*

Currencies

August 13, 2008

U.S.-dollar foreign-exchange rates in late New York trading

Country/currency	Wed in US$	Wed per US$	US$ vs, YTD chg (%)	Country/currency	Wed in US$	Wed per US$	US$ vs, YTD chg (%)
Americas				**Europe**			
Argentina peso*	.3302	3.0285	−3.8	Czech Rep. koruna**	.06201	16.126	−11.3
Brazil real	.6213	1.6095	−9.6	Denmark krone	.2001	4.9975	−2.1
Canada dollar	.9412	1.0625	6.9	Euro area euro	1.4928	.6699	−2.2
1-mos forward	.9407	1.0630	7.0	Hungary forint	.006275	159.36	−8.0
3-mos forward	.9403	1.0635	7.1	Norway krone	.1859	5.3792	−1.0
6-mos forward	.9402	1.0636	7.1	Poland zloty	.4526	2.2095	−10.5
Chile peso	.001942	514.93	3.4	Russia ruble‡	.04130	24.213	−1.5
Colombia peso	.0005410	1848.43	−8.4	Slovak Rep koruna	.04920	20.325	−11.7
Ecuador US dollar	1	1	unch	Sweden krona	.1592	6.2814	−2.8
Mexico peso*	.0985	10.1523	−7.0	Switzerland franc	.9220	1.0846	−4.3
Peru new sol	.3418	2.926	−2.4	1-mos forward	.9223	1.0842	−4.1
Uruguay peso†	.05250	19.05	−11.6	3-mos forward	.9228	1.0837	−3.9
Venezuela b.fuerte	.466287	2.1446	unch	6-mos forward	.9241	1.0821	−3.7
Asia-Pacific				Turkey lira**	.8435	1.1856	1.5
Australian dollar	.8760	1.1416	0.1	UK pound	1.8707	.5346	6.2
China yuan	.1458	6.8572	−6.1	1-mos forward	1.8664	.5358	6.4
Hong Kong dollar	.1281	7.8081	0.1	3-mos forward	1.8578	.5383	6.7
India rupee	.02350	42.553	8.0	6-mos forward	1.8469	.5414	7.0
Indonesia rupiah	.0001089	9183	−2.2				
Japan yen	.009128	109.55	−1.7	**Middle East/Africa**			
1-mos forward	.009145	109.35	−1.5	Bahrain dinar	2.6525	.3770	0.3
3-mos forward	.009179	108.94	−1.3	Egypt pound*	.1877	5.3265	−3.7
6-mos forward	.009237	108.26	−1.1	Israel shekel	.2774	3.6049	−6.5
Malaysia ringgit§	.3014	3.3179	0.3	Jordan dinar	1.4129	.7078	−0.1
New Zealand dollar	.7043	1.4198	8.8	Kuwait dinar	3.7261	.2684	−1.8
Pakistan rupee	.01330	75.188	22.0	Lebanon pound	.0006634	1507.39	−0.3
Philippines peso	.0223	44.863	8.8	Saudi Aarabia riyal	.2666	3.7509	unch
Singapore dollar	.7119	1.4047	−2.6	South Africa rand	.1273	7.8555	14.8
Soth Korea won	.0009615	1040.04	11.1	UAE dirham	.2723	3.6724	unch
Taiwan dollar	.03196	31.289	−3.5				
Thailand baht	.02970	33.670	12.1				
Vietnam dong	.00006015	16625	3.7	SDR††	1.5800	.6329	

*Floating rate †Financial §Goverment rate ‡Russian Central Bank rate **Rebased as of Jan 1, 2005
††Special Drawing Rights (SDR); from the International Monetary Fund; based on exchange rates for U.S., British and Japanese currencies.
Note: Based on trading among banks of $1 million and more, as quoted at 4p.m. ET by Reuters.

Source: Reprinted by permission of the *Wall Street Journal*,
© 2008 Dow Jones & Company, Inc. All rights reserved.

Cross exchange rate
The exchange rate
between currency
A and currency B,
given the exchange
rate of currency A
and currency B with
respect to currency C.

rate between the two currencies themselves, or cross exchange rate, can easily
be determined.

For example, if the exchange rate (R) were 2 between the U.S. dollar
and the British pound and 1.25 between the dollar and the euro, then the
exchange rate between the pound and the euro would be 1.60 (i.e., it takes
€1.6 to purchase 1£). Specifically,

$$R = €/£ = \frac{\$ \text{ value of } £}{\$ \text{ value of } €} = \frac{2}{1.25} = 1.60$$

**Effective exchange
rate** A weighted
average of the
exchange rates
between the domestic
currency and the
nation's most
important trade
partners, with
weights given by the
relative importance
of the nation's trade
with each of these
trade partners.

Since over time, a currency can depreciate with respect to some currencies
and appreciate against others, an effective exchange rate is calculated. This
is a weighted average of the exchange rates between the domestic currency
and the nation's most important trade partners, with weights given by the
relative importance of the nation's trade with each of these trade partners.
Case Study 11-4 gives the effective exchange rate of the U.S. dollar from 1972
to 2008.

Arbitrage The
purchase of a
currency in the
monetary center
where it is cheaper
for immediate resale
in the monetary
center where it is
more expensive in
order to make a
profit.

The exchange rate between any two currencies is kept the same in
different monetary centers by arbitrage. This refers to the purchase of a
currency in the monetary center where it is cheaper, for immediate resale in
the monetary center where it is more expensive, in order to make a profit. For
example, if the dollar price of the euro was $0.99 in New York and $1.01 in
Frankfurt, an arbitrageur (usually a foreign exchange dealer of a commercial
bank) would purchase euros at $0.99 in New York and immediately resell
them in Frankfurt for $1.01, thus realizing a profit of $0.02 per euro. While
the profit per euro transferred seems small, on €1 million the profit would be
$20,000 for only a few minutes' work. From this profit must be deducted the
cost of the electronic transfer and the other costs associated with arbitrage.
Since these costs are very small, we will ignore them here.

Concept
Check

How does currency
arbitrage work? What
is its effect on the
exchange rate?

As arbitrage takes place, the exchange rate between the two currencies
tends to be equalized in the two monetary centers. Continuing our example,
we see that arbitrage increases the demand for euros in New York, thereby
exerting an upward pressure on the dollar price of euros in New York. At the
same time, the sale of euros in Frankfurt increases the supply of euros there,
thus exerting a downward pressure on the dollar price of euros in Frankfurt.
This continues until the dollar price of the euro quickly becomes equal in
New York and Frankfurt (say at $1 = €1), thus eliminating the profitability
of further arbitrage.

11.5 THE EXCHANGE RATE AND THE BALANCE OF PAYMENTS

We can examine the relationship between the exchange rate and the nation's
balance of payments with Figure 11.3, which is identical to Figure 11.1, except

CASE STUDY 11-4

The Effective Exchange Rate of the Dollar

Figure 11.2 shows the effective exchange rate of the dollar (defined as the weighted average foreign-currency value of the dollar, with March 1973 = 100) from 1972 to 2008. This index is useful because the exchange rate between the U.S. dollar and the various other currencies changed by different amounts and sometimes in different directions over time. Note the sharp *appreciation* of the dollar from 1980 to 1985 and depreciation since the beginning of 2002. Note that an appreciation is here shown by an *increase* in the effective exchange rate of the dollar; that is, the effective exchange rate is usually given in *indirect* or European terms.

FIGURE 11.2. The Effective Exchange Rate of the Dollar, 1972–2008.
The effective exchange rate is defined as the weighted average of the exchange rates between the dollar and the most important U.S. trade partners, with weights given by the relative importance of the nation's trade with each of these trade partners.
Source: The Conference Board, *Business Cycle Indicators,* April 25, p. 25.

for the addition of the new demand curve for euros labeled D'_ϵ. We have seen in Chapter 10 that the U.S. demand for euros (D_ϵ) arises from the U.S. demand for imports of goods and services from the European Monetary Union (EMU), from U.S. unilateral transfers to the EMU, and from U.S. investments in the EMU (a capital outflow from the United States). These are the autonomous debit transactions of the United States that involve payments to the EMU. On the other hand, the U.S. supply of euros (S_ϵ) arises from U.S. exports of goods and services to the EMU, from unilateral transfers received from the EMU, and EMU investments in the United States (a capital inflow of the United States). These are the autonomous credit transactions of the United States that involve payments from the EMU. (We are assuming for simplicity that the United States and the European Monetary Union are

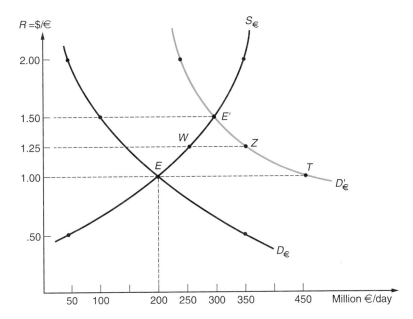

FIGURE 11.3. Disequilibrium with Flexible and Fixed Exchange Rates.
With $D_{\text{€}}$ and $S_{\text{€}}$, equilibrium exchange rate would be $R = \$/\text{€} = 1$ (point E), at which the quantities of euros demanded and supplied are equal at €200 million per day. If $D_{\text{€}}$ shifted up to $D'_{\text{€}}$, the dollar would depreciate to $R = 1.50$ (point E') if the exchange rate was allowed to vary. To keep the exchange rate at $R = 1$, the United States would have to supply the excess demand of €250 million per day (TE in the figure) out of its official euro reserves. To limit the dollar depreciation to $R = 1.25$, the United States would have to use €100 million per day (WZ in the figure) of its euro reserves.

the only two economies in the world and that all transactions between them take place in euros.)

With $D_{\text{€}}$ and $S_{\text{€}}$ the equilibrium exchange rate is $R = \$/\text{€} = 1$ (point E in Figure 11.3), at which €200 million are demanded and supplied per day (exactly as in Figure 11.1). Now suppose that for whatever reason (such as an increase in U.S. tastes for EMU products) the U.S. demand for euros shifts up to $D'_{\text{€}}$. If allowed, the exchange rate would rise (i.e., the dollar would depreciate) from $R = 1.00$ to $R = 1.50$, at which the quantity of euros demanded (€300 million per day) exactly equals the quantity supplied (point E' in Figure 11.3).

If, on the other hand, the United States wanted to maintain the exchange rate fixed at $R = 1$, U.S. monetary authorities would have to satisfy the excess demand for euros of TE (€250 million per day in Figure 11.3) out of their

official reserves of euros. Alternatively, EMU monetary authorities would have to purchase dollars (thus adding to their official dollar reserves) and supply euros to the foreign exchange market to prevent the depreciation of the dollar. In either case, the U.S. official settlements balance would show a deficit of €250 million (which equal $250 million at the official exchange rate of $R = 1$) per day, or €91.25 billion ($91.25 billion) per year.

Concept Check

What is the relationship between the exchange rate and the balance of payments?

If in the preceding example the United States wanted to limit the depreciation of the dollar to $R = 1.25$ (instead of letting the dollar depreciate all the way to $R = 1.50$), it would have to supply the remaining excess demand for euros of *WZ*, or €100 million per day, out of its official euro reserves (see the figure). In that case, part of the potential U.S. balance of payments deficit would be covered by the loss of U.S. official reserves and part would be reflected in a depreciation of the dollar.

11.6 SPOT AND FORWARD EXCHANGE RATES

The most common type of foreign exchange transaction involves the payment and receipt of the foreign exchange within two business days after the day the transaction is agreed upon. The two-day period gives adequate time for the parties to send instructions to debit and credit the appropriate bank accounts at home and abroad. This type of transaction is called a *spot transaction*, and the exchange rate at which the transaction takes place is called the spot rate. The exchange rate $R = \$/\€ = 1$ in Figure 11.1 is a spot rate.

Spot rate The exchange rate in foreign exchange transactions that calls for the payment and receipt of the foreign exchange within two business days from the date when the transaction is agreed upon.

Besides spot transactions, there are forward transactions. A *forward transaction* involves an agreement today to buy or sell a specified amount of a foreign currency, for delivery at a specified future date, at a rate agreed upon today (the forward rate). For example, I could enter into an agreement today to purchase €100 for delivery in three months at $1.01 = €1. Note that no currencies are paid out at the time the contract is signed (except for the usual 10 percent security margin). After three months, I get the €100 for $101, regardless of what the spot rate is at that time. The typical forward contract is for one month, three months, or six months, with three months the most common. Forward contracts for longer periods are not as common because of the great uncertainties involved. However, forward contracts can be renegotiated for one or more periods when they become due. In what follows, we will deal exclusively with three-month forward contracts and rates, but the procedure would be the same for forward contracts of different duration.

Forward rate The exchange rate in foreign exchange transactions involving delivery of the foreign exchange one, three, or six months after the contract is agreed upon.

The equilibrium forward rate is determined at the intersection of the market demand and supply curves of foreign exchange for *future delivery*. The demand for and supply of *forward* foreign exchange arise in the course of hedging, from foreign exchange speculation, and from covered interest arbitrage. These, as well as the close relationship between the spot rate and the forward rate, are discussed in Sections 11.9 to 11.11.

Forward discount
The percentage per year by which the forward rate on the foreign currency is below its spot rate.

At any point in time, the forward rate can be equal to, above, or below the corresponding spot rate. If the forward rate is below the present spot rate, the foreign currency is said to be at a forward discount with respect to the domestic currency. On the other hand, if the forward rate is above the present spot rate, the foreign currency is said to be at a forward premium. For example, if the spot rate is $1 = €1 and the three-month forward rate is $0.99 = €1, we say that the euro is at a three-month forward discount of 1 cent or 1 percent (4 percent per year) with respect to the dollar. On the other hand, if the spot rate is still $1 = €1 but the three-month forward rate is instead $1.01 = €1, the euro is said to be at a forward premium of 1 cent or 1 percent for three months, or 4 percent per year.

Forward premium
The percentage per year by which the forward rate on the foreign currency is above its spot rate.

Forward discounts *(FD)* or premiums *(FP)* are usually expressed as percentages per year from the corresponding spot rate and can be calculated formally with the following formula:

$$FD \text{ or } FP = \frac{FR - SR}{SR} \times 4 \times 100$$

Concept Check

What is the relationship between spot and forward rate?

where *FR* is the forward rate and *SR* is the spot rate (what we simply called *R* in the previous section). The multiplication by 4 is to express the *FD*(–) or *FP*(+) on a yearly basis, and the multiplication by 100 is to express the *FD* or *FP* in percentages. Thus, when the spot rate of the pound is *SR* = $1.00 and the forward rate is *FR* = $0.99, we get

$$\begin{aligned} FD &= \frac{\$0.99 - \$1.00}{\$1.00} \times 4 \times 100 = \frac{-\$0.01}{\$1.00} \times 4 \times 100 \\ &= 0.01 \times 4 \times 100 = -4\% \end{aligned}$$

the same as found earlier without the formula. Similarly, if *SR* = $1 and *FR* = $1.01:

$$\begin{aligned} FD &= \frac{\$1.01 - \$1.00}{\$1.00} \times 4 \times 100 = \frac{\$1.01}{\$1.00} \times 4 \times 100 \\ &= 0.01 \times 4 \times 100 = +4\% \end{aligned}$$

11.7 FOREIGN EXCHANGE FUTURES AND OPTIONS

Foreign exchange futures A forward contract for standardized currency amounts and selected calendar dates traded on an organized market (exchange).

Banks, firms, and individuals can also purchase or sell foreign exchange futures and options. A foreign exchange futures is a forward contract for standardized currency amounts and selected calendar dates. Trading in foreign exchange futures was initiated in 1972 by the International Monetary Market (IMM) of the Chicago Mercantile Exchange (CME). The currencies traded on the IMM are the Japanese yen, the Canadian dollar, the British pound, the Swiss franc, the Australian dollar, the Mexican peso, and the euro.

IMM trading is done in contracts of standard size. For example, the IMM Japanese yen contract is for ¥12.5 million, the pound contract is for £62,500, the Canadian dollar contract is for C$100,000, and the euro contract is for €125,000. Only four dates per year are available: the third Wednesday in March, June, September, and December. Buyers and sellers pay a brokerage commission and are required to post a security deposit or margin (of about 4 percent of the value of the contract). A market similar to the IMM is the Frankfurt-based Eurex.

The *futures market* differs from the forward market in that in the futures market only a few currencies are traded; trades occur in standardized contracts only, for a few specific delivery dates, and trading takes place only in a few geographical locations, such as Chicago, New York, London, Frankfurt, and Singapore. Futures contracts are usually for smaller amounts than forward contracts, and thus are more useful to small firms than to large ones, but are somewhat more expensive. Futures contracts can also be sold any time up until maturity on an organized futures market, while forward contracts cannot. Although the market for currency futures is small compared with the forward market, it has grown very rapidly in recent years.

Individuals, firms, and banks can also purchase foreign exchange options (in Japanese yen, Canadian dollars, British pounds, Swiss francs, and euros) on the Philadelphia Stock Exchange, the Chicago Mercantile Exchange, or from a bank. A foreign exchange option is a contract giving the purchaser the right, but not the obligation, to buy (a *call option*) or to sell (a *put option*) a standard amount of a traded currency on a stated date (the *European option*) or at any time before a stated date (the *American option*) and at a stated price (the *strike* or *exercise price*). Foreign exchange options are in standard sizes equal to those of futures IMM contracts (see Case Study 11-5). The buyer of the option has the choice to purchase or forgo the purchase if it turns out to be unprofitable. The seller of the option, however, must fulfill the contract if the buyer so desires. The buyer pays the seller a premium (the option price) ranging from 1 to 5 percent of the contract's value for this privilege when he or she enters the contract. For example, an American firm making a bid to take over a European firm may be required to promise to pay a specified amount in euros. Since the American firm does not know if its bid will be successful, it will purchase an option to buy the euros that it would need and will exercise the option only if the bid is successful.

Foreign exchange options A contract specifying the right to buy or sell a standard amount of a traded currency at or before a stated date.

Concept Check

What are the uses of foreign exchange futures and options?

11.8 FOREIGN EXCHANGE RISKS

Over time, a nation's demand and supply curves for foreign exchange change (shift), causing exchange rates to vary frequently. For example, if U.S. tastes for EMU products increase, the U.S. demand for euros increases (the demand curve shifts up), leading to a rise in the exchange rate (i.e., a depreciation of the dollar). On the other hand, a lower rate of inflation in the United States

CASE STUDY 11-5

Eurocurrency or Offshore Financial Market

Eurocurrency refers to commercial bank deposits outside the country of their issue. For example, a deposit denominated in U.S. dollars in a British commercial bank (or even in a British branch of a U.S. bank) is called a Eurodollar and the market in which this borrowing and lending takes place is called the Eurocurrency market. Initially, only the dollar was used in this fashion, and the market was therefore called the Eurodollar market. When British pounds sterling, Swiss francs, and euros also began being used in this way, the market was renamed *Eurocurrency market*, and with the practice spreading to Tokyo, Hong Kong, Singapore, Kuwait, the Bahamas, and the Cayman Islands, such deposits are now more appropriately called offshore deposits (the market itself, however, often continues to be called the Eurocurrency market).

With these geographical extensions, the Eurocurrency market has become an essentially 24-hour-a-day operation. Indeed, any foreign deposit made in a nation's bank (even if in the nation's currency) is considered an offshore deposit if exempted from the regulations that the nation imposes on domestic deposits. The Eurocurrency market consists mostly of short-term funds with maturity of less than six months. Offshore deposits now exceed $20 trillion ($8 trillion if interbank deposits are excluded). The creation and spectacular growth of the Eurocurrency market during the past four decades were due to (1) the higher interest rates often prevailing abroad on short-term deposits; (2) multinationals often finding it convenient to hold balances abroad for short periods in the currency in which they needed to make payments and (3) multinationals overcoming domestic credit restrictions by borrowing in the Eurocurrency market.

Besides Eurocurrencies there are also Eurobonds and Euronotes. Eurobonds are long-term debt securities that are sold outside the borrower's country to raise long-term capital in a currency other than the currency of the nation where the bonds are sold. An example is provided by a U.S. corporation selling bonds in London denominated in euros or U.S. dollars. Eurobonds differ from *foreign bonds*, which refer simply to bonds sold in a foreign country but denominated in the currency of the country in which the bonds are sold. An example is a U.S. multinational corporation selling bonds in England denominated in pounds sterling. The leading centers in the international bond market are London, Frankfurt, New York, and Tokyo.

Euronotes are medium-term financial instruments falling somewhat between short-term Eurocurrency bank loans and long-term international bonds. In 2007, corporations, banks, and countries raised about $1.5 trillion in Eurobonds and Euronotes. The incentive to issue Eurobonds and Euronotes is the lower cost of borrowing long-term funds than by available alternatives. Most Eurobonds and Euronotes are now denominated in euros and U.S. dollars. Large issues of Eurobonds and Euronotes are usually negotiated by a group of banks (called a *syndicate*) so as to spread the credit risk among many banks.

Interest rates on Eurocredits are expressed as a mark-up or spread over *LIBOR* (the London Interbank offer rate) or *EUROBOR* (the Brussels-set rate) at which Eurobanks lend funds to one another. The spread varies according to the creditworthiness of the borrower and ranges from 1 percent for best or prime borrowers to 2 percent for borrowers with weak credit ratings.

Source: G. McKenzie, *Economics of the Eurodollar Market* (London: McMillan, 1976) and D. Salvatore, *International Economics*, 9th ed., (Hoboken, N.J.: Wiley, 2007), Section 14.7.

Eurocurrency
Commercial bank deposits in a nation denominated in a foreign currency.

Eurocurrency market
The market where Eurocurrencies are borrowed and lent.

Offshore deposits
Bank deposits denominated in a currency other than that of the nation in which the deposit is held.

Eurobonds
Long-term debt securities sold outside the borrower's country to raise long-term capital in a currency other than the currency of the nation where the securities are sold.

Euronotes
Medium-term financial instruments falling somewhere between short-term Eurocurency bank loans and long-term Eurobonds.

than in the European Monetary Union leads to U.S. products becoming cheaper for EMU residents. This tends to increase the U.S. supply of euros (the supply curve shifts to the right) and causes a decline in the exchange rate (i.e., an appreciation of the dollar). Or simply the expectation of a stronger dollar may lead to an appreciation of the dollar. In short, in a dynamic and changing world, exchange rates frequently vary, reflecting the constant change in the numerous economic forces simultaneously at work.

Figure 11.4 shows the great variation in the exchange rate of the dollar with respect to the Japanese yen, the euro, the British pound, and the Canadian dollar from 1971 to 2008. Note that the exchange rate is defined here in indirect terms or from the foreign nation's point of view (i.e., it is the foreign-currency price of the U.S. dollar), so that an increase in the exchange rate refers to a depreciation of the foreign currency (it takes more units of the foreign currency to purchase one dollar), while a reduction in the exchange rate refers to an appreciation of the foreign currency (and a depreciation of the dollar).

The first panel of Figure 11.4 shows the sharp *appreciation* of the Japanese yen (depreciation of the dollar) from 360 yen per dollar in 1971 to about 100 in 2008. The second panel shows the sharp depreciation of the euro (appreciation of the dollar) from the beginning of 1999 until 2000 and then its equally large appreciation since the beginning of 2002. Note the sharp depreciation of the British pound with respect to the U.S. dollar from 1980 to 1985 in the third panel and the sharp appreciation of the Canadian dollar with respect to the U.S. dollar from 2002 to 2008 in the fourth panel.

The frequent and relatively large fluctuations in exchange rates shown in Figure 11.4 impose foreign exchange risks on individuals, firms, and banks that have to make or receive payments in the future denominated in a foreign currency. For example, suppose a U.S. importer purchases €100,000 worth of goods from the EMU and has to pay in three months in euros. If the present spot rate of the pound is $SR = \$1/€1$, the current dollar value of the payment that he or she must make in three months is $100,000. However, in three months the spot rate might change to $SR = \$1.10/€1$. Then the importer would have to pay $110,000, or $10,000 more, for the imports. Of course, in three months the spot rate might be $SR = \$0.90/€1$ so that the importer would only have to pay $90,000, or $10,000 less than anticipated. However, the importer has enough to worry about in his or her business without also having to deal with the foreign exchange risk. As a result, the importer will usually want to insure against an increase in the dollar price of the euro (i.e., an increase in the spot rate) in three months.

Similarly, a U.S. exporter who expects to receive a payment of €100,000 in three months will receive only $90,000 (instead of the $100,000 that he or she anticipates at today's spot rate of $SR = \$1/€1$) if the spot rate in three months is $SR = \$0.90/€1$. Once again, the spot rate could be higher in three months than it is today so that the exporter would receive more than

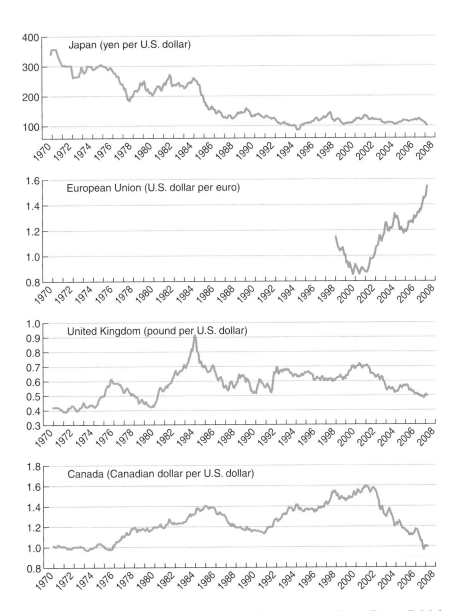

FIGURE 11.4. The Exchange Rate of the Japanese Yen, Euro, British Pound, and Canadian Dollar over Time.
The four panels show the fluctuations of the exchange rate of the Japanese yen, the euro (estimated back to 1996 from its creation at the beginning of 1999), the British pound, and the Canadian dollar. The exchange rate definition used is the foreign-currency value of the dollar, so that an increase in the exchange rate refers to a depreciation of the foreign currency and appreciation of the dollar and vice versa.
Source: The Conference Board, *Business Cycle Indicators*, April 2008, p. 25.

Foreign exchange risk The risk resulting from changes in exchange rates over time and faced by anyone who expects to make or to receive a payment in a foreign currency at a future date; also called an open position.

Concept Check

How do foreign exchange risks arise?

Hedging The avoidance of a foreign exchange risk (or the covering of an open position).

anticipated. However, the exporter, like the importer, will usually want to cover the exchange risk that he or she faces. Another example is provided by an investor who buys euros at today's spot rate in order to invest in three-month EMU treasury bills paying a higher rate than U.S. treasury bills. However, in three months, when the investor wants to convert euros back into dollars, the spot rate may have fallen sufficiently to wipe out most of the extra interest earned on the EMU bills, or even produce a loss.

These three examples clearly show that whenever a future payment must be made or received in a foreign currency, a foreign exchange risk, or a so-called open position, is involved because spot exchange rates vary over time. In general, businesspeople are risk averse and will want to avoid or insure themselves against their foreign exchange risk. (Note that arbitrage does not involve any exchange risk since the currency is bought at the cheaper price in one monetary center and *immediately resold* at the higher price in another monetary center.)

11.9 HEDGING

Hedging refers to the avoidance of a foreign exchange risk, or the covering of an open position. For example, the importer of the previous example could purchase €100,000 at the present spot rate of $SR = \$1/€1$ and leave this sum on deposit in a bank (to earn interest) for three months, until the payment is due. By doing so, the importer avoids the risk that the spot rate in three months will be higher than today's spot rate and that he or she would have to pay more than $100,000 for the imports. The exporter could borrow €100,000 today, exchange this sum for $100,000 at today's spot rate of $SR = \$1/€1$, and deposit the $100,000 in a bank to earn interest. After three months, the exporter would repay the loan of €100,000 with the payment of €100,000 he or she receives. The cost of avoiding the foreign exchange risk in this manner is equal to the positive difference between the borrowing and deposit rates of interest.

Covering the foreign exchange risk in the spot market, however, has a very serious disadvantage because the businessperson or investor must either tie up his or her own funds or borrow for three months. To avoid this, hedging usually takes place in the forward market. Thus, the importer could buy euros forward for delivery (and payment) in three months at today's three-month forward rate. If the euro is at a three-month forward premium of 4 percent per year, the importer will have to pay $101,000 in three months for the €100,000 needed to pay for the imports. Therefore, the hedging cost will be $1,000 (1 percent of $100,000 for the three months). Similarly, the exporter could sell pounds forward for delivery (and payment) in three months at today's three-month forward rate, in anticipation of receiving the payment of €100,000 for the exports. Since no transfer of funds takes place until three months have passed, the exporter need not borrow now. If the euro is at a

three-month forward discount of 4 percent per year, the exporter will get only $99,000 for the €100,000 he or she delivers in three months.

A foreign exchange risk can also be hedged and an open position avoided in the futures or options markets. For example, suppose that an importer knows that he or she must pay €100,000 in three months and the three-month forward rate of the euro $FR = \$1/€1$. The importer could either purchase the €100,000 forward (in which case he or she will have to pay $100,000 in three months and receive the €100,000) or purchase an option to purchase €100,000 in three months, say, at $1/€1, and pay now the premium of, say, 1 percent (or $1,000 on the $100,000 option). If in three months the spot rate of the pound were $SR = \$0.98/€1$, the importer would still have to pay $100,000 with the forward hedge. If the importer had instead purchased the option, he or she would let the option expire unexercised and get the €100,000 at the cost of only $98,000 on the spot market. In that case, the $1,000 premium for the purchase of the foreign currency option can be regarded as an insurance policy. Thus, the net cost of getting the €100,000 would be $99,000 with the currency option and $100,000 with the forward contract.

In a world of foreign exchange uncertainty, the ability of traders and investors to hedge greatly facilitates the international flow of trade and investments. Note that a multinational corporation that has to make and receive a large number of payments in the same foreign currency at the same time in the future need only hedge its net open position. Similarly, a bank has an open position only in the amount of its net balance on contracted future payments and receipts. The bank closes as much of its open positions as possible by dealing with other banks (through foreign exchange brokers), and it may cover the remainder in the spot, futures, or options markets. In recent years, the risks associated with all kinds of foreign exchange trading have increased significantly, but so have the awareness of them, the knowledge of how to deal with them, and the instruments available to cover them.

Concept Check

Why is it important for firms to cover their foreign exchange risks?

11.10 SPECULATION

Speculation The acceptance of a foreign exchange risk, or open position, in the hope of making a profit.

Speculation is the opposite of hedging. Whereas a hedger seeks to cover a foreign exchange risk, a speculator accepts and even seeks out a foreign exchange risk, or an open position, in the hope of making a profit. If the speculator correctly anticipates future changes in spot rates, he or she makes a profit; otherwise, he or she incurs a loss. As in the case of hedging, speculation can take place in the spot, forward, futures, or options markets—usually in the forward market. We begin by examining speculation in the spot market.

If a speculator believes that the spot rate of a particular foreign currency will rise, he or she can purchase the currency now and hold it on deposit in a bank for resale later. If the speculator is correct and the spot rate does indeed rise, he or she earns a profit on each unit of the foreign currency equal to the

spread between the previous lower spot rate at which he or she purchased the foreign currency and the higher subsequent spot rate at which he or she resells it. If the speculator is wrong and the spot rate falls, he or she incurs a loss because the foreign currency must be resold at a price lower than the purchase price.

If, on the other hand, the speculator believes that the spot rate will fall, he or she borrows the foreign currency for three months, immediately exchanges it for the domestic currency at the prevailing spot rate, and deposits the domestic currency in a bank to earn interest. After three months, if the spot rate on the foreign currency is lower, as anticipated, the speculator earns a profit by purchasing the currency (to repay the foreign exchange loan) at the lower spot rate. (Of course, for the speculator to earn a profit, the new spot rate must be sufficiently lower than the previous spot rate to also overcome the possibly higher interest rate paid on a foreign currency deposit over the domestic currency deposit.) If the spot rate in three months is higher rather than lower, the speculator incurs a loss.

In both of the preceding examples, the speculator operated in the spot market and either had to tie up his or her own funds or had to borrow to speculate. It is to avoid this that speculation, like hedging, usually takes place in the forward market. For example, if the speculator believes that the spot rate of a certain foreign currency will be higher in three months than its present three-month forward rate, the speculator purchases a specified amount of the foreign currency forward for delivery (and payment) in three months. After three months, if the speculator is correct, he or she receives delivery of the foreign currency at the lower agreed forward rate and immediately resells it at the higher spot rate, thus realizing a profit. Of course, if the speculator is wrong and the spot rate in three months is lower than the agreed forward rate, he or she incurs a loss. In any event, no currency changes hands until the three months are over (except for the normal 10 percent security margin that the speculator is required to pay at the time he or she signs the forward contract).

Stabilizing specula-tion The purchase of a foreign currency when the domestic currency price of the currency (i.e., the exchange rate) falls or is low, in the expectation that the exchange rate will soon rise, thus leading to a profit. Or the sale of a foreign currency when the exchange rate rises or is high, in the expectation that it will soon fall.

As another example, suppose that the three-month forward rate on the euro is $FR = \$1.01/€1$ and the speculator believes that the spot rate of the euro in three months will be $SR = \$0.99/€1$. The speculator then sells euros forward at the $FR = \$1.01/€$ for delivery in three months. After three months, if the speculator is correct, he or she purchases euros in the spot market at $SR = \$0.99/€1$ and immediately sells them to fulfill the forward contract at the agreed forward rate of $\$1.01/€1$, thereby earning a profit of 2¢ per euro. If the spot rate in three months is instead $SR = \$1.00/€1$, the speculator earns only 1¢ per euro. If the spot rate in three months is $\$1.01/€1$, the speculator earns nothing. Finally, if the spot rate in three months is higher than the forward rate at which the speculator sold the forward euros, the speculator incurs a loss on each euro equal to the difference between the two rates.

Destabilizing speculation The sale of a foreign currency when the exchange rate falls or is low, in the expectation that it will fall even lower in the future, or the purchase of a foreign currency when the exchange rate is rising or is high, in the expectation that it will rise even higher in the future.

Speculation can be stabilizing or destabilizing. Stabilizing speculation refers to the purchase of a foreign currency when the domestic price of the foreign currency (i.e., the exchange rate) falls or is low, in the expectation that it will soon rise, thus leading to a profit. Or it refers to the sale of the foreign currency when the exchange rate rises or is high, in the expectation that it will soon fall. Stabilizing speculation moderates fluctuations in exchange rates over time and performs a useful economic function.

On the other hand, destabilizing speculation refers to the sale of a foreign currency when the exchange rate falls or is low, in the expectation that it will fall even lower in the future, or the purchase of a foreign currency when the exchange rate is rising or is high, in the expectation that it will rise even higher in the future. Destabilizing speculation thus magnifies exchange rate fluctuations over time and can prove very disruptive to the international flow of trade and investments. Under "normal" conditions, speculation is stabilizing, and we assume so here unless specifically indicated to the contrary. In recent years, some speculators have incurred huge losses on exchange rate speculation.

Concept Check

Why do speculators willingly accept and seek foreign exchange risks?

11.11 INTEREST ARBITRAGE

Interest arbitrage The transfer of short-term liquid funds abroad to earn a higher return.

Interest arbitrage refers to the international flow of short-term liquid capital (such as the purchase of foreign treasury bills) to earn higher returns abroad. Since the transfer of funds abroad to take advantage of higher interest rates abroad involves the conversion of the domestic to the foreign currency to make the investment, and the subsequent reconversion of the funds (plus the interest earned) from the foreign currency to the domestic currency at the time of maturity, a foreign exchange risk is involved. If such a foreign exchange risk is covered, we have covered interest arbitrage; otherwise, we have uncovered interest arbitrage. Even though interest arbitrage is usually covered, we begin by examining the simpler uncovered interest arbitrage.

Uncovered interest arbitrage The transfer of short-term liquid funds to the international monetary center with higher interest rates without covering the foreign exchange risk.

Suppose that the interest rate on three-month treasury bills is 6 percent at an annual basis in New York and 8 percent in Frankfurt. It may then pay for a U.S. investor to exchange dollars for euros at the current spot rate and purchase EMU treasury bills to earn the extra 2 percent interest at an annual basis. When the EMU treasury bills mature, the U.S. investor may want to exchange the euros invested plus the interest earned back into dollars. However, by that time, the euro may have depreciated so that the investor would get back fewer dollars per euro than he or she paid. If the euro depreciates by 1 percent at an annual basis during the three months of the investment, the U.S. investor nets only about 1 percent from this foreign investment (the extra 2 percent interest earned minus the 1 percent lost from the depreciation of the euro) at an annual basis, or one-quarter of 1 percent for the three months or quarter of the investment. If the euro depreciates by 2 percent at an annual basis during the three months, the U.S. investor gains

nothing, and if the euro depreciates by more than 2 percent, the U.S. investor loses. Of course, if the euro *appreciates*, the U.S. investor gains both from the extra interest earned and from the appreciation of the euro.

Interest arbitrage, however, is usually covered. To do so, the investor exchanges the domestic for the foreign currency at the current spot rate in order to purchase the foreign treasury bills, and at the same time the investor sells forward the amount of the foreign currency he or she is investing plus the interest he or she will earn so as to coincide with the maturity of the foreign investment. Thus, covered interest arbitrage refers to the spot purchase of the foreign currency to make the investment and the offsetting simultaneous forward sale of the foreign currency to cover the foreign exchange risk. When the treasury bills mature, the investor can then get the domestic currency equivalent of the foreign investment plus the interest earned without a foreign exchange risk. Since the currency with the higher interest rate is usually at a forward discount, the net return on the investment is roughly equal to the interest differential in favor of the foreign monetary center minus the forward discount on the foreign currency. This reduction in earnings can be viewed as the cost of insurance against the foreign exchange risk.

As an illustration, let us continue the previous example where the interest rate on three-month treasury bills is 6 percent per year in New York and 8 percent in Frankfurt, and assume that the euro is at a forward discount of 1 percent per year. To engage in covered interest arbitrage, the U.S. investor exchanges dollars for euro at the current exchange rate (to purchase the EMU treasury bills) and at the same time sells forward a quantity of euro equal to the amount invested plus the interest he or she will earn at the prevailing forward rate. Since the euro is at a forward discount of 1 percent per year, the U.S. investor loses 1 percent on an annual basis on the foreign exchange transaction to cover the foreign exchange risk. The net gain is thus the extra 2 percent interest earned minus the 1 percent lost on the foreign exchange transaction, or 1 percent on an annual basis (one-quarter of 1 percent for the three months or the one-quarter of the investment). Note that we express both the interest differential and the forward discount at an annual basis and then divide by four to get the net gain for the three months, or one-quarter of the investment.

As covered interest arbitrage continues, however, the possibility of gains diminishes until it is completely wiped out. This occurs for two reasons. First, as funds are transferred from New York to Frankfurt, the interest rate rises in New York (since the supply of funds in New York diminishes) and falls in Frankfurt (since the supply of funds in Frankfurt increases). As a result, the interest differential in favor of Frankfurt diminishes. Second, the purchase of euro in the spot market increases the spot rate, and the sale of euros in the forward market reduces the forward rate. Thus, the forward discount on the euro (i.e., the difference between the spot rate and the forward rate)

Covered interest arbitrage The transfer of short-term liquid funds abroad to earn higher returns with the foreign exchange risk covered by the spot purchase of the foreign currency and a simultaneous offsetting forward sale.

Concept Check

How does covered interest arbitrage work?

Covered interest arbitrage parity (CIAP) The situation where the interest differential in favor of the foreign monetary center equals the forward discount on the foreign currency.

rises. With the interest differential in favor of Frankfurt diminishing and the forward discount on the euro rising, the net gain falls for both reasons, until it becomes zero. The euro is then said to be at covered interest arbitrage parity. Here, the interest differential in favor of the foreign monetary center is equal to the forward discount on the foreign currency (both expressed on an annual basis). In the real world, a net gain of at least one-quarter or one-eighth of 1 percent per year is normally required to induce funds to move internationally under covered interest arbitrage.

Significant unexploited covered interest arbitrage opportunities are sometimes observed in the foreign exchange market because of lack of information or fear that a foreign government might default or impose restrictions on the repatriation of profits and principal. This is one reason for the existence of the Eurocurrency or offshore financial market (see Case Study 11-5). The foreign exchange market is said to be *efficient* if the forward rate exceeds the future spot rate as often as it falls below it, so that speculators cannot earn consistent and unusual profits. Most empirical studies to date seem to indicate that the foreign exchange market is efficient for large industrial countries. Nevertheless, exchange rates have defied all attempts at being accurately forecasted. This will be the topic of the next chapter.

SUMMARY

1. Foreign exchange markets are the markets where individuals, firms, and banks buy and sell foreign currencies or foreign exchange. The foreign exchange market for any currency, say, the U.S. dollar, is composed of all the locations (such as London, New York, Zurich, Tokyo, Singapore, Sydney and Hong Kong SAR) where dollars are bought and sold for other currencies. These different monetary centers are connected by a telephone network and video screens and are in constant contact with one another. A vehicle currency is a currency, such as the U.S. dollar and the euro, that is used for international transactions and to denominate international contracts. Seigniorage refers to the benefit accruing to a nation from issuing the currency or when its currency is used as an international currency.

2. The principal function of foreign exchange markets is the transfer of purchasing power from one nation and currency to another. A nation's commercial banks operate as clearinghouses for the foreign exchange demanded and supplied. Commercial banks then even out their excess supply of or demand for foreign exchange with other commercial banks through the intermediation of foreign exchange brokers. The nation's central bank then acts as the lender or borrower of last resort.

3. The exchange rate (R) is defined as the domestic currency price of the foreign currency. If free to fluctuate, the equilibrium exchange rate is determined at the intersection of the nation's demand and supply curves for

the foreign currency. If the domestic currency price of the foreign currency rises, we say that the domestic currency depreciated. In the opposite case, we say that the domestic currency appreciated.

4. From the exchange rate between each of a pair of currencies with respect to the dollar, the cross rate between the two currencies themselves can be determined. The effective exchange rate is a weighted average of the exchange rates between the domestic currency and the nation's most important trade partners. Arbitrage refers to the purchase of a currency where it is cheaper for immediate resale where it is more expensive. This equalizes exchange rates and ensures consistent cross rates in all monetary centers.

5. If the quantity demanded of euros on U.S. private transactions exceeds the quantity supplied, the dollar would depreciate until the excess demand for euros is eliminated. To keep the exchange rate fixed, the U.S. monetary authorities would have to satisfy the excess demand for euros out of their official euro reserves (a U.S. balance of payments deficit). A potential U.S. balance of payments deficit could also be covered partly by a dollar depreciation and partly by the loss of U.S. official reserves.

6. A spot transaction involves the exchange of currencies for delivery within two business days. A forward transaction is an agreement to purchase a specified amount of a foreign currency for delivery at a future date (usually one, three, or six months hence) at a rate agreed upon today (the forward rate). When the forward rate is lower than the spot rate, the foreign currency is said to be at a forward discount of a certain percentage per year. In the opposite case, the foreign currency is said to be at a forward premium.

7. A foreign exchange futures is a forward contract for standardized currency amounts, available for specific currencies and selected calendar dates and traded on an organized exchange. A foreign exchange option is a contract specifying the right to buy or sell a standard amount of a traded currency at or before a stated date.

8. Because exchange rates usually change over time, they impose a foreign exchange risk on anyone who expects to make or receive a payment in a foreign currency at a future date.

9. Foreign exchange risks are covered by hedging. Hedging can take place in the spot, forward, future, or options markets—usually in the forward market.

10. Speculation is the opposite of hedging. It refers to the taking of an open position in the expectation of making a profit. Speculation can be stabilizing or destabilizing. Like hedging, speculation can take place in the spot, forward, future, or options markets—usually in the forward market.

11. Interest arbitrage refers to the international flow of short-term liquid funds to earn higher returns abroad. Covered interest arbitrage involves a spot purchase of the foreign currency to make the investment and a simultaneous offsetting forward sale of the foreign currency to cover the

foreign exchange risk. The net return from covered interest arbitrage is equal to the interest differential in favor of the foreign monetary center minus the forward discount on the foreign currency. As covered interest arbitrage continues, the net gain is reduced and finally eliminated. Eurocurrency refers to commercial bank deposits outside the country of their issue. There are also Eurobonds and Euronotes.

REVIEW QUESTIONS AND PROBLEMS

1. If the U.S. supply curve for euros shifted up and intersected the U.S. demand curve for euros at point B in Figure 11.1 in the text, what would be
 (a) the equilibrium exchange rate?
 (b) the equilibrium quantity demanded and supplied of euros in the United States?

2. If the U.S. supply curve for euros shifted down and intersected the U.S. demand curve for euros at point C in Figure 11.1 in the text, what would be
 (a) the equilibrium exchange rate?
 (b) the equilibrium quantity demanded and supplied of euros in the United States?

3. If the United States kept the exchange rate of the dollar fixed at $R = 0.5$ in Figure 11.1 in the text,
 (a) would the United States have a deficit or a surplus in its balance of payments?
 (b) what would be the size of the deficit or surplus?

4. Calculate the forward discount or premium for the following spot and three-month forward rates:
 (a) $SR = \$2.00/£1$ and $FR = \$2.01/£1$
 (b) $SR = \$2.00/£1$ and $FR = \$1.96/£1$

5. Assume that $SR = \$2/£1$ and the three-month $FR = \$1.96/£1$. How can an importer who will have to pay £10,000 in three months hedge the foreign exchange risk?

6. For the given in Problem 5, indicate how an exporter who expects to receive a payment of £1 million in three months can hedge the foreign exchange risk.

7. Assume that the three-month $FR = \$2.00/£1$ and a speculator believes that the spot rate in three months will be $SR = \$2.05/£1$.
 (a) How can an individual speculate in the forward market?
 (b) How much will the speculator earn if he or she is correct?

8. If the speculator of Problem 7 believes that the spot rate in three months will be $SR = \$1.95/£1$,
 (a) how can he or she speculate in the forward market?
 (b) how much will the speculator earn if he or she is correct?
 (c) what will the result be if in three months $SR = \$2.05/£1$ instead?

9. If the positive interest rate differential in favor of a foreign monetary center is 4 percent per year and the foreign currency is at a forward discount of 2 percent per year, roughly how much would an investor earn from the purchase of foreign three-month treasury bills if he or she covered the foreign exchange risk?

10. For the given of Problem 9, indicate:
 (a) How much would an investor earn if the foreign currency were at a forward premium of 1 percent per year?
 (b) What would happen if the foreign currency were at a forward discount of 6 percent per year?

SELECTED BIBLIOGRAPHY

For a problem-solving approach to the topics covered in this chapter, see:

- D. Salvatore, *Theory and Problems of International Economics*, 4th ed. (New York: McGraw-Hill, 1996), ch. 7.

The operation of the foreign exchange markets is explained in detail in:

- Federal Reserve Bank of New York, *Survey of Foreign Exchange Market* (New York: Federal Reserve Bank of New York, 1998).

On the creation of the euro and the international use of the dollar, the euro, and the yen, see:

- G. Tavlas, "The International Use of Currencies: The U.S. Dollar and the Euro," *Finance and Development*, June 1998, pp. 46–49.
- Board of Governors of the Federal Reserve System, "The Launch of the Euro," *Federal Reserve Bulletin*, October 1999, pp. 655–666.
- D. Salvatore, "The Euro: Expectations and Performance," *Eastern Economic Journal*, Winter 2002, pp. 121–136.
- D. Salvatore, "Euro," and "Vehicle Currency," *Princeton Encyclopedia of the World Economy* (Princeton, N.J.: Princeton University Press, 2008).

The classic work on the spot and forward markets for foreign exchange, hedging, and speculation is:

- P. Einzig, *The Dynamic Theory of Forward Exchange* (London: Macmillan, 1967).

For the empirical testing of covered interest arbitrage and the efficiency of foreign exchange markets, see:

- M. Taylor, "The Economics of Exchange Rates," *Journal of Economic Literature*, March 1995, pp. 13–47.
- K. Rogoff, "Monetary Models of the Dollar/Yen/Euro," *The Economic Journal*, November 1999, pp. 655–659.

- M. D. Chinn and G. Meredith, "Testing Uncovered Interest Parity at Short and Long Horizons During the Post-Bretton Woods Era," *NBER Working Paper No. 11077*, January 2005.

A discussion of the operation of the Euromarkets and international banking is found in:

- International Monetary Fund, *International Capital Markets* (Washington, D.C.: IMF, 2008).
- Bank for International Settlements, *Annual Report* (Basel, Switzerland: BIS, 2008).

INTERNet

The basics of the foreign exchange market in the United States can be found at:

http://www.ny.frb.org/education/fx/foreign.html

Data on exchange rates by country and region, cross rates, and well as the ability to calculate the exchange rate between any two currencies can be obtained by clicking on "currencies" and "currency calculator" on the Bloomberg web site at:

http://www.bloomberg.com

The monthly trade-weighted exchange rate of the dollar, as well as data on U.S. interest rates, can be obtained by clicking, respectively, on "Exchange Rates, Balance of Payments, and Trade Data" and "Interest Rates" (for covered interest arbitrage) on the Federal Reserve Bank of St. Louis web site at:

http://research.stlouisfed.org/fred2

Exchange Rate Determination

After studying this chapter, you should be able to:

- Know the different forces that affect exchange rates
- Understand how exchange rates are determined according to the elasticity approach
- Know what the purchasing-power parity theory postulates
- Understand how exchange rates are determined according to the monetary approach
- Know what the asset or portfolio approach postulates
- Know why exchange rates are very volatile
- Know how exchange rates are forecasted

CHAPTER OUTLINE

12.1 Introduction

12.2 Overview of Exchange Rate Determination

12.3 Trade or Elasticity Approach

12.4 Purchasing-Power Parity Theory

KEY TERMS

Trade or elasticity approach	Monetary model of exchange rates
Purchasing-power parity (PPP) theory	Nominal exchange rate
Absolute purchasing-power parity theory	Real exchange rate
Law of one price	Asset or portfolio approach to exchange rates
Relative purchasing-power parity theory	Exchange rate overshooting

12.1 INTRODUCTION

This chapter examines exchange rate theories or how exchange rates are determined in the real world. The exchange rate is one of the most important, if not the most important, variable in all of international finance and the exchange rate theories discussed here provide the background for all the topics examined in international finance.

We will see that exchange rates are determined by the interaction of many forces, some of a long run in nature while others of a short-run nature. We will examine international trade and price changes in the trading nations as determinants of exchange rate changes in the *long run*. Then we will focus on the importance of capital markets and international capital flows, which seek to explain the *short-run* volatility of exchange rates and their

tendency to overshoot their long-run equilibrium path or level. While both traditional or long-run and short-run forces are clearly important, we do not yet have a unified or comprehensive theory of exchange rate determination, as evidenced by the fact that we are unable to accurately forecast exchange rate, especially in the short run.

In Section 12.2, we provide an overview of the forces that affect exchange rates. Section 12.3 examines the trade or elasticity approach to exchange rate determination. Section 12.4 presents the purchasing-power parity theory, which provides the long-run framework for the monetary and asset or portfolio approach to exchange rate determination. Section 12.5 then examines the monetary approach to the balance of payments and exchange rate determination. Section 12.6 presents the asset market or portfolio approach to exchange rate determination. Section 12.7 examines exchange rate dynamics and seeks to explain the tendency of short-run exchange rates to overshoot their long-run equilibrium level. Finally, Section 12.8 deals with exchange rate forecasting.

12.2 OVERVIEW OF EXCHANGE RATE DETERMINATION

We have seen in Chapter 11 that a nation's demand for foreign exchange arises from the desire to import goods and services and invest in other nations, and from speculators when they expect the foreign currency to appreciate. The nation's supply of foreign exchange, on the other hand, results from exporting goods and services to other nations, from the inflow of foreign investments, and from the sale of the foreign currency by speculators when they expect the foreign currency to depreciate. We have seen in Chapter 11 that when exchange rates are free to fluctuate (as is the case today), the exchange rate is determined at the intersection of the market demand and supply curves of foreign exchange.

This, however, is the beginning, not the end, of the analysis. A theory of exchange rate determination must explain how the various components of the demand and supply of foreign exchange operate singly and how they interact to jointly determine exchange rates. In this section we provide an overview of the most important forces that affect exchange rates before examining each of these forces in more detail in the rest of the chapter.

Specifically, the nation's currency, say, the U.S. dollar, will depreciate if the United States experiences (1) economic growth, which increases its demand for imports, (2) an increase in its price level (inflation), (3) a reduction of its interest rate, and (4) the expectation that the dollar will depreciate. We will examine how these changes affect the dollar exchange rate by utilizing Figure 12.1, which is an extension of Figure 11.1.

In Figure 12.1, $D_{\unicode{0x20AC}}$ and $S_{\unicode{0x20AC}}$ refer to the U.S. demand and supply curves of euros ($\unicode{0x20AC}$). With the exchange rate free to fluctuate, the equilibrium exchange

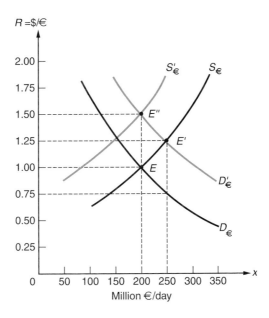

FIGURE 12.1. Forces Affecting the Dollar/Euro Exchange Rate.
With $D_{€}$ and $S_{€}$, equilibrium is at point E with €200 million per day demanded and supplied by the United States and $R = \$1 = €1$. If $D_{€}$ shifted to $D'_{€}$ with growth and an increase in the demand for U.S. imports, the new equilibrium point would be at E' with €250 million per day demanded and supplied at $R = \$1.25 = €1$ (i.e., the dollar depreciates). With inflation or a reduction in the U.S. interest rate that shift $D_{€}$ and $S_{€}$ up to $D'_{€}$ and $S'_{€}$, the equilibrium point would be at E'' at $R = \$1.50 = €1$.

rate is given at point E, where the $D_{€}$ and $S_{€}$ curves intersect. This defines the equilibrium exchange rate of $\$1 = €1$, at which €200 million per day are demanded and supplied to the United States (exactly as in Figure 11.1).

If now the rate of economic growth increases in the United States but not in the European Monetary Union (EMU), the United States will demand more imports from the EMU. This shifts $D_{€}$ up, say to $D'_{€}$, which gives the new equilibrium point E' in Figure 12.1, at which the quantity demanded and the quantity supplied of euros to the United States are in equilibrium at €250 million per day and the dollar exchange rate rises (i.e., the dollar depreciates) from $\$1 = €1$ to $\$1.25 = €1$.

Starting again from equilibrium point E in Figure 12.1, if the price level increases in the United States but does not change in the EMU, the United States will now find imports cheaper and so it demands more euros (i.e., $D_{€}$ shifts up, say, to $D'_{€}$) while EMU residents find U.S. products more expensive and so spend or supply fewer euros to the United States (i.e., $S_{€}$ shifts up and to the left, say to $S'_{€}$). $D'_{€}$ and $S'_{€}$ intersect at point E'', at which the quantity demanded and supplied of euros to the United States is in equilibrium at

€200 million per day and the exchange rate rises (the dollar depreciates) from $1 = €1 to $1.50 = €1. (Note that if D'_ϵ and S'_ϵ shifted by different amounts, the equilibrium quantity of euros demanded and supplied to the United States might be larger or smaller than €200 million per day, but the dollar will definitely depreciate.) The result would be similar if labor productivity increased in the EMU but not in the United States and this resulted in lower prices in the EMU.

If, again starting from equilibrium point E in Figure 12.1, the interest rate in the United States *fell*, there would be an increase in the U.S. demand for euros to invest in the EMU in order to earn the higher interest there. Similarly, foreign investors would reduce investments and supply fewer euros to the United States. With D_ϵ and S_ϵ shifting up to D'_ϵ and S'_ϵ, the new equilibrium point would be at E'', with €200 million per day demanded and supplied to the United States and with the exchange rate rising (i.e., the dollar depreciating) from $1 = €1 to $1.50 = €1.

Expectations will also affect the dollar exchange rate. For example, if the United States is expected to grow faster than the EMU and demand more imports, or if the United States is expected to face a higher inflation rate or a lower growth of labor productivity than the EMU in the future, then the dollar will also depreciate. In fact, the dollar will depreciate if the expectation is that it will depreciate, even if such an expectation is not based on any solid or fundamental economic reason. In financial markets, expectations have a way of becoming *self-fulfilling*.

If opposite changes than the ones examined previously were to take place, the dollar would appreciate, and if more than one change occurred at the same time, the effect on the dollar exchange rate would be the net result of all the changes taking place.

12.3 TRADE OR ELASTICITY APPROACH

One traditional and crucial model of exchange rate determination is based on the flow of goods and services and is, therefore, referred to as the trade or elasticity approach. According to this approach, the equilibrium exchange rate is the one that balances the value of the nation's imports and exports. If the value of the nation's imports exceeds the value of the nation's exports (i.e., if the nation faces a trade deficit), the exchange rate will rise (i.e., the domestic currency will depreciate). This makes the nation's exports cheaper to foreigners and imports more expensive to domestic residents. The result is that the nation's exports rise and its imports fall until trade is balanced.

Since the amount and speed of adjustment depend on how responsive (elastic) imports and exports are to price (exchange rate) changes, this approach is referred to as the trade or elasticity approach. If the nation is at or near full employment, a larger depreciation of the nation's currency is

Concept Check

What are the different forces that affect exchange rates?

Trade or elasticity approach The theory or approach that stresses the role of trade or the flow of goods and services in the determination of exchange rates. This model is more useful in explaining exchange rates in the long run than in the short run.

required to shift domestic resources to the production of more exports and import substitutes than if the nation has unemployed resources. Alternatively, domestic policies may be required to reduce domestic expenditures (absorption) to release domestic resources to produce more exports and import substitutes, and thus allow the elasticity approach to operate. The details of this trade or elasticity approach will be examined in Chapter 13, while the economic policies that a nation can undertake to influence the level of domestic economic activity (absorption) will be examined in Chapter 14.

Concept Check

How are exchange rates determined according to the elasticity approach?

Purchasing-power parity (PPP) theory The theory that postulates that the change in the exchange rate between two currencies is proportional to the change in the ratio in the two countries' general price levels.

Absolute purchasing-power parity theory Postulates that the equilibrium exchange rate is equal to the ratio of the price levels in the two nations. This version of the PPP theory can be very misleading.

Law of one price The proposition that in the absence of transportation costs, tariffs, and other obstructions to the free flow of trade, the price of each homogeneous (identical) traded commodity will be equalized in all markets by commodity arbitrage.

What is important to keep in mind here is that the elasticity approach stresses trade or the flow of goods and services in the determination of exchange rates. International capital flows are important only as passive responses (i.e., to cover or pay) for temporary trade imbalances. The trade or elasticity approach is certainly important, but it cannot explain (1) the large volatility (fluctuation) of exchange rates over the past three decades (i.e., since exchange rates were allowed to fluctuate), (2) the sharp appreciation of the dollar from 1980 to 1985 and from 1995 to 2002 (in the face of rising U.S. trade deficits), or (3) the failure of the U.S. trade deficits to decline when the dollar depreciated sharply from 1985 to 1988 and from 2002 to 2008. All of this does not mean that the trade or elasticity approach to exchange rate determination is wrong—only that it provides a fundamental part of the explanation of exchange rate determination more in the long run than in the short run, and that there must, therefore, be other important determinants of exchange rates, especially in the short run.

12.4 PURCHASING-POWER PARITY THEORY

A related exchange-rate model or approach that is also more relevant to exchange rate determination in the long run than in the short run is the purchasing-power parity (PPP) theory. There are two versions of the PPP theory, the absolute version and the relative version.

The absolute purchasing-power parity theory postulates that the equilibrium exchange rate between two currencies is equal to the ratio of the price levels in the two nations. Specifically:

$$R = \frac{P}{P*}$$

where R is the exchange rate or spot rate (defined as the domestic-currency price of a unit of the foreign currency) and P and $P*$ are, respectively, the general price level in the home nation and in the foreign nation. For example, if the price of one bushel of wheat is \$1 in the United States and €1 in the European Monetary Union (EMU), then the exchange rate between the dollar and the euro should be $R = \$1/€1 = 1$. That is, according to the law of one price, a given commodity should have the same price (so that the

purchasing power of the two currencies is at parity) in both countries when expressed in terms of the same currency. If the price of one bushel of wheat in terms of dollars were $0.50 in the United States and $1.50 in the EMU, firms would purchase wheat in the United States and resell it in the EMU at a profit. This commodity arbitrage would cause the price of wheat to fall in the EMU and rise in the United States until the prices were equal, say, $1 per bushel, in both countries. Commodity arbitrage thus operates just as does currency arbitrage in equalizing commodity prices throughout the market.

Relative purchasing-power parity theory
The theory that postulates that the percentage change in the exchange rate is equal to the difference in the percentage change in the price level in the two countries.

The absolute PPP theory, however, would hold only if there were no transportation costs, tariffs, or other obstructions to the free flow of trade; if all commodities were traded internationally; and if no structural changes (such as wars) took place in the United States and the EMU. Since these assumptions do not hold, the absolute version of the PPP cannot be taken seriously (see Case Studies 12-1 and 12-2). Whenever the purchasing-power parity theory is used, it is usually in its relative formulation.

The relative purchasing-power parity theory is potentially more useful. It postulates that the *change* in the exchange rate is equal to the difference in the *change* in the price level in the two countries. Specifically,

$$\hat{R} = \hat{P} - \hat{P}^*$$

Concept Check

Under what conditions is the relative purchasing-power parity theory useful?

where a caret (ˆ) over a variable denotes percentage change. According to this equation, the percentage change in the exchange rate (\hat{R}) should be equal to the percentage change in the domestic price level (\hat{P}) minus the percentage change in the foreign price level (\hat{P}^*). For example, starting from $R = \$1 = €1$, if prices double in the United States relative to those in the EMU, the exchange rate of the dollar with respect to the euro should also double from $R = 1$ to $R = 2$. *As long as there are no changes* in transportation costs, obstructions to trade, ratio of traded to nontraded goods, and in the structure of the two economies, the percentage change in the exchange rate should equal the difference in the percentage change in the two countries' general price levels. Since trade and commodity arbitrage respond sluggishly, however, we expect relative purchasing power-parity (PPP) to be approximated only in the long run (see Case Study 12-3).

Monetary model of exchange rates The theory that postulates that exchange rates are determined in the process of equilibrating or balancing the stock or total demand and supply of money in each nation.

12.5 THE MONETARY MODEL OF EXCHANGE RATES

In contrast to the trade or elasticity approach, in which the exchange rate is determined by the *flow* of funds (resulting from trade in goods and services and from the flow of investments), the monetary model of exchange rates

Absolute Purchasing-Power Parity in the Real World

Figure 12.2 shows the actual exchange rate of the dollar in terms of the German mark (i.e., DM/$ prevailing in the market—the color curve) and the PPP exchange rate (measured by the ratio of the German to the U.S. consumer price index—the black curve) during the flexible exchange rate period since 1973. (Since the beginning of 1999, the fluctuation of the DM/$ reflects the fluctuation of the euro with respect to the dollar.) For the absolute PPP theory to hold, the two curves should coincide. As we

can see from the figure, however, the curves diverge widely. The dollar was undervalued (the color curve was below the black curve) from 1973 to 1980, 1986 to 2000 and since 2003, and overvalued from 1981 to 1985 and from 2001 to 2002. The figure shows that at its peak (at the beginning of 1985), the dollar was overvalued by nearly 40 percent in terms of marks. Only at the beginning of 1981, 1986, 2001 and 2003 do the curves cross and the two currencies are at parity.

FIGURE 12.2. Actual and PPP Exchange Rate of the Dollar, 1973–2008.
The color curve measures the dollar exchange rate (defined as DM/$) prevailing in the market, while the black curve measures the PPP exchange rate (measured by the ratio of the German to the U.S. consumer price index) from 1973 to 2008. The figure shows that the dollar was undervalued during 1973–1980, 1986–2000, and since 2003, and overvalued during 1981–1985 and 2001–2002. (Since the beginning of 1999, the fluctuation in DM/$ reflects the fluctuation of the euro with respect to the dollar.)
Source: International Monetary Fund, *International Financial Statistics* (Washington, D.C.: IMF, various issues).

Big MacCurrencies

According to the absolute PPP theory, the dollar price of a particular product—say, the McDonald's Big Mac hamburger—should be the same in other countries as in the United States if exchange rates were equal to the ratio of the price level in the United States and other countries. From the first column in Table 12.1, however, we see that the dollar price of a Big Mac varies greatly across countries. In July 2008, the Big Mac was most expensive in Norway ($7.88) and cheapest in Malaysia ($1.70).

Since the dollar-price of a Big Mac was $7.88 in Norway as compared with $3.57 in the United States, the Norwegian Kroner was

overvalued 121 percent ($7.88/$3.57) with respect to the U.S. dollar in July 2008. The table also shows that the euro was overvalued by 50 percent, the Brazilian real by 33 percent, the British pound by 28 percent, and the Canadian dollar by 14 percent. On the other hand, the Mexican peso was undervalued by 12 percent with respect to the U.S. dollar, the Japanese yen undervalued by 27 percent, the Chinese Yuan by 49 percent, and the Malaysian Ringgit by 52 percent. Norway was thus the most expensive country for the Americans to visit and Malaysia the least expensive.

Table 12.1. *Big Mac Prices and Exchange Rates, July 2008*

Country	Price in Dollars	Local Currency Overvaluation (+) Undervaluation (−)
United States	$3.57	—
Norway	7.88	+121
Switzerland	6.36	+78
Euro area	5.34	+50
Brazil	4.73	+33
Britain	4.57	+28
Canada	4.08	+14
Argentina	3.64	+2
Poland	3.45	−3
Mexico	3.15	−12
Japan	2.62	−27
Russia	2.54	−29
South Africa	2.24	−37
China	1.83	−49
Malaysia	1.70	−52

Source: "Big Mac Index" *The Economist*, July 26, 2008, p. 88.

postulates that the exchange rate is determined in the process of equilibrating or balancing the *stock* or total demand and supply of the national currency in each nation.

The supply of money in each country is assumed to be determined or set independently by the nation's monetary authorities. The demand for money, on the other hand, depends on the level of real income in the nation, the general price level, and the interest rate. The higher are real income and prices, the greater is the demand for money balances that individuals and business demand for their day-to-day transactions (purchases). On the other hand, the higher the rate of interest, the greater the opportunity cost of holding cash or non–interest-earning demand deposits instead of interest-bearing assets or bonds. Thus, the demand for money is inversely related to the rate of interest (i.e., the higher the rate of interest, the smaller the quantity demanded of money in the nation). *For a given level of real income and prices*, the equilibrium interest rate itself is determined at the intersection of the demand and supply curves of money in each nation.

CASE STUDY 12-3

Relative Purchasing-Power Parity in the Real World

Figure 12.3 shows the relationship between changes in relative national price levels and changes in exchange rates for 18 industrial nations from 1973 to 2007 (the period of flexible exchange rates). The horizontal axis measures the average inflation rate in each country minus the average inflation rate in the United States (so that positive values refer to a higher average inflation rate in the nation than in the United States). The vertical axis measures changes in the foreign exchange rate, defined as the *foreign*-currency price of the U.S. dollar. Thus an increase in the foreign exchange rate refers to a depreciation of the *foreign* currency relative to the U.S. dollar, while a decrease in the exchange rate refers to an appreciation of the foreign currency.

According to the relative Purchasing-Power Parity (PPP) theory, nations with higher inflation rates than in the United States should experience depreciating currencies, while nations with lower inflation rates should have appreciating currencies. The figure shows that this is indeed the case over the thirty-five-year period examined. That is, countries with higher inflation rates than the United States experienced depreciating currencies with respect to the U.S. dollar, while countries with lower inflation rates experienced appreciating currencies. For the theory to hold perfectly, however, the plotted points in Figure 12.3 should fall on a straight line with a positive slope of 1. Since this is not the case, the relative PPP theory holds only approximately.

Since 1999, changes in the exchange rates of EMU countries reflect the changes in the euro/dollar exchange rate.
Source: International Monetary Fund, *International Financial Statistics*, various issues.

(continues)

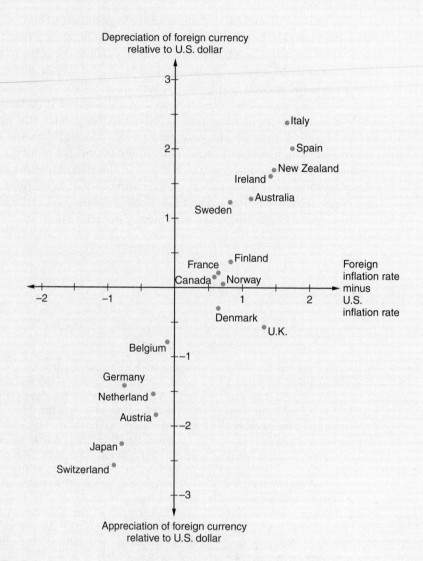

FIGURE 12.3. Inflation Differentials and Exchange Rates, 1973–2007.
Positive values along the horizontal axis refer to higher average inflation rates in the nation than in the United States. Positive values along the vertical axis refer to a depreciating currency relative to the U.S. dollar. Since nations with higher inflation rates generally experienced depreciating currencies, the relative PPP theory seems to be broadly confirmed in the long run.

According to the monetary model of exchange rates, an increase in the nation's money supply leads to a proportionate increase in prices and depreciation of the nation's currency in the long run, as postulated by the PPP theory. For example, if U.S. monetary authorities increase the money supply by 10 percent but the EMU does not, the general price level in the United States should increase by 10 percent and the dollar exchange rate increase (i.e., the dollar depreciate) by 10 percent, say from $R = 1$ to $R = 1.1$, in the long run. The nominal and real exchange rates of the dollar should then move together by the same percentage over time. The nominal exchange rate is what we have so far simply called "the exchange rate." The real exchange rate is the nominal rate adjusted for the different inflation rates in the United States and the EMU. In the real world, nominal and real exchange rates have not always moved together, however (see Case Study 12-4).

According to the monetary approach, interest rate differentials and exchange rate expectations also affect the exchange rate of a currency. For example, if the interest rate in the United States is higher than in the EMU, investment funds will flow from the EMU to the United States and lead to an appreciation of the dollar, as postulated by the uncovered interest arbitrage theory discussed in Section 11.11. But if the dollar is also expected to depreciate in the future by more than the positive interest differential in favor of the dollar, then investments funds will flow in the opposite direction, from the United States to the EMU, and the dollar will depreciate vis-à-vis the euro (see Case Study 12-5).

Nominal exchange rate The exchange rate or the domestic currency price of the foreign currency.

Real exchange rate The nominal exchange rate weighed by the consumer price index in the two nations.

Concept Check

How do expectations affect exchange rates according to the monetary approach?

12.6 ASSET OR PORTFOLIO MODEL OF EXCHANGE RATES

Asset or portfolio approach to exchange rates The theory that postulates that exchange rates are determined in the process of equilibrating or balancing the demand and supply of financial assets in each country.

Another approach that seeks to explain exchange rate movements is the asset or portfolio model. The asset or portfolio approach to exchange rates differs from the monetary approach by postulating that the exchange rate is determined in the process of equilibrating or balancing the *stock* or total demand and supply of financial assets (of which money is only one) in each country. It also brings trade explicitly into the analysis.

Starting from a position of portfolio or financial and trade balance, the asset or portfolio approach postulates that an increase in a nation's money supply leads to an immediate decline in the interest rate in the nation and a shift from domestic bonds to the domestic currency and foreign bonds. The shift from domestic bonds to domestic currency arises because the cost of holding cash has now diminished, while the shift to foreign bonds results from their relatively higher interest rates now that the domestic interest rate has fallen on domestic bonds. Holding a foreign bond, however, will lead to a foreign exchange risk. The domestic investor will, therefore, hold a foreign bond only if the return on the foreign bond, adjusted for the risk premium,

CASE STUDY 12-4

Nominal and Real Exchange Rates, and the Monetary Model

Figure 12.4 shows the nominal and the real exchange rate index (with 1973 = 100) between the U.S. dollar ($) and the German mark (DM) from 1973 to 2007. The nominal exchange rate is defined as DM/$. (From the beginning of 1999, the fluctuation of the mark reflects the fluctuation of the euro with respect to the dollar.) The real exchange rate is the nominal exchange rate divided by the ratio of the consumer price index in Germany to the consumer price index in the United States. That is, (DM/$)/(PGerm/PUS) = (DM/$)(PUS/PGerm).

If the nominal exchange rate reflected changes in relative prices in the United States and Germany (as postulated by the PPP theory), then the real exchange rate should be the same or fluctuate in the same proportion as the nominal exchange rate. The figure shows, however, that while the nominal and real exchange rates did move together over time, they became increasingly different from 1973 to 1985, 1996 to 2001, and 2004 to 2006. Thus, this crucial element of the monetary approach (i.e., the PPP theory) held reasonably well only from 1986 to 1996, 2002 to 2003, and in 2007.

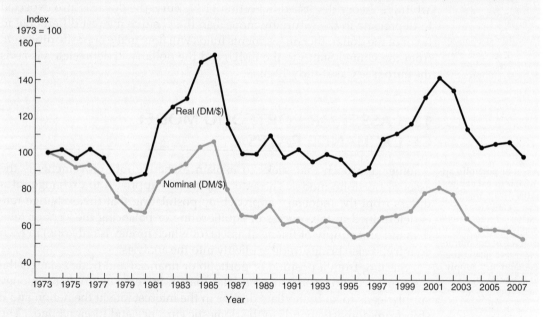

FIGURE 12.4. Nominal and Real Exchange Rate Indices between the Dollar and the Mark, 1973–2007.

The figure shows the movement in nominal and the real exchange rate indices (with 1973 = 100) between the dollar ($) and the German mark (DM) from 1973 to 2007. The nominal exchange rate is defined as DM/$ and the real exchange rate as (DM/$)(PUS/PGerm). Although the nominal and real exchange rates moved together over the period, they became increasingly different from 1973 to 1985 and from 1996 to 2001. Thus, the PPP theory, as a crucial element of the monetary approach, held reasonably well only from 1986 to 1996, 2002 to 2003, and in 2007.

exceeds the return on a domestic bond (as indicated by covered interest arbitrage theory discussed in Section 11.11).

Concept Check

What role does trade play in the asset or portfolio approach?

Assuming that this is the case, the shift from domestic to foreign bonds will then cause an immediate depreciation of the home currency as individuals and firms exchange domestic for foreign currency in order to purchase more foreign bonds. Over time, this depreciation stimulates the nation's exports and discourages the nation's imports. This leads to a trade surplus and appreciation of the domestic currency, which neutralizes part of its original depreciation. Thus, the asset or portfolio approach also explains the overshooting (i.e., the large and frequent fluctuations) in foreign exchange rates that is often observed in the real world. This is discussed next.

Exchange rate over-shooting The tendency of exchange rates to immediately depreciate or appreciate by more than required for long-run equilibrium, and then partially reversing their movement as they move toward their long-run equilibrium levels.

12.7 EXCHANGE RATE DYNAMICS

In the real world, exchange rates often exhibit a great deal of volatility and overshooting (see Case Study 12-6). Exchange rate overshooting can be explained by the asset or portfolio approach. To do so, suppose that U.S. monetary authorities suddenly increase the money supply by 10 percent. In the long run, this should lead to a 10 percent increase in domestic prices and a 10 percent depreciation of the dollar. Since the immediate depreciation of

CASE STUDY 12-5

Interest Differentials, Exchange Rates, and the Monetary Approach

Figure 12.5 shows the nominal exchange rate index between the U.S. dollar and the German mark (defined as DM/$, as in Figure 12.4) and the nominal interest rate differential between the United States and Germany from 1973 to 2007. The nominal interest rate differential (in percentage points) is defined as the U.S. treasury bill rate minus the German treasury bill rate. An increase in the U.S. interest rate relative to the interest rate in Germany should lead to an appreciation of the dollar relative to the mark, while a decrease in the interest differential in favor of the United States should lead to a depreciation (other things being equal)

as postulated by uncovered interest arbitrage. This would be reflected by the two curves in the figure below moving in the same direction. But other things do not remain equal (unchanged) in the real world, and so the relationship between interest rate differentials and exchange rates may not hold (i.e., the two curves move in opposite directions). In fact, the figure below shows that the two curves move in the same direction in some years and in opposite directions in other years over the 1973–2007 period examined.

(continues)

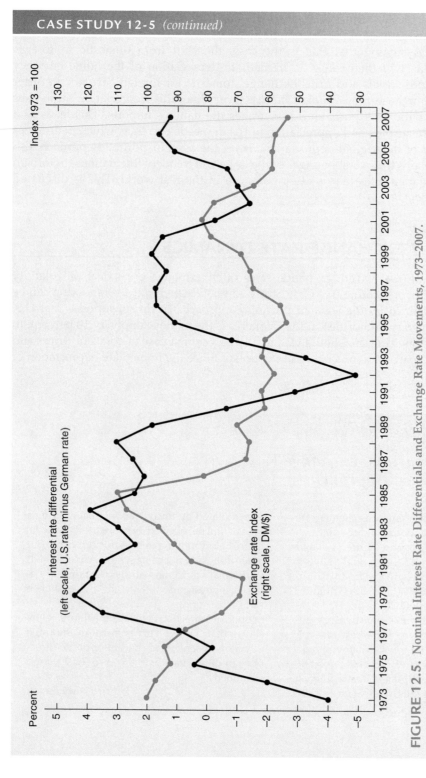

FIGURE 12.5. Nominal Interest Rate Differentials and Exchange Rate Movements, 1973–2007.

The U.S. dollar appreciated with respect to the German mark when interest rates rose in the United States relative to Germany and depreciated when the U.S. interest rate declined relative to Germany's years (i.e., the two curves move together) in only 15 of the 35-year period from 1973 to 2007.

Source: International Monetary Fund, *International Financial Statistics*, various issues.

the dollar will lead to a subsequent gradual improvement in the U.S. trade balance and dollar *appreciation*, the dollar must immediately depreciate by more than 10 percent, say, by 16 percent, if it will subsequently appreciate and if it has to end up with a net depreciation of 10 percent in the long run, as postulated by PPP theory.

The sequence of events can be summarized (and visualized in Figure 12.7) as follows: The U.S. money supply increases by 10 percent, the interest rate falls, capital flows out of the United States, and this leads to an *immediate* depreciation of the dollar of, say, 16 percent, from $R = 1.00$ to $R = 1.16$, at time t_0. Over time (i.e., in the long run), domestic prices increase by 10 percent and the dollar *appreciates* by 6 percent so as to eliminate its overshooting. Thus, the dollar exchange rate will be $R = 1.1$ (10 percent above the original exchange rate of $R = 1.00$) so as to exactly match the 10 percent U.S. inflation rate in the long run.

Concept Check

Why are exchange rates so volatile?

To summarize, we can say that since financial markets clear or adjust to disequilibria much faster than commodity markets, exchange rates are much more sensitive from day to day and from week to week to capital market imbalances than to commodity market and trade imbalances. The latter, however, are critical determinants of medium-run and long-run exchange rate trends, as postulated by the elasticity approach and the PPP theory. By considering both financial and trade adjustments, the asset or portfolio approach has become the centerpiece for the analysis of exchange rate determination. In its present form, however, the model still does not provide a complete and unified theory of exchange rate determination that fully and consistently integrates all the financial and commodity markets forces that affect exchange rates over the immediate, the short, and the long runs.

CASE STUDY 12-6

Exchange Rate Overshooting of the U.S. Dollar

Figure 12.6 shows the volatility and over-shooting of the U.S. dollar with respect to the Deutsche (German) mark and the Japanese yen from 1961 to 2007. The figure shows percent-age changes from the previous month in the units of the foreign currency per U.S. dollar. (Since the beginning of 1999, the fluctuation of the dollar/Deutsche mark exchange rate reflects the fluctuation of the euro with respect to the dollar.) Compare the small variation in the dollar exchange rates from 1961 to 1971 when exchange rates were kept officially fixed by international agreement with the wild fluctuations and overshooting since 1973 when exchange rates were allowed to fluctuate.

(continues)

CASE STUDY 12-6 *(continued)*

FIGURE 12.6. Volatility of Dollar Exchange Rates.

The wild fluctuations of the dollar exchange rate with respect to the Deutsche mark (DM) and the Japanese yen after 1973, when exchange rates were allowed to fluctuate, can be taken as evidence of exchange rate overshooting. Since the beginning of 1999, the fluctuation of the DM/$ reflects the fluctuation of the euro with respect to the dollar.

Source: International Monetary Fund, *International Financial Statistics*, various issues.

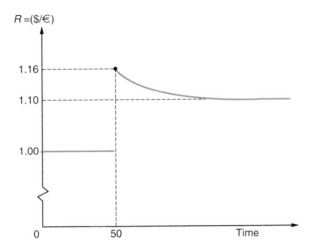

FIGURE 12.7. Overshooting of Dollar Exchange Rates.
A sudden 10 percent increase in the U.S. money supply might lead to an immediate increase in the dollar exchange rate (depreciation of the dollar), say from $R = \$1/€1$ to $R = \$1.16/€1$, thus overshooting its long-run equilibrium level of $R = \$1.10/€1$, toward which the dollar exchange rate will gradually move by subsequently appreciating (R falling) by 6 percent.

12.8 EXCHANGE RATE FORECASTING

The monetary and asset or portfolio models previously discussed have not been very successful in forecasting exchange rates, especially in the short run. There are basically two reasons for this. First, exchange rates are strongly affected by new information or "news," which is not predictable. Second, the expectations of exchange market participants often become self-reinforcing and self-fulfilling, at least for a while, thus leading to so-called *speculative bubbles*. That is, sometimes a movement of the exchange rate in a given direction leads to expectations that it will continue to move in the same direction regardless of the fundamentals. Eventually, the bubble bursts and the exchange rate movement reverses itself, with the exchange rate overcompensating in the opposite direction and overshooting its long-run equilibrium level.

Examples of exchange rate bubbles were the sharp overvaluation of the U.S. dollar in the first half of the 1980s and in 2000–2002, when the dollar was clearly overvalued, but subsequently became undervalued. Unpredictable news and bandwagon effects make it almost completely impossible to forecast exchange rates over short (less than one-year) horizons. This was clearly the case for the euro/dollar exchange rate during the euro's first five years of existence (see Case Study 12–7).

CASE STUDY 12-7

The Euro Exchange Rate Defies Forecasting

The euro was introduced on January 1, 1999 at the value of $1.17 (see Case Study 11-2) but, defying almost all prediction, it declined almost continuously to the low of $0.82 at the end of October 2000 (see Figure 12.8). The euro then appreciated to $0.95 at the beginning of 2001 only to fall again to below $0.85 at the beginning of July 2002 despite higher interest rates in the EMU than in the United States, the recession in the United States, and the terrorist attack to the World Trade Center in New York in September 2001—again defying most experts' forecasts. Starting in February 2002, however, the euro appreciated sharply, reaching parity in mid-2002 and the high of $1.57 in April 2008.

FIGURE 12.8. **The Euro/Dollar Exchange Rate Since the Introduction of the Euro.**
The euro depreciated almost continuously from the beginning of 1999 until October 2000 and remained below parity until the middle of 2002—defying most experts' forecasts. Since then, however, the euro has appreciated sharply
Source: International Monetary Fund, *International Financial Statistics*, various issues.

Thus, we can conclude that in contrast to the exciting advances in the theoretical modeling of exchange rates that have occurred over the past decades, empirical results have not provided much support for these theories, except in the long run. This does not mean that these theories are

Concept
Check

How successful
are exchange rate
theories in forecast-
ing exchange rate
changes?

wrong or useless. It simply means that they provide incomplete explanations of exchange rate determination. On an intuitive level, we do expect exchange rates to gravitate toward their PPP level in the long run and interest arbitrage to hold in the short run. What is still needed, however, is better modeling of expectations and a greater synthesis and integration of the real and the monetary forces at work. These topics are examined in the next chapter, which deals with automatic adjustments to balance of payments disequilibria under flexible and fixed exchange rates.

SUMMARY

1. Exchange rates are determined by the interaction of many forces, some of a long-run nature (trade flows and relative prices in the trading nations), others of a short-run nature (international capital flows), and still others of a very short-run or immediate nature (expectations), but there is no unified theory of exchange rate determination.

2. The U.S. dollar is expected to depreciate if the United States experiences (1) growth and an increase in its demand for imports, (2) an increase in the price level (inflation), (3) a reduction of the interest rate, and (4) the expectation that the dollar will depreciate.

3. The trade or elasticity approach postulates that the equilibrium exchange rate is the one that balances the value of the nation's imports and exports. If the value of the nation's imports exceeds the value of the nation's exports (i.e., if the nation faces a trade deficit), the exchange rate will rise (i.e., the domestic currency will depreciate) until trade is balanced.

4. The absolute purchasing-power parity (PPP) theory postulates that the exchange rate between two currencies is equal to the ratio of the price level in the two countries, so that a given commodity has the same price in both countries when expressed in terms of the same currency (the law of one price). The more refined relative PPP theory postulates that the change in the exchange rate should be equal to the change in relative prices in the two countries. Empirical tests broadly confirm the theory in the long run.

5. According to the monetary model to exchange rates, an increase in the nation's money supply leads to an equal increase in prices and depreciation of the nation's currency in the long run. Nominal and real exchange rates should then also move together over time. The expectation of changes in growth rates, inflation rates, and exchange rates should immediately lead to equal percentage changes in exchange rates. These predictions are only partially fulfilled in the real world because the monetary approach does not consider all the forces affecting exchange rates.

6. The asset or portfolio approach postulates that an increase in a nation's money supply leads to an immediate decline in the interest rate and shift from domestic bonds to the domestic currency and to foreign bonds (if the risk premium on the foreign bond does not eliminate the extra return). The

shift from domestic to foreign bonds causes an immediate depreciation of the nation's currency.

7. The shift from domestic to foreign bonds as a result of a reduction in the nation's interest rate causes an immediate depreciation of the nation's currency. Over time, this leads to a trade surplus and an appreciation of the domestic currency, which neutralizes part of its original depreciation and explains the exchange rate overshooting that is often observed in the real world.

8. Empirical tests do not provide much support for the monetary and the asset market or portfolio models of exchange rates, except in the long run. Short-run exchange rates have defied almost all attempts at accurate forecasting. One reason for this is the importance of news, which cannot be predicted. Another reason is the existence or development of speculative bubbles, which often move exchange rates away from fundamentals. This does not mean that these theories are wrong or useless, but simply that they provide incomplete explanations of exchange rate determination.

REVIEW QUESTIONS AND PROBLEMS

1. Explain what would be the effect on the dollar/euro exchange rate if economic growth increased in the EMU but not in the United States.

2. Explain what would be the effect on the dollar/euro exchange rate if the price level increased less in the United States than in the European Monetary Union (EMU).

3. Explain what would happen to the dollar/euro exchange rate if the interest rate increased in the United Sates but remained unchanged in the European Monetary Union (EMU).

4. Explain what would happen to the dollar/euro exchange rate if suddenly the expectation arises that the U.S. dollar will appreciate in the future.

5. What would happen to the dollar/euro exchange rate if growth, inflation, labor productivity, and interest rates increase in the United States but not in the European Monetary Union (EMU)?

6. (a) What is the absolute purchasing-power parity theory? Why is this not acceptable?

(b) What is the relative purchasing-power parity theory? When do we expect it to hold?

(c) Do empirical tests confirm or reject the relative purchasing-power parity theory?

7. In 1973 the Consumer Price Index was 15.9 in the United Kingdom and 29.2 in the United States (with 1995 = 100). In 2003, it was 122.4 in the United Kingdom and 121.5 in the United States. The exchange rate was £0.4304 to the dollar in 1973 and £0.5975 to the dollar in 2003.

(a) Calculate the rate of inflation in the United Kingdom minus the rate of inflation in the United States from 1973 to 2003 and compare it with the rate of depreciation of the British pound with respect to the U.S. dollar over the same period.

(b) Did the relative purchasing-power parity (PPP) theory hold between the United Kingdom and the United States between 1973 and 2003? Why?

8. (a) Explain what is the effect on the exchange rate of an increase in the nation's money supply according to the monetary model.

(b) Do empirical tests support or reject the monetary and asset market or portfolio approaches?

9. (a) Explain what is the effect on the exchange rate of an increase in the nation's money supply according to the asset market or portfolio approach.

(b) In what ways does it differ from the monetary approach?

(c) Do empirical tests support or reject the monetary and asset market or portfolio approaches?

10. How does the asset or portfolio approach explain the overshooting in exchange rates that is often observed in foreign exchange markets today?

SELECTED BIBLIOGRAPHY

For a more advanced treatment of the topics examined in this chapter, see:

- D. Salvatore, *International Economics*, 9th ed. (Hoboken, N.J.: Wiley, 2007), Chapter 15.

The purchasing-power parity theory is examined in:

- M. R. Pakko and P. S. Pollard, "Burgernomics: A Big Mac Guide to Purchasing Power Parity," *Federal Reserve Bank of St. Louis Review*, December 2003, pp. 9–28.
- A. M. Taylor and M. P. Taylor, "The Purchasing Power Parity Debate," *Journal of Economic Perspectives*, Fall 2004, pp. 135–158.
- P. Cashin and C. J. McDermott, "Parity Reversion in Real Exchange Rates: Fast, Slow, or Not at All?," *IMF Staff Papers*, Vol. 53, No. 1, 2006, pp. 89–119.

On exchange rate dynamics and overshooting, see:

- K. Rogoff, "Dornbusch's Overshooting Model After 25 Years," *IMF Staff Papers*, No. 3, 2002, pp. 1–34.

For empirical tests of the monetary and asset or portfolio models of exchange rate determination and forecasting, see:

- C. Engel, J. H. Rogers and A. K. Rose, "Empirical Exchange Rate Models," Editors, Special Issue, *Journal of International Economics*, May 2003.

- DeGrauwe, *Exchange Rate Economics: Where Do We Stand?* (Cambridge, Mass.: MIT Press, 2003).
- M. D. Evans and R. K. Lyons, "Meese-Rogoff Redux: Micro-Based Exchange-Rate Forecasting," *American Economic Review*, May 2005, pp. 405–414.

For the euro/dollar exchange rate, see:

- D. Salvatore, "The Euro, the Dollar, and the International Monetary System," Editor, Special Issue, *Journal of Policy Modeling*, June 2005, with articles by the leading economists in the field.
- Also see the references at the end of Chapters 11 and 16.

INTERNet

Data on the exchange rate of the dollar, interest rates, money supply, and inflation rate in the United States are found on the Federal Reserve Bank of St. Louis web site at:

http://www.research.stlouisfed.org/fred

Data on the exchange rates, interest rates, money supply, and inflation rates for most countries are found by following the links to the various countries' central banks on the web site of the Bank for International Settlement at:

http://www.bis.org

For a wide variety of global financial indexes on exchange rates, interest rates, inflation rates, and nominal and real GDP see the MIT web site at:

http://eh.net/hmit

Open-Economy Macroeconomics

Part Five (Chapters 13 and 14) deals with open-economy macroeconomics. Chapter 13 examines how the exchange rate affects the nation's current account and how the current account affects and is, in turn, affected by changes in the level of national income at home and abroad. Chapter 14 then deals with monetary and fiscal policies in open economies. Thus, Chapters 13 and 14 progressively build a complete model of the open economy. Specifically, Chapter 13 starts by examining the effect of exchange rate changes on the nation's current account and then extends the analysis to the economy as a whole. Chapter 14 adds the money market and international capital flows, and examines fiscal and monetary policies to achieve both internal balance (i.e., full employment without inflation) and external balance (equilibrium or sustainable balance of payments and exchange rates).

Automatic Adjustments with Flexible and Fixed Exchange Rates

After studying this chapter, you should be able to:

- Understand how the balance of payments adjusts with flexible exchange rates
- Know what a stable foreign exchange market is
- Understand how adjustment occurs under fixed exchange rates
- Know how the equilibrium level of income is determined in a closed economy
- Know how the equilibrium level of income is determined in an open economy
- Understand the meaning of foreign repercussions
- Describe how the absorption approach works
- Understand how all the automatic adjustments work together

CHAPTER OUTLINE

KEY TERMS

Stable foreign exchange market

Unstable foreign exchange market

Marshall–Lerner condition

J-curve effect

Pass-through

Gold standard

Mint parity

Gold export point

Gold import point

Price-specie-flow mechanism

Equilibrium level of income

Multiplier *(k)*

Foreign trade multiplier *(k')*

Foreign repercussions

Absorption approach

Synthesis of automatic adjustments

Quantity theory of money

Rules of the game of the gold standard

13.1 INTRODUCTION

In this chapter, we examine how a deficit in a nation's balance of payments is *automatically* corrected by price and income changes in the nation and abroad. (The opposite would be the case for a trade surplus.) For simplicity we assume that international private capital flows take place only as passive responses to cover (i.e., to pay for or finance) temporary trade imbalances, so that a balance-of-payments deficit refers to or is synonymous with a trade deficit. *Policies* to correct a balance-of-payments or trade deficit and achieve internal balance (i.e., full employment without inflation in the nation) are examined in the next chapter.

Adjustments to a balance-of-payments or trade deficit can take place automatically through price or income changes, or both, under a flexible or a fixed exchange rate system. We will examine first automatic *price* adjustments under flexible and fixed exchange rates. Then we examine adjustment through automatic *income* changes in the nation and abroad. Finally, we combine automatic *price and income* adjustments under a *flexible* and a *fixed* exchange rate system.

In Sections 13.2 and 13.3, we examine automatic adjustment with flexible exchange rates. These change the relationship between domestic and foreign prices. Section 13.4 examines automatic adjustment through price changes *within* the nation under a fixed exchange rate system, such as the gold standard. Sections 13.5 to 13.7 examine the automatic income adjustment mechanism. Section 13.8 then provides a synthesis of automatic adjustments through price and income changes. Finally, Section 13.9 presents an evaluation of automatic price and income adjustments under a flexible and a fixed exchange rate system.

13.2 ADJUSTMENT WITH FLEXIBLE EXCHANGE RATES

In this and the next section, we examine the process by which a balance of payments or trade deficit is corrected automatically by a depreciation of the nation's currency. This is shown in Figure 13.1.

In Figure 13.1, we assume that the United States and the European Monetary Union (EMU) are the only two economies in the world and that there are no autonomous international capital flows, so that the U.S. demand and supply curves for euros reflect only trade in goods and services. The figure shows that at the exchange rate of $R = \$1/€1$, the quantity of euros demanded by the United States, is €12 billion per year, while the quantity supplied is €8 billion. As a result, the United States has a balance of payments or trade deficit of €4 billion *(AB)* at $R = \$1/€1$.

If the U.S. demand and supply curves for euros are given by $D_€$ and $S_€$, a 20 percent depreciation of the dollar, from $R = \$1/€1$ to $R = \$1.20/€1$, would

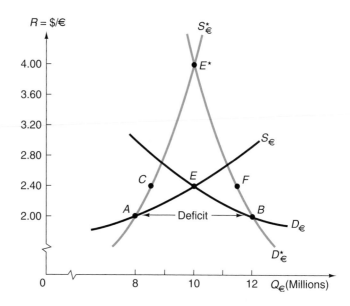

FIGURE 13.1. Balance-of-Payments Adjustments with Flexible Exchange Rates.

At $R = \$1/€1$, the quantity of euros demanded by the United States is €12 billion per year, while the quantity supplied is €8 billion, so that the United States has a balance of payments or trade deficit of €4 billion (AB). With $D_€$ and $S_€$, a 20 percent dollar depreciation would completely eliminate the deficit (point E). With $D^*_€$ and $S^*_€$, a 100 percent depreciation would be required to eliminate the deficit (point E^*).

completely eliminate the U.S. balance of payments or trade deficit. That is, at $R = \$1.20/€1$, the quantity of euros demanded and the quantity supplied would be equal at €10 billion per year (point E in the figure), and U.S. trade would be in equilibrium. If, instead, the U.S. demand and supply curves for euros were less elastic (steeper), as indicated by $D^*_€$ and $S^*_€$, the same 20 percent depreciation would only reduce the U.S. balance-of-payments or trade deficit to €3 billion (CF in the figure), and a 100 percent depreciation of the dollar, from $R = \$1/€1$ to $R = \$2/€1$, would be required to completely eliminate the deficit (point E^* in the figure).

Such a huge depreciation of the dollar would make the dollar-price of U.S. imports very high and lead to inflation in the United States, which might be an even greater problem than the trade deficit. Specifically, while a depreciation of the dollar makes U.S. products cheaper to EMU residents (because they need fewer euros to get each dollar), U.S. residents will find imports more expensive (because they need more dollars to get each euro). This may lead to an inflation problem for the United States if the U.S. demand

and supply curves for euros are steep or inelastic. Thus, it is very important to determine how elastic D_ϵ and S_ϵ are.

The U.S. demand curve for euros (D_ϵ) in Figure 13.1 is derived from the demand and supply curves of *U.S. imports* in terms of euros, while the U.S. supply curve for euros (S_ϵ) is derived from the foreign demand and supply curves for *U.S. exports* in terms of euros. The more elastic are the U.S. demand for imports (D_M) and the foreign demand for U.S. exports (D_X) in terms of euros, the more elastic are D_ϵ and S_ϵ (and the less inflationary a depreciation would be to correct a U.S. trade deficit).

The price elasticity of the *U.S. demand for imports* in euros (η_M) is equal to the percentage change in the quantity demanded of imports by the United States ($\%\Delta Q_M$) divided by the percentage change in the price of U.S. imports in euros ($\%\Delta P_M$), as indicated by the following formula:

$$\eta_M = \frac{\%\Delta Q_M}{\%\Delta P_M}$$

Similarly, the price elasticity of the *foreign demand for U.S. exports* in euros (η_X) is given by the percentage change in the quantity demanded of U.S. exports by foreigners ($\%\Delta Q_X$) divided by the percentage change in the price of U.S. exports in euros ($\%\Delta P_X$) in euros; that is:

$$\eta_X = \frac{\%\Delta Q_X}{\%\Delta P_X}$$

Since quantity and prices always move in opposite directions (i.e., an increase in price leads to a reduction in the quantity demanded, and vice versa, as dictated by the law of demand), η_M and η_X are always negative. However, in comparing price elasticities we use their absolute values (i.e., the algebraic values without the negative sign) and say that demand is elastic, inelastic, or unitary elastic, respectively, if the absolute value of $\eta > 1$, $\eta < 1$, or $\eta = 1$. When demand is elastic, a reduction in price leads to a larger proportionate increase in the quantity demanded so that expenditures on the commodity increase. If demand is inelastic, we have the opposite situation. When demand is unitary elastic, a change in price will leave expenditures on the commodity unchanged. We will make use of these concepts in the next section.

Concept Check

How do flexible exchange rates bring about balance of payments equilibrium?

13.3 STABILITY OF THE FOREIGN EXCHANGE MARKET

The U.S. demand for euros (D_ϵ), as all demand curves, is always negatively sloped, so that a reduction in the dollar exchange rate (appreciation of the dollar) leads to an increase in the quantity demanded of euros (see Figure 13.1). The U.S. supply curve of euros (S_ϵ), on the other hand, is

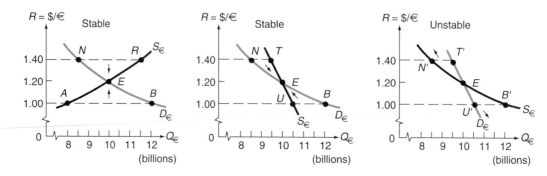

FIGURE 13.2. Stable and Unstable Foreign Exchange Markets.
In all three panels, the equilibrium exchange rate is $R = \$1.20/€1$, at which €10 billion are demanded and supplied per year. At $R = \$1/€1$, the excess demand for foreign exchange in the left and center panels will automatically push the exchange rate up toward the equilibrium rate and eliminate the U.S. trade deficit. The foreign exchange market is then said to be stable. In the right panel, an excess demand for euros (U.S. trade deficit) is found above the equilibrium. This would lead to a rise in R, which would increase the U.S. trade deficit. Here, the foreign exchange market is unstable.

usually positively sloped (so that a dollar *depreciation* leads to more euros being supplied), but it can also be vertical or negatively sloped if the foreign demand for U.S. exports in terms of euros (D_X) is sufficiently inelastic. If $S_€$ is negatively sloped and flatter than $D_€$, the foreign exchange market is unstable. In that case, a dollar depreciation would make a U.S. trade deficit worse, rather than correcting it, as explained with Figure 13.2.

The left panel of Figure 13.2 repeats $D_€$ and $S_€$ from Figure 13.1 and shows the usual situation where $D_€$ is negatively sloped and $S_€$ is positively sloped. In this case, the foreign exchange market is stable in the sense that if for whatever reason the exchange rate were below the equilibrium level of $R = \$1.20/€1$ (point E), market forces would automatically push it to equilibrium. For example, at $R = \$1/€1$, there would be an excess demand for euros (U.S. trade deficit) of €4 billion (AB), which would automatically push the exchange rate up to its equilibrium level of $R = \$1.20/€1$. On the other hand, if the exchange rate were above equilibrium, say, at $R = \$1.40/€1$, the excess supply of €3 billion (RN), would automatically push R down to its equilibrium level at point E. This is a stable foreign exchange market.

Although the middle panel of Figure 13.2 looks different from the left panel (because $S_€$ is negatively sloped, but steeper than $D_€$), the foreign exchange market is still stable because at an exchange rate other than the equilibrium rate, market forces will automatically push the exchange rate to its equilibrium level. For example, at $R = \$1/€1$, the excess demand of €1.5 billion (BU) would automatically push R up to its equilibrium level of $R = \$1.20/€1$ (point E). Similarly, if R were above equilibrium, market force would push it back to equilibrium. Thus, in this case, the foreign exchange

Stable foreign exchange market
The condition in a foreign exchange market where a disturbance from the equilibrium exchange rate gives rise to automatic forces that push the exchange rate back toward the equilibrium rate.

Unstable foreign exchange market The condition in a foreign exchange market where a disturbance from equilibrium pushes the exchange rate farther away from equilibrium.

Concept Check

What is the Marshall–Lerner condition for a stable foreign exchange market?

Marshall–Lerner condition Indicates that the foreign exchange market is stable when the sum of the price elasticities of the *demands* for imports and exports is larger than 1 (when the *supply* elasticities of imports and exports are infinite).

market is also stable. Note that here S_ϵ is negatively sloped, but steeper than D_ϵ.

The right panel of Figure 13.2 is basically different from the other two panels. Here, not only is S_ϵ negatively sloped, but it is also flatter or more elastic than D_ϵ. A U.S. trade deficit is now found above, not below, the equilibrium exchange rate of $R = \$1.20/\text{€}1$ (point E). For example, at $R = \$1.40/\text{€}1$, there would be an excess demand (U.S. trade deficit) of €1 billion ($T'N'$). The excess demand for euros would automatically lead to an increase in the dollar exchange rate and an increase in the U.S. trade deficit! Similarly, an exchange rate below equilibrium involves an excess supply of euros, which would lead to a decline in the dollar exchange rate and an even larger U.S. trade surplus. This is an unstable foreign exchange market. It occurs because S_ϵ is negatively sloped *and* flatter or more elastic than D_ϵ. With an unstable foreign exchange market, flexible exchange rates automatically lead to a perverse adjustment (i.e., to a larger trade disequilibrium). Thus, it is crucially important to determine if the foreign exchange market is stable.

The foreign exchange market is stable if the following condition is satisfied:

$$\eta_M + \eta_X > 1$$

That is, the foreign exchange market is stable or well behaved (in the sense that a trade deficit will be corrected by a depreciation of the nation's currency) if the sum of the (absolute) values of the price elasticity of the U.S. demand curve for imports and the price elasticity of the *foreign* demand for U.S. exports exceeds 1. If $\eta_M + \eta_X < 1$, the foreign exchange market is unstable and flexible exchange rates will increase rather than reduce a trade disequilibrium. If $\eta_M + \eta_X = 1$, flexible exchange rates would leave a trade disequilibrium completely unchanged. The above condition is called the Marshall–Lerner condition in honor of the two distinguished economists, *Alfred Marshall* and *Abba Lerner*, who introduced it. Real-world estimates indicate that foreign exchange markets are not only generally stable but that trade elasticities are also sufficiently large to make flexible exchange rates feasible (i.e., not too inflationary—see Case Study 13-1).

Although the foreign exchange market is stable, it usually takes a long time (as much a year-and-a-half or two) before a depreciation reduces a trade deficit significantly. The reason is that it takes time to order, ship, receive, and utilize goods. In fact, the immediate effect of a depreciation may be to worsen, rather than improve, the nation's trade balance because the price of imports usually rises sooner and faster than the price of exports. This is called the J-curve effect. Furthermore, exporting nations might not pass on to foreigners the full price increase of the trade partner's currency depreciation to avoid losing market share in their export business. For the United States, the currency pass-through (from dollar depreciation to increase in the price of U.S. imports) is about 40–60 percent. Case Study 13-2 examines the U.S. trade response to fluctuations in the effective exchange rate of the dollar.

J-curve effect The deterioration before a net improvement in a country's trade balance resulting from a depreciation or devaluation.

Pass-through The proportion of an exchange rate change that is reflected in export and import price changes.

Price Elasticities in International Trade

Table 13.1 gives the absolute value of the price elasticity of demand for imports and exports of the United States, Japan, Germany, the United Kingdom, Canada, other developed countries, less developed countries, and the Organization of Petroleum Exporting Countries (OPEC), estimated by using quarterly data from the first quarter of 1973 to the second quarter of 1985. The results show that the absolute value of the price elasticity of demand for *imports* ranges from 0.47 for the United Kingdom to 1.14 for OPEC, and it was 0.92 for the United States. On the other hand, the absolute value of the price elasticity of demand for *exports* ranges from 0.44 for the United Kingdom to 0.99 (the highest) for the United States. The last column of Table 13.1 shows that, except for the United Kingdom, the sum of the price elasticity of demand for imports and exports exceeds 1 (so that the Marshall–Lerner condition is satisfied) for all nations or groups of nations shown in the table. The trade elasticities reported here are short-run elasticities (i.e., they measure quantity responses to price changes in the year of the price change). Long-run elasticities are higher.

Table 13.1. *Estimated Price Elasticities for Imports and Exports*

Country or Group of Countries	Import Price Elasticity	Export Price Elasticity	Sum of Import and Export Elasticities
United States	0.92	0.99	1.91
Japan	0.93	0.93	1.96
Germany	0.60	0.66	1.26
United Kingdom	0.47	0.44	0.91
Canada	1.02	0.83	1.85
Other Developed Countries	0.49	0.83	1.31
Less Developed Countries	0.81	0.63	1.44
OPEC	1.14	0.57	1.71

Source: J. Marquez, "Bilateral Trade Elasticities," *Review of Economics and Statistics*, February 1990, pp. 75–76.

13.4 ADJUSTMENT WITH FIXED EXCHANGE RATES: THE GOLD STANDARD

Under a fixed exchange rate system, such as the gold standard, trade deficits are corrected by automatic changes in domestic prices. This is different than under flexible exchange rates, where a trade deficit is automatically corrected by a depreciation of the deficit nation's currency, which instead changes the relationship between domestic and foreign prices. To see how a trade deficit is corrected with fixed exchange rates, we examine the gold standard, but

Gold standard
The international monetary system operating from about 1880 to 1914 under which gold was the only international reserve, exchange rates fluctuated only within the gold points, and balance-of-payments adjustment was described by the price-specie-flow mechanism.

Mint parity The fixed exchange rates resulting under the gold standard from each nation defining the gold content of its currency and passively standing ready to buy or sell any amount of gold at that price.

much of the analysis is applicable to other types of fixed exchange rate systems.

The gold standard operated from about 1880 until the outbreak of World War I in 1914. An attempt was made to reestablish the gold standard after the war, but it failed in 1931 during the Great Depression. It is highly unlikely that the gold standard will be reestablished in the near future—if ever. Nevertheless, it is important to understand how the gold standard operated because to some extent this is how the fixed exchange rate system (the Bretton Woods system) that operated from the end of World War II also operated until it collapsed in 1971.

Under the gold standard, each nation defined the gold content of its currency and passively stood ready to buy or sell any amount of gold at that price. Since the gold content in one unit of each currency was fixed, exchange rates were also fixed. For example, under the gold standard, a £1 gold coin in the United Kingdom contained 113.0016 grains of pure gold, while a \$1 gold coin in the United States contained 23.22 grains. This implied that the dollar price of the pound, or the exchange rate, was $R = \$/£ = 113.0016/23.22 = 4.87$. This is called the mint parity. (Because the center of the gold standard was London, not Frankfurt, our discussion is in terms of pounds sterling and dollars, instead of euros and dollars.)

CASE STUDY 13-2

Effective Exchange Rate of the Dollar and the U.S. Current Account Balance

In Figure 13.3, the effective exchange rate index of the dollar (defined as the number of foreign currency units per dollar, with 1995 = 100) is measured on the right scale, while the U.S. current account balance (in billions of dollars) is measured on the left scale, from 1980 to 2007. The figure shows that the dollar appreciated by almost 40 percent on a trade-weighted basis from 1980 to 1985, but the U.S. current account balance only started to deteriorate in 1982. The U.S. trade balance then continued to deteriorate until 1987, even though the dollar started to sharply depreciate in 1985. Thus, the U.S. trade balance seemed to respond with a two-year lag to changes in the exchange rate of the dollar. From 1987 to 1991, the U.S.

current account balance improved sharply but then deteriorated until 1994, even though the exchange rate did not change very much. Obviously, other more powerful forces (discussed in Sections 13.5 and 13.6) determined the U.S. current account balance over this period.

The dollar then started to appreciate in 1995, and the U.S. current account balance resumed its sharp deterioration in 1997. The U.S. current account continued to deteriorate very rapidly (reaching the level of \$811 billion in 2006) even though the effective exchange rate of the dollar fell rapidly after 2002. Only in 2007 did the U.S. current account start to respond to the dollar depreciation and improve.

(continues)

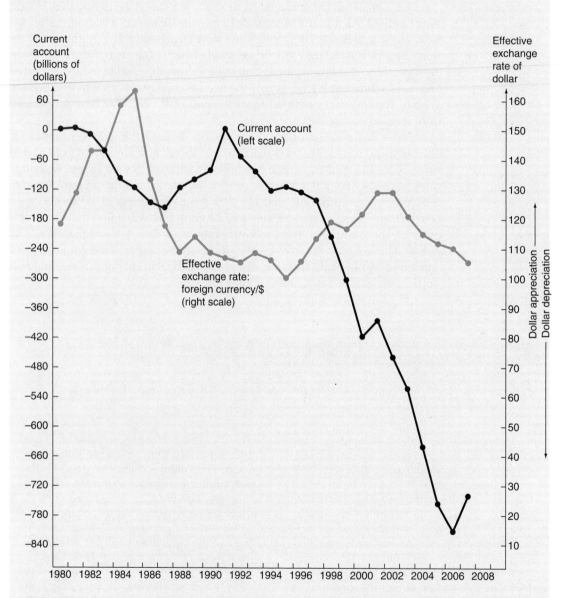

FIGURE 13.3. Effective Exchange Rate of the Dollar and U.S. Current Account Balance, 1980–2007.

Source: International Monetary Fund, *International Financial Statistics*; and Department of Commerce, *Survey of Current Business*, various issues.

Gold export point
The mint parity plus the cost of shipping an amount of gold equal to one unit of the foreign currency between the two nations.

Gold import point
The mint parity minus the cost of shipping an amount of gold equal to one unit of the foreign currency between the two nations.

Price-specie-flow mechanism The automatic adjustment mechanism under the gold standard. It operates by the deficit nation losing gold and experiencing a reduction in its money supply. This in turn reduces domestic prices, which stimulates the nation's exports and discourages its imports until the deficit is eliminated. A surplus is corrected by the opposite process.

Concept Check

How is a balance of payments deficit corrected under the gold standard?

Since the cost of shipping £1 worth of gold between New York and London was about 3 cents, the exchange rate between the dollar and the pound could never fluctuate by more than 3 cents above or below the mint parity (i.e., the exchange rate could not rise above 4.90 or fall below 4.84). The reason is that no one would pay more than $4.90 for £1, since he could always purchase $4.87 worth of gold at the U.S. Treasury (the Federal Reserve Bank of New York was only established in 1913), ship it to London at a cost of 3 cents, and exchange it for £1 at the Bank of England (the U.K. central bank). This was the U.S. gold export point.

On the other hand, the exchange rate between the dollar and the pound could not fall below $4.84. The reason for this is that no one would accept less than $4.84 for each pound he wanted to convert into dollars because he could always purchase £1 worth of gold in London, ship it to New York at a cost of 3 cents, and exchange it for $4.87 (thus receiving $4.84 net). This was the gold import point of the United States.

The exchange rate between the dollar and the pound was determined at the intersection of the U.S. demand and supply curves of pounds between the gold points, and was prevented from moving outside the gold points by U.S. gold sales or purchases. That is, the tendency of the dollar to depreciate, or the exchange rate to rise above $R = \$4.90/£1$, was countered by gold shipments from the United States. These gold outflows measured the size of the U.S. balance-of-payments deficit. On the other hand, the tendency of the dollar to appreciate, or the exchange rate to fall below $R = \$4.84/£1$, was countered by gold shipments to the United States. These gold inflows measured the size of the surplus in the U.S. balance of payments.

Since deficits were settled in gold under this system and nations had limited gold reserves, deficits could not go on forever and soon had to be corrected. The automatic adjustment mechanism under the gold standard was the price-specie-flow mechanism. This operated as follows to correct a trade disequilibrium. Since each nation's money supply under the gold standard consisted of either gold itself or paper currency backed by gold, the money supply would fall in the deficit nation and rise in the surplus nation. This caused internal prices to fall in the deficit nation and rise in the surplus nation. As a result, the exports of the deficit nation would be encouraged and its imports would be discouraged until the deficit in its balance of payments was eliminated. The reduction in the deficit nation's money supply would also increase interest rates in the nation, which induced a capital inflow that helped the nation finance its deficit. The opposite occurred in the surplus nation (a more detailed description of the operation of the gold standard is given in Appendix A13.1).

The adjustment mechanism under a fixed exchange rate system not tied to gold operates in a similar way, except that nations set exchange rates (par values) at what they believe to be the equilibrium level and the deficit nation finances or covers a trade or balance of payments deficit with its international

currency reserves instead of gold. A deficit here also reduces the nation's money supply, which tends to reduce prices relative to the surplus nation (which experiences an inflow of international currency reserves and rising money supply and prices), until the trade disequilibrium is completely corrected. The reduction in the deficit nation's money supply also tends to increase interest rates relative to the surplus nation, which induces capital inflows that help finance the deficit. Allowing the nation's money supply to change in order to correct a balance of payments disequilibrium means, however, that under a fixed exchange rate system the nation cannot conduct monetary policy.

13.5 INCOME DETERMINATION IN A CLOSED ECONOMY

The flexible exchange rate and gold standard models previously examined rely on *automatic price adjustments* to bring about equilibrium in a nation's balance of payments. But changes in a nation's balance of payments affect national income at home and abroad and these, in turn, affect the nation's balance of payments. For example, an increase in a nation's exports leads to an increase in production and income in the nation, which induces imports to rise, thus reversing some of the improvement in the nation's balance of payments that resulted from the increase in its exports. We now want to consider how these *automatic income adjustments* contribute to balance of payments adjustments. This represents the extension of *Keynesian economics* (that you studied in your principles of economics course) to the open economy.

To examine how automatic income adjustments operate we assume that all prices (exchange rates, interest rates, wages, as well as consumer prices) remain constant. These assumptions are then relaxed in the last three sections of the chapter, which examine how all automatic adjustments operate together. To study how the automatic income adjustment mechanism operates in an open economy (i.e., an economy open to world trade and finance), we begin by reviewing how the equilibrium level of national income is determined in a closed economy without a government sector (to be added in the next chapter to deal with policies adjustments).

Equilibrium level of income (Y_E) The level of income at which desired or planned expenditures equal the value of output, and desired saving equals desired investment.

In a *closed economy* without a government sector, the equilibrium level of income is determined where income (Y) is equal to desired or *planned consumption expenditures (C)* plus desired or *planned business investment (I)*. Since income (Y) is partly spent on consumption (C) and partly saved (S), we can indicate the equilibrium level of income by:

$$Y = C + S = C + I$$

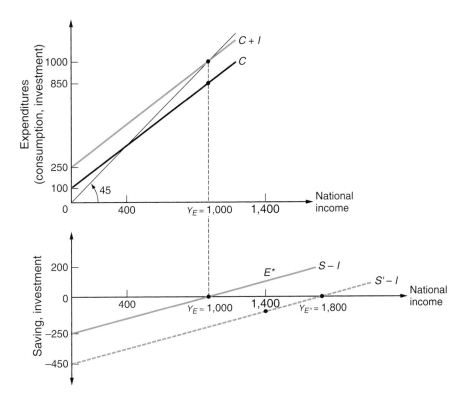

FIGURE 13.4. National Income Equilibrium in a Closed Economy.
In the top panel, the equilibrium level of income is at point E, where the $C + I$ function crosses the 45° line, so that $C + I = Y_E = 1,000$. In the bottom panel, equilibrium is given by point E, where the $(S - I)$ function crosses the horizontal axis and $S - I = 0$. The $(S - I)$ function rises because a constant I is subtracted from rising S as Y rises. If investment rises by 200 to $I' = 350$, the new equilibrium level of national income is $Y_{E'} = 1,800$, given by point E', where $S - I' = 0$.

so that

$$S = I$$

and

$$S - I = 0$$

Figure 13.4 shows all of this. The top panel measures income (Y) on the horizontal axis and planned consumption expenditures (C) and planned business investment (I) on the vertical axis. C rises as income rises, but not as much as the increase in income because part of income is saved. At $Y = 0$, $C = 100$ as consumers spend part of their savings (i.e., $S = -100$). Investment

or $I = 150$ and is *autonomous* or independent of Y. Thus, the $(C + I)$ function or line is parallel to the C function and 150 above it at every Y. The equilibrium level of income of $Y_E = 1,000$ is given at point E where the $(C + I)$ function crosses the 45° line (included as a visual aid to show the point at which $C + I = Y$).

At income levels below 1,000, $C + I > Y$ (i.e., planned consumption and investments exceed income) and this stimulates production, and so Y increases. At $Y > 1,000$, $C + I < Y$ and this leads to a reduction in production, and so Y falls toward the equilibrium level. Thus, $Y_E = 1,000$ is the equilibrium level of income in the sense that if nothing changes in the economy that level of income will persist or remain unchanged.

Concept Check

How is the equilibrium level of national income reached in a closed economy?

The equilibrium level of income is also shown in the bottom panel of Figure 13.4 where the $(S - I)$ function crosses the horizontal or Y-axis, so that $S = I$ and $S - I = 0$. $S - I = -250$ at $Y = 0$ because $S = -100$ (since $C = 100$ at $Y = 0$) and $I = 150$, so that $S - I = -100 - 150 = -250$. The $(S - I)$ function rises because we subtract a constant I from rising S as Y rises.

Savings are *leakages* out of the system because they represent income not spent on purchasing goods and services. On the other hand, investments represent *injections* into the system, which requires production (of machinery, plants, housing, etc) to carry out. The equilibrium level of national income is thus determined where leakages (S) exactly equal injections (I) into the system (i.e., where $S = I$ and $S - I = 0$) in the bottom panel of Figure 13.4.

Starting from the equilibrium level of income, if investment increases from 150 to 350, the $(S - I)$ function shifts down by the 200 increase in investment to $(S - I')$ and gives the new equilibrium level of income of $Y_{E'} = 1,800$, where $S - I' = 0$. That is, the autonomous increase in investment leads to an increase in income, which induces savings to rise until they match the new higher level of investment, so that $S - I' = 0$. Since the equilibrium level of income rises by 800 with the increase in investment of 200, the closed economy multiplier (k) is 4. That is,

Multiplier (k) The ratio of the change in income to the change in investment; in a closed economy without government, $k = 1/MPS$.

$$k = \frac{\Delta Y}{\Delta I} = \frac{800}{200} = 4$$

More generally, the value of the multiplier, k, can be determined by remembering that in order to reach the new equilibrium level of income, the *autonomous* increase in investment must equal the *induced* increase in savings. The induced increase in savings is equal to the *marginal propensity to save (s)*, or the amount of additional savings associated with each one-dollar increase in income (Y), times the increase in income (i.e., $s\Delta Y$). Thus, the condition for the new equilibrium level of income is

$$\Delta I = \Delta S = s\Delta Y$$

So that the multiplier, k, is

$$k = \frac{\Delta Y}{\Delta I} = \frac{1}{s}$$

That is, the multiplier is the inverse of the marginal propensity to save in the nation. The marginal propensity to save is given by the slope of the *savings function* (which equals to the slope of the $(S - I)$ or $(S - I')$ function since I is autonomous and does change with Y).

For example, in Figure 13.4, $s = 0.25$, which means that for every dollar increase in income, 0.75 cents are spent on consumption and 0.25 cents are saved. This gives the multiplier of $k = 1/0.25 = 4$. Then, an autonomous increase in investment of 200 leads to an increase in the equilibrium level of income in the nation of

Concept Check

$$\Delta Y = k\Delta I = 4(200) = 800$$

This increase in income induces savings to rise by

How does the multiplier affect the level of national income?

$$\Delta S = s\Delta Y = 0.25(800) = 200$$

So that $\Delta S = \Delta I$ at the new equilibrium level of income of $Y_{E'} = 1{,}800$.

13.6 INCOME DETERMINATION IN AN OPEN ECONOMY

In an open economy (i.e., an economy open to international trade and finance), the nation's imports rise as income rises. For example, as the U.S. economy grows it requires more petroleum imports. The increase in imports induced per dollar increase in income is called the *marginal propensity to import (m)*.

Imports, like savings, are *leakages* out of the system because they do not stimulate domestic production. On the other hand, exports like investment are an *injection* into the system because they stimulate production and the generation of income in the nation. The equilibrium level of income in an open economy is where total leakages $(S + M)$ equal total injections $(I + X)$; that is, where

$$S + M = I + X$$

With a change in the economy (such as an autonomous increase in investment or exports), the equilibrium condition becomes

$$\Delta S + \Delta M = \Delta I + \Delta X$$

In our analysis, we assume that exports, like investment, are autonomous and do not change with the level of income in the nation, while imports and savings are functionally related to income (i.e., rise as national income rises).

The change in the amount of savings and imports induced by a change in income in the nation are given by

$$\Delta S = s\Delta Y$$

Concept
Check

and

$$\Delta M = m\Delta Y$$

We can now use this information to derive the foreign-trade multiplier for an autonomous increase in investment or exports in the nation. Substituting the above values for ΔS and ΔM into the equilibrium condition after a change has occurred in the nation, we get

What is the condition for the equilibrium level of income in an open economy?

$$s\Delta Y + m\Delta Y = \Delta I + \Delta X$$

or

$$(s + m)\Delta Y = \Delta I + \Delta X$$

Foreign trade multiplier (k') The ratio of the change in income to the change in exports and/or investment. It equals $k' = 1/(MPS + MPM)$.

Assuming for the moment that $\Delta I > 0$ but $\Delta X = 0$, we get the foreign-trade multiplier (k') for an autonomous change in investment in the nation of

$$k' = \frac{\Delta Y}{\Delta I} = \frac{1}{(s + m)}$$

With a change in the nation's exports rather than investment, the foreign trade multiplier, k', would be the same because exports stimulate the domestic production, just like an increase in investment. That is,

$$k' = \frac{\Delta Y}{\Delta X} = \frac{1}{(s + m)}$$

For example, if $s = 0.25$ and $m = 0.25$, then k' is

$$k' = \frac{1}{(s + m)} = \frac{1}{0.25 + 0.25} = \frac{1}{0.5} = 2$$

This means that each autonomous dollar increase in either investment or exports in the nation leads to a two-dollar increase in its income. Note that with the additional leakage of M, $k' < k$. Thus, if I increases by 200, the equilibrium level of income increases by

$$\Delta Y = k'(\Delta I) = 2(200) = 400$$

This 400 increase in the equilibrium level of income induces an increase in savings and imports in the nation of

$$\Delta S = s\Delta Y = 0.25(400) = 100$$

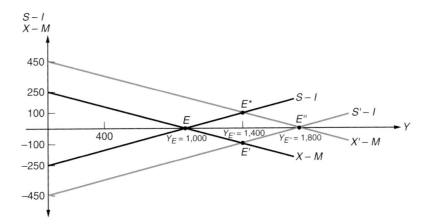

FIGURE 13.5. National Income Determination in an Open Economy.
Y is measured along the horizontal axis and $(S - I)$ and $(X - M)$ along the vertical axis. The $(S - I)$ function is that of Figure 13.4. The $(X - M)$ function falls because we subtract rising M from constant X as Y rises. The equilibrium level of income $Y_E = 1,000$ and is given at point E, where the $(S - I)$ and $(X - M)$ functions cross and $(S - I) = (X - M) = 0$. With an autonomous increase in I of 200, $Y_{E'} = 1,400$ at point E' and $S - I' = X - M = -100$. With an autonomous increase in X instead of I of 200, $Y_E{}^* = 1,400$ at point E^* and $S - I = X' - M = 100$. With an increase in both I and X of 200, $Y_{E''} = 1,800$ at point E'' and $S - I' = X' - M = 0$.

and

$$\Delta M = m\Delta Y = 0.25(400) = 100$$

Note that the nation's exports do not change because they are autonomous or independent of the level of income in the nation. Thus, if the nation started with equilibrium in the balance of payments, the autonomous increase in investment of 200 leads to a balance of payments deficit of 100. The result would be exactly the same if the nation's exports increased by 200, except that the nation would then end up with a balance of payments surplus of 100 (instead of with a 100 deficit). All of this can be seen in Figure 13.5.

In Figure 13.5, the $(S - I)$ and $(X - M)$ functions are obtained by rearranging the original equilibrium condition of

$$S + M = I + X$$

as

$$S - I = X - M$$

and assuming constant exports of $X = 300$, imports of $M = 50$ at $Y = 0$, and M rising by 25 for each 100 increase in income (since $m = 0.25$). Thus,

$X-M = 250$ at $Y = 0$ and declines as Y rises because we subtract rising M from constant X. The $(S - I)$ function, on the other hand, is the same as in the bottom panel of Figure 13.4.

Figure 13.5 shows that the original equilibrium level of income (before any increase in I or X) is $Y_E = 1,000$ and is given by point E where the $(X - M)$ and $(S - I)$ functions cross. At point E, $S = I$ and $X = M$ (i.e., the nation's balance of payments is in equilibrium).

Suppose that now I increases autonomously from 150 to 350, so that the $(S - I)$ function shifts down by 200 to $(S - I')$ as in Figure 13.4. The $(X - M)$ function now crosses the $(S - I')$ function at point E' where $Y_{E'} = 1,400$ and $S - I' = X - M = -100$ (i.e., the nation has a balance-of-payments deficit of 100).

Concept Check

What is meant by incomplete balance-of-payments adjustment?

If X instead of I increased by 200, the $(X - M)$ function would shift up by 200 to $(X' - M)$ and cross the unchanged $(S - I)$ function at point E^* where $Y_E{}^* = 1,400$ and $S - I = X' - M = 100$ (the nation has a balance of

CASE STUDY 13-3

Income Elasticity of Imports

Table 13.2 gives the values of the income elasticity of demand for imports for the United States, the United Kingdom, Germany, Canada, and Japan, the rest of the industrial or OECD (Organization for Economic Cooperation and Development) countries, LDCs (less developed countries), and OPEC (Organization of Petroleum Exporting Countries) estimated over the period from 1973 to 1985. *The income elasticity of demand for imports* (η_Y) refers to the percentage increase in imports for each percentage point increase in income. The higher is η_Y, the greater is the increase in imports for a given increase in income.

From Table 13.2, we see that the income elasticity of imports is between 1.84 and 1.94 for the United States, Germany, and Canada. It is 2.51 for the United Kingdom, 0.35 for Japan, 2.03 for other industrial countries, 0.40 for LDCs, and 1.07 for OPEC. The unusually low income elasticity of imports for Japan is

due to the fact that Japan imports mostly raw materials and spends most of its increase in income on domestic products, as compared with other industrial countries.

Table 13.2. *Income Elasticity of Imports*

Country or Group of Countries	Elasticity
United States	1.94
United Kingdom	2.51
Germany	1.88
Canada	1.84
Japan	0.35
Rest of OECD Countries	2.03
Less Developed Countries	0.40
OPEC	1.07

Source: J. Marquez, "Bilateral Trade Elasticities," *Review of Economics and Statistics*, February 1990, pp. 75–76.

payments surplus of 100—see the figure). Note that an autonomous increase in X increases Y, which induces M to rise, thus neutralizing part of the improvement in the nation's balance of payments resulting from the increase in X. Thus, we say that the automatic income adjustment mechanism has brought about *incomplete* balance-of-payments adjustment for the nation.

If both I and X increase by 200, the dashed $(S - I')$ and $(X' - M)$ functions cross at point E'', where $Y_{E''} = 1,800$ and $S - I' = X' - M = 0$ (i.e., the nation ends up with equilibrium in its balance of payments). Case Study 13-3 gives the elasticity or responsiveness of imports to income changes, while case Study 13-4 gives the savings, investment, and current account balance in various countries or groups of countries.

CASE STUDY 13-4

Savings, Investments, and the Current Account Balance in the Leading Industrial Nations

Table 13.3 shows gross national savings, gross fixed capital formation (investment), and the current account balance of the leading (G-7) industrial countries as a percentage of their gross domestic product (GDP) in 2007. The table shows that, as a percentage of GDP, savings and investment are highest in Japan and lowest in the United Kingdom; Germany has the highest current account surplus, while the United States has the largest current account deficit. Note how close the values of $S - I$ are to those of $X - M$ (current account) in the table. Equilibrium condition $(S - I = X - M)$ is not precisely met because of the missing government sector (introduced in the next chapter) and because some of the nations (such as the United States) were not in equilibrium in 2007.

Table 13.3. *Savings, Investments, and Current Account Balance as a Percentage of GDP for the G-7 Countries in 2007*

Country	Savings as a % of GDP	Investment as a % of GDP	Savings Minus Investment	Current Account Balance as a % of GDP
United States	13.6	18.7	−5.1	−5.3
Japan	28.6	23.3	5.3	4.9
Germany	23.8	18.6	5.2	5.6
United Kingdom	13.6	18.0	−4.4	−4.9
France	20.4	21.0	−0.6	−1.3
Italy	19.3	21.0	−1.7	−2.2
Canada	23.7	22.3	1.4	0.9

Source: IMF, *World Economic Outlook* and *International Financial Statistics* (Washington, D.C.: 2008).

13.7 FOREIGN REPERCUSSIONS

We have seen that an increase in a nation's exports raises the level of income in the nation by an amount equal to the increase in exports times the foreign trade multiplier (k'). We now want to extend our analysis to consider foreign repercussions. To do so, assume for simplicity a world with only two nations, Nation 1 and Nation 2. Suppose that Nation 1's exports increase as a result of a change in tastes in Nation 2 (rather than being induced by an increase in Nation 2's income). If this *autonomous* increase in Nation 2's imports comes at the expense of or replaces domestic production, Nation 2's income falls, and this *induces* a reduction in its imports, which neutralizes part of the original autonomous increase in its imports. This means that part of Nation 1's original increase in exports is subsequently reduced, thus leading to a smaller foreign trade multiplier and smaller increase in Nation 1's income. The induced fall in Nation 1's exports, which neutralizes part of its original autonomous increase in its exports, is a foreign repercussion on Nation 1. Foreign repercussions are particularly important and cannot be neglected if the nations are large.

For example, suppose that the United States develops a more advanced PC that EU citizens want to purchase at their current level of income. If these EU purchases come at the expense of PCs produced in the European Union, EU income will fall, and this induces a reduction in other EU imports from the United States. This reduction in other EU imports from the United States represents a foreign repercussion on the United States. Foreign repercussions reduce the size of the foreign multiplier and the net increase in U.S. income resulting from the original autonomous increase in U.S. exports. This dampening of the increase in U.S. income, itself dampens the induced increase in U.S. imports from the European Union and represents a foreign repercussion on the European Union. The feedback process proceeds back and forth, but diminishes over time (the formula for the foreign trade multiplier with foreign repercussions is given in more advanced texts—see the Selected Bibliography at the end of the chapter). As we will see later (in Case Study 13-5), foreign repercussions are the vehicle through which business cycles are transmitted internationally.

Foreign repercussions The effect that a change in a large nation's income and trade has on the rest of the world and which the rest of the world in turn has on the nation under consideration. This is how business cycles are transmitted internationally.

Concept Check

Why is the foreign-trade multiplier smaller with foreign repercussions?

13.8 ABSORPTION APPROACH

We now extend our analysis by combining or integrating the automatic price and income adjustment mechanisms and examining the so-called absorption approach. Specifically, we examine the effect of induced (automatic) income changes in the process of correcting a deficit in the nation's balance of payments through a depreciation of the nation's currency.

We saw in Sections 13.2 and 13.3 that a nation can correct a deficit in its balance of payments by allowing its currency to depreciate (if the foreign

CASE STUDY 13-5

Interdependence in the World Economy

Table 13.4 shows the effect of an autonomous increase in U.S. government expenditures equal to 1 percent of U.S. gross national product (GNP), on GNP, consumer price index (CPI), interest rate, currency value, and current account in the United States and OECD countries. OECD refers to the Organization for Economic Cooperation and Development, which includes all the world's industrial countries. These simulation results were obtained by using the Multi-Country Model of the Federal Reserve Board. Although the effects of an increase in government expenditures are felt over several years, the results reported in Table 13.4 show the effect in the second year after government expenditures increased.

The left part of Table 13.4 shows that the increase in U.S. government expenditures equal to 1 percent of its GNP results (through the multiplier process) in an increase of 1.8 percent in the U.S. GNP the year after the United States increased its expenditures. A longer period of time would show a larger total effect. It also leads to a 0.4 percent increase in the U.S. prices, a 1.7 percentage point increase (say, from 4 percent to 5.7 percent) in U.S. short-term interest rates, a 2.8 percent increase in the international value of the dollar (appreciation), and a (–)$16.5 billion deterioration in the U.S. current account balance. The dollar appreciates because the increase in capital inflows attracted by the increase in the U.S. interest rate exceeds the induced rise in imports resulting from the increase in U.S. GNP.

The right part of the table shows that the increase in U.S. imports resulting from the increase in its expenditures and income stimulates the growth of GNP in the rest of OECD by 0.7 percent. This, in turn, leads to an increase of 0.4 percent in prices and a 0.4 percentage point increase in short-term interest rates in the other OECD countries. The appreciation of the dollar means a depreciation of the currencies of the other OECD countries and an improvement of $8.9 billion in their current account balance. The average depreciation of the other OECD countries was not estimated, and the improvement in their current account is smaller than the increase in the U.S. current account deficit because a great deal of U.S. imports also come from OPEC (Organization of Petroleum Exporting Countries) and LDCs (less developed countries).

Table 13.4. *Estimated Effect in the Second Year of an Increase in U.S. Government Expenditure of 1 Percent of U.S. GNP*

	Effect in the United States	*Effect on Rest of OECD*
GNP	1.8%	0.7%
CPI	0.4%	0.4%
Interest rate	1.7%*	0.4%*
Currency value	2.8%	—
Current account	–$16.5 billion	$8.9 billion

* = percentage point.

Source: R. Bryant, D. Henderson, G. Holtham, P. Hooper, and S. Symansky, eds., *Empirical Macronomics for Interdependent Economies* (Washington, D.C.: Brookings Institution, 1988), p. 21.

exchange market is stable). Because the improvement in the nation's trade balance depends on the price elasticity of demand for its exports and imports, this method of correcting a deficit is referred to as the elasticity approach. The improvement in the deficit nation's trade balance arises because depreciation stimulates the nation's exports and discourages its imports (thus encouraging the domestic production of import substitutes).

However, if the deficit nation is already at full employment, production cannot rise. Then, only if real domestic absorption (i.e., expenditures) is reduced will the depreciation eliminate or reduce the deficit in the nation's balance of payments. If real domestic absorption is not reduced, the depreciation will only lead to an increase in domestic prices that will completely neutralize the competitive advantage conferred on the nation by the depreciation, with no reduction of its trade deficit.

Absorption approach
Examines and integrates the effect of induced income changes in the process of correcting a balance-of-payments disequilibrium by a change in the exchange rate.

This analysis was first introduced in 1952 by *Sidney Alexander*, who named it the absorption approach. Alexander began with the identity that production or income *(Y)* is equal to consumption *(C)* plus domestic investment *(I)* plus the trade balance or net exports *(X − M)*, all in real terms. That is,

$$Y = C + I + (X - M)$$

But then letting *A* equal domestic absorption *(C + I)* and *B* equal the trade balance *(X − M)*, we have

$$Y = A + B$$

By subtracting *A* from both sides, we get

$$Y - A = B$$

That is, domestic production or income minus domestic absorption equals the trade balance. For the trade balance *(B)* to improve as a result of depreciation, *Y* must rise and/or *A* must fall. If the nation is at full employment to begin with, production or real income *(Y)* cannot rise, and depreciation can be effective only if domestic absorption *(A)* falls.

A depreciation of the deficit nation's currency automatically reduces domestic absorption if (1) it redistributes income from wages to profits (since profit earners usually have a higher marginal propensity to save than wage earners), (2) the increase in domestic prices resulting from the depreciation reduces wealth and hence expenditures in the nation, and (3) inflation pushes people into higher tax brackets and reduces consumption. Since we cannot be certain as to the speed and size of these automatic effects, contractionary fiscal and monetary *policies* may have to be used to cut domestic absorption adequately. These are discussed in the next chapter.

✓ Concept
 Check

Why is it important to study the absorption approach?

Thus, while the elasticity approach stresses the demand side and implicitly assumes that slack exists in the economy (so as to allow it to satisfy the additional demand for exports and import substitutes), the absorption

approach stresses the supply side (i.e., that the nation can in fact produce more exports and import substitutes). It is clear, however, that both the elasticity and the absorption approaches are important and both must be considered simultaneously.

13.9 SYNTHESIS OF AUTOMATIC ADJUSTMENTS

Synthesis of automatic adjustments
The attempt to integrate the automatic price, income, and monetary adjustments to correct balance-of-payments disequilibria.

We now provide an overview or synthesis of automatic adjustments. That is, we combine automatic price and income adjustments for a nation that faces unemployment and a deficit in its balance of payments at the equilibrium level of income, under either a flexible or a fixed exchange rate system.

Under a flexible exchange rate system and a stable foreign exchange market, the nation's currency will depreciate until the deficit is entirely eliminated. A depreciation, however, stimulates production and income in the deficit nation and induces its imports to rise, thus reducing part of the original improvement in the trade balance resulting from the depreciation. This simply means that the depreciation required to eliminate a balance-of-payments deficit is larger than if these automatic income changes were not present. If the deficit nation is already at full employment, domestic absorption must be reduced to allow the nation to produce more exports and import substitutes. Otherwise, inflation in the nation will match the depreciation of the currency and there would be no correction in the nation's balance of payments deficit.

Under a fixed exchange rate system, a balance-of-payments deficit tends to reduce the nation's money supply, which induces prices to fall, thus stimulating exports and discouraging imports, until the deficit in the nation's balance of payments is corrected. Note that prices need not actually fall in the deficit nation, but only to rise less than in the surplus country. The reduction in the deficit nation's money supply also tends to increase interest rates, which discourages domestic investments and income in the nation (and thus its imports) and also attracts foreign capital (which helps finance the nation's balance of payments deficit).

When the automatic adjustment mechanisms are allowed to operate, adjustment to a balance of payments disequilibrium is likely to be complete (i.e., a deficit or surplus is likely to be completely and automatically eliminated) under a flexible or a fixed exchange rate system. The problem is that automatic adjustments frequently have serious disadvantages or negative side effects.

Flexible exchange rates may lead to erratic and wild fluctuations, which can interfere with the smooth flow of international trade (even though foreign exchange risks can often be hedged at a cost) and disrupt the pattern of international specialization. Nations may also try to keep the domestic currency undervalued in order to stimulate the domestic economy at the expense of other nations (thus inviting retaliation).

On the other hand, in order to allow a fixed exchange rate system to operate, a nation must passively allow its money supply to change and thus give up on the use of monetary policy to achieve the more important objective of full employment without inflation in the nation. Furthermore, the possibility of a devaluation of the nation's currency can lead to destabilizing international capital flows, which can also prove very disruptive (the fixed and flexible exchange rate systems are evaluated and compared in Chapter 15). For all of these reasons, nations often rely on adjustment policies to correct a balance-of-payments disequilibrium instead of relying on automatic adjustment mechanisms. These are discussed in the next chapter.

In the real world, income, prices, interest rates, exchange rates, the current account, and other variables change as a result of an autonomous disturbance (such as an increase in expenditures) in one nation, and a disturbance in one nation affects other nations, with repercussions back to the first nation. It is very difficult to trace all of these effects in the real world because of the very intricate relationships that exist among these variables and also because, over time, other changes and disturbances occur, and nations also adopt various policies to achieve domestic and international objectives. The advent of large computers led to the use of large-scale models of the economy that allow us to examine the interdependence that exists among national economies (see Case Study 13-5).

Concept Check

How do all automatic adjustment mechanisms work together in the real world?

SUMMARY

1. This chapter examined how a trade deficit is automatically corrected through price or income changes, or both, under a flexible or a fixed exchange rate system. For simplicity, we assumed no autonomous international capital flows, so that a trade deficit is the same as, or is synonymous with, a balance-of-payments deficit.

2. The more elastic are the U.S. demand for imports (D_M) and the foreign demand for U.S. exports (D_X) in terms of euros, the more elastic are the U.S. demand and supply of euros (i.e., $D_€$ and $S_€$), and the less inflationary a depreciation would be to correct a U.S. trade or balance-of-payments deficit. The price elasticity of demand for a commodity (η) is given by the percentage change in the quantity demanded of the commodity divided by the percentage change in its price.

3. The foreign exchange market is stable if the supply curve of foreign exchange is positively sloped or, if negatively sloped, is steeper (less elastic) than the demand curve of foreign exchange. According to the Marshall–Lerner condition, the foreign exchange market is stable if the (absolute value of) sum of the price elasticities of the demands for imports and exports exceeds 1. In the real world, foreign exchange markets are generally stable and demand and supply curves of foreign exchange are

fairly elastic, especially in the long run. Current account disequilibria seem to respond only with a long lag to exchange rate changes. A currency depreciation may result in a deterioration in the nation's trade balance before an improvement takes place (the J-curve effect). There is usually only a partial pass-through of a depreciation in a nation's currency to its import prices.

4. Under the gold standard, each nation defines the gold content of its currency and passively stands ready to buy or sell any amount of gold at that price. This results in a fixed exchange rate called the mint parity. The exchange rate is determined at the intersection of the nation's demand and supply curves of the foreign currency between the gold points and is prevented from moving outside the gold points by the nation's sales or purchases of gold. According to the price-specie-flow mechanism, the loss of gold by the deficit nation reduces its money supply, which causes domestic prices to fall, thus stimulating its exports and discouraging its imports until the deficit is eliminated. The opposite process corrects a surplus. Other fixed exchange rate systems operate in a similar way.

5. In a closed economy without a government sector, the equilibrium level of income is the one at which income (Y) is equal to planned consumption expenditures (C) plus planned business investment (I). Since part of income is spent on consumption (C) and part is saved (S), we have $Y_E = C + S = C + I$, so that $S = I$ and $S - I = 0$. An increase in I causes Y_E to rise by the increase in I times the multiplier (k), which is given by the reciprocal of the marginal propensity to save (s). The increase in Y_E then induces S to rise by the amount of the autonomous increase in I.

6. In an open economy, exports (X) like investment (I) are autonomous, or independent of the nation's income, and imports (M) like S depend on income. The change in M per dollar change in Y is the marginal propensity to import (m). Y_E is determined where the sum of the leakages $(S + M)$ equals the sum of the injections $(I + X)$. The condition for Y_E can also be rewritten as $S - I = X - M$. The foreign trade multiplier $k' = 1/(s + m)$ and is smaller than the corresponding closed economy multiplier (k). An autonomous increase in I and/or X causes Y_E to change by k' times ΔI and/or ΔX. The change in Y_E induces S to change by $(s)(\Delta Y)$ and M to change by $(m)(\Delta Y)$, and adjustment in the balance of payments is incomplete.

7. If nations are large, foreign repercussions cannot be ignored. Foreign repercussions refer to the feedbacks from other nations resulting from changes originating in the nation. The foreign trade multiplier and the net change in the nation's income level with foreign repercussions are smaller than those without foreign repercussions. Foreign repercussions explain how business cycles are transmitted internationally.

8. The absorption approach integrates the automatic price and income adjustment mechanisms. For example, a depreciation also stimulates the domestic production of exports and import substitutes. If the nation is at full

employment to begin with, production cannot rise, thus leaving the trade deficit unchanged, unless real domestic absorption is somehow reduced.

9. With flexible exchange rates, the currency depreciates until the deficit is eliminated, unless the nation is already at full employment. Flexible exchange rates, however, can lead to erratic fluctuations, which can interfere with the flow of international trade and disrupt the pattern of international specialization. With fixed exchange rates, a balance-of-payments deficit tends to reduce the nation's money supply, which induces prices to fall, thus stimulating exports and discouraging imports, until the deficit is corrected. The deficit nation's interest rates also tend to rise, which discourages domestic investments, income, and imports, and it also attracts foreign capital (which helps finance the deficit). The nation, however, gives control over its money supply and is unable to conduct monetary policy.

REVIEW QUESTIONS AND PROBLEMS

1. (a) Why is a depreciation inflationary?

 (b) Why is a depreciation of the nation's currency not feasible to eliminate a deficit if the nation's demand and supply curves of foreign exchange are inelastic?

2. Since the U.S. trade deficit with Japan has not been reduced as a result of the sharp depreciation of the dollar with respect to the yen during the past 10–15 years, can we conclude that the trade or elasticity approach to balance-of-payments adjustment does not work? Explain.

3. (a) What happens to the trade balance of a deficit nation if its currency depreciates from a position of full employment?

 (b) How can domestic absorption be reduced?

4. Given $C = 100 + 0.8Y$ and autonomous investment $I = 100$, draw a figure showing the equilibrium level of national income.

5. For the given in Problem 4:
 (a) Write the equation of the saving function.

 (b) Draw a figure showing the equilibrium level of national income in terms of desired saving and investment.

6. Starting from the given and figure of Problem 5, and assuming that autonomous investment expenditures increase from $I = 100$ to $I' = 200$:
 (a) Draw a figure in terms of desired saving and investment showing the new equilibrium level of national income.

 (b) Determine the value of the multiplier.

7. Given $C = 100 + 0.8Y$, $M = 150 + 0.20Y$, $I = 100$, and $X = 350$, determine Y_E algebraically.

8. For the same given as in Problem 7, show the determination of Y_E graphically as in the bottom panel of Figure 13.4.

9. Starting with the algebraic and graphical results of Problems 7 and 8, determine algebraically and determine graphically the effect on Y_E of an autonomous:

 (a) Increase in X of 200.

 (b) Increase in I of 200.

 (c) Increase in X and I of 200.

10. What is the disadvantage of each automatic adjustment mechanism?

Adjustment under the Gold Standard: The Price-Specie-Flow Mechanism

Quantity theory of money Postulates that the nation's money supply times the velocity of circulation of money is equal to the nation's general price index times physical output at full employment. With V and Q assumed constant, the change in P is directly proportional to the change in M.

The automatic adjustment mechanism under the gold standard was the *price-specie-flow mechanism*. As indicated in Section 13.4, this operated as follows to correct a balance-of-payments disequilibrium. Since each nation's money supply under the gold standard consisted of either gold itself or paper currency backed by gold, the money supply would fall in the deficit nation and rise in the surplus nation. This caused internal prices to fall in the deficit nation and rise in the surplus nation. As a result, the exports of the deficit nation would be encouraged and its imports would be discouraged until the deficit in its balance of payments was eliminated.

The reduction of internal prices in the deficit nation as a result of the gold loss and reduction of its money supply was based on the quantity theory of money. This is shown by the following equation:

$$MV = PQ$$

where M is the nation's money supply, V is the velocity of circulation of money (the number of times each unit of the domestic currency turns over on the average during one year), P is the general price index, and Q is physical output.

Classical economists believed that V depended on institutional factors and was constant. They also believed that, apart from temporary disturbances, there was built into the economy an automatic tendency toward full employment without inflation (based on their assumption of perfect and instantaneous flexibility of all prices, wages, and interests). For example, any tendency toward unemployment in the economy would be automatically corrected by wages falling sufficiently to ensure full employment. Thus, Q was assumed to be fixed at the full-employment level. With V and Q constant, a change in M led to a direct and proportional change in P (see the equation). Thus, as the deficit nation lost gold, its money supply would fall and cause internal prices to fall proportionately.

For example, a deficit in the nation's balance of payments and gold loss that reduced M by 10 percent would also reduce P by 10 percent in the nation. This would encourage the exports of the deficit nation and discourage its imports. The opposite would take place in the surplus nation. That is, the increase in the surplus nation's money supply (due to the inflow of gold) would cause its internal prices to rise, which would discourage the nation's exports and encourage its imports. The process would continue until the deficit and surplus were eliminated.

Note that the adjustment process is automatic; it is triggered as soon as the balance-of-payments disequilibrium arises and continues to operate until the disequilibrium is entirely eliminated. Note also that the adjustment relies on a change in internal prices in the deficit and surplus nations. Thus, while adjustment under a flexible exchange rate system relies on changing the external value of the national currency, adjustment under the gold standard relies on changing internal prices in each nation. Adjustment under the gold standard also relies on high price elasticities of exports and imports in the deficit and surplus nations, so that the volumes of exports and imports respond readily and significantly to price changes.

David Hume introduced the price-specie-flow mechanism in 1752 and used it to demonstrate the futility of the mercantilists' belief that a nation could continuously accumulate gold by exporting more than it imported (refer to Section 2.2). Hume pointed out that as a nation accumulated gold, domestic prices would rise until the nation's export surplus (which led to the accumulation of gold in the first place) was eliminated. The example Hume used to make this point is unsurpassed: That is, it is futile to attempt to raise the water level (the amount of gold) above its natural level in some compartment (nation) as long as the compartments are connected with one another (i.e., as long as nations are connected through international trade).

Passively allowing the nation's money supply to change for balance-of-payments considerations meant that nations could not use monetary policy for achieving full employment without inflation. Yet, this created no difficulties for classical economists, since (as pointed out earlier) they believed that there was an automatic tendency in the economic system

Rules of the game of the gold standard
The requirement under the gold standard that monetary authorities restrict credit in the deficit nation and expand credit in the surplus nation (thus reinforcing the effect of changes in international gold flows on the nation's money supply).

toward full employment without inflation. Note, however, that for the adjustment process to operate, nations were not supposed to sterilize (i.e., neutralize) the effect on their money supply of a deficit or surplus in their balance of payments. On the contrary, the rules of the game of the gold standard required a deficit nation to reinforce the adjustment process by further restricting credit and a surplus nation by further expanding credit. (The actual experience under the gold standard is discussed in Section 16.2).

SELECTED BIBLIOGRAPHY

For a problem-solving approach to the topics covered in this chapter, see:

- D. Salvatore, *Theory and Problems of International Economics*, 4th ed. (New York: McGraw-Hill, 1996), Chapter 9.

For a more advanced treatment of the topics discussed in this chapter, see:

- D. Salvatore, *International Economics*, 9th ed. (Hoboken, N.J.: Wiley, 2007), Chapters 16–17.

For a discussion of the J-curve and pass-through effects of an exchange rate change, see:

- M. D. McKinzie, "The Impact of Exchange Rate Volatility on International Trade Flows," *Journal of Economic Surveys*, February 1999, pp. 71–106.
- R. Hellerstein, D. Daly, and C. Marsh, "Have U.S. Import Prices Become Less Responsive to Changes in the Dollar?," *Current Issues in Economics and Finance*, Federal Reserve Bank of New York, September 2006.

The operation of the gold standard is discussed in:

- T. Bayoumi, B. Eichengreen, and M. Taylor, *Modern Perspectives on the Gold Standard* (Cambridge, U.K.: Cambridge University Press, 1996).

The interdependence between the current account and national income is examined in:

- OECD, *OECD Economic Outlook* (Paris: OECD, December 2003).

A discussion of the problems that might arise from the large and growing U.S. current account deficit is found in:

- C. L. Mann, "Perspectives on the U.S. Current Account Deficit and Sustainability," *Journal of Economic Perspectives*, Summer 2002, pp. 131–152.
- S. Edwards, "Is the U.S. Current Account Deficit Sustainable? If Not, How Costly Is Adjustment Likely to Be?," *Brookings Papers on Economic Activity*, No. 1, 2005, pp. 211–271.

INTERNet

Data on exchange rates (daily, monthly, and trade-weighted average from 1971 or 1973) for the U.S. and the world's most important currencies, as well as data on current account balances, that can be used to find the effect of exchange rate changes on the trade and current account balances of the United States and other nations are found on the Federal Reserve Bank of St. Louis web site at:

http://research.stlouisfed.org/fred2

Some recent studies on the effect of international trade and finance on the U.S. economy are found on the web site of the Institute for International Economics and the Council of Foreign Relations at:

http://www.iie.com

http://www.cfr.org

Data to examine the effect of changes in the trade and current account balances on the economy of the United States are found on the Bureau of Economic Analysis and the Federal Reserve Bank of St. Louis web sites, respectively, at:

http://www.bea.doc.gov

http://www.stls.frb.org

Trade data to examine the economic impact of a change in the trade and current account balances on the economies of the European Monetary Union and Japan are found on the web site of their central banks, respectively, at:

http://www.ecb.int

http://www.boj.or.jp/en/index.htm

Data for measuring the effect of exchange rate changes on trade and current account balances and inflation in Latin American and Asian countries are found on the web site of the Inter-American Development Bank and the Asian Development Bank, respectively, at:

http://www.iadb.org

http://www.adb.org

Adjustment Policies

After studying this chapter, you should be able to:

- Know what the national objectives of nations are
- Know the policy mix to achieve internal and external balance with fixed rates
- Know the effect of monetary and fiscal policies under flexible rates
- Understand what a nation can do to correct unemployment with inflation
- Describe the policy mix actually used by the United States
- Understand how direct controls work

CHAPTER OUTLINE

KEY TERMS

Internal balance	Direct controls
External balance	Trade controls
Expenditure-changing policies	Exchange controls
Expenditure-switching policies	Multiple exchange rates

14.1 INTRODUCTION

In this chapter, we examine adjustment policies to achieve full employment with price stability and equilibrium in the balance of payments. The need for adjustment policies arises because, as we have seen in Section 13.9, automatic adjustments can have some serious unwanted side effects. The economist most responsible for shifting the emphasis from automatic to policy adjustments after World War II was *James Meade*, the British economist and 1977 Nobel Prize winner.

In this chapter, Section 14.2 discusses the goals or objectives of nations and the policies available for achieving those objectives. Section 14.3 deals with the policies to achieve internal and external balance with fixed but changeable exchange rates. Section 14.4 examines the effect of monetary policy on national income and the nation's balance of payments under a fixed exchange rate system. Section 14.5 does the same for fiscal policy. Section 14.6 then deals with the appropriate mix of fiscal and monetary policies to achieve full employment with price stability and equilibrium in the balance of payments with fixed exchange rates. Section 14.7 examines the monetary and fiscal policies to achieve full employment with price stability with flexible exchange rates. Section 14.8 deals with the situation where the nation faces unemployment with inflation, as well as balance-of-payments disequilibrium. Section 14.9 examines the actual policy mix pursued by the United States and other leading industrial countries during the postwar period. Finally, Section 14.10 deals with direct (trade and exchange) controls.

14.2 NATIONAL OBJECTIVES AND POLICIES

Internal balance
The objective of full employment with price stability; usually a nation's most important economic objective.

External balance
The objective of equilibrium in a nation's balance of payments.

Expenditure-changing policies
Fiscal and monetary policies directed at changing the level of aggregate demand of the nation.

The most important economic goals or objectives of nations are (1) internal balance, (2) external balance, (3) a reasonable rate of growth, (4) an equitable distribution of income, and (5) adequate protection of the environment. Internal balance refers to full employment or a rate of unemployment of no more than, say, 4–5 percent per year (the so-called frictional unemployment arising in the process of changing jobs) and a rate of inflation of no more than 2 or 3 percent per year. External balance refers to equilibrium in the balance of payments. In general, nations place priority on internal over external balance, but they are sometimes forced to switch their priority when faced with large and persistent external imbalances. In this chapter, we will deal primarily with the goals of internal and external balance.

To achieve internal and external balance, nations have three types of policy instruments at their disposal: (1) expenditure-changing, or demand, policies, (2) expenditure-switching policies, and (3) direct controls. Expenditure-changing policies refer to fiscal and monetary policies. *Fiscal policy* refers to changes in government expenditures, taxes, or both. *Fiscal policy* is expansionary if government expenditures are increased and/or taxes reduced. These actions lead to an expansion of domestic production and income through a multiplier process (just as in the case of an increase in domestic investment or exports) and induce a rise in imports (based on the marginal propensity to import of the nation). Contractionary fiscal policy refers to a reduction in government expenditures and/or an increase in taxes, both of which reduce domestic production and income, and induce a fall in imports.

Monetary policy involves a change in the nation's money supply that affects domestic interest rates. Monetary policy is easy if the money supply

is increased and interest rates fall. This induces an increase in the level of investment and income in the nation and induces imports to rise. At the same time, the reduction in the interest rate induces a short-term capital outflow or reduced inflow. On the other hand, contractionary or tight monetary policy refers to a reduction in the growth in the nation's money supply and a rise in the interest rate. This discourages investment, income, and imports and leads to a short-term capital inflow or reduced outflow.

Expenditure-switching policies Devaluation or revaluation of a nation's currency directed at switching the nation's expenditures from foreign to domestic or from domestic to foreign goods.

Expenditure-switching policies refer to changes in the exchange rate (i.e., a devaluation or revaluation). A *devaluation* switches expenditures from foreign to domestic commodities and can be used to correct a deficit in the nation's balance of payments. But a devaluation also increases domestic production, and this induces a rise in imports, which neutralizes a part of the original improvement in the trade balance resulting from the devaluation. A *revaluation* switches expenditures from domestic to foreign products and can be used to correct a surplus in the nation's balance of payments. This also reduces domestic production and, consequently, induces a decline in imports, which neutralizes part of the effect of the revaluation.

Direct controls Tariffs, quotas, and other restrictions on the flow of international trade and capital.

Direct controls refer to trade and exchange controls on the flow of international trade and capital. These are also expenditure-switching policies, but they are usually aimed at specific balance-of-payments items (as opposed to a devaluation or revaluation, which is a general policy and applies to all items at the same time). An example of a direct control is the voluntary exports restraints (VERs) on Japanese automobiles that the United States imposed in 1981 to avoid the collapse of its auto industry (discussed in Case Study 6-1). Direct controls in the form of price and wage controls could also be used to stem domestic inflation when other policies fail.

Concept Check

What are the general goals of nations and the policies to achieve those goals?

14.3 POLICIES TO ACHIEVE INTERNAL AND EXTERNAL BALANCE WITH FIXED BUT CHANGEABLE EXCHANGE RATES

Faced with multiple objectives and with several policy instruments at its disposal, the nation must decide which policy to utilize to achieve each of its objectives. According to *Jan Tinbergen* (the 1969 economics Nobel Prize winner), the nation usually needs as many effective policy instruments as the number of independent objectives it wants to achieve. If the nation has two objectives, it usually needs two policy instruments to achieve those two objectives completely; if it has three objectives, it requires three instruments, and so on. As previously indicated, in this chapter we will deal primarily with the objectives of internal and external balance and the policy instruments to achieve them.

Under a fixed exchange rate system, the nation can use expenditure-changing policies (monetary and fiscal policies) to achieve internal balance

and expenditure-switching policies (devaluation or revaluation) to achieve external balance. As mentioned earlier, internal balance refers to full employment with price stability. There are then two types of internal imbalance: recession and inflation. We begin by assuming that inflation is of the *excess-demand* type and that prices begin to rise only after reaching full employment. In this case, inflation is the opposite of recession or unemployment (which results from inadequate demand). On the other hand, external imbalance refers to a deficit or a surplus in the nation's balance of payments. Thus, we have four different combinations or types of internal and external imbalances:

1. Inflation and surplus

2. Recession and surplus

3. Recession and deficit

4. Inflation and deficit

Sometimes a policy instrument directed at one objective also helps the nation move closer to another objective. At other times, it pushes the nation even farther away from the second objective. For example, expansionary fiscal and monetary policies to eliminate a recession will also reduce a balance-of-payments surplus (case 2), but it would increase a deficit (case 3). Similarly, a devaluation to eliminate a balance of payments deficit will also reduce domestic recession (case 3), but it would worsen inflation (case 4).

Only rarely and quite by chance would a single policy achieve both the internal and external objectives precisely. For example, the expansionary fiscal and monetary policies to correct a recession may reduce but still leave a balance of payments surplus in the nation. Then, the nation needs to revalue its currency to eliminate the remaining surplus. But the revaluation also reduces exports and increases imports, and thus neutralizes parts of the original increase in income of the expansionary fiscal and monetary policies. Thus, the nation requires stronger expansionary fiscal and monetary policies to eliminate the recession.

On the other hand, the correction of a deep recession may involve such a large increase in national income (and imports) as to turn the nation's original balance-of-payments surplus into a deficit. Then the nation must accompany expansionary fiscal and monetary policies by a devaluation of its currency to correct the deficit, but this will further stimulate national income. Thus, the expansionary fiscal and monetary policies need not be as strong to correct a recession when accompanied by a devaluation. The point is that to achieve both internal and external balance precisely, both expenditure-changing and expenditure-switching policies are usually required. Since each policy affects both targets, targets and policies cannot be viewed in isolation, but must be considered together.

Concept
Check

What policies can be used to achieve internal and external balance with fixed rates?

Nations, however, are often unwilling to change the exchange rate even in the face of a serious balance-of-payments disequilibrium. Then they would have to rely on monetary and fiscal policies to achieve both internal and external balance. Nations often want to avoid a devaluation even in cases of large and persistent (fundamental) balance of payments deficits because devaluation is regarded as a sign of weakness and an admission of failure on the part of the government. Similarly, surplus nations often avoid revaluing their currencies even when needed because of the prestige and power that increasing international reserves seem to confer on the nation. Thus, nations often are faced with the situation of having to use monetary and fiscal policies to achieve internal and external balance—or having to adopt a flexible exchange rate.

In what follows we examine the effect of monetary and fiscal policies on a nation's internal and external balance, first under fixed and then under flexible exchange rates, and then indicate the appropriate policy mix of monetary and fiscal policies to achieve both objectives simultaneously in the case where the nation is unwilling to change the exchange rate. We will originally concentrate on the case of recession and deficit (case 3 above) because it is one of the most prevalent and difficult cases to correct.

14.4 EFFECT OF MONETARY POLICY ON INTERNAL AND EXTERNAL BALANCE UNDER FIXED EXCHANGE RATES

We begin by examining the effect of an expansionary monetary policy on the internal and external balance of a nation under a fixed exchange rate system. These effects are summarized in Figure 14.1 (the outcome of a tight or contractionary monetary policy would be the opposite).

As we have seen earlier, expansionary monetary policy refers to an increase in the nation's money supply, which tends to reduce the interest rate in the nation. The fall in the interest rate leads to a capital outflow or reduced inflow from the nation and thus to a worsening of its capital account. At the same time, the fall in the interest rates stimulates domestic investments and national income (through the multiplier process), which induces imports to rise (based on the marginal propensity to import) and thus to a deterioration of the nation's current account. With both the current and capital accounts worsening, the nation's overall balance of payments worsens. Thus, expansionary monetary policy leads to an increase in investment and income in the nation but to a deterioration in its external balance.

If the nation started from recession and balance-of-payments deficit, the use of expansionary monetary policy to cure the recession would lead

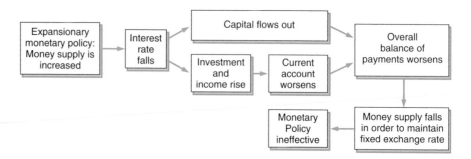

FIGURE 14.1. Monetary Policy Is Ineffective under Fixed Exchange Rates. Expansionary monetary policy (an increase in the nation's money supply) increases national income but worsens the nation's balance of payments. This leads to a reduction in the nation's money supply in order to maintain (defend) the fixed exchange rate, thus making monetary policy ineffective.

Concept Check

What is the effect of monetary policy under fixed exchange rates?

to an even greater deficit. The balance-of-payments deficit then requires official intervention in which the nation's central bank sells the foreign currency (international reserves) and buys domestic currency to pay for or cover the deficit. Otherwise, the currency depreciates and the nation would have to abandon its fixed exchange rate. But selling the foreign currency for the domestic currency reduces the nation's money supply, thus eliminating most or all of the increase in the money supply from the original expansionary monetary policy. That is, the necessity to defend the fixed exchange rate greatly constrains a nation's ability to pursue an independent monetary policy to cure a recession and achieve internal balance. As pointed out in Section 13.4, a nation essentially gives up control over its money supply (and thus on the use of monetary policy) to achieve internal balance.

The nation's monetary authorities could try to *sterilize* or neutralize the reduction in the nation's money supply arising from its balance of payments deficit by open market purchases of government bonds (which would put more money into the hands of the public). But there is a limit to how much and how long this policy could be pursued. The nation simply could not continue to run balance-of-payments deficits indefinitely because it would run out of international reserves. Eventually, the nation would face a reduction in its money supply, and this would neutralize all or most of the original increase in the nation's money supply of the expansionary monetary policy. In fact, with *perfect* capital mobility, expansionary monetary policy would be completely ineffective because any increase in the money supply would simply flow out. *Monetary policy is simply not an effective policy tool to achieve internal balance under fixed exchange rates.*

14.5 EFFECT OF FISCAL POLICY ON INTERNAL AND EXTERNAL BALANCE UNDER FIXED EXCHANGE RATES

Suppose that instead of using expansionary monetary policy to cure a recession under fixed exchange rates, the nation used expansionary fiscal policy. The effects of this on the nation's internal and external balance are summarized in Figure 14.2.

The increase in government spending and/or reduction in taxes (which would increase private spending) of an expansionary fiscal policy leads to higher interest rates as government borrowing increases. The higher interest rates induce more capital inflows (or smaller outflows), leading to an improvement in the nation's capital account. Expansionary fiscal policy also increases production and income, and can be very effective in curing a domestic recession. But it also leads to an increase in imports, which worsens the nation's current account. With the capital account improving and the current account worsening, the nation's balance of payments could improve, worsen, or remain unchanged, depending on the relative size of the change in the current and capital accounts.

With highly mobile capital, the nation's balance of payments is very likely to improve. This is the case for developed countries and is becoming increasingly so for many developing countries as they open up and liberalize their financial markets. (With perfect capital mobility the nation's balance of payments will definitely improve.) The improvement in the nation's overall balance of payments would then lead to official purchases of the foreign

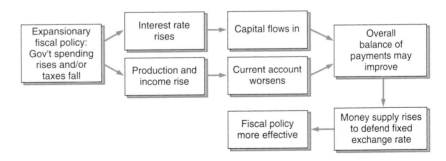

FIGURE 14.2. Fiscal Policy Is Very Effective under Fixed Exchange Rates. Expansionary fiscal policy (an increase in government spending and/or a reduction in taxes) increases the interest rate and leads to a capital inflow. By increasing production and income, expansionary fiscal policy also leads to a deterioration in the nation's current account. If the nation's overall balance of payments improves, the resulting increase in the nation's money supply (to defend the fixed exchange rate) makes fiscal policy even more effective.

currency with the domestic currency by the nation's monetary authorities in order to prevent an appreciation of the nation's currency (and thus maintain the exchange rate fixed). Official intervention increases the nation's money supply, lowers the interest rate, and stimulates production and income in the nation, thus reinforcing the effectiveness of the expansionary fiscal policy. Thus, *expansionary fiscal policy is very effective under fixed exchange rates.*

If, however, international capital flows are not very responsive to the increase in the interest rate in the nation, its overall balance of payments may deteriorate. This would require official *purchases* of the foreign currency with the domestic currency to maintain the fixed exchange rate. The resulting reduction in the nation's money supply would lead to a higher interest rate, and it would reverse some of the original increase in the nation's income from the expansionary fiscal policy.

The question of timing thus becomes important. Capital inflows usually occur very quickly in response to an increase in a nation's interest rate, while the increase in the nation's imports usually takes longer to occur as the nation's income rises. As a result, the nation's overall balance of payments can improve at first and worsen later on, and thus reinforce the effectiveness of the expansionary fiscal policy in the short run but weaken it in the long run. The overall conclusion, however, stands that *fiscal policy is effective in achieving internal balance, while monetary policy is ineffective under fixed exchange rates in the short run.* Furthermore, while an expansionary fiscal policy is likely to lead to an improvement in the nation's balance of payments in the short run, an expansionary monetary policy leads to a deterioration.

Concept Check

What is the effect of fiscal policy under fixed exchange rates?

14.6 POLICY MIX FOR INTERNAL AND EXTERNAL BALANCE UNDER FIXED EXCHANGE RATES

In Sections 14.4 and 14.5 we concluded that with fixed exchange rates, fiscal policy is very effective in correcting a recession or more generally in achieving internal balance, while monetary policy is not. Monetary policy can, however, be very effective in achieving external balance.

For example, a nation could correct a balance of payments deficit, with a tight or *contractionary* monetary policy. This involves a reduction in the nation's money supply and an increase in the interest rate, which would lead to a capital inflow (or reduced outflow) that improves the capital account. The increase in the interest rate would also cause a reduction in domestic investments and income and induce a fall in imports, so that the nation's current account also improves. With both current and capital accounts improving, the nation's overall balance of payments improves, but the nation may then face a recession—and a recession is usually considered a much worse problem than a balance-of-payments deficit.

Based on their relative effectiveness, we conclude that nations should use fiscal policy to achieve internal balance and monetary policy to achieve

external balance. If the nation did the opposite, it would move further away from internal and external balance. Specifically, since each policy affects both the internal and external balance, it is crucial that each policy be paired with or directed at the objective in which it is more effective. This is according to the *assignment rule* developed by *Robert Mundell* (the 1999 economics Nobel Prize winner). If the nation does not follow this principle, it will move farther from both balances.

We can now go back to the four different types of internal and external imbalance identified in Section 14.3 and indicate the policy mix to achieve both internal and external balance. We start by using fiscal policy to correct the internal imbalance and then use monetary policy to fill in to correct any remaining external imbalance. In doing so, we must always remember that while each policy may be more effective in correcting one type of imbalance, it will also affect the other imbalance, and so (as we will see in what follows) both policies and targets should considered together.

Case 1 (inflation and surplus): In this case, the nation should use contractionary fiscal policy to correct the inflation. Since this will make the surplus even larger, an *expansionary* monetary policy would also have to be used. Since fiscal policy is relatively more effective in correcting the internal imbalance while monetary policy is relatively more effective in correcting the external imbalance, the two contrasting policies will not completely neutralize each other, but leave a net effect of fiscal policy on the internal balance and a net effect of monetary policy on the external balance. By then applying the appropriate dosage of fiscal and monetary policy, both internal and external balance could theoretically be reached in a single bold step. However, since fiscal policy is conducted by the executive branch of government while monetary policy is conducted by the nation's central bank with usually little or no coordination, this would not be possible. However, by repeated applications of fiscal and monetary policies (with the first directed exclusively at the internal balance and the second exclusively to the external balance), the nation could gradually move closer and closer to both internal and external balance over time.

Case 2 (recession and surplus): This case is easier because the expansionary fiscal policy could also correct the surplus. Since it is unlikely, however, that the expansionary fiscal policy will also bring the nation's balance of payments exactly in equilibrium, there is room for an appropriate monetary policy to also achieve external balance.

Case 3 (recession and deficit): This is the case we have been discussing most of the time in the previous two sections, and it is the exact opposite of Case 1. Here, we would have to use expansionary fiscal policy and contractionary monetary policy to reach internal and external imbalance.

Case 4 (inflation and deficit): This is the opposite of Case 2 and would require a contractionary fiscal policy but may also require an appropriate monetary policy to fine tune the economy and eliminate both imbalances.

Concept Check

This type of analysis is also applicable to the extent that the nation *manages* its exchange rate (i.e., intervenes in foreign exchange markets) to reduce exchange rate volatility and misalignments by inducing international capital flows. Case Study 14-1 examines the relationship between U.S. current account and budget deficits since 1980.

14.7 EFFECT OF MONETARY AND FISCAL POLICIES ON INTERNAL BALANCE UNDER FLEXIBLE EXCHANGE RATES

Flexible exchange rates will automatically bring the nation's balance of payments in equilibrium. The exchange rate depreciates to correct a deficit or appreciates to correct a surplus. This frees the nation to use monetary and fiscal policies to achieve internal balance (full employment with price stability). As we will see, with flexible rates, monetary policy is effective while fiscal policy is not. This is the exact opposite of the case with fixed exchange rates, where fiscal policy was effective and monetary policy was not. Figure 14.4 summarizes the effect of monetary policy in Part (a) and of fiscal policy in Part (b) on the nation's internal balance.

Suppose that a nation with flexible exchange rates faces a domestic recession and uses expansionary monetary policy to correct the recession (the nation need not worry about its external balance because flexible rates ensure equilibrium). As shown in Part (a) of Figure 14.4, expansionary monetary policy causes the interest rate to fall. This leads to a capital outflow, a worsening of the nation's capital account, as well as to an increase in investment and income, and thus to a worsening of the nation's current account. The worsening of the nation's current and capital accounts (and hence of its overall balance of payments) leads to a depreciation of the nation's currency, which improves the current account, thus reinforcing the effect of expansionary monetary policy. With highly mobile capital, monetary policy will be very powerful indeed. As opposed to the situation with a fixed exchange rate, monetary policy becomes very effective with flexible rates. That is, flexible exchange rates enhance or reinforce the effectiveness of monetary policy on achieving internal balance.

If the nation faced inflation instead of a recession with flexible rates, the situation would be the exact opposite. The nation would pursue a contractionary monetary policy, which, on the one hand, would lead to a rise in the interest rate and capital inflows and, on the other hand, to a reduction in production and income, and an improvement in the nation's

CASE STUDY 14-1

Relationship Between U.S. Current Account and Budget Deficits

Figure 14.3 shows that from 1980 to 1989 and 2001 to 2003, the U.S. current account deficit and the U.S. budget deficit (the excess of government expenditures over taxes collected) as percentages of the U.S. gross domestic product (GDP) moved more or less together (and for that reason, they are often referred to as the *twin deficits*). This does not mean, however, that the budget deficit fully explains or causes the current account deficit because each depends on many other factors, such as rates of savings, inflation, and growth, as well as expectations about taxes, interest rates, and exchange rates in the United States and abroad. In fact, from 1989 to 2000 and 2004 to 2007, the U.S. current account deficit and the U.S. budget deficit moved in opposite directions. In 1992, the United States had the largest budget deficit (5.8% of GDP) and in 2006 the largest current account deficit (6.2% of GDP) over the 1980 to 2007 period examined.

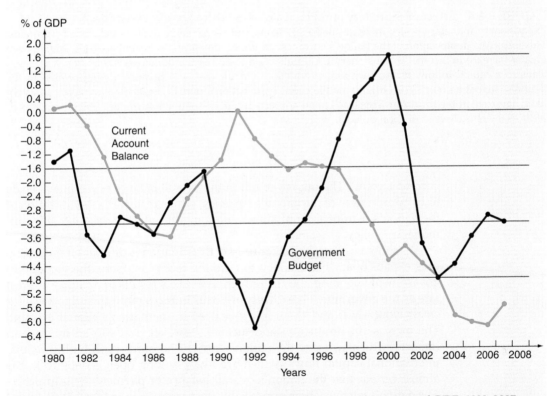

FIGURE 14.3. U.S. Current Account and Budget Deficits as a Percentage of GDP, 1980–2007.
From 1980 to 1989 and 2001 to 2003, the U.S. current account deficit and the U.S. budget deficit, as a percentage of GDP, moved together as "twins," but they moved in opposite directions in other years.
Source: OECD, *Economic Outlook* (Paris: OECD, various issues); and D. Salvatore, "Twin Deficits in the G-7 Countries and Global Structural Imbalances," *Journal of Policy Modeling*, September 2006, pp. 701–712.

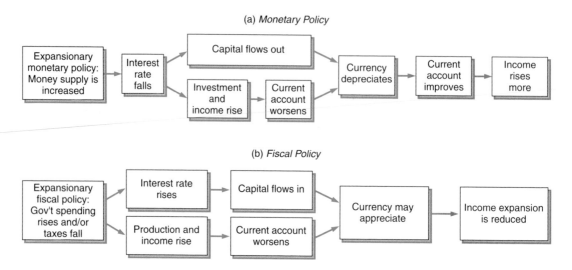

FIGURE 14.4. Effect of Monetary and Fiscal Policies with Flexible Exchange Rates.
Expansionary monetary policy increases national income but worsens the nation's balance of payments. This leads to a depreciation of the nation's currency, an improvement in its current account, and an even greater increase in income. Expansionary fiscal policy, on the other hand, increases the interest rate and leads to a capital inflow. It also increases production and income, which cause a deterioration in the nation's current account. With highly mobile capital, the nation's overall balance of payments will very likely improve in the short run. This leads to an appreciation of the nation's currency, which dampens or reduces the effectiveness of fiscal policy.

current account. The improvement in the overall balance of payments leads to an appreciation of the nation's currency, which results in a deterioration of the nation's current account, thus reinforcing the effect of the contractionary monetary policy.

As shown in Part (b) of Figure 14.4, the situation is different if the nation uses expansionary fiscal policy to cure the recession. Here, the increase in government spending and/or reduction in taxes results in a higher interest rate as the government borrows more. This induces more capital inflows (or smaller outflows) and to an improvement in the nation's capital account. The increase in production and income, however, leads to an increase in imports, which worsens the nation's current account. With highly mobile international capital flows (which are likely among open economies), it is almost certain that the nation's overall balance of payments will improve. The nation's currency then appreciates, its current account deteriorates, and the increase in income of the expansionary fiscal policy will be reduced. Thus, with highly mobile capital, fiscal policy is ineffective in the short run under flexible exchange rates.

In the long run, however, the increase in income is likely to lead to a larger deterioration in the nation's current account, as well as to a reduction in net capital inflows, a deterioration in the overall balance of payments, a depreciation of the currency, which would act as a stimulus to domestic production and income, thus reinforcing the effectiveness of the expansionary fiscal policy. But this is only in the long run. In the short run, the nation's balance of payments is likely to improve, and this dampens the effect of the expansionary fiscal policy. In fact, with perfect capital mobility, fiscal policy would be completely ineffective in the short run. If the nation faced inflation instead of recession, the situation would be the exact opposite (this is left as an end-of-chapter problem).

Thus, we can reach the following overall conclusions on the effectiveness of monetary and fiscal policies in achieving internal balance under fixed and flexible exchange rates:

Concept Check

What is the effect of monetary and fiscal policies under flexible exchange rates?

1. With fixed exchange rates, fiscal policy is effective and monetary policy is ineffective in correcting an internal imbalance.

2. If the nation is unwilling to change the exchange rate to correct an external imbalance, the nation would have to use fiscal policy to achieve internal balance and the appropriate monetary policy to correct whatever external imbalance arises or remains in the short run.

3. With flexible exchange rates, monetary policy is effective while fiscal policy is ineffective in correcting an internal imbalance in the short run.

14.8 CORRECTING UNEMPLOYMENT WITH INFLATION

During the 1970s, nations faced a serious petroleum shock and sharply higher petroleum prices, which increased costs of production and led to high inflation. The strong contractionary monetary policies pursued by industrial nations to control inflation, however, led to recession or slow growth and high unemployment. This was cost-push inflation, which is different from demand-pull type inflation that we have been discussing. With *cost-push inflation*, prices rise (inflation) in the face of high unemployment.

Concept Check

How can a nation correct unemployment with inflation?

Nations then faced three independent and important objectives: (1) full employment, (2) price stability, and (3) balance-of-payments equilibrium, requiring three different policies to achieve. Theoretically, nations could achieve all three objectives by directing fiscal policy to get to full employment, monetary policy to achieve price stability, and flexible exchange rates to reach equilibrium in the balance of payments. With full employment and price stability usually regarded as more important objectives, external balance could only be fully achieved with flexible rates or with nations willing to change the exchange rate.

This was, in fact, the situation that the United States faced in 1971. The United States, however, directed fiscal and monetary policy toward reducing unemployment and imposed *price and wage controls*, or an income policy, to control inflation, while leaving the large external imbalance uncovered (until it was forced to devalue the dollar in August 1971). Price and wage controls were not very successful in controlling inflation in the United States, however, and were later repealed.

In 2008, the United States faced very slow growth or recession as a result of the serious subprime mortgage crisis, a resurgence of inflation because of the skyrocketing price of petroleum, a huge and unsustainable trade deficit (which started to fall only in 2007 in response to the sharp depreciation of the dollar since 2005), and a budget deficit that is approaching 3 percent of GDP. Europe was afflicted by slow growth, high unemployment, and strong inflationary pressures. Japan faced slow growth and a large and persistent trade surplus. These large imbalances were not the result of policy failures but arose because of the unwillingness of the major industrial nations to undertake structural reforms. Europe needed to liberalize its labor markets to encourage growth and reduce unemployment. Japan needed structural reforms to stimulate growth and to open up its market more widely to imports to reduce its large trade surplus. The United States has to increase its rate of saving and reduce its budget deficit in order to reduce its trade deficit to sustainable levels. Case Study 14-2 examines the effect of U.S. monetary policy.

14.9 POLICY MIX IN THE REAL WORLD

During the fixed exchange rate period of the 1950s and 1960s, most of the G-7 countries (the seven largest industrial countries: the United States, Japan, Germany, France, the United Kingdom, Italy, and Canada) generally used fiscal and monetary policies to achieve internal balance and switched their aims only when the external imbalance became so critical that it could no longer be ignored. Even then, these nations seemed reluctant to use monetary policy to correct the external imbalance and instead preferred using direct controls over capital flows (discussed in the next section). During this period, the United Kingdom and France were forced to devalue their currency, while Germany had to revalue the mark. Canada, unable to maintain a fixed exchange rate, allowed its dollar to fluctuate.

During the period of flexible but managed exchange rates since 1971, the leading nations seemed content, for the most part, to leave to exchange rates the function of adjusting external imbalances and generally directed fiscal and monetary policies to achieve internal balance. During the 1970s and early 1980s, the world faced two serious petroleum crises, which sharply increased the price of petroleum. These led to huge balance of payments deficits and depreciating currencies, as well as high inflation and slow growth or

CASE STUDY 14-2

Effect of U.S. Monetary Policy

Table 14.1 shows the effect of a 4 percent increase in the U.S. money supply (expansionary monetary policy) on the gross national product (GNP), consumer price index (CPI), interest rate, currency value, and current account in the United States and other OECD countries. OECD refers to the Organization for Economic Cooperation and Development, which includes all the world's industrial countries. These simulation results were obtained by using the Multi-Country Model of the Federal Reserve Board. Although the effects of an increase in the U.S. money supply are felt over several years, the results reported in Table 14.1 show the effect in the second year after government expenditures increased.

The left part of Table 14.1 shows that a 4 percent increase in the U.S. money supply results (through the multiplier process) in a 1.5 percent increase in the U.S. GNP the year after the United States increased its money supply. A longer period of time would show a larger total effect. It also leads to a 0.4 percent increase in U.S. prices, a 2.2 percentage point decrease (say, from 7.2 percent to 5.0 percent) in the U.S. short-term interest rate, a 6 percent decrease in the international value of the dollar (depreciation), and a (–) $3.1 billion deterioration in the U.S. current account balance (because the tendency of U.S. imports to rise due to higher GNP overwhelms the tendency of the dollar depreciation to improve the U.S. current account).

The right part of the table shows that the increase in the U.S. money supply leads to a reduction in the growth of GNP in the rest of the OECD countries of 0.7 percent, a 0.6 percent fall in prices, a 0.5 percentage point reduction in the short-run interest rate, and a deterioration in the current account balance of $3.5 billion. The effect on the foreign exchange rates of the rest of OECD was not estimated. Note that both the U.S. and OECD's current accounts deteriorate. This means that the current account of the rest of the world (i.e., excluding the United States and OECD) improves.

Table 14.1. *Estimated Effect in the Second Year of a 4 Percent Increase in the U.S. Money Supply*

	Effect in the United States	*Effect on Rest of OECD*
GNP	1.5%	−0.7%
CPI	0.4%	−0.6%
Interest rate	−2.2%	−0.5%*
Currency value	−6.0%	—
Current account	−$3.1 billion	−$3.5 billion

* = percentage point.

Source: R. Bryant, D. Henderson, G. Holtham, P. Hooper, and S. Symansky, eds., *Empirical Macroeconomics for Interdependent Economies* (Washington, D.C.: Brookings Institution, 1988), p. 23.

recession, as industrial nations used highly contractionary monetary policies to bring inflation down. The United States also imposed price and wage controls. As inflationary pressures subsided during the first half of the 1980s, the leading nations continued to direct fiscal and monetary policies

to achieve internal balance but (except for the United States) sometimes switched monetary policy toward the external imbalance as they attempted to manage their exchange rates.

During the first half of the 1980s, the United States ran huge budget deficits. These kept real interest rates higher in the United States than abroad, and this attracted very large capital inflows, which resulted in a large overvaluation of the dollar, and large trade deficits and calls for protectionism (see Section 10.8). The United States then organized a coordinated international effort with four other leading industrial nations (Germany, Japan, France, and England) to jointly intervene in foreign exchange markets to correct the overvaluation of the dollar. From 1986 to 1991, the United States advocated a simultaneous, equal, coordinated reduction in interest rates in the leading nations so as to stimulate growth and reduce unemployment without directly affecting trade and capital flows.

From its peak in February 1985, the dollar depreciated until 1988, but the U.S. current account deficit did not begin to improve until the end of 1987 (refer to Figure 13.3). In 1990 and 1991, reunified Germany pushed its interest rates up to avoid inflationary pressures at home, encourage domestic savings, and attract foreign capital to help finance the rebuilding of East Germany, while the United States and other industrialized countries of Europe lowered their interest rates to fight weak economies and recession.

From 1992 to 1997, interest rates were reduced in Europe in order to stimulate anemic growth after the deep recession of the early 1990s, but increased in the United States in order to contain inflationary pressures in the face of relatively rapid growth. From 1997 to 2000, growth and interest rates were much higher in the United States than in Europe and Japan, and the United States received huge inflows of foreign financial capital and direct investments, which led to growing dollar appreciation and trade deficits. In 2001, the high-tech bubble burst and the United States fell into recession. From 2001 to 2003, the Fed sharply reduced the interest rate to 1 percent (the lowest in 40 years), and President Bush pushed a huge budget stimulus package. By fall 2003, growth had resumed in the United States but remained very low in Europe and Japan.

In 2007 and 2008, the United States, Europe and Japan faced slow growth as a result of the U.S. subprime mortgage crisis, and the United States and Europe faced increasing inflationary pressures from the skyrocketing price of petroleum. The United States also faced a huge trade deficit which led to a sharp depreciation of the dollar (especially with respect to the euro), as well as a rising budget deficit. Case Study 14-3 provides an overview of U.S. monetary policy during the past decade, while Case Study 14-4 examines the booms and busts in the U.S. economy over time.

Concept Check

What policy mix did the leading nations actually use during the postwar period?

U.S. Monetary and Fiscal Policies During the Past Decade

Table 14-2 presents U.S. macroeconomic data that summarize the course of U.S. monetary policy (measured by the growth rate of the money supply) and fiscal policy (measured by the budget balance) and their effects on other macro variables from 1997 to 2007. The first row shows that the United States experienced rapid growth from 1997 to 2000, but faced a mild recession in 2001 (but nevertheless managing a small positive growth for the year as a whole) and slow growth in 2002. Rapid growth resumed from 2003 to 2006, but slowed in 2007 as a result of the subprime housing mortgage crisis.

The second row shows a negative growth of the money supply in 2000 when the Federal Reserve Bank or Fed (the government institution entrusted with the conduct monetary policy in the United States) wrongly thought that the problem facing the U.S. economy was a resurgence of inflation. With recession hitting the U.S. economy instead, the Fed reversed course and increased the money supply very rapidly from 2001 to 2004. With rapid growth resuming in 2004 and the danger of inflation arising from the sharp increase in petroleum prices in 2006 and 2007, the Fed reduced slightly the money supply from 2005 to 2007.

The budget surplus from 1998 to 2000 shown in the third row gave way to rising budget deficits from 2001 on, which peaked at 4.8 percent of GDP in 2003, primarily as the result of the drastic tax cut legislated in 2001–2003 and the cost of the Iraq war. Row 4 shows that, as expected, the interest rate moved inversely to the rate of growth of the money supply, except in 2002 and 2003. The relationship between the current account and the exchange rate was examined in Case Study 13-2, while that between the budget deficit and the current account was discussed in Case Study 14-1.

Table 14.2. *U.S. Macroeconomic Data, 1997–2007*

	1997	1998	1999	2000	2001	2002	2003	2004	2005	2006	2007
1. Growth of real GDP (percent per year)	4.5	4.2	4.4	3.7	0.8	1.6	2.5	3.6	3.1	2.9	2.2
2. Growth of money supply (percent per year)	−0.8	2.1	2.5	−3.1	8.7	3.2	7.1	5.4	−0.1	−0.5	−0.2
3. Budget balance (as a percentage of GDP)	−0.8	0.4	0.9	1.6	−0.4	−3.8	−4.8	−4.4	−3.6	−2.6	−2.8
4. Interest rate (percent per year)	5.1	4.8	4.7	5.8	3.5	1.6	1.0	1.4	3.2	4.7	4.4
5. Inflation rate (percent per year)	2.3	1.5	2.2	3.4	2.8	1.6	2.3	2.7	3.4	3.2	2.8
6. Effective exchange rate (foreign currencies per dollar, 2000 = 100)	89.6	97.7	97.4	100.0	105.2	105.2	98.5	93.6	91.1	89.8	85.9
7. Current account balance (as percentage of GDP)	−1.7	−2.5	−3.3	−4.3	−3.8	−4.4	−4.8	−5.5	−6.1	−6.2	−5.6

Source: OECD, *Economic Outlook* (Paris: December 2007); and IMF, *International Financial Statistics* (Washington, D.C.: 2008).

CASE STUDY 14-4

Booms and Busts in the U.S. Economy

During the U.S. boom of the 1990s (the longest on record), the question arose whether the U.S. economy had become recession proof or whether recessions were a thing of the past. This discussion came abruptly to an end when growth fell sharply in fall 2000 as a prelude to recession, which officially started in March 2001. The immediate cause of the 2001 recession was the bursting of the technology and dot.com bubble. Stock prices fell sharply, industrial production and GDP declined, and unemployment rose. Although expansions have become longer and recessions fewer and milder in recent decades, excesses inevitably develop during booms and the correction of these usually leads to recession.

There are several reasons that recessions have become rarer and milder during the postwar period: (1) government insurance of bank deposits has practically eliminated bank panics, which almost always were the trigger for recessions in the past; (2) automatic stabilizers in the form of reduced income taxes and increased government expenditures on unemployment insurance and antipoverty programs are much stronger and successful today than a century ago in softening slowdowns in the economy; and (3) the Fed has done a much better job at keeping the economy on track with

monetary policy and avoiding the mistakes of the past (practically every recession since the establishment of the Fed in 1914 started with a tightening of monetary policy and higher interest rates to quell the run-up of inflation at the end of a boom).

During the past two decades, monetary and fiscal policies have become much more successful at stabilizing the economy. For example, during the 1987 stock market crash, Fed Chairman Greenspan flooded the market with liquidity to prevent the financial crisis from triggering a recession. He did the same following the September 11, 2001, terrorist attack in New York City and Washington, and so did new Fed Chairman, Ben Bernanke, in 2007 during the U.S. subprime mortgage financial crisis.

Source: "A Century of Booms and How They Ended," *The Wall Street Journal*, February 1, 2000, p. B1; "Sluggish U.S. Economy a Global Concern," *The New York Times*, September 27, 2002, p. 14; "On the Roll," *U.S. News and World Report*, January 12, 2004, pp. 32–39; and C. Reinhart and K. Rogoff, "Is the 2007 U.S. Sub-Prime Financial Crisis So Different? An International Historical Comparison," *American Economic Review*, May 2008, pp. 339–344.

14.10 DIRECT CONTROLS

Direct controls
Tariffs, quotas, and other restrictions on the flow of international trade and capital.

Direct controls to affect the nation's balance of payments can be subdivided into trade controls (such as tariffs, quotas, and other quantitative restrictions on the flow of international trade), financial or exchange controls (such as restrictions on international capital flows and multiple exchange rates), and others. In general, trade controls are both less important and less acceptable than exchange controls. As we have seen in Section 14.8, direct controls can also take the form of *price and wage controls* in an attempt to restrain domestic

Trade controls
Tariffs, quotas, advance deposits on imports, and other restrictions imposed by a nation on international trade.

Exchange controls
Restrictions on international capital flows, official intervention in forward markets, multiple exchange rates, and other financial and monetary restrictions imposed by a nation.

inflation when more general policies have failed or nations are unwilling to pursue them.

One of the most important trade or commercial controls is the import tariff. This increases the price of imported goods to domestic consumers and stimulates the domestic production of import substitutes. On the other hand, export subsidies make domestic goods cheaper to foreigners and encourage the nation's exports. In general, an import tariff and an export subsidy of a given percentage applied across the board on all commodities are equivalent to a devaluation of the nation's currency by the same percentage. However, import duties and export subsidies are usually applied to specific items rather than across the board. Both are expenditure-switching policies, just as devaluation, and both stimulate domestic production. In general, nations today are not allowed to impose new import tariffs and quotas except temporarily, when in serious balance-of-payments difficulties.

Turning to financial, or exchange, controls, we find that developed nations imposed restrictions on capital exports when in balance-of-payments deficit and on capital imports when in surplus. For example, in 1963, the United States imposed the Interest Equalization Tax on portfolio capital exports in order to reduce its balance-of-payments deficit. On the other hand, West Germany and Switzerland sought to discourage capital imports by allowing lower or no interest on foreign deposits in the face of large balance-of-payments surpluses, in order to insulate their economies from worldwide inflationary pressures. In the late 1960s and early 1970s, France and Belgium established a two-tier foreign exchange market and allowed the exchange rate on capital transactions to fall (appreciate) to limit speculative capital inflows, while keeping the exchange rate higher on current account transactions in order not to discourage their exports and encourage their imports. With the rapid globalization and integration of capital markets that took place since the 1980s, however, developed nations abolished most restrictions on international capital flows.

Multiple exchange rates The different exchange rates often enforced by developing nations for each class of imports depending on the usefulness of the various imports as determined by the government.

Most developing nations, on the other hand, have some type of exchange controls. The most common is multiple exchange rates, with higher exchange rates on luxury and nonessential imports (in order to discourage these types of imports) and lower rates on essential imports, such as machinery and raw materials. An extreme form of exchange control requires exporters and other earners of foreign exchange to turn in all their exchange earnings to monetary authorities (in exchange for the domestic currency), who then proceed to allocate the available supply of foreign exchange to importers through import licenses and at various rates, depending on how important the monetary authorities consider the particular import commodity to be. This, however, encourages black markets and corruption. Case Study 14-5 summarizes the prevalence of exchange controls among the 186 members of the International Monetary Fund.

Direct Controls on International Transactions Around the World

Table 14.3 summarizes data on the different types direct controls that various countries had on international transactions in 2007. From the table, we see that the most common forms of direct controls or international transactions around the world are payment restrictions on capital transactions of commercial banks and other credit institutions, direct investments, real estate transactions, and capital market securities.

Table 14.3. *Direct Controls on International Transactions by IMF Members in 2007*

Type of Restriction	Number of Countries
A. Exchange rate structure	
1. Dual exchange rates	12
2. Multiple exchange rates	5
B. Arrangements of payments and receipts	
1. Bilateral payments arrangements	64
2. Payment arrears	42
C. Controls on proceeds from exports and/or invisible transactions	
1. Repatriation requirements	89
2. Surrender requirements	59
D. Capital transactions	
1. Capital market securities	137
2. Money market instruments	113
3. Collective investment securities	113
4. Derivatives and other instruments	90
5. Commercial credits	88
6. Financial credits	120
7. Guarantees, securities, and financial backup facilities	81
8. Direct investments	145
9. Liquidation of direct investments	46
10. Real estate transactions	140
11. Personal capital transactions	92
12. Commercial banks and other credit institutions	159
13. Institutional investors	119

Source: IMF, *Exchange Arrangements and Exchange Restrictions* (Washington, D.C.: IMF, 2008).

Government authorities sometimes impose direct controls to achieve a purely domestic objective, such as inflation control, when more general policies have failed. For example, as indicated in the previous section, the United States imposed price and wage controls, or an income policy, to

control inflation in 1971. From an efficiency point of view, however, monetary and fiscal policies and exchange rate changes are to be preferred to direct controls on the domestic economy and on international trade and finance. The reason is that direct controls often interfere with the operation of markets, while the more general expenditure-changing and expenditure-switching policies work through the market. Nevertheless, when these general policies take too long to operate, when their effect is uncertain, and when the problem affects only one sector of the economy, nations may turn to direct controls as temporary measures to achieve specific objectives. An example is the "voluntary" export quotas on Japanese automobiles negotiated by the United States in 1981.

In general, for direct controls and other policies to be effective, international cooperation is required. For example, the imposition of an import quota by a nation may result in retaliation by the other nations affected (thus nullifying the effect of the quota) unless these nations are consulted and understand and agree to the need for such a temporary measure. International policy coordination is examined in the next chapter.

Concept Check

How has the United States used direct controls to reduce its trade deficits?

SUMMARY

1. Adjustment policies are needed because automatic adjustments often give rise to unwanted side effects.

2. The most important economic goals or objectives of nations are internal and external balance. Internal balance refers to full employment with price stability. External balance refers to equilibrium in the balance of payments. To reach these goals, nations have at their disposal expenditure-changing policies (i.e., fiscal and monetary policies), expenditure-switching policies (devaluation or revaluation), and direct controls.

3. There are four different combinations of internal and external imbalances: (1) inflation and surplus, (2) recession and surplus, (3) recession and deficit, and (4) inflation and deficit. The nation could use expenditure changing (i.e., fiscal and monetary policies) to achieve internal balance, and expenditure switching (i.e., devaluation or revaluation) to achieve external balance. When nations are often unwilling to change their exchange rate, they have to utilize fiscal and monetary policies to achieve both balances.

4. Expansionary monetary policy (an increase in the nation's money supply) increases national income but worsens the nation's overall balance of payments with fixed exchange rates. This leads to a reduction in the nation's money supply in order to maintain (defend) the fixed exchange rate, thus making monetary policy ineffective in achieving internal balance. With perfect capital mobility, monetary policy is completely ineffective.

5. Expansionary fiscal policy (an increase in government spending and/or a reduction in taxes) increases the interest rate and leads to a capital inflow. The increase in production and income can be very effective

in curing a domestic recession, but it leads to deterioration in the nation's current account. If the nation's overall balance of payments improves (which is likely to be the case for developed countries in the short run), the resulting increase in the nation's money supply (to defend the fixed exchange rate) makes fiscal policy even more effective in the short run. With perfect capital mobility, fiscal policy becomes very powerful.

6. Since fiscal policy is relatively more effective in correcting an internal imbalance while monetary policy in correcting external imbalances, the nation should use fiscal policy to achieve internal balance and correct whatever external imbalance remains with the appropriate monetary policy.

7. With flexible exchange rates, monetary policy is effective while fiscal policy is ineffective (the exact opposite of the case under fixed exchange rates). Flexible rates enhance the effectiveness of monetary policy but reduce or completely destroy (with perfect capital flows) the effectiveness of fiscal policy in the short run.

8. The existence of inflation at less than full employment adds price stability as an important third objective of nations. Three policy instruments are then usually required to achieve all three objectives completely. Nations could direct fiscal policy to reach full employment, monetary policy to achieve price stability, and exchange rate changes or flexible exchange rates to achieve external balance. Sometimes, nations use price and wage controls to achieve price stability. But these almost always fail and they also lead to large market inefficiencies.

9. During the 1950s and 1960s, the G-7 countries used fiscal and monetary policies for internal balance and switched their aims only when the external imbalance became critical. The United Kingdom and France were forced to devalue and Germany to revalue, while Canada had flexible rates. During the 1970s and early 1980s, nations faced sharply higher petroleum prices, inflation, slow growth, or recession, and adopted flexible but managed rates. The United States faced large dollar overvaluation and trade deficits during the 1980s. From 1991 to 1993, the G-7 countries experienced recession or slow growth. Growth was rapid in the United States, but low in Europe and Japan during the second half of the 1990s. The United States faced a mild recession in 2001 but rapid growth resumed in 2004. Most G-7 countries faced slow growth in 2007 and 2008 primarily as a result of the U.S. subprime mortgage crisis. The United States and Europe also faced inflationary pressures resulting in skyrocketing petroleum prices and the United States a huge and unsustainable trade deficit and a depreciated dollar.

10. Direct controls can be subdivided into trade controls, exchange controls, and others. Trade controls refer to tariffs, quotas, advance deposits on imports, and other selective restrictions on the flow of international

trade. Exchange controls include restrictions on international capital movements, and multiple exchange rates. In general, direct controls lead to economic inefficiencies. For direct controls and other policies to be effective, international cooperation is often essential.

REVIEW QUESTIONS AND PROBLEMS

1. Under what conditions and why do nations need policies to adjust a balance-of-payments disequilibrium?

2. (a) Which are the most important objectives of nations?

 (b) Which of the most important objectives of nations are primarily dealt with in international economics? Why? How are they ranked?

3. (a) What policies can nations utilize to achieve internal and external balance when the nation is willing to change the exchange rate when facing a large and persistent balance-of-payments disequilibrium?

 (b) How do these policies operate to achieve the intended objectives?

4. (a) How can fiscal and monetary policies be used to cure recession and balance-of-payments deficit when the nation is not willing to change the exchange rate even when facing a large and persistent balance-of-payments disequilibrium?

 (b) How do these policies operate to achieve the intended objectives?

 (c) Is there a conflict between the policies used? If so, how is this resolved?

5. What is meant by the "assignment problem"? Why is it crucial that nations follow this principle?

6. Why is monetary policy completely ineffective in achieving internal balance with perfect international capital mobility under fixed exchange rates?

7. How can a nation use fiscal and monetary policies to correct a recession or unemployment with flexible exchange rates and
 (a) imperfect capital mobility?
 (b) perfect international capital mobility?

8. How can a nation correct the problems of recession and deficit when the additional objective of price stability is recognized as a separate goal when operating under a system of
 (a) flexible exchange rates?
 (b) fixed exchange rates?

9. What are some of the difficulties in utilizing policies in trying to achieve internal and external balance?

10. (a) What are the advantages and the disadvantages of direct controls?

 (b) Why do direct controls which affect a nation's balance of payments require international cooperation to be effective?

SELECTED BIBLIOGRAPHY

For a problem-solving approach to the topics covered in this chapter, see:

- D. Salvatore, *Theory and Problems of International Economics*, 4th ed. (New York: McGraw-Hill, 1996), Chapter 10.

For a more advanced treatment of the topics discussed in this chapter, see:

- D. Salvatore, *International Economics*, 9th ed. (Hoboken, N.J.: Wiley, 2007), Chapters 18–19.
- M. Fratianni and D. Salvatore, *Handbook of Monetary Policies in Developed Economies* (Amsterdam and Westport, Conn.: North-Holland and Greenwood Press, 1993).
- M. Fratianni, D. Salvatore, and J. von Hagen, *Handbook of Macroeconomic Policy in Open Economies* (Westport, Conn.: Greenwood Press, 1997).
- B. T. McCallun, "Recent Developments in the Analysis of Monetary Policy," *Federal Reserve Bank of St. Louis Review*, November/December, 1999, pp. 3–12.
- D. Salvatore, "Global Imbalances," *Princeton Encyclopedia of the World Economy* (Princeton, N.J.: Princeton University Press, 2008).

For a review of economic policies in the United States and around the world, see:

- D. Salvatore, ed., "U.S. Trade Deficits, the Dollar, and International Monetary Stability," "Twin Deficits, Growth and Stability in the U.S. Economy," and "Growth, Productivity and Wages in the U.S. Economy," Special Issues of the *Journal of Policy Modeling*, respectively, of September 2006, 2007, and 2008, with the participation of William Baumol, Guillermo Calvo, Richard Cooper, Sebastian Edwards, Barry Eichengreen, Martin Feldstein, Jeffrey Frankel, Glenn Hubbard, Dale Jorgenson, Lawrence Klein, Greg Mankiw, Ronald McKinnon, Robert Mundell, Kenneth Rogoff, John Taylor, and others.
- Council of Economic Advisors, *Economic Report of the President* (Washington, D.C.: U.S. Government Printing Office, 2008).
- IMF, *World Economic Outlook* (Washington, D.C., IMF, April 2008).
- OECD, *Economic Outlook* (Paris: OECD, December 2008).

For information on direct controls, see:

- IMF, *Exchange Rate Arrangements and Exchange Rate Restrictions* (Washington, D.C.: IMF, 2007).

INTERNet

Data on the current account, budget balance, and growth of the GDP of the United States that can be used to examine the relationship among them are found on the Bureau of Economic Analysis, the Penn World Table, and the Federal Reserve Bank of St. Louis web sites, respectively, at:

http://www.bea.doc.gov

http://pwt.econ.upen.edu

http://research.stlouisfed.org/fred2

Information and data on the conduct and effectiveness of fiscal and monetary policy in industrial nations can be found on the web sites of the Bank for International Settlements (BIS), the Organization for Economic Cooperation and Development (OECD), and the National Bureau of Economic Research (NBER), respectively at:

http://www.bis.org

http://www.oecd.org/home

http://www.nber.org

The International Monetary System: Past, Present, and Future

Part Six (Chapters 15 and 16) deals with the international monetary system. It examines how the international monetary system operated in the past, how it operates today, and the demands for reforms for the future. Chapter 15 evaluates and compares the advantages and disadvantages of a flexible as opposed to fixed exchange rate system, as well as the merits and drawbacks of hybrid systems that combine various characteristics of flexible and fixed systems. It also discusses optimum currency areas, the European Monetary Union, and international macroeconomic policy coordination. Chapter 16 then reviews the actual operation of the international monetary system from the time of the gold standard to the present. It also examines the problems facing the present international monetary system and evaluates proposals for reforms.

Flexible versus Fixed Exchange Rates, European Monetary Systems, and Macroeconomic Policy Coordination

After studying this chapter, you should be able to:

- Identify the benefits of flexible and fixed exchange rates
- Understand the meaning of an optimum currency area
- Describe the creation of the euro and the operation of the European Central Bank
- Describe the operation of a currency board
- Understand why some nations have adopted the U.S. dollar as their currency
- Understand the meaning of adjustable and crawling pegs, and managed floating
- Know the meaning and importance of macroeconomic policy coordination

CHAPTER OUTLINE

KEY TERMS

Freely floating exchange rate system or clean float

Optimum currency area or bloc

European Monetary System (EMS)

European Currency Unit (ECU)

Exchange Rate Mechanism (ERM)

European Monetary Cooperation Fund (EMCF)

European Monetary Institute (EMI)

Maastricht Treaty

Growth and Stability Pact (GSP)

European Monetary Union (EMU)

Euro

European Central Bank (ECB)

Currency board arrangements (CBAs)

Dollarization

Adjustable peg system

Crawling peg system

Managed floating exchange rate system or dirty float

International macroeconomic policy coordination

15.1 INTRODUCTION

In Chapters 13 and 14, we examined separately the process of adjustment to balance-of-payments disequilibria with flexible and fixed exchange rates. In this chapter, we evaluate and compare the advantages and disadvantages of

a flexible as opposed to a fixed exchange rate system, as well as the merits and drawbacks of hybrid systems that combine various characteristics of flexible and fixed rates.

Section 15.2 provides an overview of the debate on flexible versus fixed exchange rates. Sections 15.3 and 15.4 examine, respectively, the case for flexible and fixed exchange rates. Section 15.5 then presents the closely related theory of optimum currency areas, while Sections 15.6 and 15.7 present, respectively, the European Monetary System and the creation of the euro and the European Central Bank. Section 15.8 deals with currency board arrangements and dollarization. Section 15.9 examines the advantages and disadvantages of hybrid systems that combine some of the characteristics of flexible and fixed exchange rates in various degrees. These include adjustable pegs, crawling pegs, and managed floating. Finally, Section 15.10 deals with international macroeconomic policy coordination.

15.2 FLEXIBLE VERSUS FIXED EXCHANGE RATES: AN OVERVIEW

In general, advocates of flexible exchange rates argue that by allowing a nation to achieve external balance easily and automatically flexible rates facilitate the achievement of internal balance and other economic objectives of the nation. Advocates of fixed exchange rates respond that by introducing a degree of uncertainty not present under fixed rates, flexible exchange rates reduce the volume of international trade and investment, are more likely to lead to destabilizing speculation, and are inflationary.

A careful review of these arguments does not lead to any clear-cut conclusion that one system is overwhelmingly superior to the other. To be sure, at the time of the collapse of the fixed exchange rate system in the early 1970s, the majority of economists seemed to lean toward flexible exchange rates. However, as a result of the great volatility in exchange rates experienced over the past three decades, the balance today seems to be toward fixed or managed rates. It seems that economists often compare the painfully obvious weaknesses of whatever the prevailing exchange rate system is to an idealized alternative system. This is contrasted to the more or less consistent preference of businesspeople, bankers, and government officials for fixed rates, or at least greatly restrained fluctuations.

No one can deny the important benefits of having a single currency throughout a nation and thus *permanently* fixed exchange rates between the various areas of the nation. For example, a dollar in New York can be exchanged for a dollar in San Francisco or in any other part of the United States. But then the debate over fixed versus flexible exchange rates becomes essentially a debate over what is an *optimum currency area*, or how large the area covered by permanently fixed exchange rates can be before the benefits of fixed rates are overwhelmed by their drawbacks.

Concept
Check

Why is the choice
of fixed versus
flexible exchange
rate important?

In the final analysis, whether flexible or fixed exchange rates are better may very well depend on the nation or region involved and the conditions under which it operates. We will see that, in general, a fixed exchange rate (or a greater degree of fixity) is preferable if disturbances are predominantly monetary (such as inflation). On the other hand, a flexible exchange rate (or a greater degree of flexibility) is preferable if disturbances are predominantly real (such as a change in technology) and originate abroad.

15.3 THE CASE FOR FLEXIBLE EXCHANGE RATES

We saw in Chapter 13 that under a truly flexible exchange rate system, a deficit or surplus in the nation's balance of payments is automatically corrected by a depreciation or appreciation of the nation's currency, respectively, without any government intervention and loss or accumulation of international reserves by the nation. On the other hand, pegging or fixing the exchange rate at one level usually results in excess demand or excess supply of foreign exchange (i.e., a deficit or a surplus in the nation's balance of payments), which can only be corrected by a change in economic variables other than the exchange rate. That is, it is alleged that a fixed exchange rate system is (1) inefficient, (2) requires the use of policies (such as monetary policy) that, therefore, are not available to achieve purely internal economic objectives, and (3) can lead to policy mistakes. Let us examine each of these points.

Under a flexible exchange rate system, only the exchange rate needs to change to correct a disequilibrium in the nation's balance of payments instead of all prices in the nation having to change as under a fixed exchange rate system. Thus, it is argued that it is more efficient or less costly to change only one price (i.e., the exchange rate) than to rely on all internal prices changing in order to bring about adjustment in the balance of payments. The reasoning is the same as that for changing to daylight saving time during the summer months rather than rescheduling all events one hour earlier. Furthermore, internal prices are sticky and far from perfectly flexible in today's world, especially downward.

According to its advocates, a flexible exchange rate system also corrects balance-of-payments disequilibria smoothly and continuously, as they occur. This results in stabilizing speculation, which dampens fluctuations in exchange rates. Whatever fluctuations in exchange rates remain can then be hedged at a small cost. On the other hand, the inability or unwillingness of a nation to adjust the exchange rate when out of equilibrium under a fixed exchange rate system is likely to lead to destabilizing speculation and eventually force the nation to make a large discrete change in its exchange rate, which interferes with the smooth flow of international trade and investments.

A flexible exchange rate system also means that the nation need not concern itself with its external balance and is free to utilize all policies at its disposal to achieve its purely domestic goals of full employment

with price stability. For example, we saw in Chapter 14 that under a fixed exchange rate system, the nation could use fiscal policy to achieve internal balance and monetary policy to achieve external balance. Other things being equal, the achievement of internal balance would certainly be facilitated if monetary policy were also free to be used alongside fiscal policy to attain this goal. Or monetary policy could be utilized to achieve other purely internal objectives, such as growth. In view of the limited number of effective policy instruments usually available to nations, this is no small benefit. In addition, the possibility of policy mistakes and delays in achieving external balance would be minimized under a flexible exchange rate system.

Flexible exchange rates would also prevent the government from setting the exchange rate at a level other than equilibrium in order to benefit one sector of the economy at the expense of another or to achieve some economic objective that could be reached by less costly means. For example, developing nations usually maintain an overvalued exchange rate so as to keep the price of imported capital goods needed for development cheaper. Since this discourages exports of agricultural and traditional commodities, the government then uses a maze of exchange and trade controls to eliminate the excess demand for foreign exchange. Other things being equal, it would be more efficient to allow the exchange rate to find its own equilibrium level and give a subsidy to the nation's industrial producers.

This represents the strongest possible case for flexible exchange rates, and while generally correct in its broad outlines, it needs to be greatly qualified. This is undertaken in the next two sections in the context of making a case for fixed exchange rates and in examining the theory of optimum currency areas. Also to be pointed out is that we are here examining the case for a freely floating exchange rate system or clean float in which there is no government intervention at all in foreign exchange markets. A system that permits even a minimum of government intervention in foreign exchange markets to support a specific exchange rate or even to simply smooth out excessive short-run fluctuations does not qualify as a truly flexible exchange rate system. This is referred to as managed or dirty floating and will be examined in Section 15.9.

Concept Check

What are the benefits of flexible exchange rates?

Freely floating exchange rate system or **clean float** The flexible exchange rate system under which the exchange rate is always determined by the forces of demand and supply without any government intervention in foreign exchange markets.

15.4 THE CASE FOR FIXED EXCHANGE RATES

The case for fixed exchange rates rests on (1) the alleged smaller degree of uncertainty that fixed exchange rates introduce into international trade and finance, (2) being more likely to lead to stabilizing speculation, and (3) the greater price discipline (i.e., less inflation) than under flexible rates.

According to its advocates, a fixed exchange rate system avoids the wild day-to-day fluctuations that are likely to occur under flexible rates (refer to Figure 12.6), which discourage specialization in production and the flow of international trade and investments. Furthermore, they believe that

speculation is more likely to be stabilizing under fixed than under flexible exchange rates.

Advocates of flexible exchange rates disagree. They point out that destabilizing speculation is less likely to occur when exchange rates adjust continuously than when they are prevented from doing so until a large discrete adjustment can no longer be avoided. Anticipating a large change in exchange rates, speculators will then sell a currency that they believe is going to be devalued and buy a currency that they believe is going to be revalued (destabilizing speculation), and their expectations often become self-fulfilling. It must be pointed out, however, that this would not be the case under a *truly* fixed exchange rate system, such as the gold standard, when exchange rates are kept fixed no matter what. But then that is also likely to be the case under a *truly* flexible exchange rate system. Under the managed floating exchange rate system in operation over the past three decades, speculation has often been destabilizing during times of financial crisis, but has usually been stabilizing under "normal" conditions.

Finally, advocates of fixed exchange rates believe that fixed exchange rates impose a price discipline on the nation not present under flexible exchange rates. That is, a nation with a higher rate of inflation than the rest of the world is likely to face persistent deficits in its balance of payments and loss of reserves under a fixed exchange rate system. Since deficits and reserve losses cannot go on forever, the nation needs to restrain its inflation, thus facing some price discipline. There is no such price discipline under a flexible exchange rate system, where balance-of-payments disequilibria are, at least in theory, automatically and immediately corrected by changes in the exchange rate. Knowing this, elected officials are more likely to overstimulate the economy in order to increase their chances of reelection.

In fact, managed floating since 1973 has coincided with sharp inflationary pressures throughout the world until the early 1980s, but not afterward. Furthermore, the inflationary pressures during the 1970s were primarily the result of the sharp increase in petroleum prices and excessive money creation in most nations rather than due to flexible exchange rates, as such. However, even if we exclude the more unstable years of the 1970s, we find that the economic performance of the leading industrial countries was better during the 1960s than during the 1980s and 1990s, except for inflation (see Case Study 15-1).

Flexible exchange rates to a large extent insulate the domestic economy from *external* shocks much more than fixed exchange rates do. As a result, flexible rates are particularly attractive to nations subject to large external shocks. For example, a large exogenous increase in the nation's exports will lead to an appreciation of the nation's currency, which reduces the original increase in its exports. On the other hand, a fixed exchange rate system provides more stability to an open economy subject to large *internal*

Concept Check

What are the benefits of fixed exchange rates?

Macroeconomic Performance under Fixed and Flexible Exchange Rate Regimes

Table 15.1 presents some indicators of the macroeconomic performance of the leading industrial (G-7) countries during the last 14 years of the fixed exchange rate period (i.e., from 1960 to 1973) and the 24 years from 1983 to 2007 of the present flexible (managed) exchange rate period. The years from 1974 to 1982 were excluded because the petroleum crises of 1973–1974 and 1979–1980 (and their aftermath) made this period quite unusual. The table shows that the rate of growth or real GDP was much higher (almost double), the rate of inflation was 50 percent higher, and the rate of unemployment was much lower (less than half) during the fixed exchange rate period as compared with the flexible exchange rate period examined.

We cannot, however, attribute the better macroeconomic performance during the 1960–1973 period entirely or even primarily to fixed exchange rates because economic performance depends on many other factors, such as flexibility of labor markets, rate of technological change, and globalization. For example, rapid globalization may be responsible for the lower inflation rate during the managed exchange rate regime (despite the fact that we would expect the former to be less inflationary than the latter). In fact, when all the sources affecting economic performance are taken into consideration, it becomes difficult to say which system is better. It really depends on the nation and the circumstances under which it operates. In the final analysis, no exchange rate regime can substitute for sound economic policies.

Table 15.1. *Macroeconomic Performance under Fixed and Flexible Exchange Rates, 1960–1973, 1983–2007*

Country	Real GDP Growth		Inflation Rate		Unemployment Rate	
	1960–1973	*1983–2007*	*1960–1973*	*1983–2007*	*1960–1973*	*1983–2007*
United States	3.7	3.4	2.8	3.1	4.9	5.9
Japan	11.0	2.4	5.6	0.7	1.2	3.4
Germany	5.5	2.1	2.9	2.0	0.6	7.8
United Kingdom	2.9	2.5	4.5	3.3	2.8	7.6
France	6.0	2.1	4.3	2.8	1.8	10.0
Italy	5.7	1.8	3.8	4.7	3.1	9.4
Canada	5.0	3.1	2.8	2.9	5.1	8.8
Weighted average	5.7	2.9	3.8	2.5	2.8	6.2

Source: OECD, *Economic Outlook* (Paris, December 2007); and A. Ghosh, G. A. Gulde, and H. Wold, *Exchange Rate Regimes* (Cambridge, Mass.: MIT Press, 2002).

shocks. For example, an autonomous increase in investment in the nation increases the level of national income and induces imports to rise, thus possibly leading to a deficit in the nation's balance of payments. The loss on international reserves reduces the nation's money supply and contains domestic expansion. Under a flexible exchange rate system, on the other hand, the nation's currency will automatically depreciate and stimulate the nation's exports, thus reinforcing the tendency for the nation's income to rise (i.e., enhancing the original shock from the increase in domestic investment).

To summarize: A flexible exchange rate system does not seem to compare unfavorably to a fixed exchange rate system as far as the type of speculation to which it gives rise and the degree of uncertainty that it introduces into international transactions when all factors are considered. Furthermore, flexible exchange rates are generally more efficient and do give nations more flexibility in pursuing their own stabilization policies. At the same time, they are more inflationary than fixed exchange rates and less suited for nations facing large internal shocks. The greatest attraction of flexible exchange rates is that they allow the nation to retain greater control over its money supply than fixed exchange rates. This benefit, however, is greatly reduced in today's world of high international capital flows. The greatest disadvantage of flexible exchange rates is the lack of price discipline and the large day-to-day volatility and overshooting of exchange rates. In general, a fixed exchange rate system is preferable for a small open economy that trades mostly with one or a few larger nations and in which disturbances are primarily of a monetary nature. On the other hand, a flexible exchange rate system seems superior for a large, relatively closed economy with diversified trade and facing primarily disturbances originating in the real sector abroad.

15.5 OPTIMUM CURRENCY AREAS

The theory of optimum currency areas developed by *Robert Mundell* and *Ronald McKinnon* during the 1960s can shed some light on the conflict between fixed versus flexible exchange rates. An optimum currency area or bloc refers to a group of nations whose national currencies are linked through *permanently* fixed exchange rates and the conditions that would make such an area optimum. The currencies of member nations could then float jointly with respect to the currencies of nonmember nations.

The formation of an optimum currency area eliminates the uncertainty that arises when exchange rates are not permanently fixed, thus stimulating specialization in production and the flow of trade and investments among member regions or nations. The formation of an optimum currency area also encourages producers to view the entire area as a single market and to benefit from greater economies of scale in production.

With permanently fixed exchange rates, an optimum currency area is likely to experience greater price stability than if exchange rates could

Optimum currency area or bloc Refers to a group of nations whose national currencies are linked through permanently fixed exchange rates and the conditions that would make such an area optimum.

change among the various member nations because random shocks in different nations tend to cancel out each other. This greater price stability encourages the use of money as a store of value and as a medium of exchange, and discourages inefficient barter deals arising under more inflationary circumstances. An optimum currency area also saves the cost of official interventions in foreign exchange markets involving the currencies of member nations, the cost of hedging, and the cost of exchanging one currency for another to pay for imports of goods and tourist services (if the optimum currency area also adopts a common currency).

Perhaps the greatest disadvantage of optimum currency areas is that each member nation cannot pursue its own independent stabilization and growth policies attuned to its particular circumstances. For example, one nation within an optimum currency area might require expansionary fiscal and monetary policies to reduce an excessive unemployment rate, while another nation might require contractionary policies to curb inflationary pressures. To some extent, this cost of an optimum currency area is compensated by the ability of workers to emigrate from the poorer to the richer members and by greater capital inflows into the poorer members. Despite the fact that national differences are likely to persist, few would suggest that poorer nations or regions would do better by not entering into or seceding from an optimum currency area or nation. Furthermore, poorer nations or regions usually receive investment incentives and other special aid from richer members or areas.

The formation of an optimum currency area is more likely to be beneficial on balance under the following conditions: (1) the greater is the mobility of resources among the various member nations, (2) the greater their structural similarities, and (3) the more willing they are to closely coordinate their fiscal, monetary, and other policies. An optimum currency area should aim at maximizing the benefits from permanently fixed exchange rates and minimizing the costs. It is not easy, however, to actually measure the net benefits accruing to each member nation or region from joining an optimum currency area.

To be noted is that some of the benefits provided by the formation of an optimum currency area can also be obtained under the looser form of economic relationship provided by fixed exchange rates. Thus, the case for the formation of an optimum currency area is to some extent also a case for fixed as opposed to flexible exchange rates. The theory of optimum currency areas can be regarded as the special branch of the theory of customs unions (discussed in Chapter 7) that deals with monetary factors.

Concept Check

What are the benefits and costs of belonging to an optimum currency area?

European Monetary System (EMS) The organization formed by the members of the European Union (EU) in 1979 based on the creation of the European currency unit (ECU) of account, the exchange rate mechanism (ERM), and formation of the European Monetary Fund (EMF).

15.6 EUROPEAN MONETARY SYSTEM AND TRANSITION TO MONETARY UNION

In March 1979, the European Union or EU (then called the European Economic Community or EEC) announced the formation of the European Monetary System (EMS) as a first step toward a common currency and

European Currency Unit (ECU) The unit of account defined by the European Monetary System, based on the weighted average of the currencies of the EU members.

Exchange Rate Mechanism (ERM) The mechanism that allowed the currency of each EMS nation to fluctuate by a maximum of 2.25 on either side of its central rate or parity.

European Monetary Cooperation Fund (EMCF) The institution of the European Monetary System that provides short-term and medium-term balance-of-payments assistance to member nations.

European Monetary Institute (EMI) The forerunner of the European Central Bank that was set up in January 1994 by the Maastricht Treaty of December 1991 to further centralize members' macroeconomic policies and reduce exchange rate fluctuation margins.

Maastricht Treaty The treaty that called for the creation of the European Monetary Institute as a forerunner of the European Central Bank and monetary union by the European Union by 1999.

central bank. The main features of the EMS were: (1) creation of the European Currency Unit (ECU), defined as the weighted average of the currencies of the member nations. (2) The Exchange Rate Mechanism (ERM), which allows the currency of each EU member to fluctuate by a maximum of 2.25 percent on either side of its central rate or parity and jointly floating against the dollar. (3) The establishment of the European Monetary Cooperation Fund (EMCF) to provide short- and medium-term balance-of-payments assistance to its members that needed it.

When the fluctuation of a member nation's currency reached 75 percent of its allowed range, a *threshold of divergence* was reached, and the nation was expected to take a number of corrective steps to prevent its currency from fluctuating outside the allowed range. If the exchange rate did reach the limit of its range, intervention burdens were to be shared symmetrically by the weak- and the strong-currency member. For example, if the French franc depreciated to its upper limit against the German mark, then the French central bank had to sell Deutsche mark (DM) reserves and the German central bank (the Bundesbank) had to lend the necessary DM to France.

From March 1979 to September 1992, there were a total of 11 currency realignments of the EMS as high-inflation countries, such as Italy and France, had to periodically devalue their currency with respect to the ECU in order to maintain competitiveness in relation to a low-inflation country, such as Germany. The range of allowed fluctuation of the exchange rate of member countries was also increased to 15 percent in August 1993, after the system came under attack. The amount of ECUs grew rapidly as member nations converted more and more of their dollars and gold into ECUs and the ECU became an important international asset and intervention currency. At the beginning of 1998, the value of the ECU was $1.1042.

In June 1989, a committee headed by *Jacques Delors*, the president of the European Commission, recommended a three-stage transition to the goal of monetary union. The first stage, which started in July 1990, called for convergence of economic performance and cooperation in monetary and fiscal policy, as well as the removal of all restrictions to intra-community capital movements. The second stage, approved at a meeting in the Dutch city of Maastricht in December 1991, called for the creation of a European Monetary Institute (EMI) as the forerunner of a European Central Bank (ECB) by 1994. The third stage was to involve the completion of the monetary union by 1999, with the establishment of a single currency and a European Central Bank. This meant that member nations would relinquish their sovereign power over their money supply and monetary policy. In addition, they would no longer have full freedom over their budget (fiscal) policies. With a common central bank, each national central bank would assume functions not unlike those of Federal Reserve banks in the United States.

The Maastricht Treaty set several conditions before a nation could join the monetary union: (1) an inflation rate not exceeding 1.5 percentage points

the average rate of the three Community nations with the lowest rate; (2) a budget deficit not exceeding 3 percent of GDP; (3) overall government debt not exceeding 60 percent of GDP; (4) long-term interest rates not exceeding two points more than the average interest rate of the three countries with the lowest inflation rates; and (5) the average exchange rate not falling by more than 2.25 percent of the average of the EMS for the two years before joining. By 1991, only France and Luxembourg had met all of these criteria. Because of the cost of reunification, Germany could not meet all conditions, and Italy met none. By 1998, however, most member countries had met most of the Maastricht criteria (see Case Study 15-2) and the stage was set for true monetary union.

Stability and Growth Pact (SGP) The pact that requires members of the European Monetary Union to keep their budget deficits not exceeding 3 percent of their GDP.

In 1997, the Stability and Growth Pact (SGP) was negotiated to further tighten the fiscal constraint of participating countries. The SGP required member countries to aim at budget deficits smaller than 3 percent of GDP, so that in case of recession the nation could conduct expansionary fiscal policy and still remain below the 3 percent guideline. Nations that violated the fiscal indicator would be subject to heavy fines. Germany demanded the pact in order to make sure that fiscal discipline would prevail in the monetary union so as to avoid excessive money creation, inflation, and a weak euro. The irony was that it was precisely Germany (and France) that was unable to meet the SGP in 2003, when its budget deficit reached 4 percent of its GDP, and this led to the relaxation of the SGP's rules by adding some loopholes in 2005.

Concept Check

How does the European monetary system work?

Throughout the negotiations, the United Kingdom tried consistently to slow the EU's moves toward greater economic and political union in order to limit further loss of sovereignty. Differences in culture and language made progress toward monetary union difficult, and the admission of the new democracies of Eastern and Central Europe greatly complicated matters. Nevertheless, the Maastricht Treaty operated as the bridge that led to true monetary union in Europe at the beginning of 1999, when the ECB (created in 1998) began to operate and the euro came into existence.

European Monetary Union (EMU) The 12 members of the European Union that adopted the euro as their common currency and established the European Central Bank to conduct their common monetary policy.

15.7 CREATION OF THE EURO, THE EUROPEAN CENTRAL BANK, AND THE COMMON MONETARY POLICY

Euro (€) The common currency adopted at the beginning of 1999 by 11 of the 15 member countries of the European Union.

At the beginning of 1999, the European Monetary System became the European Monetary Union (EMU) with the introduction of the euro and the adoption of a common monetary policy by the European Central Bank. On January 1, 1999, the euro (€) came into existence as the common currency of eleven countries of the euro area (Austria, Belgium, Germany, Finland, France, Ireland, Italy, Luxembourg, Spain, Portugal, and the Netherlands). Greece was admitted on January 1, 2001 (see Figure 15.1). Britain, Sweden,

CASE STUDY 15-2

Maastricht Convergence Indicators

Table 15.2 gives the value of four of the five Maastricht indicators for the 15 member countries of the European Union in January 1998. This information, together with the exchange rate indicator (not shown in the table), is what the European Commission used to determine which member nations were eligible to participate in the single currency. From the table we see that all countries, except Greece, satisfied the inflation, public deficit, and long-term interest indicators, but eight countries did not satisfy the public debt criteria. Furthermore,

Ireland did not meet the exchange rate indicator. The European Commission, however, ruled that all countries (except Greece) had made sufficient progress for all to participate in the single currency. The United Kingdom, Denmark, and Sweden, however, chose not to participate at the start, but they reserved the right to join later. Greece was admitted on January 1, 2001, Slovenia in 2007, Cyprus and Malta in 2008, and Slovakia in 2009—thus increasing to 16 the number of Eurozone countries (see Figure 15.1).

Table 15.2. *EU Members' Maastricht Convergence Indicators, January 1998*

	Inflation Rate (%)	Public Deficit as % of GDP	Public Debt as % of GDP	Long-Term Interest Rate (%)
Germany	1.4	2.5	61.2*	5.6
France	1.2	2.9	58.1	5.5
Italy	1.8	2.5	118.1*	6.7
United Kingdom	1.8	0.6	52.3	7.0
Austria	1.1	2.3	64.7*	5.6
Belgium	1.4	1.7	118.1*	5.7
Denmark	1.9	−1.1	59.5	6.2
Greece	5.2*	2.2	107.7*	9.8*
Finland	1.3	−0.3	53.6	5.9
Ireland	1.2	−1.1	59.5	6.2
Luxembourg	1.4	−1.0	7.1	5.6
Netherlands	1.8	1.6	70.0*	5.5
Portugal	1.8	2.2	60.0	6.2
Spain	1.8	2.2	67.4*	6.3
Sweden	1.9	0.5	74.1*	6.5
EU average	1.6	1.9	70.5	6.1
Reference value	2.7	3.0	60.0	7.8

*Country not satisfying criteria.

Source: European Commission, *Convergence Report 1999* (European Commission: Brussels, 1998).

FIGURE 15.1. The Eurozone Countries as of January 1, 2009.

Source: http://uk.encarta.msn.com/media_122600895_781530385_-1_1/the_euro_zone.html

and Denmark chose not to participate. The creation of the euro is one of the most important events in postwar monetary history: Never before had a large group of sovereign nations voluntarily given up their own currency for a common currency.

From January 1, 1999, euros were traded in financial markets, new issues of securities were denominated in euros, and official statistics in the euro area were quoted in euros, but euro bank notes and coins were not introduced until the beginning of 2002. That is, until that date, the euro was only a unit of account and not an actual physical circulating currency. From January 1 until July 1, 2002, euros and national currencies circulated together for nations

Table 15.3. *Official Conversion Rates for the Euro*

Country	National Currency	Currency Units per Euro
Austria	schilling	13.7603
Belgium	Belgian franc	40.3399
Finland	markka	5.94573
France	French franc	6.55957
Germany	Deutsche mark	1.95583
Ireland	punt	0.787564
Italy	Italian lira	1936.27
Luxembourg	Luxembourg franc	40.3399
Netherlands	guilder	2.20371
Portugal	escudo	200.482
Spain	peseta	166.386

Source: "The Launch of the Euro," *Federal Reserve Bulletin*, October 1999, pp. 655–666.

that so chose, but by July 1, 2002, all national currencies were phased out (taken out of circulation) and euro paper currency and coins became the sole legal tender in the 11 participating members of the euro area.

The value of the euro in terms of the participating currencies was decided in the fall of 1998 and became rigidly fixed (i.e., it could not be changed). The official euro conversion rates for the currencies of the participating countries are given in Table 15.3.

Until January 1, 2002, the euro fluctuated in terms of other currencies, such as the U.S. dollar and the Japanese yen, but the value of each participating currency remained rigidly fixed in terms of euros. This meant that the exchange rate of the currencies participating in the euro fluctuated in relation to other currencies only to the extent that the euro fluctuated in relation to those other currencies. A limit was also imposed on the fluctuation of currencies of the United Kingdom, Sweden, and Denmark vis-à-vis the euro. The euro was introduced on January 1, 1999, at the exchange rate of €1 = $1.17, but fluctuated down to a low of $0.82 at the end of October 2002 before returning to near parity with the dollar by the middle of 2002 and then rising to $1.56 in June 2008 (see Case Study 12-7). The creation of the euro provides major benefits to euro-area countries but also imposes significant costs, especially in the short run (see Case Study 15-3).

In 1998, European Central Bank (ECB) was established as the operating arm of the *European System of Central Banks (ESCB)*, a federal structure of the national central banks of the European Union. Since January 1999, the ECB assumed responsibility for the common EMU monetary policy. ECB's monetary decisions are made by a majority vote of the governing council, composed of a six-member executive board (including the President of the ECB, who was *Willem F. Duisenberg* of the Netherlands until fall 2003, when

Concept Check

How much has the dollar–euro exchange rate fluctuated?

European Central Bank (ECB) The institution similar to the Federal Reserve System in the United States that would control the money supply and issue the single currency of the European Union.

CASE STUDY 15-3

Benefits and Costs of the Euro

The adoption of the euro as the common currency of the euro-area countries confers major benefits on the participating countries, but it will also lead to significant costs. The benefits are: (1) elimination of the need to exchange currencies among euro-area members (this has been estimated to save as much as $30 billion per year); (2) elimination of exchange rate volatility among the currencies of participating countries; (3) more rapid economic and financial integration of participating nations; (4) the participation of each member nation in determining the common monetary policy; (5) greater economic and budgetary discipline for member countries; (6) seigniorage from the use of the euro as an international currency (see Case Study 11-1); (7) reduced cost of borrowing in international financial markets; and (8) increased economic and political importance for the EMU in international affairs.

The most serious problem created by the adoption of the euro for the participating countries arises when only one or a few of them face a recession or some other asymmetric shock. In that case, the nation or nations can use neither exchange rate nor monetary policy to overcome the problem and (as indicated) fiscal policy is also severely constrained or limited. The nation or nations must then passively wait for the problem to be resolved by itself, gradually, over time. In a more fully integrated economy, such as the United States, if a region is in recession, some labor will immediately move out and the region will also benefit from a great deal of fiscal redistribution (such as greater unemployment insurance receipts). In the EMU, instead, labor mobility is much lower than in the United States and so is fiscal redistribution. Thus, it will be much more difficult for a EMU nation to deal with an asymmetric shock. It is true that economic integration will encourage intra-EMU labor mobility, but this is a slow process that is likely to take years to complete. Capital mobility within the euro area, however, can to some extent substitute for inadequate labor mobility in overcoming the problem.

Source: G. Fink and D. Salvatore, "Benefits and Costs of European Economic and Monetary Union," *The Brown Journal of World Affairs*, Summer/Fall 1999, pp. 187–194; and D. Salvatore, "The Unresolved Problem with the EMS and EMU," *American Economic Review*, May 1997, pp. 224–226; and D. Salvatore, "Euro," *Princeton Encyclopedia of the World Economy*, 2008.

he was succeeded by *Jean-Claude Trichet* of France) and the heads of the participating national central banks.

The Maastricht Treaty entrusted the ECB with the sole goal of pursuing price stability and made it almost entirely independent of political influences. The ECB is only required to regularly brief the European Parliament on its activities, but the European Parliament has no power to influence ECB decisions. While the U.S. Congress could pass laws reducing the independence of the Federal Reserve Board, the Maastricht Treaty itself would have to be amended by the legislatures or voters in every member country for the ECB's statute to be changed. The almost total independence of the ECB from political influences was deliberate so as to shield the ECB from political influences that might force it to provide excessive monetary

stimulus, and thus lead to inflation. But this also led to the criticism that the ECB is distant and undemocratic, and not responsive to the economic needs of the citizens.

The first year of operation of the EMU in 1999 was somewhat turbulent, with politicians demanding lower interest rates to stimulate growth, and with the ECB resisting for fear of resurgent inflation and in order to establish its credibility. The conflict also arose because in 1999 nations such as Ireland and Spain faced excessive growth and the danger of inflation (and hence required a more restrictive monetary policy), while other nations (such as Germany and Italy) faced anemic growth (and hence required lower interest rates). As it was, the ECB adopted an intermediate monetary policy, with interest rates possibly too low for Ireland and Spain and too high for Germany and Italy.

Concept Check

What monetary policy did the European Central Bank pursue?

15.8 CURRENCY BOARD ARRANGEMENTS AND DOLLARIZATION

Currency board arrangements (CBAs) The exchange rate arrangement whereby the nation rigidly fixes the exchange rate and its central bank loses its ability to conduct an independent monetary policy by allowing the nation's supply to increase or decrease only in response to balance-of-payments surpluses or deficits.

Currency board arrangements (CBAs) are the most extreme form of a fixed exchange rate system, short of adopting a common currency or dollarizing (i.e., adopting the dollar as the nation's currency). Under CBAs, the nation rigidly fixes (often by law) the exchange rate of its currency to a foreign currency or basket of currencies and thus gives up control over its money supply (so that its central bank can no longer conduct an independent monetary policy). With a CBA, the nation's money supply increases only by the amount of a balance-of-payments surplus and inflow of international reserves, and decreases only by the amount of a balance-of-payments deficit and outflow of international reserves. As a result, the nation's inflation and interest rates will be similar to those in the country against whose currency the nation pegged or fixed its currency.

A nation usually makes this extreme arrangement when in a financial crisis and as a way to effectively combat inflation. CBAs have been in operation in several countries or economies, such as Hong Kong (since 1983), Argentina (from 1991 to the end of 2001), Estonia (since 1992), Lithuania (since 1994), Bulgaria (since 1997), and Bosnia and Herzogovina (since 1997). The key conditions for the successful operation of CBAs are a sound banking system (since the central bank cannot be the "lender of last resort" or extend credit to banks experiencing difficulties) and a prudent fiscal policy (since the central bank cannot lend to the government). The main advantage of CBAs is the lower interest rates and lower inflation in the nation. The cost of CBAs is the inability of the nation's central bank to (1) conduct its own monetary policy, (2) act as a lender of last resort, and (3) collect seigniorage from independently issuing its own currency. Case Study 15-4 examines Argentina's experience with CBAs during the 1990s.

Concept Check

What are the advantages and disadvantages of establishing a currency board?

CASE STUDY 15-4

Argentina's Currency Board Arrangements and Crisis

Argentina had a currency board from 1991 until the end of 2001, when it collapsed in the face of a deep economic crisis. Argentina CBAs operated reasonably well until Brazil was forced first to devalue its currency (the real) in 1999 and then allow it to sharply depreciate. With the peso rigidly tied to the dollar, Argentina suffered a huge loss of international competitiveness vis-à-vis Brazil (its largest trade partner) and plunged into recession. Having a grossly overvalued currency was not, however, the only reason for Argentina's economic crisis. Even more serious was its out-of-control budget deficit. Argentina was simply living beyond its possibilities and this was unsustainable.

The overvaluation of the peso only made the crisis deeper. Tightening up its public finances in order to encourage foreign investments deepened the recession and led to riots in the streets without attracting new foreign investments. Foreign investors feared that Argentina would be forced to abandon its currency board and devalue the peso, which would lead to losses and possibly even restrictions on repatriation of the capital invested.

This left Argentina only two choices: devalue the peso or full dollarization. Argentina

was very reluctant to abandon its CBA and devalue the peso for fear of returning to the condition of hyperinflation of the late 1980s. Dollarization was not without risks either. Specifically, while it would eliminate the foreign exchange risk and very likely attract more foreign investments, dollarization would not eliminate Argentina's international competitiveness problem, especially with respect to Brazil, nor would it solve Argentina's budget problems. As it was, in January 2002, Argentina defaulted on its huge foreign debt and was forced first to abandon its currency board and devalue the peso, and then let it float. By fall 2002, the peso had depreciated from 1 peso to the dollar under the CBA to more than 3.5 pesos per dollar (a 250 percent depreciation). Argentina eventually repaid only 25 cents on the dollar to foreign holders of its bonds.

Source: A. de la Torre, E. Yeyati, and E. Talvi, "Living and Dying with Hard Pegs: The Rise and Fall of Argentina's Currency Board," in G. von Furstenberg, V. Alexander, and J. Melitz, eds., *Monetary Unions and Hard Pegs* (New York: Oxford University Press, 2004), pp. 183–230.

Dollarization The situation whereby a nation adopts another nation's currency as its legal tender.

Some nations go even further than creating a CBA by adopting another nation's currency as its own legal tender. This process is usually referred to as dollarization, even when the currency adopted is not the dollar (the term *euroization*, however, is now also used if the country adopts the euro). Nations that are fully or officially dollarized are Panama, Ecuador, and El Salvador. Guatemala is nearly fully dollarized, and Honduras, Nicaragua, and Costa Rica are seriously considering it. Some of the new entrants into the EU are considering unilateral euroization, before being formally admitted into the EMU.

The benefits and costs of dollarization are similar to those arising from adopting a CBA, only they are more pronounced because dollarization involves an even more complete renouncement of the nation's monetary

sovereignty by practically giving up an "exit option" to abandon the system. The benefits of dollarization arise from the nation (1) avoiding the cost of exchanging the domestic currency for dollars and the need to hedge foreign exchange risks; (2) facing an inflation and interest rate similar to that of the United States (except for any remaining country risk); (3) avoiding foreign exchange crises and the need for foreign exchange and trade controls; and (4) fostering budgetary discipline and encouraging more rapid and full international financial integration.

Dollarization, however, also imposes some costs on the dollarizing country. These are: (1) the cost of replacing the domestic currency with the dollar (estimated to be about 4 to 5 percent of GDP for the average Latin American country); (2) the loss of independence of monetary and exchange rate policies; and (3) the loss of its central bank as a lender of last resort to bail out domestic banks and other financial institutions in case of a crisis.

Good candidates for dollarization are small open economies for which the United States or Europe is the dominant economic partner and that have a history of poor monetary performance. Most of the small countries of Latin America, especially those in Central America and the Caribbean, fit this description well. Once we move to large countries (such as Argentina or Mexico), however, it becomes more difficult to come up with clear-cut answers as to whether dollarization would be a net benefit to the nation.

Concept Check

What are the advantages and disadvantages of dollarization?

15.9 ADJUSTABLE PEGS, CRAWLING PEGS, AND MANAGED FLOATING

We have seen in Section 13.4 that all fixed exchange rate systems allow a small band of fluctuations of exchange rates about the par value. The actual exchange rate is then determined by the forces of demand and supply (as explained in Chapter 11) within the allowed band of fluctuation, and it is prevented from moving outside this band by official interventions in foreign exchange markets. The band of allowed exchange rate fluctuation could be made larger, however. The wider the band of allowed fluctuation, however, the more the system assumes the characteristic of a flexible exchange rate system, where there are no official interventions in foreign exchange markets.

Adjustable peg system The system under which exchange rates or par values are periodically changed to correct balance-of-payments disequilibria.

An adjustable peg system is a fixed exchange rate system where the band of allowed fluctuation is very narrow (say, 1 percent on ether side of parity). Under such a system, the nation facing a large and persistent (fundamental) balance-of-payments deficit is allowed and even encouraged to devalue the currency and a nation with a fundamental surplus to revalue, so as to correct the balance-of-payments disequilibrium. The Bretton Woods system, which operated from 1947 until 1971 (discussed in Chapter 16), was originally set up as an adjustable peg system, but collapsed essentially because nations were not willing to devalue even when facing a fundamental deficit. As pointed

out in Section 14.3, devaluation was regarded as a sign of failure and the fear was that it would cause destabilizing speculation.

Crawling peg system
The system under which par values or exchange rates are changed by very small preannounced amounts at frequent and clearly specified intervals until the equilibrium exchange rate is reached.

It is to avoid the disadvantage of relatively large changes in par values and possibly destabilizing speculation that the crawling peg system or system of "sliding or gliding parities" was devised. Under this system, par values are changed by small *preannounced* amounts or percentages at frequent and clearly specified intervals (say, every month) until the equilibrium exchange rate is reached. The nation could prevent destabilizing speculation by manipulating its short-term interest rate so as to neutralize any profit that would result from the scheduled change in the exchange rate. For example, an announced 2 percent devaluation of the currency would be accompanied by a 2 percent increase in the nation's short-term interest rate. Nations wanting to use a crawling peg need to decide the frequency and amount of the changes in their par values, as well as the width of the allowed band of fluctuation. A crawling peg seems best suited for a developing country that faces real economic shocks and different inflation rates than elsewhere.

Managed floating exchange rate system
or **dirty float** The policy of intervention in foreign exchange markets by monetary authorities to smooth out short-run fluctuations without attempting to affect the long-run trend in exchange rates.

Under a managed floating exchange rate system or dirty float, the nation's monetary authorities are entrusted with the responsibility of intervening in foreign exchange markets to smooth out short-run fluctuations in exchange rates without attempting to affect their long-run trend. The nation can do this by adopting a policy of *leaning against the wind*. This requires the nation's monetary authorities to supply, out of international reserves, a portion (not all) of any short-run excess demand for foreign exchange in the market (thus moderating the tendency of the nation's currency to depreciate) and absorb (and add to its reserves) a portion of any short-run excess supply of foreign exchange in the market (thus moderating the tendency of the nation's currency to appreciate). This reduces short-run fluctuations without affecting the long-run trend in exchange rates.

Concept Check

How do adjustable pegs, crawling pegs, and managed rates work?

There is, however, the danger that if the rules of leaning against the wind are not spelled out precisely (as has been the case since 1973), a nation might be tempted to keep the exchange rate high (i.e., its currency at a depreciated level) in order to stimulate its exports. In recent years, Japan seems to have been following this policy. This *dirty floating* is a disguised beggar-thy-neighbor policy and invites retaliation by other nations.

The world has had a floating exchange rate system of sorts since 1973. To be sure, this system was not deliberately chosen but was imposed by the collapse of the Bretton Woods system under chaotic conditions in foreign exchange markets and unbearable destabilizing speculation. In the early days of the managed floating system, serious attempts were made to devise specific rules for managing the float to prevent dirty floating and the inevitable conflicts that would follow. These attempts generally failed. What is true is that neither the best expectations of those who favored flexible rates in the early 1970s, nor the worst fears of those who opposed flexible

rates, have in fact materialized over the past three decades or so of the managed float.

Nevertheless, the large appreciation of the U.S. dollar from 1980 to 1985 and again from 1995 to 2001 and the equally large subsequent depreciation clearly indicate that large exchange rate disequilibria can arise and persist over several years under the present managed floating exchange rate system. This interferes with international specialization and can lead to protectionism and calls for reform of the present international monetary system and more international cooperation and coordination of policies among the leading nations.

The present managed floating system exhibits a large degree of flexibility by more or less allowing each nation to choose the exchange rate regime that best suits its preferences and circumstances (see Case Study 15-5). In general, large industrial nations and nations suffering from stronger inflationary pressures than the rest of the world have opted for greater exchange rate flexibility than smaller developing nations or highly specialized open economies.

15.10 INTERNATIONAL MACROECONOMIC POLICY COORDINATION

During recent decades, the world has become much more integrated, and industrial countries have become increasingly interdependent. International trade has grown twice as fast as world output, and the international capital mobility has increased even faster, especially since the early 1970s. Today, the ratio of international trade to GNP in the seven largest industrialized (i.e., G-7) countries is twice as large as in 1960, and the world is rapidly moving toward truly integrated, global international capital markets.

The increased interdependence in the world economy has sharply reduced the effectiveness of national economic policies and increased their spillover effects on the rest of the world. For example, an easy monetary policy to stimulate the U.S. economy will reduce interest rates in the United States and lead to capital outflows. This undermines some of the expansionary effect of the easy monetary policy in the United States and results in dollar depreciation (other things equal). Other nations face a capital inflow and appreciation of their currencies as the direct result of monetary expansion in the United States, and this may undermine their own fight against specific national objectives. A U.S. expansionary fiscal policy would similarly have important spillover effects on the rest of the world (refer to Section 13.7).

International macroeconomic policy coordination
The modifications of national economic policies in recognition of international interdependence.

With increased interdependence, international macroeconomic policy coordination becomes more desirable and essential. Specifically, nations can do better by setting policies cooperatively than by acting independently. International macroeconomic policy coordination thus refers to the modifications

Exchange Rate Arrangements of IMF Members

Table 15.4 gives the distribution of exchange rate arrangements of the 185 member countries of the International Monetary Fund as of April 30, 2008. The table shows that about half of the countries operated under a fixed exchange rate system of some type, while the other half operated with some kind of exchange rate flexibility. The countries that had fixed exchange rates included those that adopted the currency of another country (such as Ecuador, El Salvador, and Panama), those that had a common currency (such as the members of the European Monetary Union), those that adopted currency board arrangements (Bulgaria, Estonia, Hong Kong, and Lithuania), and those that

adopted other fixed-peg arrangements (such as Argentina and the Russian Federation).

Of the countries that operated with some exchange rate flexibility, 8 had crawling pegs (such as China), 43 had managed floating (such as India, Indonesia, and Thailand), and the remaining 40 countries were independently floating their currency (these included the United States, Japan, the United Kingdom, Canada among the developed countries, and Brazil, Korea, and Mexico among the developing countries). Thus, we see that there was a wide variety of exchange rate arrangements in existence at the end of April 2008.

Table 15.4. *Exchange Rate Arrangements of IMF Members as of April 30, 2008*

Exchange Rate Regime	Number of Countries
No separate legal tender	10
Currency board arrangements	12
Other fixed peg arrangements	70
Total pegged	92
Crawling pegs	10
Managed floating	43
Independent floating	40
Total with some flexibility	93
Total	185

Source: IMF, *Annual Report, 2008.*

of national economic policies in recognition of international interdependence. For example, with a worldwide recession, each nation may hesitate to stimulate its economy to avoid a deterioration of its trade balance. Through a coordinated, simultaneous expansion of all nations, however, output and employment can increase in all nations without any of them suffering deterioration in trade balance. Similarly, international policy coordination

Concept Check

Why is international policy coordination needed?

can avoid competitive devaluations by nations in order to stimulate their exports (beggar-thy-neighbor policies).

International policy coordination under the present international monetary system, however, has occurred only occasionally and has been limited in scope. One episode of limited international policy coordination was the Plaza Agreement of September 1985 under which the G-5 countries (the United States, Japan, Germany, France, and the United Kingdom) agreed to jointly intervene in foreign exchange markets to induce a gradual depreciation or "soft landing" of the dollar in order to correct its large overvaluation. Other examples are given by the quick coordinated response of the United States, Japan, and Germany to the October 1987 worldwide equity-market crash, and September 11, 2001 terrorist attack on the United States, and the subprime mortgage crisis in 2007.

These instances of policy coordination were sporadic and limited in scope, however. The coordination process seems also to have deteriorated since 1990. For example, in December 1991, Germany sharply increased interest rates to their highest level since 1948 in order to stem inflationary pressures fueled by the rebuilding of East Germany, even though the United States and the rest of Europe were in or near recession (and therefore required lower interest rates). The United States did in fact lower its interest rate to pull out of recession, but this led to a sharp depreciation of the dollar vis-à-vis the German mark. The other countries of the EU were instead forced to follow the German lead and raise interest rates in order to keep their exchange rates within the allowed 2.25 percent band of fluctuation, as required by the European Monetary System, and thus had to forgo easy monetary policy to stimulate their weak economies. This total German disregard for the requirements of other leading nations was a serious setback for international monetary cooperation and coordination and led to the serious crisis of the ERM in September 1992 and August 1993.

There are several obstacles to successful and effective international macroeconomic policy coordination today. One is the lack of consensus about the functioning of the international monetary system. For example, the U.S. Fed may believe that monetary expansion would lead to expansion of output and employment, while the ECB may believe that it only will result in inflation. Another obstacle arises from the lack of agreement on the precise policy mix required. For example, different macroeconometric models give widely different results as to the effect of a given fiscal stimulus. There is then the problem of how to distribute the gains from successful policy coordination among the participants, and how to spread the cost of negotiating and policing agreements. Empirical studies indicate that most of the time nations gain from international policy coordination, but that the gains are not very large. These empirical studies, however, might not have captured the full benefits from successful international policy coordination.

Concept Check

How much international policy coordination has taken place?

SUMMARY

1. In this chapter we evaluated and compared the advantages and disadvantages of a flexible as opposed to a fixed exchange rate system, as well as the merits and drawbacks of hybrid systems combining various characteristics of flexible and fixed exchange rates.

2. Whether flexible or fixed exchange rates are better depend on the nation or region involved and the conditions under which it operates. In general, a fixed exchange rate is preferable if disturbances are predominantly monetary (such as inflation), while a flexible exchange rate is preferable if disturbances are predominantly in the real sector (such as a change in technology) and originate abroad.

3. The case for a flexible exchange rate system rests on its alleged greater market efficiency and its policy advantages. A flexible exchange rate system is said to be more efficient than a fixed exchange rate system because it (1) relies on exchange rate changes instead of on changing all internal prices, to bring about balance-of-payments adjustment; (2) makes adjustment smooth and continuous rather than occasional and large; (3) frees monetary policy for domestic goals; and (4) removes the danger that the government will use the exchange rate to reach goals that can be better achieved by other policies.

4. The case for a fixed exchange rate system rests on (1) more stable exchange rates, (2) the belief that speculation is more likely to be stabilizing, and (3) being less inflationary than flexible exchange rates.

5. An optimum currency area or bloc refers to a group of nations whose national currencies are linked through permanently fixed exchange rates. This offers important advantages but also leads to some costs for the participating nations.

6. The European Monetary System (EMS) was started in 1979 and involved creating the European Currency Unit (ECU), keeping exchange rates of member countries fluctuating within a 2.25 percent band, and establishing the European Monetary Cooperation Fund (EMCF) to provide members with short- and medium-term balance-of-payments assistance. The Maastricht Treaty set five conditions before a nation could join the monetary union. In 1997, the Stability and Growth Pact (SGP) was negotiated to further tighten the fiscal constraint of member countries.

7. In June 1989, a three-stage transition to the goal of monetary union was started with the aim of establishing a single currency and a European Central Bank (ECB) by 1999. The euro was created on January 1, 1999, and began circulating on January 1, 2002 as the currency of the 12 member nations of the European Monetary Union (EMU). In January 1999 the European Central Bank (ECB) assumed responsibility for EMU monetary policy.

8. Under currency board arrangements (CBAs), the nation rigidly fixes the exchange rate, and its central bank loses control over the nation's money

supply, its ability to conduct an independent monetary policy, and to be the lender of last resort. With a CBA the nation's money supply increases or decreases, respectively, only in response to balance-of-payments surpluses or to balance-of-payments deficits. The main advantages of CBAs are lower inflation and interest rates. Dollarization refers to a nation adopting the currency of another nation (most often the dollar and the euro) as its legal tender. The benefits and costs of dollarization are similar to those arising from adopting a CBA, only they are more pronounced because the nation gives up its "exit option."

9. An adjustable peg system requires nations to periodically change their exchange rates when facing serious balance-of-payments disequilibria. Since nations are usually not willing to devalue or revalue, they may face destabilizing speculation. This disadvantage can be overcome by a crawling peg system, where par values are changed by small amounts at frequent, specified intervals. Under a managed exchange rate system or dirty floating, monetary authorities intervene in foreign exchange markets to smooth out excessive exchange rate volatility. About half of the 185 members of the International Monetary Fund operated under a fixed exchange rate system of some type, while the other half had some exchange rate flexibility in 2007.

10. During recent decades the world has become increasingly interdependent, thus making international policy coordination desirable. International policy coordination under the present international monetary system has occurred only occasionally and been limited in scope because of the lack of consensus about the functioning of the international monetary system, the precise policy mix required, and on how to distribute the gains and spread the costs.

REVIEW QUESTIONS AND PROBLEMS

1. (a) What are the alleged advantages of a fixed over a flexible exchange rate system? How do advocates of flexible exchange rates respond?

 (b) What overall conclusion can be reached on whether flexible or fixed exchange rates are preferred?

2. Draw a figure showing the fluctuation in the exchange rate over the business cycle without speculation, with stabilizing speculation, and with destabilizing speculation.

3. (a) Explain the difference between an optimum currency area and a fixed exchange rate system.

 (b) What are the main advantages and disadvantages of an optimum currency area?

 (c) What are the requirements for a well functioning optimum currency area?

4. Indicate the benefits and costs of EMU member countries from the establishment of the euro.

5. Indicate the difference among a
 (a) fixed exchange rate system
 (b) currency board arrangement
 (c) dollarization

6. What is meant by a crawling peg system? How can such a system overcome the disadvantage of an adjustable peg system?

7. (a) What is meant by a managed floating exchange rate system?
 (b) How does the policy of leaning against the wind operate?
 (c) What is the advantage of a managed floating system with respect to freely floating and fixed exchange rates?

8. A flexible exchange rate system will insulate the economy from international disturbances and, therefore, eliminate the need for international policy coordination. True or false? Explain.

9. Explain why each nation might pursue a loose fiscal policy and a tight monetary policy in the absence of international policy coordination, but the opposite with policy coordination.

10. (a) Why would more international macroeconomic policy coordination among the leading industrial countries during the past two decades be useful?
 (b) What conclusion can you reach regarding the possibility of much greater international macroeconomic policy coordination among the leading industrial countries of the world today?

SELECTED BIBLIOGRAPHY

The debate over flexible versus fixed exchange rates is found in:

- A. Ghosh, A. M. Gulde, and H. Wold, *Exchange Rate Regimes: Choices and Consequences* (Cambridge, Mass.: MIT Press, 2002).
- J. A. Frankel, "Experience and Lessons from Exchange Rate Regimes in Emerging Market Economies," *NBER Working Paper 10032*, October 2003.
- IMF, *Exchange Rate Arrangements and Foreign Exchange Markets* (Washington, D.C.: IMF, 2008).

Regional monetary integration and the European Monetary System are discussed in:

- R. Dornbusch, P. Kenen, R. McKinnon, R. Mundell, M. Mussa, and D. Salvatore, "Common Currencies vs. Currency Areas," *American Economic Review*, May 1997, pp. 208–226.

- D. Salvatore, "The Euro, the European Central Bank, and the International Monetary System," *Annals of the American Academy of Political and Social Science*, January 2002, pp. 153–167.
- D. Salvatore, "The Euro: Expectations and Performance," *Eastern Economic Journal*, Winter 2002, pp. 121–136.
- D. Salvatore, "Can NAFTA Be a Stepping Stone to Monetary Integration in North America?" *Economie Internationale*, Vol. 105, No. 3, 2006, pp. 135–149.
- P. Lane, "The Real Effect of the European Monetary Union," *Journal of Economic Perspectives*, Fall 2006, pp. 47–66.
- P. Kenen and E. Meade, *Economic and Monetary Union in Europe* (Cambridge: Cambridge University Press, 2008).

The present managed floating system is discussed and evaluated in:

- D. Salvatore, "Problems and Reforms of the International Monetary System," in M. Fratianni, P. Savona, and J. Kirton, eds., *Assembling a New Financial Architecture: The Deeper Challenges* (Aldershot, Hempshire, U.K., Ashgate, 2002), pp. 103–115.

Currency boards, dollarization and euroization are discussed in:

- D. Salvatore, J. Dean, and T. Willett, *The Dollarization Debate* (New York: Oxford University Press, 2003).
- D. Salvatore, "Euroization, Dollarization and the International Monetary System," in G. von Furstenberg, V. Alexander, and J. Melitz, eds., *Monetary Unions and Hard Pegs* (New York: Oxford University Press, 2004), pp. 27–39.

International macroeconomic policy coordination is examined in:

- P. B. Kenen, ed., *Understanding Interdependence: The Macroeconomics of Open Economies* (Princeton, N.J.: Princeton University Press, 1995).
- R. C. Bryant, *International Coordination of National Stabilization Policies* (New York: Oxford University Press, 1996).
- IMF, *World Economic Outlook* (Washington, D.C.: IMF, October 2008).

INTERNet

The International Monetary Fund (IMF), the Organization for Economic Cooperation and Development (OECD), and the Bank for International Settlements (BIS) regularly review the monetary, fiscal, and exchange rate policies of various nations and other economic units and post many of their results on their web sites, which are:

http://www.imf.org

http://www.oecd.org

http://www.bis.org

The central banks of the leading nations (the Board of Governors of the Federal Reserve Bank and the Federal Reserve Bank of New York for the United States and the European Central Bank for the European Monetary Union) include on their web sites a great deal of information on national economic and financial policies. The web sites for the United States, the European Union, the Bank of England, the Bank of Japan, and the Bank of Canada, are:

http://www.federalreserve.gov/policy.htm

http://www.ny.frb.org

http://www.ecb.int

http://www.bankofengland.co.uk

http://www.boj.or.jp/en/index.htm

http://www.bankofcanada.ca/en/intro-e.html

The link to most of the world's central banks is found on the web site of the Bank for International Settlements (BIS) at:

http://www.bis.org/cbanks.htm

Analyses of monetary and other economic policies of the leading nations are also provided in *The Economic Report of the President*, the Federal Reserve Bank of St. Louis, the European Commission (EC), National Bureau of Economic Research (NBER), Institute for International Economics (IIE). The web sites for these organizations are:

http://www.gpoaccess.gov/eop

http://www.stls.frb.org

http://europa.eu.int

http://nber.org

http://www.iie.com

The International Monetary System: Past, Present, and Future

After studying this chapter, you should be able to:

- Understand the meaning of an international monetary system
- Understand how the gold standard worked
- Know what the Bretton Woods System is
- Describe how the Bretton Woods System operated
- Understand how U.S. trade deficits contributed to the collapse of the system
- Know how the present international monetary system works
- Understand the causes and effects of financial crises in emerging markets
- Identify the major international economic problems facing the world today

CHAPTER OUTLINE

KEY TERMS

International monetary system

Adjustment

Liquidity

Confidence

Bretton Woods System

Intervention currency

International Monetary Fund (IMF)

Fundamental disequilibrium

Currency convertibility

International Bank for Reconstruction and Development (IBRD or World Bank)

International Development Association (IDA)

International Finance Corporation

Gold tranche

Credit tranches

Net IMF position

General Arrangements to Borrow (GAB)

Standby arrangements

Swap arrangements

Special Drawing Rights (SDRs)

Dollar shortage

Seigniorage

Smithsonian Agreement

Dollar standard

Dollar glut

Jamaica Accords

Benign neglect Substitution account

First credit tranche Target zones

New Arrangement to Borrow (NAB) Subprime mortgage crisis

IMF conditionality Sovereign wealth funds

Dollar overhang

16.1 INTRODUCTION

In this chapter, we examine the operation of the international monetary system from the gold standard period to the present. Some of these experiences were presented as examples when the various mechanisms of balance-of-payments adjustment were examined. We now bring it all together and evaluate the process of balance-of-payments adjustment and, more broadly, open-economy macroeconomic policies and performance under the various international monetary systems that existed from 1880 to the present. Although the approach is historical, the evaluation of the operation of the various international monetary systems will be conducted in terms of the analytical framework developed in Chapters 13 through 15.

In Section 16.2, we define the meaning of an international monetary system. Section 16.3 examines the gold standard as it operated from about 1880 to 1914 and the experience between World War I and World War II. The gold standard was a fixed exchange rate system with gold as the only international reserve asset. The interwar period was characterized first by a system of flexible exchange rates and subsequently by the attempt to reestablish the gold standard—an attempt doomed to failure. Sections 16.4–16.6 examine the establishment, operation, and collapse of the Bretton Woods system, the fixed or adjustable peg gold-exchange standard that operated from the end of World War II until August 1971. From then through March 1973, an adjustable-peg dollar standard prevailed. Section 16.7 and 16.8 examine, respectively, the problems facing the present managed floating exchange rate system and proposals for reform. Sections 16.9 and 16.10 deal with financial crises in emerging market economies and other current international economic problems.

16.2 MEANING OF INTERNATIONAL MONETARY SYSTEM

International monetary system The rules, customs, instruments, facilities, and organizations for effecting international payments.

An international monetary system (sometimes referred to as an international monetary order or regime) refers to the rules, customs, instruments, facilities, and organizations for effecting international payments. International monetary systems can be classified according to the way in which exchange rates

are determined or according to the form that international reserve assets take. Under the exchange rate classification, we can have a fixed exchange rate system with a narrow band of fluctuation about a par value, a fixed exchange rate system with a wide band of fluctuation, an adjustable peg system, a crawling peg system, managed floating, or a freely floating exchange rate system. Under the international reserve classification, we can have a gold standard (with gold as the only international reserve asset), a pure fiduciary standard (such as a pure dollar or exchange standard without any connection with gold), or a gold-exchange standard (a combination of the previous two).

The various classifications can be combined in various ways. For example, the gold standard is a fixed exchange rate system. However, we can also have a fixed exchange rate system without any connection with gold, but with international reserves composed of some national currency, such as the U.S. dollar, that is no longer backed by gold. Similarly, we can have an adjustable peg system or a managed float with gold and foreign exchange or with only foreign exchange as international reserves. Under a freely floating exchange rate system, there is theoretically no need for reserves since exchange rate changes automatically and immediately correct any balance-of-payments disequilibrium as it develops. Throughout the period of our analysis, most of the international monetary systems possible were in operation at one time or another or for some nations, as described in this chapter.

A good international monetary system is one that maximizes the flow of international trade and investments and leads to an "equitable" distribution of the gains from trade among the nations. An international monetary system can be evaluated in terms of adjustment, liquidity, and confidence. Adjustment refers to the process by which balance-of-payment disequilibria are corrected. A good international monetary system is one that minimizes the cost of and the time required for adjustment. Liquidity refers to the amount of international reserve assets available to settle temporary balance-of-payments disequilibria. A good international monetary system is one that provides adequate international reserves so that nations can correct balance-of-payments deficits without deflating their own economies. Confidence refers to the knowledge that the adjustment mechanism is working adequately and that international reserves will retain their absolute and relative values.

Adjustment The process by which balance-of-payments disequilibria are corrected.

Liquidity The amount of international reserve assets available to nations to settle temporary balance-of-payments disequilibria.

Confidence The knowledge that the balance-of-payments adjustment mechanism is working adequately and that international reserves will retain their absolute and relative values.

Concept Check

What is an international monetary system? How can it be evaluated?

16.3 THE GOLD STANDARD AND THE INTERWAR EXPERIENCE

The *gold standard* operated from about 1880 to 1914. As explained in Section 13.4, under this standard each nation defined the gold content of its currency and passively stood ready to buy or sell any amount of gold at that price. Since the gold content in one unit of each currency was fixed, exchange rates were also fixed. This was called the *mint parity*. The exchange

rate could then fluctuate above and below the mint parity (i.e., within the gold points) by the cost of shipping an amount of gold equal to one unit of the foreign currency between the two monetary centers. A deficit nation would lose gold, its money supply would fall, and so would its prices. This would stimulate the nation's exports and discourage its imports until the balance-of-payments deficit was eliminated. The opposite occurred in the surplus nation.

Passively allowing its money supply to reflect balance-of-payments conditions meant that a nation could not use monetary policy for achieving full employment without inflation. But this created no difficulties for classical economists since they believed that there was an automatic tendency in the economic system toward full employment without inflation. For the adjustment process to operate, nations were not supposed to *sterilize* (i.e., neutralize) the effect of a balance-of-payments deficit or surplus on the nation's money supply. On the contrary, the *rules of the game* of the gold standard required a deficit nation to reinforce the adjustment process by further restricting credit and a surplus nation to further expand credit.

This is how the adjustment mechanism was supposed to work under the gold standard. In reality, balance-of-payments disequilibria were settled mostly by international capital flows rather than through gold shipments. That is, when the United Kingdom had a balance-of-payments deficit, its money supply fell, interest rates rose, and this attracted a short-term capital inflow to cover the deficit. With the pound sterling as the only important international currency and London the only international monetary center, international capital movements were stabilizing. With conditions vastly different today, it is most unlikely that the gold standard or anything closely resembling it will be reestablished.

With the outbreak of World War I, the classical gold standard came to an end. Between 1919 and 1924, exchange rates fluctuated wildly, and this led to a desire to return to the stability of the gold standard. In April 1925, the United Kingdom reestablished the convertibility of the pound into gold *at the prewar price*. Other nations followed the United Kingdom's lead and went back to gold. The new system, however, was a gold-exchange standard because both gold and currencies convertible into gold (mostly pounds but also U.S. dollars and French francs) were used as international reserves. Since the United Kingdom had lost a great deal of its competitiveness and had liquidated a substantial portion of its foreign investments to pay for the war effort, reestablishing the prewar parity left the pound grossly overvalued and led to large balance-of-payments deficits and gold losses until the United Kingdom was forced to abandon the system in 1931 (the United States followed suit in 1933).

There followed, from 1931 to 1936, a period of great instability and competitive devaluations as nations tried to "export" their unemployment. The United States even devalued the dollar (by increasing the dollar price

of gold from $20.67 to $35 an ounce) in 1933–1934, from a position of balance-of-payments *surplus*, in order to stimulate its exports. Needless to say, this was a serious policy mistake. Expansionary domestic policies would have stimulated the U.S. economy and at the same time corrected or reduced its balance-of-payments surplus. By 1936, exchange rates among the major currencies were approximately the same as they had been in 1930, before the cycle of competitive devaluations began.

This was also a period when nations imposed very high tariffs and other restrictions on imports that sharply reduced world trade. For example, in 1930 the United States passed the *Smoot–Hawley Tariff Act*, which raised U.S. import duties to an all-time high (see Section 6.7). By 1939, depression gave way to full employment—and war. The unstable and chaotic conditions of the interwar experience strongly influenced the Allies at the close of World War II to establish an adjustable peg system after the war.

16.4 THE BRETTON WOODS SYSTEM

At 1944 meetings in Bretton Woods, New Hampshire, representatives of the United States, the United Kingdom, and other allies decided on the establishment of a gold-exchange standard after the war. Under this system, which became known as the Bretton Woods system, the United States was to maintain the price of gold fixed at $35 per ounce and be ready to exchange on demand dollars for gold at that price without restrictions or limitations. Other nations were to fix the price of their currencies in terms of dollars (and thus implicitly in terms of gold) and intervene in foreign exchange markets to keep the exchange rate from moving by more than 1 percent above or below the par value. Within the allowed band of fluctuation, the exchange rate was determined by the forces of demand and supply.

Specifically, a nation would have to use its dollar reserves to purchase its own currency to prevent it from depreciating by more than 1 percent from the agreed par value, or the nation had to purchase dollars with its own currency (adding to its international reserves) to prevent an appreciation of its currency by more than 1 percent from the par value. Until the late 1950s and early 1960s, when other currencies became fully convertible into dollars, the U.S. dollar was the only intervention currency, so that the new system was practically a gold-dollar standard.

Nations were to finance temporary balance-of-payments deficits out of their international reserves and by borrowing from the International Monetary Fund (IMF), a new international institution created for that purpose. Only in a case of fundamental disequilibrium was a nation allowed, with IMF approval, to change the par value of its currency. Fundamental disequilibrium was nowhere defined, but referred broadly to large and persistent balance-of-payments deficits or surpluses. Exchange rate changes of less than 10 percent were, however, allowed without IMF approval. Thus,

Concept Check

How did the gold standard operate?

Bretton Woods system The gold-exchange standard that operated from the end of World War II until 1971.

Intervention currency A convertible national currency (primarily the U.S. dollar) used by nations' monetary authorities to intervene in foreign exchange markets in order to keep the exchange rate from moving outside the allowed or desired range of fluctuation.

International Monetary Fund (IMF) The international institution created under the Bretton Woods system for the purposes of (1) overseeing that nations followed a set of agreed-upon rules of conduct in international trade and finance and (2) providing borrowing facilities for nations in temporary balance-of-payments difficulties.

Fundamental disequilibrium Large and persistent balance-of-payments deficits or surpluses.

Currency convertibility The ability to exchange one national currency for another without any restriction or limitation.

International Bank for Reconstruction and Development (IBRD or World Bank) The international institution established after World War II to provide long-run development assistance to developing nations.

International Development Association (IDA) The affiliate of the International Bank for Reconstruction and Development set up in 1960 to make loans at subsidized rates to poorer developing nations.

International Finance Corporation (IFC) The affiliate of the International Bank for Reconstruction and Development set up in 1956 to stimulate *private* investments in developing nations from indigenous and foreign sources.

Concept Check

What is the Bretton Woods system?

the Bretton Woods system was set up as an adjustable peg system, combining general exchange rate stability with some flexibility.

Besides providing borrowing facilities for nations in temporary balance of payments difficulties, the IMF was also to oversee that nations followed a set of agreed-upon rules of conduct in international trade and finance. The IMF opened its doors on March 1, 1947, with a membership of 30 nations. By 2004, IMF membership had reached 185. Only a few countries, such as Cuba and North Korea, are not members.

After a period of transition following the war, nations were to remove all restrictions on the convertibility of their currencies into other currencies and into the U.S. dollar. Nations were forbidden to impose additional trade restrictions (otherwise currency convertibility would not have much meaning), and existing trade restrictions were to be removed gradually in multilateral negotiations under the sponsorship of GATT (see Section 6.8). Restrictions on international liquid capital flows were, however, permitted to allow nations to protect their currencies against large destabilizing, international money flows.

Borrowing from the IMF was to be repaid within three to five years. *Long-run* development assistance was to be provided by the International Bank for Reconstruction and Development (IBRD or World Bank) and its affiliates, the International Development Association (established in 1960 to make loans at subsidized rates to the poorer developing nations) and the International Finance Corporation (established in 1956 to stimulate *private* investments in developing nations from domestic and foreign sources).

Upon joining the IMF, each nation was assigned a quota based on its economic importance and volume of international trade. The size of a nation's quota determined its voting power and its ability to borrow from the IMF. The total subscription to the IMF was set in 1944 at $8.8 billion. The United States was assigned by far the largest quota, 31 percent. Every five years, quotas were to be revised to reflect changes in the relative economic importance and international trade of member nations. By June 2008, the total subscription of the Fund had grown to $352 billion through increases in membership and periodic increases in quotas. The U.S. quota had declined to 17.1 percent of the total, the quota of Japan and Germany was, respectively, 6.1 and 6.0, and that of France and the United Kingdom 4.9 percent. China, with 9.7 percent of the global economy, had a quota of 3.7 percent.

Upon joining the IMF, a nation was to pay 25 percent of its quota to the IMF in gold and the remainder in its own currency. In borrowing from the Fund, the nation would get convertible currencies from the IMF in exchange for depositing equivalent (and additional) amounts of its own currency into the IMF. Under the original rules, a member nation could borrow no more than 25 percent of its quota in any one year, for up to a total of 125 percent of its quota over a five-year period. The nation could borrow the first 25 percent of its quota, the so-called gold tranche, almost automatically, without any

Gold tranche The 25 percent of a nation's quota in the IMF that the nation was originally required to pay in gold and could then borrow from the Fund almost automatically.

Credit tranche The amount that a member nation could borrow from the IMF, subject to conditions, over and above the gold tranche.

Net IMF position The size of a nation's quota in the IMF minus the Fund's holdings of the nation's currency.

restrictions or conditions. For further borrowings (in subsequent years), the credit tranches, the IMF charged higher and higher interest rates and imposed more and more supervision and conditions to ensure that the deficit nation was taking appropriate measures to eliminate the deficit. A nation's gold tranche minus the amount of its borrowing (if any) is called the nation's net IMF position.

16.5 OPERATION AND EVOLUTION OF THE BRETTON WOODS SYSTEM

While the Bretton Woods system envisaged and allowed changes in par values in cases of fundamental disequilibrium, industrial nations were very reluctant to change their par values until such action was long overdue and practically forced upon them by the resulting destabilizing speculation. Deficit nations regarded devaluations as a sign of national weakness, while surplus nations preferred to continue accumulating international reserves instead of revaluing. Thus, from 1950 until August 1971, the United Kingdom devalued only in 1967; France devalued only in 1957 and 1969; West Germany *revalued* in 1961 and 1969; and the United States, Italy, and Japan never changed their par values. Meanwhile, Canada (defying the rules of the IMF) had fluctuating exchange rates from 1950 to 1962 and then reinstituted them in 1970. Developing nations, on the other hand, devalued all too often.

The unwillingness of industrial nations to change their par values as a matter of policy when in fundamental disequilibrium robbed the system of the mechanism for balance-of-payments adjustment and gave rise to destabilizing international capital flows, which eventually led to the collapse of the system. Specifically, facing large trade deficits, the United Kingdom experienced huge capital outflows in the expectation that the pound would be devalued, until it was indeed forced to do so in 1967. On the other hand, West Germany received huge capital inflows in the expectation that it would revalue the mark. This made revaluation of the mark inevitable in 1961 and again in 1969. Convertibility of the dollar into gold resumed soon after World War II. Formal convertibility for current account transactions was achieved in 1961 for major European currencies and in 1964 for the Japanese yen. Capital account restrictions were permitted to allow nations some protection against destabilizing capital flows.

Under the *Trade Expansion Act of 1962* and *GATT* auspices (see Section 6.7), the United States initiated and engaged in wide-ranging multilateral trade negotiations (the *Kennedy Round*), which lowered average tariffs on manufactured goods to less than 10 percent. Many nontariff barriers remained, however, especially in agriculture, which are of special importance to developing nations. Several attempts were made at economic integration during this period, the most successful being the European Common Market (see Section 7.5).

General Arrangements to Borrow (GAB) The arrangements under which the IMF negotiated to borrow from the "Group of Ten" (most important industrial nations) and Switzerland to augment its resources if needed to help nations with balance-of-payments difficulties.

Standby arrangements The arrangements under which member nations negotiate with the IMF for advance approval for future borrowings from the Fund so they will be immediately available when needed.

Swap arrangements The arrangements under which national central banks negotiate to exchange each other's currency to be used to intervene in foreign exchange markets to combat international hot money flows.

Special Drawing Rights (SDRs) International reserves created by the IMF to supplement other international reserves and distributed to member nations according to their quotas in the Fund.

Concept Check

How did the Bretton Woods system operate?

Over the years, the Bretton Woods system evolved in several ways in response to changing conditions. In 1962, the IMF negotiated the General Arrangements to Borrow (GAB) up to $6 billion from the so-called Group of Ten most important industrial nations (the United States, the United Kingdom, West Germany, Japan, France, Italy, Canada, the Netherlands, Belgium, and Sweden) and Switzerland to supplement its resources, if needed, to help nations facing balance-of-payments difficulties. GAB was renewed and expanded in subsequent years.

Starting in the early 1960s, member nations began to negotiate standby arrangements. These refer to advance permission for future borrowings by the nation at the IMF. Once a standby arrangement was negotiated, the nation paid a small commitment charge on the amount earmarked and was then able to borrow up to this additional amount *immediately* when the need arose at a 5.5 percent charge per year on the amount actually borrowed. Standby arrangements were usually negotiated by member nations as a first line of defense against anticipated destabilizing hot money flows. After several increases in quotas, the total resources of the IMF reached $28.5 billion by 1971. By the end of 1971, the IMF had lent about $22 billion, of which about $4 billion was outstanding. Member nations were also allowed to borrow up to 50 percent of their quotas in any one year (up from 25 percent).

National central banks also began to negotiate so-called swap arrangements to exchange each other's currency to be used to intervene in foreign exchange markets to combat hot money flows. Swap arrangements were negotiated for specific periods of time and with an exchange rate guarantee. When due, they could either be settled by a reverse transaction or renegotiated for another period. The United States and European nations negotiated many such swap arrangements during the 1960s.

The IMF also created Special Drawing Rights (SDRs) to supplement the international reserves of gold and foreign exchange. Sometimes called *paper gold*, SDRs are accounting entries in the books of the IMF. SDRs are not backed by gold or any other currency, but represent genuine international reserves. Their value arises because member nations have so agreed. SDRs can be used only in dealings among central banks to settle balance-of-payments deficits and surpluses, not in private commercial dealings. A total of $9.5 billion SDRs were created from 1970 to 1972, and these were distributed to member nations according to their quotas in the IMF. Further allocations of SDRs were made in the 1979–1981 period. The value of one SDR was originally set equal to one U.S. dollar, but rose above $1 as a result of the devaluations to the dollar in 1971 and 1973. Starting in 1974, the value of SDRs was tied to a basket of currencies and was $1.58 at the end of 2007.

Overall, the Bretton Woods system served the world well, particularly until the mid-1960s, with international trade growing faster than (and therefore stimulating) world output (see Case Study 16-1).

CASE STUDY 16-1

Macroeconomic Performance under Different Exchange Rate Regimes

Table 16.1 presents some indicators of the macroeconomic performance of the United Kingdom and the United States under the gold standard, interwar period, and post-World War II period, under fixed and flexible exchange rates. The table shows that growth in per capita income in both the United Kingdom and the United States was higher during the post-World War II period than during the gold standard period, inflation was higher, and unemployment was lower, except for the United Kingdom during 1973–2007. Thus, aside from the lower inflation rate, the macroeconomic performance of both countries was not better during the gold standard period compared with the post-World War II period. On the other hand, the interwar period was dominated by the Great Depression and characterized by a worse macroeconomic performance than either under the gold standard or in the post-World War II period. The only exception was that the relatively high growth in real per capita income during the interwar period (despite the Great Depression) in the United States exceeded its growth during the gold standard period. Caution should be exercised, however, in comparing pre- to post-World War II performance because data for the former period are of poor quality.

Table 16.1. *Macroeconomic Performance of the United States and the United Kingdom under Different Exchange Rate Regimes, 1870–2007*

	Average Growth in Real per Capita per Year	Rate of Inflation	Rate of Unemployment
Gold standard			
United Kingdom (1870–1913)	1.0	−0.7	4.3[a]
United States (1879–1913)	1.4	0.1	6.8[b]
Interwar period			
United Kingdom (1919–1938)	0.6	−4.6	13.3
United States (1919–1940)	1.6	−2.5	11.3
Post-World War II period—			
Fixed exchange rate period			
United Kingdom (1946–1972)	1.7	3.5	1.9
United States (1946–1972)	2.2	1.4	4.6
Post-World War II period—			
Flexible exchange rate period			
United Kingdom (1973–2007)	2.2	6.3	7.6
United States (1973–2007)	3.0	4.4	6.3

[a]1888–1913;
[b]1890–1913.

Source: M. Bordo, "The Classical Gold Standard: Some Lessons for Today," in *Readings in International Finance* (Chicago: Federal Reserve Bank of Chicago, 1987), pp. 83–97; M. Friedman and A. Schwartz, *A Monetary Theory of the United States* (Princeton, N.J.: Princeton University Press, 1963), p. 243; and International Monetary Fund, *International Financial Statistics Yearbook*, 2007.

16.6 U.S. BALANCE-OF-PAYMENTS DEFICITS AND COLLAPSE OF THE BRETTON WOODS SYSTEM

Dollar shortage The inability of war-torn nations during the late 1940s and early 1950s to accumulate substantial dollar reserves.

Seigniorage The benefit accruing to a nation from issuing the currency or when its currency is used as an international currency and reserve.

Smithsonian Agreement The agreement reached in December 1971 in Washington under which the dollar was devalued by about 9 percent (by increasing the dollar price of gold from $35 to $38 an ounce), other strong currencies were revalued by various amounts with respect to the dollar, the dollar convertibility into gold remained suspended, and exchange rates were allowed to fluctuate by 2.25 percent on either side of the new par values.

Concept Check

How did the U.S. trade deficits contribute to the collapse of the system?

From 1945 to 1949, the United States ran huge balance-of-payments surpluses with Europe and extended Marshall Plan aid to help in its reconstruction. With European recovery more or less complete by 1950, the U.S. balance of payments turned into deficit. Up to 1957, U.S. deficits were small and allowed European nations and Japan to build up their international reserves. This was the period of the dollar shortage. The United States settled its deficits mostly in dollars. Surplus nations were willing to accept dollars because (1) the United States stood ready to exchange dollars for gold at the fixed price of $35 an ounce, making the dollar "as good as gold"; (2) dollars could be used as an international currency to transactions with any other nation; and (3) dollar deposits earned interest while gold did not.

Starting in 1958, U.S. balance-of-payments deficits increased sharply, first because of the huge capital outflows (mostly direct investments in Europe) and then because of the high U.S. inflation rate (during the Vietnam War). By 1970, foreign official dollar holdings were more than $40 billion, up from $13 billion in 1949 in the face of U.S. gold reserves declining from $25 billion in 1949 to $11 billion in 1970.

Because the dollar was an international currency, the United States felt that it was unable to devalue to correct its balance-of-payments deficits. Instead, it adopted a number of other policies, with limited success. The United States tried to encourage exports, reduced military and other government expenditures abroad, tied most of its foreign aid, and imposed some direct controls over capital outflows. As U.S. balance-of-payments deficits continued to rise over time, U.S. gold reserves declined to the point where they were only about one-quarter of foreign-held dollar reserves by 1970.

In 1970 and early 1971, the expectation was that the United States would soon have to devalue the dollar, and this led to huge destabilizing capital movements out of dollars. On August 15, 1971, President Nixon was forced to suspend the convertibility of dollars into gold. The Bretton Woods System was dead. At the same time, the United States imposed wage and price controls, as well as a temporary 10 percent import surcharge, to be lifted after the required currency realignment took place. For the benefit of seigniorage from the use of the dollar as an international currency, the United States had paid a heavy price by being unable to devalue, even though it was clearly in fundamental disequilibrium. The irony was that the dollar remained an international currency without any backing of gold.

With the Smithsonian Agreement in December 1971, representatives of the Group of Ten nations agreed to increase the dollar price of gold from $35 to $38 an ounce. This implied a devaluation of the dollar of about 9 percent. At the same time, the German mark was revalued by about 17 percent, the

Dollar standard
The international monetary system that emerged from the Smithsonian Agreement in December 1971 under which the U.S. dollar remained an international currency and reserve without any gold backing.

Dollar glut The excess supply of dollars in the hands of foreign monetary authorities that developed during the late 1950s and early 1960s.

Japanese yen by about 14 percent, and other currencies by smaller amounts. In addition, the band of fluctuation was increased from 1 percent to 2.25 percent on either side of the new central rates, and the United States removed its 10 percent import surcharge. Since the dollar remained inconvertible into gold, the world was now essentially on a dollar standard.

However, with another huge U.S. balance-of-payments deficit in 1972, it was felt that the Smithsonian Agreement was not working and that another devaluation of the dollar was required. This expectation led to renewed speculation against the dollar and became self-fulfilling in February 1973, when the United States was once again forced to devalue the dollar, this time by about 10 percent (achieved by increasing the official price of gold to $42.22 an ounce). When speculation against the dollar flared up again in March 1973, monetary authorities in the major industrial nations decided to let their currencies float. The present managed floating exchange rate system was born.

While the immediate cause of the collapse of the Bretton Woods system was the huge balance-of-payments deficits of the United States in 1970 and 1971, the *fundamental* cause was the lack of a workable balance-of-payments adjustment mechanism. Under the Bretton Woods system, most international reserves were provided by U.S. balance-of-payments deficits, but the longer these deficits persisted and the more unwanted dollars accumulated in foreign hands, the greater was the expectation that the dollar would be devalued. The dollar shortage of the 1950s had given way to the dollar glut of the 1960s. It was in response to this problem and in the hope that the United States would soon be able to correct its deficits that the IMF decided to create $9.5 billion of SDRs in 1970–1972. As it was, persistent U.S. balance-of-payments deficits undermined confidence in the dollar and led to its collapse.

Jamaica Accords
The agreements reached in January 1976 and ratified in April 1978 that recognized the managed float and abolished the official price of gold.

Benign neglect
The policy of nonintervention in foreign exchange markets followed by the United States from March 1973 until the end of 1977 and from 1981 to 1985.

16.7 OPERATION OF THE PRESENT INTERNATIONAL MONETARY SYSTEM

Since March 1973, the world has had a managed floating exchange rate system. Under such a system, nations' monetary authorities can intervene in foreign exchange markets to smooth out short-run fluctuations in exchange rates usually without attempting to affect long-run trends. This could be achieved by a policy of leaning against the wind (see Section 15.9).

The 1976 Jamaica Accords (ratified in 1978) formally recognized the managed floating system and allowed nations the choice of foreign exchange regime as long as their actions were not disruptive to trade partners. At the beginning of 2008, about half of the 185 members of the IMF adopted some form of exchange rate flexibility (see Case Study 15–5). From 1974 to 1977, again from 1981 to 1985, and since the early 1990s, the United States generally followed a policy of benign neglect by not intervening in foreign exchange

Table 16.2. *International Reserves in 2007 (billions of U.S. dollars, at year end)*

	Reserves
Foreign exchange	$6,393.0
SDRs	29.1
Reserve position in the IMF	21.7
Total minus gold	6,443.8
Gold at official price	47.9
Total with gold at official price	6,491.7

Source: IMF, *International Financial Statistics*, May 2008.

First credit tranche
The 25 percent of a nation's quota in the IMF that the nation is required to pay in SDRs or in the currencies of other members selected by the Fund and could then borrow from the Fund almost automatically.

New Arrangement to Borrow (NAB)
The arrangement negotiated by the International Monetary Fund at the beginning of 1997 under which 25 participant countries and institutions agreed to lend up to SDR34 billion (about $47 billion) to supplement the General Arrangements to Borrow (GAB) for a period of five years (subject to renewal).

IMF conditionality
The conditions imposed by the IMF on members' borrowings from the Fund.

markets to stabilize the value of the dollar. In March 1979, the European Monetary System (EMS) was formed and in January 1999 the European Monetary Union (EMU) came into existence with the creation of the euro (which began actual circulation at the beginning of 2002) and the European Central Bank (ECB) starting to operate (see Sections 15.6 and 15.7).

Under the present managed float, nations still need international reserves in order to intervene in foreign exchange markets to smooth out short-run fluctuations in exchange rates. At present, such interventions are still made mostly in dollars. In January 1975, U.S. citizens were allowed for the first time since 1933 to own gold (other than in jewelry). The price of gold temporarily rose above $800 an ounce in January 1980, but it soon fell and stabilized at less than half of its peak price. The price of gold reached the all-time high of $1,000 in April 2008 but it was about $850 in June 2008. The official price of gold was abolished and the IMF suspended all gold transactions with member nations. The old gold tranche at the IMF was renamed the first-credit tranche. The IMF continued to value its gold holdings at the pre-1971 official price of $35 an ounce. Table 16.2 shows the composition of international reserves at the end of 2007.

The IMF renewed and expanded the General Arrangements to Borrow (GAB) and in 1997 extended it with the New Arrangement to Borrow (NAB) that provided the IMF with an additional $49 billion in lending capability in 2003 (on top of $24 billion on GAB). Central bankers also expanded their swap arrangements to $54 billion and their standby arrangements, $50 billion in 2007. Borrowing rules at the IMF were also relaxed and new credit facilities were added that greatly expanded the overall maximum amount of credit available to a member nation. There is an initial fee for borrowing, and the interest charged is based on the length of the loan, the facility used, and prevailing interest rates. Besides the usual surveillance responsibilities over the exchange rate policies of its members, the IMF has in recent years broadened its responsibilities to include help for members to overcome their structural problems. As of June 2008, the IMF had loans outstanding to 64 countries of $19.4 billion.

Concept
Check

What is the present
international mone-
tary system? How is
it working?

Dollar overhang
The large amount
of foreign-held
dollars resulting
from past U.S.
balance-of-payments
deficits, the move-
ment of which from
monetary center to
monetary center
can lead to large
exchange rate fluc-
tuations and which
complicates the con-
duct of monetary
policies.

Substitution account
The account pro-
posed to be used
to exchange all
foreign-held dollars
for SDRs at the IMF
to solve the prob-
lem of the dollar
overhang.

Target zones The
system in which the
leading industrial
nations estimate the
equilibrium exchange
rate and agree on
the range of allowed
fluctuation.

Concept
Check

What are the major
problems with the
current international
monetary system?

Since 1982, the IMF has engaged in a number of debt rescheduling and rescue operations. As a condition for the additional loans and special help, the IMF required reductions in government spending, growth of the money supply, and wage increases in order to reduce imports, stimulate exports, and make the country more nearly self-sustaining. Such IMF conditionality, however, proved very painful and led to riots and even the toppling of governments. Partly in response to these accusations, the IMF has become more flexible in its lending activities. By way of summary, Table 16.3 presents the most important dates in modern monetary history.

16.8 PROBLEMS WITH THE PRESENT INTERNATIONAL MONETARY SYSTEM AND PROPOSALS FOR REFORMS

The present international monetary system faces the problems of large volatility and misalignments of exchange rates. As discussed in the next section, it has also been unable to prevent international financial crises in emerging market economies or to adequately deal with them when they do arise.

We have seen in Sections 11.8 and 12.7 that since 1973 exchange rates have been characterized by very large volatility and overshooting. Volatility discourages the flow of international trade and investments. More serious are large exchange rate disequilibria (misalignments) that arise and can persist for years. Examples are the very large appreciation of the dollar from 1980 to 1985 and from 1995 to 2001, and its large subsequent depreciations (see Section 15.9 and Case Study 16–2). These disrupt the pattern of trade and comparative advantage, and lead to trade disputes and protectionism.

A related problem of the present international monetary system is the huge dollar overhang or large quantity of dollars held by foreigners and ready to move from monetary center to monetary center in response to variations in international interest differentials and expectations of exchange rate changes. One proposal of long standing aimed at eliminating this problem involves converting all foreign-held dollars into SDRs by the introduction of a substitution account by the IMF. No action, however, has been taken on this proposal.

Several proposals have been advanced to reduce exchange rate volatility and avoid large exchange rate misalignments. One proposal, originally advanced by *John Williamson*, is based on the establishment of target zones, whereby the leading industrial nations estimate the equilibrium exchange rate and agree on the range of allowed fluctuation (say, 10 percent above and below the equilibrium exchange rate). The exchange rate is then determined by the forces of demand and supply within the allowed band of fluctuation and prevented from moving outside the target zones by official intervention

Table 16.3. *Important Dates in Modern Monetary History*

1880–1914	Classical gold standard period
April 1925	United Kingdom returns to the gold standard
October 1929	U.S. stock market crashes
September 1931	United Kingdom abandons the gold standard
February 1934	United States raises official price of gold from $20.67 to $35 an ounce
July 1944	Bretton Woods Conference
March 1947	IMF begins operation
September 1967	Decision to create SDRs
August 1971	United States suspends convertibility of dollar into gold—end of Bretton Woods system
December 1971	Smithsonian Agreement: official price of gold raised to $38 an ounce; band of allowed fluctuation increased to 4.5 percent
February 1973	United States raises official price of gold to $42.22 an ounce
March 1973	Managed floating exchange rate comes into existence
October 1973	OPEC selective embargo of petroleum exports and start of sharp increase in petroleum prices
January 1976	Jamaica Accords (agreement to recognize the managed float and abolish the official price of gold)
April 1978	Jamaica Accords take effect
March 1979	Establishment of European Monetary System (EMS)
Spring 1979	Second oil shock
January 1980	Gold price temporarily above $800 an ounce
September 1985	Plaza Agreement to intervene to lower value of dollar
Fall 1986	New round of GATT multilateral trade negotiations begins
October 1987	New York Stock Exchange collapses and spreads to other stock markets around the world
1989–1990	Democratic and market reforms begin in Eastern Europe and German reunification
December 1991	Maastricht Treaty approved; called for European Union to move toward monetary union by 1999
December 1991	Soviet Union dissolved and Commonwealth of Independent States (CIS) formed
December 1993	Uruguay Round completed and World Trade Organization replaces GATT
January 1, 1994	North American free Trade Agreement (NAFTA) comes into existence
January 1, 1999	Introduction of euro; European Central Bank (ECB) begins operation
October 2000	Euro falls to lowest level with respect to dollar
January 1, 2002	Euro begins circulation as the currency of the 12-member European Monetary Union (EMU)
April 23, 2008	Euro reaches the all-time high of $1.59

in foreign exchange markets. The target zone would be changed when the underlying equilibrium exchange rate moves outside of or gets near the boundaries of the target zone. Critics, however, feel that target zones embody the worst characteristics of fixed and flexible exchange rate systems. As in the case of flexible rates, target zones allow substantial fluctuation and volatility in exchange rates and can be inflationary. As in the case of fixed exchange rates, target zones can only be defended by official intervention in foreign exchange markets, which reduce the monetary autonomy of the nation.

Other proposals seek to limit exchange rate volatility and misalignments by greater *macroeconomic policy coordination* among the leading industrial countries. *Ronald McKinnon* proposed that the United States, Japan, and Germany (now the European Monetary Union or EMU) fix the exchange rate among their currencies at the equilibrium level (determined by purchasing-power parity) and then closely coordinate their monetary policies to keep exchange rates fixed. A tendency for the dollar to depreciate vis-à-vis the euro would signal that the United States should reduce the growth rate of its money supply, while the EMU should increase it. The net overall increase in the money supply of these three economies would then be expanded at a rate consistent with the noninflationary expansion of the world economy.

Another proposal advocated by the *IMF Interim Committee* was based on the development of *objective indicators* of economic performance to signal the type of coordinated macropolicies for nations to follow, under the supervision of the IMF, in order to keep the world economy growing along a sustainable noninflationary path. These objective indicators are the growth of

CASE STUDY 16-2

Exchange Rate Volatility and Misalignments

Figure 16.1 shows the percentage deviations of the exchange rate (defined in U.S. cents per unit) of the major currencies with respect to U.S. dollar parities of October 1967. The symbols for the various currencies are: DM for the Deutsche mark or German mark, Y for the Japanese yen, £ for the British pound, FF for the French franc, SF for the Swiss franc, C$ for the Canadian dollar, Gld for the Dutch guilder, and L for the Italian lira. The figure clearly shows the large volatility and misalignments of exchange rates and gives the chronology of the major exchange rate changes from 1967 to 1991. From the figure

we can see that during the 1980s the value of the Japanese yen fluctuated from between 35 and 190 percent of its 1967 dollar value, while the appreciation of the Deutsche mark ranged from 20 to 170 percent. Exchange rate volatility and misalignments, though not as spectacular, have also been very large since 1991 (see Figure 11.4). Such large exchange rate volatility and misalignments represent one of the major international monetary problems facing the present floating exchange rate system.

(continues)

FIGURE 16.1. Exchange Rates of Major Currencies against the Dollar.

Source: OECD, *OECD Economic Outlook* (Paris: OECD, December 1991), p. 151.

Concept Check

What are the major proposals for improving the operation of the present system?

GNP, inflation, unemployment, trade balance, growth of the money supply, fiscal balance, exchange rates, interest rates, and international reserves. A rise or fall in these objective indicators in a nation would signal the need for restrictive or expansionary policies for the nation. Stability of the index for the world as a whole would be the anchor for noninflationary world expansion. So far, however, the leading nations have not been willing to give up some of their autonomy in order to achieve greater policy coordination (see Section 15.10).

Still another proposal (advanced by *James Tobin*) is based on restricting international speculative capital flows (regarded as the primary cause of exchange rate instability and misalignments) by a transaction tax that would become progressively higher the shorter the duration of the transaction. But this would be difficult to implement and may not solve the problem. Finally, there is the single world currency advanced by *Robert Mundell*.

16.9 FINANCIAL CRISES IN EMERGING MARKET ECONOMIES

Another serious problem facing the present international monetary system is its seeming inability to prevent international financial crises, especially in emerging markets. There have been six such crises since the mid-1990s: Mexico in 1994–1995, Southeast Asia in 1997–1999, Russia in summer 1998, Brazil in 1999, and Turkey and Argentina in 2001–2002 (see Case Studies 16.3 and 16.4). The IMF estimated that the cumulative loss of output as a percentage of GDP over the years of the most recent crisis was 82 for Indonesia, 57 for Thailand, 39 for Malaysia, 30 for Mexico, and 27 for Korea (there are no estimates for Brazil, Russia, Turkey, and Argentina).

Although the fundamental cause of these crises was different, the process was similar. Each crisis started as a result of a massive withdrawal of short-term liquid funds at the first sign of financial weakness in the nation. Foreign investors poured funds into many emerging markets during the early 1990s when these nations liberalized their capital markets in order to take advantage of high returns and for portfolio diversification, but immediately withdrew their funds on a massive scale at the first sign of economic trouble in the nation—thereby precipitating a crisis. The danger is that such crises could spread to the rest of the world, including industrial countries.

A number of measures have been proposed, and some steps have already been taken to avoid or minimize such crises in the future and thus greatly strengthen the *architecture of the present international monetary system* and improve its functioning. These include: (1) increasing transparency in international monetary relations, (2) strengthening emerging markets' banking and financial systems, and (3) promoting greater private sector involvement.

CASE STUDY 16-3

The Anatomy of a Currency Crisis: The Collapse of the Mexican Peso

In December 1994, Mexico found itself in the grip of an intense financial crisis that led to the deepest recession the country had faced in decades. The immediate cause of the crisis was the sharp increase in U.S. interest rates during 1994, which reversed the large U.S. capital flow to Mexico. This was aggravated by the political crisis triggered by the armed rebellion in the southern state of Chiapas in January 1994 and the murder of two high political officials later in 1994.

In order to reverse the resulting massive capital outflows, Mexico started to issue short-term, dollar-denominated securities and sharply increased domestic interest rates. Fearful that Mexico would not be able to service its loan obligations, however, foreign investors continued to pull funds out of Mexico. This forced Mexico to devalue the peso by 15 percent from 3.5 pesos to the dollar to 4.0 on December 20, 1994. But this was too little and

too late, and in the face of continued loss of international reserves, Mexico was forced to let the peso float. The peso then depreciated to 7 pesos to the dollar by March 1995 and reached nearly 8 pesos to the dollar in December 1995.

In order to help Mexico and to prevent the spread of the financial crisis to other emerging markets (particularly Argentina and Brazil), the United States organized an international support package of nearly $48 billion through the IMF in January 1995, which succeeded in calming financial markets and containing the crisis to Mexico. But very high interest rates and deep budget deficit cuts plunged Mexico into a deep recession in 1995. It was only in 1996 that the bottom of the recession was reached and growth resumed in Mexico.

Source: Federal Reserve Bank of Atlanta, "A Predictable and Avoidable Mexican Meltdown," *Economics Update*, December 1996, pp. 1–3.

CASE STUDY 16-4

Chronology of Economic Crises in Emerging Market Economies: From Thailand to Argentina

Table 16.4 presents the chronology of economic crises in emerging markets from the late 1990s to the present. The latest round of economic crises in emerging markets started in Thailand in July 1997. By fall 1997, the crisis had spread to the Philippines, South Korea, Indonesia, and Malaysia; by summer 1998 to Russia; and in January 1999 to Brazil. It also affected China, Taiwan, Hong Kong, Singapore, as well as Mexico and Argentina and, to some extent, most other developing countries. Developed countries were also affected. By the end of

1999, the crisis was more or less over and growth resumed in most emerging markets, except Indonesia and Russia. A new banking and financial crisis erupted in Turkey and Argentina in 2001, and in 2002 Argentina faced a financial, economic and political collapse. Both of these crises, however, were more or less resolved by 2003. Emerging markets were not much affected by the subprime mortgage crisis that started in the United States in 2007 and spread to several other advanced countries.

(continues)

Table 16.4. *Chronology of Economic Crises in Emerging Markets from the Late 1990s*

1997

May 15	Thailand announced capital controls in an effort to ease the pressure on its currency (the baht).
July 2	Thailand devalues the baht by 15–20%.
July 14	Philippines and Indonesia devalue the pesos and the rupiah, respectively.
August 20	Thailand and the IMF agree on a $17-billion financial stabilization package.
October 27	Dow Jones Industrial Average falls 554 points amid Asian fears.
October 31	Indonesia and the IMF agree on a $23-billion financial support package.
November 7	Financial markets in Argentina, Brazil, Mexico, and Venezuela fall sharply.
November 17	South Korea abandons its defense of the won.
December 3	South Korea and the IMF agree on a $57 billion financial assistance package.
December	South Korean won and Indonesian rupiah collapse; other Asian currencies continue to decline.
December 30	Foreign banks agree to roll over South Korea's $100 billion short-term debt.

1998

January	Value of the Indonesian rupiah falls even further.
January 15	Indonesia and IMF agree on revised economic program to enact promised reforms.
Early March	Indonesian economy verges on hyperinflation; rioting erupts. Government subsidizes food imports, violating IMF program.
April 10	Indonesia signs new letter of intent with IMF for a new reform program.
Early May	Economic situation in Indonesia deteriorates; more frequent and larger riots.
May 19	Markets in Russia fall sharply amid fears of spreading financial contagion.
May 21	Suharto resigns as president of Indonesia; B. J. Habbie takes over.
May 26	South Korea stock market hits an 11-year low.
May 27	Russian Central Bank triples interest rates to 150 percent to encourage foreign capital to stay.
July 13	Russia and IMF agree on an emergency $22.6-billion financial stabilization package.
August 17	Russia devalues the ruble and defaults on payments on its short-term debt.
Late August	Russia's economy collapses.
Late September	The New York Federal Reserve Bank coordinates a bailout of "Long-Term Capital Management," a hedge fund with some $100 billion in liabilities.
November 13	Brazil negotiates a $41.5-billion IMF/World Bank/multicountry rescue package.

1999

January 8	Brazil devalues the real by 8 percent in the face of large capital outflows.
January 15	Brazil allows the real to float freely on world markets and the real declines by 35 percent.
January 27	China rejects rumors that it will devalue the yuan; China's growth rate declines.
Late 1999	Financial crises in emerging markets declared over; growth resumes.

(continues)

Table 16.4. *(Continued)*

2001	
February	Banking crisis in Turkey; nation lets the currency (the lira) float.
December	Argentina defaults on its debt (largest in history).
2002	
January	Argentina ends currency board arrangements and devalues peso; nation plunges into financial, economic, and political turmoil; IMF refuses to grant loans without credible restructuring plan.
February 4	Turkey receives IMF loan of $12.8 billion.
August 7	Brazil receives $30-billion grant to help it avoid new financial crisis.
2005	
June	Argentina restructures its foreign debt with about 75 percent of its bond holders by paying 25 cents to the dollar.
July	China revalues its currency by 2 percent and breaks its exchange rate peg to the dollar.
November	Brazil pays off its outstanding IMF debt early.
2006	
December	Brazil and Argentina pay off outstanding IMF debt early.
2007	
August	Emerging market economies not much affected by the breakout of the subprime mortgage crisis in the United States.
2008	
June	Price of petroleum reaches $139 per barrel and the price of food skyrockets, resulting in inflation and reduced growth rates in emerging markets and advanced countries, and increased poverty in poorest countries.

Source: Inter-American Development Bank, 1999; updated by the author.

Increased transparency is essential because markets cannot work efficiently without adequate, reliable, and timely information. *Early-warning financial indicators,* such as budget and current account deficits, long-term and short-term foreign debts, and international reserves as percentages of GDP could signal which emerging country or countries might be heading for trouble. The hope is that foreign investors would take note of the potential problem and avoid pouring excessive funds into the nation, thus possibly avoiding the crisis.

Strengthening emerging markets' banking and financial systems is also essential. Weaknesses in the banking systems were common to all emerging markets that were involved in financial crises during the past decade. The IMF has been formulating standards or codes of good practice in accounting, auditing, corporate governance, payments and settlements systems, insurance, and banking. Some of these are already being implemented as part of the IMF surveillance function.

It is also essential to have greater involvement of the private sector in sharing the burden of resolving financial crises in emerging markets by rolling over and renegotiating loans or providing new money rather than rushing for the exit, as a precondition for IMF official assistance. The logic is that lenders should be compelled to take some responsibility for the crisis by having lent too much short-term funds for nonproductive purposes to an emerging market.

Concept Check

What are the causes of emerging market crises? How can they be minimized?

In the final analysis, however, we must realize that even if all the reforms being considered were adopted, these would not eliminate all future crises. All that we can hope is that reforms would reduce the frequency and severity of financial crises in the future. Some international financial instability and crisis may be the inevitable result of liberalized financial markets and the cost that we need to pay for the benefits that liberalized financial markets provide to industrial and emerging market economies alike. And financial crises are not limited to emerging markets (see Case Study 16-5).

16.10 OTHER CURRENT INTERNATIONAL ECONOMIC PROBLEMS

The problems arising from present exchange rate arrangements discussed above are closely related to other serious economic problems facing the world today. These are: (1) trade protectionism in advanced countries in the context of a rapidly globalizing world; (2) deep structural imbalances in the United States, slow growth in Europe and Japan, and insufficient restructuring in transition economies of Central and Eastern Europe; (3) deep poverty in many developing countries; and (4) resource scarcity, environmental degradation, and climate change and the danger that they pose for continued growth and sustainable world development. Let us examine each of these interrelated problems and see what can be offered in the way of analysis and possible solution to them after this introductory study of international economics.

1. Trade Protectionism in Advanced Countries in the Context of a Rapidly Globalizing World

We have seen in Section 6.8 that since the mid-1970s, there has been a rapid proliferation of nontariff trade barriers (NTBs), to the point where

CASE STUDY 16-5

The U.S. Subprime Mortgage Crisis and Sovereign Wealth Funds

The U.S. subprime mortgage crisis started in the United States in mid-2006, spread to the rest of the U.S. financial sector in mid-2007, and then to the rest of the world later in 2007 and in 2008. This is the first global financial crisis of the 21st century and the most serious financial crisis in a generation. The losses from the crisis have been estimated at between $400 billion to $1 trillion.

Subprime mortgages are housing loans issued to borrowers facing a high risk of being unable to meet their mortgage payments. Many of these subprime mortgages were made at variable rates in 2003 and 2004 when the lending rate was the lowest in 50 years and led to a serious housing bubble (home prices rising very rapidly and excessively). When the Fed started to increase interest rates in June 2004 to fight inflationary pressures, many of subprime borrowers defaulted on their mortgages, housing prices fell, and financial institutions faced huge losses, writedowns, and failures. Banks were willing to make subprime loans because they were able quickly to sell those loans to financial firms which proceeded to bundle them into securities (collateralized debt obligations) and sell them to the public after receiving high (triple AAA) ratings from rating agencies, such as Moody's and Standard & Poor, despite the high (but now hidden to the public) risk on which they were based.

As the Fed increased interest rates from 2004 to 2006, as many as 10 million homeowners

faced default and foreclosures, housing prices started to fall, financial institutions incurred billions of dollars of losses, banks started to make fewer loans, consumers started to spend less, and what started as a purely financial crisis spread to the real sector, causing growth to fall sharply in 2007 and pushing the U.S. economy to the brink of recession in 2008. In the meantime, the housing bubble also burst in other advanced countries, such as Spain and the United Kingdom, affected the entire financial sector of advanced countries, and had negative repercussions for emerging markets as well.

The need to raise capital by financial institutions in advanced countries in order to overcome the subprime crisis lead to a new problem—that of sovereign wealth funds. These are state-owned asset companies, mostly from emerging markets economies (such as the United Arab Emirates, Singapore, Saudi Arabia, China, Singapore, Kuwait, Russia, Brazil, but also Norway and Australia) that invest in financial and technological firms of advanced nations, causing anxieties and fears of financial dependence and loss of technology in these nations.

Source: "Putting Hard Numbers on a Bad Practice," *The Wall Street Journal,* April 9, 2009, p. A1; R. Lowenstein, "Triple A Failures," *The New York Times Magazine,* April 27, 2008, pp. 36–41; and "Governments as Global Investors," *Forbes,* May 19, 2008, p. 25.

Subprime mortgage crisis The financial crisis that started in the U.S. housing market and spread to the entire U.S. financial sector in 2007 resulting from the bursting of the housing bubble.

they now represent the most serious threat to the postwar trading system and the world's welfare. By interfering with the flow of international trade, rising protectionism leads to a misallocation of resources internationally, a slowdown in structural adjustments in mature economies and growth in developing economies, and it raises the specter of trade wars. This problem has been rendered more complex by the breakup of the world into three major trading blocs: the North American Free Trade Agreement (NAFTA,

Sovereign wealth funds State-owned asset companies, mostly from emerging market economies that invest in financial and technological firms of advanced nations.

including the United States, Canada, and Mexico), the European bloc or European Union (EU), and a much less defined and looser Asian bloc (see Sections 7.7 to 7.9).

The successful completion of the Uruguay Round in December 1993 went a long way toward reducing or at least putting an end to increased protectionism in the world today. As pointed out in Section 9.7b, however, many serious trade problems remain. Some sectors (such as insurance) were not included in the agreement, agricultural subsidies remain high, patent protection for pharmaceuticals is disappointing, and trade in computer chips is still subject to tariffs. Although tightened, antidumping action and safeguards are still possible, and so the potential for serious trade disputes remains. These problems were to be addressed in a new round of multilateral trade negotiations (the Doha Round) launched in November 2001 in Doha, Qatar, but which failed in July 2008. Regional trade agreements are no substitute for true multilateralism.

Technological change, globalization, and increased competition from the manufactured exports of emerging market economies, especially China, are held responsible for widespread firm downsizing, job insecurity, and stagnant wages in the United States and other advanced countries. But the solution to these problems is not to restrict trade and reduce international competition but to increase job training and create a labor force more skilled and prepared for the new information-age jobs that open up in telecommunications, computers, biomedical, and other high-tech fields. Only if workers in the United States and other advanced countries continuously upgrade the skills required for these new high-tech jobs, are willing to move to where the jobs are created, and accept more skilled immigrants will the United States and other advanced economies remain internationally competitive. This is the price that workers in rich countries have to pay for the higher productivity, wages, and standards of living that the "new economy" brings.

2. Structural Imbalances in the United States, Slow Growth in Europe and Japan, and Insufficient Restructuring in Transition Economies

Today, the United States faces deep structural imbalances in the form of excessive spending and inadequate national saving. This means that the United States is simply living beyond its means by borrowing excessively abroad. The result is huge and unsustainable trade deficits, a depreciated dollar, and unstable financial conditions (see Case Study 16-6). Being such a huge economy, U.S. economic problems quickly become global economic problems in our interdependent world. The United States thus needs to cut its spending deeply and sharply increase its savings rate in order to overcome its serious structural imbalance. While this cannot be easily or quickly

CASE STUDY 16-6

Trade Imbalances of the Leading Industrial Nations

One of the most serious global imbalances facing the world economy today is the large and chronic trade deficits of the United States and surpluses of Japan and Germany. Table 16.5 shows that the U.S. trade deficit increased from $25.5 billion in 1980 to $110.3 billion in 1990, $449.8 billion in 2000, to a high of $834.6 billion in 2006, and it was $815.3 billion in 2007. Japan's trade surplus rose from $2.1 billion in 1980 to the all-time high of $131.8 billion in 1995, and it was $104.8 billion in 2007. Germany's trade surplus rose from $7.9 billion in 1980 to the all-time high of $278.7 billion in 2007. In 2007, the United Kingdom had a trade deficit of $179.3 billion, France had a trade deficit of $54.9 billion, Canada had a trade surplus of

$45.8 billion, while Italy trade was practically balanced.

The U.S. dollar appreciated by nearly 40 percent on a trade-weighted basis from 1981 to 1985, but then depreciated by a similar amount from 1985 to 1988, but the U.S. trade deficit started to decline only in 1988. Despite record trade deficits, the U.S. dollar appreciated sharply from 1995 until 2001 because rapid growth attracted huge amounts of foreign capital to the United States. The U.S. trade deficit continued to increase until 2006 even though the dollar started to depreciate in mid-2005. The current U.S. trade deficit is unsustainable in the long run and so are the large trade surpluses of Japan and Germany.

Table 16.5. *Trade Imbalances of the Leading Industrial Countries, 1960–2007, Selected Years (in billions of U.S. dollars)*

Country	1960	1970	1980	1990	1995	2000	2005	2006	2007
United States	4.9	2.6	−25.5	−110.3	−172.3	−449.8	−783.4	−834.6	−815.3
Japan	0.3	4.0	2.1	69.3	131.8	116.7	94.0	81.3	104.8
Germany	2.1	5.7	7.9	68.5	65.1	57.5	194.3	200.9	278.7
United Kingdom	−1.1	0.0	3.4	−32.5	−19.0	−45.9	−125.1	−142.9	−179.3
France	0.6	0.3	−14.1	−13.3	11.0	−3.6	−27.8	−36.9	−54.9
Italy	−0.6	−0.2	−15.9	−1.5	39.7	9.5	0.6	−12.5	4.2
Canada	−0.2	3.0	7.9	9.5	25.9	45.6	52.7	45.1	45.8

Source: International Monetary Fund, *International Financial Statistics Yearbook,* various years; and D. Salvatore, "Global Imbalances," *Princeton Encyclopedia of the World Economy* (Princeton University Press, 2008).

accomplished, the United States does not seem to be trying sufficiently hard to resolve its problem.

During the past decade, European unemployment averaged 8 percent of the labor force, as compared to about 5 percent in the United States. Worse still, almost half of Europe's jobless have been unemployed for over a year, as compared with 11 percent in the United States. Unemployment is clearly Europe's major economic problem. Although conditions have improved somewhat since the beginning of this decade, the problem persists. The

European unemployment problem is mostly structural or long term in nature and is due, in large part, to overgenerous social security benefits and inflexible labor markets, which discourage work and job creation in the face of globalization and international competition. With high unemployment, Europe imports less than it would otherwise and tends to restrict trade in the vain effort to protect jobs. Again, we see how in our interdependent world, a national or regional problem quickly becomes a general global problem. The emerging consensus is that solving Europe's unemployment problem requires scaling down social security benefits and eliminating the regulations that hinder labor market flexibility. (If it is very difficult to fire workers, employers will think twice before hiring them.) But this is more easily said than done, especially since Europeans are justifiably proud of their high wages and comprehensive social-labor legislation.

Japan is only now emerging from a decade-long stagnation. It suffered three recessions and anemic growth from the early 1990s when the real estate bubble burst and left many banks with huge noncollectible loans. Banks then stopped making loans even to deserving businesses and the nation plunged into economic stagnation. Japan tried almost everything to overcome its problem. It lowered interest rates to practically zero to stimulate privates investments; it undertook huge public works to build roads and other infrastructures (often not needed) in order to jump-start and stimulate the economy, and it kept the exchange rate undervalued to stimulate exports—but the nation remained in a crisis. It is only since 2004 that Japan seems to have finally emerged from economic crisis, but growth remains too slow primarily due to Japan's inefficient distribution system.

Although considerable progress has been made in restructuring and establishing market economies in transition economies (the former centrally planned economies of Central and Eastern Europe and the Soviet Union), the process is far from complete. As pointed out in Section 7.9, these countries need massive amounts of foreign capital and technology, as well as more liberal access to Western markets in order to establish full-fledged market economies. Slow growth and high unemployment in Western Europe, however, have somewhat retarded progress. Ten transition economies (eight in Central and Eastern Europe plus Cyprus and Malta) were admitted into the European Union in 2004, Bulgaria and Romania entered in 2008, and others are in line for admission. This is facilitating their process of economic restructuring and integration into the world economy, and helping them to close their large gap in standard of living with other advanced countries.

3. Deep Poverty in Many Developing Countries

Even though many developing countries, especially China and India, are now growing very rapidly, many of the poorest developing nations, particularly those of sub-Saharan Africa, face deep poverty, unmanageable international

debts, economic stagnation, and widening international inequalities in living standards. These conditions pose serious problems for the world economy. An international economic system that has spread the benefits from international trade and specialization so unevenly can hardly be said to be functioning properly—not to mention equitably. And a world where millions of people starve not only is unacceptable from an ethical point of view, but also can hardly be expected to be a peaceful and tranquil world. Chapter 8 examined the reasons that international inequalities in standards of living between the rich and many of the poorest developing countries of the world are so large and widening, and what can be done to overcome them.

Over the years, the United Nations Conference on Trade and Development (UNCTAD) and other international forums have advanced many proposals to improve conditions in developing nations and stimulate their development. These proposals lost some of their immediacy during the 1980s and 1990s because developed countries (especially Western Europe, Japan, and the United States) were absorbed with their own domestic problems of monetary and exchange rate instability, slow growth, structural imbalances and high unemployment. As part of the demands for a New International Economic Order (NIEO—see Section 8.10), developing countries have been demanding both greater access for their exports to developed country markets and much greater flow of aid. The successful completion of the Uruguay Round in December 1993 only partially addressed the trade problems facing developing countries. The foreign aid granted by developed countries has stagnated despite the fact that the problems faced by the poorest developing countries remain oppressively high (see Table 8.6 and Case Study 8-6). The hope was that the Doha Round would address the trade problems of developing countries and truly be a development round, but it failed in July 2008.

4. Resource Scarcity, Environmental Degradation, Climate Change and Sustainable Development

Growth in rich countries and development in poor countries are today threatened by resource scarcity, environmental degradation, and climate change. In the face of rapidly growing demand, particularly by China and India, and supply rigidities in producing nations, the price of petroleum and other raw materials has risen sharply during the past few years, and so has the price of food. In many leading emerging market economies protection of the environment takes a back seat to the growth imperative. Environmental pollution is dramatic in some parts of China and the Amazon forest is rapidly being destroyed. And we are witnessing very dangerous climate changes that may have increasingly dramatic effects on life on earth. These problems, however, can be only adequately analyzed and addressed by a joint effort of all the sciences together, a major worldwide cooperative effort, and a change in world governance.

It is clear from the above discussion that the international economic problems facing the world today are closely interrelated. For example, excessive U.S. trade and budget deficits lead to protectionism and dollar depreciation, which affect all countries, developed and developing. They also shows the strong links between international trade discussed in the first half of the text (Chapters 2–12) and international finance discussed in the second half (Chapters 13–21).

Despite their seriousness, the world has faced similar, and sometimes even worse, problems in the past. The hope is that the world can tackle the current economic, financial, social, political, and environmental challenges in the spirit of cooperation and mutual understanding.

SUMMARY

1. In this chapter, we examined the operation of the international monetary system from the gold standard period to the present.

2. An international monetary system refers to the rules, customs, instruments, facilities, and organizations for effecting international payments. International monetary systems can be classified according to the way in which exchange rates are determined or according to the form that international reserve assets take. A good international monetary system is one that maximizes the flow of international trade and investments and leads to an equitable distribution of the gains from trade among nations. An international monetary system can be evaluated in terms of adjustment, liquidity, and confidence.

3. The gold standard operated from 1880 to 1914. Most of the adjustment under the gold standard took place through stabilizing short-term capital flows, rather than through changes in internal prices. From 1919 to 1924, exchange rates fluctuated wildly. Starting in 1925, Britain and other nations attempted to reestablish the gold standard. This attempt failed with the deepening of the Great Depression in 1931. There followed a period of competitive devaluations as each nation tried to "export" its unemployment, which cut international trade almost in half.

4. The Bretton Woods system, agreed upon in 1944, called for the establishment of the International Monetary Fund (IMF) and a gold-exchange standard with exchange rates allowed to fluctuate by 1 percent above and below par values. Par values were to be changed only in cases of fundamental disequilibrium. Each nation was assigned a quota into the IMF, 25 percent to be paid in gold and 75 percent in its currency. The nation could borrow 25 percent of its quota each year for five years.

5. Under the Bretton Woods system, industrial nations in fundamental disequilibrium were reluctant to change par values. The convertibility of the dollar into gold was resumed soon after the war and that of other industrial nations' currencies in the early 1960s. Tariffs on manufactured

goods were lowered to less than 10 percent by 1971. The IMF negotiated the General Arrangements to Borrow to further augment its resources. Nations negotiated standby arrangements with the IMF and swap arrangements with other central banks. The IMF created $9.5 billion of Special Drawing Rights in 1970–1972 to supplement international reserves. World output grew rapidly and international trade even faster.

6. For the seigniorage benefit from the use of the dollar as the principal international currency, the United States paid by being unable to devalue to correct its balance-of-payments deficits. The immediate cause of the collapse of the Bretton Woods system was the huge U.S. trade deficits, which led to massive destabilizing speculation, suspension of dollar convertibility into gold (August 1971), and currency realignment (December 1971). The fundamental cause of the collapse of the Bretton Woods system was lack of an adequate adjustment mechanism. The dollar was devalued again in February 1973 and in March 1973 the major currencies were allowed to fluctuate.

7. Since March 1973, the world has operated under a managed float. This has been formally recognized in the 1976 Jamaica Accords. The European Monetary System was formed in 1979, the European Central Bank began operating, and the euro was introduced at the beginning of 1999. The euro began circulating in 2002. Borrowing at the IMF has been relaxed, and significant new credit facilities have been created.

8. The most significant monetary problems facing the world today are the excessive fluctuations and large misalignments in exchange rates. Target zones and greater international macroeconomic policy coordination have been advocated to overcome them.

9. During the past decade, there was a series of financial and economic crises in Mexico, Southeast Asia, Russia, Brazil, Turkey, and Argentina. Proposed solutions involve increased transparency in financial relations, strengthening the emerging markets' banking and financial systems, and greater private sector involvement in rescue programs. The subprime mortgage crisis started in the United States in 2006 but it then spread to the entire financial sector and to other advanced countries facing a housing bubble in 2007.

10. Other serious international economic problems are: (1) trade protectionism in advanced countries in the context of a rapidly globalizing world; (2) deep structural imbalances in the United States, slow growth in Europe and Japan, and insufficient restructuring in transition economies of Central and Eastern Europe; (3) deep poverty in many developing countries; and (4) resource scarcity, environmental degradation, and climate change and the danger that they pose for continued growth and sustainable world development.

REVIEW QUESTIONS AND PROBLEMS

1. Explain:
 (a) How economic conditions today differ from those prevailing under the gold standard period.
 (b) Why the different economic conditions today would make the reestablishment of a smoothly working gold standard impossible.

2. (a) With respect to a nation with a $100-million quota in the IMF, indicate how the nation was to pay in its quota to the IMF and the amount that the nation could borrow in any one year under the original rules.
 (b) How are the rules different today?

3. (a) Explain how a nation could attempt to discourage large destabilizing international capital inflows under the Bretton Woods system by intervening in the spot market.
 (b) Can the same be done under the present international monetary system?

4. Explain the role of the dollar under the Bretton Woods system.

5. Explain with respect to the Bretton Woods system:
 (a) The immediate cause of its collapse.
 (b) The fundamental cause of its collapse.

6. Explain briefly the operation of the present international monetary system.

7. (a) Explain the fundamental reason for the Mexican currency crisis of December 1994.
 (b) How does the International Monetary Fund propose to avoid the recurrence of similar crises in the future?

8. With regard to the Mexican crisis of December 1994, indicate the lesson that it provides
 (a) for developing countries relying heavily on short-term capital inflows.
 (b) on how to deal with a currency crisis once it starts.

9. (a) Explain the fundamental causes of the economic crises in emerging markets in the second half of the 1990s.
 (b) What is being proposed to avoid similar crises in the future?

10. Identify the most significant international economic problems facing the world today.

SELECTED BIBLIOGRAPHY

The operation of the gold standard is examined in:

• R. I. McKinnon, *The Rules of the Game* (Cambridge, Mass.: MIT Press, 1996).

For the interwar experience, see:

- R. Nurkse, *The Interwar Currency Experience: Lessons of the Interwar Period* (Geneva: United Nations, 1944).

An examination of the post-World War II international monetary experience is found in:

- R. Triffin, *Gold and the Dollar Crisis* (New Haven, Conn.: Yale University Press, 1961).
- M. de Vries, *The IMF in a Changing World* (Washington, D.C.: IMF, 1986).
- M. Fratianni, D. Salvatore, and P. Savona, eds., *Ideas for the Future of the International Monetary System* (Boston: Kluwer, 1999).
- J. Boughton, *Silent Revolution: The International Monetary Fund, 1979–1989* (Washington, D.C.: IMF, 2001).
- D. Salvatore, "Liquidity" and "Reserve Currency," *Princeton Encyclopedia of the World Economy* (Princeton University Press, 2008).

Reforms of the international monetary system are examined in:

- J. Williamson, "Target Zones and the Management of the Dollar," *Brookings Papers on Economic Activity*, No. 1, 1986, pp. 165–174.
- R. McKinnon, "Monetary and Exchange Rate Policies for International Financial Stability: A Proposal," *Journal of Economic Perspectives*, Winter 1988, pp. 83–104.
- P. Kenen, *The International Financial Architecture* (Washington, D.C.: Institute for International Economics, 2001).
- D. Salvatore, "The Architecture and Future of the International Monetary System," in A. Arnon and W. Young, eds., *The Open Economy Macromodel: Past, Present, and Future* (New York: Kluwer, 2002), pp. 310–330.
- R. Rajan, "The Future of the IMF and the World Bank," *American Economic Review*, May 2008, pp. 110–115.

The current trade problems and reforms are examined in:

- D. Salvatore, ed., *Protectionism and World Welfare* (New York: Cambridge University Press, 1993).
- C. L. Mann, *Is the U.S. Trade Deficit Sustainable?* (Washington, D.C.: Institute for International Economics, 1999).
- D. Salvatore, "Currency Misalignments and Trade Asymmetries among Major Economic Areas," *The Journal of Economic Asymmetries*, Vol. 2, No. 1, 2005, pp. 1–24.

For the debt and growth problems, as well as financial crises in developing countries, see:

- E. Grilli and D. Salvatore, eds., *Handbook of Development Economics* (Westport, Conn., and Amsterdam: Greenwood Press and North-Holland, 1994).
- D. Salvatore, "Could the Financial Crisis in East Asia Have Been Predicted?" *Journal of Policy Modeling*, May 1999, pp. 341–348.
- "Symposium: The Origin and Management of Financial Instability," *The Economic Journal*, January 2000, pp. 235–362.
- D. Reagle and D. Salvatore, "Forecasting Financial Crises in Emerging Market Economies," *Open Economies Review*, August 2000, pp. 247–259.
- R. Dornbusch, "A Primer on Emerging Market Crises," *NBER Working Paper No. 8326*, June 2001.
- IMF, *Fiscal Vulnerability and Financial Crises in Emerging Market Economies* (IMF: Washington, D.C., 2003).
- G. Schinasi, Preserving Financial Stability, *IMF Economic Issues* No. 35, September 2005.

INTERNet

Data and analyses of the operation of the present international monetary and trading systems are regularly conducted by the International Monetary Fund (IMF), the Organization for Economic Cooperation and Development (OECD), the Bank for International Settlements (BIS), the World Trade Organization (WTO), and the World Bank (WB). Many of these are posted on their web sites at:

http://www.imf.org

http://www.oecd.org

http://www.bis.org

http://www.wto.org

http://www.worldbank.org

For historical exchange rate, interest rate, and price of gold data during the gold standard, see:

http://nber.nber.org/databases/macrohistory/contents/index.html

For the operation of the international monetary system and International Monetary Fund, as well as proposals for reforms of the international monetary system, see:

http://www.imf.org/external/pubs/ft/weo/2008/01/index.htm

To compare price discipline under fixed and flexible exchange rate systems, examine historical CPI data for various countries at:

http://www.economagic.com/blsint.htm

For the Special Drawing Rights (SDR) "valuation basket: percentage weights," see:

http://www.imf.org/external/np/exr/facts/sdr.htm

GDP and trade data are found in:

http://www.worldbank.org

http://www.wto.org

Financial data on emerging markets and their crises as well as studies on the global financial structure and issues are found in:

http://www.worldbank.org/data/jointdebt.html

http://www.emgmkts.com

http://www.fdi.net

Glossary

A

Absolute advantage The greater efficiency that one nation may have over another in the production of a commodity. This was the basis for trade for Adam Smith.

Absolute purchasing-power parity theory Postulates that the equilibrium exchange rate is equal to the ratio of the price levels in the two nations. This version of the PPP theory can be very misleading.

Absorption approach Examines and integrates the effect of induced income changes in the process of correcting a balance-of-payments disequilibrium by a change in the exchange rate.

Accommodating transactions Transactions in official reserve assets required to balance international transactions; also called below-the-line items.

Ad valorem tariff A tariff expressed as a fixed *percentage* of the value of a traded commodity.

Adjustable peg system The system under which exchange rates or par values are periodically changed to correct balance-of-payments disequilibria.

Adjustment The process by which balance-of-payments disequilibria are corrected.

Adjustment in the balance of payments The operation and effects of the mechanisms for correcting balance-of-payments disequilibria.

Adjustment policies Specific measures adopted by a nation's monetary authorities for the primary purpose of correcting a balance-of-payments disequilibrium.

Aggregate demand (AD) curve The graphical relationship between the total quantity demanded of goods and services at various prices.

Aggregate supply (AS) curve The graphical relationship between the nation's output and the price level over a given time period.

Anti-globalization movement The loose organization which blames globalization for many human and environmental problems throughout the world and for sacrificing human and environmental well-being to the corporate profits of multinationals (Sect. 1.5).

Antitrade production and consumption Increases in production and consumption that lead to a smaller than proportionate increase (or even an absolute decline) in the volume of trade.

Appreciation A decrease in the domestic currency price of the foreign currency.

Arbitrage The purchase of a currency in the monetary center where it is cheaper for immediate resale in the monetary center where it is more expensive in order to make a profit.

Asset or portfolio approach to exchange rates The theory that postulates that exchange rates are determined in the process of equilibrating or balancing the demand and supply of financial assets in each country.

Autarky The absence of trade, or isolation.

Autonomous transactions International transactions that take place for business or profit motives (except for unilateral transfers) and independently of balance-of-payments considerations; also called above-the-line items.

B

Balance of payments A summary statement of all the international transactions of the residents of a nation with the rest of the world during a particular period of time, usually a year.

Balanced growth Equal rates of factor growth and technological progress in the production of both commodities.

Baltic Free Trade Area (BFTA) The agreement signed by Estonia, Latvia, and Lithuania in 1992 calling for the establishment of free trade among its members in preparation for admission into the European Union.

Basis for trade The forces that give rise to trade between two nations. This was absolute advantage according to Adam Smith and comparative advantage according to David Ricardo.

Benign neglect The policy of nonintervention in foreign exchange markets followed by the United States from March 1973 until the end of 1977 and from 1981 to 1985.

Bilateral agreements Agreements between two nations regarding quantities and terms of specific trade transactions.

Bilateral trade Trade between any two nations.

Brain drain The migration of highly skilled and trained people from developing to developed nations and from other industrial nations to the United States.

Bretton Woods system The gold-exchange standard that operated from the end of World War II until 1971.

BRICs Brazil, Russia, India, and China, the new economic giants that provide increasing competition to the traditional giants (the United States, the European Union, and Japan).

Buffer stocks The type of international commodity agreement that involves the purchase of the commodity (to be added to the stock) when the commodity price falls below an agreed minimum price, and the sale of the commodity out of the stock when the commodity price rises above the established maximum price.

Bulk purchasing An agreement to purchase a specified amount of a commodity for a year or a number of years.

C

Capital account The change in U.S. assets abroad and foreign assets in the United States, other than official reserve assets.

Capital inflow An increase of foreign assets in the nation or a reduction in the nation's assets abroad.

Capital outflow A decrease of foreign assets in the nation or an increase in the nation's assets abroad.

Central and Eastern European Countries (CEEC) Includes Albania, Bosnia and Herzegovina, Bulgaria, Croatia, the Czech Republic, the Federal Republic of Yugoslavia, Hungary, the former Yugoslav Republic (FYR), Macedonia, Poland, Romania, the Slovak Republic, and Slovenia.

Central European Free Trade Association (CEFTA) The agreement signed by Poland, Hungary, the Czech Republic, and Slovakia in 1992 calling for the establishment of free trade among its members within ten years (subsequently anticipated for 1997).

Centralized cartel An organization of suppliers of a commodity that behaves as a monopolist.

Centrally planned economies Economies in which factors of production are owned by the government and prices are determined by government directives.

Closed economy An economy in autarky or not engaging in international transactions.

Cobb–Douglas production function The production function exhibiting a unitary elasticity of substitution between labor and capital.

Commercial policies The regulations governing a nation's commerce or international trade.

Commodity, or net barter, terms of trade The ratio of the price index of the nation's exports to the price index of its imports times 100.

Common market Removes all barriers on trade among members, harmonizes trade policies toward the rest of the world, and also allows the free movement of labor and capital among member nations. An example is the European Union (EU) since January 1, 1993.

Commonwealth of Independent States (CIS) The organization formed by most of the former Soviet Republics when the Soviet Union was dissolved at the end of 1991.

Community indifference curve The curve that shows the various combinations of two

commodities yielding equal satisfaction to the community or nation. Community indifference curves are negatively sloped, convex from the origin, and should not cross.

Complete specialization The utilization of all of a nation's resources in the production of only one commodity with trade. This usually occurs under constant costs.

Compound tariff A combination of an ad valorem and a specific tariff.

Confidence The knowledge that the balance-of-payments adjustment mechanism is working adequately and that international reserves will retain their absolute and relative values.

Constant elasticity of substitution (CES) production function The production function exhibiting a constant (but not necessarily unitary) elasticity of substitution between labor and capital.

Constant opportunity costs The constant amount of a commodity that must be given up to produce each additional unit of another commodity.

Consumer surplus The difference between what consumers are willing to pay for a specific amount of a commodity and what they actually pay for it.

Consumption effect of a tariff The reduction in domestic consumption of a commodity resulting from the increase in its price due to a tariff.

Council of Mutual Economic Assistance (CMEA or COMECON) The organization of Communist bloc nations formed by the Soviet Union in 1949 to divert trade from Western nations and achieve a greater degree of self-sufficiency among Communist nations.

Countervailing duties (CVDs) Tariffs imposed on imports to offset subsidies by foreign governments.

Covered interest arbitrage The transfer of short-term liquid funds abroad to earn higher returns with the foreign exchange risk covered by the spot purchase of the foreign currency and a simultaneous offsetting forward sale.

Covered interest arbitrage margin (CIAM) The interest differential in favor of the foreign monetary center minus the forward discount on the foreign currency, or the interest differential in

favor of the home monetary center minus the forward premium on the foreign currency.

Covered interest arbitrage parity (CIAP) The situation where the interest differential in favor of the foreign monetary center equals the forward discount on the foreign currency.

Crawling peg system The system under which par values or exchange rates are changed by very small preannounced amounts at frequent and clearly specified intervals until the equilibrium exchange rate is reached.

Credit tranche The amounts that a member nation could borrow from the IMF, subject to conditions, over and above the gold tranche.

Credit transactions Transactions that involve the receipt of payments from foreigners. These include the export of goods and services, unilateral transfers from foreigners, and capital inflows.

Cross exchange rate The exchange rate between currency A and currency B, given the exchange rate of currency A and currency B with respect to currency C.

Currency board arrangements (CBAs) The exchange rate arrangement whereby the nation rigidly fixes the exchange rate and its central bank loses its ability to conduct an independent monetary policy by allowing the nation's supply to increase or decrease only in response to balance-of-payments surpluses or deficits.

Currency convertibility The ability to exchange one national currency for another without any restriction or limitation.

Current account The account that includes all sales and purchases of currently produced goods and services, income on foreign investments, and unilateral transfers.

Customs union Removes all barriers on trade among members and harmonizes trade policies toward the rest of the world. The best example is the European Union (EU).

D

Debit transactions Transactions that involve payments to foreigners. These include the import of goods and services, unilateral transfers to foreigners, and capital outflows.

Deficit in the balance of payments The excess of debits over credits in the current and capital accounts, or autonomous transactions; equal to the net *credit* balance in the official reserve account, or accommodating transactions.

Deindustrialization The decline in the relative importance of manufacturing and in the share of manufacturing employment.

Depreciation An increase in the domestic currency price of the foreign currency.

Destabilizing speculation The sale of a foreign currency when the exchange rate falls or is low, in the expectation that it will fall even lower in the future, or the purchase of a foreign currency when the exchange rate is rising or is high, in the expectation that it will rise even higher in the future.

Devaluation A deliberate (policy) increase in the exchange rate by a nation's monetary authorities from one fixed or pegged level to another.

Differentiated products The somewhat different products (such as automobiles, cigarettes, and soaps) produced by different manufacturers in the same industry or general product group.

Direct controls Tariffs, quotas, and other restrictions on the flow of international trade and capital.

Direct investments Real investments in factories, capital goods, land, and inventories where both capital and management are involved and the investor retains control over the use of the invested capital.

Dirty floating Managing the nation's exchange rate to achieve aims other than simply the smoothing out of short-term fluctuations, for example, keeping the nation's currency undervalued so as to stimulate exports.

Doha Round The multilateral trade negotiations launched in November 2001 in Doha (Qatar) with the aim of providing greater trade access by developing countries in developed countries' markets, but which failed in July 2008.

Dollar glut The excess supply of dollars in the hands of foreign monetary authorities that developed during the late 1950s and early 1960s.

Dollar overhang The large amount of foreign-held dollars resulting from past U.S. balance-of-payments deficits, the movement of which from monetary center to monetary center can lead to large exchange rate fluctuations and complicates the conduct of monetary policies.

Dollar shortage The inability of war-torn nations during the late 1940s and early 1950s to accumulate substantial dollar reserves.

Dollar standard The international monetary system that emerged from the Smithsonian Agreement in December 1971 under which the U.S. dollar remained an international currency and reserve without any gold backing.

Dollarization The situation whereby a nation adopts another nation's currency as its legal tender.

Domestic value added Equals the price of a final commodity minus the cost of the imported inputs going into the production of the commodity.

Double-entry bookkeeping The accounting procedure whereby each (international) transaction is entered twice, once as a credit and once as a debit of an equal amount.

Double factoral terms of trade The ratio of the price index of the nation's exports to the price index of its imports times the ratio of the productivity index in the nation's export sector to the productivity index in the nation's import-competing sector.

Dumping The export of a commodity at below cost or at a lower price than sold domestically.

Duty-free zones or free economic zones Areas set up to attract foreign investments by allowing raw materials and intermediate products duty free.

Dynamic Asian economies (DAEs) Includes Korea, Taiwan (Chinese Taipei), Hong Kong, Singapore, Thailand, and Malaysia. (China is also sometimes included.)

Dynamic external economies The decline in the average cost of production as cumulative industry output increases and firms accumulate knowledge over time.

E

Economic integration The commercial policy of discriminatively reducing or eliminating trade barriers only among the nations joining together.

Economic union Removes all barriers on trade among members, harmonizes trade policies toward the rest of the world, allows the free movement of labor and capital among member nations, and also harmonizes or unifies the monetary, fiscal, and tax policies of its members.

Edgeworth box diagram The diagram constructed from the isoquants of two commodities and the given quantities available of two factor inputs.

Effective exchange rate A weighted average of the exchange rates between the domestic currency and the nation's most important trade partners, with weights given by the relative importance of the nation's trade with each of these trade partners.

Elasticity approach The change in the trade balance resulting from a depreciation or devaluation and depending on the price elasticity of demand for the nation's exports and imports.

Elasticity of substitution The degree or ease with which one factor can be substituted for another in production when the price of the factor declines.

Endogenous growth theory The theory that seeks to identify in detail and rigorously the actual channels or the ways by which freer trade leads to faster long-run economic growth and development.

Engine of growth The view that exports were the leading sector that propelled the economies of the regions of recent settlement into rapid growth and development during the nineteenth century.

Environmental standards The level of pollution accepted in various countries.

Equilibrium level of income (Y_E) The level of income at which desired or planned expenditures equal the value of output, and desired saving equals desired investment.

Equilibrium-relative commodity price in isolation The relative commodity price at which a nation is maximizing its welfare in isolation. It is given by the slope of the common tangent to the nation's production frontier and indifference curve at the autarky point of production and consumption.

Equilibrium-relative commodity price with trade The common relative commodity price in two nations at which trade is balanced.

Escape clause A protectionist device that allowed any industry that claimed injury from imports to petition the International Trade Commission, which could then recommend to the president to revoke any negotiated tariff reduction.

Euler's theorem The theorem that postulates that if constant returns to scale prevail in production and each factor is rewarded (paid) according to its productivity, the output produced is exhausted.

Euro The common currency adopted at the beginning of 1999 by 11 of the 15 member countries of the European Union.

Eurobonds Long-term debt securities sold outside the borrower's country to raise long-term capital in a currency other than the currency of the nation where the securities are sold.

Eurocurrency Commercial bank deposits in a nation denominated in a foreign currency.

Eurocurrency market The market where Eurocurrencies are borrowed and lent.

Euronotes Medium-term financial instruments falling somewhere between short-term Eurocurrency bank loans and long-term Eurobonds.

European Central Bank (ECB) The institution similar to the Federal Reserve System in the United States that would control the money supply and issue the single currency of the European Union.

European Currency Unit (ECU) The unit of account defined by the European Monetary System, based on the weighted average of the currencies of the EU members.

European Economic Area (EEA) The free trade area formed by the 12 members of the EU and 5 of the 7 members of the EFTA on January 1, 1994.

European Free Trade Association (EFTA) The free trade area that was formed in 1960 by the United Kingdom, Austria, Denmark, Norway, Portugal, Sweden, and Switzerland, with Finland an associate member in 1961. Iceland acceded in 1970. In 1973, the United Kingdom and Denmark left the EFTA to join the EU. Finland became a full member of the EFTA in 1986 and Liechtenstein in 1991. In 1995, Austria, Finland, and Sweden left the EFTA and joined the EU.

European Monetary Cooperation Fund (EMCF) The institution of the European Monetary System that provides short-term and medium-term balance-of-payments assistance to member nations.

European Monetary Institute (EMI) The forerunner of the European Central Bank that was set up in January 1994 by the Maastrich Treaty of December 1991 to further centralize members' macroeconomic policies and reduce exchange rate fluctuation margins.

European Monetary System (EMS) The organization formed by the members of the European Union (EU) in 1979 based on the creation of the European currency unit (ECU) of account, the Exchange rate mechanism (ERM), and formation of the European Monetary Fund (EMF).

European Monetary Union (EMU) The 12 members of the European Union that have adopted the euro as their common currency and have established the European Central Bank to conduct their common monetary policy.

European Union (EU) The customs union formed by West Germany, France, Italy, Belgium, the Netherlands, and Luxembourg that came into existence in 1958, and expanded to 15 nations with the joining of the United Kingdom, Denmark, and Ireland in 1973, Greece in 1981, Spain and Portugal in 1986, and Austria, Finland, and Sweden in 1995.

Exchange controls Restrictions on international capital flows, official intervention in forward markets, multiple exchange rates, and other financial and monetary restrictions imposed by a nation.

Exchange rate The domestic currency price of the foreign currency.

Exchange Rate Mechanism (ERM) The mechanism that allowed the currency of each EMS nation to fluctuate by a maximum of 2.25 on either side of its central rate or parity.

Exchange rate overshooting The tendency of exchange rates to immediately depreciate or appreciate by more than required for long-run equilibrium, and then partially reverse their movement as they move toward their long-run equilibrium levels.

Expansion path The line joining the origin with points of producer's equilibrium obtained by increasing expenditures on inputs with input prices constant.

Expected prices The prices that are believed will prevail.

Expenditure-changing policies Fiscal and monetary policies directed at changing the level of aggregate demand of the nation.

Expenditure-switching policies Devaluation or revaluation of a nation's currency directed at switching the nation's expenditures from foreign to domestic or from domestic to foreign goods.

Export controls The type of international commodity agreement that seeks to regulate the quantity of the commodity exported by each nation.

Export-Import Bank A U.S. government agency that extends subsidized loans to foreigners to finance U.S. exports.

Export instability Short-run fluctuations in export prices and earnings.

Export-oriented industrialization The policy of industrialization pursued by some developing nations that involves increasing the output of manufactured goods for export.

Export pessimism The feeling that developing countries' exports to developed countries cannot grow rapidly because of the latter's increased protectionism.

Export subsidies The granting of tax relief and subsidized loans to potential exporters, and low-interest loans to foreign buyers of the nation's exports.

Export tariff A tax or duty on exports.

External balance The objective of equilibrium in a nation's balance of payments.

F

Factor endowments See factor abundance.

Factor-intensity reversal The situation where a commodity is L intensive when the relative price of labor is low and K intensive when the relative price of capital is low. If prevalent, this would lead to rejection of the H–O trade model.

Factor-price equalization theorem The part of the H–O theory that predicts, under highly restrictive assumptions, that international trade will

bring about equalization in relative and absolute returns to homogeneous factors across nations.

Factor-proportions or **factor-endowment theory** See Heckscher–Ohlin theory.

First credit tranche The 25 percent of a nation's quota in the IMF that the nation is required to pay in SDRs or in the currencies of other members selected by the Fund and could then borrow from the Fund almost automatically.

Foreign debt The hundreds of billions of dollars that developing countries owe to commercial banks in developed countries and that they find difficult to repay or even service (i.e., pay interest on).

Foreign exchange futures A forward contract for standardized currency amounts and selected calendar dates traded on an organized market (exchange).

Foreign exchange markets The framework for the exchange of one national currency for another.

Foreign exchange option A contract specifying the right to buy or sell a standard amount of a traded currency at or before a stated date.

Foreign exchange risk The risk resulting from changes in exchange rates over time and faced by anyone who expects to make or to receive a payment in a foreign currency at a future date; also called an open position.

Foreign repercussions The effect that a change in a large nation's income and trade has on the rest of the world and which the rest of the world in turn has on the nation under consideration. This is how business cycles are transmitted internationally.

Foreign Sales Corporations (FSC) The overseas subsidiaries set up by U.S. corporations to take advantage of partial exemption from U.S. tax laws.

Foreign trade multiplier (k') The ratio of the change in income to the change in exports and/or investment. It equals $k' = 1/(MPS + MPM)$.

Forward discount The percentage per year by which the forward rate on the foreign currency is below its spot rate.

Forward premium The percentage per year by which the forward rate on the foreign currency is above its spot rate.

Forward rate The exchange rate in foreign exchange transactions involving delivery of the foreign exchange one, three, or six months after the contract is agreed upon.

Freely floating exchange rate system The flexible exchange rate system under which the exchange rate is always determined by the forces of demand and supply without any government intervention in foreign exchange markets.

Free trade area Removes all barriers on trade among members, but each nation retains its own barriers on trade with nonmembers. The best examples are the EFTA, NAFTA, and Mercosur.

Fundamental disequilibrium Large and persistent balance-of-payments deficits or surpluses.

G

Game theory A method of choosing the optimal strategy in conflict situations.

General Agreements on Tariffs and Trade (GATT) An international organization devoted to the promotion of freer trade through multilateral trade negotiations.

General Arrangements to Borrow (GAB) The arrangements under which the IMF negotiated to borrow from the "Group of Ten" (most important industrial nations) and Switzerland to augment its resources if needed to help nations with balance-of-payments difficulties.

General equilibrium model An economic model that studies the behavior of all producers, consumers, and traders simultaneously.

Globalization The increasing integration of economies around the world, particularly through trade and financial flows, but also through the movement of ideas and people, facilitated by the revolution in telecommunications and transportation.

Gold export point The mint parity plus the cost of shipping an amount of gold equal to one unit of the foreign currency between the two nations.

Gold import point The mint parity minus the cost of shipping an amount of gold equal to one unit of the foreign currency between the two nations.

Gold standard The international monetary system operating from about 1880 to 1914 under which gold was the only international reserve, exchange rates fluctuated only within the gold

points, and balance-of-payments adjustment was described by the price-specie-flow mechanism.

Gold tranche The 25 percent of a nation's quota in the IMF that the nation was originally required to pay in gold and could then borrow from the Fund almost automatically.

H

Heckscher–Ohlin (H–O) theorem The part of the Heckscher–Ohlin theory that postulates that a nation will export the commodity intensive in its relatively abundant and cheap factor and import the commodity intensive in its relatively scarce and expensive factor.

Heckscher–Ohlin (H–O) theory The theory that postulates that (1) a nation exports commodities intensive in its relatively abundant and cheap factor and (2) international trade brings about equalization in returns to homogeneous factors across countries.

Hedging The avoidance of a foreign exchange risk (or the covering of an open position).

High-performance Asian economies (HPAEs) Hong Kong, Korea, Singapore, and Taiwan; characterized by rapid growth in gross domestic product (GDP), in industrial production, and in manufactured exports; also called newly industrialized economies (NIEs).

Homogeneous of degree 1 A production function exhibiting constant returns to scale.

Horizontal integration The production abroad of a differentiated product that is also produced at home.

Human capital The education, job training, and health embodied in workers, which increase their productivity.

I

IMF conditionality The conditions imposed by the IMF on members' borrowings from the Fund.

Immiserizing growth The situation where a nation's terms of trade deteriorate so much as a result of growth that the nation is worse off after growth than before, even if growth without trade tends to improve the nation's welfare.

Import-substitution industrialization (ISI) The industrialization policy that many developing nations followed during the 1950s, 1960s, and 1970s involving the replacement of imports of industrial goods with domestically produced goods.

Import tariff A tax or duty on imports.

Income terms of trade The ratio of the price index of the nation's exports to the price index of its imports times the index of the nation's volume of exports.

Incomplete specialization The continued production of both commodities in both nations with increasing costs, even in a small nation with trade.

Increasing opportunity costs The increasing amounts of one commodity that a nation must give up to release just enough resources to produce each additional unit of another commodity. This is reflected in a production frontier that is concave from the origin.

Increasing returns to scale The production situation where output grows proportionately more than the increase in inputs or factors of production. For example, doubling all inputs more than doubles output.

Industrial policy An activist policy by the government to stimulate the development and growth of some industry (usually a high-tech industry) in an industrial nation.

Infant-industry argument The argument that temporary trade protection is needed to set up an industry and to protect it during its infancy against competition from more established and efficient foreign firms.

Interdependence The (economic) relationships among nations.

Interest arbitrage The transfer of short-term liquid funds abroad to earn a higher return.

Internal balance The objective of full employment with price stability; usually a nation's most important economic objective.

International Bank for Reconstruction and Development (IBRD or World Bank) The international institution established after World War II to provide long-run development assistance to developing nations.

International cartel An organization of suppliers of a commodity located in different nations (or a group of governments) that agrees to restrict

output and exports of the commodity with the aim of maximizing or increasing the total profits of the organization. An international cartel that behaves as a monopolist is called a centralized cartel.

International commodity agreements Organizations of producer and consumer nations attempting to stabilize and increase the prices and earnings of the primary exports of developing nations.

International debt The hundreds of billions of dollars that developing countries owe to commercial banks in developed countries and that they find difficult to repay or even service (i.e., pay interest on).

International Development Association (IDA) The affiliate of the International Bank for Reconstruction and Development set up in 1960 to make loans at subsidized rates to poorer developing nations.

International economies of scale The increased productivity resulting from the firm's integration of its entire system of manufacturing operations around the world.

International finance The study of foreign exchange markets, the balance of payments, and adjustment to balance-of-payments disequilibria.

International Finance Corporation (IFC) The affiliate of the International Bank for Reconstruction and Development set up in 1956 to stimulate *private* investments in developing nations from indigenous and foreign sources.

International investment position The total amount and the distribution of a nation's assets abroad and foreign assets in the nation at year-end; also called the balance of international indebtedness.

International macroeconomic policy coordination The modifications of national economic policies in recognition of international interdependence.

International Monetary Fund (IMF) The international institution created under the Bretton Woods system for the purposes of (1) overseeing that nations followed a set of agreed-upon rules of conduct in international trade and finance and (2) providing borrowing facilities for nations in temporary balance-of-payments difficulties.

International monetary system The rules, customs, instruments, facilities, and organizations for effecting international payments.

International trade policy Examines the reasons for and effects of trade restrictions.

International trade theory Analyzes the basis and the gains from trade.

Intervention currency A convertible national currency (primarily the U.S. dollar) used by nations' monetary authorities to intervene in foreign exchange markets in order to keep the exchange rate from moving outside the allowed or desired range of fluctuation.

Intra-industry trade International trade in the differentiated products of the same industry or broad product group.

Isocost A line showing the various combinations of two inputs that a firm can hire for a given expenditure and factor prices.

Isoquant A curve showing the various combinations of two factors or inputs that a firm can use to produce a specific level of output.

J

Jamaica Accords The agreements reached in January 1976 and ratified in April 1978 that recognized the managed float and abolished the official price of gold.

J-curve effect The deterioration before a net improvement in a country's trade balance resulting from a depreciation or devaluation.

K

Kennedy Round The multilateral trade negotiations that were completed in 1967 (under the authority of the 1962 Trade Expansion Act) under which agreement was reached to reduce average tariff duties on industrial products by 35 percent.

L

Labor theory of value The theory that the cost or price of a commodity is determined by or can be inferred exclusively from its labor content.

Laissez-faire The policy of minimum government interference in or regulation of economic activity, advocated by Adam Smith and other classical economists.

Law of comparative advantage Explains how mutually beneficial trade can take place even when one nation is less efficient than, or has an absolute disadvantage with respect to, another nation in the production of all commodities. The less efficient nation should specialize in and export the commodity in which its absolute disadvantage is smaller (this is the commodity of its comparative advantage), and should import the other commodity.

Law of one price The proposition that in the absence of transportation costs, tariffs, and other obstructions to the free flow of trade, the price of each homogeneous (identical) traded commodity will be equalized in all markets by commodity arbitrage.

Learning curve The curve showing the degree by which average costs of production decline as cumulative industry output increases over time.

Leontief paradox The empirical finding that U.S. import substitutes were more K intensive than U.S. exports. This is contrary to the H–O trade model, which predicts that, as the most K-abundant nation, the United States should import L-intensive products and export K-intensive products.

Liquidity The amount of international reserve assets available to nations to settle temporary balance-of-payments disequilibria.

Long-run aggregate supply (LRAS) curve The fixed relationship between the nation's price level and its natural level of output, which depends on the availability of labor, capital, natural resources, and technology in the nation.

M

Maastricht Treaty The treaty that called for the creation of the European Monetary Institute as a forerunner of the European Central Bank and monetary union by the European Union by 1999.

Macroeconomics The study of the whole or the aggregate, such as the total receipts and payments of a nation and the general price index.

Managed floating exchange rate system The policy of intervention in foreign exchange markets by monetary authorities to smooth out short-run fluctuations without attempting to affect the long-run trend in exchange rates.

Marginal rate of substitution (MRS) The amount of one commodity that a nation could give up in exchange for one extra unit of a second commodity and still remain on the same indifference curve. It is given by the slope of the community indifference curve at the point of consumption and declines as the nation consumes more of the second commodity.

Marginal rate of technical substitution of labor for capital in production (MRTS) It shows how much capital a firm can give up by increasing labor by one unit and still remain on the same isoquant.

Marginal rate of transformation (MRT) The amount of one commodity that a nation must give up to produce each additional unit of another commodity. This is another name for the opportunity cost of a commodity and is given by the slope of the production frontier at the point of production.

Marketing boards National schemes set up by several developing nations after World War II to stabilize export prices for individual producers of an agricultural commodity.

Marshall–Lerner condition Indicates that the foreign exchange market is stable when the sum of the price elasticities of the *demands* for imports and exports is larger than 1 (when the *supply* elasticities of imports and exports are infinite).

Mercantilism The body of writings prevailing during the seventeenth and eighteenth centuries that postulated that the way for a nation to become richer was to restrict imports and stimulate exports. Thus, one nation could gain only at the expense of other nations.

Mercosur The South American, or Southern Cone, Common Market that was formed in 1991 by Argentina, Brazil, Paraguay, and Uruguay.

Microeconomics The study of individual units, such as a particular nation and the relative price of a single commodity.

Mint parity The fixed exchange rates resulting under the gold standard from each nation defining the gold content of its currency and passively standing ready to buy or sell any amount of gold at that price.

Monetary model of exchange rates The theory that postulates that exchange rates are determined in the process of equilibrating or balancing the stock or total demand and supply of money in each nation.

Most-favored-nation principle The extension to all trade partners of any reciprocal tariff reduction negotiated by the United States with any other nation.

Multilateral trade negotiations Trade negotiations among many nations.

Multinational corporations (MNCs) Firms that own, control, or manage production and distribution facilities in several countries.

Multiple exchange rates The different exchange rates often enforced by developing nations for each class of imports depending on the usefulness of the various imports as determined by the government.

Multiplier (k) The ratio of the change in income to the change in investment; in a closed economy without government, $k = 1/MPS$.

N

National security clause A protectionist device that prevented any tariff reduction (even if already negotiated) that would hurt industries important for national defense.

Natural level of output (Y_N) The fixed level of output that a nation can produce in the long run with its given quantity of labor, capital, natural resources, and technology.

Net IMF position The size of a nation's quota in the IMF minus the Fund's holdings of the nation's currency.

Neutral production and consumption In creases in production and consumption that lead to proportionate increases in the volume of trade.

New Arrangement to Borrow (NAB) The arrangement negotiated by the International Monetary Fund at the beginning of 1997 under which 25 participant countries and institutions agreed to lend up to SDR34 billion (about $47 billion) to supplement the General Arrangements to Borrow (GAB) for a period of five years (subject to renewal).

New Independent States (NIS) Includes Armenia, Azerbaijan, Belarus, Estonia, Georgia, Kazakh-

stan, the Kyrgyz Republic, Latvia, Lithuania, Moldova, Russia, Tajikistan, Turkmenistan, Ukraine, and Uzbekistan.

New International Economic Order (NIEO) The demands made by developing nations as a group at the United Nations for the removal of the alleged inequities in the operation of the present international economic system and for specific steps to be taken to facilitate their development.

Newly industrialized economies (NIEs) Hong Kong, Korea, Singapore, and Taiwan; characterized by rapid growth in gross domestic product (GDP), in industrial production, and in manufactured exports; also called high-performance Asian economies (HPAEs).

Nominal tariff A tariff (such as an ad valorem one) calculated on the price of a final commodity.

Nominal exchange rate The exchange rate or the domestic currency price of the foreign currency.

Nontariff trade barriers (NTBs) Trade restrictions other than tariffs, such as voluntary export restraints; technical, administrative, and other regulations; as well as those arising from international cartels, dumping, and export subsidies.

Nontraded goods and services Those goods and services that are not traded internationally because the cost of transporting them exceeds the international price difference.

North American Free Trade Agreement (NAFTA) The agreement to establish a free trade area among the United States, Canada, and Mexico that came into existence on January 1, 1994.

O

Offer curve A curve that shows how much of its import commodity a nation demands to be willing to supply various amounts of its export commodity, or the willingness of the nation to import and export at various relative commodity prices.

Official reserve account It measures the change in U.S. official reserve assets and the change in foreign official reserve assets in the United States.

Official settlements balance The net credit or debit balance in the official reserve account.

Offshore deposits Bank deposits denominated in a currency other than that of the nation in which the deposit is held.

Offshoring It refers to a firm producing in its own plants abroad some of the parts and components that it uses in its products.

Omnibus Trade and Competitiveness Act of 1988 Through its Super 301 provision, the Act requires curbing imports from countries that do not remove major barriers to the U.S. exports.

Open-economy macroeconomics The study of foreign exchange markets, the balance of payments, and adjustment to balance-of-payments disequilibria.

Opportunity cost theory The theory that the cost of a commodity is the amount of a second commodity that must be given up to release just enough resources to produce one more unit of the first commodity.

Optimum currency area or bloc Refers to a group of nations whose national currencies are linked through permanently fixed exchange rates and the conditions that would make such an area optimum.

Optimum tariff The rate of tariff that maximizes the benefit resulting from improvement in the nation's terms of trade against the negative effect resulting from reduction in the volume of trade.

Outsourcing It refers to a firm's purchase of parts and components abroad, rather than itself producing them at home, in order to keep its costs down in a global world economy.

P

Pass-through The proportion of an exchange rate change that is reflected in export and import price changes.

Pattern of trade The commodities exported and imported by each nation.

Peril-point provisions A protectionist device that prevented the president from negotiating any tariff reduction that would cause serious damage to a domestic industry.

Persistent dumping The *continuous* tendency of a domestic monopolist to maximize total profits by selling the commodity at a lower price abroad than domestically; also called international price discrimination.

Portfolio investments The purchase of purely financial assets, such as bonds and stocks (if the stock purchase represents less than 10 percent of the stock of a corporation), usually arranged through banks and investment funds.

Portfolio theory Maintains that by investing in securities with yields that are inversely related over time, a given yield can be obtained at a smaller risk or a higher yield can be obtained at the same level of risk for the portfolio as a whole.

Predatory dumping The *temporary* sale of commodity at a lower price abroad in order to drive foreign producers out of business, after which prices are raised to take advantage of the newly acquired monopoly power abroad.

Preferential trade arrangements The loosest form of economic integration; provides lower barriers to trade among participating nations than on trade with nonparticipating nations. An example is the British Commonwealth Preference Scheme.

Price-specie-flow mechanism The automatic adjustment mechanism under the gold standard. It operates by the deficit nation losing gold and experiencing a reduction in its money supply. This in turn reduces domestic prices, which stimulates the nation's exports and discourages its imports until the deficit is eliminated. A surplus is corrected by the opposite process.

Producer equilibrium The tangency point where a producer reaches the highest isoquant possible with a given isocost line.

Product cycle model The hypothesis, advanced by Vernon, that new products introduced by industrial nations and produced with skilled labor eventually become standardized and can be produced in other nations with less skilled labor.

Production contract curve The curve joining points at which the isoquants of two commodities are tangent and factor inputs are used most efficiently.

Production effect of a tariff The increase in domestic production of a commodity resulting from the increase in its price due to a tariff.

Production function A relationship showing the maximum quantities of a commodity that a firm can produce with various amounts of factor inputs.

Production possibility frontier A curve showing the various alternative combinations of two commodities that a nation can produce by fully utilizing all of its resources with the best technology available to it.

Prohibitive tariff A tariff sufficiently high to stop all international trade so that the nation returns to autarky.

Protection cost or **deadweight loss of a tariff** The real losses in a nation's welfare because of inefficiencies in production and distortions in consumption resulting from a tariff.

Protrade production and consumption Increases in production and consumption that lead to greater than proportionate increases in the volume of trade.

Purchase contracts Long-term multilateral agreements that stipulate the minimum price at which importing nations agree to purchase a specified quantity of the commodity and a maximum price at which exporting nations agree to sell specified amounts of the commodity.

Purchasing-power parity (PPP) theory The theory that postulates that the exchange rate depends on relative prices in the two countries.

Q

Quantity theory of money Postulates that the nation's money supply times the velocity of circulation of money is equal to the nation's general price index times physical output at full employment. With V and Q assumed constant, the change in P is directly proportional to the change in M.

Quota A direct *quantitative* restriction on trade.

R

Rate of effective protection The tariff calculated on the domestic value added in the production of a commodity.

Real exchange rate The nominal exchange rate weighed by the consumer price index in the two nations.

Reciprocal demand curve Another name for the offer curve.

Regions of recent settlement The mostly empty and resource-rich lands that Europeans settled during the nineteenth century, such as the United States, Canada, Argentina, Uruguay, Australia, New Zealand, and South Africa.

Relative commodity prices The price of one commodity divided by the price of another commodity. This equals the opportunity cost of the first commodity and is given by the absolute slope of the production possibility frontier.

Relative factor prices The ratio of the price of one factor of production to the price of the other factor. With labor and capital as the factors of production, the relative price of labor is w/r and the relative price of capital is the inverse, or r/w.

Relative purchasing-power parity theory The theory that postulates that the percentage change in the exchange rate is equal to the difference in the percentage change in the price level in the two countries.

Rent or producer surplus A payment that need not be made in the long run in order to induce producers to supply a specific amount of a commodity or factor services.

Reserve-currency country (RCC) A country, such as the United States, whose currency is held by other nations as international reserves.

Revealed comparative advantage The revealed comparative advantage of a nation or region is measured by the excess in the percentage of total exports over the percentage of total imports in each major commodity group for the nation or region (Case Study 3-1, p. 67).

Revenue effect of a tariff The revenue collected by the government from the tariff.

Risk diversification Investments in securities with yields that are inversely, or negatively, correlated or investments in different lines or products in order to spread and thus reduce the overall risks of the total investments.

Rules of the game of the gold standard The requirement under the gold standard that monetary authorities restrict credit in the deficit nation and expand credit in the surplus nation (thus reinforcing the effect of changes in international gold flows on the nation's money supply).

Rybczynski theorem Postulates that at constant commodity prices, an increase in the endowment of one factor will increase by a greater proportion the output of the commodity intensive in that factor and will reduce the output of the other commodity.

S

Scientific tariff The tariff rate that would make the price of imports equal to domestic prices so as to allow domestic producers to meet foreign competition.

Seigniorage The benefit accruing to a nation from issuing the currency or when its currency is used as an international currency.

Shared Foreign Sales Corporations U.S. tax legislation aimed at stimulating U.S. exports by reducing the effective rate of taxation on export income.

Short-run aggregate supply (SRAS) curve The temporary positive relationship between the nation's output and the price level resulting from imperfect information or market imperfections.

Single factoral terms of trade The ratio of the price index of the nation's exports to the price index of its imports times the productivity index in the nation's export sector.

Small-country case The situation where trade takes place at the pretrade-relative commodity prices in the large nation so that the small nation receives all of the benefits from trade.

Smithsonian Agreement The agreement reached in December 1971 in Washington under which the dollar was devalued by about 9 percent (by increasing the dollar price of gold from $35 to $38 an ounce), other strong currencies were revalued by various amounts with respect to the dollar, the dollar convertibility into gold remained suspended, and exchange rates were allowed to fluctuate by 2.25 percent on either side of the new par values.

Smoot-Hawley Tariff Act Raised average import duties in the United States to the all-time high of 59 percent in 1932.

Sovereign wealth funds State-owned asset companies, mostly from emerging markets economies that invest in financial and technological firms of advanced nations.

Special Drawing Rights (SDRs) International reserves created by the IMF to supplement other international reserves and distributed to member nations according to their quotas in the Fund.

Specific-factors model The model to analyze the effect of a change in commodity price on the returns of factors in a nation when at least one factor is not mobile between industries.

Specific tariff A tariff expressed as a fixed *sum* per unit of a traded commodity.

Speculation The acceptance of a foreign exchange risk, or open position, in the hope of making a profit.

Sporadic dumping The *occasional* sale of a commodity at a lower price abroad than domestically in order to sell an unforeseen and temporary surplus of the commodity abroad without having to reduce domestic prices.

Spot rate The exchange rate in foreign exchange transactions that calls for the payment and receipt of the foreign exchange within two business days from the date when the transaction is agreed upon.

Stability and Growth Pact (SGP) The pact that requires members of the European Monetary Union to keep their budget deficits not exceeding 3 percent of their GDP.

Stabilizing speculation The purchase of a foreign currency when the domestic currency price of the currency (i.e., the exchange rate) falls or is low, in the expectation that the exchange rate will soon rise, thus leading to a profit. Or the sale of a foreign currency when the exchange rate rises or is high, in the expectation that it will soon fall.

Stable foreign exchange market The condition in a foreign exchange market where a disturbance from the equilibrium exchange rate gives rise to automatic forces that push the exchange rate back toward the equilibrium rate.

Stagflation The combination of recession or stagnation and increasing prices or inflation.

Standby arrangements The arrangements under which member nations negotiate with the IMF for advance approval for future borrowings from the Fund so they will be immediately available when needed.

State trading companies The state organizations in centrally planned economies handling trade in specific product lines.

Statistical discrepancy The entry made in a nation's balance of payments to make total credits equal to total debits, as required by double-entry bookkeeping.

Stolper–Samuelson theorem It postulates that free international trade reduces the real income of the nation's relatively scarce factor and increases the real income of the nation's relatively abundant factor.

Strategic trade policy The argument that an activist trade policy in oligopolistic markets subject to extensive external economies can increase a nation's welfare.

Subprime mortgage crisis The financial crisis that started in the U.S. housing market and spread to the entire U.S. financial sector in 2007 resulting from the bursting of the housing bubble.

Substitution account The account proposed to be used to exchange all foreign-held dollars for SDRs at the IMF to solve the problem of the dollar overhang.

Surplus in the balance of payments The excess of credits over debits in the current and capital accounts, or autonomous transactions; equal to the net *debit* balance in the official reserve account, or accommodating transactions.

Swap arrangements The arrangements under which national central banks negotiate to exchange each other's currency to be used to intervene in foreign exchange markets to combat international hot money flows.

Synthesis of automatic adjustments The attempt to integrate the automatic price, income, and monetary adjustments to correct balance-of-payments disequilibria.

T

Target zones The system in which the leading industrial nations estimate the equilibrium exchange rate and agree on the range of allowed fluctuation.

Tariff factories Direct investments made in a nation or other economic unit (such as a customs union) to avoid import tariffs.

Technical, administrative, and other regulations Nontariff trade barriers such as safety, health, and labeling requirements, and border taxes.

Technological gap model The hypothesis that a portion of international trade is based on the introduction of new products or processes.

Terms of trade The ratio of the index price of a nation's export to its import commodities.

Terms of trade effect of a tariff The reduction in the price of the import commodity that results when a large nation imposes an import tariff.

Theory of the second best Postulates that when all of the conditions required to reach maximum social welfare or Pareto optimum cannot be satisfied, trying to satisfy as many of these conditions as possible does not necessarily or usually lead to the second-best welfare position.

Tokyo Round The multilateral trade negotiations that were completed in 1979 (under the authority of the 1974 Trade Reform Act) in which agreement was reached to cut average tariff rates by about 30 percent and to adopt a uniform international code of conduct for applying nontariff trade barriers.

Trade Adjustment Assistance The provision of the Trade Expansion Act of 1962 (and continued in subsequent Trade Acts), which provides to assist displaced workers and firms injured by trade liberalization.

Trade Agreements Act of 1934 Authorized the President to negotiate with other nations mutual tariff reductions of up to 50 percent under the most-favored-nation principle.

Trade and Tariff Act of 1984 Authorized the President to negotiate the lowering of trade barriers in services and a free trade agreement with Israel, and extended the Generalized System of Preferences (GSP) until 1993.

Trade controls Tariffs, quotas, advance deposits on imports, and other restrictions imposed by a nation on international trade.

Trade creation Results when higher priced imports from a nonunion member nation (subject to an import tariff) are replaced by lower priced imports from a member nation (not subject to the import tariff). Trade creation increases the welfare of member nations because it increases international trade and specialization.

Trade deflection The entry of imports from the rest of the world into the low-tariff member of a free trade area to avoid the higher tariffs of other members.

Trade diversion Results if lower cost imports from outside the customs union are replaced by higher cost imports from a union member because of the preferential trade treatment given to member nations. Trade diversion, by itself, reduces welfare.

Trade effect of a tariff The reduction in the volume of trade in the commodity resulting from a tariff.

Trade Expansion Act of 1962 Granted the President authority to negotiate across-the-board tariff reductions of up to 50 percent of their 1962 level and replaced the no-injury principle with adjustment assistance.

Trade indifference curve The curve showing the various trade situations that provide a nation equal welfare.

Trade or elasticity approach The theory or approach that stresses the role of trade or the flow of goods and services in the determination of exchange rates. This model is more useful in explaining exchange rates in the long run than in the short run.

Trade policies The regulations governing a nation's commerce or international trade.

Trade promotion authority or "fast track" Legislation granting to the president of the United States the right to negotiate global trade agreements with other nations that allowed no amendments, but only an up-or-down vote by Congress to ratify or reject the agreement (Sect. 9.7A).

Trade Reform Act of 1974 Granted the President authority to negotiate tariff reductions of up to 60 percent of their post-Kennedy Round level and to negotiate reductions in nontariff trade barriers.

Transfer pricing The overpricing or underpricing of products in the intrafirm trade of multinational corporations in an attempt to shift income and profits from high- to low-tax nations.

Transfer problem Deals with the conditions under which a large and unusual capital transfer is actually accomplished by an export surplus of the paying nation and an equal import surplus of the receiving nation.

Transport or logistics costs Freight charges, warehousing costs, costs of loading and unloading, insurance premiums, and interest charges while goods are in transit (Sect. 6.6).

Trigger-price mechanism The antidumping mechanism introduced by the United States in 1978 to protect its steel industry by imposing a duty on underpriced imported steel to make its price equal to that of the lowest cost foreign producer.

U

Uncovered interest arbitrage The transfer of short-term liquid funds to the international monetary center with higher interest rates without covering the foreign exchange risk.

Unilateral transfers Gifts or grants extended to or received from abroad.

United Nations (UN) The international organization to facilitate cooperation in international law, international security, economic development, social progress, and human rights issues.

United Nations Conferences on Trade and Development (UNCTAD) Special conferences held under the auspices of the United Nations in 1964, 1968, 1972, 1976, 1979, 1983, 1987, and 1992 at which developing nations advanced their demands to improve the operation of the present international economic system to facilitate their development.

Unstable foreign exchange market The condition in a foreign exchange market where a disturbance from equilibrium pushes the exchange rate farther away from equilibrium.

Uruguay Round The multilateral trade negotiations started in 1986 and completed at the end of 1993 aimed at reversing the trend of rising nontariff trade barriers. It replaced the GATT with the World Trade Organization (WTO), brought services and agriculture into the WTO, and improved the dispute settlement mechanism.

V

Variable import levies The import duties levied by the EU on imports of agricultural commodities and equal to the difference between the high farm prices established by the EU and the lower world prices.

Vehicle currency A currency, such as the U.S. dollar and the euro, that is used for international transactions and to denominate international contracts.

Vent for surplus The view that exports could be an outlet for the potential surplus of agricultural commodities and raw materials in some developing countries.

Vertical integration The expansion of a firm backward to supply its own raw materials and intermediate products and/or forward to provide its own sales or distribution networks.

Voluntary export restraints (VERs) Refer to an importing country inducing another country to "voluntarily" reduce its exports of a commodity to the importing nation under the threat of higher all-around trade restrictions.

W

World Bank See International Bank for Reconstruction and Development (IBRD).

World Trade Organization (WTO) The organization set up at the Uruguay Round to replace the General Agreement on Tariffs and Trade (GATT) secretariat with authority over trade in industrial goods, agricultural commodities, and services, and with greater authority to settle trade disputes.

Name Index

Subject Index